D0396412

GETTYSBURG

ALSO BY NOAH ANDRE TRUDEAU

GETTYSBURG

A Testing of Courage

NOAH ANDRE TRUDEAU

HarperCollins*Publishers*

HarperCollins books may be purchased for educational, business, or sales promotional use. For information, please write: Special Markets Department, HarperCollins Publishers Inc., 10 East 53rd Street, New York, NY 10022.

FIRST EDITION

Library of Congress Cataloging-in-Publication Data is available upon request.

ISBN: 0-06-019363-8

02 03 04 05 06 NMSG/RRD 10 9 8 7 6 5 4 3

When I was younger I could remember anything, whether it happened or not. But as I grew older, it got so I only remembered the latter.

—MARK TWAIN

CONTENTS

Acknowledgments xiii

Preface xv

Author's Note xvii

List of Maps xix

PROLOGUE: May 15–18, 1863   1

PART ONE: Confluence

  1. "I wish I could get at those people. . . ."   11
  2. ". . . we were taking a lot of chances"   22
  3. "Lee's army . . . is your true objective"   34
  4. "Push on"   41
  5. "I hope . . . to end the war if Providence favors us"   50

PART TWO: Roads to Gettysburg

  6. ". . . I can throw Genl Hooker's army across the Potomac"   67
  7. "We were all scared"   77
  8. ". . . I . . . request that I may at once be relieved"   88
  9. "It was my firm determination . . . to give battle"   102
10. "I am going straight at them"   116
11. "It begins to look as though we will have a battle soon"   127

PART THREE: Battle

NOCTURNE: Night, Tuesday, June 30   144

12. July 1, 1863   152
Predawn–7:30 A.M.   152
7:30 A.M.–10:45 A.M.   161
10:45 A.M.–11:15 A.M.   185
11:15 A.M.–2:45 P.M.   197
2:45 P.M.–5:45 P.M.   221
5:45 P.M.–Midnight   251

NOCTURNE: Night, Wednesday, July 1   273

13. July 2, 1863   277
Midnight–Sunrise   277
Dawn–3:40 P.M.   282
3:40 P.M.–4:10 P.M.   328
4:10 P.M.–10:00 P.M.   334
10:00 P.M.–Midnight   410

NOCTURNE: Night, Thursday, July 2   423

14. July 3, 1863   427
Midnight–Sunrise   427
Sunrise–1:07 P.M.   434
1:07 P.M.–2:40 P.M.   464
2:40 P.M.–2:55 P.M.   476
2:55 P.M.–3:15 P.M.   484
3:15 P.M.–3:40 P.M.   494
3:40 P.M.–Midnight   509
15. "I thought my men were invincible"   530

PART FOUR: Endings and Beginnings

16. Pursuit to a Personal Crossroads   543
August 8, 1863: Orange, Virginia   543
March 5, 1864: Washington, D.C.   546
17. Judgments   550

The People: Afterward 557

The Opposing Armies 565

Chapter Notes 597

Bibliography 643

Index 679

ACKNOWLEDGMENTS

First and foremost, this book is a tribute to the many historians who have produced sharply focused studies of the campaign and battle of Gettysburg over the last three decades. These scholars have stripped away the many layers of varnish that were applied to the Gettysburg story in the seventy-five years or so following the battle. Thanks to their dedicated work, our understanding of the events surrounding, and the motivations behind, virtually every phase of this engagement possesses a clarity that is without parallel in the field of U.S. military history. Even on the international stage, there are only a handful of military encounters whose understanding has been so remarkably enhanced and sharpened over the years. The bibliography at the back of this volume acknowledges the books and articles I have found most useful and stimulating.

This book is also a tribute to the individuals and organizations dedicated to the preservation and interpretation of the Gettysburg battlefield. Not long after I began working on it, the last telephone pole was removed from the stretch of the Emmitsburg Road that crosses the ground of major fighting on July 2 and 3. As I was reaching the end of the project, I was able to enjoy the view from Oak Hill along the Mummasburg Road for the first time in the many years I've been tramping the battlefield. The hard work of organizations such as the Friends of the National Parks at Gettysburg, and others, continually rejuvenates the story told by the land.

As always, there are individuals whose assistance, guidance, and suggestions were invaluable to me. Once more, my principal researcher, Bryce Suderow, mined the Washington, D.C., libraries and archives on my behalf, not only producing the items I requested, but many times coming forward with material that I had not known to ask for but was very glad to have. Along the way, I received other research help from Chris Hunter as well as from James W. and Paula Stuart Warren. My chief research base away from home was the United States Army Military History Institute, where David Keogh now presides over the archival collections, though Dr. Richard Sommers continues to make regular and welcome appearances. There I became acquainted with the immense collection of Gettysburg-related materials assembled by naval officer Robert L. Brake in anticipation of the history he never wrote. Other archives also played their part; I am grateful, in particular, for the fine services rendered by John M. Coski of the Museum of the Confederacy and Edward Varno of the Ontario County Historical Society and Museum.

I would be remiss if I did not mention the wonderful collection of primary materials maintained by Robert K. Krick at the Fredericksburg-Spotsylvania National Park. My access was through ranger-historian Donald Pfanz, who was helpful above and beyond the call. D. Scott Hartwig of the Gettysburg National Park somehow found the time in the midst of a busy schedule to review the manuscript and provide thoughtful corrections and gentle suggestions when I wandered too far astray. My friend Kee Malesky went over the first section of the typescript to help me catch errors missed by the spell checker. Copy editor Dorothy Straight was, once again, indefatigable in her quest to tighten up wayward sentences, find the right word when I could not, correct my woeful efforts at addition, and ensure name spelling was consistent.

Finally, a tip of the hat to my literary agent, Raphael Sagalyn, who managed my transition from one publishing home to another; and to my editors at HarperCollins, who turned the manuscript into the book you're holding. Tim Duggan stood watch over the final phase and was present at the delivery.

As always, I much appreciated the thoughts and ideas offered by others throughout the project's gestation, though again, as always, the final product reflects my judgments and choices, good or bad.

PREFACE

There is a hallowed tradition in the Gettysburg battle-book industry of beginning each new work by apologizing for adding to the congestion of so many previous studies on the subject, and explaining why the latest effort is justified. I have no apologies to offer, and only the briefest of explanations: a fresh look needs to be taken at this most emblematic military campaign and combat of the Civil War. The last overall treatment of length and substance was Edwin B. Coddington's justly lauded *The Gettysburg Campaign: A Study in Command,* which first appeared in 1968. Since then, writing about the battle has been constant, so much so that several small publishing houses specialize in it as a genre. A new breed of Gettysburg scholar has emerged: the microspecialist. The event has been broken down into every conceivable subtopic, from the experiences of individual regiments, soldiers, or combat arms, to medical and civilian histories, to second-by-second accounts of its individual days (or even portions of individual days). The sum total is that a powerful refinement of Gettysburg's story has emerged. Many cherished tales were found to be fables, while other, long-overlooked acts of heroism and courage were revealed. This book synthesizes those discoveries and my own into a comprehensive narrative of one of the most unforgettable sagas in United States history. It is time.

AUTHOR'S NOTE

A basic understanding of Civil War military organization, tactics, and weapons is assumed in the text that follows, so a brief primer may not be out of place here. For the most part, the military forces of each side were organized according to the same hierarchy, by corps, divisions, brigades, regiments, and companies (in descending order of size). It was common in the Confederate army to refer to units above the regimental level by the names of their commanders (present or past); I have followed that practice and capitalized accordingly (e.g., Longstreet's Corps, Rodes' Division, Archer's Brigade). Union forces, in contrast, tended to follow a numbering system (e.g., Third Corps, First Division, Second Brigade), so when I refer to those units with the names of their commanders I have *not* capitalized the result (e.g., Wadsworth's division, Vincent's brigade). A few Federal units achieved an identity that transcended the military numerology, most notably Iron Brigade and the Irish Brigade. With a few exceptions, regiments are always referred to by their number and state: the 154th New York, for instance, or the 26th North Carolina.

The two essential unit formations, at least so far as this book is concerned, are column and line. A column was a marching formation; with three or four men abreast, it packed a regiment into as compact a space as was practicable for rapid movement along a road or across open ground. Once engaged in combat, columns transformed into lines of battle—usually at least two and sometimes three, with the third standing by as a reserve. These lines, each containing perhaps three hundred men or more, were jointed by companies, allowing one section of the line to face one way while another portion faced in a different direction. The ends of a line were its flanks; the process of bending back a segment of the line so that the men stood at an angle to their original orientation was referred to as refusing the flank.

The standard combat formation relied on a massing of rifles and the resultant firepower for its effect. Often positioned in advance of the compact lines of battle were more widely dispersed and irregular detachments known as skirmish lines. Their purpose was to harry the enemy, break up advancing formations, and provide the main body with ample warning when trouble was coming. Skirmish units could take many forms, from small cells of three or four men to widely strung lines consisting of individual soldiers posted several yards apart.

Most of the weapons used at Gettysburg were muzzle loaders—that is, their powder and shot were loaded through the front of the barrel. Also on the field were some breech-loading weapons, whose munitions were inserted into the barrel from the side, top, or rear. Cannon fired three basic types of ordnance: solid shot, case shot, and canister. Solid shot, the traditional cannon ball, was generally reserved for long-distance counterbattery shooting. Case shot was a fuzed shell that exploded into deadly particles either on contact or after a timed fuse ignited the charge. Canister consisted of a coffee-can-like casing holding golf-ball-sized metal spheres. The casing disintegrated upon firing, scattering the spheres like shotgun pellets. Canister was an antipersonnel munition, typically saved for fairly close-in work.

Directional references in the text are always from the point of view of the side under discussion. When it comes to spelling from original sources, especially manuscripts, I have used a variable standard in an effort to eliminate the qualifier *sic* from the text. Where I feel a particular spelling conveys a vivid sense of character, I have preserved the original; otherwise I have engaged in some judicious editorial cleaning-up of manuscript passages.

LIST OF MAPS

The Strategic Picture: May 15–16, 1863   3
June 3–9, 1863   23
Brandy Station: June 9, 1863   31
June 10–13, 1863   35
Winchester: June 14–15, 1863   44
June 14–15, 1863   47
June 15–17, 1863   51
June 18–24, 1863   56
June 25, 1863   68
June 26, 1863   78
Gettysburg: June 26, 1863   83
June 27, 1863   89
June 28, 1863   103
June 29, 1863   117
June 30, 1863   128
Hanover: June 30, 1863   134
Ewell (Lines of March Ordered for July 1)   139
Gettysburg 1863   142
The Pipe Creek Line   151
July 1: Morning Positions   155
July 1: Heth's Advance   167
July 1: Entering the Herbst Woods/Action North
     of the Railroad Cut   177
July 1: Action in the Herbst Woods   183
July 1: Mixed Fortunes on McPherson's Ridge   189
July 1: Fight for the Railroad Cut   193
July 1: Union First Corps at Midday   199
July 1: First Fight for Oak Hill   210
July 1: Attack on Blocher's Knoll   223

July 1: Afternoon Assault on McPherson's Ridge 227
July 1: Early Sweeps the Field 229
July 1: Second Fight for Oak Hill 234
July 1: Assault on Seminary Ridge 238
July 1: Coster's Last Stand 242
July 1: Reinforcements Arriving 265
Gettysburg 1863 274
July 2: The Bliss Farm 285
July 2: Lower Seminary Ridge Deployments 291
July 2: Morning Deployment by Sickles 295
July 2: Encounter in the Pitzer Woods 309
July 2: Longstreet's Flank Attack: Three Scenarios 323
July 2: Sickles and Longstreet Deploy 329
July 2: Robertson's and Law's Scrambled Advance 338
July 2: Benning and Anderson Strike Sickles 350
July 2: Action on Little Round Top 361
July 2: Caldwell Sweeps the Wheat Field 366
July 2: Barksdale Sweeps the Peach Orchard 369
July 2: Benner's Hill and Brinkerhoff's Ridge 374
July 2: Action near the Trostle Farm 387
July 2: Attack and Counterattack along Cemetery Ridge 389
July 2: Action on Culp's Hill 399
July 2: Action on Cemetery Hill 406
July 3: Preparing for More Combat 422
July 3: Early-Morning Action on Culp's Hill 435
July 3: Artillery Positions 445–46
July 3: Midmorning Action on Culp's Hill 448
July 3: The Cemetery Ridge Assault: The Confederate Plan 482
July 3: The Cemetery Ridge Assault: Brockenbrough/Davis 492
July 3: The Cemetery Ridge Assault: Pettigrew/Fry/
    Garnett/Kemper 498
July 3: The Cemetery Ridge Assault: Lane/Scales/Armistead 503
July 3: The Cemetery Ridge Assault: Flags Lost 512
July 3: East Cavalry Battlefield 515
July 3: South Cavalry Battlefield 517
July 4: Positions of the Armies 528
July 5–15, 1863 544

GETTYSBURG

Prologue

The dawn light came up behind Richmond's imposing statehouse, spreading inexorably across the eight marble columns fronting the building. Already the streets around Capitol Square were stirring with slow-moving figures and horse-drawn wagons that clattered on the cobblestones. Dark rectangles on the faces of a hundred nearby houses glowed from within as the population roused itself to face another day at war. This one was Friday, May 15, 1863.

Thousands were soon making their way to government and industrial offices, a daily ritual necessary to administer and supply the field armies fighting for the Confederacy. Those entering the Tredegar Iron Works passed the still-smoldering ruins of the Crenshaw Mill. This neighboring five-story brick building had burst into flame at around two o'clock that morning, sending "volumes of sparks far away through the night." Some 140 workers, men and women, now discovered that they were without jobs.

The hardship their families would suffer through this loss would be exacerbated by the price inflation then gripping the Confederate States of America, or C.S.A. By 1863 it took ten dollars to buy what one dollar had purchased just three years earlier. Nearly lost among the worried minions entering their workplaces this day was a clerk in the Confederate War Department named John Beauchamp Jones. Jones scrutinized his finances constantly, fearful and wary of what he called the "gaunt form of wretched famine," which hung about the city like the odor of burned wood from the overnight conflagration.

Jones had been with the War Department long enough to know many important military men by sight. Today he spotted a number of such notables, among them major generals Samuel Gibbs French and James Ewell Brown ("Jeb") Stuart and General Robert E. Lee. Lee had come to symbolize both the hopes and the grim resignation of Richmond's citizenry. In the first week of May he had commanded the Army of Northern Virginia as it defeated a much larger enemy force at Chancellorsville, near Fredericksburg. The details of this action had reached the city largely through Lee's dispatches, adding in no small measure to the celebrity of the otherwise unassuming officer.

Any public commemoration of this incredible victory had been instantly muted, however, by the news that Lee's charismatic second in command, Major General Thomas J. "Stonewall" Jackson, had been seriously wounded in the fighting. Even so, his recovery had seemed assured until pneumonia-like complications set in; on May 8, Jackson died. All of Richmond had turned out for the funeral four days later, including the ubiquitous Jones. "The grief is universal," he noted, "and the victory involving such a loss is regarded as a calamity." The prospects of renewed fighting had kept Lee near Fredericksburg while the capital mourned. Perhaps his knowledge of that fact colored Jones's view of Lee this day: the War Department clerk thought the general appeared "thinner, and a little pale."

The man on whose shoulders so much of the war now rested had been, in 1861, just another Southern former army officer in search of an appointment. His first assignments, in western Virginia and along the lower Atlantic coast, had been competently managed, if nothing more. Then, in March 1862, C.S.A. President Jefferson Davis had brought Lee to Richmond and made him his military adviser, a position with little actual authority. But fate had intervened in late May of the same year, when a massive Union army under Major General George B. McClellan bulled its way to Richmond's gates. After General Joseph E. Johnston, then commanding the Confederate forces defending the capital, was wounded, Davis had surprised everyone by putting his military adviser in charge. Lee had immediately transformed Johnston's defensive program into a series of costly offensives that turned back McClellan's grand army. There had followed a sequence of hard-fought battles—Second Manassas, Sharpsburg, Fredericksburg, Chancellorsville—most of which were Southern victories. Lee was now hailed as "one of the great military masters."

Although he did not often display a sense of irony, Lee must have reflected on the paradox that his "victory" at Chancellorsville threatened him more than a defeat might have. He had won the battle with almost 16,000 out of his 72,000-man army on detached service below Richmond. In the minds of some in the government, this suggested that Lee's soldiers might be better employed elsewhere in the Confederacy—a speculation that would have been a pointless rhetorical exercise had there not been another military front then in desperate need of more Southern fighting men.

That place was Vicksburg, Mississippi, the fortress city representing the South's grip on a stretch of the Mississippi River adjoining the C.S.A.'s eastern and western wings. The river port's defenders had already repelled several attempts on the part of Federal land and naval forces to capture it. Now a fresh campaign was under way, and this time the prognosis was not good for the Confederates. On May 14, word reached Richmond that Vicksburg's vital inland link, the city of Jackson, had been taken by Union forces under a general named Grant. "This is a dark cloud over the hopes of patriots," John Beauchamp Jones noted. He added in his diary that Vicksburg's loss "would be the worst blow we have yet suffered."

Men were so urgently needed on that front that a number of government officials wondered aloud if Lee might not be able to spare some troops. Among the prominent figures demanding such reassignment was

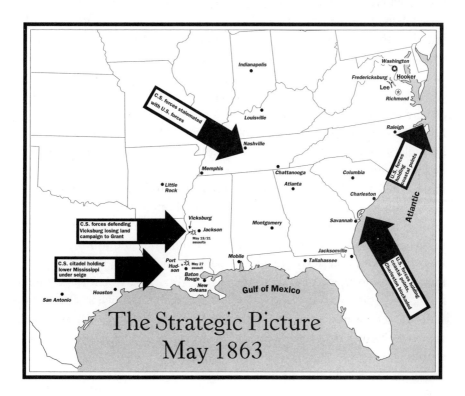

The Strategic Picture
May 1863

the Confederate secretary of war, James Seddon, a man consumed by inner fires. War Department clerk Jones mused that Seddon looked like a "dead man galvanized into muscular animation." But if his body was failing, the forty-seven-year-old's determination was firm. Even before the Chancellorsville battle, Seddon had suggested to Lee that he ought to part with "two or three brigades" that could then be combined with others to create "an encouraging re-enforcement to the Army of the West."

Lee had not rejected Seddon's request outright; he had simply enumerated all the things that could go wrong with such a complicated troop transfer. Then the army's adjutant and inspector general had entered the arena on Seddon's side, and in so doing had upped the bidding to a full division from Lee's army. Lee had countered by proposing that he make an aggressive move into the North, thereby remedying the problem by drawing the enemy's potential western reinforcements toward him. It almost came as a relief when the Federals launched their operation at Chancellorsville.

Just two days after the fighting ended, Lee had resumed the telegraphic exchange. He tried to turn everyone's attention deeper to the south, where General P. G. T. Beauregard commanded Confederate forces defending the Atlantic coast from South Carolina to Florida. Arguing that the summer swamp fevers common to the coastal lowlands would prevent the Federals there from mounting any major operations, Lee suggested that Beauregard's troops might be better deployed closer to Richmond. This in turn would free up units from Lee's army that were assigned to the capital's defenses, which could then be returned to him. Lee invited himself to Richmond to meet with C.S.A. officials, but before he could set out for the capital, there was another telegraphic exchange as Seddon renewed his original request.

Having already pointed out the risks of transferring troops via the South's undependable rail system, and having hinted that units elsewhere were more disposable, Lee now prophesied disaster. Any such reduction in the size of his army, he said, would force him to relinquish the line he was holding at Fredericksburg and fall back on Richmond, thus abandoning much of northern Virginia to the enemy. War Department clerk Jones monitored this exchange and recorded its conclusion, when President Jefferson Davis intervened with the opinion that it was "just such an answer as he expected from Lee, and he approves it. Virginia will not be abandoned."

Lee met with President Davis and Secretary Seddon throughout the afternoon of May 15. No notes have survived regarding this discussion, but we know that Lee was not by nature given to making specific promises or outlining his intentions in any detail. He would later summarize his argument by saying, "An invasion of the enemy's country breaks up all of his preconceived plans, relieves our country of his presence, and we subsist while there on his resources." Lee undoubtedly reitcrated his claim to Major General George E. Pickett's division, then detailed to Richmond's defense. Seddon likely restated his concerns about the growing crisis in the West and the need to direct scarce Southern military manpower to Vicksburg.

Jefferson Davis was no pushover, despite his still being weak from a recent illness. At first, as Lee would much later relate, "Mr. Davis did not like the [prospect of the] movement northward." The Confederate president worried about Richmond's safety were it to lose its principal shield. But Lee expressed his belief that "by concealing his movements and managing well, he could get so far north as to threaten Washington before they could check him, & this once done he knew there was no need of further fears about their moving on Richmond." With his army moving, Lee was confident he could "baffle and break up" any enemy schemes. Davis listened, then decided: Lee could reinforce his army for a northward advance.

The next day, Saturday, May 16, Davis called in his full cabinet to discuss the Vicksburg matter. Only Postmaster General John H. Reagan left an account of this session, which was held in the second-floor council room of Davis's house. Reagan was from the west side of the Mississippi and understood more clearly than most the importance of holding Vicksburg. Everyone present, Reagan would later declare, "realized the grave character of the question to be considered." The cabinet members, he recalled, "assembled early . . . and remained in session in the anxious discussion of that campaign until after nightfall." To his dying day the Texan would believe that a critical decision was made during this meeting, though in fact everything important had already been decided during Lee's May 15 conference with Davis and Seddon. The army commander was not present during the cabinet discussions; he did not have to be. War Department clerk Jones knew immediately who had won as he watched the "long column" of Pickett's Division marching "through the city northward," even as Reagan and his colleagues struggled for consensus. "Gen. Lee," Jones noted, "is now stronger than he was before the battle [of Chancellorsville]." When Lee paid a social call that evening, he seemed anything but thin or pale. One young man who saw him would never forget the "superb figure of our hero," and judged Lee the "most noble looking mortal I had ever seen."

It is impossible to know precisely what Lee's thoughts may have been concerning his next operation. Many of the arguments he had used to win its approval were more opportunistic than real. It would not be unfair to suggest that he considered a range of possibilities at that moment, varying only in their probability. At worst, a march into Maryland and beyond would significantly alleviate his logistical difficulties. By taking his army into the enemy's breadbasket, Lee could help himself to a rich larder of livestock and grains, as well as a large, ambiguous category of goods euphemistically termed "military supplies." Drawing the point of battle away from northern Virginia would also allow Old Dominion farmers to harvest their crops free of enemy interference.

But there was another, even more important reason for Lee to move north. While a later generation of writers would tout Chancellorsville as "Lee's greatest victory," there is evidence that its principal architect did not see it that way. He had, in a postbattle proclamation to his men, pronounced the results a "glorious victory," but such occasions always demanded inflated language. More likely, he would have agreed with the reporter covering the campaign for the *Richmond Enquirer,* who wrote, "I believe General Lee expected a more brilliant result." Lee said as much when he berated one of his subordinates for failing to press the enemy at the end of the fighting: "You have again let these people get away . . . ," he exclaimed. "Go after them! Damage them all you can!" He was equally candid when he reviewed the results of Chancellorsville with an aide sent by President Davis. The Confederate "loss was severe," Lee said, "and again we had gained not an inch of ground and the enemy could not be pursued."

He had taken great risks with his army at Chancellorsville. Time and again he had opened himself to the possibility of destruction by stripping his defensive strength in one sector to reinforce an offensive movement in another. His goal throughout had been not merely to drive the enemy force back across the Rappahannock River but to destroy its military effectiveness. In the next campaign he hoped to find the battle of annihilation he had tried and failed to manage at Chancellorsville. All other reasons proffered for his intended operation were inconsequential. Accord ing to the recollection of a staff officer, Lee "knew oftentimes that he was playing a very bold game, but it was the only *possible* one."

How deep into the North he would march, and where he would meet the enemy, would be determined as events unfolded. The important preliminary step had been taken: he had won Richmond's grudging permission to make the effort. Still, Lee recognized that the sufferance could be taken from him at any time. Postmaster Reagan had in fact renewed his arguments during an impromptu caucus with other cabinet members in Davis's office on May 17, though nothing had come of that discussion because not enough had changed on the Vicksburg front to alter the president's decision. Lee worried that the next dawn would bring news from the West that might upset everything. As he left Richmond on May 18, the general knew one thing for certain: he would have to act quickly. On his way to rejoin his army, Lee breakfasted with a family friend who was "very glad to see that the great and good man was so cheerful."

Some fifty-five miles north of Richmond, on the same day Lee met with Seddon and Davis, Union military engineers watched in grim silence as ambulances bearing the last gatherings from the Chancellorsville battlefield creaked painfully across the pontoon bridge laid at Banks' Ford. An assistant surgeon on the scene was satisfied with the manner in which his staff had handled these wounded men, some of whom had lain untended for days. "The complicated injuries . . . were placed in proper supports, firmly bound, and the men were then well supported in the ambulances by pads and blankets," he reported. "In this manner, we were enabled to transport the wounded with comparatively little suffering." Nevertheless, reflected a soldier, "more than one poor fellow died on the way from loss of blood."

A short distance south along the Rappahannock River, near Falmouth, the man who had commanded the Army of the Potomac at Chancellorsville was suffering his own torments. If ever an officer had set himself up for ridicule, Major General Joseph Hooker provided an object lesson. The forty-eight-year-old West Pointer had risen steadily through the ranks thanks to solid performances in combat, some valuable political connections, and a willingness to intrigue. The sharp criticisms he had voiced regarding his superior's mishandling of his men at the Battle of Fredericksburg had tagged him for dismissal, but then the superior had been relieved instead, and Joe Hooker had found himself commanding the Army of the Potomac.

Sure of himself to the point of arrogance, Hooker had undertaken the Chancellorsville campaign absolutely confident of success. To the reporters he made welcome around headquarters, Hooker had boasted that Lee's army was the "legitimate property of the Army of the Potomac." Even Lincoln, always anxious to encourage aggressiveness in his generals, worried to a friend, after hearing Hooker's predictions, that "he is overconfident."

Hooker's plan *had* been brilliant. While one Union corps of more than 23,600 men kept Lee's attention riveted at Fredericksburg, Hooker had marched the rest of his infantry undetected upstream to cross behind the Rebel army. His flanking force numbered about 72,300 men at that point and would eventually grow to nearly 80,000. However, the Confederate commander refused to play according to Hooker's script, even when the Union corps that had been left behind to divert attention actually crossed the river to occupy Fredericksburg. Instead of falling back toward Richmond, Lee divided his outnumbered command and struck at Hooker's main force in a series of ragged, desperate actions that suddenly metamorphosed into a powerful, stunning flank attack. In an instant, Hooker's posture changed from a bold offensive stance into a confused and hesitant defensive. While Hooker fretted, Lee struck hard against the lone Federal corps that had moved inland from Fredericksburg, threatening it with annihilation. Stung, and ignoring subordinates who were prepared to fight where they stood, the Union commander ordered his army to retire to the northern side of the river, which it did by May 6. Even though he would always refuse to label Chancellorsville a defeat, Hooker would admit that its aftermath was a time "when the nation required a victory."

Hooker's failure at Chancellorsville had been compounded by many factors, including leadership lapses on the part of several of his leading corps officers, some instances of plain bad luck, and a number of poor command decisions that were his alone to make. Most damning was the fact that he never used all his available units in the fight: while three of his seven corps were heavily engaged, the other four were only partially involved. It was not without some justification that one of Hooker's officers declared that the "Army of the Potomac did not fight at Chancellorsville."

Most observers saw only Hooker's failings. Newspapers that had bannered his predictions of victory in their headlines now turned on him, with the *New York Herald* leading the pack that trumpeted for his dismissal. Certain bars in Washington and New York were even said to be promoting a new concoction dubbed "Hooker's Retreat."

Most unseemly to some was Hooker's selective memory regarding the council of war he had called on the evening of May 4 (the fourth day of battle), during which several of his corps commanders, especially the Fifth Corps' Major General George G. Meade, had urged that the attack be renewed. Meade now learned that Hooker was characterizing his objections to a retreat as conditional, implying that once his conditions had been met, the Pennsylvanian favored the withdrawal. This prompted the austerely professional Meade to solicit statements from others who had been present disputing Hooker's version. In the end, the testimonials would prove unnecessary, as Hooker would never write up a final report of the Chancellorsville campaign.

President Abraham Lincoln had visited Hooker's headquarters on May 7, not to apportion blame but to assess matters. Lincoln had confided to George Meade that this reverse, in terms of its effect on both Northern morale and international opinion, "would be more serious and injurious than any previous act of the war." At the end of his one-day visit, the president had given Hooker a personal note in which he urged the officer to consider soon making "another movement" but cautioned him not to undertake any initiative out of "desperation or rashness." Lincoln had also posed the most painful question of all: "What next?" he asked. "Have you already in your mind a plan wholly, or partially formed?"

In response, Hooker had assured Lincoln that he indeed had in mind "the plan to be adopted in our next effort, if it should be your wish to have one made." After a week's further consideration, Hooker had informed Lincoln of his intention to move soon, even though his total force had been reduced by casualties and the expiration of enlistments to around 80,000. Lincoln replied on May 14. The time to strike the enemy, he told Hooker, "has now passed away. . . . It does not now appear probable to me that you can gain anything by an early renewal of the attempt to cross the Rappahannock."

Far more chilling, though, was the president's closing comment: "I must tell you," he wrote, "that I have some painful intimations that some of your corps and division commanders are not giving you their entire confidence. This would be ruinous, if true. . . ." The news that some of his key officers were speaking against him did not come as a complete surprise, but to hear it from the commander in chief was especially galling.

Even as Robert E. Lee headed back to Fredericksburg with a blank check of limited term, his opposite number faced a public pillorying and a revolt in his command ranks. Perhaps most discomforting was President Lincoln's blunt question: "What next?" Joseph Hooker had to admit to himself that he had no good answer.

ONE

"I wish I could get at those people. . . ."

Following the Battle of Chancellorsville, the Union Army's seven infantry corps had returned to their winter encampments along the Rappahannock River's northern bank, near Fredericksburg. Their positions covered likely crossing points and protected the logistical arteries connecting them to supply sources via the Potomac River. Morale among many Federals was low. Private Theodore Garrish—whose Fifth Corps regiment, the 20th Maine, had seen action during the battle—deemed Hooker's performance at Chancellorsville a "fearful shock" to the army. Meanwhile, in the 7th Indiana, a First Corps regiment that had missed the combat, a lieutenant diagnosed the Army of the Potomac as being "in a comatose state." That opinion was seconded and elaborated on by Robert K. Beecham, an infantryman in the 2nd Wisconsin (First Corps), who declared, "The Chancellorsville campaign pretty thoroughly demonstrated the fact that as a general in the field at the head of an army, Gen. Joseph Hooker was no match for Gen. R. E. Lee."

Not everyone shared this pessimistic outlook, however. "The army is neither disorganized, discouraged, or dispirited," insisted a soldier in the 14th Connecticut (Second Corps). "As far as spirits are concerned, the army was never more jubilant; it thinks with Joe Hooker that 'it can take care of itself, move when it wishes to; fight when it sees fit; retreat when it deems it best.' " This determination was reflected in a letter sent by the officer commanding the 20th Maine to his six-year-old daughter: "There has been a big battle," explained Joshua Chamberlain, "and we had a great many men killed and wounded. We shall try it again soon, and see if we cannot make those Rebels behave better, and stop their wicked works in trying to spoil our Country, and making us all so unhappy."

A Pennsylvanian in the 102nd regiment (Sixth Corps) minced no words: "The talk about demoralization in this army is all false. The army is no more demoralized to-day than the day it first started out, although God knows it has had, through the blundering of inefficient commanders and other causes too numerous to mention, plenty of reason to be." A soldier in the Third Corps by the name of John Haley weighed the moment with the fatalistic outlook of a veteran: he was certain, he wrote, that the army was "again buoyant and ready to be led to new fields of conquest—or defeat."

A member of the 1st United States Sharpshooters marveled at the way the men put defeat out of their thoughts and "turned their minds and hands to the duties and occupations of the present." For Wilbur Fisk, a private in the 2nd Vermont (Sixth Corps), those duties included standing guard in a position so far to the rear that "the prospect of seeing an enemy was about equal to the prospect of taking Richmond." Oliver Norton, a Fifth Corps orderly, found time between assignments to enjoy the performance of a mockingbird that was housekeeping in a nearby apple tree. "He combines in one the song of every bird I ever heard and many I haven't," Norton enthused. "One minute he's a bobolink, the next a lark or a robin, and he's never tired of singing."

The mood was far less upbeat in the camps of the Eleventh Corps, situated along the railroad connecting the army to its supply base at Aquia Landing. The May 2 Confederate flank attack had fallen squarely on the poorly positioned Eleventh, whose commander had chosen to ignore the warning signs, leaving his men to their fate. They had fought better than might have been expected, but few outside the corps gave them much credit for that.

Nearly half of the soldiers in the Eleventh Corps hailed from Germany, a circumstance that made them handy scapegoats. Sergeant Benjamin Hirst, a member of the Second Corps, expressed a not-untypical opinion when he described to his wife how "the whole 11th Army Corps, gave way almost without firing a shot, the Panic stricken runing about in hundreds and thousands." Similar contempt was voiced by Lieutenant Frank Haskell, an otherwise perceptive Second Corps officer, who noted that the "Dutchmen . . . ran . . . before they had delivered a shot." "As for this last defeat they lay it all to the Dutch. 11th Army Corps," reported a Third Corps soldier. "They runn like sheep."

All of this contumely came as a rude surprise to the Eleventh Corps soldiers themselves, who had suffered about three-fourths of the Union losses on May 2 while delaying the enemy advance until nightfall ended the combat. One of the corps' brigade commanders was visited by a delegation of soldiers bearing copies of newspapers heaping scorn on the Eleventh. The men bluntly asked "if such be the reward they may expect for the sufferings they have endured and the bravery they have displayed." A few outside the corps' German community managed to see past the filters of prejudice. One such was Robert K. Beecham, who avowed, "The fault was not in the troops, but in the generalship that could not provide against such a surprise."

The Eleventh Corps was under the overall command of Major General Oliver Otis Howard. A deeply religious man who had lost his right arm in battle in 1862, Howard had been brought in to replace the extremely popular (but in military terms notably unsuccessful) Fritz Sigel just a few months before Chancellorsville. When Howard failed to acknowledge the indignation that was coursing through the ranks of his German regiments, and carefully dodged any personal blame for his own leadership failures, the mood of some under his command darkened. "It is only the miserable setup of our Corps because of General Howard that we had to retreat in such a shameful way," swore one soldier in the 26th Wisconsin. "In time the truth will come out," promised another in the same regiment. "It was all General Howard's fault. He is a Yankee, and that is why he wanted to have us slaughtered, because most of us are Germans. He better not come into the thick of battle a second time, then he won't escape."

One of the officers whom Howard counted among his friends was Major General John Fulton Reynolds, commanding the First Corps. Reynolds, Howard would later proclaim, "secured reverence for his serious character, respect for his ability, care for his uniform discipline, admiration for his fearlessness, and love for his unfailing generosity." Like Howard, Reynolds was a West Point graduate and a veteran of some of the toughest campaigns undertaken by the Army of the Potomac. Unlike several of his fellow corps commanders, Reynolds kept himself apart from the political intrigues that were an inevitable fact of life for an army posted so near the capital.

A professional soldier to the core, Reynolds had come to view almost all instruction from Washington as interference. He was firm in his belief, as he said, that "no one can conduct a campaign at a distance from the field or without being in the presence of operating armies." Such conviction made it all the more ironic, then, that John Reynolds should find himself away from the Fredericksburg camps in early June on a visit to the very seat of that interfering power, being sized up by President Lincoln as Joe Hooker's possible replacement.

In a later conversation with George Meade about this interview, Reynolds would indicate that it was wrong to think that Abraham Lincoln had been seeking to drop Hooker. According to Reynolds, Lincoln said "he was not disposed to throw away a gun because it missed fire once; that he would pick the lock and try again." Nevertheless, Reynolds was clearly invited to state his conditions for taking over the Army of the Potomac. Not long after he returned to Fredericksburg, one of his aides was told that the major general had been offered the command and had "refused it on the ground that there was too much interference from Washington."

Although he would later claim to have had no specific knowledge of these conversations, Hooker was too astute a political creature to have missed the signs. Brigadier General John Gibbon, who led a division in the Second Corps, believed that Hooker had entered the Chancellorsville campaign "possessed of the very decided confidence of both the officers and men of his army" but emerged with "a very decided loss of this confidence." For his part, Gibbon began the month of June "with some apprehension [as] to the renewal of hostilities."

Hooker, himself apprehensive about Lee's next moves, turned all his energies toward divining them. From the commander of Union forces on the lower Virginia peninsula came word on June 2 that sizable bodies of Rebel troops were moving toward Fredericksburg, "and that the idea prevails over the lines that an invasion of Maryland and Pennsylvania is soon to be made." At the same time, Hooker's own chief of cavalry was certain that Lee's army "has been weakened by troops sent west and south." Fortunately for Hooker, one of his first reorganizational steps upon taking over the Army of the Potomac had been to improve both the gathering and the assessment of military intelligence.

To this end, Hooker had established the Bureau of Military Information, headed by Colonel George H. Sharpe, a well-schooled New York lawyer and combat veteran who was fluent in several languages. Prior to the creation of the bureau, intelligence regarding the enemy had come to headquarters through dozens of different channels, and there had been no systematic means for sorting the useful from the useless. An important part of the brief for Sharpe and his staff was to collate these various sources, compare the information they provided, and weigh the veracity of interrogation subjects, all the while looking for patterns that might reveal enemy intentions. The colonel also directed a small group of "scouts" who operated in hostile territory. Like any truly new idea, Sharpe's role was not well understood by many army officers, some of whom refused to cooperate with him or his agents.

Sharpe's men were at present focusing on several assignments. They were trying to pin down the location of two of Lee's divisions (Hood's and Pickett's) that had been noticeably absent at Chancellorsville and were now believed to be rejoining the Army of Northern Virginia. At the same time, they were working to compile a fresh table of organization for Lee's army. Because units tended to operate in connection with their parent organizations—regiments with their brigades, brigades with their divisions, divisions with their corps—a precise knowledge of the Army of Northern Virginia's "family tree" enabled Union officers in the field to deduce the presence of a corps through the affiliation of prisoners taken from just a few regiments. Immediately prior to Chancellorsville, Sharpe and his staff had developed just such a chart, which had proved amazingly accurate. But now it was apparent that Lee's army was undergoing major changes, so everyone at the bureau was scrambling to construct a revised Confederate organizational chart.

Sharpe had only just delivered his first strategic summary since Chancellorsville. Among its key points was a seemingly trivial tidbit offered by a Confederate deserter, who reported that Lee's men had been warned to prepare for a "campaign of long marches & hard fighting." Another task that Sharpe and his unit had yet to complete was drawing up an estimate of enemy strength. That pending status suited Joe Hooker just fine, since for the moment he preferred that there be no data contradictory to the numbers he was forwarding to Washington.

This was part of a dangerous game that Hooker was playing with his commander in chief and, more especially, with the president's chief military adviser, Major General Henry W. Halleck. Hooker and Halleck were antagonists, neither liking nor respecting the other. Their mutual disdain predated the war, and the exigencies of the conflict had done little to mute them. On first taking command of the Army of the Potomac,

Hooker had insisted on reporting directly to Lincoln, bypassing Halleck in the chain of command. Hooker was convinced that Halleck so favored operations in the Western theater (where his career had been made) that neither the Army of the Potomac "nor its commander expected justice at his hands." Although the dispute never erupted into a public squabble, men in the ranks sensed the unhealthy tensions between the two leaders. The chaplain of a First Corps regiment accepted as fact the "bad blood between Hooker and General Halleck," while a German baron serving as an aide in the Eleventh Corps was told that Halleck "worked against" Hooker.

Halleck was now in a perfect position to impede what Hooker felt was the absolutely necessary reinforcement of his command. To bolster his case for more troops, and to offset what he saw as Halleck's certain opposition, Hooker accepted without question estimates that made the Army of Northern Virginia larger than the Army of the Potomac. He did so in the personal belief, as he told his chief of staff, that "the rebellion rested upon that army, and when it was destroyed the end was at hand."

The first day of June 1863 found Private Leander Huckaby of the 11th Mississippi on picket duty below Fredericksburg. His regiment was posted along the river's southern bank, or what the young soldier referred to as the "Dixie side of the rappahannock." Experience had taught the citizen-soldier how to gauge terrain, so he looked with plea-sure on the broad, open river bottom that stretched before him. There was no place for the enemy to hide, Huckaby observed, and should the Yankees attempt to advance, he knew that the Confederate artillery would "shel them as they come across to death." For the moment, though, it was live and let live. Continuing his improvisational spelling, Huckaby noted, "i can get up on our brest works an see the enemy on there brest works any time in the day."

It would become common for postwar Southern writers to proclaim that Lee's army was nearly bursting with confidence following Chancel-lorsville, and indeed, there were strong optimistic currents in the ranks. Major Charles Marshall reflected the view from Lee's headquarters when, comparing the army that had marched into Maryland in 1862 with the one gathered around Fredericksburg in 1863, he judged the latter "bet-ter disciplined and far more efficient." Private David E. Johnston of George Pickett's division was certain that the Army of Northern Virginia was then "composed of the best fighting material that General Lee ever led to battle." A South Carolina surgeon fully expected that Lee's men would henceforth "fight better than they have ever done, if such a thing is possible."

Yet there were other, more sober perspectives as well. "I do not think it will be long before we will have another row here," brooded a lieutenant in the 34th North Carolina. "I see no prospect for peace." It was a view shared by one of Lee's most promising young officers, Colonel Henry King Burgwyn Jr., who commanded the 26th North Carolina. "God alone knows how tired I am of this war," he wrote to his mother, "& He alone knows when it will end." Brigadier General William Dorsey Pender, the very capable commander of one of Lee's brigades (who would soon be raised to divisional command), had "not much doubt but that a fight is on hand." Unlike many of his colleagues, who dismissed the combat qualities of the Yankee army, Pender worried that when they met again, the enemy would "fight as well even as they did at Chancellorsville, which was bad enough."

Since his return from Richmond, Robert E. Lee had been laboring with little rest to implement a plan he had been considering for some while, which called for his army to be reorganized from two infantry corps into three. As he had explained to Jefferson Davis, the old setup, in which each corps numbered about 30,000 muskets, gave the corps commanders "more than one man can properly handle & keep under his eye in battle." Under Lee's new scheme, as recalled by his aide Major Walter Taylor, each of the "corps embraced three divisions; one of the divisions of the Second Corps and one of the Third had five brigades; all the others had four brigades. The artillery was also reorganized. To each corps there were attached two or three battalions of four batteries each, under the command of a chief of artillery for that corps; these three divisions and the reserve artillery were under the command of the chief of artillery of the army." Lee's cavalry corps, though not reorganized to any significant degree, was meanwhile increased in size with the addition of six regiments and a battalion.

Lee met with his top leadership on June 1. The trio he had selected to head his restructured infantry corps would be vital to the success of his forthcoming campaign. When it came to his personal command style, Lee took a decentralized approach: his role, as he saw it, was to prescribe the overall shape, broad direction, and desired objectives of an operation, which his subordinates would then implement as the situation allowed.

Rather than issue direct orders, Lee preferred to suggest the most reasonable course of action, trusting that his generals would share his vision. Lee and the late Stonewall Jackson had been a well-matched pair; it remained to be seen if the new team would work together as well.

Lee's anchor in the reorganized army was Lieutenant General James Longstreet. Under the previous system, he and Jackson had each commanded half of Lee's force, and Longstreet retained most of his old units in the newly shaped First Corps. Born in South Carolina and raised in Georgia, the forty-two-year-old officer had initially favored tolerating a stalemate in the East while reinforcements were sent west. A lengthy discussion with Lee, however, had changed his mind. Even as Lee traveled to Richmond for his showdown with Davis and Seddon, Longstreet was advising an influential Confederate senator that "we can spare nothing from this army to re-enforce in the West." Longstreet tried to persuade Lee that the upcoming campaign ought to be essentially defensive in nature. It would be unwise to wage offensive operations, he thought, because "our losses were so heavy when we attacked that our Army must soon be depleted to such an extent that we should not be able to hold a force in the field sufficient to meet our adversary." He argued that instead, "we should work so as to force the enemy to attack us, in such good position as we might find in his own country . . . which might assure us of a grand triumph." Longstreet would later summarize his conception of the campaign as "one of offensive strategy, but defensive tactics." Lee listened to Longstreet's arguments but made no firm commitment either way—though Longstreet believed otherwise.

The Army of Northern Virginia's revamped Second Corps was basically Jackson's old command. To lead it, Lee tapped Virginian Richard Stoddert Ewell, a forty-six-year-old professional officer who had served with distinction under Jackson, and had in August 1862 suffered a wound that had cost him his left leg in fighting near Manassas. An artilleryman recalled Ewell as being "a queer character, very eccentric, but upright, brave and devoted. He had no high talent but did all that a brave man of moderate capacity could." Lee himself publicly described his Second Corps commander as an "honest, brave soldier, who had always done his duty well." Privately, though, he worried about Ewell's state of mind, specifically his periods of "quick alternations from elation to despondency." Lee made it a point to speak "long and earnestly" with Ewell about the great responsibilities he was accepting. Partly because Ewell's prewar U.S. Army service had included a posting to southern Pennsylvania, Lee decided that Jackson's old corps would lead the way in the upcoming operation.

The new Third Corps was constructed of elements drawn from the First and Second, along with other units that had recently been added to the Army of Northern Virginia. Ambrose Powell Hill, the thirty-seven-year-old Virginian picked to command the corps, had a reputation as a hard fighter, both on and off the battlefield. He had locked horns more than once with Stonewall Jackson; for a short while a malicious rumor even circulated that Jackson had used some of his last words to blackball Hill as his successor. In Lee's opinion, however, A. P. Hill was simply "the best soldier of his grade with me."

The restructuring of the Army of Northern Virginia from two corps into three was just part of the transformation that Lee completed in record time. Out of the nine infantry divisions in the new scheme, three were led by men untried at that level, and out of the thirty-seven brigades within the nine divisions, thirteen were entrusted to officers with no previous command experience. At any other juncture, such wholesale changes would have required an extended shakedown period before the army was committed to a major campaign. But Lee could not wait. The situation at Vicksburg had continued to deteriorate, and the possibility that Jefferson Davis might revisit his decision not to send reinforcements to the West loomed larger with each passing day.

Caught between events that he could not control and the struggle to rebuild his army, Lee felt stymied, and his diplomacy and tact began to wear thin. Two days before he met with his corps commanders, he fired off a pair of petulant notes to Richmond. To Jefferson Davis, he complained that Major General Daniel Harvey Hill had refused his request to release troops to him from those assigned to defend North Carolina. This action, Lee claimed, had so compromised his buildup that should the Federal army again come at him, there "may be nothing left for me to do but fall back [toward Richmond]." To Secretary of War Seddon, Lee griped that some of the troop transfers that D. H. Hill had approved were nothing more than administrative smoke screens. An experienced brigade in Pickett's Division had been replaced by a makeshift one that had in turn been dispersed back to its original command, leaving Pickett with three brigades instead of four.* "I . . . dislike to part with officers & men

---

*A fifth brigade assigned to Pickett had been detached for the defense of Richmond.

who have been tried in battle and seasoned to the hardships of the campaign in exchange for wholly untried troops," Lee grumbled.

He shared none of these frustrations with his corps commanders. Nor did he likely give them any specific orders beyond designating routes for the first stage of the coming movement. Of the campaign's overall shape, Longstreet recollected it thus: "The enemy would be on our right flank while we were moving north. Ewell's corps was to move in advance to Culpeper Court House, mine to follow, and the cavalry was to move along on our right flank to the east of us. Thus by threatening his rear we could draw Hooker from his position . . . opposite Fredericksburg." The bulk of Lee's army would enter the Shenandoah Valley, taking full advantage of the screen provided on its right flank by the rugged Blue Ridge Mountains. In a communication sent to Richmond on June 2, Lee maintained the impression that he had not yet made up his mind whether or not to advance. Wrote Lee, "If I am able to move, I propose to do so cautiously, watching the result, and not to get beyond recall until I find it safe."

At the less rarefied levels of the Army of Northern Virginia, life went on. John O. Casler was a private in the 33rd Virginia (Ewell's Corps) whose easygoing view of army discipline had landed him on a work detail. This punishment turned out just fine on the evening of June 1, when Casler and twenty others were sent to draw rations. While standing in the inevitable line, Casler and a buddy spotted a large and unguarded pile of hams. The two spread the word, and by the time the detail returned to camp, they had their own rations plus nine unauthorized hams. "We never let an opportunity pass to get extra rations," Casler would later recall, "no matter if we had to steal them."

For Robert T. Douglass, a private in the 47th Virginia (Hill's Corps), the first days of June were pleasant ones; in his diary he recorded picking strawberries with a friend, playing baseball, and fishing in the river. An artilleryman whose battery was attached to the First Corps remembered how on these evenings "we listened to the music of [the Yankee] . . . bands, [and] at night could see the glow of their campfires for miles around."

Near Fredericksburg, the encampments occupied by McLaws' Division of Longstreet's Corps were astir on June 3 with the arrival of orders putting the men in motion to Culpeper. Lee would wait no longer. Colonel E. P. Alexander, a gifted young artillery commander, would never forget "the hurried preparations, the parting with my wife & little daughter." Alexander lingered as the column shuffled forward, "looking back as long as even the tops of the locust trees & oaks about the house [where the family had wintered together] could be seen."

As McLaws's men marched, those in Ewell's Corps were readying themselves to follow the next day. Among them was a Maryland staff officer named Randolph McKim. Before the war, his Baltimore family had befriended Lee, then a U.S. Army officer assigned to that post. That prior acquaintance had led to a recent dinner invitation from the army commander, which the young officer had happily accepted. Afterward they had taken a walk near the Rappahannock River. McKim noted the hungry look in Lee's eyes as he gazed at the enemy's campfires and then said quietly, "I wish I could get at those people over there."

TWO

"... we were taking a lot of chances"

Once again Robert E. Lee was gambling on what he assumed his opponent would or would not do. The entire Army of the Potomac was encamped along the northern bank of the Rappahannock, opposite Fredericksburg. Facing it along the heights west and south of the town were two full infantry corps from Lee's army, along with one division from his third corps. Following his orders, that lone division marched off toward Culpeper on June 3. On the night of June 4, Lee also began to move almost all of Ewell's Corps to that same point, leaving only A. P. Hill's men—perhaps 20,000 in all—to confront Hooker's 80,000.

If Lee's plan was to work, the Yankee observers had to be fooled. Most bothersome in this regard were the two balloons that soared up into the sky nearly every day, bearing officers with powerful telescopes who were intent on piercing the screen of secrecy that Lee had thrown over the operation. The best Lee's men could do was to shoot at the balloons, which rarely ventured within easy range but whose operators nonetheless tended to be so skittish that even a wide miss might result in a rapid descent. The corps commanders also relied on other tricks to help cover the troops' movement. George W. Nichols, a Georgia soldier in Ewell's Corps, remembered setting out at midnight: "We marched all night and camped just before day in very thick woods," he wrote. "We were not permitted to have any fire. Ewell did this to keep Hooker's balloon spies from seeing us moving."

The night tramp not only hid Lee's movements from enemy spotters but also kept his own men confused. The diary of a North Carolina soldier in Ramseur's Brigade (Rodes' Division, Ewell's Corps) reads: "June 4 broke camp near Gracie's church for God knows where." Another Tarheel reported that "various were the conjectures among the men as to our probable destination."

While still holding his cards close to his vest, Lee was providing Richmond with broad hints. From his headquarters at Fredericksburg, he sent a telegram to the War Department requesting that all convalescents and other soldiers returning from leave "be forwarded to Culpeper Court House instead of this place."

"The rascals are up to something," noted a staff officer in Reynolds' First Corps on June 4. Even though most of Ewell's men were waiting until dark, the passage of McLaws' Division on June 3 had not gone unnoticed. "Balloon reports from Banks' Ford two camps disappeared and several batteries in motion," declared a headquarters circular issued at

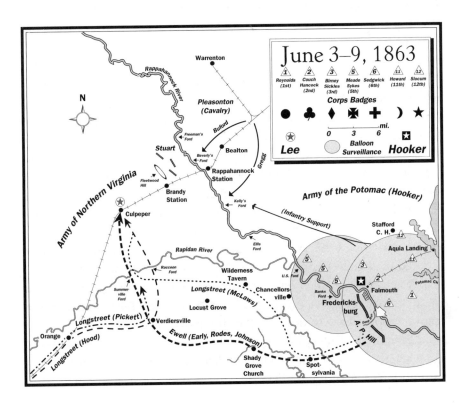

10:00 A.M. Another sighting recorded a "line of dust" just west of Fredericksburg and "20 wagons moving northerly." Just in case, Hooker's men were ordered to take down their tents and be ready to march. When the day brought no further signs of enemy activity, the soldiers, in the words of one Michigan man, "were directed to pitch tents and quiet ourselves down into the routine we have pursued for the past month."

Hooker's intelligence chief, George Sharpe, had one of his better agents posted to the cavalry headquarters of Brigadier General John Buford, then located near Warrenton Junction, some thirty miles north of Fredericksburg. "There is a considerable movement of the enemy," Sharpe advised his agent on June 4. "Their camps are disappearing at some points. We shall rely on you to tell us whether they go your way or towards the [Shenandoah] Valley. You must be very active in the employment of everybody and everything."

At ten o'clock in the morning on June 5, Robert E. Lee's cavalry commander indulged himself in the pomp and pageantry of war by having his mounted command pass in review. Major General Jeb Stuart understood how the romantic currents of the age could help to mute some of the harsh realities of the soldier's life. A formal review presented just such an opportunity, and besides, he wanted to take full advantage of the fact that, thanks to Lee's efforts, the cavalry arm was larger than it had ever been before.

The review was held in a big open field near a stop on the Orange and Alexandria Railroad known as Brandy Station. "Behind the reviewing stand there was an audience of admiring ladies and gentlemen from all over the countryside," a young North Carolina cavalryman recalled with forgivable pride. "They saw a magnificent sight: well-groomed horses mounted by the finest riders to be found on earth. Eight thousand cavalry . . . passed in review first at a walk and then at a thundering gallop. The massed horse artillery fired salutes." A trooper in a Virginia regiment declared the whole affair "one of the grandest sights I had ever beheld." Only when the horsemen returned to their camps did they learn that the guest of honor, Robert E. Lee, had not been able to make it, meaning that they would have to do the whole thing over again.

Closing on Culpeper were McLaws' and Hood's divisions of Longstreet's Corps as well as all three divisions of Ewell's Corps. It was a hard go for some of the artillery units, whose forage-starved horses were barely up to the task. A cannoneer in the much-lauded Washington Artillery of New Orleans explained in his diary that because they had brought along only five pounds of corn for each of the horses, he and his comrades were compelled to "stop early to let them graze." Major General Jubal Early's division had marched just beyond Spotsylvania Court House on June 4, and the next day the cantankerous Virginian expected his men to do a lot better. It was not to be, however. At some point in the afternoon, as Early would later recount, "during the march, I received an order to halt and wait for further orders, as the enemy had crossed a force [over the Rappahannock River] at Fredericksburg in front of [A. P.] Hill." Similar messages went to Johnson's and Rodes' divisions, stopping all of Ewell's Corps in its tracks.

Robert E. Lee had remained at Fredericksburg even as the last of Ewell's men (belonging to Major General Edward Johnson's division) marched off. Early on Friday, June 5, Lee provided A. P. Hill, whose Third Corps alone faced Hooker's entire army, with instructions: Hill was to do everything possible "to deceive the enemy, and keep him in ignorance of any change in the disposition of the army." Should Lee's bluff fail, and Hill be forced away from Fredericksburg's heights, he was to fall back south to the North Anna River, where he would find Pickett's Division.

Lee may have begun to have doubts around midday, when reports arrived that the enemy was massing a force just south of Fredericksburg, at a narrow point on the river. Shortly after 5:00 P.M., the hitherto quiet Union army was suddenly all sharp edges and thunder. Lee later described the action: "After driving back our sharpshooters [posted at the river's edge], under a furious cannonade from their batteries, by a force of skirmishers, they crossed a small body of troops and occupied the [southern] bank of the river."

Many of the Yankee soldiers camped near Fredericksburg were itching to move on. A member of the 4th Ohio (Second Corps) noted on June 5 that "our camp was becoming bare and dusty, and the leaves of the pine boughs dropping, became a nuisance, as they mixed too freely with rations and clothing; camp-life became once more intolerably monotonous." Regiments, brigades, and divisions were called out several times and lined up to march, only to be told to stand down hours later. Sergeant Benjamin Hirst of the 14th Connecticut (Second Corps) complained about such false starts in a letter written this Friday. He also mentioned the mosquitoes, and how much he hated waking up at night to "find them sucking away."

Joseph Hooker was having his own problems. Shortly before noon he composed a telegram to President Lincoln outlining his dilemma. He had noted the changes in the enemy's camps but was not sure what they meant. He reminded Lincoln of his standing instructions to shield Washington at all times, and wondered how loosely he might interpret this directive. If the enemy was moving northward and leaving only a small rear guard at Fredericksburg, Hooker believed he had an obligation to "pitch into" that force, even if that meant that the head of Lee's column might threaten Washington without the Army of the Potomac to block it. Hooker respectfully asked for Lincoln's opinion on the matter.

The president's answer crackled back four and a half hours later. Given the Union army's recent lack of success in attacking Fredericksburg's heights, Lincoln was not keen on Hooker's attempting that objective a second time. Hoping to make his point with one of his colorful analogies, Lincoln cautioned Hooker against becoming "like an ox jumped half over a fence and liable to be torn by dogs front and rear, without a fair chance to force one way or kick the other." Then came words that were bitter ashes to Hooker: Lincoln added that he had passed his memo on to Henry Halleck for his comments.

The hated Halleck finished writing his own reply to Hooker forty minutes after the president. Reiterating that Washington's defense depended upon the supporting presence of the Army of the Potomac, the Union general in chief suggested (it was not Halleck's style to state things with specificity) that it would "seem perilous to permit Lee's main force to move upon the Potomac [River] while your army is attacking an intrenched position on the other side of the Rappahannock."

Even as these messages were being exchanged, Hooker was undertaking a Rappahannock crossing to determine the enemy's disposition. Orders issued early this morning alerted Federal engineers, infantry, and artillery to be ready to move. The engineers set out first, stopping when they reached a somewhat sheltered bend in the river near a point they knew as Franklin's Crossing. There they waited in the hot sun while Rebel pickets on the opposite bank jeered them. At around 4:00 P.M., the leading elements of Brigadier General Albion P. Howe's Second Division of Sedgwick's Sixth Corps arrived on the scene, and four artillery batteries (twenty-four guns) unlimbered for action. Shortly after 5:00 P.M., the cannon opened fire.

The Federal engineers tried to push a pontoon bridge across using preset sections, but Rebel sharpshooters drove them back. Under a heavy covering fire from the artillery, a storming party of Vermont and New Jersey troops paddled in pontoon boats to the opposite bank. A New York soldier standing in support watched in amazement as "the whole plain, on the further side, . . . [became] a sheet of flame from the bursting shells, and huge clouds of dust, plowed up by the shrieking missiles, rose so as to obscure [the river bluff]." The Federals landed and swept over the rifle pits dug along the river's edge. Then, reinforced, they charged up the height to overrun a stronger series of Confederate works located there. By dusk, a shallow perimeter had been established, with pickets pushed out almost a mile from the river. At very little cost, Joe Hooker had grabbed a jumping-off point on the southern side of the Rappahannock River for whatever purpose he had in mind.

Robert E. Lee spent all of June 6 observing the troops that Hooker had landed on the southern bank. If the Union commander became uncharacteristically aggressive, Lee would have to reevaluate all his plans. But Lee's intuition was right on the mark. He soon reported to Richmond, "After watching the enemy's operations Saturday, and being unable to discover more troops [across the Rappahannock] than could be attended to by [A. P.] Hill, and no advance having been made by them, I sent for word to Gen[era]l Ewell to resume his march, and left Fredericksburg myself in the evening."

Ewell, anxious to prove himself in his new position, had his men moving quickly. The soldiers slogged through a heavy thundershower that left them, in the words of one, "wet and very cold." Most marched for six hours, camping at around 10:00 P.M. Still, spirits were high, and when Ewell's men spotted him watching them cross the Rapidan River on June 7, they "began to cheer him as had been their habit with Gen. Jackson," observed a Second Corps staff officer. It was a good omen.

Lee reached Culpeper "early on Sunday morning, June 7." Hood's and McLaws' divisions of Longstreet's Corps were on hand to greet Ewell's men, who would continue to arrive throughout the day. The status report that Lee sent to Richmond this day was disingenuous, to say the least. In it he implied that the movement of so many Confederate troops to Culpeper had been prompted by the need to match a similar Federal redeployment, rather than to prepare for a raid into Maryland and Pennsylvania. He also urged that the repositioning of troops defending Richmond be completed so that Pickett's Division, now holding north of the capital at Hanover Junction, could fill out Longstreet's Corps. He closed by renewing his argument that troops from Beauregard's coastal command should either "be sent to re-enforce Johnston in the west, or be ordered to re-enforce this army." Next, in the same breath, he sent orders directing one detached cavalry brigade (then in southwestern Virginia) to be ready to link up with his vanguard when it entered the Shenandoah Valley, and instructing a second detached mounted brigade to undertake a diversionary raid into northwestern Virginia.

Reports from Fredericksburg indicated that Hooker's bridgehead across the Rappahannock remained in place. For a while on June 6, Lee had contemplated returning the favor by dispatching Hood's Division to force a river crossing below Culpeper at Ellis Ford, but he had decided against the move shortly after midnight. Artilleryman E. P. Alexander had helped to scout this operation with John B. Hood. "I remember on this trip talking a great deal with Hood about our chances in an invasion of the enemy's territory," Alexander would recollect, "& the impression I gathered of Hood's view was that we were taking a lot of chances."

On June 8, Jeb Stuart restaged his grand review, this time with Lee present. During his ride from Culpeper to the reviewing field, Lee passed a column of Longstreet's troops that included the 17th Mississippi. The general was roughly dressed for travel and, surrounded by his mounted detail, looked for all the world like a man under arrest. The spectacle caused one Mississippian to call out, "Boys, where did you get that bushwhacker? . . . He looks like a good old man. . . . Turn him loose." According to Sergeant C. C. Cummings, Lee beamed when he heard the remark. "His bright smile," Cummings would write in 1915, "haunts me still."

Conscious of the need to preserve horseflesh and gunpowder for the upcoming operation, Lee forbade any mock charges or massed cannon firing. Nonetheless, Stuart managed to put on a good show. An officer on Longstreet's staff swore it was a "sight . . . not soon to be forgotten." Lee concurred, describing the review as "a splendid sight" and noting that "Stuart was all in his glory."

Lee returned to his headquarters already thinking about his next move. In a letter written earlier that day to Secretary of War Seddon, he had urged that "every exertion [be] made to obtain some material advantage in this campaign." The next steps were fixed: Ewell would march north into the Shenandoah Valley, with Longstreet following after Pickett arrived; Stuart's horsemen would screen the eastern side of the movement. It was all timed to get under way on June 9.

By June 6, George Sharpe and his staff at the Bureau of Military Information had worked up revised organizational tables for Lee's army. Among those briefed on the changes was Hooker's provost marshal, whose notes indicated that "Longstreet's & Jackson's Old Corps are divided into 3, Ewell taking Jackson's and A. P. Hill having added to his Division to make up a . . . Corps." Ironically, this intelligence coup would help to mislead Hooker into accepting the testimony of prisoners captured by Sedgwick's men, who provided a ready explanation for the disappearance of the bivouacs. According to Hooker's interrogation summary, "The changes remarked in the camps proceeded from the reorganization of their army, and the assignment of them to new camps."

In ordering the probe across the Rappahannock, Hooker had authorized John Sedgwick to throw his entire "corps over the river, if necessary," but the cautious Sixth Corps commander was having none of that. He limited the number of men holding the bridgehead to about a division's worth, advising Hooker that any further effort would ignite "a general fight." New information that had come in was demanding Hooker's complete attention, so he allowed Sedgwick to maintain what he held. To the Sixth Corps infantrymen posted on the southern bank, the sudden inactivity made no sense. "If we were going to attack, why wait?" wondered a Vermont soldier. "If not, what are we going to do?"

The new intelligence that Hooker was pondering concerned the concentration of Confederate cavalry near Culpeper. The usually perceptive George Sharpe badly misread the situation this time. He was convinced, as he told Hooker on June 7, that Stuart was preparing for a big cavalry raid—"the most important expedition ever attempted in this country." At the same time, Sharpe predicted that Lee's infantry (most of which he believed to be still near Fredericksburg) would soon "fall back upon Richmond and thence reinforce their armies in the west." Forgotten in the processing of all the new data was Sharpe's own previous conclusion that a northward movement of Lee's army was in the offing. Hooker sent Sharpe's assessment to Washington with a covering note suggesting that he was planning a preemptive "bust . . . up" of Stuart's concentration.

On June 7, Hooker sent detailed instructions to his cavalry commander, Major General Alfred Pleasonton. Using all his mounted units, Pleasonton was to "cross the Rappahannock at Beverly and Kelly's Fords, and march directly on Culpeper." His objective was "to disperse and destroy the rebel force assembled in the vicinity of Culpeper." To ensure that all mounted units could participate, Hooker dispatched a picked force of infantry to protect the fords behind the cavalry. Pleasonton was primed for action: "My people are all ready to pitch in," he assured Hooker.

Throughout the morning of June 8, as Lee watched Stuart's cavalry pass in review, the Yankee horsemen made ready for battle. At 2:00 P.M., the mounted columns were formed and moved up close to their assigned crossing points. The hard-marching infantry arrived as scheduled. Everything was set.

It was an uncomfortable night for the Union soldiers. No fires were allowed, so the men ate their rations cold and tried to sleep on the hard ground. Whispered orders brought the riders to horse at 2:00 A.M., June 9. By 4:00 A.M., the lead regiments were at the fords, ready to go.

Robert E. Lee may have had his own plans for June 9, but Joseph Hooker's would supersede them.

Everybody was surprised at Brandy Station, though for different reasons: Stuart because he had never imagined that the Yankee cavalry would attack, and Pleasonton because Stuart was not where he was supposed to be. The Union plan called for two columns to cross the Rappahannock, unite at Brandy Station, and then attack the Rebel cavalry camps, which were thought to be near Culpeper. But Stuart was actually bivouacked around Brandy Station, so the Federal columns hit enemy strength immediately upon crossing the river, prompting Pleasonton to notify Hooker that their plans had been compromised. Nevertheless, the Union troopers did have the advantage of striking first.

Just after dawn, Pleasonton's northern column, an augmented division under John Buford, rolled over a company of Virginia cavalry posted at Beverly's Ford before drawing up near St. James Church, where a hastily cobbled together defensive line, spiked with artillery and bolstered by several costly counterattacks, brought the advance to a halt. Pleasonton's two-division southern column, using Kelly's Ford, delayed crossing until nearly 9:00 A.M. because the leading unit was late. Once across, the Federals, commanded by Brigadier General David McMurtrie Gregg, separated, with one portion pushing due west to Stevensburg while the other took a road leading north to Brandy Station.

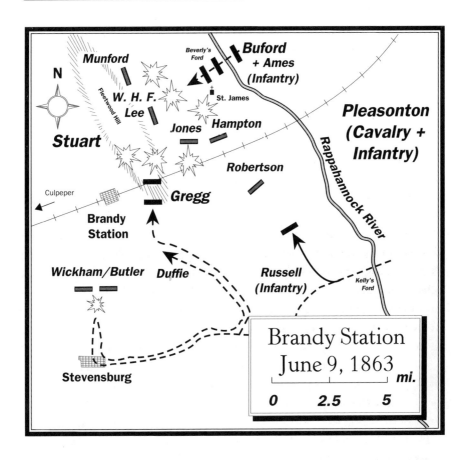

Brandy Station
June 9, 1863
0 2.5 5 mi.

As soon as he got over his initial surprise, Jeb Stuart was cool enough. He sent his wagons back to Culpeper, ordered some units to Kelly's Ford, and then rode to St. James Church with reinforcements. What Stuart could not have anticipated was that the troopers he had sent to Kelly's Ford would, by taking the direct road, miss the Federal column moving in the opposite direction on a secondary lane. Lee's cavalry chief got his next jolt when frantic couriers arrived around noon with word that the Yankee riders were well in his rear and closing on Brandy Station.

Stuart promptly released regiments from the St. James front, sending them off to the threatened point. The two sides met at Fleetwood Hill, where, for the next few hours, mounted charge was met by mounted charge as men on horseback flailed, stabbed, slashed, and shot at one another. The broad slope of Fleetwood Hill presented a churning panorama of small units engaged in clanging combat while around them terrified, riderless horses reared and galloped in every direction. The portion of Gregg's force that had marched west to Stevensburg was bluffed into retreating by a smaller enemy party and then countermarched to add its strength to the efforts at Fleetwood.

Stuart's northern flank began to collapse at about 3:30 P.M. as the alert Buford, sensing that his enemy was weakening, increased the pressure and began to make gains. But even as his men approached victory on the northern slope of Fleetwood Hill, Buford received orders from Pleasonton to break off the action. The Federal cavalry commander was satisfied that he had carried out his mission. By 9:00 P.M., the last bluecoat soldier capable of doing so had retired to the opposite bank of the Rappahannock.

Stuart had managed matters fairly well. He had been surprised but had regained sufficient poise effectively to handle each crisis in turn. Even though thousands of Rebel infantrymen had been positioned just a few miles west of the fighting, none had been brought into action. Lee had moved some units to within easy supporting distance, but in the end Stuart had handled the affair using solely his own resources. The best guess on his casualties was about 523 killed, wounded, missing, or captured.

In a terse summary of the day's events that was telegraphed to Richmond, Lee omitted any mention of his preparations to move north, or of the one-day delay imposed by Pleasonton's incursion. Instead, he reported that prisoners from two Union infantry corps had been captured in the fighting, and that there were unconfirmed indications of two more corps nearby. Once again, the implication was that his movements had been undertaken more to counter these Federal deployments than to pursue any initiative of his own. But few in Richmond were buying what Lee was selling. War Department clerk Jones, writing on June 9 and knowing only of the river crossing at Fredericksburg, observed that "Lee is 'marching on,' northward, utterly regardless of the demonstration of Hooker."

Pleasonton, the Union cavalry commander, would later recount his version of the Brandy Station engagement with the full benefit of hindsight. His sole object had been reconnaissance, he would insist, so his failure to break up the Rebel concentration was in fact no failure at all. Pleasonton would also claim to have captured documents disclosing Lee's intention to invade the North. This evidence existed only in Pleasonton's mind, however, for an examination made long afterward found nothing in this material to substantiate his statement. One partial bit of intelligence did come from David Gregg, who spotted Southern railroad cars suitable for carrying infantry. Union losses in all categories were tallied at 866.

Back at Fredericksburg, Hooker maintained Sedgwick's position on the southern side of the river. While the Sixth Corps men exchanged sniper fire with the Confederates who were hemming them in, Hooker finished his Brandy Station summary. In a report sent directly to President Lincoln, he predicted that the Rebel cavalry "raid" would be delayed at least a "few days." He remained convinced that Ewell's and Hill's troops faced him at Fredericksburg, though he was now willing to concede that another infantry corps was likely stretched out between Gordonsville and Culpeper. He thought he might be able to use the Sixth Corps bridgehead to "throw a sufficient force over the river to compel the enemy to abandon his present position," and from there threaten Richmond. Hooker wondered if such a course would be within the ground rules imposed on him by Washington.

Lee, meanwhile, was wasting no time. The day after Brandy Station, the lead elements of Ewell's Corps left Culpeper, heading north.

THREE

"Lee's army . . . is your true objective"

Lee's buildup near Culpeper had not gone unnoticed by Northern civilian authorities. Pennsylvania's governor, Andrew W. Curtin, pressed the War Department for action. On June 10, having decided that a single command embracing the entire southern portion of Curtin's state was too unwieldy, Washington split the region into two smaller military districts: the Department of the Monongahela for the western half (including Pittsburgh) and the Department of the Susquehanna for the eastern side. Major General Darius N. Couch, a Pennsylvanian then unhappily commanding the Army of the Potomac's Second Corps (he was no friend of Hooker's), was tapped for the eastern department and left at once. Responsibility for the capable Second Corps passed to Major General Winfield Scott Hancock, an aggressive, popular officer.

On June 12, Curtin alerted Pennsylvanians that "a large rebel force" was poised to raid the state. In measured tones, Curtin urged his citizens to fill the ranks of the militia units then being organized for the "defense of our own homes, firesides, and property." Few of his constituents took the threat seriously. That complacency, coupled with enlistment terms that many found unappealing, resulted in a response that was, in the words of one resident, "not . . . as general and prompt as desired."

In Washington, Lincoln's response to Hooker's telegram seeking permission to march on the Rebel capital was lukewarm at best. In a coded message sent on June 10, Lincoln advised Hooker that "Lee's army, and not Richmond, is your true objective." The following day, Lincoln showed Hooker's dispatch to Henry Halleck, who promptly telegraphed the Army of the Potomac commander seconding everything the president had said. In reply, Hooker again claimed that he was outnumbered. On June 12, he informed Halleck that the enemy at Fredericksburg "has been greatly reinforced." Two days later he estimated Lee's infantry strength at about 100,000.

Lincoln planned to meet with Hooker late on June 13, ostensibly to witness testing of a new incendiary shell. The tug carrying the president left Washington at 1:00 P.M. that day and had reached Alexandria, Vir-

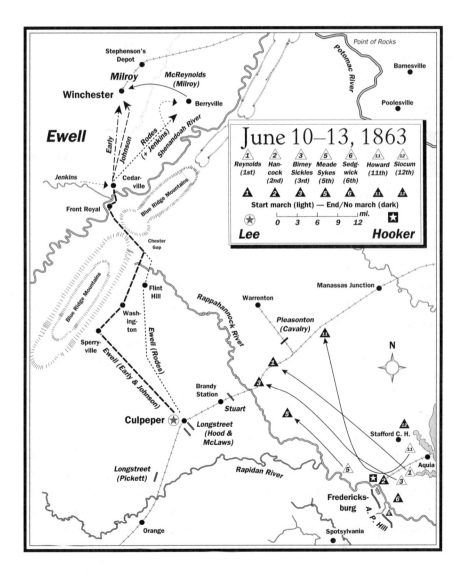

ginia, when a frantic message from shore halted the journey: Joe Hooker was putting his army in motion.

Except for the Sixth Corps' scrap near Franklin's Crossing, June 10 was another routine day. An Eleventh Corps officer charted the pattern in his Wednesday journal entry: 5:00 A.M. up and dressed, 6:00 A.M. breakfast and camp inspection, 7:00 A.M. battalion drill, 8:00 A.M. guard mounting, 9:00 A.M. noncommissioned officer drill, 10:00 A.M. to 4:00 P.M. various camp duties, 4:00 P.M. more drill, and 6:00 P.M. dress parade, "which ends the day." Things were much the same in the First Corps, where the 16th Maine added a bit of horsing around to the combat practice. A diarist in the regiment wrote that the men "charge[d] double quick, the band [got in the way, and the players] . . . climb[ed] trees and skedadled, spoiled one drum."

Even in the midst of such routines, men died. The gunners of the 9th Massachusetts Battery recalled June 10 as the day they buried Edwin H. Balson, a victim of lung congestion. "He was nineteen years old, an excellent soldier, liked by officers and men," recalled a batterymate. Balson was laid to rest at sundown, under an apple tree, with a final ceremonial volley fired by the artillerymen from their standard-issue revolvers.

Another death that many would long remember took place two days after Balson's. This time the cause was military justice. Parts of Hooker's army were moving just then, as their commander repositioned his strength northward, fretting about a Rebel retaliatory strike for Brandy Station. John Reynolds' First Corps was one of the units involved. Among its best-known components was the brigade that was all number one: First Brigade, First Division, First Corps. Its men hailed from the states of Indiana, Michigan, and Wisconsin. They sported a distinctive bit of headgear, a black (Hardee) hat with a brim that many wore turned up on one side. Their stubborn courage at the Battle of Antietam had earned the Indiana and Wisconsin boys (the Michigan regiment had not yet joined at that point) a proud sobriquet: they were known as the Iron Brigade.

On June 12, these mostly combat-tested veterans marched under orders to kill one of their own. John P. Woods, a private in the 19th Indiana's Company F, had three times absented himself from the ranks on the eve of an engagement. Twice he had returned or been brought back, but the third time he had changed into a Confederate uniform in an attempt to pass himself off as a Rebel deserter. At his court-martial, Woods tried to explain his actions: "I cannot stand it to fight," he said. The court,

finding him guilty, sentenced him to death. After the judgment was confirmed, orders were issued calling for the punishment to be carried out on
June 12, between noon and 4:00 P.M. That the First Corps was marching
that day made no difference: the condemned man was hauled along in an
ambulance, under guard, his hands and feet shackled.

Lieutenant Clayton Rogers of the 6th Wisconsin was provost marshal
for the First Division, which was commanded by Brigadier General James
S. Wadsworth. It was Rogers' responsibility to perform the execution. "I
had a rough box prepared for [Woods'] remains," he would recall after
the war, "and [I selected] a detail of twelve men for guard and firing."
The First Corps tramped all morning, then halted for dinner about midday. John Reynolds had a schedule to keep, so he sent an aide to
Wadsworth "to have the affair hurried up." The officer hastened away
after delivering the message, grateful that he did not have to witness the
event. "It seemed rather hard to march a man all the morning and then
shoot him at noon," he reflected.

Wadsworth took Reynolds' hint. The four regiments of the Iron
Brigade were formed in a hollow square, a U-shaped formation with one
side left open, between 1:00 and 2:00 P.M. The rude coffin had been
placed on the ground at the square's open end. The ambulance was driven to that point, and Woods was pulled out, allowed a last moment with
the chaplain, and seated on the box. The firing squad was drawn up. As
Clayton Rogers remembered it, Woods "requested me not to bandage his
eyes, a request that was not granted"; he opened the condemned man's
shirt to expose his chest to the executioners. The chaplain who accompanied Woods declared that his "firmness, composure and naturalness . . . [were] astonishing." A soldier watching from the ranks marveled
that the doomed private sat waiting patiently, as one might wait for a
photographer to prepare his equipment.

Wadsworth gave the firing squad a few words of encouragement
before the men filed into line some thirty feet from their target. Eight
stood ready to carry out the death sentence, while four more waited in
reserve. Rogers called out "Attention!" and then lifted his hat. A quick
glance showed him that the men were set. The hat came down, and the
eight fired a ragged volley. The impact of the large-caliber bullets
punched Woods back over the coffin but failed to kill him. The first pair
of the reserve stepped up and grimly fired into the body, finishing the
job. "We left the men digging his grave," wrote an Iron Brigade soldier,
"and resumed the march as if nothing had happened."

At Army of the Potomac headquarters, near Falmouth, the cloudy crystal ball was clearing. George Sharpe and his staff were close to having a trustworthy sense of Lee's troop positions. Cavalry prisoners taken at Brandy Station had helped to confirm the presence of Hood's Division in Culpeper. The intelligence officers strongly suspected that McLaws was there, too, with Pickett's Division also close at hand. And Robert E. Lee himself had been reliably spotted near Culpeper. Yet it was not until the afternoon of June 13 that Sharpe was able to verify to his satisfaction the interrogation reports of two blacks who had just passed through Culpeper. One of them knew what Richard Ewell looked like and was certain he was there.

That was the final piece of the puzzle. For the first time, Hooker now had persuasive evidence that Lee had moved most of his army from Fredericksburg to Culpeper. Couriers began to stream out of headquarters with messages for the various corps commanders, instructing them to be ready to move. It would take until nightfall for Hooker to remove Sedgwick's men from the southern bank, but that was just the beginning: no sooner had the weary soldiers recrossed the Rappahannock than they were ordered to set out at once on roads leading north.

Richard S. Ewell began marching his corps north from Culpeper on June 10. An artilleryman in one of the long, snaking columns described it as a "very hot and dusty day." Regardless, the men were primed for what lay ahead. "We had but few stragglers," wrote George W. Nichols, a Georgia private. "We made excellent time." Johnson's and Early's divisions tramped along the foot of the Blue Ridge Mountains, while Rodes' men followed on a parallel route farther east. On June 11, after meeting with Lee, Ewell himself would ride out of Culpeper, eventually catching up with Johnson and Early about half a day's march from Chester Gap. Once his troops were through the Blue Ridge and into the Shenandoah Valley, Ewell would face his first testing as a corps commander. The town of Winchester, sitting astride several important valley roads, was occupied by a 6,000-man Union garrison commanded by Major General Robert H. Milroy, whose iron-fisted military rule oppressed local Virginians loyal to the Confederacy. Clearing this obstacle was Ewell's task.

For Hill's troops, patiently watching over the dormant Union incursion near Franklin's Crossing, June 10 was, in the words of one diarist, "all quiet along our lines." The lull gave soldiers of all ranks a chance to write home, and the boy colonel of the 26th North Carolina took full advantage of it. In a note to his family, Henry King Burgwyn Jr. displayed some of the ambition that had helped to make him one of the Confederacy's youngest colonels. Looking ahead to the prospect of an active campaign, Burgwyn wrote that it would inevitably create "sufficient vacancies & sufficient opportunities."

Robert E. Lee spent part of June 10 in Culpeper composing a long, reflective letter to Jefferson Davis. He offered no information regarding his troop movements but instead took to task Confederate politicians and newspaper editors who had been pouring public scorn on various Northern peace movements. As Lee saw it, the South's armies were "growing weaker" for the lack of fresh recruits, so anything that divided Northern opinion seemed to him a good thing. He urged Davis to "give all the encouragement we can . . . to the rising peace party of the North." Lee also sent a heartfelt note to his son, Rooney, who had been wounded at Brandy Station. "I wish I could see you," he wrote, "but I cannot."

On June 11, the first of Ewell's troops passed through Chester Gap to reach Front Royal, tucked along the southern fork of the Shenandoah River. It was a pleasant day's march. A North Carolina soldier under Early enjoyed hearing a band play "Bonnie Blew Flag" and did his share of gawking at the "pritty and kind ladies" in the small town of Washington who provided fresh water to the passing soldiers. Lee penned a letter of concern to his wife, then suffering through an arthritic episode that kept her confined to her room. "I grieve I fear too much over my separation from you, my children & friends," he wrote.

Ewell made plans on June 12 to knock out Winchester. Two of his divisions, Johnson's and Early's, would march directly on the town, while his third, Rodes', would tackle a small Federal force posted at Berryville. By 4:30 A.M. on June 13, all three were in motion.

Even as his infantry columns were heading into battle, Robert E. Lee crossed swords again with James Seddon. On June 9 and 10, the secretary of war had sent notes to Lee that, while professing support for his "aggressive movements," also painted a dire picture of Richmond's defenses. Union forces garrisoned on Virginia's eastern peninsula were stirring, causing Seddon considerable anxiety. "Our great want here is some cavalry, to scout and give timely notice," Seddon had complained to Lee. In his reply, Lee made it clear that he could not both undertake an "offensive movement" and "cover Richmond." After downplaying the threat posed by Federal troops on the peninsula, Lee proclaimed that he barely had enough cavalry to cover his *own* operations. Were he forced to weaken that screen, he feared that a "heavier calamity may befall us."

The fight for Winchester began at around noon on June 13, a few miles south of town, along the road to Front Royal. Virginia troops moving ahead of Johnson's Division contended with Yankee outposts. As more of Johnson's brigades arrived on the scene, they found the well-positioned Federals not inclined to give way. Johnson decided to wait and see if Early had any better luck. For their part, Early's soldiers ran into stiffer opposition blocking the Valley Pike, so they likewise held back. Off to the east, Rodes advanced to Berryville only to discover that the Federals posted there had slipped away to reinforce Milroy at Winchester.

Everything pointed to June 14 as a day of decision.

FOUR

"Push on"

There was little acknowledgment of Sunday's pastoral character within the Army of the Potomac. Hooker's headquarters was transferred to Dumfries even as the Sixth and Twelfth corps vacated the Fredericksburg area, leaving Hancock's Second Corps as their rear guard. A severe thunderstorm rumbled through the region on the night of June 13, messing up the dirt roads and making the march "tedious and toilsome," according to one of Sedgwick's soldiers. It was no simple task to move more than 80,000 men with their wagons and animals. Mistakes were made. Someone neglected to dismantle the tent-city hospital at Aquia Landing, an oversight that Hooker's fuming chief of staff termed a "shameful waste and abandonment of property." He ordered that the matériel be salvaged, even "if the surgeons have to pack [it all] on their own horses."

Four of Hooker's corps were now operating along the line of the Orange and Alexandria Railroad, tramping eastward the better to cover Washington. John Reynolds, in charge of this wing, was not sparing the shoe leather: "We marched Sunday morning and all day Sunday and all night," wrote an Iron Brigade officer, adding, "Our army is in a great hurry for something." Howard's Eleventh Corps had a great distance to cover, though a Wisconsin officer in its ranks still found time for observation and reflection. "We passed over farms where rich clover was growing," he noted, "but deserted ruins only mark the spots where the Virginia husbandman and his family once were happy."

* * *

Richard S. Ewell spent the first part of Sunday morning planning his attack on Winchester. The Yankee troops holding the town were concentrated in a series of strong points located on high ground northwest of the settled areas. Any force attempting an assault from the south would be first scrambled by having to move through the town streets and then chopped up on exposure to the enemy's fields of fire beyond. Ewell was so discouraged by his initial assessment that he sent a message to Lee concluding that Milroy's position was "too strong to be attacked." Lee did the best he could from a distance: his reply expressed confidence in Ewell's on-site judgment and offered the corps commander the option of holding Milroy in place with one division while moving the other up to the Potomac. By the time this exchange was completed, however, Ewell had come up with a viable plan of his own.

A dominating hill that the enemy had not fortified, rising just west of the Federal positions, provided the key. Jubal Early, recognizing the opportunity it presented, suggested a movement that Ewell approved of. By 11:00 A.M., a strong column was in motion on a wide flanking swing to the west while everyone else held position south of Winchester. At about the same time, another of Ewell's division commanders, Major General Robert Rodes, having frightened a small Union garrison out of Berryville, was marching his men north toward Martinsburg, close to the Potomac River.

That there were any Union troops at all in Winchester was the result more of bad decisions than of any positive purpose. Robert Milroy, in charge of the Federal forces in the town, got his orders through Major General Robert C. Schenck, headquartered in Baltimore, Maryland. The two shared the mistaken belief that Stuart's concentration near Culpeper portended a cavalry raid, an offensive tactic that would pose little danger to a fortified garrison. Confident in their misapprehension, they ignored clues that something far more serious was in fact in the offing. Thus, on June 11, when the War Department ordered Schenck to evacuate Winchester, he conveyed the order to Milroy as an instruction to *prepare* for a withdrawal. It was June 13 before Schenck realized that much more than a mere cavalry raid was under way. He sent an urgent message ordering Winchester's evacuation, but it never reached its destination because Ewell's men cut the telegraph wires as they closed in. Milroy was left with no option but to stand fast.

President Lincoln, monitoring the situation through the War Department, could not believe what was happening. At 1:14 P.M. on June 14, he queried Hooker, "Do you consider it possible that 15,000 of Ewell's men can now be at Winchester?" Hooker's answer, received at 5:40 P.M., was unhelpful, as it was based on information now twenty-four hours old. Ten minutes later, the line at Hooker's Dumfries headquarters was clacking again. If Milroy's men could hold out for a few days, Lincoln was asking, "can you help them? If the head of Lee's army is at Martinsburg and the tail of it . . . between Fredericksburg and Chancellorsville, the animal must be very slim somewhere. Could you not break him?"

Robert E. Lee attended Sunday services at Culpeper's Episcopal Church, where he was seen by a young artilleryman in Parker's Virginia Battery. James Longstreet was with Lee, underscoring the fact that his men had no marching orders for this day. They were holding at Culpeper, as were Stuart's horsemen at Brandy Station, just in case the Federal forces clustered to the east intended to cross the Rappahannock.

At Fredericksburg, A. P. Hill sent Anderson's Division of his corps off toward Culpeper. A Georgia soldier marching in Anderson's column recalled it as a "hot day" and noted that "many were stricken by the intense heat." The continued presence of Union troops across the river (Hancock's rear guard) gave Hill enough pause that he kept Heth's and Pender's divisions in place.

Lee sent no communication to Richmond this Sunday. Neither did the Confederate War Department have any news from Vicksburg. Perhaps for this reason, a petty squabble regarding control of the local militia units assigned to defend the capital commanded war clerk Jones' full attention. Jefferson Davis and the C.S. War Department were claiming suzerainty over troops said to fall under the control of Virginia authorities. Jones simply could not comprehend how so many important people could be caught up in this affair "when the common enemy is thundering at all our gates!"

The flanking attack designed by Jubal Early and approved by Richard S. Ewell began with a bang at 6:00 P.M., when a line of twenty guns that had been quietly rolled into place opened a furious cannonade against the Yankee forts west of Winchester. A staff officer who was present thought it a "rapid and well directed fire." He watched with satisfaction as "some of the shells [exploded] . . . in the [enemy's] work[s], while others struck

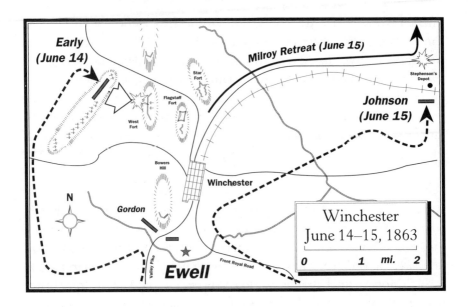

the [enemy fort's] parapet making great holes in it [and] sending the dirt high up in the air." Forty-five minutes later, Louisiana troops charged across two hundred yards of exposed ground, clawed their way through the fort's protecting entanglements, and overran the position. Ewell, who was cheering his men on from a hill just south of Winchester, staggered as a spent bullet thumped his chest. The one-legged general was lucky this time: he was only bruised, and determined to remain in touch with the action. His frustrated surgeon took away his crutches, but even that did not keep Ewell from propping himself up and continuing to direct affairs. Suspecting that the Federal general would try to evacuate after dark, Ewell put units in motion to cut him off, even as he sent a note outlining his success to Lee at Culpeper.

Joe Hooker spent most of June 15 in the dark, at least regarding matters at Winchester. His forces remained concentrated along the Orange and Alexandria Railroad, largely between Manassas Junction and Fairfax Station. Army headquarters was moved this day to that latter place. Most of the Second Corps began to close the distance, leaving part of its force to watch over the stores still stacked at Aquia Landing. The Fifth, Sixth, and Twelfth corps joined the First, Third, and Eleventh, while the cavalry left Warrenton for the same area of concentration.

The weather and poor road conditions made Hancock's tramp hard on the men. "The day was very hot, the roads were filled with dust, and the march of twenty-eight miles was so oppressive that a number of the men fell from sunstroke and exhaustion," complained a Pennsylvania soldier. Those in the Sixth and Twelfth corps had a lot of ground to cover as well. As a weary New Jerseyman in the 15th Regiment collapsed in camp that evening, he had enough strength left to scribble in his diary, "They came verry near Marched us to death." "The men carried heavy loads with them," noted a New York comrade in the Twelfth Corps. "All through the long day they dragged themselves along."

One unplanned casualty of the movement was the town of Stafford Court House. The 1st Minnesota, part of Hancock's rear guard, reached it at about 9:00 A.M. "Here the court house was in flames," observed a soldier, "having been fired by some wretches from the preceding column." "I wondered at this act of vandalism," declared a member of the 148th Pennsylvania. A soldier in the First Corps was particularly incensed at the consequent loss of so many historic documents: "The destruction of such relics I consider an act of vandalism far beneath the dignity of our American soldier in this enlightened age," he wrote.

Early on June 15, President Lincoln issued a proclamation calling for states throughout the region threatened by Lee's raid to provide 100,000 militia for local defense. "This call is made from outside pressure . . . ," fumed Navy Secretary Gideon Welles, "and not from the War Department or Headquarters."

Shortly after 9:00 P.M., Joseph Hooker, at Fairfax Station, received a presidential message that succinctly summarized the known situation. "Winchester and Martinsburg were both besieged yesterday," Lincoln reported, adding that the Federal troops there had been driven off, so that "the enemy [now] holds both places." Even more chilling was Lincoln's statement that Confederate troops were "crossing the Potomac at Williamsport." The president ended his brief message with the words "I would like to hear from you."

Just as Ewell had predicted, Robert Milroy tried to retreat after darkness fell on June 14. In the early-morning hours of June 15, the Yankee soldiers ran into what one of them called a "murderous trap" at a place named Stephenson's Depot, where they were attacked by elements from Johnson's Division, sent there by Ewell for just that purpose. It was a night fight, marked by confusion on both sides, but by dawn, several thousand Yankee soldiers had been taken prisoner, and most of the rest were scattered across the countryside, seeking escape. Among those slipping through the net was the hated Milroy, who reached the friendly garrison at Harper's Ferry. It was a grand victory for Confederate arms, and Ewell was the man of the hour. An officer on Ewell's staff who had served with the great Stonewall wrote that if the "spirits disembodied can see what goes on in this world, I am sure that General Jackson has felt unfeigned pleasure since yesterday."

Going almost unnoticed amid all the celebration was the activity of Ewell's third division, commanded by Robert Rodes. On June 14, Rodes' men had marched virtually unchallenged through Martinsburg; the next day they continued north for fifteen miles to the Potomac River. There Rodes spent the following two days crossing his three brigades into Maryland. Tarheel Louis Leon recorded that the river was "knee-deep" where they forded it, and that the Maryland citizens they met on the other side were "mixed in their sympathies, some Confederates and some Yankees."

Taking the point on Rodes' advance was a small cavalry brigade commanded by Brigadier General Albert G. Jenkins. The thirty-two-year-old Virginian (who habitually tucked his long beard into his belt when the wind blew) was a competent warrior, though out of his depth directing men in such an operation. On the evening of June 14, Rodes had instructed Jenkins to press ahead the next day as far as Chambersburg, Pennsylvania. Accordingly, his four mounted regiments were called to horse while it was still dark, and set off at 2:00 A.M.

Refugees had already sounded the alarm in Chambersburg. This prosperous Pennsylvania town had been visited by Confederate raiders in 1862, so the local merchants knew just what to do. One such merchant, Jacob Hoke, would later recollect, "The usual work of sending away and secreting merchandise and other valuables was begun." The packing, shipping, and hiding took place against an unsettling cavalcade of refugees displaced by recent events. "Horses, wagons, and cattle crowded every avenue of escape northward," Hoke explained. The worst moment came when a military supply train fleeing Winchester tumbled into town, its half-crazed animals lashed by panic-stricken teamsters. Chaos threatened, but a Federal officer who was on hand with a small cavalry patrol stopped the drivers and forced them to continue their journey at a more

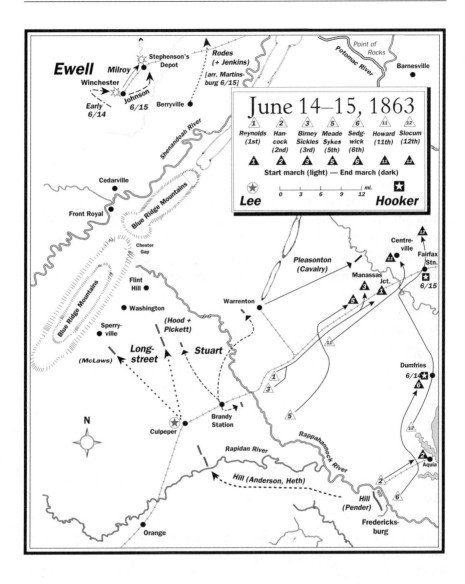

measured pace. By the time evening came on June 15, the streets were mostly empty.

Albert Jenkins was endowed with a quality not usually associated with dashing cavalrymen: an excess of caution. He eased his brigade along the road from Williamsport to Chambersburg, taking great care whenever they encountered any sign of resistance. The undefended town of Greencastle was captured by two columns, one charging in while the other swept through from the flank. A small Federal patrol caught there was easily routed, and its officer taken prisoner. Hermann Schuricht, riding in one of Jenkins' regiments, recorded this day's events in his diary, from "destroying the railroad depot" to "cutting the telegraph wires." He also indicated that the Rebel advance "had several skirmishes with the retreating enemy." The Yankee force comprised only about forty riders, but Jenkins was a cautious man. It took his mounted column ten hours to cover the twenty-two miles between Greencastle and Chambersburg. The sun set long before the first of his scouts poked into the latter town.

While certain chronicles of the Gettysburg campaign have held that Pennsylvania's citizens meekly capitulated to the Rebel raiders, events in Chambersburg on the evening of June 15 suggest that some, at least, gave them a different sort of welcome. Two Confederate officers who galloped in first to intimidate the civilian population into compliance were instead taken prisoner by a pair of residents recently discharged from military service. The Southerners might have been hustled off for interrogation had they not been freed by the large squadron following them, whose arrival suddenly filled the main street with sweating, darkly threatening men.

Watching it all from the second floor of his now empty store, merchant Jacob Hoke found few to argue with him when he declared that June 15 brought Chambersburg "the greatest excitement which had occurred up to that time during all the history of the war."

A. P. Hill, still headquartered in Fredericksburg, continued his disengagement on June 15 by sending Heth's Division off to follow Anderson's toward Culpeper. Before they left, some of Heth's men scouted the opposite bank. Private G. W. Bynum and two others from the 2nd Mississippi waded the river near where Hooker's headquarters had been. "When we appeared in the streets of Falmouth I never saw a happier people," Bynum later recalled. "The old men and ladies happily met us with a cordial handshake, their eyes brimming with tears of joy."

Heth's departure meant that only Pender's Division was left to watch over the largely empty Union encampments on the Rappahannock's northern bank. This gave Pender time to compose a note to his wife. "Thus far Gen. Lee's plans have worked admirably, so says Gen. Hill who I suppose knows them," he wrote. "May God in his goodness be more gracious than in our last trial. We certainly may be allowed to hope as our mission is one of peace altho' through blood."

With Hill's men converging on Culpeper, it was time for Longstreet's command to join Ewell's. "My corps left Culpeper on the 15th," recorded the general, "and with a view of covering the march of Hill and Ewell through the [Shenandoah] Valley, moved along the east side of the Blue Ridge." His men were no more immune to the weather than were their foes. "The heat is frightful," noted Virginian John Dooley, "and the road in many places is strewn with the sunstruck." Colonel William C. Oates of the 15th Alabama affirmed that: "A good many of the men fainted or had sunstroke on the march, yet the morale of the army was never better."

Still monitoring matters from Culpeper, Lee sent a situation report to Richmond at 7:00 A.M. In it he recapped Ewell's success at Winchester, adding somewhat disingenuously that he presumed that Ewell had subsequently "advanced toward the Potomac." Relaying Hill's information about the enemy's pullout from Fredericksburg, he confirmed that large numbers of Union troops were known to be in the Warrenton area. Then, reviving his argument with Richmond, Lee complained that the reluctance of the government to bring troops up from North Carolina to enable him to complete his divisions "has caused delay in the movements of this army, and it may now be too late to accomplish all that was desired." A message that Lee sent to Ewell at the same time conveyed a very different outlook: "Longstreet started today," Lee informed his Second Corps commander. "Hill is in motion. Push on."

FIVE

"I hope . . . to end the war if Providence favors us"

George Sharpe was stumped. After locating most of Lee's army near Culpeper, he and his staff had been flooded with conflicting reports that put paralyzing question marks at the end of what had lately seemed to be conclusive statements. Provost Marshal Marsena Patrick tracked the confusion in his diary entry for June 17: "There seems to be doubt as to Lee's Movements and it is understood that A. P. Hill remains near Frederic[k]sburg, Ewell's Position undetermined, and Longstreet investing Harper's Ferry."

Most of Hooker's men, having marched hard to reach blocking positions southwest of Washington, had lesser distances to cover on June 16 and 17, giving many time to ingest the latest rumors. "News that the 'Rebs' are in Pennsylvania [causes] great sensation," wrote a Sixth Corps staff officer on Tuesday, June 16. The same information reached the Third Corps. "Reported rebbels in Md. & Pa.," noted a diarist in the 86th New York. An officer in that corps' Second Division recorded the rumor as fact: "The Rebels are in Pennsylvania," he scribbled. "We seem to be completely Isolated from the world . . . ," complained an officer in the 154th New York (Eleventh Corps), "as we get neither mails or Newspapers here. . . . To be thus cut off from the world at a time when of all others one wants to know what is transpiring outside, When each day is developing anew what may decide the fate of a World, is to say the least anything but pleasant."

There was one arena where Union fact-finding was working well.

Pennsylvania. Jenkins' movement into Chambersburg had triggered a response by a variety of intelligence-gathering groups. Working in parallel to the traditional military patrols, operating as part of the Department of the Susquehanna, were a cadre of scouts deployed by the two railroads most threatened by the Southern incursion, the Pennsylvania Central and Northern Central lines. Included in this latter group were several specialists equipped with portable field-telegraph keys. To transmit information to Harrisburg, these operators had only to find a point clear of where the Rebels had cut the lines and patch in. Also reporting to the capital were another group of civilian spies, under the direction of a prominent Pennsylvania citizen named David McConaughy. McConaughy controlled this activity from his home, located in the town of Gettysburg.

June 16 brought a dramatic change in Joe Hooker's command relationships. Shortly before noon, he sent a message to Abraham Lincoln in hopes of getting Henry Halleck off his back. "You have long been aware, Mr. President," asserted Hooker, "that I have not enjoyed the confidence of the major-general commanding the army, and I can assure you so long as this continues we may look in vain for success." At the same time, Hooker foolishly allowed himself to be maneuvered by Halleck into following a course of action that would undermine Lincoln's support. It had to do with the Union garrison at Harper's Ferry, which Hooker believed was about to suffer the same fate as Milroy's unit at Winchester. The succession of messages sent on June 16 tells the story.

HALLECK TO HOOKER, 3:50 P.M.
THERE IS NO DOUBT THAT THE ENEMY IS SURROUNDING HARPER'S FERRY, BUT IN WHAT FORCE I HAVE NO INFORMATION.

HOOKER TO HALLECK, 4:00 P.M.
PLEASE INFORM ME . . . FROM WHAT DIRECTION IS THE ENEMY MAKING HIS ATTACK?

HOOKER TO HALLECK, 7:30 P.M.
IN COMPLIANCE WITH YOUR DIRECTIONS, I SHALL MARCH TO THE RELIEF OF HARPER'S FERRY.

HALLECK TO HOOKER, 8:20 P.M.
INFORMATION OF ENEMY'S ACTUAL POSITION AND FORCE IN FRONT OF HARPER'S FERRY IS AS INDEFINITE AS THAT IN YOUR FRONT. NEARLY EVERYTHING IS CONJECTURE.

HOOKER TO LINCOLN, 9:50 P.M.
MY ORDERS ARE OUT TO MARCH* [TO HARPER'S FERRY] AT 3 O'CLOCK TO-MORROW MORNING. IT WILL BE LIKELY TO BE ONE OF VIGOR AND POWER.

LINCOLN TO HOOKER, 10:00 P.M.

TO REMOVE ALL MISUNDERSTANDING, I NOW PLACE YOU IN THE STRICT MILITARY RELATION TO GENERAL HALLECK OF A COMMANDER OF ONE OF THE ARMIES TO THE GENERAL-IN-CHIEF OF ALL THE ARMIES. I HAVE NOT INTENDED DIFFERENTLY, BUT AS IT SEEMS TO BE DIFFERENTLY UNDERSTOOD, I SHALL DIRECT HIM TO GIVE YOU ORDERS AND YOU TO OBEY THEM.

HALLECK TO HOOKER, 10:15 P.M.

I HAVE GIVEN NO DIRECTIONS FOR YOUR ARMY TO MOVE TO HARPER'S FERRY. . . . WITH THE REMAINDER OF YOUR FORCE IN PROPER POSITION TO SUPPORT THIS, I WANT YOU TO PUSH OUT YOUR CAVALRY, TO ASCERTAIN SOMETHING DEFINITE ABOUT THE ENEMY.

Throughout June 17, even though Hooker kept in close contact with Halleck, the two remained at cross purposes. For a while Hooker believed that Halleck was telling him that the Union post at Harper's Ferry had been abandoned. It was early evening before Lincoln's general in chief explained that he had been referring to a repositioning of troops in that location, not to the post's abandonment.

Hooker's focus on Halleck left his chief of staff, Major General Daniel Butterfield, to handle almost all other army communications. Alfred Pleasonton was told it was "better that we should lose men than to be without knowledge of the enemy." Accordingly, horse soldiers from New York, Massachusetts, Maine, and Ohio were sent into the Loudoun Valley through the gateway village of Aldie. They were met on its outskirts by equally determined troopers from Virginia, who battled them throughout the day. At dusk the grim-faced Federals, still holding the valley portal, watched the sun set behind the Blue Ridge Mountains. In his final message to Halleck this day, Hooker pondered reports that no Rebel infantry had been spotted in the Loudoun Valley, and questioned whether all the cavalry fighting might not be "a cover to Lee's re-enforcing Bragg or moving troops to the west."

Hooker's contretemps with Washington was costing him respect and credibility. Provost marshal and diarist Brigadier General Marsena Patrick noted that "Halleck is running the Marching and Hooker has the role of a subordinate—He acts like a man without a plan and is entirely at a loss what to do, or how to match the enemy, or counteract his movements."

The marching on June 17 was especially hard on the Second Corps, which was still trying to close on the rest of the army. "The weather is very hot," wrote a Pennsylvanian in the 140th, adding that the "Dust [is] shoe mouth deep." Sergeant Benjamin Hirst, of the 14th Connecticut, was no longer edgy about mosquitoes; now it was the interminable marching that galled him: "We seemed to be suffocating at each step," he related, ". . . strong men wilted as though blasted by something in the air."

The movement into this area brought Army of the Potomac veterans into contact with some of Washington's garrison troops, many of whom were on short-term enlistments. Private John Haley of the 17th Maine (Third Corps) took stock of some of these "sunshine" soldiers: "They look very nice, as if they are just out of the bureau drawer and intend to return there immediately," he noted. "We are lousy and filthy and, curious to say, not ashamed of either condition."

Even though Washington lay just to the east, the state was still Virginia, part of the Confederacy, and few Union troops felt any compunction about helping themselves to civilian property. When the colonel commanding the 24th Michigan (First Corps) wondered why his drummer was not beating the march cadence, he was shown the confiscated geese that were being stored in the instrument. "Well, if you're sick and can't play, you needn't," he said, securing himself a main course for that evening's dinner. In the Eleventh Corps, a 136th New York foot soldier named John T. McMahon watched his regiment decimate a flock of sheep. "The boys went out and killed them without leave or license," he remembered. In an effort to halt such practices, some officers spread stories about guerrillas' murdering unsuspecting foragers. Although these contrived warnings would become enshrined as fact in some postwar writings, few soldiers took them seriously at the time: "They fear nothing so much as an empty stomach," one averred.

After completing his capture of Winchester and then pushing Rodes' Division across the Potomac at Williamsport, Richard S. Ewell was uncertain what he should do next. Lacking the instinctive understanding of Lee's greater goals and objectives that might have enabled him to propose some further action, Ewell instead finished cleaning up the task he had been assigned. Jubal Early's division remained at Winchester to han dle the aftermath of the victory, while Edward Johnson's men marched to Shepherdstown, where they prepared to cross the Potomac.

Any chance that Robert Rodes and his division, already in Maryland, might act more aggressively was eliminated on June 18, when Albert Jenkins returned to report that his occupation of Chambersburg, Pennsylvania, had lasted only until June 17, when a large enemy force had been observed approaching from the north. Not seeking a fight, Jenkins' entire command had fallen back. Rodes suspected that Jenkins had been spooked, and his suspicion would prove to be right: the "large enemy force" turned out to be a crowd of citizens from neighboring towns who converged on Chambersburg to gawk at the invaders.

Nevertheless, the time Rodes spent in Williamsport and Jenkins' sojourn (however brief) in Pennsylvania were not without benefit. As Rodes would later report, his food and livestock quartermasters were able to seize "large supplies in their respective departments." It was the first trickle in what would become a great flood of matériel. Men in the ranks were already beginning to enjoy the fruits of this windfall. If "an old soldier is ever happy," declared an Alabama man in O'Neal's Brigade, "it is when grub is plentiful and [there is] no fighting."

The men of Pickett's Division (Longstreet's Corps) had some ground to cover today. Virginian Randolph Shotwell was angry that so little allowance had been made for the men's previous assignment. Most of them, he noted, were "just out of winter-quarters, where they were well screened from the sun, and now under the combined effect of heat, fatigue, thirst, and intolerable dust they wilt and drop like wax-figures in a fiery furnace."

Hill's Corps, now fully gathered around Culpeper, was preparing to follow Longstreet. William Dorsey Pender, whose division had been the last to leave Fredericksburg, had shaken off his previous pessimism: "Everything thus far has worked admirably," he wrote to his wife on June 17, "and if the campaign goes on as it has commenced it will be a telling one." The boy colonel, Henry King Burgwyn Jr., was also brimming with optimism. Lee's army, he reported on June 17, "is admirably organized & officered & has the most implicit confidence in him. The men are all in good spirits & the whole army expects to go into Pennsylvania."

On June 19, Ewell met with Longstreet to coordinate their movements. That same morning, Lee felt he had to chastise his Second Corps commander for not bringing his divisions together and pushing on. "I very

much regret that you have not the benefit of your whole corps," he wrote
to Ewell at 7:00 A.M., "for, with that north of the Potomac, should we be
able to detain General Hooker's army from following you, you would be
able to accomplish as much, unmolested, as the whole army could perform
with General Hooker in its front." This time, Ewell got the message. That
same day, Rodes' Division marched out of Williamsport toward Hagerstown, while Johnson's men crossed the Potomac at Shepherdstown and
proceeded as far as Sharpsburg. By the time Early's men came in behind
Johnson's, they found the Potomac at flood level from recent rains, mak-

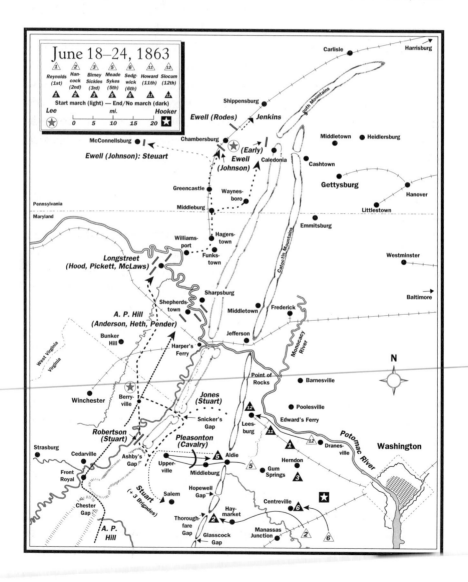

ing it impossible to cross. Not wanting to let his divisions become danger-ously separated, Ewell held everyone in place for the next two days.

There was more fighting in the Loudoun Valley, as Union cavalrymen kept pressing toward the gaps in the Blue Ridge Mountains, and Jeb Stu-art's riders battled to block them. Combat flared at Middleburg on June 19 and then at Upperville on June 21. By the latter day's end, the Feder-als had battered their way to the eastern slopes of the Blue Ridge, and a few bold patrols had even penetrated to the dominating ridge line. Then, just as he had done at Brandy Station, Alfred Pleasonton backed off, satis-fied that he had carried out the letter of his orders. He was certain there was no Rebel infantry in the Loudoun Valley.

Hooker was meanwhile using Washington's intense interest in these actions to bulk up his army. He was now operating within the capital's defensive zone, which had its own units assigned to it, and he promptly began to appropriate these troops for his purposes. Henry Halleck offered no objection; in fact, on June 22, he placed all of Robert C. Schenck's men under Hooker's direct command.

By now everyone at headquarters knew that Hooker was inflating his estimates of the enemy's strength. "We get accurate information," Provost Marshal Patrick complained, "but Hooker will not use it and insults all who differ from him in opinion." Hooker was also engaging in some curi-ous speculations: speaking with newly arrived Brigadier General Samuel W. Crawford on June 21, for example, he wondered aloud if Lee's objective might not be to capture Pittsburgh.

While Hooker busied himself with getting reinforcements, George Sharpe got very little sleep. The information-gathering network he had created worked best when the army was at rest; now that it was on the move, Sharpe found his apparatus straining to keep up. Frustrations mounted as opportunities were lost due to the absence of simple, com-monsense field practices. Prisoner interrogations were haphazard, and little effort was made to assess captured enemy documents in terms of their intelligence value. In one case reported to Sharpe, an operative watched a group of Federal officers have "a right jolly time" reading Rebel material. The next day, Sharpe's agent picked up a discarded scrap that proved to be a recent and informative muster roll for a Virginia cavalry company.

There were times, these days, when Sharpe even considered returning to line command. One of his biggest headaches was Alfred Pleasonton, whose position as cavalry chief also made him a key figure for intelligence gathering. Unfortunately, the general showed neither any gift for performing this activity himself nor any skill in assessing the information his troopers brought in, and the often wide discrepancies in his reporting made Sharpe's job even more complicated. Then, too, aside from the problems inherent in gathering and evaluating intelligence, Sharpe was catching some of the fallout from Hooker's losing exchanges with Halleck. Provost Marshal Patrick, always on the alert for good camp gossip, wrote in his diary on June 17 that Hooker had treated Sharpe "with indifference at first, & now with insult."

But despite all that, Sharpe and his staff had still managed to piece together a fairly complete picture of the disposition of Lee's army. From the Union garrison at Harper's Ferry had come information that placed most, if not all, of Ewell's Corps in Maryland, with advance units already in Pennsylvania. Confederate cavalrymen taken prisoner in the Loudoun Valley had related that Longstreet's Corps was holding Ashby's and Snicker's gaps. That left Hill's Corps to be located. The best guess Sharpe could hazard was that it was en route to the Potomac. As late as June 20, he had sensed that Lee intended to concentrate just south of the Potomac in order to fight Hooker somewhere near Manassas. In a letter to his uncle, Sharpe ventured the opinion that Lee "must whip us before he goes in force to Md. or Penna."

While Sharpe struggled to bring light into the darkness, Hooker was marking time. Having transferred his Army of the Potomac from the Fredericksburg area to the region just west of Washington, he now made only minor adjustments in position. A nagging suspicion at headquarters that Lee might be seeking to reach Manassas, the scene of two previous Confederate victories, helped keep the majority of the Federal units fixed in place. The exceptions were George Meade's Fifth Corps, which had been sent into the Loudoun Valley to support Pleasonton's troopers, and Hancock's Second with Sedgwick's Sixth Corps, assigned to monitor the southwestern approaches to Washington through Thoroughfare Gap.

The movements of the Second and Sixth corps had brought the men past the old Bull Run battlefields. "Have we seen some sights," wrote Private William Penn Oberlin. "In many cases or most all where these soldiers were buried, we could see their heads, arms, hands, and feet sticking out of the grave." John F. L. Hartwell observed, "We found plenty of signs of the battle that was fought here last summer. . . . Shots in trees, earth works, &c." J. W. Muffley of the 148th Pennsylvania claimed that he and his comrades had located "several grinning skeletons still entire, lying on the surface of the ground still partially clothed in the blue uniforms."

It was after sunset on June 20 by the time Hancock's advance reached Thoroughfare Gap. According to a soldier in the 19th Maine, "While the Regiment was plodding along, slowly picking its way in the dark, one of the boys fell into a deep ditch and when inquired of as to what he was doing down there he answered back, 'Boys, here's the gap. I've stopped it up.'"

Fifth Corps infantry marching to support Pleasonton's troopers in the Loudoun Valley had encountered carnage of more recent vintage. "Wounded men lay upon litters of straw near the roadside and in the yards of the houses," recorded a member of the 118th Pennsylvania. "Dead horses were scattered about, and lost and abandoned arms and trappings were numerous." The Twelfth Corps had made its own additions to the morbid debris when, on June 19, troops were formed into the ominous hollow square to witness the executions of three of their number found guilty of desertion. "I hope it will have a good effect on those who saw it," reflected a Connecticut soldier. "I did not care about seeing it at all."

Particularly poignant were the small groups of escaping slaves who made their way through the Federal lines. "It is really affecting to see a mother with little children . . . , marching along fatigued and poorly clad," testified Private Oberlin, "the mother unable to carry them much on account of the heavy load she has to carry of clothing to keep them warm after night." When one black elder asked a Federal if Mr. Lincoln was nearby, the amused soldier pointed toward Washington. "Yes," the Yankee replied, "he's in his chariot forty miles back the road."

On June 18, Hooker sent a letter "confidentially to the [newspaper] editors throughout the country," imposing restrictions on press coverage of the campaign. From this point on, correspondents would no longer be allowed to identify the "location of any corps, division, brigade, or regiment" or, especially, the placement of army headquarters. Moreover, the newspapermen could print only those official reports that had been cleared by the War Department. "These rules being observed," Hooker concluded with a touch of gallows humor, "every facility possible will be given to reporters and newspapers in this army, including the license to abuse or criticize me to their heart's content."

At the time Hooker's advisory was sent out, representatives from all the major metropolitan newspapers were spread throughout the army.

They were an unusual band of brothers: comrades and competitors, mere scribblers and sound wordsmiths, open-minded and utterly opinionated. Their status was often what they could make of it. Many found ways to attach themselves to various headquarters, where they could count on having some access to supplies and communications. Most existed on sufferance: one unflattering observation, and a reporter might find himself without a tent flap to cover him at night, and no place set for him at the dinner table.

The best of this breed were proud of their efforts to bring war news and human-interest stories to the home front. Perhaps the most active reporters tagging along with Hooker's army were the group representing James Gordon Bennett's *New York Herald*. And one of the busiest of the *Herald* men was Thomas M. Cook, who on June 18 had provided his New York editors with a remarkably prescient assessment of the situation: "There is very large reason for doubt whether any considerable body of the rebels have yet passed beyond the Potomac northward," he wrote. "Their main force of infantry is yet in the Shenandoah Valley and about Winchester."

The newsmen's occupation had its dangers, of course—a fact that became evident on June 22. Lynde W. Buckingham had drawn the *Herald*'s assignment to cover the cavalry actions in the Loudoun Valley. Having gathered his notes about the June 21 fight at Upperville, Buckingham was riding toward the nearest telegraph connection to Washington when he ran into a band of Confederate irregulars near Aldie. His horse bolted at the first shots, galloped headlong down a steep hill, and threw its rider heavily to the ground. Union soldiers from a nearby picket post took the unconscious correspondent to a field hospital located in a church, but Buckingham died the following morning. His close associate Alfred Waud arrived too late to see him alive. Waud, a talented artist whose specialty was sketching battle scenes, "himself dug the grave for the burial of his old friend in a little graveyard adjoining the church, where the remains were interred."

In Richmond, news of Lee's advances and successes arrived in penny packets. Rumors of the Winchester fight had begun trickling in on June 16, a day before Lee's official report reached the capital. "It is believed Hooker's army is utterly demoralized, and that Lee is *going on*," wrote War Department clerk John Beauchamp Jones on June 18. It was Jones' hope that the "long longed-for day of retributive invasion may come at last."

On this day, Jones also came across a memorandum concerning an interview between a Confederate official and a prominent Northern peace activist named Clement Vallandigham, who had been banished to the Confederacy for speaking out against Lincoln's war policies. Before he left the South for Canada, the Ohio politician wanted to offer some tactical advice. Jones' eyes must have widened considerably when he read that the well-known dove had cautioned "strongly against any invasion of Pennsylvania, for that would unite all parties at the North, and so strengthen Lincoln's hands."

There was little apprehension in the ranks of Lee's army, however, as the various columns approached and crossed the Potomac. "I do not suppose any army ever marched into an enemies country with greater confidence in its ability to [conquer] and with more reasonable grounds for that confidence than the army of Gen. Lee," declared Brigadier General Abner Perrin of Hill's Corps. A surgeon who served under Perrin wrote, "Our army is very large now, and if . . . Hooker engages us you may be certain that he will be severely whipped." A South Carolina soldier in Kershaw's Brigade (Longstreet's Corps) predicted, "We will march to Philadelphia (if Hooker will allow us) and I think we will end the War by the time we get back."

Any doubt his men may have harbored was almost always overcome by Robert E. Lee's charisma. "I could not get over the feeling that an invasion of the enemy's territory, however tempting, was the wrong policy for us," Maryland staff officer Henry Kyd Douglas would later recall, "but at the same time I believed that General Lee must know better than I did." By now, William Dorsey Pender of Hill's Corps had become a true believer: "Gen. Lee has completely outgeneraled Hooker thus far and then our numbers are more equal than they have been," he assured his wife. "The General says he wants to meet [Hooker] . . . as soon as possible and crush him." Lest he become too serious, Lee joked with Pender that he was going to begin shooting stragglers if the men did not keep up. Pender related his retort: "I told him if he gave us authority to shoot those under us he might take the same privilege with us."

The members of Louisiana's Washington Artillery Battalion were buoyed by the rumors they heard. "Yankee papers say that Johnston & Pemberton are driving Grant before them at Vicksburg," noted gunner Edward Owen. "Also say that our Cavalry is in Harrisburg, Pa. & that the

Pa. Dutchmen refuse to respond to the call . . . for 100,000 more troops." A. D. Betts, a Confederate chaplain, was pleased that a number of his flock had been moved by events to make a personal commitment to God. In his diary entry for June 21, he noted with pride the newly baptized: "Several are immersed in p.m."

All of Ewell's infantry were now across the Potomac. A lieutenant in the 49th Virginia would later remember that the river was running "up to our hips" as the troops waded to the Maryland side. Louisiana soldiers under Brigadier General Harry T. Hays stripped to the buff when their turn came. "It was amusing," wrote a staff officer who was present, "to see the long lines of naked men fording [the river]—their clothing and accouterments slung to their guns and carried above their heads to keep them dry." There was a bit more ceremony when the 38th Georgia made the crossing, at least according to the recollection of Private F. L. Hudgins, who described "flags fluttering and bands playing 'Maryland, My Maryland.' "

Before he went across, gunner Henry Robinson Berkeley of the Amherst (Virginia) Artillery enjoyed his last breakfast as the guest of a farm woman who admitted to being a Union sympathizer. "She said she felt very sorry for the soldiers on both sides," Berkeley reported, "and fed both alike."

For his part, Abraham Lincoln now found himself mediating between Henry Halleck and Joseph Hooker. The president's telegram of June 16, firmly placing Hooker under Halleck in the chain of command, had been his official statement, but that same day, Lincoln had also penned a private letter to the Army of the Potomac commander, seeking to mitigate the sting of that other communiqué. "I need and must have the professional skill of both [of you]," Lincoln wrote, "and yet these suspicions tend to deprive me of both. . . . Now, all I ask is that you will be in such mood that can get into our action the best cordial judgment of yourself and General Halleck, with my poor mite added."

In the days that followed, Lincoln juggled other matters of government with a steady concern over the events transpiring just to the west of the capital. On June 23, Hooker took advantage of his proximity to Washington to pay a visit to the White House. It was a day on which Lincoln, in the opinion of one cabinet member, looked "sad and careworn." No record was kept of any discussion between the two. Hooker departed as quickly as he had arrived, leaving behind a growing unhappiness regarding his handling of the situation. "What disgust there is everywhere about Hooker and the [Lincoln] administration," exclaimed the officer commanding Washington's defenses on June 24. Word began to spread that Hooker was drinking a great deal.

Also on June 24, Hooker sent Halleck his assessment of the strategic picture. Ewell's Corps, he conceded, "is over the river . . . for purposes of plunder," but he was sanguine that Pennsylvania's militiamen "should be able to check any extended advance of that column." He had no news to convey about the rest of Lee's army. Provided that Lee did not heavily reinforce Ewell, Hooker felt it would make sense for the Army of the Potomac to "strike for his line of retreat in the direction of Richmond." Also included in Hooker's note were complaints about officers serving in the Washington defenses who were not cooperating with him. Until Halleck issued definitive orders placing him in overall command, the Army of the Potomac commander claimed not to know whether he was "standing on [his] . . . head or feet."

Robert E. Lee set up his headquarters just outside Berryville, Virginia, on June 20. Straightaway he dashed off a letter to the officer in charge of the Confederate Department of Western Virginia, urging him to "threaten Western Virginia [so that] . . . you may at least prevent the [U.S.] troops in that region from being sent to reinforce other points." The officer commanding the Southern cavalry operating in western Maryland was advised to concentrate his force and advance along the flank of the Army of Northern Virginia as it moved north. Writing to the C.S. president, Lee once more asked that the brigades that he had been promised, but that Davis was still holding near Richmond, "be sent to me."

Lee returned to some of his favorite subjects in a June 23 dispatch to Davis. He argued yet again that the hot summer made it impossible for the enemy to "undertake active operations on the Carolina and Georgia coast," and suggested that "a part . . . of the troops . . . can be employed at this time to great advantage in Virginia." Lee reminded Davis of an idea he had broached at the May meeting, proposing that instead of being sent to him, or even being used to replace troops intended for him, this force "be organized under the command of General [P. G. T.] Beauregard, and pushed forward to Culpeper Court-House, threatening Washington from that direction."

Lee also tried to lower expectations regarding what he might achieve in his current campaign. If he was successful, and Davis went along with the Beauregard ploy, then Lee felt they "might even hope to compel the recall of some of the enemy's troops from the west." In a private conversation he had this day with Major General Isaac R. Trimble, present at headquarters as a supernumerary, Lee hinted that his personal aspirations had not waned. "We have again out-maneuvered the enemy," he told Trimble, adding that the great lead he enjoyed over Hooker would force the Yankee general "to follow us by forced marches. I hope with these advantages to accomplish some signal result, and to end the war if Providence favors us."

Getting Ewell's Corps to move deeper into Pennsylvania was the first item on Lee's agenda. He was confident that he could hold Hooker off and thereby afford Ewell considerable freedom of action, but he had no control over the weather. The Potomac was still running high, keeping Early's Division stranded on the Virginia side as late as June 21. However, the indications pointed to its being fordable within twenty-four hours. On June 22, Lee ordered Ewell to advance into Pennsylvania and then spread his force eastward in three separate columns to maximize the area he could scour for supplies, his ultimate objective being the Susquehanna River. Lee gave Ewell wide discretion: "If Harrisburg comes within your means, capture it," he instructed. Of course, everything depended on what Lee termed the "development of circumstances."

Lee also wanted Stuart's cavalry to lend direct support to Ewell's advance by operating just off its right flank. Delays incurred in fending off the Union thrusts into the Loudoun Valley had permitted Hill's and Longstreet's corps to pass behind Stuart, creating a logistical problem. For Stuart's riders, getting to their proper place with Ewell's men would mean having to work their way forward using roads already clogged with columns of infantry and slow wagon trains. Stuart had another idea.

His plan had originated with Major John S. Mosby, one of Stuart's most trusted officers, who had been on detached service throughout the greater Loudoun Valley, conducting a highly effective harassment campaign against Union outposts and supply lines. Mosby had a good sense of troop dispositions and a boldness that recognized opportunities. He knew from personal observation that Hooker's army was "spread out like a fan—his left being at Thoroughfare Gap and his right on the Potomac at Leesburg." Mosby had conveyed this information to Stuart, who had then decided that "with the approval of General Lee, [he would move] to pass around, or rather through them, as the shortest route to Ewell." Lee, meeting with Stuart on June 21, had given his cavalry commander provisional orders allowing him the freedom to move in any way practicable to achieve his objective of closing on Ewell's flank. Lee and Stuart had planned this kind of movement before; neither anticipated any serious problems.

Located some twenty-five miles east of Chambersburg, through a pass in the South Mountains called the Cashtown Gap, the town of Gettysburg (population approximately 2,400) endured the great uncertainties of the times. Communications reaching the Adams County seat may have been garbled, but they were swift. On June 15, the same day Jenkins rode into Chambersburg, Gettysburg diarist Sarah Broadhead had written that the "Rebels were crossing the river in heavy force and advancing on this state." The town's merchants were soon taking the same precautions as their Chambersburg counterparts. Every traveler was grilled about what he knew or had heard.

Jenkins' abrupt pullback from Chambersburg had left residents breathing easier. Another Gettysburg citizen, Fannie Buehler, would note that "it grew to be an old story. We tried to make ourselves believe that they would never come." There was hard evidence to the contrary, however. On June 17, a small crowd had seen off a group of eighty-three men, volunteers from Gettysburg's college and seminary, who were heading to Harrisburg in response to Governor Curtin's call for militiamen. Two days later, a mounted local defense force was organized under Captain Robert Bell and immediately set about patrolling the Chambersburg Pike.

There had been a further portent of things to come on June 22. A band of Gettysburg men who had offered to help fell trees to block the Cashtown Gap were fired on as they approached that place. The axmen returned with their job undone. On June 24, word spread that the state militia unit that included Gettysburg's young men would arrive in town the next day. Sarah Broadhead mentally compared the known fighting qualities of Lee's veterans with those of the hastily trained, untested militia. "We do not feel much safer," she concluded.

June 23 was a clear day, perfect for the Federal observers posted on high ground near Harper's Ferry. The men sharpened the focus on their binoculars as they peered toward Sharpsburg and Shepherdstown. The Rebels who had been camped at the former location were gone, their passage marked by a line of supply wagons slowly trailing behind them. A large number of Confederate troops could be seen gathering at the Shepherdstown river crossing. Identifying these units now became objective number one for George Sharpe and his staff at the Bureau of Military Information.

After collating information from several sources, Sharpe felt certain that all of Ewell's Corps was now in Pennsylvania, with cavalry detachments fanning out ahead of it. The troops preparing to cross the Potomac must be Longstreet's, as Sharpe figured it. The enemy First Corps had been second in the line of march since the movement began, and a Rebel courier who had been taken near Harper's Ferry claimed to be from that corps. Williamsport was too far away to be monitored from Harper's Ferry, but Sharpe had received data via Harrisburg that placed Hill's men over the river. In one of those sudden moments of brutal clarity, George Sharpe realized that everything pointed to the conclusion that Lee's entire army, or most of it, was north of the Potomac.

Even with this assessment in hand, Hooker held off on moving his army. He also had a report from his Twelfth Corps commander at Leesburg that 6,000 Rebels, said to be commanded by Longstreet, were in the Loudoun Valley. Not until Sharpe provided additional confirmation from Harper's Ferry (in the form of more prisoners' professing to belong to Longstreet's Corps), along with word from his officer in Frederick, Maryland, that "the last of Lee's entire army has passed through Martinsburg towards the Potomac," was Hooker convinced. At 11:35 P.M. on June 24, orders were sent to Oliver Otis Howard and his Eleventh Corps to cross the Potomac the next morning. The rest of the Army of the Potomac would follow.

It was one of the grand ironies of this operation that Hooker's most critical and best decision was based on incorrect data. Longstreet's Corps was not across the Potomac by June 24, nor was it anywhere near Shepherdstown. Because they had stopped to hold the Blue Ridge Mountain gaps behind Stuart's cavalry, Longstreet's troops had been leapfrogged by Hill's men, who were then routed to Shepherdstown. All the intelligence supporting the Longstreet identification had been either planted by the Confederates, as deliberate misinformation, or else plucked from the rumor pit to bolster prior assumptions. Joe Hooker was making his most important move of the campaign for all the wrong reasons.

SIX

". . . I can throw Genl Hooker's army across the Potomac"

A t about 1:00 A.M. on June 25, in the village of Salem, Virginia, Jeb Stuart made a final, satisfied survey of the long, dark columns of mounted troops awaiting his word of command. Anxious to preserve some modicum of deception regarding what he was about to attempt, Stuart said loudly enough for those nearby to hear, "Ho! for the Valley!," and waved his riders in the direction of the Blue Ridge Mountains.

The misdirection, if that was what it was, did not last long. Just outside Salem, he turned the column south and then east. By early morning, his scouts had secured passage through Glasscock Gap in the Bull Run Mountains. Jeb Stuart was now committed to what would become the most controversial operation of his military career.

The three days following his and Lee's decision to undertake a possible ride around the Union forces had been marked by efforts on the part of several individuals to refine the operational orders so there could be no misunderstandings. Lee began the exchange by advising Stuart, in a note sent on June 22, that if he found Hooker's army "moving northward," he could march three brigades "into Maryland, and take position on General Ewell's right," which "will probably move toward the Susquehanna [River] by the Emmittsburg . . . [or] Chambersburg [routes]." This set an overall objective and provided a triggering action.

To further clarify one of the cavalryman's options, Lee's First Corps commander, James Longstreet, sent Stuart a message at 7:00 P.M. that same day, summarizing a conversation he had just had with Lee. In it, the army chief had described Stuart's action as "passing by the rear of the enemy," and specified a route through Hopewell Gap. Longstreet seconded Lee's choice of route but cautioned that Stuart's moving directly north would "disclose our plans."

Then, at 5:00 P.M. on June 23, Lee sent Stuart orders that were slight refinements of the instructions of the day before. "If General Hooker's army remains inactive," the dispatch read (removing the need for a triggering action), "you can leave two brigades to watch him, and withdraw with the three others"—but if at any time before the operation began, the

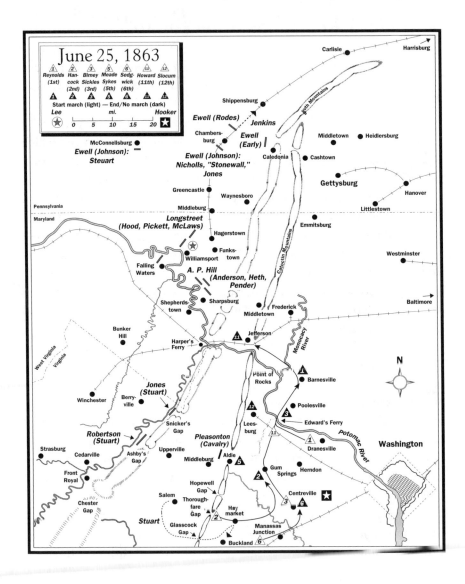

enemy appeared to be "moving northward,"* Lee advised, "I think you had better withdraw this side of the mountain to-morrow night, cross at Shepherdstown next day, and move over to Frederick." Thus, if the Federals were on the move, Lee preferred Stuart take the more congested route.

Yet another message from Lee to Stuart arrived at the cavalryman's headquarters that evening implying that Lee had changed his mind. Although the communiqué was later lost, the staff officer who received it would never forget its contents: "The letter suggested that, as the roads leading northward from Shepherdstown and Williamsport were already encumbered by the infantry, the artillery, and the transportation of the army, the delay . . . in passing by these would, perhaps, be greater than would ensue if General Stuart passed around the enemy's rear." The city of York, Pennsylvania, was named by Lee as the most likely place for Stuart to connect with Ewell's right flank.

Stuart made his first mistake in this operation on June 24. Faced with the task of deciding which two brigades would remain behind and which three would undertake the movement, Stuart chose the best to accompany him. Left with the army were the brigades of Brigadier Generals Beverly H. Robertson and William E. ("Grumble") Jones. Robertson had muffed an important assignment at Brandy Station on June 9, and Jones and Stuart were barely on speaking terms. Neither was well known to Lee, nor did either enjoy his confidence or comprehend his expectations. Although he was following his instructions to the letter, Stuart had badly misread the degree of personal connection his superior required. Longstreet understood this about Lee, and so had specifically requested that Stuart select an officer whom Lee knew and trusted, Brigadier General Wade Hampton, to coordinate the cavalry remaining with the army. Stuart's failure to comply embittered Longstreet. The infantryman's later recollections would roundly condemn the cavalryman's vainglorious ride, and not always fairly so.

Stuart had valid reasons for being where he was on the morning of June 25, and he had Lee's sanction to "judge whether you can pass around their army without hindrance, doing them all the damage you can, and cross the [Potomac] river east of the [Blue Ridge] mountains."

---

*The text printed in the *Official Records* reads "*not* moving northward," a curious contradiction of Lee's previous instruction. The original message was lost, and the version in the *Official Records* was derived from a copy. I surmise that the copy was in error and that the words should actually be "*now* moving northward."

Once his scouts had cleared the way through Glasscock Gap, his riders continued toward Centreville, where John Mosby's information suggested they might find easy passage through Hooker's rear echelon.

Joseph Hooker's troop movements this day were essentially defensive in nature. Three corps (the First, Third, and Eleventh), under the overall command of John Reynolds, were ordered to the northern side of the Potomac. Their objective was to take control of Crampton's and Turner's gaps through the South Mountains in order to prevent Confederate forces from interdicting the Army of the Potomac's crossing. Hooker was not expecting a fight. "My advices of last night inform me that the rebels do not hold [the passes]," he assured Reynolds. Provost Marshal Patrick caught something of the sudden urgency in the air as he noted in his diary, "Genl. Hooker intends that *all* shall be over the River by tomorrow night."

The first Eleventh Corps soldiers began to cross the Edward's Ferry pontoon bridge a little before 4:00 A.M. A member of the 107th Ohio judged the river at that point to be "about one-fourth of a mile wide." Private John T. McMahon, a witness to the June 17 sheep slaughter, would remember this day for its long tramp, with rain in the afternoon. The weary boys got some encouragement as they passed through Poolesville: "The women cheered us and waved their handkerchiefs [as] well," McMahon recollected. Also on the Eleventh Corps' line of march today was the village of Jefferson, where, recalled an Ohio soldier, "we stopped and got lots of good things to eat."

After Howard's men had cleared out, shortly after midday, Reynolds' First Corps made the river crossing, followed later in the afternoon by the Third. A Pennsylvania sergeant marching in the Third Corps paid especial attention to the pontoon bridge. As he explained it, "First, boats are built with flat bottoms about twenty feet long and three or four feet wide. . . . When it is desired to lay a bridge these boats are . . . placed in the water about six to eight feet apart, with the ends up and down stream, where they are securely anchored from both ends. Then timbers already fitted are laid across these boards from shore to shore, furnishing stringers upon which planks are laid, just as in any bridge."

The route taken by the Third Corps, once it was across the river, ran parallel to the Potomac, following the towpath for the Chesapeake and Ohio Canal. It was anything but pleasant. "No man who participated in that march can ever forget the driving rain, the slippery and narrow pathway, with water to the right of us, water to the left of us, water above, water below," complained a Pennsylvania soldier in the 26th regiment. A weary private John Haley grumbled that "we slipped back as fast as we could proceed." A more cynical Massachusetts man thought he knew why this route had been selected: "As the General commanding desired to make the [mouth of the] Monocacy [River] before stopping, he had the shrewdness to take the towpath . . . from which there was no egress till we arrived at that place—no houses or barns, no woods for men to straggle off to, out of sight of the Provost Guard; so they were obliged to keep along."

Robert E. Lee planned to cross the Potomac himself this morning. Just before and just after he did so, he penned letters to Jefferson Davis. In the first (written "opposite Williamsport"), Lee worried that his thrust into the North might prove *too* successful. He mentioned the militia forces that Lincoln had called out, and passed along rumors he had heard of Union troop transfers that all seemed to be aimed at stopping him. "It is plain that if all the Federal Army is concentrated upon this [army]," Lee asserted, "it will result in our accomplishing nothing, and being compelled to return to Virginia."

He restated his scheme to have P. G. T. Beauregard establish "an army, even in effigy, . . . at Culpeper Court-House." Claiming that his need to have every musket in line was such that he could not spare the men necessary to maintain direct communication with Richmond, Lee announced that he was going to break the link. He concluded with a statement evidently intended to limit expectations for his current campaign: "I think I can throw Genl Hooker's army across the Potomac and draw troops from the south, embarrassing their plan of campaign in a measure, if I can do nothing more and have to return."

Lee's second note this day (headed "Williamsport") presented his strategic views. Referencing Union news reported in Richmond papers, he cited stories of a yellow fever outbreak along the North Carolina coast to buttress his contention that the "enemy contemplates nothing important in that region." Lee urged Davis to send Confederate troops from that area to Culpeper and place them under Beauregard. Unconfirmed reports of Federal pullbacks in Kentucky suggested to Lee that a thrust there by Confederate forces could "render valuable service by collecting and bringing out supplies," as well as preventing Union "troops now there from being sent to other points." Of course, he added, those Confederate troops could always be moved back into Virginia to help bulk up the Beauregard force. "It should never be forgotten that our concentration at any point compels that of the enemy, and, his numbers being limited, tends to relieve all other threatened localities," Lee lectured.

In between writing these notes, Lee crossed the Potomac. Artilleryman Francis W. Dawson remembered it as a "dreary day," with rain "falling in torrents." He saw "Genl Lee, Genl Longstreet and Genl Pickett . . . riding together followed by their staffs." As the group reached the Maryland side, they were met by "several patriotic ladies with small feet and big umbrellas," who insisted on presenting Lee with a large wreath. A bit of delicate negotiation ended with a courier's taking the bulky offering and conveying the general's thanks. All around them, recalled one of Longstreet's officers, "the inspiriting strains of 'Dixie' burst forth from bands of music."

As the twisting files of Lee's army began to spread into Pennsylvania, the men kept a nervous watch over their shoulders—a detail that in later years they would omit from their storytelling. Most recollections of the Confederate march into the Keystone State treated the civilian population with bemused indifference, but that seemingly docile populace had a dark side that few Southerners cared to remember. The danger they felt from civilian snipers was real. One North Carolina soldier described how the men in his unit "were bound to form squads of some strength to prevent 'bushwhackers' and the enraged citizens from attacking us on the road." A member of Pickett's Division, recalling the march from Chambersburg toward Gettysburg, noted that his "command was frequently fired on during the day by bushwhackers." A cavalryman preceding the foot soldiers into the same region observed that it "seems to be full of 'bushwhackers.'" The threat posed was more than theoretical: in nearby McConnellsburg, a pair of Rebel stragglers, rounded up without arms, "were simply led out and shot."

Those four of Hooker's infantry corps that did not cross the Potomac today formed a long screen stretching from Slocum's Twelfth, near the river at Leesburg; through Meade's Fifth, holding position near Aldie; down to Hancock's Second and Sedgwick's Sixth, watching for any enemy movement from the southwest. Throughout the day, all these units started to fall back slowly toward Edward's Ferry.

Hancock's men had begun backing away from Thoroughfare Gap in the early morning. It was around noon when Harrow's Brigade of Gibbon's Division reached what one soldier called the "insignificant hamlet" of Haymarket, where the line of march turned to the north. What happened next was scribbled down later this day by Corporal Stephen E. Martin of the 1st Minnesota, writing in his diary: "After marching 2 miles the [Rebel] cavalry got on a knoll and when the troops came along the road comenced to shell us[.] [T]he 1st shells was at our Regt." Another Minnesota diarist, Private Isaac Lyman Taylor, provided a bit more detail: "At 12 m.," he wrote, "as we approach Haymarket some cavalry appear on a bluff south of us & while the boys are earnestly arguing the question 'Are they our men?', a white puff of smoke and the unearthly screech of a shell closes the debate & a unanimous decision is rendered in the Neg[ative]."

"There were several casualties," affirmed Lieutenant William Lochren of the 1st, "and Colonel [William] Colvill's horse was killed under him." "The exploding shells put to flight and into a great panic a crowd of sutlers, negroes, and other camp followers that were lingering in the rear of Gibbon's Division," reported the 1st Minnesota's historian, "and it is said that there were some ludicrous scenes."

The 1st was not the only unit targeted. One of the exploding shells struck Private Israel D. Jones of the 19th Maine, who became the first man of his regiment to be killed by enemy action. "In less than ten minutes from the time that Mr. Jones was chatting cheerfully with the man marching at his side, he was buried by the roadside," observed the regiment's historian. "The forming of Harrow's brigade and the advance of Webb's [Brigade] caused [the Rebel cavalry] . . . to leave the field," related a 1st Minnesota man.

The Rebel cavalry that ambushed Hancock's men near Haymarket was in fact the head of Stuart's 4,000-man column. After transiting Glasscock Gap, Stuart had intended to march through that hamlet to Gum Springs, where he expected to find John Mosby and information about usable

Potomac fords. In place of a clear road, however, he encountered what one aide described as "long lines of wagons and artillery; and behind these came on the dense blue masses of infantry, the sunshine lighting up their burnished bayonets." As Stuart later reported, "I chose a good position, and opened with artillery on his passing column with effect, scattering men, wagons, and horses in wild confusion." According to another aide, the artillery fire "was continued until the enemy moved a force of infantry against the guns. Not wishing to disclose his force, Stuart withdrew from Hancock's vicinity after capturing some prisoners and satisfying himself concerning the movement of that corps."

Scouts sent out to ascertain the extent of the Federal column returned with disheartening news. Instead of the widely spaced deployment of relatively stationary units that he had hoped to exploit, Stuart was facing an entire corps on the move, one that was filling the available roads with men and matériel, making it impossible for him to slip through as he had planned.

Stuart sent off a sighting report to Lee* and pondered his options. He could sit tight until the enemy troops cleared the roads, or he could backtrack into the Shenandoah Valley and try to squeeze past Longstreet's men, or he could swing farther east in the hope of finding an open route to the Potomac. "He consulted with no one concerning the decision," recalled an aide, "and none is authorized to speak of the motives which may have presented themselves to his mind." In his official report, Stuart wrote that he "determined to cross Bull Run lower down, and strike through Fairfax for the Potomac the next day."

In Washington, Major General Samuel P. Heintzelman was fuming. As the officer responsible for defending the capital, he had fought a losing bureaucratic skirmish against Hooker, who was successfully using the current emergency to appropriate as many of Heintzelman's troops as possible. "Since Hooker's appearance on my front," the general scratched in his diary, "he had taken from me 6,000 cavalry and at least 15,000 infantry." His sense of injury made the rumors Heintzelman had heard about Hooker all the more satisfying. One officer swore that Hooker had been seen drunk at his headquarters that very day. "I learn also that when

---

*This is one of the unsolved mysteries of the Gettysburg campaign: Stuart's message never reached Lee.

he left town the day before that, he was not sober," Heintzelman noted with smug piety.

At almost the same time, Lincoln's navy secretary, Gideon Welles, was responding to public fears excited by Lee's raid. Officials at Havre de Grace, Maryland, near the mouth of the Susquehanna River, were worried for the safety of government property; they had asked for, and now got, a gunboat to protect the town. Welles had also heard stories that had Ewell's and Longstreet's corps passing through Hagerstown, headed north. His pen inscribed the burning question that was on everyone's mind: "Where, in the mean time," Welles asked, "is Genl Hooker and our army?"

The rain had finally subsided, but the mood was no less dismal, thanks to the sound of a band playing the death march. In a large open field near Hagerstown, Maryland (their bivouac for the night), the men of George Pickett's division formed a hollow square with one side left open. A member of the 18th Virginia, one John E. Riley, a hired substitute* and convicted deserter, had been condemned by a court-martial and was now to pay the price. A soldier in the 18th's Company E was unlucky enough to be selected for the firing squad. "It was very trying to me," he confided in a letter written a few days later, "but I am here for duty." The sad procession circled the drawn-up division, then halted while a chaplain offered "a long and beautiful prayer."

Just before the condemned man was blindfolded, he looked at his executioners and said, "Good-bye boys." Then the firing squad did its duty. "In twenty seconds the prisoner was dead," the soldier recalled. A staff officer who heard the shots from a comfortable distance was told that there were "four like executions" that took place at this time. Another observer suggested that the spectacle had a deterrent effect that was "beneficial to other substitutes, whose only object was to secure the pay and desert."

"Every one is asking, Where is our army, that they let the enemy scour the country and do as they please?" wrote Gettysburg resident Sarah Broadhead in her diary. The promised militia troops had been held up

---

*Both sides allowed drafted individuals to pay for a substitute to serve in their place.

when their train engine struck a cow and derailed. No soldiers were injured, but neither was the unit going to get any closer this day. The mood throughout Gettysburg was tense. Sharp-eyed citizens spotted a smattering of campfires in the hills framing the Cashtown Pass. Those distant, flickering flames spoke louder than any headline.

SEVEN

"We were all scared"

In his official report of the operation, Jeb Stuart wrote of this Friday, June 26, "We marched through Brentsville to the vicinity of Wolf Run Shoals, and had to halt . . . in order to graze our horses, which hard marching without grain was fast breaking down. We met no enemy to-day." Stuart's animals found little relief. "Had very poor grazing for horses," recorded a Virginian riding under Fitzhugh Lee, "this being a miserably poor country & the armies having entirely consumed it."

Some forty miles to the west, the two cavalry brigades under Beverly H. Robertson stolidly watched over Ashby's and Snicker's gaps. Before setting off, Stuart had left Robertson with very detailed instructions directing him to "hold the Gaps" as long "as the enemy remains in your front." Robertson, taking his time completing this determination, kept his units immobile. One of his troopers noted that "there were no skirmishes, [and] no enemy in sight."

Armed men in blue uniforms marched through Gettysburg this morning. There were 743 in the ranks, a militia unit designated the 26th Pennsylvania Emergency Infantry. "The men upon whom this duty was imposed, coming from the field, the college, and the home, had been in the service just four days," remembered one of them: "not long enough to have acquired a knowledge of the drill, hardly long enough to have learned the names of their officers and comrades." Commanding them was Colonel William W. Jennings. The militia regiment reached town at about 9:00

A.M. to find that the forewarned citizens had prepared a tasty breakfast of pies, sandwiches, and coffee for the novice soldiers.

The fun part of this outing ended after about ninety minutes, when Major Granville O. Haller, acting on the authority of the Department of the Susquehanna commander Darius Couch, ordered a protesting William Jennings to march his regiment toward Chambersburg. The men fell into ranks,

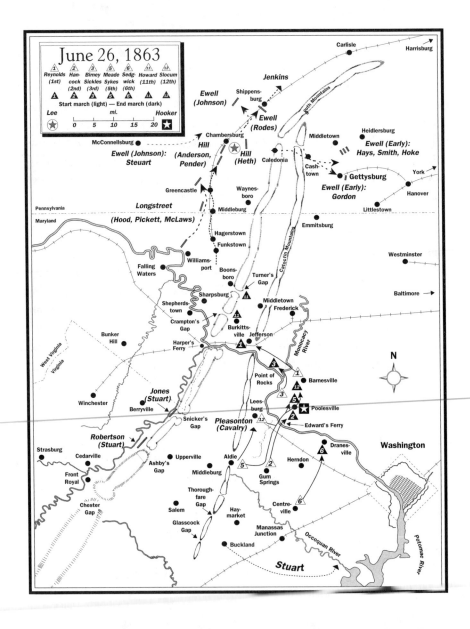

their dour mood not improved by the drizzling rain that began to fall. The little cavalry squadron under Robert Bell accompanied the foot soldiers. Three and a half miles passed slowly under the wet feet of these emergency troops before Jennings halted his column along a ridge overlooking Marsh Creek, where he and Bell, finding a little high ground, peered through the mist toward the mountains. After a while they could make out some movement in the distance. Before very long, the tiny suggestions of activity coalesced into something larger and definitely more dangerous.

In Gettysburg, twelve-year-old Mary Fastnacht looked on in innocent wonder as the town's handful of African American residents* reacted to events. "They, of course, were badly frightened and, with their bundles tried to leave town," she recollected. Two of the refugees, a widow and her daughter, appealed to Fastnacht's mother because "they were alone and did not know what to do." Recalling this moment many years later, Mary Fastnacht would be unable to restrain her pride as she related how "Mother told them to come to our house, that she would hide them in the loft over the kitchen, take the ladder away and they would be safe."

The experiences of Gettysburg's blacks were typical of those suffered by the thousands of African Americans[†] who lived in the path of Lee's advance. Although no formal orders were ever issued directing a general roundup of black civilians encountered in Pennsylvania, such actions were carried out with an openness and on a scale that suggest, at the very least, tacit knowledge at the highest command levels.

A soldier-correspondent who went by the initials W.K., riding with Jenkins' command, reported to the *Richmond Enquirer* that the Rebel troopers had appropriated "many 'contrabands' and fine horses." An individual named William Brown was said by the Georgia soldier Alfred Zachry to have been "arrested . . . as a contraband, supposed to be a slave." Perhaps most chilling were the words penned on June 28 by a Confederate officer named William S. Christian: "We took a lot of negroes yesterday," he wrote. "I was offered my choice, but as I could not get them back home I would not take them. In fact, my humanity revolted at taking the poor devils away from their homes."

---

*There were about 190 in total.
[†]According to the 1860 census, there were 5,622 blacks settled in the counties directly threatened by the Rebel raiders.

The exodus of so many blacks before the advancing gray tide cast an eerie pall over the surroundings. "The free negroes are all gone," wrote a surgeon in Hill's Corps at the end of June. "My servant, Wilson, says he 'don't like Pennsylvania at all,' because he 'sees no black folks.' " Not all of those who fled were Northern freemen: a member of the 14th North Carolina (Ewell's Corps) noted that right after his regiment entered Pennsylvania, "Ben, the negro cook of Lieutenant Liles, took French leave for the Yankees—never heard of him afterwards." Most of the African Americans who stayed behind were those with little to fear. A Louisianian under Ewell reported that on the "entire line of march I saw only two negroes, and they were a very old couple, man and woman, standing on the roadside as the army passed. One of my company asked the negro man if he was 'secesh,' and he replied, 'Yes, sir, massa; I sees you now.' "

Throughout this day, Joseph Hooker continued to move his Army of the Potomac across its namesake river, until, as darkness closed down operations, he had all but the Sixth Corps and his cavalry on the northern side. In the evening, he designated Frederick, Maryland, as his new concentration point by directing that all supplies be sent there. The army's First, Third, and Eleventh corps remained grouped under John Reynolds, charged with covering the gaps piercing the South Mountain chain. "A steady and continuous rain has made the roads very disagreeable for marching," observed a Michigan man in the Iron Brigade, "but has at the same time saved us from the heat and dust and consequent exhaustion of our previous march from the Rappahannock." In the 136th New York, one of Howard's regiments in the Eleventh Corps, the men resorted to odd tactics to ward off the rain. "We had our knapsacks on our shoulders and placed our rubber blankets over all," remembered a New Yorker. "This shut out what little air we otherwise might have got."

The toils of his soldiers must have been on Lincoln's mind for at least part of this day. Using his presidential authority, he commuted six military death sentences that had been sent to him for review. He was also thinking about Joe Hooker. To Navy Secretary Gideon Welles, Lincoln said, "We cannot help beating them, if we have the man. How much depends in military matters on one master mind. Hooker may commit the same fault as [previous Army of the Potomac commander George B.] McClellan and lose his chance. We shall soon see, but it appears to me he can't help but win." It was in these comments, Welles believed, that Lincoln first "betrayed doubts of Hooker, to whom he is quite partial."

Robert E. Lee broke camp near Williamsport early this morning, rode through Hagerstown, crossed the Pennsylvania border, and reached Chambersburg at around 9:00 A.M. Merchant Jacob Hoke was on hand to view the Rebel chief. "He was at that time about fifty-two years of age," Hoke later recounted, "stoutly built, of medium height, hair strongly mixed with gray, and a rough, gray beard. . . . His whole appearance indicated dignity, composure, and disregard for the gaudy trappings of war."

Hoke was convinced that the direction Lee took once he reached the town square would reveal much about his plans. If he continued northward, "then Harrisburg and Philadelphia are threatened," Hoke told one of the town's unofficial scouts. If, however, Lee turned east toward the Cashtown Gap, "Baltimore and Washington are in danger." Lee made a right-hand turn to the east and the scout hurried away to take word of it to officials in Harrisburg. For the rest of his life, Hoke would feel certain that he had seen through to Lee's real purpose, but it was really more a matter of hindsight. Lee rode only a short distance out of town before making camp. He set up his headquarters in a pleasant grove that was a local favorite for picnics. His only orders today for Longstreet and Hill were to rest their corps as the men arrived from the south.

A Georgia soldier in Longstreet's Corps would recall the sojourn in Chambersburg as having been devoted to "testing the qualities of Pennsylvania poultry, which proved to have a very palatable flavor. Many of the men seemed to consider the private impressment of supplies an imperative duty incumbent upon us in retaliation for the marauding of the Yankees in our country." In some cases, officers tried to offset the chilling effect of the rain by letting their men help themselves to the whiskey that was freely offered and readily available. Another of Longstreet's Georgians thought that the drunken boys made for a "jolly set." A member of one unit that began its day in Virginia and ended it near Chambersburg bragged that the men "marched in four states that day, the fourth in a state of intoxication."

By the time Longstreet's Mississippi soldiers of Brigadier General William Barksdale's brigade reached the Pennsylvania line, they were far from being the first of Lee's legions to enter the North. Nonetheless,

Sergeant C. C. Cummings, whose friend had jokingly called Robert E. Lee a bushwhacker, decided that some sort of ceremony was in order. Marching at the head of the column as it entered the town of Middleburg,* through which the Mason-Dixon line ran, Cummings spotted an old man watching the troops pass and instructed him to drag his cane across the dirt street to replicate the border. "He did so," Cummings related, "and with a running jump I bounded over into Pennsylvania."

With Longstreet's and Hill's men now arriving in Chambersburg, it was time for Ewell to push on. Contrary to the modern perception that Lee's infantry vanguard was groping blindly forward in Stuart's absence, Ewell was in fact operating with cavalry covering his front. A mounted brigade from western Virginia, under the command of Albert Jenkins, had been riding with the Second Corps since June 12. Jenkins' Brigade, comprising three regiments, two battalions, and a horse battery, may have lacked the combat experience and discipline of Stuart's outfit, but it performed generally effective advance duties as Ewell moved deeper into Pennsylvania. Extra help had arrived on June 25 in the form of the 35th Battalion Virginia Cavalry, under the capable Colonel Elijah V. White, detached from "Grumble" Jones' command. Ewell appended White's men plus one of Jenkins' regiments to Early's Division, while the rest swept ahead of Rodes and Johnson.

Ewell's advance was planned along two different axes. Two of his divisions—Rodes' and Johnson's—pressed northward to the town of Shippensburg. One of Johnson's brigades, commanded by Brigadier General George R. Steuart, had been dispatched westward to gather supplies around McConnellsburg. That unit was now hustling to catch up with its parent division, bringing along with it, as staff officer Randolph McKim noted approvingly, "60 head of cattle, 40 horses, [and] a few mules." A Tarheel soldier under Rodes penned a brief eulogy for the bountiful harvest being decimated: "Our camp was in a wheat field," he explained. "What a pity for the wagons, artillery, the horses and ourselves to destroy it. [But] it could not be avoided."

Jubal Early's division was sent off in a different direction, due east. As his columns entered the western approaches to the Cashtown Gap, their route took them past a sizable iron foundry owned and operated by the

*Modern State Line.

abolitionist U.S. congressman Thaddeus Stevens. Stevens' outspoken advocacy of a vigorous prosecution of the war was well known to Early, who decided to exact a little Southern justice of his own. He ordered the iron works burned and the supplies stored there seized, then turned a blind eye to his troops' vandalism of workers' housing. Early believed that these actions were more than justified. In part they were simple retaliation for the "various deeds of barbarity perpetuated by Federal troops in some of the Southern states," and in part they were a message aimed right at Stevens for his "most vindictive spirit toward the people of the South."

Once through the pass, Early learned that a Yankee force of unknown composition was holding position west of Gettysburg. He decided to flank the Federals by sending three of his brigades on a northerly swing through Mummasburg, while ordering the remaining one (John Gordon's) plus Elijah White's cavalry to push ahead and develop the enemy's strength, location, and intentions.

Approaching Cashtown, the head of Gordon's column was fired upon from an ambush staged by four locals. Only one of them was armed, but he mortally wounded a Georgia soldier, so infuriating Jubal Early that he dispatched White's troopers to find the bushwhackers. Although the quartet successfully eluded capture, the shooter, one Henry

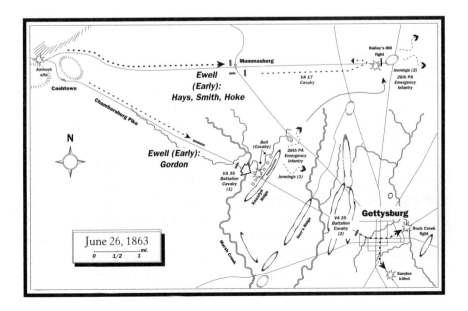

Hahn, would come to regret his act of murder so deeply that when he died, in 1879, many would say it was his conscience that had killed him.

Back along Marsh Creek, William Jennings became convinced that the trouble headed his way was more than his raw militiamen could handle. "It has always seemed to me that the situation had in it much of the heroic," one of the emergency soldiers would later suggest. "Untrained, untried, and unused to war, they were sent to meet an overwhelming and disciplined force, not in some Grecian pass . . . , but in the open field with the certainty that they could make no effectual resistance." "Our colonel, left to his own resources, wisely decided to make an effort to return to Harrisburg, and immediately struck off from the [Chambersburg] pike," remembered another militiaman. Jennings left behind a picked squad to serve as a rear guard while the bulk of his command hurried off to the northeast at various speeds. It was this delaying force, along with Robert Bell's mounted squadron, that White's cavalry encountered at around 2:00 P.M.

It was no contest. Bell's thin screen was ripped to tatters, while many in Jennings' rear guard were overrun and captured. "It was well that the regiment took to its heels so quickly," an amused Jubal Early later reported, "or some of its members might have been hurt."

The twelve companies that Jennings had withdrawn regrouped on Bailey's Hill, four miles north of Gettysburg. There they made a last stand, holding against Early's infantry and cavalry for perhaps thirty minutes before retreating for good. Those not captured or felled by exhaustion (about a hundred men) eventually made it back to Harrisburg. "I never thought I could bear what I have gone through," one survivor wrote afterward. "Old soldiers, nine-month men, say they never experienced anything like it."

Once through Jennings' ineffective roadblock, the Virginia cavalrymen continued along the pike. Deciding that shock tactics would suppress any further opposition, they charged into Gettysburg yelling and firing their pistols in the air. The strategy worked, for the most part: "It seemed as if Pandemonium had broken loose," recalled townswoman Lydia Catherine Ziegler. Sarah Broadhead thought it was "enough to frighten us all to death." "We were all scared," avowed Elizabeth Thorn, then six months pregnant, "and wished for them to go." A few, however, took it less seriously: in the house where Gates D. Fahnestock lived, the "boys looking through the slatted shutters [from the] second story saw and enjoyed it as they would a wild west show."

White's riders had a brief skirmish with a company that had been detailed from Jennings' emergency regiment and posted on the eastern side of town, along Rock Creek. This small force was scattered, and a few of the hapless Yankees were taken prisoner. The "wild west show" turned deadly when some of the Virginia troopers flushed out a couple of Bell's pickets, left behind when the squadron rode west. Two tried to escape on horseback, but one of them was thrown off at a fence, and when he confronted his pursuers with a pistol in hand, he was gunned down. Private George W. Sandoe thus earned the doleful distinction of being the first Union soldier to die by enemy action at Gettysburg. A hired substitute, he had been in the company just three days.

For a while, the Rebel cavalry had free rein in everything. A woman resident vividly recollected the raiders' "ransacking the barns, stores and chicken coops." Fourteen-year-old Tillie Pierce ran home from school and arrived in time to see a Confederate lead away her favorite mount. "I began to plead for the horse," she would write years later. "As I stood there begging and weeping, I was so shocked and insulted, I shall never forget it." Young Leander Warren's mother got the surprise of her life when a mounted Rebel banged on the house shutters and demanded some matches. " 'Oh, are you going to burn the old barn?' " she asked. " 'No,' " replied the Confederate, " 'we want to shoe our horses in the Blacksmith Shop.' " Leander "was not long in getting him some matches."

Things became a bit more orderly after John Gordon's infantry marched into town. "These Confederates were very firm and businesslike in their attitude toward the townspeople," reported Henry Jacobs, whose father taught at Gettysburg's Pennsylvania College. Businesslike though they may have been, however, "I never saw a more unsightly set of men," swore Fannie Buehler, a mother of six whose postmaster husband was in hiding. She described Gordon's men as being "dirty, . . . hatless, shoeless, and footsore." In hiding like Postmaster Buehler was spymaster David McConaughy, whose third son chose this day to be born.

Not long after Gordon's men secured the area, Jubal Early rode in from Mummasburg, where he had parked the rest of his division. Early was feeling like a beneficent conqueror. The crestfallen survivors of the 26th Pennsylvania Emergency Infantry were gathered in the town square, where the Confederate general addressed them. According to one resident, "He suggested the propriety of returning them to their mothers." Early provided the town authorities with a list of supplies that he expected to be furnished to him. If the foodstuffs were not available, he said, he would take five thousand dollars instead. In a somewhat truculent response, Gettysburg's borough council president, David Kendlehart, declared that neither food nor cash would be forthcoming, though the town merchants would open their doors "to furnish whatever they can of such provisions."

Early had a timetable to keep and may have wanted to rehabilitate his image somewhat after burning Stevens' ironworks. Rather than losing his temper, he sent squads off in a halfhearted search of the town that managed to turn up 2,000 military rations in a rail car intended for the militia. After seeing that Gordon's men got the food, Early rode away to his headquarters to plan the next day's march. Among the units spending this night in Gettysburg was the band attached to Gordon's Brigade. Fifteen-year-old Albertus McCreary would never forget how "exasperating" it had been to hear those musicians "through the night playing 'Dixie' and other Confederate airs."

Joseph Hooker took the offensive this evening—not against the men in gray but against Henry Halleck. After losing his special place in the president's chain of command, Hooker had regained ground by using the urgency of Lee's close passage to Washington to draw reinforcements from the capital's garrison—troops that Halleck had promptly surrendered. Halleck had sent him the best units assigned to Washington's protection, including a large brigade of short-term Vermont men under Brigadier General George J. Stannard; two brigades of Pennsylvania Reserves led by Samuel Crawford; another brigade commanded by Brigadier General Alexander Hays, an experienced combat leader; an entire division of cavalry; plus several batteries and other miscellaneous units. But even this infusion was not enough for Hooker.

Now he had set his sights on the Union forces holding Harper's Ferry. Once more he made claims not supported by the intelligence he was receiving from George Sharpe's bureau. At 7:00 P.M., Hooker wired Halleck seeking authority over the Harper's Ferry troops. "It must be borne in mind that I am here with a force inferior in numbers to that of the enemy," Hooker insisted, "and must have every available man to use on the field."

Just one hour before sending Halleck this demand, Hooker had received a curious note from Abraham Lincoln, who wished to know if a news report placing the general in Washington on the night of June 25 was true. "You need not believe any more than you choose," Hooker responded at 8:00 P.M. He asked for Lincoln's help in identifying the source for the story. Lincoln's reply came twelve hours later: "It did not come from the newspapers," the president wrote, "nor did I believe it, but I wished to be entirely sure it was a falsehood."

EIGHT

"... I ... request that I may at once be relieved"

Jeb Stuart continued his passage through the abandoned Union rear areas this Saturday, though the march was not without incident. Once across the Occoquan at Wolf Run Shoals, he divided his command, sending a brigade off on a side expedition with orders to rejoin the main body at Fairfax Court House. As that larger group approached the rail station servicing the courthouse, some of Stuart's men bumped into a Federal cavalry patrol, which they overwhelmed, but at a cost: Major John H. Whitaker of the 1st North Carolina Cavalry, whom one of Stuart's aides termed "a most gallant officer," died in the action. During this brief melee, Stuart himself was surprised by a squad of Federal troopers and almost captured; it was not the first time that his superb horse-handling skills had saved him from harm.

They were now passing through what one member of Stuart's staff described as a "wild and desolate locality, swarming with abandoned cabins and army *debris*." Stuart had hoped to contact John Mosby, who was, however, nowhere to be found.* When the detached brigade arrived, bringing news that the Yankees had cleared the area and were said to be

---

*When Stuart failed to arrive on schedule, Mosby—taking notice, as well, of the sudden increase in activity on the part of the Federal soldiers camped around him—assumed that the operation had been called off. He then returned to his hit-and-run raids, completely unaware of what his intelligence report had set in motion. After the war, he would become a vigorous defender of Stuart's decisions and actions during this campaign.

off toward Leesburg, Stuart was faced with some important decisions. As a staff officer later articulated it, the question was, "What would Stuart do—what route would he now follow?"

The two brigades that Stuart had left behind to watch over Ashby's and Snicker's gaps remained in place. Given a choice between displaying some possibly insubordinate initiative and strictly following orders, Bev-

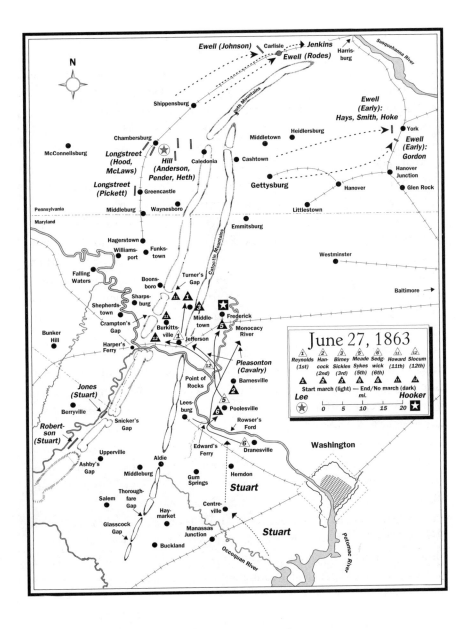

erly H. Robertson was content to do the latter. "The orders left with me
by General Stuart . . . ," he would later protest, "were exactly obeyed by
me." What Robertson knew about the situation in his front has always
been a matter of conjecture, but a scout from the 7th Virginia Cavalry
(part of Grumble Jones' Brigade) spent most of this day in Leesburg,
where it was obvious that the Federal infantry had departed.

With Stuart's cavalry off on its ride, Robertson's and Jones' troopers tied
down watching vacated mountain gaps, and Jenkins' small mounted brigade
screening Ewell's advance, there was painfully lax security along the main
line of Lee's march. The implications of this were demonstrated today when
two wagonloads of Hagerstown refugees came unimpeded into the Union
lines. "They unite in saying that . . . Ewell's, Longstreet's and Hill's corps
have passed through Hagerstown," reported the Eleventh Corps' provost
marshal. The fleeing civilians also testified that Rebel foraging "parties were
going in every direction, picking up cattle and sheep and other supplies."
Another who slipped easily through Lee's ineffective security this day was a
perceptive blacksmith named Thomas McCammon, who arrived on horseback from Hagerstown. He and two friends had made a careful accounting
of the numbers of Rebels passing through the town, and they tallied the
enemy artillery strength at 275 guns. The testimony of these citizens added
important details to the picture of Lee's army being put together by George
Sharpe and his Bureau of Military Information.

In Chambersburg today, Robert E. Lee kept his small headquarters staff
busy making copies for distribution of his General Orders number 73. The
document began with praise for the "high spirit" and "fortitude" his men
had shown, before gently taking them to task for "instances of forgetful-
ness" involving the "destruction of private property." It concluded with an
earnest exhortation urging the men "to abstain with most scrupulous care
from unnecessary or wanton injury to private property," and enjoining
officers to inflict "summary punishment" on violators.

  "Our orders are very strict here," noted a North Carolina soldier in
Ewell's Corps. "Nothing is wantonly destroyed, no private seizures are
allowed, and nothing taken without due orders and authority." A Georgian under Longstreet later maintained that the "people of Pennsylvania

were as safe in their homes, their persons and property, whilst the country was occupied by Lee's army, as was any territory in the South within the Confederate lines." This assertion was seconded by an officer with Hill, who swore that "no depredations were committed by our troops on the march, no one (citizens) were molested." "The greater part of the supplies that found their way into camp were paid for in Confederate money," claimed a Texas soldier with Longstreet, adding that "the rest were voluntary offerings."

"The infantry did not have much chance to plunder, as we were kept close in ranks and marched slowly," recalled Texan John Casler. "Of course we could go to the houses and get all we wanted to eat without money, for they did not want our money, and were glad to give us plenty through fear." A Virginia soldier in Ewell's Corps penned in his diary, with improvised spelling, "Morning. Went out a foraging. Sitisons scared nearly to death. Give the last thing they have If we only spare there lives." Another forager was well pleased with the results of his efforts: "The people are scared into fits and break their necks nearly to wait on me," he wrote.

While Lee's General Orders number 73 prohibited personally injurious and wanton acts, it legitimized whole categories of confiscation. A Georgia private named I. G. Bradwell observed that the "quartermasters and the small cavalry force with us were busy collecting horses, cattle, and sheep for the use of the army." "Our army is pressing in provision and horses by the whole sale and some of the finest horses I ever saw," marveled a fellow Georgia native in Hill's Corps. "We have provisions in abundance," recorded yet another Georgian. "The boys have played havoc with hogs, sheep, poultry, &c." "I heard one man say there were ninety-five sheep skins in [our] . . . camp," related a Texas infantryman, "and when some one spoke to him about it, he said that no man's sheep could bite his men without getting hurt." A juridically inclined officer in Ewell's command argued that his men had applied the "Confederate 'conscript law'" in drafting Pennsylvania horses into service."

There was a dark foundation beneath these carefully legitimized and seemingly benign activities. "I hope the officers will devastate the territory and give the enemy a taste of the horrors of war," wrote a grim North Carolina man. The sentiment was loudly echoed by a Virginia soldier who vowed, "The wrath of southern vengeance will be wreaked upon the pennsilvanians & all property belonging to the abolition horde which we cross." A member of the Stonewall Brigade* declared that "the people in this state did not know any thing of war times only what they herd and read . . . but they feel the effects of war at this time."

"Our men did very bad in M.D. and Penn.," a North Carolina soldier confessed in a letter to his sister. "They robed every house about such battle field not only of eatables but of everything they could lay their hands on. They tore up dresses to bits and broke all the furniture." Another roughly tutored North Carolinian wrote to his wife from "Franklin County, the State of Pennsylvania": "We are now in the enemy country we know not what will befall us for some of our solders have done mity bad since they have ben here." "The most of our Virginia boys treat [the Northern civilians] verry kind though there is some [of] our extreams southern troops has treated the people badley," observed a private in the 38th Virginia. "I treated everybody like I do at home, if anything better," an Alabama soldier swore to this sister. "But some of the army treated the citizens very badly."

Headquarters for the Army of the Potomac was moved today from Poolesville to Frederick, Maryland. In making the ride between those two places, Provost Marshal Marsena Patrick was able to indulge his dislike of the army's commander. "We started & came on 6 or 8 miles before being overtaken by Head Quarters," he recorded in his diary. "I never ride with Head Quarters longer than I am obliged to and held back." Joseph Hooker passed Patrick on his way to visit Harper's Ferry. Hooker rode as far as Point of Rocks, where he sent a message back to his chief of staff, Daniel Butterfield, holding station in Poolesville. "Direct that the cavalry be sent well to the advance of Frederick, in the direction of Gettysburg and Emmitsburg," Hooker ordered, "and see what they can of the movements of the enemy."

Before closing up shop in Poolesville, Hooker had sent a note to Halleck in which he tallied his current strength at not more than 105,000 men. "I state these facts that there may not be expected of me more than I have material to do with," Hooker had declared for the record. He had also taken care to copy President Lincoln on his note. Hooker's sights were now set on appropriating the garrison at Harper's Ferry. Halleck had seen this coming, however, and even before Hooker reached that

---

*This brigade in Johnson's Division of Ewell's Corps was previously commanded by the late Stonewall Jackson and so bore his name.

point, there was an answer waiting for him. The fortified heights at Harper's Ferry, Halleck explained, "have always been regarded as an important point to be held by us. . . . I cannot approve their abandonment, except in the case of absolute necessity."

The battle of wills between Hooker and Halleck was joined again, in full force. Soon after arriving at Harper's Ferry, Hooker sent Halleck his unsolicited assessment of conditions there: "I find 10,000 men here, in condition to take the field. Here they are of no earthly account. . . . Now they are but a bait for the rebels, should they return. I beg that this may be presented to the Secretary of War and His Excellency the President."

Hard on the heels of this memo came a second from Hooker, suggesting that he had been handed Halleck's message after dispatching his first note. The refusal of Lincoln's general in chief to let Hooker absorb that garrison pushed the Army of the Potomac commander to declare a situation of "absolute necessity":

HOOKER TO HALLECK—1 P.M. (RECEIVED 3 P.M.)
MY ORIGINAL INSTRUCTIONS REQUIRE ME TO COVER HARPER'S FERRY AND WASHINGTON. I HAVE NOW IMPOSED UPON ME, IN ADDITION, AN ENEMY IN MY FRONT OF MORE THAN MY NUMBER. I BEG TO BE UNDERSTOOD, RESPECT-FULLY, BUT FIRMLY, THAT I AM UNABLE TO COMPLY WITH THIS CONDITION WITH THE MEANS AT MY DISPOSAL, AND EARNESTLY REQUEST THAT I MAY AT ONCE BE RELIEVED FROM THE POSITION I OCCUPY.

To a friend and officer serving with the Harper's Ferry garrison, Hooker muttered, " 'Halleck's dispatch severs my connection with the Army of the Potomac.' " In later testimony before Congress, Hooker would charge that it had been "expected of me by the country that I would not only whip the army of the enemy, but prevent it from escaping. This I considered too much for the authorities to expect with the force I had."

The precise role that Henry Halleck played in bringing affairs to this pass may never be fully known. Halleck was a deeply flawed individual invested with enormous authority. His position at the president's right hand made him indispensable, even as his unwillingness and inability to take charge of situations rendered him simultaneously undependable and unpredictable. While his advice could be astute and insightful, it could also be specious and spurred by panic. Navy Secretary Gideon Welles deemed Halleck "offusticated, muddy, uncertain and stupid." In any event, Halleck's known animosity toward Hooker must cast a veil of suspicion over his motivations and actions in this case. There is some evidence that the general in chief was not alone in his feelings: referring to this period, his chief of staff, Brigadier General George Washington Cullum, would later brag to a friend, " 'I did my share in getting rid of Hooker, in whom I never had confidence.' "

HALLECK TO HOOKER—8 P.M.

YOUR APPLICATION TO BE RELIEVED FROM YOUR PRESENT COMMAND IS RECEIVED.

AS YOU WERE APPOINTED TO THIS COMMAND BY THE PRESIDENT, I HAVE NO POWER TO RELIEVE YOU. YOUR DISPATCH HAS BEEN DULY REFERRED FOR EXECUTIVE ACTION.

Isaac R. Trimble had fought with distinction under Stonewall Jackson at Second Manassas, in which battle he had been seriously wounded. After a determined recuperation, he had taken a largely administrative post in the Shenandoah Valley, where he had remained until the passage of Lee's forces through his district persuaded him that an important campaign was under way. Because sitting on the sidelines would never do for a man of action, Trimble appended himself to Lee's headquarters, hoping for a combat posting. He got one of sorts this afternoon, when Lee asked him to ride ahead and advise Richard Ewell regarding the lay of the land around Harrisburg—something Trimble knew about from his work in the region before the war, as a civil engineer. During his briefing, Trimble found Lee uncharacteristically loquacious.

" 'Our army is in good spirits, not over fatigued, and can be concentrated on any one point in twenty-four hours or less,' " Lee stated. The absence of any positive reports from his cavalry (Stuart and Robertson) indicated that Hooker's army was not yet across the Potomac. " 'When they hear where we are they will make forced marches to interpose their forces between us and Baltimore and Philadelphia,' " Trimble recalled Lee's saying. " 'They will come up, probably through Frederick, broken down with hunger and hard marching, strung out on a long line and much demoralized, when they come into Pennsylvania. I shall throw an overwhelming force on their advance, crush it, follow up the success, drive one corps back on another, and by successive repulses and surprises before they can concentrate, create a panic and virtually destroy the army.' "

While these two were conversing, more of Longstreet's men were passing through Chambersburg. The promising artillery officer E. P. Alexander could not help but see the United States flags defiantly displayed by some of the town's residents. It was a point of pride for him, however, that his well-disciplined men "took not the slightest notice" of this provocation. A "stout" girl, taking their indifference as a challenge, began waving a small Union flag "almost in the faces of the men, marching on the side walk." The protest action came to an abrupt halt when one of Alexander's gunners stopped in front of the girl and shouted "Boo!" "A roar of laughter & cheers went up along the line," Alexander recounted, "under which the young lady retreated to the porch."

Today's marching orders for the Army of the Potomac kept most of its strength covering the South Mountain passes. Pleasonton's cavalry and Sedgwick's Sixth Corps completed the crossing of Hooker's force to the northern bank of the Potomac, while George Meade's Fifth Corps followed army headquarters from Poolesville to Frederick. The intermittent rainshowers of days past stopped by noon, and the sky began to clear.

Many of Meade's men marveled at the countryside around them. "For miles in every direction this beautiful country was replete with cereal and vegetable products," exclaimed a Massachusetts man. "Vast fields of wheat, oats, barley, etc., flourished and grew under the hands of the husbandman, and delighted the eyes of a hurrying, tramping army of men who had just left the barren fields of war-stricken Virginia." A Michigan soldier in Strong Vincent's brigade wrote in his diary, "Passed through the finest part of Maryland. Wheat ready for harvesting."

Just outside Frederick, George Meade's columns reached the near bank of the Monocacy River, which an officer in the 16th Michigan reckoned to be "about two hundred feet wide; water was about waist deep." Recollections of the crossing varied. While staff officer John W. Ames described the men as being "in a gale of good spirits and laughter," a foot soldier in the 44th New York remembered only that they all "got thoroughly wet." For his part, Captain Francis Adams Donaldson of the 118th Pennsylvania was annoyed that no one had bothered to bridge the river. "This extreme haste," he declared, "portend[s] an anxiety to reach the 'rebellious,' most gratifying to the powers that be at Washington if they are aware of it, but extremely ruffling to the temper of us dough bellies as we poor infantrymen are called by those chicken thieves, the cavalry. . . .

"Hooker has lost all command over the army," Donaldson continued, "and I doubt very much indeed whether a successful battle can be fought under him." The officer felt sorry for his corps commander, George Meade: " 'Old Four Eye,' as General Meade is termed by the men," Donaldson wrote, "appears to be a man universally despised in the Corps. He certainly cares little for the rank and file, and cries loud and deep are hurled at him, (for obeying instructions, as he must be doing), in marching us so tremendously." Had Donaldson been able to register his complaint directly, he would have found George Meade equally unhappy. "I hear nothing whatever from headquarters," Meade grumbled to his wife on June 25, "and am as much in the dark as to proposed plans here on the ground as you are in Philadelphia. This is what Joe Hooker thinks profound sagacity—keeping his corps commanders, who are to execute his plans, in total ignorance of them until they are developed in the execution of orders."

The Fifth Corps commander was not one to underestimate Robert E. Lee. "That he has assumed the offensive and is going to strike a blow there can be no doubt," Meade mused, "and that it will be a very formidable [blow] is equally certain." Given the air of intrigue that was swirling around the Army of the Potomac during this campaign like a dust cloud along the line of march, Meade felt obliged to ease his wife's mind with regard to another matter. "I see you are still troubled with visions of my being placed in command [of the army]," he wrote to her. "I thought that had all blown over, and I think it has, except in your imagination, and that of some others of my kind friends."

This became a day of personal satisfaction for Richard S. Ewell. Lee's Second Corps commander was traveling with Rodes' and Johnson's divisions, whose line of march brought them to Carlisle, Pennsylvania, a training site for the U.S. Cavalry before the war. It was here, more than twenty years earlier, that a Virginia boy just graduated from West Point had had his first posting. Ewell now established his headquarters at Carlisle Barracks, using the same building he had previously occupied as a second lieutenant in the United States Dragoons. When staff officer

Henry Kyd Douglas stopped in, Ewell was "in a talkative mood" and eager to reminisce about his youthful experiences.

For Colonel John H. S. Funk, commanding the 5th Virginia in the Stonewall Brigade, this day was a run-on sentence punctuated only by little misspellings: "I have nothing of interest to write you since we have been in Pennsylvania," he informed his mother, "we have fared verry well we are now in the richest part of the state the people through here hardly know that the war is going on but I think they will find it out before we leave we are within 20 miles of the state capital so you may [believe] the excitement is great some of the Duch that has seen our army corps pass think we will all be captured before we leave the state the Coper Heads seem glad to see us as we save them from being drafted, the girls are all Duch and in for the Union." A North Carolina soldier under Rodes agreed with Funk on one point concerning the Pennsylvanians: "The war had not hurt them like it had us."

The remaining third of Ewell's Corps—Jubal Early's division—was now closing on York, Pennsylvania. Uncertain as to the condition of the town's defenses, Early prudently halted his march a few miles short of the place. Muddy roads and city defenses were not the only things slowing him down: in moving through the Gettysburg area, Early's Louisiana troops had uncovered caches of whiskey and were none the better for it. "Many of them were drunk," groused a brigade staff officer. His remedy was to load the worst offenders into the cooks' wagons, "where they had a rough and disagreeable ride on the sharp sides and projecting legs of the pots and kettles, which sobered them speedily."

Scouting reports and other intelligence suggested to Early that he would have little trouble taking York on Sunday, June 28. Anticipating an easy conquest, he rode over to the camp of John Gordon's brigade and sought out its commander. He gave Gordon verbal orders to move out at dawn and strike for Wrightsville, where there was a large covered bridge across the Susquehanna River. Ewell's instructions to Early had been to burn that span, but Early's orders to Gordon modified the directive in one important aspect: Gordon was told to "get possession of [the bridge] . . . at both ends and hold it until I came up," Early later recollected. The ambitious division commander believed that having a foothold on the eastern bank of the Susquehanna would provide significant tactical and strategic advantages—advantages that he was determined to realize.

In their march around Pennsylvania, Ewell's troops encountered a number of civilians who proceeded to gesticulate to them in a way that seemed intended to convey some message. The gestures puzzled Jubal Early, who described them only as "mysterious signs." A staff officer with one of Early's brigades investigated the matter and learned that it was all one grand con. A pair of enterprising Yankees, he discovered, had kept pace ahead of Ewell's advance and presented themselves to the Pennsylvanians as members of a pro-South secret society. For a mere five dollars a piece, they had offered to teach the frightened and gullible residents special hand signals that "would be respected by the Confederate Army. In this way, thousands of people were induced to pay their money for the privilege of being accounted as friends of the South," Early's man informed him.

Back at Carlisle, Richard Ewell's reveries about the old days were interrupted by a visit from a delegation of ministers seeking permission to conduct church services on Sunday. After Ewell agreed, the clerics made one more petition. It was not unusual for them to offer prayers for the president in this time of crisis, they said; would Ewell object to their continuing this practice?

"Certainly not," the Rebel general replied. "Pray for him. I'm sure he needs it."

Joseph Hooker's calculated request to resign was not a welcome development for Abraham Lincoln. The officer had powerful friends on the congressional Committee on the Conduct of the War who would be certain to make trouble for the administration. Lincoln had been hoping that his personal appeals to Hooker might help mend the rift. In truth, he liked Hooker's spirit—the man had great ambitions, which could be the stuff of great victories—but it was clear from their telegraphic exchange that he and Halleck would never reconcile their differences. Because Lincoln was not prepared to dispense with Halleck's services, he was left with two equally unhappy alternatives: he could refuse Hooker's resignation and send him into battle with his self-doubts and suspicions intact, or he could accept it and risk the political and military consequences that would accompany an abrupt change in leadership.

As was his custom, Lincoln sought the advice of others. Given the explosive nature of this issue, he limited his discussions to just two advisers: Henry Halleck and Secretary of War Edwin Stanton. Halleck, not surprisingly, thought Hooker should go. Stanton agreed and suggested that either George Meade or John Sedgwick would be a good choice to replace him. Meade's record was free of the intrigues that called into question the integrity of others eligible for the position, and the fact that he was a Pennsylvanian, Stanton believed, meant that he would be highly motivated now that Lee seemed poised to fight on that front. Sedgwick had possibilities as well, but he had been decidedly lukewarm when sounded out about the prospect. Lincoln let his confidants continue talking for a while and then called for a nonbinding vote.

"We were up bright and early on York street that morning," recalled a Gettysburg resident, "but not a tent or Rebel was in sight." People stood about in small groups wondering where the Confederate soldiers had gone. Sarah Broadhead was told that a trio of Yankee scouts had poked into town just as the Rebels were leaving. The scouts, she learned, "report a large force of our soldiers near, making all feel much safer."

This afternoon, a wayward Confederate chaplain, on his way to join Early's command, rode innocently into town. Before he could quite comprehend his situation, he was taken prisoner by a furloughed Union soldier. The cleric was divested of whatever interesting papers he had and then was "paroled and allowed to go home." There were more visitors before nightfall, in the form of a squad of Federal cavalry. After being informed that there were Rebel infantry to the east, north, and west, the troopers hurriedly withdrew southward.

Jeb Stuart's crossing of the Potomac was suitably dramatic. Having decided to use Rowser's Ford, he sent Wade Hampton's brigade ahead to secure it. Hampton had good news and bad to report. The good was that there were no Federal pickets along the northern bank, so the Confederate crossing would be unopposed. The bad was that the river was running two feet above normal. Men on horseback would be able to make it, but the caissons carrying powder for the horse batteries would be completely submerged.

A quick check confirmed that this was indeed the best place to ford the Potomac. Lacking any better option, Stuart ordered that the cannon powder be unpacked and hand-carried across the river by the mounted men. Then came the wagons and the artillery tubes. Fortune favored the bold this night: not a man nor a single piece of equipment was lost. "By three o'clock on the morning of the 28th of June," wrote one of Stuart's staff officers, "we all stood wet and dripping on the Maryland shore."

Once he reached the army headquarters now established at Frederick, Maryland, Joe Hooker realized that his offer to resign might actually be accepted by the president. He poured out a torrent of self-justification and self-defense to his surprised chief of staff, Daniel Butterfield. Recalled Butterfield,

> He said that . . . it was a very . . . critical period in the campaign, one bearing an important influence upon the whole country, he said that if every available man could not be concentrated and used against Lee, . . . the consequences would be most disastrous; that he felt General Halleck did not give him that cordial assistance and co-operation which he had a right to expect; . . . that he had too much respect for the position of general of the army of the Potomac to continue to hold it when he was not allowed to exercise all its powers fully; that he would wait for history to do justice to him and his motives; but now he must look only to the good of the country.

This night also threw an obscuring mantle over the movements of two men, each of whom possessed information that would dramatically change the campaign. One was a lone figure on horseback, riding slowly and cautiously on a westerly course from Frederick. He expected to avoid Federal pickets and patrols but had a story ready if chance played otherwise. He also had the skills to carry off the deception: Henry T. Harrison was an actor by trade, though circumstances and opportunities had led him to seek adventure and earn welcome cash payments by serving as a "scout" in the Confederate service. At present he was on James Longstreet's payroll, dispatched on a freelance assignment to pick up information about the Federal units opposing Lee's raid. Endowed with the acute sense of timing so essential to his craft, the actor-turned-spy had deemed that the moment was right for him to make his appearance and report his findings. He was now bound for Longstreet's headquarters.

The other anxious traveler this night was far less concerned with stealth, though secrecy was also foremost in his thoughts. Just a few hours earlier, Colonel James A. Hardie had been looking forward to another evening in Washington, where he was posted on Henry Halleck's War Department staff. His plans had changed abruptly when he was summoned to the department's conference room to find his boss waiting for him with the secretary of war and the president. Hardie was told that he had been selected to carry the orders that would change the leadership of the Army of the Potomac. His protests swept aside by the urgency of the moment, he was hastily briefed, given the written orders and some cash for emergencies, and sent to the rail station, where a special locomotive was ready with its steam up. There was just enough time for him to slip into civilian clothes before the train pulled out.

The route ran toward Baltimore, then along a spur line that connected into Frederick. Hardie arrived in the latter town just after midnight. No one seemed to be in charge, so the officer banged on doors until he found a local willing (at a price) to provide him with a buggy and driver. Then, with only the sketchiest idea of where they were headed, Hardie and his new companion rattled off into the night.

NINE

"It was my firm determination . . . to give battle"

A t "3 A.M., I was aroused from my sleep by an officer from Washington entering my tent," George Meade wrote to his wife, "and after waking me up, saying he had come to give me trouble. At first I thought that it was either to relieve or arrest me, and promptly replied to him, that my conscience was clear, void of offense towards any man; I was prepared for his bad news. He then handed me a communication to read; which I found was an order relieving Hooker from the command and assigning me to it."

Meade's account suggests an equanimity that may have been more imagined than real. According to the messenger, James A. Hardie, Meade at first "became much agitated." He protested that John Reynolds should have been chosen instead; that he, Meade, "was totally ignorant of the positions and dispositions of the army he was to take in charge"; and that it would only make sense for him to refuse the assignment. Hardie patiently explained that all of Meade's arguments had already been taken into consideration, and the president's decision was final. As Meade absorbed this, some of his dry humor returned: " 'Well, I've been tried and condemned without a hearing,' " he told Hardie, " 'and I suppose I shall have to go to the execution.' "

Once Jeb Stuart had successfully waded his command across the Potomac River at Rowser's Ford, he encountered his next problem. The Chesapeake

and Ohio boat canal ran alongside the river at this point, effectively presenting a water-filled ditch that would have to be traversed if the cavalry unit was
to continue on its mission. The narrow canal lock gates could accommodate
just a few men and horses at a time—not good enough for a situation that
required speedy movement. The problem was solved when Stuart's men
located some canal boats. The craft (forty boats altogether) were pivoted
crosswise in the channel with gangplanks laid over them. Using this improvised span, Stuart finally got his men on firm and open ground. "The sun

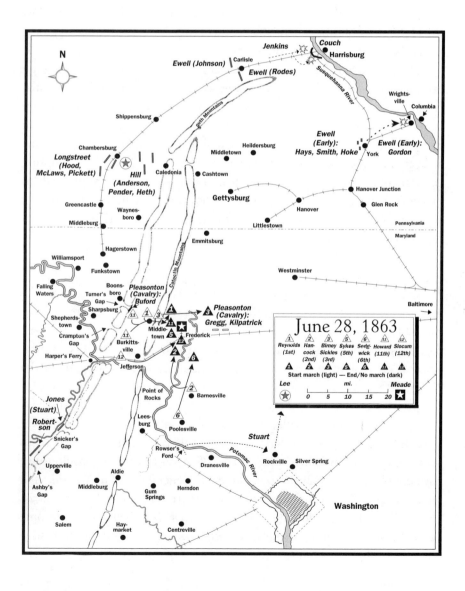

was several hours high before the command left the Potomac," wrote one of the cavalry chief's staff officers.

For three days, Colonel Jacob Frick had been trying to figure out how he could possibly protect the formidable covered bridge that spanned the Susquehanna River at Wrightsville. Frick commanded some of Pennsylvania's militia units—primarily the 27th Pennsylvania Emergency Infantry—and had been posted in Columbia, opposite Wrightsville, since June 24. He had marched his regiment across the river to defend the bridge against Rebel cavalry, but he knew that confronting an enemy infantry force would be another matter altogether.

He had taken some steps by ordering earthworks dug along high ground just west of Wrightsville, overlooking the bridge. While his men worked and guarded, they were also witness to a seemingly endless stream of refugees carrying belongings and herding animals over the bridge. On Saturday night, June 27, Frick had met with Granville O. Haller, who had seen the 26th Pennsylvania Emergency Infantry swept aside attempting to "defend" Gettysburg, and now feared the worst. Frick reinforced his entrenched position with more militia companies (including an all-black one), prepared a section of the almost mile-long span for demolition, and did the only other thing he could do: he waited.

Robert E. Lee's progress into Pennsylvania had followed a prudent pattern. As he had explained to Jefferson Davis on June 2, "If I am able to move, I propose to do so cautiously, watching the result." For the past few days, he had allowed Ewell's Corps to move toward Harrisburg, while holding Hill and Longstreet at Chambersburg as he gauged the Federal reaction. The relative ease with which Ewell had carried out his instructions convinced Lee that the time was right to take the next step.

Toward evening he called in his chief of staff, Charles Marshall, and gave him instructions. As Marshall later recalled: "General Ewell [was] to move directly upon Harrisburg, and . . . General Longstreet would move the next morning, the 29th, to his support. General A. P. Hill was directed to move eastward to the Susquehanna and cross the river below Harrisburg. . . ." While writing out these directives, Marshall indulged some fantasies. At that moment, he truly believed that "there would be such alarm created by those movements that the Federal Government would be obliged to withdraw its army from Virginia."

The transition from Hooker to Meade was relatively brief because it had to be—there just wasn't much time. The sun was not up long before Meade and Hardie arrived at Hooker's headquarters tent, where Hooker was formally relieved of his command. Key staff members were brought in, told the news, and asked to brief Meade on the overall situation. As Meade later related, "I received from [Hooker] . . . no intimation of any plan, or any views that he may have had up to that moment." With the exception of some personal aides, Meade kept Hooker's command staff unchanged. That included the important position of chief of staff. Meade did attempt to recruit several candidates for the post, but each officer he approached had compelling reasons not to change positions at this critical time. So Meade retained Hooker's man, Daniel Butterfield, a civilian-turned-officer and Hooker confidant. George Meade was very much on his own. "The order placing me in command of this army is received," Meade wired Halleck at 7:00 A.M. "As a soldier, I obey it, and to the utmost of my ability will execute it."

The orders that Meade pledged to obey had been written by Henry Halleck. "Your army is free to act as you may deem proper under the circumstances as they arise," Halleck directed. "You will, however, keep in view the important fact that the Army of the Potomac is the covering army of Washington as well as the army of operation against the invading forces of the rebels. You will, therefore, maneuver and fight in such a manner as to cover the capital and also Baltimore, as far as circumstances will permit."

Within the ranks, the reaction to Meade's appointment was thoroughly mixed. A captain in the Fifth Corps described the new army commander as a "grumpy, stern, severe and admirable soldier." Some wanted Hooker back, while a few others wished that George B. McClellan had been reinstated. What seemed to worry everyone was the timing of the change. "I was taken by surprise at this announcement . . . ," admitted a Pennsylvania soldier. "It did seem so strange that now for the 3rd or 4th time the General, commanding, should be suddenly relieved . . . in the very midst of most important operations." Reporter T. C. Grey, in a private letter to his *New York Tribune* editor, noted that the news had been "received with a kind of apathetic indifference by the army although many are loud in denouncing the act *at this particular moment.*"

Meade was provided with a remarkably accurate outline of Lee's movements, drawn up by George Sharpe. Scouts and agents operating out of Gettysburg had identified Gordon's Brigade as the body that had occupied the town on June 26, suggesting that the rest of Early's Division was not far away. Also recorded in the intelligence report was the presence of a strong column (Rodes' and Johnson's divisions) near Carlisle. So certain was Sharpe that Lee had all his infantry with him, in fact, that when Henry Halleck later this day reported Stuart's presence near Washington and credited the Rebel force with more than just cavalry, Meade firmly corrected the misconception.

"What Meade will do is a question," observed Provost Marshal Marsena Patrick, "but he has taken hold of work with a will." The new officer in charge of the Army of the Potomac turned his attention to the garrison at Harper's Ferry and effected a neat compromise that might have saved Joe Hooker his job. Rather than advocating that the place be abandoned, Meade requested permission to reduce the number of troops there, taking care to leave some to hold the key position of Maryland Heights. Permission was granted. One part of the Hooker legacy that Meade did accept without question was his predecessor's generous estimate of the enemy's strength. Even when testifying before Congress many months later, Meade would still insist that Lee's army facing him had numbered "about 110,000 men."*

"The 28th and 29th were exciting days in Gettysburg for we knew the Confederate army, or a part of it at least, was within a few miles of our town," recalled Daniel Skelly. It was about 10:00 A.M. Sunday when, as Sarah Broadhead inscribed in her diary, "a large body of our cavalry began to pass through town." "We were delighted to see them," declared Agnes Barr. "All along the street the people were out with their buckets of water and tin cups."

The troopers belonged to the 5th and 6th Michigan Cavalry regiments, units that had formerly been assigned to Washington's defenses but were now operating in concert with the Army of the Potomac. The young troopers enjoyed the moment. "Lines of men stood on either side

---

*Lee's total force at Gettysburg did not exceed 71,000 men.

[of the road] with pails of water or apple butter," in one rider's description. "Others held immense platters of bread. . . . The people were overjoyed and received us with an enthusiasm and hospitality born of full hearts." Lydia Ziegler would reminisce, "How well do I remember the happiness it gave me to hand out the cakes and pies that our kind mother made until late at night."

None of the cavalrymen wished to spoil the moment by informing the townspeople that they were following a patrol route and had no instructions to remain. The two regiments camped outside the town in a field knee-high in clover and posted pickets on the main roads converging on Gettysburg. For its residents, ignorance was bliss. "We now felt assured that our Government were keeping an eye on us," remembered Catherine Foster.

In the 116th Pennsylvania (Second Corps), news of Hooker's replacement arrived just as the soldiers were "listening to the very unusual sound of the church bells coming over the fields from Frederick town." War or no, it was Sunday, and throughout that part of Maryland, congregations were summoned to worship, no matter how incongruous it might seem. For a New Jersey native in the Third Corps near Burkettsville, the tolling bells "vibrating upon the calm morning air, redolent with all the odors of queenly June, and re-echoing from the green mountain-sides, seemed sadly at variance with the marching columns, the glittering rifles and frowning cannons around."

Church bells also sounded throughout southern Pennsylvania, where a different army covered the land. Near Chambersburg, the chaplain of the 26th North Carolina delivered a sermon on the text "The harvest is passed, the summer is ended and we are not saved." The regiment's boy colonel was in attendance and watched closely for clues about upcoming events. The friend of a musician in the 26th left the service shaking his head. "Did you notice Col. Burgwyn during the preaching?" he asked. "He seemed to be deeply impressed. I believe we are going to lose him on this trip."

Now definitively on the northern side of the Potomac, Jeb Stuart was beginning to realize that rather than running alongside the Union army, he was in fact well behind it. His intention may have been to press on, but circumstances conspired to slow him down. His troopers were helping themselves to the rich spoils of the Maryland farms: "There is plenty of grass and grain here," a Virginia cavalryman wrote to his father this Sunday. And then things became much worse by becoming better still.

Stuart's course took his command north and east, to the village of Rockville, outside Washington. While his outriders traded shots with Yankee patrols, his main column enjoyed a warm welcome from the residents, who plied the men with food and keepsakes. When a long, fully packed supply train began to enter the town from the south, bearing goods for the Army of the Potomac, Stuart's veterans were swarming after the booty in a flash. Chaos ensued as the pursuit became a free-for-all. "Did you ever see anything like that in all your life!" Stuart exclaimed. Some U.S. wagons were caught, others were smashed up, and a few escaped. Even Stuart's chief engineer, Captain William W. Blackford, was swept up in the moment: "It was as exciting as a fox chase for several miles," he later wrote, "until when the last was taken I found myself on a hill in full view of Washington."

When it was all over, Stuart was gorged on his victory: he had prisoners, supplies, and some 125 wagons. He gave brief consideration to actually attacking the U.S. capital but in the end decided against it. It took him a while to reorganize his command, so it was later in the afternoon by the time his column was finally under way once again. Still hoping to make contact at some point with Ewell's Corps, the Confederate horsemen, with their captured wagons and prisoner coffle, moved slowly northward on the Baltimore Road.

The result of today's movements by the Army of the Potomac was the concentration of its corps around Frederick, Maryland. That end necessitated some fair tramping for the Second and Sixth corps, but for once, all the conditions were right. A New Yorker under Hancock marveled that he was "marching through a land of beauty and loveliness. . . . Maids and pretty girls smile approvingly as our war-worn veterans march on." There was time for reflection. A Pennsylvania enlisted man felt sure that he was involved in the "campaign of the war, and the rebs have staked their all upon it."

The officer commanding the Second Corps' 5th New Hampshire was also thinking. An aide, concerned that Colonel Edward E. Cross was "in a sort of abstracted mood that was not usual for him," listened in as the popular officer spoke with a signal corps captain about various matters of the moment. After a time, the conversation turned to the battle that everyone sensed was coming. The aide was shocked and horrified to hear Cross, speaking in a "grave, decided way," confide to the captain, " 'It will be my last battle.' " What unsettled the aide most of all was that the colonel's statement sounded so matter-of-fact: the thirty-one-year-old veteran commander seemed at once at peace and resigned to the knowl edge that he would not survive his regiment's next fight.

The same special train that had carried James A. Hardie to Frederick had also brought Major General Daniel E. Sickles back to take charge of the Third Corps. In the community of officers commanding corps in the Army of the Potomac, Sickles stood apart as the only one who had not attended West Point or served in the military prior to the war. He stood apart in other ways as well, not many of which would be considered flattering. A scarred veteran of New York City's political brawls, Sickles had thrived in the army, thanks especially to his fierce ambition, which was wedded to a reckless determination to prevail.

His instinct to act first and think afterward had already made him notorious. As a congressman in 1859, Sickles had stalked and publicly killed his wife's lover. At his trial, one of the most closely followed of its time, he had set the legal world on its ear using the first-ever successful plea of temporary insanity. With the advent of the Civil War, Sickles had proved so effective a recruiter and organizer that he had entered the ranks as a general.

Daniel Sickles owed his elevation to corps command to the patronage of his friend Joe Hooker. When he reported to Hooker for duty after returning to Frederick, he was informed of the change at the top. Worse yet, at least from Sickles' point of view, was that the man who had been handed the reins exemplified everything he despised most about the cliquish, cautious, calculating West Pointers. That his associate and mentor was to be replaced at this critical time struck Sickles as madness. As he would later declare, "I should always regard it as a most hazardous expedient to change the commander of an army in such exigencies as then existed."

While many of the West Point officers serving in the Third Corps regarded Sickles' military acumen with the greatest skepticism, many in the volunteer ranks were of a different mind. "Sickles is a great favorite with this corps," asserted Private John Haley of the 17th Maine. "The men fairly worship him. He is every inch a soldier and looking like a game cock. No one questions his bravery or patriotism. Before the war he killed a man who seduced his wife. A person who has the nerve to do that might be expected to show good qualities as a general where daredeviltry is a factor."

Sickles had rejoined his command against his doctor's orders, and indeed, a reporter who saw him around this time described him as being "in delicate health." Partly for this reason, some on the general's staff had counseled him to resign from the corps. Then, too, Sickles himself believed that his new superior, George Meade, harbored animosity toward him "dating from several incidents in the Chancellorsville campaign." Accordingly, during the same meeting with Hooker in which he learned of the change, Sickles asked his former commander if he should also step down. " 'You cannot ask to be relieved on the eve of battle,' " Hooker told him. " 'Wait at least until after the engagement.' " Sickles agreed: he would wait, bide his time. And watch George Meade very carefully.

The sun was decidedly post meridiem as John B. Gordon looked down at the defenses of Wrightsville and its still-intact covered bridge across the Susquehanna River. He held a note that had been surreptitiously passed to him by a civilian as his command marched through York,* describing in good detail the layout of Wrightsville's defenses. As best Gordon could tell from where he was standing, the intelligence was correct in every aspect.

Key to his plan of attack was a "deep gorge or ravine" mentioned in the message, which was said to offer a protected approach to the town's southern side. Once the existence of this feature had been confirmed, it became a simple matter for Gordon's combat veterans to occupy the attention of the enemy militia in their front while a select strike force infiltrated their flank. What Gordon had not counted upon, however, was the inability of the green defenders to withstand even a probing effort. Hardly had his artillery batteries begun their part of the program when the Yankee troops began to flee across the bridge. Unwilling to see his undertrained men sacrificed for no purpose, Jacob Frick had ordered them to fall back.

---

*The city of York had surrendered quietly to Jubal Early, who would use it as his base of operations until June 30.

Before Gordon's men could get in position to rush the bridge, one of its spans was set on fire. As the Rebel general watched, the flames spread until the entire thing was ablaze. No civilians volunteered to help fight the bridge fire, but when the flames actually threatened Wrightsville, bucket brigades appeared. It was a point of pride for John Gordon that his men "labored as earnestly and bravely to save the town as they did to save the bridge."

But if the public-relations part of this operation could be deemed a success for the Confederates, no advantage was achieved from a military point of view. Quite the opposite, in fact: Jubal Early's hope of using the bridge to gain a jumping-off point across the Susquehanna was reduced to ashes, like the structure itself. Ewell's ambitious division commander arrived on the scene just after the fire had done its job. "I regretted this very much," Early would later admit. Only in retrospect would it become evident that the long line of march laid out by Lee, which had begun at Fredericksburg twenty-four days earlier, had reached its climax along the banks of the Susquehanna, in the smoldering wreckage of a once-famous span.

In addition to George Sharpe's Bureau of Military Information, there was another group—this one outside the military or government—tracking the movements of Lee's army with a determined exactitude. At newspaper editorial offices throughout the East, amateur strategists stuck pins into maps and tried to figure out where the next big battle story would happen. The newspaper that got there first with the best men would also get the glory. For the longest time, the betting had been divided among Baltimore, Washington, and Philadelphia; now, increasingly, Harrisburg seemed to be the focal point. Every editor was scrambling to put his top war correspondent in the field.

Whitelaw Reid, a prized reporter for the *Cincinnati Gazette*, was resting in Washington following what he termed "a flying visit to Frederick, Maryland." Even though he had left there before the Union army settled in, Reid's nose for news did not fail him: "The week," he wrote today, "it would seem, must bring a battle; two days may do it." Reid was looking forward to getting a good night's sleep in a decent bed when he was handed a note from the manager of his paper's Washington bureau. "Would like you (if you feel able) to equip yourself with horse and outfit, put substitutes in your place in the office, and join Hooker's army in time for the fighting," it read. With that, any thought of a soft bed was gone. Whitelaw Reid was going to find the war.

Charles Carleton Coffin was another member in good standing of the veteran correspondents' club. He prowled his beat for the *Boston Journal*. The wily Coffin was where Reid wanted to be, in Frederick, with the Army of the Potomac clustered all around him. "Cavalry, infantry, and artillery were pouring through the town," Coffin scribbled, "the bands playing, and the soldiers singing their liveliest songs." The reporter knew for a fact that Hooker was out and Meade in. He saw the Army of the Potomac's new commander, a "tall, slim, gray-bearded man, wearing a slouch hat, a plain blue blouse, with his pantaloons tucked in to his boots." The experienced Coffin took a hard look at the man in those clothes. "There was no elation," he noted, "but on the contrary he seemed weighed down with a sense of the responsibility resting on him."

By the end of this day, George Meade had a plan. He mapped it out in a memo to Henry Halleck, and later he would put it into words for a congressional committee: "I determined," he said, ". . . I should move my army as promptly as possible on the main line from Frederick to Harrisburg, extending my wings on both sides of that line as far as I could consistently with the safety and the rapid concentration of that army, and should continue that movement until I either encountered the enemy, or had reason to believe that the enemy was about to advance upon me, my object being at all hazards to compel him to loose his hold on the Susquehanna and meet me in battle at some point. It was my firm determination . . . to give battle wherever and as soon as I could possibly find the enemy."

At times, the journey had seemed impossibly long and filled with obstacles too great to overcome, but Arthur J. L. Fremantle, of the British Coldstream Guards, was not a man to be deterred by such things. He had read all about the American war during his boring outpost duty at Gibraltar, in the process becoming a long-distance admirer of the "gallantry and determination of the Southerners." Fremantle had subsequently wrangled a leave of absence, hopped a blockade runner that got him in through Brownsville, Texas, and then followed endless roads on a trip that had carried him through nine Confederate states and introduced him to some of the Southern Republic's most powerful figures, including Jefferson Davis.

Fremantle had chased after Lee's army for seven days, passing from one contact to the next, enduring bad horses, bad manners, and abominable roads. He had finally caught up with Longstreet's headquarters on Saturday, June 27, and gratefully attached himself to that command.

Today he met Major General John B. Hood, one of Longstreet's division commanders, whom he described as a "tall, thin, wiry-looking man, with a grave face." Fremantle spent part of the day in Chambersburg, whose natives were greatly bemused by his presence. They refused to believe that he was a noncombatant Englishman, insisting he "must be either a Rebel or a Yankee"; only when he showed that he had some gold to spend did they become "quite affable." He recounted the story of his journey to Pennsylvania and was amazed to discover how parochial the townsfolk were: "They seemed very ignorant," he wrote afterward, "and confused Texans with Mexicans."

This was a day for rumors in Richmond, and C. S. War Department clerk Jones heard them all. "There are two reports of important events current in the streets: first, that Lee's army has taken and destroyed Harrisburg, Pennsylvania; and second, that Vicksburg has fallen," he noted. Jones was properly skeptical of both stories, though he very much wanted to believe the first. Thomas Cooper DeLeon, a Confederate officer stationed in the capital, thought he knew why: "Such . . . was the universal belief of the southern people . . . ," he observed around this time, "and so great was their reliance in the army that was to accomplish the brilliant campaign, that they looked upon it already as a fixed fact."

There was considerable puzzlement in the office of Jefferson Davis as the Confederate president pondered Lee's June 23 note suggesting the establishment of a mock army corps under Beauregard at Culpeper. "This is the first intimation that he has had that such a plan was ever in contemplation," avowed presidential adviser Samuel Cooper. Davis today penned a response that carefully sketched out the strategic picture (nowhere as positive as it had been portrayed by Lee in his note) and itemized the troops that were needed to defend Richmond and therefore not accessible to Lee. "Do not understand me as balancing accounts in the matter of brigades," Davis concluded. "I only repeat that I have not many to send you, and [not] enough to form an army to threaten, if not capture, Washington as soon as it is uncovered by Hooker's army." He hoped his message was clear this time: Lee could expect no further help from Richmond.

At today's cabinet meeting, Abraham Lincoln revealed that Joseph Hooker had requested to be relieved, and that he had obliged him. There was some discussion regarding the choice of his successor, but it soon became apparent that the decision had already been made. "We were consulted after the fact," lamented Navy Secretary Gideon Welles. After the meeting, Welles asked around about Hooker's replacement, George Meade. "He is not great," Welles heard. "His brother officers speak well of him, but he is considered rather a 'smooth bore' than a rifle. It is unfortunate that a change could not have been made earlier."

The time was about 10:00 P.M.

Robert E. Lee was inside his headquarters in the woods east of Chambersburg when he heard a respectful rap on the tent pole. It was Major John W. Fairfax of Longstreet's staff, with important news: a scout employed by Longstreet, a man named Harrison, had been brought in from the picket line with a remarkable report regarding the enemy's real position. As Fairfax later recollected their conversation, Lee "questioned me about my opinion of Harrison's veracity. My answer was General Longstreet has confidence in him." Lee sent the aide away and considered this development. He was not overly fond of civilian scouts and preferred to seek independent verification of any intelligence they provided, but with Stuart not yet back in contact and no word from Robertson, who was supposed to be watching for such enemy movements, there was no immediate means of checking Harrison's information. All Lee could do was look the man in the eye and trust his own instincts.

Another member of Longstreet's staff, Colonel G. Moxley Sorrel, brought the scout around. According to Sorrel, Lee listened to what Harrison had to say "with great composure and minuteness." After questioning him closely, the general felt convinced that the man was proffering an honest and perceptive analysis. He called in his chief of staff, Charles Marshall, who had only just sent off orders to Ewell and Hill concerning the movement against Harrisburg. Remembered Marshall, "I found [Lee] . . . sitting in his tent with a man in citizen's dress, whom I did not know to be a soldier, but who, General Lee informed me, was a scout of General Longstreet's, who had just been brought to him. He told me that this scout . . . had brought information that the Federal army had crossed the Potomac, and that its advance had reached Frederickstown, and was moving thence westward toward the mountains."

The intelligence supplied by Harrison was significant, but it was also flawed. It suggested that the Union army was attempting to break into the Shenandoah Valley and from there come up behind Lee. If that was true, he risked being caught at a disadvantage, with fully one third of his army (Ewell's Corps) spread off to the east. Lee now needed to accomplish two objectives: he must stop the enemy from pushing westward, and he must bring his own army together. There would be more work for Marshall this night.

As the chief of staff later summarized these new instructions, Lee "determined to move his own army to the east side of the Blue Ridge so as to threaten Washington and Baltimore, and detain the Federal forces on that side of the mountains to protect those cities. He directed me to countermand the orders to General Ewell and General Hill. . . . He ordered General Longstreet to prepare to move the next morning, following Hill." In addition to calling off Ewell's advance, Lee instructed his Second Corps commander to "move your forces to this point"— meaning Chambersburg.

TEN

"I am going straight at them"

Every decision Jeb Stuart made on June 29 cost him a measure of his most important commodity: time. After leaving Rockville the previous evening, he had marched slowly with his men, prisoners, and captured wagons. The procession had covered only a few miles when the cavalry commander gave in to entreaties by Federal officers among the POWs and decided to parole the lot. It took hours to record the name of each of the more than four hundred Yankees and to issue parole slips for everyone. The job was not finished until early in the morning, at which point the column again headed north.

At a place called Hood's Mill, Stuart's riders crossed the Baltimore and Ohio Railroad line running east–west. Stuart now knew, as he would later admit, that the supposedly inert Union army had in fact been "ascertained to be moving through Frederick City northward." Nor had he forgotten that his orders were to "reach our [main] column . . . [in order to] acquaint the commanding general with the nature of the enemy's movements." Still, there were temptations along the way. The tracks, station buildings, and miscellaneous rolling stock at Hood's Mill proved just too inviting to resist, so Stuart set his troops to the task of destroying them—an activity that would keep them occupied until midday. All of this was taking its toll. As he led his men forward again, the cavalry chief fell asleep in the saddle, noticeably swaying from side to side as his horse plodded on.

Other large columns of Confederate cavalry were also moving today. Beverly H. Robertson, having at last concluded that the enemy was no longer intent on passing through Ashby's or Snicker's Gap, was carrying out the part of Stuart's orders that instructed him to "follow the army, keeping on its right and rear." Even though fully two thirds of Lee's infantry had crossed the Potomac at Shepherdstown, Robertson set his own route via Berryville and Martinsburg, bound for a more distant crossing at Williamsport. In following this course, the cavalryman swung over to the left and rear of Lee's army—a track that would later inspire a

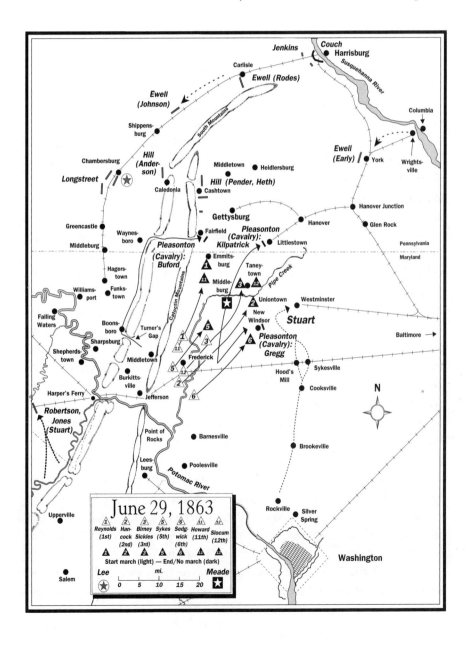

June 29, 1863

critical John S. Mosby to quip that "Stuart had ridden around General Hooker while Robertson was riding around General Lee." For his part, Robertson would never waver from his contention that he had obeyed Stuart's instructions "literally and promptly."

The orders from Henry Halleck placing George Meade in charge of the Army of the Potomac had also granted him a free hand to "appoint to command [any officers] you may deem expedient." Meade exercised that prerogative today by promoting three promising young officers in one jump from the rank of captain to brigadier general. They were Elon J. Farnsworth, Wesley Merritt, and George Armstrong Custer. "George A. Custer was, as all agree, the most picturesque figure of the Civil War," recollected a trooper in the Michigan Cavalry Brigade, which Custer now took over. The same soldier noted that the colorful boy general "acted like a man who made a business of his profession; who went about the work of fighting battles and winning victories, as a railroad superintendent goes about the business of running trains."

George Meade also began dramatically to reposition his army. With confirmed reports of a Confederate presence as far east as the Susquehanna River, Meade felt he had to move his forces in such a way as to challenge the enemy advance while at the same time protecting Washington and Baltimore. That meant deploying his troops across a broad front up to the Pennsylvania line—no small task for a force this large, requiring Meade to spend much of his time on June 28 charting the routes and drawing up the orders. Long marches lay ahead for everyone, as Meade was hoping to close in one day a distance that it would normally have taken his infantry two to cover.

The eastern edge of this new line was assigned to the Sixth Corps, which had more than twenty-five miles to travel. The men were roused at 2:30 A.M., given no time for breakfast, and forced to tramp seventeen miles before a stop was ordered for coffee. "This was taking morning exercise with a vengeance," reflected a Maine volunteer. Each soldier walked this distance, recalled another Sixth Corps member, "carrying rifle, knapsack and contents, accouterments, haversack containing rations and sixty rounds of cartridges—over fifty pounds."

Filling in the line to the west of the Sixth Corps were the Fifth and Second. The men of the Fifth had a march of some twenty miles. Captain

Francis Adam Donaldson of the 118th Pennsylvania was struck by the curious spectacle of it all: "The several divisions are stretched, one after another, along the road like a huge snake, and when the head of [the] column halts, the balance keeps closing in mass until there are thousands upon thousands of men jammed close together, stretched at full length upon the ground resting. . . . As the different regiments [in the rear] close up and rest, the head of the column [is] moving off again, so that both ends of the snake are moving at the time the other part is resting." Another Pennsylvanian, this one with Hancock's Second Corps, described it as a "hard, hard march. Many a brave boy was obliged to stop by the wayside to be driven up by wretched provost guards." The men were subjected to extreme pressure from their commander, who was trying to make up for time lost when a mistake at his headquarters had resulted in the corps' starting out several hours late.

Moving along parallel roads to the west of these two corps were the columns of the Twelfth and Third, which also had in excess of twenty miles to cover. The Twelfth was joined on its march by reinforcements sent out from Baltimore. The sight of the army in motion was unforgettable for these soldiers, most of whom had never seen any force larger than their regiment. One of the new men would remember that "as far as the eye could reach, the hills seemed to be covered with a moving mass of soldiers, together with horses, army wagons, artillery, and the general paraphernalia of an army, with flags flying at every quarter."

The rank and file of the Third Corps were heartened by the return of their absent commander. "General Sickles . . . ," wrote a Massachusetts officer, "was welcomed with great enthusiasm by the old 3d Corps as he passed along the line." More than a few of his supporters happily improved their reputations today as the bad boys of the Army of the Potomac: a Pennsylvania officer in charge of the rear guard recalled having to herd forward "a considerable number of the men [who] . . . got their canteens filled with whiskey [and] . . . were left behind because they were too drunk to travel." For his part, Sickles himself was slow getting his wagon train moving, an oversight that provoked a sharp rebuke from Meade, who seemed to be especially impatient with the civilian general in the club. It was little wonder that one of Sickles' staff observed that "Meade is not liked in the Corps."

Taking up the line of advance farthest to the west, brushing along the foot of the Catoctin Mountains, were the First and Eleventh corps.

Because this portion of Meade's long line was closest to the largest known concentration of the enemy, and Meade himself was miles away, at Middleburg, First Corps commander John Reynolds was given considerable latitude in controlling the movements of the two corps. Both of them moved up from Frederick, covering a distance of twenty miles or more. "Marched all day through the mud & rain," griped a Connecticut soldier in the Eleventh, "very hard walking."

Reynolds' blue columns wound through some very rich farmland. A member of one of Howard's (Eleventh Corps) Ohio regiments marveled that the civilians did not seem at all apprehensive; rather, "they only exhibited curiosity and wonder of seeing so many soldiers; and, from their remarks, evidently thought our force was abundantly able to annihilate the rest of the human family." At day's end, many of the weary soldiers found themselves near a Catholic convent. "The beauty and tranquility of the place, so strikingly in contrast with the military tumult which suddenly invested it, are vividly remembered," wrote an Illinois officer.

Pennsylvanian John Reynolds was pushing his men. "Marched us too fast," complained a New Yorker in the First Corps ranks. "Men played out." Added another, "It rained all day, and many of the men were obliged to march barefoot for want of shoes." The First Corps (and now left wing) commander rode ahead of his columns to reach Emmitsburg, Maryland, in the early afternoon. In a note sent from there at 3:15 P.M., he summarized for Meade the intelligence he had gathered. A scout in George Sharpe's employ had located positions for Ewell's Corps and placed Hill's men near Chambersburg. Reynolds wrote that he planned to recruit some bold locals to slip through the Catoctin gaps and "learn what they can of the enemy."

Even as Reynolds was assessing his information and planning the next day's march, some of his men were in Mechanicstown,* having bread tossed to them by a farmer and his wife. "Oh, boys, you don't know what's before you," the woman sobbed as she worked. "I'm afraid many of ye'll be dead or mangled soon, for Lee's whole army is ahead of ye and there'll be terrible fighting." Seeing the effect the woman's words were having on his men, one officer clambered onto the wagon and began tossing the loaves himself. "Walk up, boys, and get your rations!" he called out. "Bread and tears, tears and bread."

*Modern Thurmont.

* * *

Robert E. Lee was also making some moves this day. Couriers had left his headquarters early, bearing orders for Beverly H. Robertson, still in Virginia, to join the main body at Chambersburg. During the night, Lee had reconsidered his instructions to Richard Ewell and decided to modify them. Instead of marching his Second Corps to Chambersburg, Ewell was now to "move in the direction of Gettysburg, via Heidlersburg [, from where] . . . you can either move directly on Gettysburg, or turn down to Cashtown."*

A. P. Hill's corps now began to ease its way through the Cashtown Gap, while Longstreet spread his units more evenly around the Chambersburg area. During this repositioning, some of George Pickett's men passed through town in a southerly direction, brightening some civilian "faces thinking we were retreating." When a woman in the crowd asked why they were not going on to Harrisburg, a Virginia soldier named William Henry Cocke felt compelled to reply. "I told her to keep quiet," he recalled, "[that] we had not gone yet & it was too soon for her to crow." A soldier-correspondent for the *Savannah Republican,* writing under the moniker "Tout le Monde," mused this day that the townspeople's attitude was the "offspring of an education from the miserable abolition sheets and anti-slavery speeches which had been ding-donged into them from time immemorial."

It was Henry Heth's division of Hill's Corps that led the way through the mountain pass, heading east. To guard his flank, Heth sent a detachment of North Carolina troops and a Mississippi regiment south toward Fairfield with orders to watch the Emmitsburg approaches. "On June the 29th," Heth later recollected, "I reached Cashtown, eight miles from Gettysburg. . . . My men were sadly in want of shoes. I heard that a large supply of shoes were stored in Gettysburg." Barefoot or not, Hill's troops were in high spirits. When the 55th North Carolina reached Cashtown this night, it was, in the estimation of a member of the regiment, "in splendid condition." The only unsettling words were heard by a gunner in one of Hill's batteries, when a woman watching from the roadside shouted, " 'You are marching mighty proudly now, but you will come back faster than you went.' " One officer could not help but ask the woman why she thought so. " 'Because you put your trust in General Lee and not in the Lord Almighty,' " she answered.

*This is another message written down after the fact from memory and garbled. From Heidlersburg, Ewell's options would actually be to move directly on *Cashtown* or turn down to *Gettysburg.*

* * *

An unrecorded act by an unnamed trooper riding with Jeb Stuart accomplished one strategic objective this day. By pulling down the telegraph wires running between Baltimore and Frederick, Stuart's men cut off the Army of the Potomac from timely contact with Washington and Harrisburg.* A courier service was established between Meade's headquarters and the nearest operating point on the telegraphic route, but the flow of valuable intelligence coming from Harrisburg slowed to a trickle. Even more than Hooker before him, Meade now had to depend on George Sharpe and his Bureau of Military Information for help in discerning the enemy's intentions.

Robert E. Lee was beginning to manifest some anxieties that his most trusted staff found disquieting. This morning he had occasion to speak with a late-arriving officer on Ewell's staff who was passing through Chambersburg on his way to rejoin his command. At one point during their discussion, Lee asked if the officer had heard anything of Jeb Stuart. The young captain replied that he had met a pair of cavalrymen who had told him that Stuart was still in Virginia on June 28. "The General was evidently surprised and disturbed" by this news, Ewell's officer later noted. Lee waved over one of his staff officers, Walter Taylor, and had the story repeated for him. A few moments later, standing alone with Taylor, the captain inquired about Lee's obvious concern. Taylor explained "that General Lee expected General Stuart to report before that time in Pennsylvania, and that he was much disturbed by his absence, having no means of information about the movements of the enemy's forces."

This seems to have been the day on which Lee learned that George Meade now commanded the Army of the Potomac.† Precisely how this information reached him is unclear, but with tens of thousands of Union soldiers suddenly in the know, its transmission to Confederate headquarters was inevitable. Equally inevitable was that someone should ask Lee

*The Frederick-to-Washington line had been cut on June 28.
†Although this revelation is often included among the intelligence bounty delivered by the spy Harrison, it seems unlikely that he could have conveyed the information. The news was not generally circulated in the Union army until midday on June 28, making it unlikely that Harrison (who by then must have been on his way to find Longstreet) could have heard it. Moreover, an important communication sent by Lee this morning referred to "General Hooker" in a way that implied he was still commanding the Union army.

what effect he thought the change would have on for his plans. He responded, "General Meade will commit no blunder in my front, and if I make one he will make haste to take advantage of it." Lee revealed some more of his thinking today when he greeted John B. Hood of Longstreet's Corps with the words "Ah, General, the enemy is a long time finding us; if he does not succeed soon, we must go in search of him."

An artilleryman marching with Longstreet recalled that during their sojourn in Chambersburg, he and his batterymates got accustomed to "living upon the fat of Pennsylvania." While no thorough accounting was ever made, the amount of matériel removed from the Keystone State by Lee's soldiers was unquestionably prodigious. One observer cataloged the spoils simply as "great quantities of horses, mules, wagons, beefs, and other necessaries." A South Carolina surgeon was certain that the number of rustled Pennsylvania beeves was in the "thousands . . . enough to feed our army until cold weather." And in a letter published in a Richmond newspaper, "an intelligent young officer" advised readers, "You can form no idea of the immense droves of cattle and horses that are being sent to the rear from our advanced forces in Pennsylvania."

The Michigan cavalry regiments, whose arrival in Gettysburg had so boosted everyone's spirits on June 28, left without fanfare this morning. "Quiet has prevailed all day," Sarah Broadhead wrote. Most felt as if they were in the eye of some terrible storm. An editorial writer for the town newspaper complained, "It is annoying to be thus isolated."

As evening came on, a bold resident named Samuel Herbst, who had successfully hidden his horse from Gordon's searches, rode the animal south toward Emmitsburg. Herbst returned after dark with word that there were thousands of Federal troops on the way. "The news flew through the town like wildfire," recalled another in Gettysburg.

During the time it took for Lee's mounted couriers to cover the distance from Chambersburg to Carlisle, Richard Ewell continued to operate on the assumption that he was to move against Harrisburg. On his orders, Captain H. B. Richardson, an engineer, went out with some of Jenkins' cavalry to scout the capital's defenses. Their approach ignited brief skirmishes at all the various points of contact, especially near a road intersection known as Oyster's Point. But "on Monday morning, June 29," claimed an officer with Jenkins, ". . . we . . . viewed the city of Harrisburg and its defenses."

"About 9 A.M. received orders to march back to Chambersburg," noted a staff officer with Johnson. "Great surprise expressed." Whatever frustration he may have felt, Ewell acted promptly to carry out his new instructions. A rider was dispatched with orders for Jubal Early, at York, directing him to move the next day, when Robert Rodes would also be in motion. It was just past noon when Ewell sent Johnson's Division off toward Chambersburg with all the corps supply wagons and two battalions of reserve artillery. "The people seemed delighted at our going," reported a soldier in the 4th Virginia. The only Confederate smiles were cracked when one of the columns passed a file of captured Pennsylvania militiamen: a Virginia cannoneer observed that "all of them [were] barefooted, their shoes and stockings having been appropriated by needy rebels."

As Ewell's troops marched out of Carlisle, someone asked a civilian, If you could have peace by letting the South secede, what would you do? "I would let you'ins go," was the reply. When the long files of soldiers turned back onto the route they had come in by the day before, the men's "disappointment and chagrin were extreme," confessed one of them. Still, their dismay did not come close to matching Ewell's. "The General was quite testy and hard to please," grumbled an officer at headquarters, adding that he "became disappointed, and had every one flying around." Preoccupied by his personal turmoil, Ewell dropped an important stitch. Although a number of couriers left his headquarters today with changed directions for his infantry commanders, no one thought to notify Albert Jenkins, in charge of the cavalry force operating with the Second Corps, that Harrisburg was no longer the target. As a result, the mounted units that might have effectively screened Ewell's movements over the next two days remained in contact with Harrisburg's defenders for another twenty-four hours.

Jeb Stuart's destructive midday sojourn at Hood's Mill blocked Ohio reporter Whitelaw Reid's efforts to catch up with the Army of the Potomac. The train on which Reid was riding, along with fellow corre spondents Sam Wilkeson (*New York Times*) and Uriah H. Painter (*Philadelphia Inquirer*), stopped just outside Baltimore, where the passengers were told that service to Frederick had been interrupted. The three newsmen had no choice but to return to Washington. The *Boston Journal*'s Charles Coffin was having better luck: already in Frederick, he had been able to find a horse and spent this day riding along the line of march taken by the Second and Fifth corps.

Sometime this evening, George Meade penned a letter to his wife. "We are marching as fast as we can to relieve Harrisburg," he informed her, "but have to keep a sharp lookout that the rebels don't . . . get . . . in our rear. They have a cavalry force in our rear, destroying railroads, etc., with the view of getting me to turn back, but I shall not do it. I am going straight at them and will settle this thing one way or another."

Time and circumstances were still conspiring against Jeb Stuart. After investing several hours in prying up the rails running into and out of Hood's Mill, the Confederate cavalry chief now had his men back on roads leading north. Their destination this time was Westminster, Maryland. Because this stop on the Western Maryland Railroad would soon be a forward supply base for the Army of the Potomac, a guard of ninety-five Delaware cavalrymen was posted in the town.

With the odds at 4,000 to 95, the fight at Westminster was never in doubt, though its brevity belied its ferocity. The Union riders were routed in a series of small-scale but savage combats that left two of Stuart's promising young lieutenants—St. Pierre Gibson and John W. Murray—sprawled dead on the side of the road. The victorious Confederate troopers rounded up the Federal survivors and located what Stuart would later describe as a "full supply of forage," though he would also concede that, "the delay and difficulty of procuring it kept many of the men up all night." "We left that town that night," remembered one of the general's aides, "bivouacked in the rain by the roadside [at Union Mills, and] pushed on at dawn."

It was a long day in the saddle for the men of the First and Second brigades of John Buford's division, who rode a weary circuit today covering the western flank of George Meade's long infantry line. The troopers had broken camp at Middletown (about ten miles west of Frederick) at 9:00 A.M., headed west through Turner's Gap in the South Mountains, and then turned north to follow the mountain range. "Traveled near forty miles thro' a most beautiful country," one Yankee rider recorded in his diary. Another was less complimentary, declaring that the town of Boonsboro seemed "to be mostly occupied by Secessionists." Either way, it was hardly a pleasure ride: a New York cavalryman noted that the blue-coats "heard of the movements of the enemy all the way."

A touch of fanfare marked the moment when the columns crossed the state line. A trooper in the 17th Pennsylvania would long remember the "responsive and ringing cheers of the gallant soldiers as they marched past the trooper of Company G, who stood with streaming guidon, on the boundary line of the state, indicating our exit from doubtful Maryland into loyal Pennsylvania." Buford's command then swung back east through the mountains at Waynesboro to camp at Fountaindale, near the eastern end of the pass, about four miles south of Fairfield. The warm reception they were given here was invigorating, and all the more so for the contrast with their experience in Maryland. "The citizens were overjoyed to see us and we were enthusiastically welcomed," wrote an Indiana trooper. For him, this Monday in late June would go down as "one of life's grandest days."

ELEVEN

"It begins to look as though we will have a battle soon"

While the main body of John Buford's division rested at Foun-taindale, an advance party took station at Fairfield, where the mood was decidedly cooler. "The whole community seemed stampeded, and afraid to speak or to act," Buford observed. What it was that the townsfolk were unwilling to reveal became evident soon after his column set out this foggy morning on a northward course toward Cash-town, from which it would turn toward Gettysburg. Buford's scouts had not gone more than a half mile when gunfire popped and then crackled in the gloom: the Yankee advance had run into the small Confederate force that Henry Heth had dispatched from Cashtown the night before.

The combative Buford fed more men into the skirmish line before he was satisfied as to the size and composition of the enemy force blocking him. With typical staccato terseness, he reported, "Resolved not to dis-turb them. . . . Fairfield was 4 or 5 miles west of the route assigned to me, and I did not wish to bring on an engagement so far from the road I was expected to be following." He would take a more direct route to his prescribed destination. Buford's men backed away from this fight and passed through Emmitsburg, then occupied by portions of John Reynolds' First Corps. Although there is no record of their having met, it seems unlikely that Buford would have ridden through the area without speaking to Reynolds. The infantry officer had more up-to-date informa-tion and was in touch with Meade's headquarters, affording Buford an opportunity to pass along word of his encounter with some of Lee's foot

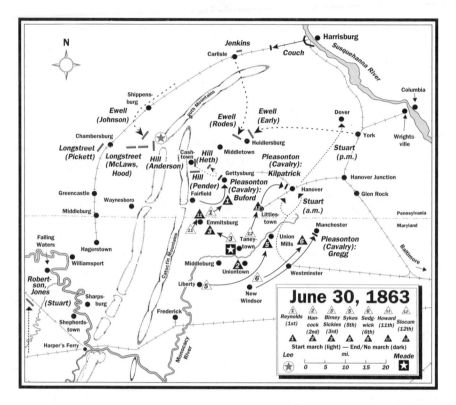

soldiers.* Perhaps coincidentally, Reynolds sent off a courier to Meade at about the time Buford was there.

After clearing Emmitsburg, Buford turned north, heading for the point designated in his orders as his objective for this day: Gettysburg.

Henry Heth was looking for Brigadier General J. Johnston Pettigrew, who commanded one of the four brigades in his division, all now camped around Cashtown. Lieutenant Louis G. Young was standing within earshot as Heth found Pettigrew, and later recalled their conversation: "General Pettigrew was ordered by General Heth," recollected Young, "to go to Gettysburg with three of his four regiments present, three field pieces of the Donald-sonville Artillery, of Louisiana, and a number of wagons, for the purpose of collecting commissary and quartermaster stores for the use of the army." Pettigrew's instructions allowed for the usual latitude, but on one point

---

*There is no evidence that the Confederate soldiers informed Heth about their skirmishing with Buford's horsemen.

Heth was very specific: "It was told to General Pettigrew that he might find the town in possession of a home guard, . . . but if, contrary to expectations, he should find any organized troops capable of making resistance, or any portion of the Army of the Potomac, he should not attack it."

Drums soon began to beat throughout the brigade camps, and by 6:30 A.M., Pettigrew had his 2,000 men marching east on the Chambersburg Road. As his column passed through Heth's picket line, manned by the 55th Virginia, Pettigrew used a little gentle persuasion on the officer commanding the regiment, successfully convincing him to append his more experienced unit to the expedition.

It was just as well that Pettigrew brought help, because after marching on a short distance, his advance party was approached by a friendly scout who warned that a large force of Yankee cavalry was already at Gettysburg. This was disincentive enough for the cautious Pettigrew, who held up the advance until a courier could make the round trip to Heth's headquarters, returning with orders to continue.

The next incident on this mission occurred not far from Gettysburg, when a sniper took a shot at the 47th North Carolina. The officer in charge of the regiment prudently eased back from the gunman, who had failed to hit anyone. Pettigrew pressed on. By about 9:45 A.M., his leading scouts had a clear view of the town of Gettysburg.

It was a sign of trouble to come, as sure as anything. At first Mary Fastnacht was perplexed that the black mother and daughter whom her own mother had hidden from John Gordon's Confederates on June 26 had packed up and left town. The tension of having to hide at a moment's notice was just more than they could face, evidently; Mary remembered very clearly the young girl's telling her that "she couldn't be paid to put in such another night." Now they were gone—nimble, defenseless creatures fleeing before a fire.

When Sarah Broadhead stepped outside this morning, she was feeling less anxious than she had felt in days. Her husband had come home the night before, after being stranded in Harrisburg when the trains stopped running. Her relief was short-lived, though: glancing westward, she at once saw the "Rebels [who] came to the top of the hill overlooking the town on the Chambersburg pike, and looked over our place. We had a good view of them from our house, and every moment we expected to hear the booming of cannon, and thought they might shell the town."

* * *

Jeb Stuart's column—cavalry, some prisoners, and those captured wagons—finished unwinding from last night's camps near Union Mills at around 8:00 A.M. Stuart's intention was to march through the town of Hanover and from there angle to York, where he hoped to find Ewell's Corps. Something new began slowing him down today: the moment his riders passed into Pennsylvania, recalled one aide, "details were immediately sent out to seize horses." Stuart's scouts had reported enemy cavalry a few miles to the west, at a place called Littlestown. Despite the equine distractions, Stuart pushed on, hoping to get past Hanover before the Federals arrived. As they drew near the town, however, riders brought back word that Union troopers had been encountered; in the words of Stuart's aide, "We stirred up the Hornets." It was approaching 10:00 A.M.

J. Johnston Pettigrew was a prudent man. He halted his command along Seminary Ridge, just west of Gettysburg, and sent forward a line of skirmishers to ascertain what might be lurking in the town. He was quite conscious of his orders from Henry Heth, which, as his aide Louis Young doubtless reminded him, "were peremptory, not to precipitate a fight." Every available telescopic glass was turned on Gettysburg. The skirmish line had disappeared into the town below when, at about 10:30 A.M., someone told Pettigrew that Yankee cavalry had been spotted. Another report indicated that drumming could be heard in the distance—which might mean infantry nearby, since cavalry generally used only bugles. That was all Pettigrew needed to know: he issued orders for his column to return to its camps. The slow countermarch began at around 11:00 A.M.

The long column of Union cavalry that eased out of Littlestown starting at 8:00 A.M. had, until June 28, been assigned to the defenses of Washington. The units had been vacuumed up by Hooker as he passed through that zone, to be added to the Army of the Potomac's cavalry corps as its Third Division. The original commander of these troops was thought to be too timid for combat, so, in one of his first administrative moves, George Meade had installed Brigadier General Judson Kilpatrick at the head of the new unit. Flamboyant in appearance, conniving in manner, and possessed of boundless ambition, Kilpatrick was described by a fellow cavalryman as a "brave, injudicious boy, much given to blow-ing." These characteristics, translated into action, had his men calling him "Kill-cavalry."

Most of Kilpatrick's men rode through Hanover before 10:00 A.M., on their way toward York. The column's tail, its supply wagons followed by a security detachment from the 18th Pennsylvania, began to enter the town from the west as the rear guard, the 5th New York, held position near the town square—partly to watch over the wagons and partly to enjoy the food and other delicacies provided by Hanover's grateful citizens.

Suddenly, a band of some sixty Confederate horsemen moved to cut off the Pennsylvanians trailing the wagons. This time, the Rebels' opponents were no less combative than they: the smaller Yankee detail charged, burst through the enemy cordon, and was chased by the Confederate riders into the town's center, where the New York troopers were waiting. The Battle of Hanover—waged between two cavalry commands forced to fight largely in the streets and alleys of a Pennsylvania town—was under way.

George Meade's marching plan for this day was a hostage to circumstances. No longer was the army commander thrusting his corps forward in hopes of disrupting enemy schemes. At 11:30 A.M., he sent a summary to John Reynolds: "We are as concentrated as my present information of the position of the enemy justifies," he declared. "I have pushed out the cavalry in all directions to feel for them, and so soon as I can make up any positive opinion as to their position, I will move again."

Meade had to consider what he would do if Lee concentrated his forces quickly and moved against the Army of the Potomac. The Union commander needed a place to make a stand, so throughout this day, staff officers under the supervision of his chief engineer, Brigadier General Gouverneur K. Warren, were kept in the saddle scouting out just such a contingency location. Warren's crew identified a position that followed a twenty-mile-long chain of hills rising along the southern side of Big Pipe Creek. This line would afford Meade excellent high ground and offer the added advantage of positioning his army directly astride three major avenues of approach from south-central Pennsylvania to Baltimore and Washington. In later testimony before Congress, Warren would voice a concern then current at Meade's headquarters, which argued against concentrating the army into too tight a position: "If [Lee] . . . could get off on our right, he could go down to Baltimore," said Warren. "If to the left, he might escape us and go to Washington."

There was some confusion today as Meade learned to handle all the component parts of his army. He had earlier reconfirmed the authority of John Reynolds to direct the marches of the First, Third, and Eleventh corps,* but this seems to have slipped his mind when, around midday, without first checking with Reynolds, he issued marching instructions to Daniel Sickles. The problem was that Sickles had already received different orders from Reynolds. Any thoughts the Third Corps commander may have had about West Pointers at this moment went unrecorded; instead, Sickles sent a note to Meade, informing him of the conflicting orders and requesting clarification. None of this did anything to improve his opinion of his new superior.

First off, small parties of Federal scouts poked around the town's outskirts. Then, a little after 10:00 A.M., a more formidable squadron from the 8th Illinois Cavalry eased into Gettysburg. It did not take the riders long to spot the powerful formations denoting Pettigrew's men on a ridge west of town. To the surprise and relief of the advance parties, the Confederates slowly turned away; by the time the main body of John Buford's division arrived, at about 11:00 A.M., they were well out of sight.

Since June 26, Gettysburg's citizens had been seeing Rebel troops come and go, and Union detachments do the same—but this was the first time the appearance of the Federals had caused the Confederates to retire. The advance parties were an undeniable harbinger of larger U.S. forces in the area. That, plus the blessed comfort of having those young, confident Union soldiers in their midst, was more than enough to lift the spirits of even the most dour residents.

Ten-year-old Charles McCurdy clambered atop a rail fence to get a better view of the horsemen. As he later recalled it, the "perfectly accoutered troops" provided "a strong contrast to the Rebel cavalry I had seen a week before." Tillie Pierce pronounced the procession of riders "a novel and grand sight. . . . I knew then we had protection; and I felt they were our decent friends." A trooper riding with the 8th New York Cavalry was pleasantly surprised at "receiving the most enthusiastic welcome from the

*Meade had also placed the Fifth and Twelfth corps under Major General Henry W. Slocum.

citizens, who hailed us as their deliverers; cheers, bouquets and refreshments were tendered us on all sides, accompanied in many cases, by the tears of tender hearted women." Tillie Pierce joined a group of girls who tried to sing "The Battle Cry of Freedom." "As some of us did not know the whole of the piece we kept repeating the chorus," she admitted.

Robert E. Lee moved his headquarters today from the pleasant grove outside Chambersburg to the village of Greenwood, at the western entrance to the Cashtown Gap. James Longstreet reported that he rode along "with General Lee most of the day." Once Lee's new headquarters had been established, artilleryman E. P. Alexander came calling to catch up on news with some friends of his who served on the general's staff. Alexander found the mood at army headquarters "unusually careless & jolly."

The Cashtown Gap itself was becoming something of a choke point. At midday, Longstreet discovered that his corps' line of march was "blocked by [Anderson's Division of] Hill's Corps and Ewell's wagon train, which had cut into the road from above." Just two of Longstreet's divisions were involved; George Pickett's men remained near Chambersburg, charged with watching over the army's supplies until some cavalry units could relieve them.

No sooner were Longstreet's headquarters established than he had a visitor of his own. Fitzgerald Ross was an English-born Scotsman and something of a soldier of fortune, having spent much of his professional life officering in the Austrian Army. Ross passed this afternoon "very pleasantly" with Longstreet's staff. His fellow soldier-tourist Arthur Fremantle, meanwhile, had just been introduced to Robert E. Lee. It took only that one meeting for Fremantle to become an unabashed admirer of the general: "He is a perfect gentleman in every respect," Fremantle noted. "I imagine no man has so few enemies, or is so universally esteemed."

Jeb Stuart had not wanted a fight at Hanover; his objective was to link up with Ewell's men at York and, through them, reconnect with Lee's army. However, once his aggressive point brigade attacked, Stuart had no recourse but to press the matter. The confused fighting continued for a while in the town's streets as both sides sent supporting units into the

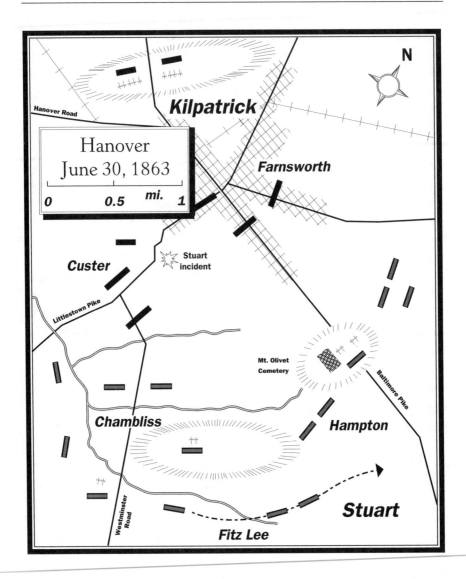

Hanover
June 30, 1863

0   0.5   mi.   1

Kilpatrick

Farnsworth

Custer

Stuart
incident

Littlestown Pike

Mt. Olivet
Cemetery

Baltimore Pike

Chambliss

Hampton

Westminster
Road

Stuart

Fitz Lee

struggle.* Stuart had to keep up the pressure on the Federals to prevent them from maneuvering against him and his vulnerable wagon train.

As a rule, Stuart preferred to lead from the front, but today he was directing affairs from a point on the outskirts of the town, near a farm owned by a family named Forney. For the second time in this campaign, he was nearly captured, in this instance when a squad of Federals broke

*Important to the Union success in this fight was the leadership of newly minted brigadiers Elon Farnsworth and George Custer.

out of the whirling combat and charged for the headquarters guidon. The cavalry commander and a few aides galloped for safety, only to find their escape blocked by a gully fifteen feet wide. The mounted aide leading the group took the gap in one grand jump and then turned to see what his general's horse would do. "I shall never forget the glimpse I then saw of this beautiful animal up in mid-air over the chasm and Stuart's fine figure sitting erect and firm in the saddle," he marveled.

Stuart's efforts had their desired effect, so that by early afternoon the two sides were essentially glaring at each other, the Confederates on the high ground along an arc south of Hanover, and the Federals in the town itself.

In his official report, John Buford would claim that his men had met the "enemy entering the town, and in good season to drive him back before his getting a foothold." The truth was less dramatic. Louis Young of Pettigrew's staff, with a fellow mounted officer, constituted the brigade's visible rear guard. As their unit pushed on, the two took care always to stop on high ground that would afford them a "perfect view of the movements of the approaching [Yankee] column. Whenever it would come within three or four hundred yards of us we would make our appearance, mounted, when the column would halt until we retired. This was repeated several times."

Pettigrew moved his brigade across Marsh Creek and left the 26th North Carolina to picket its western bank. The rest of his command marched a short distance farther toward Cashtown and then camped for the night. The unofficial army grapevine crackled with news: the word, noted in one Rebel diary, was that Pettigrew's soldiers, "in coming in contact with the enemy, had quite a little brush, but being under orders not to bring a general engagement fell back, followed by the enemy."

George Meade's thinking regarding the position of Lee's forces changed throughout this day. For much of the morning, his attentions were focused on the enemy units said to be along the Susquehanna River, to counter which he planned to move his army more strongly toward the northeast. Then, about midday, news came in from John Reynolds of Buford's clash with Rebel infantry at Fairfield. This information, coupled with rumors that Confederates were advancing on Gettysburg, persuaded Meade "to hold this army pretty nearly in the position it now occupies."

As late as 4:30 P.M., the Union commander still believed that Ewell's Corps was in strength "in the vicinity of York and Harrisburg." By the time evening orders were issued to all commands, however, further information had been received that put Ewell "at Carlisle and York." This latest intelligence compelled Meade to reconsider his balance of forces. He had already sent Sickles' Third Corps toward Emmitsburg to support Reynolds and Howard—both of whom were scheduled to reach Gettysburg the next day, July 1—but even more weight was clearly needed on the left. Accordingly, Meade made sure that three of his remaining seven corps were also placed on roads leading directly to Gettysburg. Only Sedgwick's Sixth Corps, holding position near Manchester, was not fitted into this scheme.

These directives meant relatively normal marches for the men. John Reynolds' First Corps left the Emmitsburg area and proceeded north as far as Marsh Creek, about five miles from Gettysburg. Just before they quit the Maryland town, some of the boys in the 90th Pennsylvania partook of food freely offered by an old couple who told them, " 'We'll give you all we have if you will drive the rebels off, and hope you'll not get killed.' " When this regiment crossed the line into its home state, the men sent up "nine cheers."

As the 12th Massachusetts settled into its night bivouac at Marsh Creek, the regiment's colonel was approached by one of his company captains, who had a boyish-looking civilian in tow. The stranger said he lived close by and was desperate to "fight the rebels." The colonel reluctantly accepted this impromptu volunteer, who was allowed to join Company A. "After an extended search," recalled a member of that company, "a cap, blouse, musket, and roundabout were secured, together with a supply of ammunition, and thus equipped he took his place in the ranks."

Once the First Corps had cleared Emmitsburg, the Eleventh moved up from south of the village and set up all around it. The soldiers of the 26th Wisconsin were lucky enough to be assigned to camp on the grounds of the Saint Joseph Academy, operated by the Sisters of Charity. "The Sisters gave us a very good dinner today," wrote an officer in the unit, "which all enjoyed heartily." A staff officer with Major General Carl Schurz performed a little recital on the academy's chapel organ, "to the edification of all who heard him."

Not everything was so placid. A soldier in the 154th New York observed that "Lee's troops cannot be far off, from reports and the number of aid[e]s ... flying in all directions." Another of Howard's men, this one from the 107th Ohio, was "told this evening that there was not much doubt but that the engagement would begin sometime within the next day or two."

It was not long after sunset when the Eleventh Corps' commander, Oliver Otis Howard, received a note from John Reynolds, now in charge of the left wing, asking him to pay him a visit. When Howard arrived at his headquarters, Reynolds greeted him warmly and showed him a copy of a circular that Meade had ordered to be read to the troops. "The enemy are on our soil," it declared. "The whole country now looks anxiously to this army to deliver it from the presence of the foe." The message ended by advising that officers were "authorized to order the instant death of any soldier who fails in his duty at this hour." After Reynolds' visitor digested this, the two men "sat down ... to study the maps of the country," Howard later recollected, "and we consulted upon those matters till eleven o'clock at night."

As Howard prepared to return to his own headquarters, one of his aides scrutinized Reynolds closely. "General Reynolds was a tall, vigorous man of quick motion and temperament," he observed. "That night he was somewhat paler than usual and seemed to feel anxious or at least to be keenly alive to the responsibility resting upon him." Howard likewise noted his colleague's mood: "Probably he was anxious on account of the scattered condition of our forces, particularly in view of the sudden concentration of the enemy," he remarked.

Jeb Stuart sweated out the rest of the daylight at Hanover, worrying all the while that the Federals might renew the combat, and concerned about rumors of Union regular infantry in the neighborhood. When darkness finally fell, he wasted little time in getting out of harm's way, sending his wagons swinging off to the east of the town and following soon after with the rest of his command.

"Kilpatrick," a Confederate headquarters aide reported with great relief, "showed no disposition to hinder Stuart's withdrawal." Jeb Stuart was beginning to wish he had never captured that Yankee wagon train at Rockville. The lumbering prize, he later conceded, "was now a subject of

serious embarrassment, but I thought . . . I could save it. . . . I was satisfied, from every accessible source of information . . . that the Army of
Northern Virginia must be near the Susquehanna."

Reporter Whitelaw Reid would always think of it as one of the great untold
stories of this military campaign. Not twenty-four hours earlier, legions of
Rebel cavalrymen had been swarming over the Baltimore–Frederick rail
line, ripping out, burning, tearing up, and generally destroying things to
the best of their abilities. And now here he was, approaching Frederick on
that very same line, aboard a train pulling "cars crowded to overflowing
with citizens and their wives and daughters willing to take the risk rather
than lose a train."

Reid's more resourceful and luckier rival Charles Coffin was at this
moment on horseback, trying to navigate by the sound of the guns. His
ride would bring him this evening to Hanover, where he would see "dead
horses and dead soldiers in the streets lying where they fell. The wounded
had been gathered into a schoolhouse and the warm-hearted women of
the place were ministering to their comfort."

When Reid finally reached Frederick, he would find there only the
basest detritus of Meade's military machine. The fighting soldiers of the
Army of the Potomac had departed northward to seek their foe, leaving
behind mobs of the outfit's undesirables. "Frederick is Pandemonium,"
reported Reid. "The worst elements of a great army are here in their
worst condition; its cowards, its thieves, its sneaks, its bullying
vagabonds, all inflamed with whiskey, and drunk as well with their freedom from accustomed restraint." It would be several days before the
army's hard-pressed provost marshal could restore order to the city.

Richard Ewell met with two of his three division commanders this
evening near Heidlersburg, Pennsylvania. Present were Robert Rodes
and Jubal Early, the latter only just arrived from York. Also with them
was the unrequested adviser sent to Ewell by Robert E. Lee. Fresh from
army headquarters and confident that he was better informed about the
overall state of affairs than Ewell, Isaac Trimble did not hesitate to offer
his opinions.

Ewell was frowning at two communications he had received from
headquarters, trying to reconcile them with the information he was get-

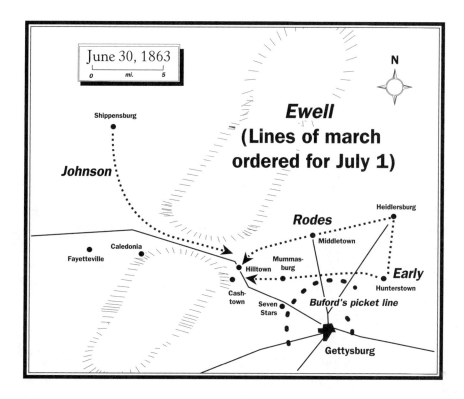

June 30, 1863

0   mi.   5

N

Ewell
(Lines of march
ordered for July 1)

Shippensburg

Johnson

Heidlersburg

Rodes

Middletown

Caledonia

Fayetteville

Hilltown

Mummas-
burg

Early

Cash-
town

Seven
Stars

Hunterstown

Buford's picket line

Gettysburg

ting from his scouts. One note, from Lee, modified Ewell's initial instructions. Instead of heading for Chambersburg, the Second Corps was now to proceed to "Cashtown, near Gettysburg," or else just to the latter if the situation warranted it. A follow-up memo from A. P. Hill advised that the Third Corps was already at Cashtown, where Hill had heard rumors that Federal infantry were posted in Gettysburg.

Still unhappy about being recalled before he could take Harrisburg, Ewell did not feel that Lee was giving him the whole picture. As he reread Lee's message to the officers present, he could not refrain from criticizing its "indefinite phraseology." He asked each man what he thought might decide the matter between Cashtown and Gettysburg. Rodes and Early had nothing to contribute, but Trimble was more than happy to weigh in. He recounted in detail Lee's expressed wish to beat the enemy and concluded that it meant Ewell should head for Gettysburg, where the Federal infantry were said to be. "This explanation," Trimble later wrote, "did not satisfy Gen'l Ewell."

From a mounted patrol he had sent off to scout south, Ewell had reports that there were no Yankee foot soldiers in Gettysburg, only cavalry. Given that he was supposed to avoid any fight, he therefore opted for Cashtown. Johnson's Division was too far along on the road to Chambersburg to be recalled, so those men would continue to that point. In the meantime, Robert Rodes was directed to march due west through Middletown,* while Early was to drop down to Hunterstown and then move parallel to Rodes, via Mummasburg. As the officers left the meeting, Trimble could still hear Ewell muttering, " 'Why can't a commanding General have some of his staff who can write an intelligent order?' "

Back at his own headquarters, Jubal Early did two things. First, he sent a message via mounted courier to the officer in charge of the Virginia troopers who were scouting for his division: "A small band of Yankee cavalry has made its appearance between Gettysburg and Heidlersburg," he wrote. "See what it is." And then he had a look at some maps of the area. As he had suspected, his assigned route to Hunterstown was more circuitous than one that carried traffic more directly toward Gettysburg. Early decided to shift his line of march to that shorter route.

It was evening before J. Johnston Pettigrew was able to locate his division commander, Henry Heth, and brief him on the results of his foray toward Gettysburg. In later years, Heth would recall the conversation with several variants. What seems indisputable is that Pettigrew told him "that he had not gone to Gettysburg; that there was evidently a cavalry force occupying the town," and that there was some indication that infantry might be nearby. Heth was saved from having to take notes on his subordinate's report when A. P. Hill rode up, giving Pettigrew the opportunity to tell him in person. Hill listened to his story and then remarked that what Pettigrew had encountered was only "cavalry, probably a detachment of observation." The best information that Hill had from Lee put the enemy almost sixteen miles farther south, or about a day's march away.

Something about Hill's and Heth's smug assurance prompted Pettigrew to wave Louis Young up to join the group. Under questioning, Young offered his opinion that the enemy riders had been not militia scouts but "well-trained troops." Hill, however, either would not or could not accept that the Army of the Potomac might be that close. Even if Young's surmise was true, he said, there was no place he would rather

*Modern Biglerville.

have the Yankee infantry than in front of him at Gettysburg. At this point, Heth spoke up.

"If there is no objection," he said, "I will take my division to-morrow and go to Gettysburg."

Hill thought for a moment. With Ewell's troops passing north of Gettysburg from east to west, it made sense to try to keep the Federal riders from using the town as a base from which they could harass the Second Corps' march. Besides, he needed to know what was in his front.

Hill had his answer. Any objection? "None in the world," he said.

On June 29, John Buford had received orders from Alfred Pleasonton, directing him to proceed "to Gettysburg" no later than the night of June 30. He had accomplished that task with hours to spare. Buford knew from his brief meeting with John Reynolds in Emmitsburg that the whole army was moving slowly forward along a front perhaps twenty-five miles long. If all went according to program, the marching orders for July 1 would bring that line up so that its left flank (Reynolds' First Corps, supported by Howard's Eleventh and Sickles' Third) was at Gettysburg. It was Buford's responsibility to secure the place to ensure that the foot soldiers would arrive unmolested. This he now set out to do.

"The night of the 30th was a busy night for the division," he would later write. Buford had with him perhaps 2,750 men in two brigades, plus one six-gun battery. After setting up his headquarters at the Eagle Hotel, he had made contact with what he later termed some "reliable men"— very likely belonging to the intelligence network operated by David McConaughy—who helped fill in some of the details. The cavalry officer had also spent the remaining daylight hours riding about the area to gauge the lay of the land. He was observed at around 4:00 P.M. by Daniel Skelly, who would never forget Buford's "calm demeanor and soldierly appearance." As the general seemed to be "in profound thought," Skelly did not bother him.

In the absence of further orders either to move on in the morning or to withdraw, Buford saw it as his duty to hold the approaches from the west, north, and even east until the infantry came up. But the more he thought about the problem he faced, the more impossible it all seemed. Members of his staff would later recall that they "had never seen him so apprehensive[,] so uneasy about a situation as he was at this time." A signal officer concurred that John Buford seemed very "anxious."

By the time Buford met with his two brigade commanders, Colonels William Gamble and Thomas C. Devin, he had settled on a plan. He would post a strong series of vedettes to the west and north. All the intelligence Buford had gathered suggested that the whole of Hill's Corps was "massed back of Cashtown" to the west, but there were also clear indications that Ewell's Corps was "coming over the mountains from Carlisle," to the north. Having decided that Hill represented the more immediate

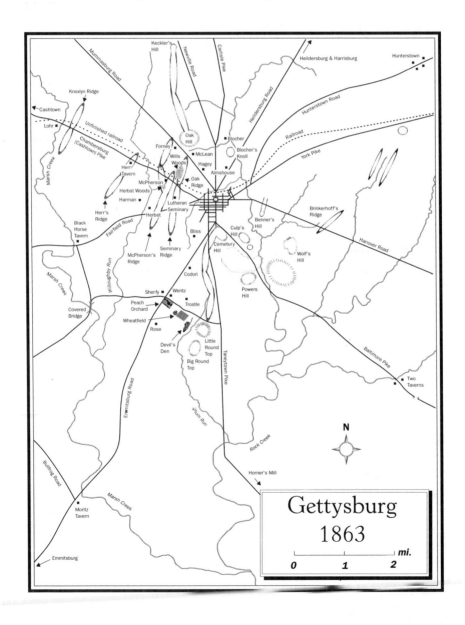

threat, Buford resolved to concentrate most of his strength west of the town, along McPherson's Ridge, and assigned Gamble to that sector. Devin was to cover Gamble's right as well as the roads leading into Gettysburg from the north and east.

Buford was determined not to be caught napping. The most advanced posts in his screen formed an arc from west to north more than three miles from the town's center. It would take a column of infantry at least an hour to march that distance unopposed. And John Buford had every intention of providing some opposition.

No single mood characterized the citizens of Gettysburg this night. True, many were reassured by the presence of Buford's men: young Daniel Skelly remarked that the townsfolk went to bed "with a sense of security they had not enjoyed for days," and Catherine Foster was certain that with the "cavalry between us and the enemy, . . . the battle was good as begun, fought and won." A few felt, like Tillie Pierce, that luck was with them and that "some great military event was coming pretty close to us." But others expected the worst. "It begins to look as though we will have a battle soon," wrote Sarah Broadhead, "and we are in great fear."

NOCTURNE
Night, Tuesday, June 30

The sunset at 7:24 P.M. By 9:00 P.M., any light on the land was man-made and hard to find. The moon, rising just after midnight, was almost full, though its reflected illumination was muted by rain clouds. Lanterns laboriously hauled along lit select tents at various headquarters, but for the most part, the men spread across the landscape for miles around Gettysburg did without and went to sleep.

Along the western bank of Marsh Creek where it crossed the Chambersburg Pike, perhaps three miles from Gettysburg's town square, Lieutenant Colonel John R. Lane was kept busy setting up the picket line for Pettigrew's Brigade. The large (800-strong) 26th North Carolina had drawn this night's assignment. It was standard procedure for the regiment's colonel to oversee this important task, but Henry King Burgwyn Jr. had let his second in command take over so he could "sleep sound" and be ready for whatever tomorrow morning might bring.

While there was still sufficient light, Lane had mapped out the area his men would cover following the creek bed and selected the all-important reserve posts that would provide support for the widely spaced string of men. Hardly had the line been set when it snagged two women trying to reach their houses, which lay just outside Lane's perimeter. Offering the gracious explanation that "the Confederate soldier did not make war upon women and children," Lane not only let the ladies pass but obligingly extended that part of his picket line to include their homes. Otherwise it proved to be a quiet night, with an occasional spattering of light rain. It would also be the last night for 588 men of the regiment, who by the end of tomorrow would be lying dead or wounded on the wooded slopes of a gentle ridge a few miles distant.

In the fields near Heidlersburg, Pennsylvania, the nearly 1,400 North Carolinians of Brigadier General Alfred Iverson's brigade (Rodes' Division, Ewell's Corps) camped for the night, reasonably tired but likely content. Their march south from Carlisle had covered some twenty miles, along a route running through areas not previously swept by passing Rebel columns. "Cherries were ripe along the rock-walled lanes," recounted a member of the 23rd North Carolina. "Bringing camp hatchets out, fruit-ladened limbs were severed and we regaled ourselves as we swung onward."

What general unhappiness there was in this brigade centered on its Georgia-born commander. Alfred Iverson was a competent professional soldier who had resigned a U.S. Army commission to serve the Confederacy. He had helped to organize the 20th North Carolina and had led it with distinction during the Seven Days' Campaign outside Richmond and in one of the battles preliminary to bloody Antietam; it was after that latter costly engagement that he had succeeded his fallen brigade commander. Iverson's once-happy relationship with his men was an early casualty of his promotion. Many of his officers had turned on him when he tried to fill a vacant colonelcy with an outside candidate—not only outside the understaffed regiment itself but outside the *brigade*. After Chancellorsville, the brigadier had been stigmatized for his conspicuous absence at the height of the fighting, a lapse he had officially ascribed to the effects of being hit by a spent bullet. And during his outfit's more recent sojourn at Carlisle, Iverson (who, like Ewell, had been posted there before the war) had gotten quite obviously drunk. Less than a day into the future, his men would march into the bloodiest ambush at Gettysburg, confirming forever, in the minds of many in the brigade, the character of the man they had come so to despise.

Commanding another brigade, this one in William Dorsey Pender's division of Hill's Corps, was Colonel Abner Perrin, who counted himself something of a thinking man. Like most of his rank in Lee's army, he had been told little about the current situation overall, beyond whatever route information he needed for each day's march. Had he been asked on the morning of June 30 to describe the campaign plan, he would have answered that "Gen Lee expected to concentrate his army at Chambersburg & give the enemy battle there." Perrin was just as surprised as the other 1,900 South Carolinians constituting the five regiments in his brigade when orders came for them to march toward the mountain gap to their east.

The day was wet and rainy, but the men had some luck: the going was not as bad as it might have been. "But for the firm mountain pike," recalled an officer in the 1st South Carolina (Provisional Army), "we should scarcely have been able to move." And pleasure in some cases was more than just a macadamized road. Resourceful officers such as Surgeon Spencer Glasgow Welch, of the 13th South Carolina, found the few homesteaders in the hills eager to share all they had, which for Welch and his companions meant generous main courses washed down with coffee and sweet milk. "None but a soldier who has experienced a hard campaign could appreciate such a meal," Welch declared.

The regular foot soldiers did well, too. "That night whiskey was again issued to us," remarked a line officer. The men were told to prepare rations enough to last them through the next day, an order that "at once aroused our suspicions, for we concluded we were about to meet the enemy," recollected Surgeon Welch. His surmise was more accurate than he could have guessed, for in less than a day, Perrin's Brigade would charge into a wheel-to-wheel phalanx of Yankee cannon that would smash down nearly 600 of its men.

Northeast of Gettysburg, John B. Gordon's six regiments of Georgia troops (slightly more than 1,800 men) were the last of Jubal Early's units to pull into the division's encampments near Heildersburg. Gordon had marched his men over from York, where they had enjoyed a bounty that few of their fellows would have imagined possible. "Even when our men awoke [to march this morning] they paid no attention to the great piles of supplies we had brought them," grumbled one Georgia soldier, "and marched away, leaving their portions for anybody who might find them."

As two weary companies from the 38th Georgia trudged off to take up their assigned picket posts, Gordon tried hard to shake off a curious premonition. It was his brigade that had marched through Gettysburg on June 26, on which occasion he had briefly surveyed the area and noted the dominating presence of Cemetery Hill. As Gordon later remembered it, "I expressed to my staff the opinion that if the battle [we all expected] should be fought at Gettysburg, the army which held the heights would probably be the victor." Ahead for Gordon's Brigade was a moment of pure glory in the fields north of the town, a hard-fought victory that would cost the brigadier more than 500 of his men and present Robert E. Lee with the intoxicating prospect of the battle of annihilation he was seeking.

Lee himself fell asleep satisfied that his instructions to consolidate the army were being carried out with few hitches. Given another day without incident, he would be ready for anything Meade might send his way. Sleep did not come so easy to Lee's Third Corps commander, A. P. Hill.

Hill was not an especially stolid campaigner, and his health had been compromised by a youthful bout with a sexually transmitted disease. He would be quite unwell on the morning of July 1, so it is likely that he suffered through this night. For his part, Hill's confident subordinate Henry Heth *should* have spent some sleepless hours worrying about all the little details involved in an operation as tricky as a reconaissance in force. The evidence of his actions in the next morning's events, however, suggests that he neglected to do so.

Perhaps half to three quarters of a mile east of Lane's North Carolina pickets were the most advanced vedette posts in the wide, watchful screen set out by John Buford. These Yankee boys came from Company E of the 8th Illinois Cavalry. Whereas as much as six hundred yards separated the outposts along some portions of Buford's perimeter, the observers positioned on either side of the Chambersburg Pike were only about two hundred yards apart, attesting to the roadway's importance.

Each vedette post, typically numbering four or five men, was located on a prominent point or near some important strategic feature such as a water crossing or an accessible passage. A short distance behind the forward outposts were the vedette reserves, made up of men from the same company as those assigned to the front. To ensure alertness and guard against surprises, small roving squads periodically checked the stations. In the main compounds spread along McPherson's Ridge, half of the horses were kept fully bridled, and a third of the men remained awake and ready for quick deployment if needed.

The man commanding the vedettes and their reserves was spending this night at the Eagle Hotel with his staff. Buford had decided that if the enemy advanced on Gettysburg in the morning, he would make a fight of it with his two brigades. Relief, he knew, was on its way: the infantry marches ordered for July 1 should bring the First Corps into town and put the Eleventh nearby. At 10:30 P.M., he sent off a situation report to John Reynolds, headquartered just south of town. Ever the practical warrior, Buford closed his note with a request: "Should I have to fall back [in the morning], advise me by what route."

Just ten minutes after dispatching that message, Buford composed another summary, this one for his immediate superior, Alfred Pleasonton. After noting with a touch of poetic license that Hill's pickets "are in sight of mine," he reported that the roads north of town were "terribly infested with roving detachments of [enemy] cavalry." Buford could breathe a little easier now, thanks to the arrival in Gettysburg, just before dark, of Lieutenant John Calef's six-gun Battery A, 2nd United States Light Artillery, whose three-inch ordnance cannon added some welcome punch to his carbines. But still, the combat-experienced cavalry commander was far from overconfident. In a briefing with one of his brigade commanders, Buford offered a sober assessment of the coming day: " 'You will have to fight like the devil to hold your own until [infantry] supports arrive.' "

The man immediately responsible for bringing those supports to Buford was wrapped in a blanket on the floor of Moritz Tavern, trying to sleep. John Reynolds had fretted throughout the day that the Rebels might push through Gettysburg, sweep south with the mountain passes safely behind them, and smash his exposed flank, itself the extreme left wing of the Army of the Potomac. Reynolds had kept that thought in mind as he selected the camps for his First Corps divisions,* and when he advised Oliver Otis Howard on where to position the Eleventh Corps outside Emmitsburg. While their commander lay awake worrying about the next morning's possibilities, Reynolds' military aides, young men with a spirit of adventure, snored away in another room of the tavern, deep in the sleep of the innocent.

This night found James Wadsworth's two-brigade division of the Union First Corps camped between Moritz Tavern and Gettysburg, where the Emmitsburg Road crossed Marsh Creek. Nothing in their orders, or even in the rumors they had heard, gave the approximately 1,800 men of Wadsworth's celebrated First Brigade any indication that a desperate struggle awaited them just a few hours into the future. As so often was the case, the bliss of ignorance offered these soldiers their only protection: by sunset tomorrow, nearly 1,200 members of the cocky black-hatted Iron Brigade would be dead, wounded, or captured by the enemy.

Lieutenant Loyd G. Harris of the 6th Wisconsin seemed to have not a care in the world as he entertained his fellow lieutenant Orrin Chapman with a harmonica rendition of "Home, Sweet Home." A mile or so closer to Gettysburg, the division's picket line, manned by four companies of the 19th Indiana, stretched across the gently rolling Pennsylvania land-

*When Reynolds bore the responsibilities of left wing commander, Major General Abner Doubleday commanded the First Corps.

scape. The rest of the regiment was settled down in reserve near the tiny village of Green Mount, where the men were made welcome. "We lived high here," recalled Lieutenant George H. Finney. "People brought in everything in the way of eatables."

A few letters were started, and some even finished in the fading light. Lieutenant Colonel Rufus Dawes' missive fell into the former category. "I am kept full of business . . . ," he scribbled, "scarcely from morning to night getting a moment I can call my own." Lieutenant Colonel William Dudley of 19th Indiana was able to complete his message: "[We] shall soon be engaged," he prophesied, "deciding this thing one way or the other."

Brigadier General John C. Robinson's First Corps division was camped a few miles west of Moritz Tavern, covering a road that led to Fairfield, just in case the Rebels tried to use it. The division's First Brigade, commanded by Brigadier General Gabriel R. Paul, included the nearly 300-strong 16th Maine. The next afternoon, the New Englanders would make a suicidal last stand that would save their division while costing them more than 230 casualties. This night, however, they were savoring the moment. They had marched only a short distance today, getting into camp around noon. Lieutenant George D. Bisbee was grateful for the "much needed rest" everyone got. One exception was the regimental adjutant, Major Abner R. Small, who took the opportunity to catch up on his paperwork and file away a copy of George Meade's stirring address to the army. "If we had any lingering doubts about the probability of a battle in the near future . . . ," he later reflected, "they were promptly dispelled."

The 157th New York, part of Carl Schurz's division in the Eleventh Corps, was among the units camped on the northern side of Emmitsburg, near St. Joseph's College. The regiment's members hailed mostly from the middle part of New York, especially Cortland and Madison counties. When the 157th had first marched off to war, its proud ranks had counted 1,000 souls, but this night, after less than a year of service, fewer than 400 were ready to advance in the morning. At the end of the next day's road for these boys lay a nondescript field north of Gettysburg, where more than 300 of them would fall. Most of the veterans likely gave little thought to that possibility. A few shared a survivor's sense of invincibility, as voiced by the regiment's second in command, Lieutenant Colonel George Arrowsmith: "I have come to feel that the bullet is not molded which is to kill me."

Fellow New Yorkers in the 154th Regiment (Steinwehr's division, First Brigade) had enjoyed the hospitality of Emmitsburg's nuns after their arrival on June 29. Today they marched closer to the Pennsylvania line. These Yankees came from the southern part of their state, primarily Cattaraugus and Chautauqua counties. This relative proximity prompted one lovesick private to write to his wife this day, "We are within two miles of [the] Pennsylvania line . . . so you see that I am not more than 300 miles from you (maybe, much less), so you can get a horse and buggy and drive down to see me. It would not take you only *3 or 4 days!!*" In store for these Union boys was an intersection with fate near a brick-making plant in Gettysburg. There they would help save their corps and in doing so lose 200 out of 239 men. Among those destined to fall was Sergeant Amos Humiston, whose deep love for his children, while not sparing his life, would make them national celebrities.

The man whose orders meant life or death for all these soldiers got little sleep this night at army headquarters, now located in Taneytown, Maryland. George Gordon Meade had spent the day studying reports from his engineers regarding the placement of a possible defensive line, which he finally resolved to adopt if Lee began to move south looking for a fight. Meade's weary aides were subsequently kept busy drafting copies of an important circular intended for all corps commanders. It identified what would become known as the Pipe Creek Line and spelled out the specific conditions that would trigger a general retrograde movement to that position. The plan had been conceived to address something that Meade saw as a very real concern: the danger that his widely spaced corps alignment could be chewed up in a piecemeal fashion if the Rebel army moved against any discrete portion of it. The Pipe Creek trigger would allow any corps commander subjected to such pressure to initiate the withdrawal process. Once that process was begun, all other corps commanders would be compelled to follow suit.

These instructions would not be distributed until after dawn on July 1. Several hours before sunrise, a bone-tired telegrapher arrived from Frederick with an important message from Harrisburg, sent via Washington.* "Lee is falling back suddenly from the vicinity of Harrisburg, and is concentrating all his forces," it read. "The concentration appears to be at or near Chambersburg." Meade likely felt a surge of relief at this news, for it validated his decision to allow John Reynolds to continue to advance the

*The lines cut by Stuart's raiders had by now been restored

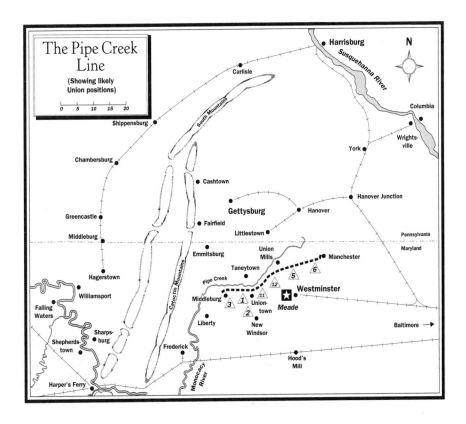

The Pipe Creek
Line
(Showing likely
Union positions)

0   5   10   15   20

Harrisburg   N

Susquehanna River

Carlisle

Columbia

Shippensburg

Wrights-
ville

Chambersburg   York

Cashtown

Hanover Junction

Gettysburg   Hanover

Greencastle   Fairfield

Littlestown   Pennsylvania

Middleburg   Maryland

Emmitsburg   Union
                   Mills   Manchester

Hagerstown   Taneytown

Pipe Creek   ⑤   ⑥

Williamsport   Middleburg   ⑫
                            ⑪   ★ Westminster
Falling   ③ ① Union-   Meade
Waters   ② town

Shepherds- Sharps-   Liberty   New   Baltimore →
town   burg   Windsor
                   Frederick

Hood's
Mill

Harper's Ferry

Monocacy River

South Mountains

Catoctin Mountains

left wing as far as Gettysburg. The chance of a fight's erupting and getting out of hand before all his corps commanders received the Pipe Creek circular now seemed very remote.

What Meade could not know was that a follow-up message, written less than two hours after the first, was also on its way to him. Unfortunately, it was being held in Frederick until a courier could be found to carry it, and would not reach him until late in the afternoon of July 1. This note, from the same source as the first, began, "Information just received . . . leads to the belief that the concentration of forces of the enemy will be at Gettysburg rather than Chambersburg."

TWELVE

July 1, 1863

(Predawn–7:30 A.M.)

John Reynolds had been asleep for perhaps four hours when an aide just returned from army headquarters regretfully woke him. Reynolds did not get up immediately but instead lay quietly with one hand under his head while Meade's orders were read aloud, a recitation he had repeated twice to make sure all the details had registered. The most important item was the final confirmation of today's left wing movements: First Corps backed by Eleventh to Gettysburg, Third Corps to Emmitsburg. The next nearest unit would be the Twelfth Corps, marching to a hamlet named Two Taverns.

Meade's intelligence assessment put two Rebel corps between Chambersburg and the area west of Gettysburg. Ewell's Corps was likely spread north and east of the town. While the orders seemed clear enough, their intent was less so. On the one hand, Meade believed that his broad front advance had arrested the enemy's reach toward Harrisburg, so the urgency of past days was abated. On the other hand, his instructions contained the unmistakable warning that each corps should be "ready to move to the attack at any moment." That latter advice matched Reynolds' sense of the situation. He waved away a fourth reading as he got to his feet. There was much to be done.

Men were moving about the encampments of Henry Heth's division well before the sun rose at 4:36 A.M. Already it was not Heth's day. Either forgotten from the previous evening's discussions with A. P. Hill or only just received were orders to begin the march at 5:00 A.M. There was a haste to the early morning's preparations that caught some off guard. Notable in this category was Colonel John A. Fite of the 7th Tennessee, in Brigadier General James J. Archer's brigade. Fite went out to his picket line while it was still dark for a home-cooked breakfast at the farmhouse being used by his outpost officers. He was enjoying a chat with the farmer's daughter when, as he later recalled, "a courier came and ordered all of my pickets in." After making hasty apologies, Fite hurried off.

Not stirring this morning was A. P. Hill. Lee's Third Corps commander lingered indoors, and even when he felt well enough later to move about, he looked, according to one observer, "very delicate." For reasons that he never explained, Hill had resolved that this day's expedition to Gettysburg was not going to be a halfhearted affair. On his orders, Pender's entire division would follow Heth's, boosting the force committed to this reconnaissance to almost 15,000 men.

The mixed signals Hill was sending perhaps reflected his own confusion and uncertainty. The very size of the force and the nature of the troops he assigned indicated that the Gettysburg foray would not be easy. Yet Hill's admonition to Heth was clear: "Do not bring on an engagement." Managing the fine balance between aggressively executing the assignment and avoiding a full-blown encounter would have taxed the judgment of the most experienced combat officer, and Henry Heth was not at that level.

Hill's incapacity left Heth without any sage counsel, and he promptly made his first bad decision of the day. Even though Pettigrew's Brigade was camped closest to Gettysburg, Heth decided it would remain in place until most of the division had marched past. He saw no reason to take advantage of Pettigrew's recent familiarity with the terrain; possibly he was still smarting over the lack of initiative Pettigrew had shown the day before, in not more actively challenging the enemy. The capstone to Heth's morning arrived with a message that, when recollected years later, would be wrapped up in the pleasant mythology of his search for shoes. As Heth remembered it, "A courier came from Gen. Lee, with a dispatch, ordering me to get the shoes even if I encountered some resistance." This unsubstantiated exhortation meshed well with Heth's understanding of Lee's prime motive for entering Pennsylvania: "General Lee's . . . intention was to strike his enemy the very first available opportunity that offered—believing he could, when such an opportunity offered, crush him."

* * *

The first small engagements around Gettysburg began some thirty minutes after sunrise. A few miles north, a Carlisle Road outpost manned by
17th Pennsylvania cavalrymen traded shots with Rebel riders likely probing out from Ewell's columns. A short time later, in Hunterstown, northeast of Gettysburg, a pair of 9th New York scouts were surprised and
chased by four mounted Confederates, who were themselves captured
after the Yankees enlisted the help of a friendly patrol. Neither event signaled the start of any substantial action, but like heat lightning, the activity presaged increasing turbulence.

Smoke curled from Gettysburg's chimneys as the town's citizens prepared
to entertain even more Union troops. "The members of our household
were all up bright and early," remarked Catherine Ziegler, "for much was
to be done for the comfort of the soldiers." "I got up early this morning
to get my baking done," Sarah Broadhead recorded. A number of cavalrymen were roaming the town on personal errands. A few residents living
on the north side heard the outpost carbines crack. "Gettysburg awoke,
but was not alarmed," noted Henry Jacobs. "We felt no apprehension; at
worst, the town thought there might be a skirmish."

The mood was decidedly nonchalant among the bivouacs of Buford's
troopers, one of whom would remember that "the camp was astir; men
prepared and partook of the morning meal; horses were fed and
groomed, arms cleaned and burnished." Young Leander Warren was having the time of his life. He and a couple of other boys went out to
Buford's camps, where they pitched in by "riding the cavalry horses to
the creek for water."

A newspaper reporter's reputation depended on reliable sources of information and a little timely luck. After arriving in Frederick, Maryland, veteran correspondents Samuel Wilkeson (*New York Times*), Uriah H.
Painter (*Philadelphia Inquirer*), and Whitelaw Reid (*Cincinnati Gazette*)
had gone to work locating army headquarters. Everyone they contacted
confirmed that George Meade had gone to Westminster, making that
where their story would be. Wilkeson and Painter hustled to secure rail
passage back to Baltimore, where they would hop a government train to

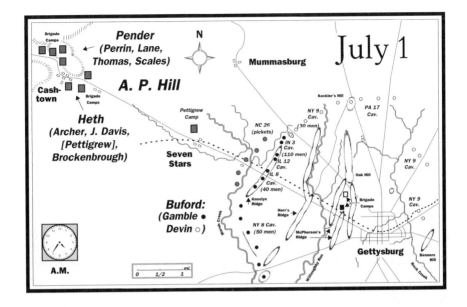

Westminster. Reid bade his companions farewell, determined to reach that same point overland.

The Cincinnati newsman managed to obtain some breakfast shortly after dawn. Showing little concern for the modest limits of his expense account, he purchased a horse and all the equipment he would need "for the campaign." And then some of that luck came his way: even as he was setting out in the company of "a messenger for one of the New York papers," Reid encountered an army courier who helpfully revealed that headquarters were not at Westminster but at Taneytown. Reid immediately smelled gunpowder, believing "it was fair to suppose that our movements to the northwest were based upon news of a similar concentration by the rebels. The probabilities of a speedy battle were thus immensely increased, and we hastened the more rapidly on."

Henry Heth's marching column got under way at roughly the appointed hour of 5:00 A.M. For some reason—perhaps because the morning's assembly was so rushed, or maybe because Heth wanted mounted men leading the march—Major William Pegram's artillery battalion was allowed to precede the column, followed by the 1,200 Alabama and Tennessee foot soldiers of Archer's Brigade. Next came Brigadier General

Joseph R. Davis' brigade, or at least part of it. Ironically, it was Davis' two untested regiments, the 42nd Mississippi and the 55th North Carolina, that tramped along while his veteran pair—the 2nd and 11th Mississippi—stayed behind to guard army stores. The 2nd would be relieved in time to rejoin the brigade before it deployed for action, but the 11th would not. Colonel John M. Brockenbrough's all-Virginia brigade marched next, though once the column reached Pettigrew's camps, the Tarheels would fill in between Davis and Brockenbrough.

One of Pegram's officers later recalled, "We moved forward leisurely smoking and chatting as we rode along, not dreaming of the proximity of the enemy."

After handling some necessary headquarters business, John Reynolds headed north from Moritz Tavern to the area where James S. Wadsworth's division was camped. "He rode up to my headquarters . . . ," Wadsworth later testified, "and asked what orders I had received from General Doubleday, who then commanded the corps. . . . I told him that I was waiting for the other divisions to pass, as I was ordered to move in rear of the other two divisions. He said that this was a mistake, and that I should move on directly."

While Wadsworth went about getting his division on the road, Reynolds returned to the tavern, where acting corps commander Abner Doubleday was waiting to meet with him. "General Reynolds read his telegrams to me," Doubleday would recollect, "showing where our troops were, and what they were doing." Reynolds had decided that Buford should have infantry support at once. "He told me that he had already ordered Wadsworth's division to go forward," continued Doubleday. "He then instructed me to draw in my pickets, assemble the artillery and the remainder of the corps, and join him as soon as possible." There was nothing subtle about Reynolds' plan. His intention, as Doubleday later expressed it, "was . . . to fight the enemy as soon as he could meet him."

Of all John Buford's vedette posts, the one most likely to see trouble was located on the Chambersburg Pike, about three quarters of a mile east of where the road crossed Marsh Creek. A little after 6:00 A.M., two privates from the 8th Illinois Cavalry, Thomas B. Kelley and James O. Hall, relieved the pair who had been standing watch. Soon after taking over, the fresh sentries observed a sizable dust cloud rising from the road, maybe three miles away. Something large was heading right toward them.

The Eleventh Corps' encampments around Emmitsburg were stirring by first light. The members of one unlucky regiment, the 41st New York, had already been up for hours patrolling the roads, under orders to detain any civilians they encountered. Also feeling unlucky were 200 soldiers from the four regiments of Colonel Charles R. Coster's brigade, assigned to scout six miles west; included in this group, which set off at 5:00 A.M., were 50 men from the 154th New York. Nor was it a particularly auspicious morning for those remaining in camp. A diarist in the 153rd Pennsylvania noted that "it is still cloudy," while another, from the 136th New York, described the conditions in a single word: "Rainy."

Oliver Otis Howard shook off his weariness by charting a route for his units that would enable them to avoid likely congestion with the First Corps. Reflecting the lack of urgency everyone felt, his instructions to his supply trains were to march in tandem with the infantry. Howard sent a summary of his planned movements to Reynolds at 6:00 A.M.

Since breaking contact with Kilpatrick's cavalry at Hanover, Pennsylvania, an immensely tired Jeb Stuart had led his likewise exhausted column first east and then north, expecting to cut Ewell's trail near York. "Whole regiments slept in the saddle, their faithful animals keeping the road unguided," Stuart later reported. "In some instances they fell from their horses, overcome with physical fatigue and sleepiness."

Once his men reached the town of Dover, Stuart let them rest while he pondered his situation. His unwavering objective throughout the operation had been to join up with Ewell's Corps. Now here he was, near York, but there was no sign of Ewell—though there was plenty of evidence that he had recently been in the area. The most Stuart could glean from scouting reports and local newspapers was that the Confederate Second Corps was concentrating near Shippensburg.

While his men slept away the daylight hours of the morning, Stuart did something he should have done sooner: he dispatched his staffer Major Andrew R. Venable and a small escort with orders to find Ewell. At about the same time, Brigadier General Fitzhugh Lee, then holding Stuart's western flank, ordered one of his aides, Captain Henry Lee, to try to locate the Army of Northern Virginia.

At 7:00 A.M. George Meade sent a brief situation report to Henry Halleck. "The point of Lee's concentration and the nature of the country, when ascertained, will determine whether I attack him or not," he declared. By now, Meade's Pipe Creek instructions had begun circulating among his corps commanders.

The cannoneers at the head of Heth's reconnaissance column had crossed the western outskirts of Pettigrew's camps a little after 6:00 A.M., and reached the picket line on their eastern side before 7:00. At some point—either as his command party rode slowly through the camp or (as most historians have suggested) the previous evening—Pettigrew had briefed James Archer about Gettysburg. According to his aide Louis Young, Pettigrew "told General Archer of a ridge some distance west of Gettysburg on which he would probably find the enemy, as this position was favorable for defense."

Archer's leading regiment was the 13th Alabama. The men halted as they got to the swampy land fringing Marsh Creek, beyond which the ground angled up in a single gentle swell to a ridge line. A light and misty rain blurred faraway objects, making it impossible to identify the mounted men an artillerist spotted to the east of the creek. A brief argument ensued when a few present insisted that the strangers must belong to Longstreet, who was rumored to be marching on a parallel course. The discussion ended abruptly, however, when a trustworthy sergeant spoke up, saying that as he had ridden through the pass the day before, he had seen Longstreet's men camped west of the mountains. "That decided the question," recorded one gunner, "and at a word from Colonel Pegram the leading gun, a three-inch rifle piece of accuracy and long range, was at once unlimbered and swung around."*

Colonel Birkett D. Fry, commanding the 13th Alabama, had eased ahead to find out why the artillery had stopped. Seeing one of the guns deploying, he hurriedly returned to his regiment. According to a private

*In fact, William Pegram was not promoted to the rank of colonel until *after* the Gettysburg campaign. In such cases, however, fellow officers writing after the war tended to refer to their comrades by the superior rank, more as an honorific than as a statement of fact.

in the ranks, Fry "rode back to the color bearer and ordered him to uncase the colors, the first intimation that we had that we were about to engage the enemy." A skirmish line was quickly established south of the pike, consisting of four companies from the 5th Alabama Battalion (135 men) and two from the 13th Alabama (70 men).

The cupola of the Lutheran seminary offered a fine vantage point for viewing the landscape west and northwest of Gettysburg. A Union signal corps officer, Lieutenant Aaron B. Jerome, had climbed to the rooftop platform early this morning to establish an observation post. It was around 7:00 A.M. when he spied the leading elements of Heth's column approaching on the Chambersburg Pike and immediately notified John Buford. The cavalry commander kept a cool head, holding off for the moment on sounding an alert. Until he knew in what strength the enemy was advancing from Cashtown, Buford did not wish to commit his main forces either west or north.

Oliver Howard's proposed order of march reached John Reynolds by 7:00 A.M. The left wing commander wanted all the fighting troops to be up front, so he instructed Howard not to intermingle his supply wagons with his infantry. Similar instructions had been given to Abner Doubleday, to ensure that the First Corps wagons would wait until the Eleventh Corps foot soldiers had passed.

Reynolds took these steps merely as a precaution, not because he had positive information that any special effort was necessary. To the contrary: Colonel Charles Wainwright, commanding the First Corps artillery, remembered Reynolds' telling him that "he did not expect any [trouble], that we were only moving up so as to be within supporting distance to Buford, who was to push out farther."

Amid all the activity, Reynolds' assistant adjutant general failed to collect a more personal message that Meade had sent on the heels of the morning's orders. In it the Army of the Potomac commander shared some of the conflicting intelligence he had been given and offered his thoughts on the likely options. The note closed with the words "You have all the information which the general has received, and the general would like to have your views." Also not delivered to Reynolds was Meade's Pipe Creek circular.

*   *   *

Kelley and Hall, the Illinois privates on vedette duty, would recall that it was around 7:00 A.M. when they sighted the flash of red indicating "the old Rebel flag"—the colors leading Archer's section of the column. The two soldiers looked for Sergeant Levi S. Shafer, to whom they were supposed to report, but he was nowhere to be found. Kelley decided to ride to the reserve position, and either there or somewhere on the way, he met Private George Heim, who in turn located Lieutenant Marcellus E. Jones, commanding the detail. Jones had been expecting just such a report, so as he mounted his horse to investigate, he issued a preliminary order: "Get the entire command to the outpost."

On reaching the advanced vedettes, Jones dismounted, confirmed the sighting, and dispatched a report to the regimental commander. By now Sergeant Shafer had appeared. Jones asked the noncom for his carbine and, propping it on the fork of a handy rail fence, sighted toward the enemy column, a good half mile distant. Jones aimed at a man on horseback near the Confederate flag, knowing he had virtually no chance of hitting him.

At about 7:30 A.M., a moment he would never forget, Marcellus E. Jones fired a single shot.

The cannoneers assigned to Captain Edward A. Marye's Fredericks-burg Artillery knew their business. Per Pegram's orders, the first gun in the Virginia battery was quickly set up for firing in the yard of the Lohr farm. Seeing the commotion, the farmer ran out of his house and exclaimed, in what would prove to be a grand understatement, "My God, you are not going to fire here, are you?" The gunners ignored the inter-ruption and hurriedly finished their preparations. At a nod from the bat-tery commander, the cannon flashed flame, hurling the first shell into the sticky morning air.

Columns of troops were moving all across the region. Even though none had yet been summoned to Gettysburg, most were already headed in that direction. From camps around Scotland, Pennsylvania, northeast of Chambersburg, Johnson's Division of Ewell's Corps headed toward the Cashtown Gap. "Reveille at 5 a.m. Marched at 7," scribbled a Stonewall Brigade diarist. "The weary miles were slowly unreeled that hot July day, for the road was blocked by a long train of wagons," noted a Maryland soldier, "but finally that obstruction was passed and the march became easier." North of Gettysburg, Rodes' Division (also in Ewell's Corps) was in motion as well. "We left camp at 6 a.m.," a Tarheel foot soldier wrote. A brigade staff officer would recollect that the men marched "without thinking any danger was at hand."

On the Union side, the First Division of the First Corps was bustling. Because Cutler's brigade was camped nearest to Wadsworth's headquar-ters, its troops were on the road before the Iron Brigade (which was actu-ally camped closer to Gettysburg) could draw in its pickets to get off. Of the six regiments under Cutler, one, the 7th Indiana, remained behind to guard the wagons. As the other men started out, a soldier in the 84th New York (whose members preferred to call their unit the 14th Brooklyn, after its initial state militia designation) announced to anyone who would listen that the red sunrise was "the prophecy of a hot July day."

Even as Pegram's gunners loosed a second and then a third round at the Federals scattered ahead of them, skirmishers from Archer's Brigade were pushing through the tangled, swampy underbrush along Marsh Creek. If any of them noted that first shot fired by Marcellus E. Jones, none ever mentioned it. Coming up behind them on their left was a spread-out line from Davis' Brigade, about two hundred picked men forming a sharp-shooter battalion.

The combined force was more than Jones could manage, so the officer ordered his vedettes to retreat, working their carbines with care.* They had not backed up far when reinforcements arrived from the 8th Illinois Cavalry's Company E, under Captain Amasa E. Dana, who now took charge. The captain estimated that the Rebel skirmish line covered "a distance of a mile and a half, concealed at intervals by timber."

The tactics employed by this vedette line differed markedly from usual practice. The widely dispersed and unsupported outposts were normally expected to "fire and flee" upon the enemy's approach, but this morning Buford's troopers were being stubborn. Dana ordered his men "to throw up their carbine sights and [we] gave the enemy the benefit of long range practicc[;] the firing was rapid from our carbines, and at the distance induced the belief of four times our number of men actually present. . . . This was evident because the [enemy skirmish] line in our front halted."

Henry Heth's string of command errors continued. Even though his skir-mish line was engaged and some of his artillery were already in action, Heth decided to keep most of his troops in column rather than deploy them into lines of battle. Still anxious to effect a quick passage into Get-tysburg, he was reluctant to shift his men out of the compact marching formation that would enable him to accomplish his objective. Sooner or later, he reasoned, the Yankee cavalry would have to withdraw, leaving the road wide open; he wanted to be ready when that happened.

*One of Gettysburg's enduring myths is that Buford's men were armed with seven-shot Spencer guns. Ordnance reports indicate, however, that most of the Union troopers carried an assortment of single-shot, breech-loading weapons

Well back along the pike, Heth's smallest brigade, John M. Brocken-brough's all-Virginia unit, was completing the column. A chaplain riding near the 47th Virginia's Colonel Robert M. Mayo, who was accompanying Brockenbrough, saw one of Henry Heth's staff officers gallop up. According to the cleric, the aide reported, "General Heth is ordered to move on Gettysburg, and fight or not as he wishes." After the man passed along, the chaplain heard one of the officers say, "We must fight them; no division general will turn back with such orders."

More and more units were in motion by 8:00 A.M. The Union Iron Brigade marched about fifteen minutes behind Cutler's men. The 2nd Wisconsin led the way, followed by the 7th Wisconsin, the 19th Indiana, the 24th Michigan, the 6th Wisconsin, and a brigade guard of one hundred men (twenty from each regiment). As the Michigan regiment was getting ready, its cleric held a prayer meeting. "During Chaplain [W. C.] Way's invocation," recollected one soldier, "cartridges and hardtack were distributed among the men." Rufus Dawes of the 6th Wisconsin pronounced the boys "in the highest spirits." When some Milwaukee Germans in one of Dawes' companies lustily sang a "soul stirring song," they were cheered by their comrades and answered by boys from Juneau County who offered a humorous army ditty. A Wisconsin soldier thought it "odd for men to march toward their [possible] death singing, shouting and laughing as if it were [a] parade or holiday."

Perhaps a mile west, the Third Division of the First Corps was on a parallel track. One New York officer noted that "a hundred rumors circulated through the camp as to what was going on or what would happen." Some members of the 80th New York had discovered to their astonishment that the locals were not disposed to be generous toward outsiders. So this day the New Yorkers had a plan: they would tell anyone they met on the march that they were a Pennsylvania regiment.

Miles south of the First Corps, the Eleventh was on the march by 8:30 A.M. A small band of precipitation must have been targeting these troops, for a diarist in the 154th New York recorded that they "traveled very hard in the rain and mud." Word of the march was slow in getting to the gunners of Battery I, 1st Ohio Light Artillery, known as Dilger's Battery after their commander. Roused late, the men hurried but did not rush. The feeling was that they would meet Rebels today, and no one wanted to go into action unprepared.

Powerful Confederate columns were also stirring. North of Gettysburg, following the less circuitous track he had preferred, Jubal Early led
his division toward Heidlersburg, where he picked up the Harrisburg
Road on his way to a more direct route to Cashtown.* There was no
urgency to Early's pace. It was nearly 8:00 A.M. before the main column
uncoiled; while some units had started earlier, others would not move
until after 9:00 A.M.

Eight miles west of the front of Heth's procession, Pender's Division
was joining the line. The hasty departure bothered at least one of Pender's brigade commanders. Watching his men scramble into columns,
Colonel Abner Perrin of South Carolina concluded "from the hurried &
confused manner of our getting out of camp that the enemy was not far
off." A Georgia soldier described this day as "warm," with "some rain."
He noticed that the supply wagons were being left behind, which usually
meant that an engagement was anticipated.

Officers with Henry Heth's advance would later refer to the process of
pushing back the Yankee vedettes this morning as "driving" them. It was
at best a slow, cautious drive, however. The Illinois troopers were hard to
move, forcing Heth's skirmishers to undertake the time-consuming task
of fixing the enemy line in place, then working parties around its flanks or
into any other chinks they could find. The steady pressure in front coupled with the deadly threat posed by flanking or infiltration parties invari-
ably compelled the outnumbered, dismounted troopers to retreat. While
the cavalrymen's breech-loading carbines gave them a slightly faster rate
of fire than their opponents, they were outranged by the infantry's muz-
zle-loading rifles. But even when they were rousted, Buford's men never
left the field; instead they merely sifted back a short distance to take
another stand.

Illinois Cavalry Captain Amasa Dana later recounted the action from
his point of view: "The true character and length of our line soon became
known to the enemy, and they promptly moved upon our front and
flanks. We retired and continued to take new positions, and usually held
out as long as we could without imminent risk of capture. We were driven
from three positions successively in less than one hour." One of Dana's

*Ten miles northeast of Gettysburg, the Harrisburg Road became the Heidlersburg
Road.

soldiers remembered that the Federal vedettes "fought with the enemy overwhelming us in numbers and pressing us at every point."

On the Chambersburg side of the Cashtown Pass, James Longstreet's corps was starting its passage east. A soldier who saw Lee this morning thought he "was looking in perfect health & seemed happy as the troops cheered him." Longstreet remembered that Robert E. Lee "was in his usual cheerful spirits . . . , and called me to ride with him."

As the command group approached the western entrance to the pass, it became apparent to the generals that the single roadway through could not sustain all the traffic at once. Johnson's Division of Ewell's command, under orders to join its parent unit, was already waiting impatiently. Lee decided that allowing Ewell to complete his concentration near Cashtown was more important than interposing the First Corps, so he told Longstreet to hold back until the Second Corps infantry and wagons had cleared out. The officers dismounted and stood for a while, watching the columns pass. Then, as Longstreet recalled, "General Lee proposed that we should ride on."

It was about 8:00 A.M. when Captain Daniel W. Buck of the 8th Illinois Cavalry rode into Buford's field headquarters looking for the general. Buford was in town, so Major John L. Beveridge received Buck's report that "the enemy was advancing in force in two columns." Beveridge ordered out reinforcements to the picket line and told the bugler to sound "Boots and Saddles." The commotion brought Buford back from town, along with William Gamble, who approved Beveridge's actions.

At Buford's direction, Gamble began to deploy his entire brigade to meet Heth's advance. The native Irishman and veteran of the British Army was a stern taskmaster whose well-drilled unit was ready for combat. A main line of battle was established along McPherson's Ridge, while John Calef's six cannon were rolled into firing positions astride the pike. Couriers raced off to spread the news along the chain of command.

Gamble had another scheme up his sleeve. Having delayed the Rebel advance by repeatedly holding until they were forced to retreat, his backpedaling vedettes were almost at Herr's Ridge, the best defensible location west of McPherson's Ridge. Their commander now turned Herr's Ridge into a strong point by sending forward some 400 men to form a thick skirmish line there. Gamble was matched to his right by Thomas Devin, who bolstered his advance with another 100 cavalry. "Our orders were to hold [the enemy] back," recollected one of Gamble's men.

The sudden appearance of the Federal line caused the Rebel skirmishers to stop and request further instructions. Discounting horseholders,* perhaps 550 Union troopers now confronted 400 Confederate voltigeurs. Henry Heth considered the changed odds before deciding fully to deploy his two leading brigades. Aides rode along the halted columns with the new orders as bugles blared and drums rattled.

Once the heretofore fluid skirmishing lines were locked into firm contact, serious casualties began to occur.† On Gamble's front, an unidentified trooper riding a gray horse galloped beyond the cover of his skirmishers and was dropped by alert Alabama riflemen. Several in the 5th Alabama were hit, including Private C. L. F. Worley, who lost a leg.

To help protect the helpless columns while they were reforming into battle lines, William Pegram set his cannon working from whatever positions the cannoneers could find. As Archer's men deployed, the 7th Tennessee established the line with its left resting on the pike. The spaces to its right were then filled by the 14th Tennessee, the 1st Tennessee, and the 13th Alabama, while the 5th Alabama Battalion kept up skirmishing duty. Davis' Brigade was meanwhile filing into the fields on the northern side of the pike, with the 42nd Mississippi setting its right on the road, followed by the 2nd Mississippi (which had hustled to catch up) and finally the 55th North Carolina. It was a slow process, taking the better part of an hour to complete.

John Calef was moving his six guns into their appointed place, straddling the Chambersburg Pike on the western spur of McPherson's Ridge. He deemed the position "a good one for artillery, with the exception that a railway cut existed near the right flank." Then new instructions came from John Buford, who had conceived a different strategy. Buford wanted Calef to post only four of his cannon by the pike and instead send the other two south along the eastern spur of the ridge, to a point just

*During dismounted fighting, every fourth cavalryman in four was detailed to hold the others' horses, keeping station a few hundred feet to the rear of the firing line.
†The surgeon of the 17th Pennsylvania would later declare that he had been treating minor combat wounds since the skirmishing began

southeast of the Herbst Woods. "It was part of General Buford's plan to cover as large a front as possible with my battery (his only artillery) for the purpose of deceiving the enemy as to his strength," Calef later recalled. Two cannon under Sergeant Charles Pergel started off toward the designated position.

Harriet Bayly, who lived on a farm north of Gettysburg, was overcome by curiosity. Accompanied by her uncle Robert, she walked along a ridge line that ran southwest, hoping to find something interesting. After half an hour the two met a weary squad of Federal cavalrymen, one of whom asked Harriet if she had seen any Rebels. Before she could answer, there was a distant cannon boom that seemed to tell the riders all they needed to know. Suddenly many more men rose from the fields on either side, readying themselves for combat. Someone yelled to Harriet that it was not safe for her to be here.

But Harriet Bayly had not come all this way just to turn tail at the first sign of danger. She and her uncle pressed on toward the Chambersburg Pike and before long encountered another mounted party. This time the riders were Confederate soldiers, who promptly focused their attention on Robert, permitting Harriet to sidle away without challenge. She had almost made it past the group when she heard one of their number

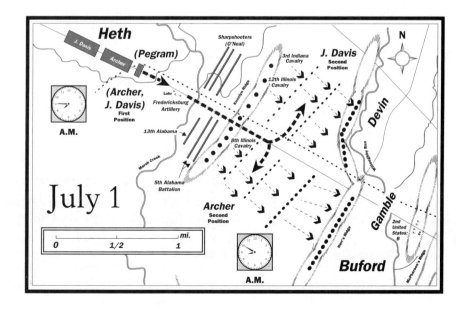

ask her uncle what he knew about Yankees ahead of them. Harriet could not help herself: "You go on and you will soon find out," she said with some spunk. "I didn't stop to count them." A bemused officer finally waved the pair off toward the north, where he said they would be out of harm's way.

On the western slope of Herr's Ridge, skirmishers from the 5th Alabama Battalion passed a small wooden cabin guarded by an aggressive dog. A few of the Alabama boys were trying to quiet the animal when its owner appeared and asked, "What are you here for?" The riflemen told the farmer that a battle was about to be fought. "By whom?" the man asked. "By General Lee and the Yankees," was the reply. "Tell Lee to hold on just a little until I get my cow in out of the pasture," the man shouted as he ran off.

The members of the 5th Alabama Battalion laughed and moved along. A follow-up wave from the 13th Alabama was less accommodating: when the dog snarled at the soldiers, one of them shot it.

Obeying John Buford's instructions to disperse his firepower, Lieutenant John Calef escorted two of his guns to a position southeast of the Herbst Woods. Once there, he could clearly hear "the enemy's skirmishers open upon our pickets, who were retiring." A noise coming from much closer snapped Calef's head toward the Chambersburg Pike, where Lieutenant John Roder, left in charge of the four guns, had caught sight of a mounted Rebel party off to the north, at extreme range. Roder commanded that one gun be fired. With that, Buford's force was fully engaged.

Signalman Aaron Jerome was enjoying his bird's-eye perspective from the cupola of the Lutheran seminary. He had sent an initial sighting report to Buford at about 7:00 A.M.; now he could impart the positive news that help was on its way. It was around 9:15 A.M. when Jerome turned his telescopic glasses toward Emmitsburg and spied what he recognized as "an army corps advancing some two miles distant." The wind threw the unit's flag broad to view, allowing Jerome to identify it as the insignia of Reynolds' First Corps. He sent word to Buford.

* * *

When they later reflected on this morning, the young members of John Reynolds' staff would agree that it seemed as if a tremendous weight had been lifted from their commander's shoulders. Some of this could be credited to Reynolds' trust in and respect for George Meade, but a greater share stemmed from his having discovered a kindred spirit in John Buford. Noted one First Corps staff officer, "Buford and Reynolds were soldiers of the same order, and each found in the other just the qualities that were most needed to perfect and complete the task entrusted to them." It was a composed and confident John Reynolds who rode at the head of Wadsworth's leading brigade (Cutler's) and at one point took part in an impromptu strategy session, studying some maps while being briefed on scouting reports. A sergeant standing nearby heard the general react to news that Rebel troops had been seen near Gettysburg; he remembered Reynolds' saying "they were probably after cattle."

Reynolds nevertheless gestured for his First Division commander to join him. "It was a matter of momentary consultation between General Reynolds and myself," Wadsworth later testified, "whether we would go into the town or take a position in front. . . . He decided that if we went into the town the enemy would shell it and destroy it, and that we had better take a position in front." Also around this time, Reynolds detailed his aide Captain Joseph G. Rosengarten to gallop ahead and warn Gettysburg's citizens to remain indoors.

Reynolds and his party had covered about half the distance between Moritz Tavern and Gettysburg when they saw a rider approaching from the town. As Reynolds' orderly Charles H. Veil remembered it, the courier brought a note from John Buford to the effect "that the enemy was advancing on the Cashtown road, [though Buford] did not state what the force was supposed to be." This was intelligence that Reynolds could not ignore. Riders were dispatched with messages for George Meade (providing a hasty summary) and Oliver Howard (telling him to hurry). Then, wrote Veil, "the Genl sent an aid[e] to Genl Wadsworth . . . to close up his div[isio]n and come on, while the Genl rode to the front." Probably included with the hurry-on message to Wadsworth was a directive to halt his command near the Codori farm and await further instructions.

The routes that Richard S. Ewell had selected for his corps' march toward Cashtown would allow him to alter course to the south if necessary. Just before Ewell passed through Middletown* with Robert Rodes' division, a courier from A. P. Hill's headquarters rode up, bringing word that the Third Corps was marching against Yankee cavalry at Gettysburg. Although he had no solid information regarding the enemy's strength, Ewell wasted little time in deciding that his place was with Hill. While riders carried new orders to Rodes and Early, one aide was sent to tell Hill and another—Ewell's stepson, Campbell Brown—dispatched to inform Robert E. Lee.

Henry Heth's decision fully to deploy his two leading brigades was having its desired effect. It was convincing proof that he meant business, and it amplified the pressure exerted by Archer's skirmishers, who began to force Buford's men off the crest of Herr's Ridge.

Union officer John Beveridge watched the determined Rebel advance. "Presently the boys of the 8th Illinois with the led horses were seen coming over the ridge west of Willoughby Run, in our immediate front," he recalled. "Then a line of smoke along and beyond the crest of the hill; then our pickets; then another line of smoke, then the (enemy) skirmishers; then twelve guns wheeled into line, unlimbered, and opened fire." Wanting at once to shield his two deployed brigades and to unnerve the opposition, Henry Heth had instructed William Pegram "to fire at the woods in his front for half an hour."

North of the Chambersburg Pike, another, similar effort undertaken by Davis' Brigade was causing Thomas Casimir Devin's dismounted cavalrymen to scramble back. A former housepainter who had found his true calling leading men in combat, Devin was tagged by some "Buford's Hard Hitter." He was known to all as a man who could be counted on to make the most of what he had. McPherson's Ridge offered fewer defensive possibilities north of the pike than it did to the south, so Devin resolved to make his stand in front of the Wills Woods, on the northern branch of Seminary Ridge, also known as Oak Ridge. As Devin's men began to concentrate, John Buford sought out his Second Brigade leader. Striving to impress upon his subordinate the strategic importance of that post, Buford confided, " 'Devin, this is the key to the army position. We must hold this if it cost every man in our command.' "

*Modern Biglerville.

*   *   *

Once Heth's skirmishers had cleared Herr's Ridge and Pegram's cannon could unlimber, the Confederates achieved an artillery superiority that they would not relinquish this day. There were five batteries under Pegram's command, totaling nineteen or twenty guns. With one exception—the Pee Dee Artillery of South Carolina—these were Virginia gunners belonging to Crenshaw's, Letcher's, Purcell's, and Marye's Fredericksburg batteries. Despite their sheer numerical advantage, the artillerists encountered stubborn resistance from the four Yankee guns posted along the Chambersburg Pike. Giving credit where it was due, one of Marye's men conceded that the enemy's shooting was "steady and well aimed, though none of our battery was struck in this position."

There was little that John Calef could do to better the odds. "Seeing the battery so greatly outnumbered," he later wrote, "I directed the firing to be made slowly and deliberately and reported to Buford what was in my front. The battle was now developing, and the demoniac 'whir-r-r' of the rifled shot, the 'ping' of the bursting shell and the wicked 'zip' of the bullet, as it hurried by, filled the air."

This first artillery exchange marked the start of the battle for many of Gettysburg's citizens. Northwest of the town square, Sarah Broadhead was in her kitchen when she heard the cannon fire. "People were running here and there, screaming that the town would be shelled," she later remembered. "No one knew where to go or what to do." Recollected Salome Myers, "Many of us sat on our doorsteps, our hearts beating with anxiety, looking at one another mutely."

A small group of spectators gathered on the southern reach of Oak Ridge, near a cut that had been made for the proposed railroad extension. Enough wood had been cleared to provide a relatively open observation area on high ground. That was not good enough, however, for Daniel Skelly, who climbed up a tree and got a view of Pegram's guns arrayed against Calef's. Evidently no one in the crowd was aware that it was not uncommon for the cannon to overshoot their targets. Suddenly a shell whizzed by, seemingly only inches over the onlookers' heads. Then "there was then a general stampede toward the town," according to Skelly.

Leander Warren, who earlier had helped water the cavalrymen's horses, had prudently left the immediate area when the assembly bugles sounded, though he had retreated only as far as the railroad cut. He would recall that there were a number of boys in the trees when that first rogue shell screamed past. The boys "did not climb down, but some fell down," he declared. A lawyer named William McClean, standing with the observers, admitted that the overshoot "had the effect of utterly removing all the curiosity I had entertained, and I beat a hasty retreat, not in the best order either, to my home, where I found my wife and children in tears over my absence, and in fear for my safety."

Not far from Gettysburg, a panicked civilian waved down John Reynolds. By Charles Veil's account, the noncombatant "stated that our Cavalry was fighting." Another staffer, Captain Stephen Weld, recorded the message slightly differently, as "The rebels are driving in our cavalry pickets." After hearing this information, Reynolds and his party set off again at "a fast gallop." They stopped at the first occupied house to get directions to the Lutheran seminary. The instructions led the riders toward the center square, and as they entered the town, Veil noted that "there was considerable excitement." Anxious not to make a wrong turn, Reynolds asked a local named Peter Culp to guide them.

Still posted in the seminary's cupola, Aaron Jerome spotted Reynolds and his party and sent word to John Buford, who rode over from McPherson's Ridge. Arriving before Reynolds, Buford improved the moment by making his own survey from the cupola. He was doing this when the left wing commander came riding up below.

" 'What's the matter, John?' " Reynolds called up to him.

" 'The devil's to pay,' " Buford responded before descending to ground level. Reynolds needed to be briefed on the tactical situation, so Buford summarized it, in words that likely echoed those he used in a message sent this morning to George Meade: "The enemy's force (A. P. Hill's) are advancing on me at this point, and driving my pickets and skirmishers very rapidly." Reynolds indicated that his men were still two, maybe three miles away. Could Buford hold until they arrived? " 'I reckon I can,' " Buford replied.

Reynolds now had to decide whether to hold here or fall back. The evidence suggests that he barely hesitated. According to Charles Veil, "The Genl ordered Genl Buford to hold the enemy in check as long as possible, to keep them from getting into town and at the same time sent orders to Genl Sickles . . . & Genl Howard to come on as fast as possi ble." A staff officer riding with Reynolds this morning recalled that "all his remarks and appearance gave me the impression that he had gone there to stay."

John Reynolds turned to Stephen Weld and directed him to find Meade's headquarters, "to say that the enemy was coming on in strong force, and that he was afraid they would get the heights on the other side of the town before he could; that he would fight them all through the town, however, and keep them back as long as possible." Recognizing the young officer's nervousness, Reynolds carefully explained where he would find the road to Taneytown, "and told me to ride with the greatest speed I could, no matter if I killed my horse."

Then John Reynolds and John Buford rode out to McPherson's Ridge to plan their next moves.

Almost from the moment Cutler's brigade halted near John Sherfy's peach orchard, it became apparent that there was trouble ahead. Hardly had the men gotten their bearings when, recalled one, "the sound of artillery firing was borne to them on the morning wind, and the whitish colored puffs of smoke dotted the faces of the distant hills." The commander of the 14th Brooklyn could plainly see the "shells burst[ing] a little to the left of the road we were marching on." In anticipation of an overland push, the call "Pioneers to the front!" rippled along the ranks, summoning the labor gangs forward in readiness to knock openings in the fences west of the road.

The 76th New York had stopped near some cherry trees ripe with fruit. Major Andrew J. Grover turned a blind eye while his men helped themselves to the sweet bounty. It helped divert their attention from the sight of a small procession of civilians leaving Gettysburg—"gray-haired old men tottering along; women carrying their children, and children leading each other, while on the faces of all were depicted the indices of the terror and despair which had taken possession of them."

Cutler's pause allowed the Iron Brigade to close some of the gap. The same cannon fire that Cutler's soldiers were seeing could be heard by Brigadier General Solomon Meredith's men as a dull, distant thumping. Veteran Loyd Harris joked to a fellow officer that the "Pennsylvanians have made a mistake and are celebrating the 4th three days ahead of time." Someone in authority, hoping to strengthen the men's determination, started a rumor that a former, very popular commander of the Army of the Potomac—Major General George B. McClellan—had been put back in charge of the forces. "Our fellows cheered like mad," recollected a 6th Wisconsin soldier.

While Calef's and Pegram's cannon continued their unequal duel, a small but bitter close-in combat flared along Willoughby Run as the dismounted Yankee horsemen stiffened their resistance, knowing that the main line was just behind them. It was likely during this phase that the greatest number of cavalry casualties occurred; among the fallen was Major Charles Lemon of the 3rd Indiana, cited by some as the first Union officer mortally wounded in this action.

Even as he was working his guns, John Calef spotted Generals Buford and Reynolds riding along McPherson's Ridge, "conferring . . . as to the lay of the land and other military points of pressing interest." An aide was sent on a direct route to the Codori farm to guide Wadsworth's men, and Reynolds and his party returned to the seminary, where the general met one of Abner Doubleday's staff officers, come in search of fresh orders. "I . . . received instructions to hurry forward the other two divisions of the corps as fast as possible," the officer later remembered. There was a hard clarity to all of Reynolds' actions now. He was determined to stop the enemy west of the town.

Meredith's Iron Brigade had closed to within a quarter mile of Cutler's unit, when James Wadsworth, at the head of the column near the Codori farm, saw a mounted man approaching across the fields to the west. Suspecting it was something important, Wadsworth rode out to meet the courier, who was in fact bringing orders from the wing commander: " 'Gen. Reynolds desires you to turn your leading brigade into the field, following along the ridge at the double [quick] toward the wood yonder,' " the messenger told him. " 'Hall's Battery will strike across to relieve Calef's guns, which are overmatched and have suffered severely. The General will meet the column and himself place the troops and guns. He wishes you, General, to hasten forward your other brigade.' "

Cutler's column, with the 76th New York leading, drew even with the farm and from there began angling off the road, moving crosslots to the northwest. As the New Yorkers passed out of the area cleared by the brigade pioneers, they were "obliged to remove fences as they led the army through fields, gardens and yards." When the third-in-line 147th New York reached the turnoff and broke into a trot, officers shouted at the men to load their rifles. "Then was heard the wild rattle of jingling ramrods, as we moved toward the sound of the cannon," recalled one soldier. Behind the 147th came the 95th New York and then the 14th Brooklyn, followed by the six guns of Hall's 2nd Maine Battery.

After granting Johnson's Division the right-of-way over Longstreet's Corps and then themselves riding ahead, Robert E. Lee and his party had worked their way slowly past the files of men ascending the western side of the Cashtown Gap. According to one of Lee's staff officers, they were near the crest when "firing was heard from the direction of Gettysburg. This caused Lee some little uneasiness . . . [, but he was] persuaded that the firing indicated a cavalry affair of minor importance." Still, an engineer officer who saw Lee at about this time thought he looked "much older and somewhat careworn." The army commander kept on at the same pace toward Cashtown, where he expected to find A. P. Hill.

At Army of the Potomac headquarters in Taneytown, Maryland, George Meade was waiting for an update. In a communication sent off at an early hour to John Sedgwick, whose Sixth Corps represented the army's extreme right, Meade had outlined the likely scenarios. He was anticipating that John Reynolds would find the Rebels already in control of Gettysburg, in which case "he is instructed to hold the enemy in check, and fall slowly back." That would trigger the actions mandated in the Pipe Creek circular. However, Meade also allowed for the possibility that Reynolds would find a battle, which would mean he would have to be reinforced. Meade's best advice for Sedgwick was to be ready "to move in such direction as may be required at a moment's notice."

John Reynolds rode south along Seminary Ridge until he could see Cutler's men approaching. He dispatched his escort to help speed their way by knocking down nearby fences. While he was waiting, the aide he had sent into town to urge the civilians to seek shelter returned and reported that his warnings had been ignored. Reynolds frowned, then nodded toward the staff officer's binoculars, which were spattered with mud from his ride. " 'Oh, they have been throwing dirt in your eyes,' " he said in a wan attempt at humor.

Reynolds had started to attract a crowd. James Wadsworth rode over, followed by Captain James A. Hall, commanding the 2nd Maine Battery. Not far away was John Buford, whose exhausted cavalrymen were by now reaching the limits of their endurance. Reynolds instructed Hall to relieve Calef's battery and then sketched out for Wadsworth where he wanted the first infantry regiments placed. Buford took it all in before spurring off to get Calef pulled back and his own troopers set to withdraw.

Henry Heth was no longer completely in the dark. Now poised to enter Gettysburg, he was convinced "that the enemy was in the vicinity of the town in some force." Although he could only guess at what might be waiting for him on McPherson's Ridge, any hope that it was merely militia was long gone. "I . . . supposed it consisted of cavalry, most probably supported by a brigade or two of infantry," Heth would later report. Interviewed after the war, he would add, "I did some lively work to get my artillery, and advance troops in position, fearing that I might be attacked in force before proper dispositions could be made."

Riders confirmed that both Archer's and Davis' Brigades were ready to go. Possibly because they had been less disrupted by Pegram's exchange with Calef's guns, or perhaps due to the eagerness of their commander, the three regiments constituting Davis' Brigade jumped off first. Since the ground along Willoughby Run north of the pike offered few defensive possibilities, Thomas Devin had pulled most of his strength back to the Wills Woods, leaving only a thin screen. Once this force had been sent packing, the Mississippi and North Carolina troops found little to impede their way beyond the "thick underbrush and briars" near the creek.

Cutler's column (1,600 strong) wriggled along the western base of Seminary Ridge, canteens clanking and arms pumping as guns were loaded. The leading three regiments reached the Chambersburg Pike just after John Calef withdrew his four cannon; together these actions attracted enemy artillery fire to the packed columns, prompting Colonel J. William Hofmann of the 56th Pennsylvania to order his men to lie down. The respite was momentary. Hall's guns were due to take over the position vacated by Calef's, so Wadsworth instructed Cutler to put three regiments on the battery's right.

These units were in the process of crossing the pike when Hall, anxious to get his guns into action, cut off the 147th New York, the third in line. This incident, plus harassing fire from Confederate skirmishers, delayed the regiment's deployment. Two other regiments trailing the 147th were headed for positions on the battery's left; when the 147th halted, this pair left-faced and proceeded west, past the McPherson farm

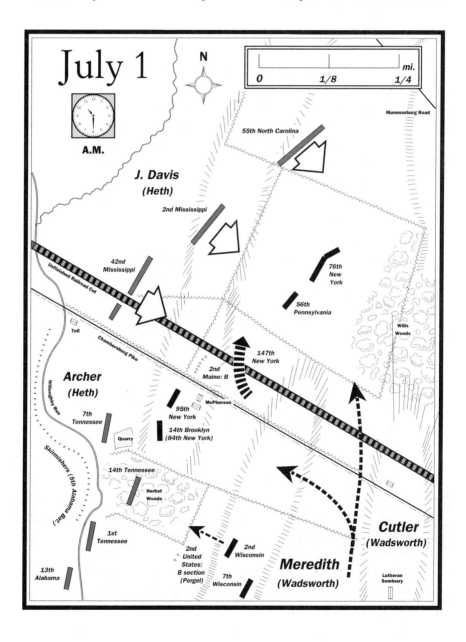

buildings and through a small orchard, to form a line of battle along the western spur of McPherson's Ridge. John Reynolds met these two units on their way up the slope so he could give instructions to the 14th Brooklyn's Colonel Edward B. Fowler.

Although Joseph Davis began the advance with his three regiments carefully aligned, it took only a few minutes for the formation to spread apart. Wary of the killing power of the Federal cannon along the pike, Davis' right regiment, the 42nd Mississippi, eased away from the road to follow what one soldier in the brigade described as "a railroad which had been graded but not ironed." The left regiment in Davis' line, the 55th North Carolina, stuck with its skirmishers, who were drawn off toward the Mummasburg Road. The experienced 2nd Mississippi, for its part, settled into a position about midway between the other two. With the least opposition confronting them, the Tarheels got ahead of their brigade mates.

Lysander Cutler's two leading regiments were still in marching formation as they crossed into the open fields north of the unfinished railroad. Cutler ordered them deployed from column into line. The 56th Pennsylvania got the word first and completed its transformation just as the 76th New York was beginning to reform. A Pennsylvanian recalled that the men "could see a line of battle in front and to the right, distant perhaps 450 yards."

"Is that the enemy?" asked William Hofmann, commanding the 56th. When Cutler answered that it was, Hofmann barked the commands, "Ready, right oblique, aim, fire!" The first controlled volley of the battle sparked from the regiment's 250 rifles, aimed at the 55th North Carolina. "Two men of the color guard of the regiment were wounded by this volley," attested a Tarheel. The Confederate formation at once returned the fire, in an exchange that constituted the 640 rifles' first combat. The bullets knocked down men and animals, among the latter Lysander Cutler's horse.

Archer's Brigade was also moving, though it had been slowed by stiff resistance from cavalry skirmishers pocketed along Willoughby Run. In the words of one of Archer's embattled voltigeurs, "Just before [we reached] Willoughby's Run, the cavalry began to get stubborn." When the heavy lines of battle crested the ridge, Pegram's cannon ceased firing as the grime-streaked gunners waited for the infantry to clear their front. The two pieces with John Calef, southeast of the Herbst Woods, were under no such restriction. The artillery officer allowed himself a brief moment to observe that the enemy's "battle-flags looked redder and bloodier in the strong July sun than I had ever seen them before"; then he gave the order to fire.

Calef's little bombardment put a hurry-up into Archer's men. An Alabama private thought his fellows "moved somewhat faster, attempting to run from under the shells, which were just falling behind us." Once the infantry had cleared out of the way, Pegram's guns reengaged, throwing shells toward McPherson's Ridge with a hiss that one of Archer's soldiers judged to be "the sweetest music I had ever heard." Assaulted from all sides by these projectiles, spiteful shots taken by the slowly retiring cavalry skirmishers, and the prickly underbrush along Willoughby Run, Archer's line finally reached the small valley of the creek. "We halted to reform, reload, catch our breath, and cool off a little," related a member of the 13th Alabama.

Although later writers would make a habit of excoriating James Archer for stumbling blindly into the Battle of Gettysburg, there was nothing foolhardy in his decision to halt his line of battle once he reached the stream. A glance behind him showed the empty slope of Herr's Ridge, devoid of supports, while the topography of the bank and hillside opposite effectively obscured what might lie ahead. Archer sensibly resolved to hold there until some backup arrived or the situation in his front became more comprehensible.

Henry Heth could not understand why Archer had stopped. He believed that his best chance to knock the enemy back on his heels was slipping away, and that now was the time to take risks. Davis was already engaging north of the pike, so the sooner Archer closed with the enemy, the better. According to Captain Jacob B. Turney of the 1st Tennessee, Heth rode up to his brigade commander and ordered him to resume his movement. Archer, recalled Turney, "suggested that his brigade was light to risk so far in advance of support." Heth reiterated his orders for Archer to advance and determine the "strength and line of battle of the enemy." Stifling any residual protest, Archer made sure his entire command was aligned before he ordered it forward.

* * *

In the open field north of the Chambersburg Pike, Davis' three regiments exchanged fire with Cutler's. The 56th Pennsylvania and 76th New York had been belatedly joined off to their left by the 147th New York, which now held the undivided attention of the 42nd Mississippi. The Southern unit was itself attracting artillery and rifle fire, causing Captain Leander Woollard to station himself behind his men with his sword drawn, his intention obvious. Perhaps unsurprisingly, Woollard later recounted that "not a man showed a willingness to go back but rather an anxiety to go ahead." The 2nd Mississippi advanced to support the 55th North Carolina. When the 76th New York reformed into battle line, it had to refuse one flank to confront the gunfire coming from the west (the 2nd Mississippi) and northwest (the 55th North Carolina).

"After we got into the musketry the men fell like sheep on all sides of me," a sergeant in the 76th New York remembered. Among the fallen was Andrew Grover, who had let his waiting men feast on cherries. Another in the regiment believed that "no body of men ever withstood a more terrible shower of lead." It was just as hellish, however, on the other side. Colonel John K. Connally of the 55th North Carolina, wanting to wheel his regiment to the right to achieve a solid enfilade on the two Yankee units in the field, took position in front of his men, holding the regimental flag. Almost immediately he was hit twice. When his second in command asked if he was badly wounded, Connally gasped, " 'Yes, but do not pay any attention to me; take the colors and keep ahead of the Mississippians.' "

Oliver Howard had his Eleventh Corps tramping toward Gettysburg on parallel routes: Barlow's division was using the well-traveled Emmitsburg Road, while the divisions led by Schurz and von Steinwehr were marching a few miles farther east, intending to hook onto the less congested Taneytown Road. Riding well ahead of Barlow's columns, Howard and his staff had reached a point that an aide recalled as being not far from Marsh Creek when "heavy firing began to be heard in the direction of Gettysburg." It was likely here that Howard encountered the first orderly sent by John Reynolds, who urged him to hurry. Since his troops were already in motion, though, Howard took no special action.

The party continued as far as the Sherfy peach orchard, where Howard met the staff officer dispatched by Reynolds from the seminary. The new message modified Howard's original orders to bring his men near the town: " 'Come quite up to Gettysburg,' " the messenger said. Glancing to his left front, the Eleventh Corps commander saw the tail end of one of Wadsworth's brigades (most likely the Iron Brigade), which he remembered as "moving along northwesterly across the open fields toward the seminary."

When Howard asked where Reynolds wanted the Eleventh Corps placed, the officer indicated Sherfy's peach orchard, possibly because it lay at the intersection of the Emmitsburg and Millerstown Roads and thus offered a ready jumping-off place from which to support Reynolds' left if necessary. Howard sent some of his aides back along the road to speed up the pace of both columns, and at the same time ordered Captain Daniel Hall forward "to find Reynolds and bring me word that I might go to him."

Oliver Otis Howard now undertook a curious odyssey. Believing that it was more important for him to familiarize himself with the area than to make personal contact with John Reynolds, the one-armed general rode with his party "from place to place, first visiting the high portion of a cross ridge to my left, near the Emmitsburg Road." Anxious to find a good view, Howard moved on "to the highest point of the Cemetery Ridge." Although he was not the first superior officer on the scene to appreciate the strategic importance of the height,* Howard does seem to have been the first to fix it in his mind as too critical to risk losing.

Turning to his adjutant general, Theodore A. Meysenburg, Howard declared, "This seems to be a *good position,* colonel."

Meysenburg replied without skipping a beat. " 'It is the *only* position, general,' " he said.

As he held station not far from Charles Pergel's two cannon, John Reynolds was still being visited by aides sent forward by his corps commanders. Daniel Hall, in a letter written afterward to Oliver Otis Howard, noted that he had found Reynolds "nearly at the extreme advance of our troops, where the skirmishers and some regiments were already hotly engaged." Reynolds, the officer continued, "told me to inform you . . . to bring your Corps forward as rapidly as possible." To an

*There is convincing evidence that both John Buford and John Reynolds also recognized the tactical significance of Cemetery Hill.

officer reporting the Third Corps' arrival at Emmitsburg, Reynolds said, " 'Tell General Sickles I think he had better come up.' "

Yet another staff rider brought word that Abner Doubleday was on the field seeking orders. "I . . . received instructions to hurry forward the other two divisions of the [First] corps as fast as possible," the division commander recollected. As Doubleday's messenger rode from the Chambersburg Pike toward the Fairfield Road, Reynolds called after him, " 'Tell Doubleday I will hold on to this road, and he must hold on to that one.' " Reynolds also directed his personal aides to ride to the various regiments that were just reaching the field and advise them "to charge as fast as they arrived."

In the advance east from Willoughby Run, the alignment of Archer's Brigade was quickly broken. The left regiment, the 7th Tennessee, was slowed by a small quarry, then stung to a halt by disciplined volleys from the 14th Brooklyn and the 95th New York, underscored by Hall's cannon. The next in Archer's line, the 14th Tennessee, kept pushing steadily through the Herbst Woods, well screened from Cutler's men. Archer's two right regiments, the 1st Tennessee and 13th Alabama,* further dispersed the formation: the 1st went to ground to avoid the canister blasts coming from Charles Pergel's guns, while the 13th eased south to take the guns from their unprotected side. James Archer, who had begun the advance dismounted, now found himself between these latter units.

Any hope the brigadier might have had of powering through the enemy with his entire command was lost to the terrain and the effective enemy defenses. The sheer force of Archer's advance, however, was having its own effect. As the 13th Alabama sidled over to threaten the two Yankee cannon, John Calef decided it was time to go. His gunners frantically limbered their hot tubes and pulled back, leaving Cutler's battle line wide open to a crushing flank attack.

The Iron Brigade was approaching at a run. The Western soldiers had followed the same course as Cutler's men but were making better time as the way was cleared. When the black-hatted columns began snaking across the seminary grounds, the 2nd Wisconsin, in the lead, was met by Lieutenant Colonel John Kress, who yelled for the men to fix bayonets and get into combat formation. "You have not a second to lose," Kress

*The 5th Alabama Battalion was fully deployed in skirmishing

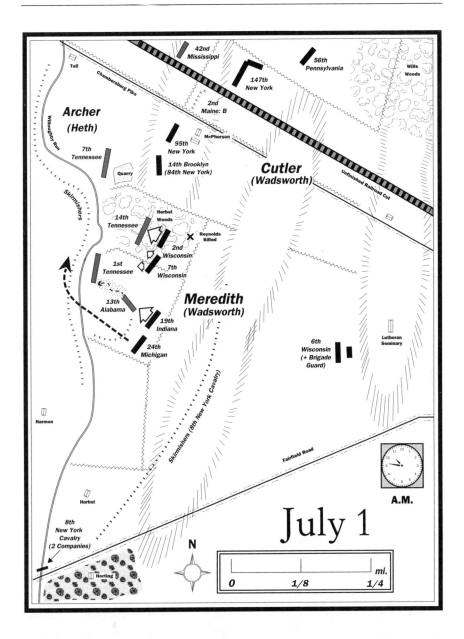

shouted. "The enemy are upon you!" To Colonel Lucius Fairchild, commanding the 2nd, Kress gave a more specific order to "form his regiment forward into line, double-quick," adding that Fairchild could expect to encounter the enemy "in his immediate front as soon as he could form."

On getting clear of the seminary buildings, each regiment in Meredith's Iron Brigade had to slow down to transform from column into line, a procedure that forced the units to enter into action one by one instead of all together. "We were immediately thrown forward into line and at a double quick advanced upon [the enemy] loading our guns as we went," wrote a 2nd Wisconsin sergeant. "We ascended a slight elevation, entered a piece of woods and when on the top received a full volley from the Rebel infantry which at the same time was advancing towards us."

Entering the Herbst Woods, the 2nd Wisconsin ran straight into the 14th Tennessee, which won the race with enough time left over to get set, aim carefully, and fire a killing volley. A Wisconsin captain in the eye of the bloody storm later claimed that this initial blast "cut down 30 per cent of the rank and file." Lucius Fairchild reported that "officers and men fell killed or wounded with terrible rapidity." An untested regiment would have been shattered, but the proud veterans in black hats kept their formation. "We held our fire until within 10 yards of Archer's line, and then gave them a volley that counted," recollected Robert Beecham. For minutes that seemed like hours, the two regiments gouged slashes from each other's ranks. Fairchild fell in one of the first exchanges, with a wounded arm that would require amputation. His next in command, Lieutenant Colonel George Stevens, was killed.

John Reynolds was sitting on his horse just east of the Herbst Woods when the 2nd Wisconsin surged past on its way into the inferno. " 'Forward men, forward, for God's sake, and drive those fellows out of the woods,' " he called out. As he watched, the woods exploded with gunfire. Knowing that this one regiment could not sustain itself without help, he turned his mount to look for the next unit coming forward, the 7th Wisconsin. Both sides were firing furiously, and the air buzzed with bullets. Reynolds' orderly Charles Veil was eyeing his commander when, as he wrote less than a year later, "a Minnie ball struck him in the back of the neck, and he fell from his horse dead. He never spoke a word, or moved a muscle after he was struck. I have seen many man killed in action but never saw a ball do its work so *instantly* as did the ball which struck General Reynolds."

The man whose determination and decisions had brought a battle to Gettysburg was dead, with the day's outcome very much in doubt.*

---

*Reynolds' body was carried first to the seminary, then to the George house on the Emmitsburg Road, near Cemetery Hill. From there it was transferred to an ambulance that conveyed it to Westminster, where it was put on a train to Baltimore and then to Lancaster, where John Reynolds was finally buried.

(10:45 A.M.–11:15 A.M.)

The dissection of Archer's Brigade proceeded with a slow precision that seemed almost stage-managed. It was a meeting in combat of two veteran units, each instinctively seeking the weak point of the other, but in this deadly game of musical chairs it would be the last standing that would win.

Archer's left regiment, the 7th Tennessee, was nullified by the difficult terrain and the steady fire from the Yankee troops (Cutler's) stationed by the McPherson farm. Next in line, the 14th Tennessee was locked in a deadly embrace, first with the 2nd Wisconsin alone and then with the 2nd joined by the 7th Wisconsin. The 1st Tennessee, which should have supported the 14th, was hung up along Willoughby Run, initially by canister blasts from Pergel's two cannon, then by volleys from the 7th Wisconsin. That left the 13th Alabama.

After giving up its quest for Calef's guns, this unit pivoted north to take advantage of the open flank of the 7th Wisconsin. In doing so, however, it exposed its own flank to the just-arriving 19th Indiana, which promptly slammed lead into it. By the time the 24th Michigan moved up, there were only Rebel skirmishers ahead, who were easily scattered, allowing this last Yankee regiment to drive down to Willoughby Run and cross it. Now Henry Heth's failure to bring his next brigades close enough to render aid was paying a bitter dividend.

The better-coordinated Iron Brigade broke up Archer's three right regiments, then herded the increasingly disorganized mass down the western slope of McPherson's Ridge and into the Willoughby Run lowlands. A private in the 13th Alabama swore that "there were 20,000 Yanks down in among us hallowing surrender." When a bewildered Jacob B. Turney of the 1st Tennessee ducked briefly under the gunpowder fog that enveloped his regiment, he saw "the feet and legs of the enemy moving to our left." James Archer dismissed Turney's observations, but matters were worse than he imagined: under a steady pressure from the 2nd and 7th Wisconsin, the 14th Tennessee was slipping back toward the north, opening a fatal gap in Archer's line.

The Westerners of the Iron Brigade paid a stiff price for their advantage. As the 19th Indiana surged into contact with the 13th Alabama, the men in Company C gasped in horror at seeing Corporal Andrew J. Wood blasted three feet into the air: a freak hit by a Rebel minié ball had exploded his cartridge box, leaving the corporal flash-burned and unconscious. When the regiment's flag bearer fell, Corporal Abram Buckles realized a martial fantasy by grasping the Stars and Stripes and leading the rush down the slope toward Willoughby Run. Buckles enthusiasm propelled him so far out in front of the regiment that the 19th's commander had to yell repeatedly, "Come back with that flag!"

Confederate command and control collapsed as Archer's three regiments (the 7th Tennessee had retreated out of harm's way) stumbled backward from the advance of the Iron Brigade, which was now closing from the north, east, and south. A brief free-for-all ensued along Willoughby Run, just at the northwest corner of the Herbst Woods. Whatever hopes James Archer might have harbored of restoring some semblance of organization vanished the instant a soldier from the 2nd Wisconsin confronted him with a demand to surrender. Archer resisted at first, but he was just too tired and too shaken by his abrupt reversal of fortune to go on fighting, and soon enough he joined the steady procession of Rebel POWs wending their way eastward.

The Union regiments were nearly as disorganized in victory as their Confederate counterparts were in defeat, but no matter. Henry Heth had no intention of counterpunching with either Pettigrew's or Brockenbrough's Brigade, both of which stood in combat formation behind Herr's Ridge, too far away to do anything more than collect the remnants of Archer's command.

Although some Federal reports would claim that as many as 1,000 of Archer's men were taken or killed in this engagement, a thoughtful modern accounting reckons that out of Archer's 1,197 men, some 373 were July 1 casualties. The Iron Brigade had about 1,400 engaged, of which perhaps 300 lay still or writhing on the Pennsylvania soil this morning. An Indiana boy later summed up the action simply: "We went down at them pretty lively and captured a good many, the rest ran away."*

*Just one Iron Brigade soldier was rewarded with a Medal of Honor for the Herbst Woods fight: Sergeant Jefferson Coates of the 7th Wisconsin was cited for displaying

* * *

Ten-year-old Gates Fahnestock was enjoying the view from the roof of his family's home, slightly east of the town square. "Could see the fighting off on Seminary Ridge," he would recollect years later. "We were not in direct line of fire, but [saw an] occasional shell go over [the] house. Having a good time." Catherine Ziegler was not having so good a time. The young girl, whose family occupied part of one of the Lutheran seminary buildings, had slipped away from her worried parents to observe the Herbst Woods fighting. It was, she would remember, an "awe-inspiring scene." The deadly hiss of minié balls passing near and a warning shout from a Union soldier perched in the cupola sent her running back home, where she found "that all the family had repaired to the cellar for safety."

Already some parts of Gettysburg were being transformed into military aid stations. Surgeon A. S. Cox of Cutler's brigade commandeered "a large hotel on the north side of the town, opposite to the railroad depot, for a hospital. At the time we took possession of the building it was filled with guests, and no one seemed to expect much of a battle; but in a very short time the wounded were brought in in great numbers and the guests and proprietors left without much order in going, leaving us in quiet and undisputed possession."

After observing the general skedaddle of civilians near the lower Oak Ridge railroad cut, Daniel Skelly walked toward the town's square, finding "the streets full of men, women and children, all under great excitement." Still anxious to see what was happening to the west, Skelly remembered a store two blocks south of the square that boasted a railed observatory on its roof. He made his way there and joined some others who had had the same idea. They were all still trying to make some sense out of the smoke and the movements near the Chambersburg Pike when Skelly looked toward the south and spotted "a general and his staff coming."

It was Oliver Howard, still embarked on his personal reconnaissance of the vicinity. He had been drawn here by the prospect of gaining the view from the courthouse belfry, but the building was secured and his staff was reluctant to destroy private property by breaking in. Daniel Skelly came tumbling down the stairs from the store roof to trumpet its suitability. "The general dismounted and with two of his aides went with me up onto the observatory," Skelly recalled.

"a courage . . . that [was] seldom equaled." Coates was wounded and blinded in the struggle.

Howard later pronounced himself "delighted with the open view. . . . Wadsworth's infantry, Buford's cavalry, and one or two batteries were nearest, and their fighting was manifest," he wrote. "Confederate prisoners were just then being sent to the rear in large groups from the Seminary Ridge down the street past my post of observation." Howard was completely engrossed in his field orientation when a mounted soldier called up to him from the street below, " 'General Reynolds is wounded, sir.' " " 'I am very sorry,' " Howard replied. " 'I hope he will be able to keep the field.' " The Eleventh Corps commander then returned to his scrutiny, only to be interrupted by another aide. " 'General Reynolds is dead,' " was this one's message, " 'and you are the senior officer on the field.' "

The 6th Wisconsin and the hundred-man brigade guard had been the last units in line as the Iron Brigade deployed along McPherson's Ridge. Lieutenant Colonel Rufus Dawes was preparing to order his men forward into position to the left of the 24th Michigan when a mounted staff officer ordered him to halt. The sweating, panting files drew back from their rush, dressed their lines, and watched their comrades diminish into the distance. Hardly had the 6th settled into its stationary line when Lieutenant Loyd Harris, directing the brigade guard, ran over to Dawes for instructions. He was told to split his command in half and place one detachment on each flank of the regiment.

In any war, the combat death of a high-ranking field officer begins an immediate process of succession that unfolds only as smoothly as circumstances allow. The killing of John Reynolds had elevated Abner Doubleday to control of the scene, which in turn caused other changes as his subordinate commanders shifted places. Orders were given, countermanded, and reaffirmed. Dawes experienced his share of this confusion when a rider brought orders from his brigade commander to move forward, only to be overruled moments later by another mounted officer who announced, " 'General Doubleday is now in command of the First Corps, and he directs that you halt your regiment.' " Dawes yelled out the command, and the files again jerked to a stop.

Abner Doubleday was adjusting to the "great responsibilities" thrust on him by virtue of Reynolds' death. The Union line south of the Chambersburg Pike was in reasonably good shape following Archer's repulse, but a crisis loomed north of the road. The unequal contest between Cutler's three regiments and those of Davis' Brigade lasted about thirty minutes before James Wadsworth decided to pull the former out. Members of the 56th Pennsylvania and the 76th New York would later tend to portray a more orderly withdrawal than was witnessed by others present. In a nonstandard formation incapable of immediate further service, the battered survivors of the two regiments tumbled back into the Wills Woods on Oak Ridge, some of them not stopping until they neared the town's western edge.

A variety of reasons were subsequently offered to explain why Cutler's third regiment north of the pike—the 147th New York—did not receive the word to retreat. Until the abrupt departure of the other two regiments, the 147th had been slowly shredding the 42nd Mississippi,

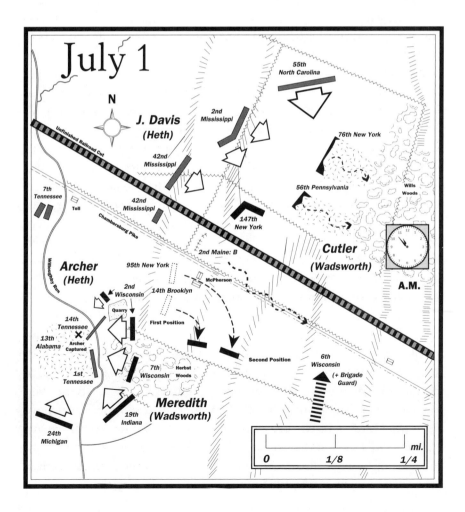

but with that flank cover gone, first the 2nd Mississippi and then the 55th North Carolina turned their hot rifles on the lone Yankee unit still in action against them. The New Yorkers refused their flank to meet the new threat, but the combined musketry was exacting a brutal toll. "It was a hot place, and no mistake," a member of the regiment recalled. Said another, "The scourge of lead that passed over was terrible, and could almost be felt—not the zip of bullets, but a rushing, forcing sound." "The fighting was at very short range and very destructive," attested the regiment's adjutant.

The dramatic change of fortune north of the pike threatened James Hall's six cannon, which had been shoveling canister at the Rebel infantry even as they dealt with the deadly projectiles sent against them by Pegram's Battalion. With no infantry protection to the north, Hall's guns were doomed. After seeing the two regiments in the field clear out, and having lost sight of the 147th New York in the gunpowder smog, Hall "ordered the battery to retire by sections, although having no order to do so," as he later conceded.

His intention was to leapfrog one pair of guns past the next until all had reached the relative safety of Seminary Ridge. The plan might have worked on a parade ground, but when the first covering section pulled back seventy-five yards, it found itself right in the sights of the 55th North Carolina, whose riflemen dropped all the horses pulling one cannon and kept the gunners so busy ducking that they could not set either tube to fire. This pair promptly resumed their retrograde movement, with the motive power for one cannon coming from its two-legged battery members. The crews assigned to the other four guns somehow hooked the cannon to their limbers and then lashed the animals into a wild gallop across the narrow, open field between the pike and the railroad bed. The last gun to leave did not make it clear and was left behind.

Even as James Hall completed his untidy withdrawal, the last stand of the 147th New York was reaching its climax. The regiment had stood against its massed enemies for perhaps ten minutes before word percolated among the ranks that it was time to go. The officer in charge gave the improvised order "In retreat, double quick, run," and those who could hear him fled for their lives. "We was ordered to retreat, which we did at a fast rate," wrote a private in the ranks. "We left [an] awful sight of dead and wounded on the field as we retreated."

The impending collapse of Cutler's line north of the pike next threatened the two regiments arrayed just south of the road by the McPherson farm, facing west. Disaster was averted when Edward Fowler, in tactical control of both units, bawled out orders that reoriented the battle lines 90 degrees, so that the pair now faced north, with the 14th Brooklyn on the left and the 95th New York on the right. Still, so convinced was James Wadsworth that the Chambersburg Pike position was compromised that he reportedly told James Hall "to lose no time, but get my battery in position near the town on the heights, to cover the retiring of the troops." Lysander Cutler was meanwhile advised "to fall back to the town and barricade the streets."

North of Gettysburg, Richard Ewell's decisiveness was beginning to pay off for the Confederate cause. Union cavalry outposts located three miles out from the town's square, near Keckler's Hill, suddenly came under fire from the advanced elements of Robert Rodes' division, now marching south instead of west, as initially ordered. Brigadier General Alfred Iverson's all–North Carolina brigade had the point, and once contact had been made, the call went out for the sharpshooters to come forward. "I went," recalled one of them, "and very soon we commenced shooting at the Yankees." In a pattern similar to that established a few hours earlier, infantry skirmishers took on cavalry vedettes, who stuck in place as long as they could. The difference now was that Rodes' men were driven by an urgency such as had never possessed Heth's troops, for they could hear the distant sounds of combat, signaling that their comrades were fighting.

The news of John Reynolds' death, and with it the realization that he was now in command of the Union forces engaged at Gettysburg, hit Oliver Howard hard. "Is it confessing weakness to say that when the responsibility of my position flashed upon me I was penetrated with an emotion never experienced before or since?" he later asked. But in almost the same instant, his trepidation turned to a hard resolve to hold the position that his fallen predecessor had staked out. Couriers began to stream out from Howard's location with a passel of messages: one to Carl Schurz putting him in charge of the Eleventh Corps, one to Doubleday telling him to hold his position, one to John Buford directing him to remain with Doubleday, and one to Daniel Sickles at Emmitsburg, "ordering him up" (with instructions for the courier to carry the message on to Meade at Taneytown). Finally, a dispatch was sent to Henry Slocum, commanding the Twelfth Corps, supposedly camped near Two Taverns. Before throwing himself into demands of the moment, the deeply religious Howard allowed himself the briefest of prayers: " 'God helping us, we will stay here till the [rest of the] army comes.' "

After riding down the eastern slope of the Cashtown Pass, Robert E. Lee and his staff reached Cashtown proper at about 11:00 A.M. According to one of the officers with Lee, "The sound [of firing coming from the direction of Gettysburg] had become heavy and continuous, and indicated a severe engagement." Lee met with A. P. Hill, who had no details about any action involving Heth's Division; he could confirm only that Heth's instructions had been "to ascertain what force was at Gettysburg, and, if he found infantry opposed to him, to report the fact immediately, without forcing an engagement." Fully cognizant of how inadequate his report was, Hill sought and received permission to ride toward the town to find out what the situation was.

Shortly after the ailing Third Corps commander departed, Lee learned that R. H. Anderson's division of that corps was nearby. He summoned the general, hoping that *someone* had news of what was happening, but Anderson could add nothing to what little Lee already knew. Nevertheless, his presence occasioned a monologue from the army commander: " 'I cannot think what has become of [General] Stuart,' " Lee said ("more to himself than me," Anderson noted). " 'In the absence of reports from him, I am in ignorance as to what we have in front of us here. It may be the whole Federal army, or it may be only a detachment. If it is the whole Federal force, we must fight a battle here.' "

Rufus Dawes and the 6th Wisconsin (plus the brigade guard) had been standing in reserve on southern Seminary Ridge for no more than a few minutes when a First Corps staff officer galloped up and shouted, " 'General Doubleday directs that you move your regiment at once to the right.' " The well-drilled soldiers evolved smoothly into a column of fours that wriggled north along the western base of the ridge. Another staff officer now reined up alongside Dawes and breathlessly summarized the disaster that had befallen Cutler's brigade north of the pike. The officer looked ahead, then turned to Dawes again and spoke with redoubled urgency: " 'Go like hell. It looks as though they are driving Cutler.' "

Nothing Dawes could see in front of him was encouraging. "The guns of Hall's battery could be seen driving to the rear," he wrote afterward, "and Cutler's men were manifestly in full retreat." A sergeant in Company C recognized the 147th New York "flying before the enemy," while the two regiments in the field north of the road were "scattering like sheep, . . . and outrunning" the Rebels. Reacting to the situation unfolding before his eyes, Dawes called out orders that brought the 6th Wisconsin into a line of battle "parallel to the turnpike and R.R. cut, and almost directly upon the flank of the enemy." With their commander leading on horseback, the double-ranked line advanced toward the Chambersburg Pike.

All at once a rifle ball hit Dawes' horse in the chest, causing it to fall heavily onto its haunches. Dawes was able to scramble clear even as his regiment passed him in grim combat formation. " 'I am all right, boys,' " he called out. By the time he made it back to its front, the line had reached a rail fence that ran along the pike's southern side. The open field

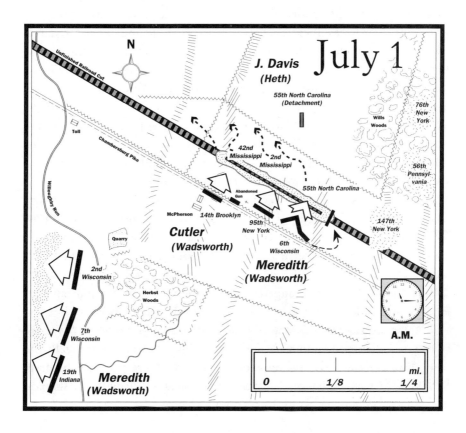

beyond the railroad cut seemed to be full of enemy soldiers. " 'Fire by file, fire by file,' " Dawes yelled.

The success enjoyed by Joe Davis' three regiments north of the Chambersburg Pike had not come without cost. Most critical was the loss of two of the three regimental commanders. The 55th North Carolina's John Connally had fallen early on in the fight with the two Yankee units in the field, while Colonel John Marshall Stone of the 2nd Mississippi had been punched down by a bullet soon after. In the absence of these strong leaders, the two regiments had fallen prey to the heady tonic of victory, letting discipline fall away as they chased after the beaten Yankees. Davis, in the midst of the delirium, was unable to rein in his men, so it was something approaching an armed mob that swept Cutler's rear guard from the field. In that context, the ordered, raking fire that tore into the mass from along the Chambersburg Pike came as a rude shock.

Wisconsin officer Loyd Harris later recalled that when "the enemy discovered us coming, they gave up the pursuit of Cutler's men and wheeled to the right to meet [us]. . . . I could not help thinking, now, for once, we will have a square 'stand up and knock down fight.' No trees, nor walls to protect either, when presto! their whole line disappeared as if swallowed up by the earth." Rushing to meet this new threat, the Mississippi and North Carolina troops had come upon the unfinished railroad cut, which offered all the security of a good trench. Few hesitated to avail themselves of its cover; the senior officer in the Confederate mass, Major John A. Blair of the 2nd Mississippi, would later write that "all the men were jumbled together without regard to regiment or company." Jumbled they might be, but they still could shoot, and soon, recollected a Wisconsin soldier, "they opened a tremendous fire on us."

The soldiers of the 6th Wisconsin either scaled or wiggled through the fence lining the southern side of the pike, then knocked down most of the one that paralleled it across the road. The Union line of battle pushed slowly into the open ground between the pike and railroad bed, advancing in bloody half steps, firing the whole time. Rufus Dawes glanced to his left, saw a ragged line of battle taking shape, and ran over to its commander, Major Edward Pye of the 95th New York.

" 'Let's go for them, Major!' " Dawes yelled. Pye nodded: " 'We are with you,' " he shouted in reply, signaling to his men to make ready. By the time Dawes returned to his regiment, several in the ranks were chanting, " 'Charge! Charge! Charge!' " " 'Forward!' " Dawes called out. " 'Align on the Colors!' " The battle line surged forward, straight into the sheets of gunfire that rippled from the improvised trench. "Men were being shot by twenties and thirties and breaking ranks by falling or running," remembered a Wisconsin boy. All, wrote another, "seemed to be trying to see how quick they could get to the railroad cut."

Wounded Badgers propped themselves up to take another shot or two at the Rebel line, even as enemy bullets continued to knock down their comrades. Lieutenant Orrin Chapman, who had so enjoyed Loyd Harris' harmonica performance of "Home, Sweet Home," was writhing in mortal agony, and Harris himself was bleeding from a neck wound. The first Wisconsin color-bearer was shot, then the second, then the third. Dawes later recalled that the once-neat battle line became a "V-shaped crowd of men, with the colors at the point, moving hurriedly and firmly forward, while the whole field behind [was] streaming with men plunging in agony to the rear or sinking in death upon the ground." Some Rebel officer in the railroad cut got things organized so the men delivered one solid volley that exploded in the faces of the yelling Wisconsin soldiers when they were no more than thirty-five feet away. "The volley had been so fatal that it seemed half our men had fallen," wrote one survivor.

Then suddenly the Wisconsin troops, who were soon joined on their left by the 95th New York, were at the cut's edge. Soldiers clubbed, stabbed, and shot one another at close range. "The men [were] black and grimy with powder and heat," remembered one of them. "They seemed all unconscious to the terrible situation, they were mad and fought with a desperation seldom witnessed." More and more Yankee voices repeated the chant: "Throw down your muskets!" An alert Wisconsin officer directed a dozen or so men to close off the eastern end of the cut and begin shooting into the mob. There were more Confederates than Wisconsin men in the melee, but the Union troops had the initiative.

" 'Where is the colonel of this regiment?' " Rufus Dawes shouted. John Blair identified himself, then asked Dawes who *he* was. " 'I command this regiment,' " Dawes responded. " 'Surrender or I will fire.' " Blair hesitated a moment and then handed over his sword, prompting the men around him to fling down their muskets. Even as this was happening, not twenty-five feet away soldiers were locked in a vicious melee for the flag of the 2nd Mississippi. The Confederate color guard were all shot down, and the standard's staff was hit two or three times. Several Wisconsin soldiers lost their lives grabbing for the flag before Corporal Francis A. Waller of Company I, who at five foot eight and a half was considered a big man in the regiment, finally enveloped the color-bearer and the colors.*

The 95th New York, followed by the 14th Brooklyn, joined the 6th Wisconsin at the railroad cut, but not before a large number of Mississippi and North Carolina soldiers fled out its western end. The Confederate effort that might have compensated for Archer's disaster had itself been rebuffed, leaving the Federals in possession of McPherson's Ridge. When Joe Davis reassembled his brigade, he would have 600 fewer men than had marched with him this morning. Cutler, for his part, had lost perhaps 660 in this action, with the 6th Wisconsin and its brigade guard adding another 190 or so to the casualty list.

"This success," Abner Doubleday later wrote, ". . . enabled us to regain the gun which Hall had been obliged to abandon. The enemy having vanished from our immediate front, I withdrew the Iron Brigade from its advanced position beyond the creek, reformed the line on the ridge where General Reynolds had originally placed it, and awaited a fresh attack, or orders from General Meade."

*Corporal Waller would later receive a Medal of Honor for his "conspicuous bravery on the battlefield."

Stephen Weld, carrying the message entrusted to him by John Reynolds, located George Meade's Taneytown headquarters at 11:20 A.M. According to Weld, Meade "seemed quite anxious about the matter." When he conveyed Reynolds' uncertainty about holding the "heights on the other side of the town," Meade exclaimed, " 'Good God! if the enemy get Gettysburg we are lost!' " In almost the next breath, the army commander "roundly damned the Chief of Staff . . . for his slowness in getting out orders." Weld finished his report by relaying Reynolds' determination to fight street by street if necessary. This seemed to settle Meade, who remarked, " 'Good! This is just like Reynolds.' " He immediately sent orderlies riding with messages for all his other corps commanders, urging them—especially Hancock—to hurry along. He had no message, however, for Weld to take back to Reynolds—or if he did, the officer did not remember it.

Carl Schurz's Eleventh Corps division was on the Taneytown Road, just crossing the Pennsylvania state line, when its bespectacled commander received Oliver Howard's order "to hurry my command forward as quickly as possible." Suspecting this meant trouble ahead, Schurz gave the necessary instructions, then rode on with his staff to investigate. As he and his party drew closer to Gettysburg, they encountered clots of civilians, most beset by fear and uncertainty. One woman gestured for the uniformed men to halt, crying loudly, " 'Hard times at Gettysburg! They are shooting and killing! What will become of us!' "

Schurz reached Cemetery Hill at about 11:30 A.M. There he found Oliver Howard and learned that since his superior had assumed overall command of the field, he himself (as senior officer) was now in charge of the Eleventh Corps. The fighting along McPherson's Ridge was over for the moment, with at least one report from that sector (Schurz recalled it as coming from James Wadsworth) indicating that the enemy was threatening the right flank of the Union line. Working with the information in hand, Howard and Schurz settled on a plan. As Schurz remembered it, he was to take the "First and Third Divisions of the Eleventh Corps through the town and . . . place them on the right of the First Corps, while he [Howard] would hold back the Second Division . . . and the reserve artillery on Cemetery Hill and the eminence east of it, as a reserve." A staff officer present recollected Howard's saying quite clearly, " 'We must hold this hill.' "

Robert Rodes had a decision to make. The handsome and likable Confederate officer, commanding one of the two divisions that Ewell had moving toward Gettysburg from the north, reached Keckler's Hill (by now cleared of Yankee cavalry vedettes) at about 11:30 A.M. This was Rodes' first action as a division commander, and fate had placed him at a critical juncture. From Keckler's Hill the road stretched down a gentle slope to Gettysburg, but a ridge line branched off toward the southwest, in the direction of the gunfire he and his men had been hearing for more than half an hour. Rodes' dilemma was this: should he remain on the road and march into Gettysburg, or angle off toward the sound of the guns?

As Rodes later explained it, "By keeping along the wooded ridge . . . I could strike the force of the enemy with which General Hill's troops were engaged upon the flank, and [I reasoned] that, besides moving under cover, whenever we struck the enemy we could engage him with the advantage in ground." Richard Ewell, who was riding with him, concurred, so as Rodes' units reached Keckler's Hill, they peeled off to their right, making their way warily along the wooded ridge.

Abner Doubleday's resolution to maintain the position selected by John Reynolds seemed to be validated by events. The enemy showed no inclination to renew the infantry fight (though the Rebel artillery never let up), and shortly after 11:30 A.M., the rest of the First Corps began to reach McPherson's Ridge.

Charles Wainwright arrived at the head of the corps' artillery. Wainwright was a difficult man to please, and he had little confidence in Doubleday's leadership skills. With John Reynolds dead, Wainwright felt that his successor "would be a weak reed to lean upon; that it would not do for me to wait for orders from him, but that I must judge and act for

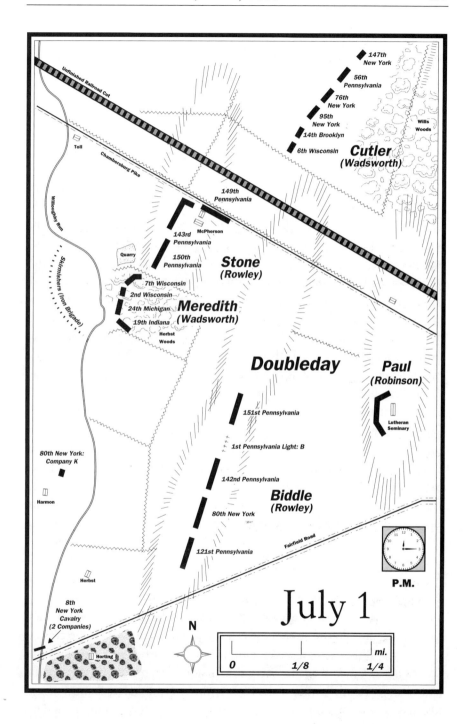

Unfinished Railroad Cut

147th
New York

56th
Pennsylvania

76th
New York

95th
New York

14th Brooklyn

6th Wisconsin

Cutler
(Wadsworth)

Wills
Woods

Toll

Chambersburg Pike

149th
Pennsylvania

McPherson

143rd
Pennsylvania

Willoughby Run

Quarry

150th
Pennsylvania

Stone
(Rowley)

Skirmishers (Iron Brigade)

7th Wisconsin

2nd Wisconsin

24th Michigan

19th Indiana

Meredith
(Wadsworth)

Herbst
Woods

Doubleday

Paul
(Robinson)

151st Pennsylvania

Lutheran
Seminary

1st Pennsylvania Light: B

80th New York:
Company K

142nd Pennsylvania

Biddle
(Rowley)

80th New York

Harmon

121st Pennsylvania

Fairfield Road

Herbst

P.M.

8th
New York
Cavalry
(2 Companies)

July 1

Horting

N

0   1/8   1/4   mi.

myself." After making a hurried mounted survey of the area, Wainwright concluded that Seminary Ridge offered the best available positions for his artillery. He also decided that the Rebel cannon so effectively dominated McPherson's Ridge that no Union battery posted near the Chambersburg Pike could hope to stand for very long. Despite repeated pleas from infantry officers along the rise, Wainwright would send guns forward only under peremptory orders to do so.

The two brigades constituting Brigadier General Thomas A. Rowley's Third Division were next on the scene. They had spent the previous night a few miles west of Moritz Tavern, then marched north together until they were across Marsh Creek. Colonel Roy Stone's all-Pennsylvania Second Brigade reached the battlefield first, having turned east after the creek crossing to connect with the well-trod Emmitsburg Road. Like Wadsworth's men before them, Stone's troops moved crosslots at the Codori farm to reach McPherson's Ridge through the seminary's grounds. In his regrouping of units following this morning's fight, Doubleday had clustered Cutler's regiments north of the pike, in the Wills Woods, leaving open the space formerly occupied by the 14th Brooklyn and the 95th New York. Stone's three regiments now took up that position, which put them directly under the artillery fire coming from Herr's Ridge.

The First Brigade of Rowley's division, Colonel Chapman Biddle's New York and Pennsylvania outfit, came next, but from a completely unexpected direction. After splitting off from Stone's command at Marsh Creek, Biddle had led his men north on a series of country lanes that had eventually landed them at the Fairfield Road, near Black Horse Tavern. Although he did not realize it at the time, his approach had brought him to the right and rear of the Confederate line along Herr's Ridge. While his scouts reported the presence of Rebel artillery ahead, Biddle himself had no clear picture of where the enemy strength lay, so he gratefully followed the guides sent out by John Buford to lead him to the battlefield. On his arrival from the west, Biddle was instructed to cover the open southern portion of McPherson's Ridge, which he accomplished by first forming his lines in the swale between the seminary and the ridge crest.

Even as Biddle's men were being positioned, Brigadier General John C. Robinson's two-brigade Second Division began coming up via the Emmitsburg Road. Under orders from Abner Doubleday, Robinson was "directed . . . to station his division in reserve at the seminary, and to throw up some slight intrenchments, to aid me in holding that point in case I should be driven back."

Doubleday's recollection was that the realignment of the First Corps and the placement of the reinforcements were undertaken entirely on his initiative. The aide whom Oliver Otis Howard remembered sending to let Doubleday know that he was assuming overall command had apparently never delivered that message. "I was not aware, at this time, that Howard was on the ground, for he had given me no indication of his presence," Doubleday declared; in testimony given not long after the battle, he avowed that "General Howard arrived at Gettysburg about the same time with the 11th corps." What was more, he even questioned Howard's right to take up the mantle of left wing commander, a not-so-subtle dig that further diluted any unity of purpose that might have existed between the two of them.

Henry Heth summarized the effects of the disastrous morning probes undertaken by Archer's and Davis' Brigades with the comment that the "enemy had now been felt, and found to be in heavy force in and around Gettysburg." Even as Abner Doubleday reset his defense, Heth, too, reorganized. He kept Davis' Brigade north of the pike "that it might collect its stragglers," while south of the road, along Herr's Ridge, he positioned Brockenbrough's Virginians with their left on it, he placed Pettigrew's large North Carolina brigade next running south, and deployed what remained cohesive of Archer's Brigade (now led by Colonel Birkett D. Fry) as a screen to protect Pettigrew's right.

Shortly after noon, Pender's Division (6,500 strong) came in behind Heth's men. These soldiers could have been on hand much sooner had anyone thought to ask them to hurry. But as his infantry deployed in the area where Heth's skirmishers had earlier scrapped with Buford's vedettes, Pender did manage to send forward Major David McIntosh's artillery battalion, which added some significant weight to the Confederate advantage. Together Pegram's and McIntosh's batteries totaled some thirty-three guns, a virtual guarantee that no Yankee cannon could survive long on most of McPherson's Ridge.

Lost to history is any account of what transpired when A. P. Hill was briefed by Heth. The after-action reports submitted by both men skip directly from the repulse of Archer and Davis to the renewal of the offensive several hours later. The confused summary of events provided in Hill's report suggests that his mental cloud had not lifted by the time he reached the scene. It seems quite possible that Heth may have carried the discussion by claiming that his reconnaissance mission, though roughly handled, had been successfully completed. As Heth later wrote, "This was the first intimation that General Lee had that the enemy had moved from the point he supposed him to occupy, possibly thirty miles distant." Equally important was that Heth had completely disengaged. Robert E. Lee was not irrevocably committed to a serious fight this day at Gettysburg.

The midday period was anything but peaceful across McPherson's and Herr's Ridges. The infantries may have fought each other to the point of exhaustion, but the artilleries were evidencing no such fatigue. With the advent of McIntosh's guns, the Confederates had in place a powerful array of field ordnance that was making life hell for the bluecoats across the way.

The high water of Davis' Brigade had driven Hall's six guns away from their post alongside the pike on the western spur of McPherson's Ridge. If Abner Doubleday felt some relief with the arrival of the First Corps artillery, he had not reckoned with Charles Wainwright, who obstinately refused to send any guns up to Hall's old position. Only on the southern end of Doubleday's line, where Biddle's brigade stood, was one battery able to operate. Himself frustrated with Wainwright's refusal to cooperate, James Wadsworth even tried to shanghai John Calef's battered unit for the job; when Calef initially refused, Wadsworth threated to arrest him.

Whether in obeisance to this show of authority or out of his own sense of duty, Calef finally ordered his guns to return to their morning position. This time, however, it was impossible to hold. Rebel skirmishers had the range, and the diligent Confederate gunners soon caught the Federals in a vicious crossfire. Calef's men fell back to a position near the point Pergel held and remained there for the moment.

Wadsworth meanwhile had pulled rank in front of Doubleday, leaving Wainwright little choice but to move more guns into the shooting gallery. He picked the 1st New York Light Artillery, Battery L, under Captain Gilbert H. Reynolds, and personally accompanied the guns into position. It was very nearly a fatal gesture: Reynolds was soon struck on his left side and in the face by shell fragments, and another shot nearly claimed Wainwright's left leg. Lieutenant George Breck took over the battery and pulled it back five hundred yards. The First Corps infantry spread across

McPherson's Ridge were forced to find whatever cover they could to shield themselves from the shelling that continued without pause.

The steady bass thumping of the Confederate artillery lent credence to civilian fears that the town of Gettysburg was itself the target. "How shall I describe my feelings as the booming of cannon waked that mournful sound! 'Tis impossible, utterly impossible!" declared one resident. Near the central square, Charles J. Tyson, a businessman and photographer, heard a Federal officer loudly "warning all women, children and non-combatants to leave the town, as General Lee intended to shell it." Charles McCurdy's mother was advised to evacuate her family from their home on the east-west-running Chambersburg Pike and "to go into the side streets where they would be out of line of the firing, and less subject to danger." Mrs. McCurdy packed a few necessities, locked the house, and then hustled the rest of her clan four blocks to the more protected house of Charles' grandmother.

At least one Gettysburg civilian was resolutely heading *into* the fray, toward McPherson's Ridge. John Burns, soon to be enshrined in folk, official, and commercial legend, was nearly seventy years old. A former Gettysburg constable and self-proclaimed veteran of the War of 1812, he had been a background figure throughout the troubled days of June. By all indications he was a stubborn patriot, a man not unused to combat, and, on the morning of July 1, one mad enough to fight.

He was spotted on his way to McPherson's by several staff officers who would happily expand their memories of the incident in later years. Burns presented himself to one of the regimental commanders of Stone's brigade, located in the McPherson farm sector, and requested permission to fight with the men. The colonel commanding suggested that he would be better off under the cover of the nearby Herbst Woods, in the company of the Iron Brigade. The old man obligingly trundled over there and soon hooked up with the 7th Wisconsin. Its commander tried to disuade the senior volunteer, but once he saw how determined Burns was, he reluctantly allowed him to stick around. A cleric with the regiment recalled that Burns wore "a bell-crowned hat, a swallow tail coat with rolling collar and brass buttons and a buff vest." After standing and talking with the boys in the main position for a while, John Burns went out to the Iron Brigade skirmish line, where he was soon potting away at any Rebel target that presented itself.

*   *   *

While Henry Heth is usually credited with initiating the Battle of Gettysburg, the distinction more properly belongs to Richard S. Ewell. Heth's
assignment had been to probe aggressively into Gettysburg, determine
the enemy's strength, and back out if a significantly larger action loomed.
He had accomplished his mission and then pulled back, so that by midday
on July 1 he was only in skirmishing contact with the enemy, well
shielded by the corps' artillery and under no practical imperative to
restart serious fighting. Had Heth held his position until nightfall to
cover the near passage of Ewell's two divisions, and then fallen back to a
more fully consolidated Confederate army near Cashtown, his actions
early that first day might well have been totted up as a costly reconnaissance rather than the prelude to a great battle.

The decision of whether or not to escalate the combat at Gettysburg
this day was made not by Henry Heth or even by Robert E. Lee. Instead,
it rested on the shoulders of Richard Ewell, who around midday was with
Robert Rodes under the cover of the woods on Oak Hill, looking southward across the fields where Joseph Davis had fumbled. His gaze carried
past the bloody railroad cut to the Chambersburg Pike, which marked
what his eyes told him was the exposed right flank of the Union line. As
Ewell was making this survey, Rodes was completing the deployment of
his five brigades.

Rodes' resolve to follow Oak Hill's ridge had placed him in a somewhat awkward position. Prudence and the need to cover the impending
arrival of Jubal Early's division had forced him to spread across a wide
front. His advance on the ridge was led by Iverson's Brigade. To prevent
the enemy from turning him to the east via either the Carlisle or the Heidlersburg Road, Brigadier General George Doles' all-Georgia brigade
had been assigned to cover the plain north of Gettysburg, screened by a
skirmish line of Alabama troops under Major Eugene Blackford. Doles'
eastward orientation disconnected him from Rodes' main body on Oak
Hill, the closest link being Colonel Edward A. O'Neal's Alabama brigade.

On examining the situation from Oak Hill, Rodes had realized that
the only route to the enemy flank that was so enticingly visible near the
McPherson farm was directly across the fields in his front. He determined
that he would have to assemble his attack force in the woods behind a
western spur of Oak Ridge. Iverson's Brigade would become his first
wave, backed up by other all–North Carolina brigades commanded by
Brigadier Generals Junius Daniel and Stephen Dodson Ramseur.

Even as the deployment was proceeding, Richard Ewell made the decision to push out Lieutenant Colonel Thomas H. Carter's artillery battalion. Whatever tactical advantage of surprise Rodes' movement might have achieved was squandered the instant Carter's guns began shelling Doubleday's McPherson Ridge line. With Rodes' infantry not yet ready to advance, and Heth's line under no pressure, Ewell's move succeeded only in spoiling the opportunity.

By this time Ewell had also decided to disregard Lee's prime directive to avoid a general battle. Perhaps, like Rodes, he thought "that Hill had blundered, and . . . feared [that blunder] w[oul]d bring on a general engagement before anybody was up." Certainly he believed that Heth was directly threatened and Rodes too deeply committed to withdraw now. "It was too late to avoid an engagement without abandoning the position already taken up, and I determined to push the attack vigorously," Ewell later reported.

The first Eleventh Corps regiments began to arrive shortly after noon. They were anything but martial in appearance: the soldiers of the 45th New York, who had been double-quicking for several miles, reached Cemetery Hill "panting and out of breath," their historian remembered. Following the rough plan hashed out by Howard and Schurz, the men continued marching into town. Behind them came Captain Hubert Dilger's battery (which paused at Cemetery Hill), followed by portions of Colonel George von Amsberg's First Brigade (Third Division). These regiments, too, recorded one member, were "much fatigued with a rapid march on a mid-summer day." Their division commander, Brigadier General Alexander Schimmelfennig (elevated to replace Carl Schurz, the new corps commander), was told by Schurz to use his men to extend the right flank of the First Corps as far as Oak Hill.

The 45th New York moved through Gettysburg via Washington Street, which, on the northern side of town, connected with the Mummasburg Road. As his New Yorkers poked out from the town's built-up area, von Amsberg spread out a four-company skirmish line as far east as it would reach. The open formation pushed toward Oak Hill, each man moving with cover as it suited him. The widely spaced line had advanced only a short distance, however, when it was subjected to a slow shelling from Confederate cannon (Captain R. C. M. Page's Morris Artillery) located near the Moses McLean farm, at the eastern base of the hill. Since skirmish lines were hardly bothered by long-range shelling, the New York soldiers continued their dodging, ducking advance until they were stopped by direct rifle fire from Alabama sharpshooters belonging to O'Neal's Brigade. Oliver Otis Howard's plan to anchor a new line on Oak Hill had never had a chance of succeeding.

The decision to maintain the First Corps' line on McPherson's Ridge after Ewell's arrival was Abner Doubleday's. While he would later offer a variety of military reasons for not withdrawing, his essential motivation was emotional. In his after-action report, he explained that "to fall back without orders from the commanding general might have inflicted lasting disgrace upon the corps, and as General Reynolds, who was high in the confidence of General Meade, had formed his lines to resist the entrance of the enemy into Gettysburg, I naturally supposed that it was the intention to defend the place."

Although he had been amply warned of Ewell's approach by Buford's scouts, Doubleday had assumed that Howard would deal with it, so he was surprised when the threat actually materialized. In a memoir written many years after the war, he noted that the "first indication I had that Ewell had arrived, and was taking part in the battle, came from a battery posted on an eminence called Oak Hill, almost directly in the prolongation of my line, and about a mile north of Colonel Stone's position."

This rude awakening prodded Doubleday into an immediate series of countermoves. Cutler's brigade, which was closest to Carter's guns and at that point deployed in a line of battle facing west, refused its right flank to face north before slowly backpedaling into the cover provided by the Wills Woods. Doubleday then turned to his reserve division at the seminary, ordering John C. Robinson to send a brigade to the threatened flank. Robinson had one brigade already set in place and another in the process of arriving, so he kept the one that was in motion moving along to the north. This was Brigadier General Henry Baxter's brigade of Massachusetts, New York, and Pennsylvania regiments. Baxter dispatched the 11th Pennsylvania and the 97th New York to screen ahead while he followed with the other four. As the Federal skirmishers approached the Mummasburg Road, they encountered several Union cavalrymen, who shouted, " 'You stand alone between the Rebel army and your homes. Fight like hell!' "

* * *

It was about 1:00 P.M. when the First Corps staff officer bringing the news of John Reynolds' death reached Taneytown. George Meade later testified:

> The moment I received this information I directed Major General [Winfield S.] Hancock, who was with me at the time, to proceed without delay to the scene of the contest, and, . . . I directed him to make an examination of the ground in the neighborhood of Gettysburg and to report to me, without loss of time, the facilities and advantages or disadvantages of that ground for receiving battle. I furthermore instructed him that in case, upon his arrival at Gettysburg—a place which I had never seen in my life . . . —he should find the position unsuitable and the advantages on the side of the enemy, he should examine the ground critically as he went out there and report to me the nearest position in the immediate neighborhood of Gettysburg where a concentration of the army would be more advantageous than at Gettysburg.

The written orders that Meade issued to Hancock (time-dated 1:10 P.M.) directed him temporarily to turn over command of the Second Corps to Brigadier General John Gibbon and then to proceed to Gettysburg, where, "in case of the truth of General Reynolds's death, you assume command of the corps there assembled." Hancock had some qualms about taking over, given that at least one other senior officer (Howard) was already on the scene, but Meade assured him that he had the necessary authority to put him in charge.

Meade's decision to stay behind in Taneytown would later be questioned. A newspaperman sympathetic to his case offered this rationale: "It was impossible for Meade to go to the battlefield at once. Only two of his infantry corps were at that place. The great bulk of his army . . . [was] many miles from Gettysburg; and it was therefore necessary for the army headquarters to remain near the center, from which point all the parts of the army could be readily communicated with." Besides, in selecting Hancock to precede him to Gettysburg, Meade had anointed a proxy who, as he later explained, "understood and could carry out my views."

Hancock and his staff left Taneytown at about 1:30 P.M. In order to familiarize himself with the Gettysburg area, Hancock rode part of the way in an ambulance so that he could study maps of the region.

* * *

German by birth and trained at the Karlsruhe Military Academy in
Baden, Hubert Dilger had been pursuing an honorable military career in
the Grand Duke of Baden's horse artillery when an invitation from a distant uncle lured him to America to put into practice the war-making he
had previously only rehearsed. Dilger had proven to be an apt and talented soldier. Handsome, well mustached, and fluent in four languages,
the born artillerist had soon been made captain of Battery I, 1st Ohio
Light Artillery. The unit he commanded in the advance of the Eleventh
Corps this day was arguably the best-trained one of its kind, and Dilger,
in the words of an observer, "one of the bravest, coolest and most clear-
headed of battery commanders developed in the Civil War."

By the time Dilger's artillery reached Cemetery Hill, the skirmish
action along the Mummasburg Road north of town had cranked up several notches. The four companies from the 45th New York that had been
committed to the fight were making little headway against the Alabama
soldiers screening Rodes on Oak Hill, who were themselves backed by
the four guns of Page's Virginia Battery posted near the McLean farm. As
long as the Rebel pieces could fire with impunity across the open fields
between Oak Hill and Rock Creek, it would be both difficult and costly
to deploy the Eleventh Corps.

A two-gun section of Dilger's battery, commanded by Lieutenant
Clark Scripture, were the first Union tubes to challenge Page. The Confederates knew their business, however, and quickly began making things
uncomfortable for Scripture. As soon as he was apprised of his subordinate trouble, Dilger brought the rest of his battery forward from Cemetery Hill. On his way he passed the 157th New York, one of whose members would never forget the sight of the artillery unit, "its cannoniers
bouncing high in their seats as the wheels revolve[d] rapidly over obstructions in the roadway."

Once in position east of the Mummasburg Road, Hubert Dilger
promptly demonstrated what a true professional could accomplish.
According to one admiring witness,

> The first shot from the Ohio Battery flew over the Confederate Bat-
> tery. At this the rebels yelled in derision. Capt. Dilger now sighted the
> gun himself and fired it. The shot dismounted a rebel gun and killed
> the horses. Capt. Dilger tried it a second time, sighting and firing the

gun. No effect being visible with the naked eye, Col. [Philip] Brown [commanding the 157th New York], . . . asked, "what effect Capt. Dilger?" Capt. Dilger, after looking through the glass, replied, "I have spiked a gun for them plugging it at the muzzle."*

There was something almost intoxicating about the view of the battlefield from Oak Hill. It revealed at once the position of the Union First Corps, the cautious deployment under way by the Eleventh, and the presence of A. P. Hill's divisions along Herr's Ridge. "It seemed like some grand panorama with the sounds of conflict added," marveled one Rebel soldier. Rodes himself would later report that "the whole of that portion of the force opposing General Hill's troops could be seen." His analysis of the situation was based on these observations, which, tragically for many of his North Carolina troops, had one failing. From his position Rodes could not see well along the eastern base of Oak Ridge, nor could he adequately assess how many Federal troops had traversed the ridge as far as the Mummasburg Road. His guess was, not many.

His attack plan had the benefit of simplicity. He would advance south from Oak Hill on a two-brigade front: O'Neal's Alabama unit along the eastern slope of the hill, and Iverson's North Carolinians moving in tandem south from the hill crown. Part of O'Neal's job was to clear away the Yankee skirmishers on the eastern ridge slope near the Mummasburg Road, while Iverson was to target the more substantial enemy line in the Wills Woods. Iverson, with the more difficult assignment, was backstopped by Junius Daniel's North Carolina brigade. Rodes' methodical preparations were upset, however, by the appearance along the Mummasburg Road of the two regiments screening the Union advance of Baxter's brigade from Robinson's division, which persuaded Rodes "that the enemy was rash enough to come out from the woods to attack me." He at once ordered Iverson and O'Neal to begin the assault.

Rodes' hopes of a united assault were dashed almost immediately. O'Neal wasn't going anywhere; his first effort exposed him to long-range musketry from the 45th New York soldiers, closer-range musketry from

*For the record, a Union soldier captured later this day, in a letter home on July 3, wrote that he had seen "a rebel cannon which had been struck in its mouth by one of our shots and flattened out." What he saw may actually have been an imperfect shell jammed in the barrel during firing, an anomaly noted several times in the course of this battle.

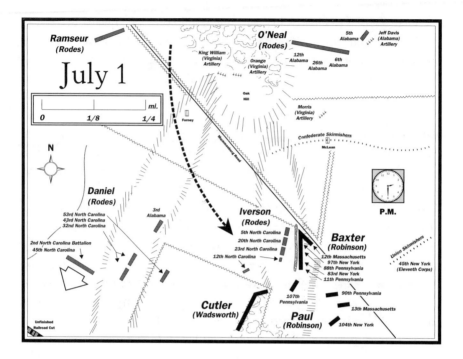

First Corps units along the Mummasburg Road, and Hubert Dilger's murderous artillery.* The few of his men who made it as far as the McLean farm were swarmed by the alert New Yorkers, who took many prisoners. So quickly was O'Neal's first attack squashed, in fact, that it has been questioned whether he really made any effort at all at this time. Only the 3rd Alabama, stationed on O'Neal's right, joined the advance, as its position in the woods shielded it from much of the disruptive fire.

Iverson's four regiments were ready to go; the one thing missing was the brigade commander. Alfred Iverson had some queries about the battle plan, and he had also learned at the last moment that he was expected to coordinate the movements of Daniel's Brigade. Possibly to clarify these matters, he left his men for the rear, where he was given the false intelligence that O'Neal's Brigade was in action. Iverson sent orders for his own brigade to advance, then went to find Junius Daniel to confirm that he could rely on his support.

As Iverson's line of battle (without Iverson) moved out to the open

*Major Alfred J. Sellers of the 90th Pennsylvania would be awarded a Medal of Honor in recognition of his efforts directing the brigade's fire against O'Neal.

fields south of the Mummasburg Road, the men rapidly realized that O'Neal's troops were nowhere in sight to their left. The North Carolina regiments veered eastward in a vain attempt to locate O'Neal's right. In doing so, they separated themselves from Daniel's supporting regiments and came more directly against the Oak Ridge crest line, with no support on either flank.

Bad luck (on the Confederate side) and solid initiative (on the Union) combined to spell disaster for Iverson's men. What Rodes had assumed to be only a small group of Federals on Oak Ridge near the Mummasburg Road was actually closer to a full brigade in size. Most of Baxter's Second Brigade was there, soon to be joined by portions of Brigadier General Gabriel R. Paul's First Brigade (both from the Second Division of the First Corps), sent along by Abner Doubleday from their reserve position near the Lutheran seminary. A providential stone wall that ran along the ridge perpendicular to the road furnished sufficient cover that five regiments were able to ease into firing positions unseen by most of Iverson's men. In a final error of judgment that would soon cost many lives, Iverson had not deployed any skirmishers, so his men marched in an orderly fashion across an open field, guided only by what little they could see.

The Federals showed deadly patience. The steady Tarheels reached a point between eighty and a hundred yards from the concealed Yankee line before the Union officers yelled for their men to "up and fire." A survivor from the 23rd North Carolina later recollected that "when we were in point blank range the dense line of the enemy rose from its protected lair and poured into us a withering fire." Another member of the 23rd, who was marching in the second rank at that instant, would later tell his brother that he had been "sprayed by the brains of the first rank." The once-neat lines shuddered as if struck by lightning; the advance "staggered, halted, and was swept back as by an irresistible current," declared a Federal officer. Those Confederates who had the presence of mind to do so dropped to the ground and tried to find enough cover from behind which to shoot back; others attempted to return the musketry from an erect position, as they had been trained. "I believe every man who stood up was either killed or wounded," noted an officer in the 20th North Carolina.

The slaughter continued for some minutes. Finally, several groups of Federals charged out to capture dazed bunches of Rebels, allowing other Confederates to fall back under a covering fire from different parts of

Rodes' Division.* Alfred Iverson suffered something approaching a nervous breakdown, swore that his brigade had endeavored to surrender en
masse, "and became unfit for further command."

Not long after his conversation with Richard Anderson, Robert E. Lee
rode toward Gettysburg in search of A. P. Hill. The steady drumming of
artillery fire from ahead was unsettling evidence that his army was in a
fight of some considerable size. When Lee reached the hamlet of Seven
Stars, the site of Pettigrew's morning encampment, he was met by
Richard Ewell's aide Campbell Brown. "Troops came up while I was talking with Gen'l Lee and passed by toward Gettysburg," the young officer
later recalled. After informing Lee of Ewell's decision to alter his course
and move for Gettysburg instead of Cashtown, Brown was surprised to
be asked by the general if his commander had heard anything from Jeb
Stuart. When he answered in the negative, Lee appeared to grow both
anxious and angry. "This from a man of Lee's habitual reserve surprised
me at the time," Brown remembered. Lee issued instructions for Ewell to
make every effort "to open communications with Gen'l Stuart," then dismissed the aide to return to his corps.

From Seven Stars, Lee rode on over Knoxlyn Ridge (the site of the
morning's skirmishing) and continued until he reached a slight rise just
west of Herr's Ridge and north of the Chambersburg Pike. There he met
A. P. Hill, who still could provide no more than a sketchy situation
report. It was around the time when Iverson's Brigade was being shredded near Oak Hill that Henry Heth located the two generals. Protocol
called for Heth to deliver his report to Hill, but something—the look in
Lee's eyes, perhaps, or the pallor of Hill's skin—prompted him instead to
speak directly to the army commander.

" 'Rodes is very heavily engaged, had I not better attack?' " Heth asked.

" 'No,' " Lee replied, " 'I am not prepared to bring on a general
engagement today—Longstreet is not up.' "

Robert Rodes' first attack, though a bloody debacle for Iverson's
Brigade, nonetheless marked the beginning of an increasing desperation

*Sergeant Edward L. Gilligan of the 88th Pennsylvania, who helped his captain wres-
tle away the flag of the 23rd North Carolina in this action, would later receive a
Medal of Honor for his deed.

on the part of the Union First Corps and its commander, Abner Doubleday. To meet the threat posed by Ewell's arrival on Oak Hill, Doubleday committed virtually his entire reserve, Robinson's two-brigade division, to succor his northern flank. The tentative initial shelling by the Rebel cannon on Oak Hill was quickly augmented by Pegram's and McIntosh's gunners, all of whom lavished special attention on the McPherson farm area, where Roy Stone's three Pennsylvania regiments held the ground. The barrage of hissing and exploding shells became severe enough that Stone turned one regiment, the 149th Pennsylvania, to front north and pulled most of the other two back a bit to gain some cover from the farm buildings.

In facing north, however, the 149th presented its left flank to the gunners on Herr's Ridge, who promptly took advantage of the situation. After seeing several of his men get pulped into a fleshy mash by this enfilading fire, the regiment's commander decided to break a few rules. Normally a regiment's flags were its most prized possession, ever to be kept in a well-guarded position. But in this instance, realizing that those standards were providing handy targeting poles for the Rebel gunners, Lieutenant Colonel Walton Dwight ordered the flags and color guard to a point about fifty yards north of where the main body of the regiment lay. The men assigned to this detail made their way forward and located a small fence-rail breastwork that they used for cover while the Confederate cannoneers dutifully shifted their fire to the new target.

It was from their position along the Chambersburg Pike that a number of Stone's men engaged in some long-distance sniping at Iverson's struggling command. But Iverson's men were not entirely alone; moving to support them off to the west was Daniel's Brigade. Daniel had detached three regiments to help provide covering fire for Iverson's withdrawal, while keeping the remaining two focused on his principal objective: attaining the Chambersburg Pike. Those latter regiments, the 2nd North Carolina Battalion and the 45th North Carolina (about 810 men in all), had reached the area previously occupied by Cutler's 147th New York when Stone's line erupted with disciplined volleys. The musketry, aided by supporting cannon fire from Seminary Ridge, pummeled the Rebel battle lines until a countercharge ordered by Stone sent the Tarheels scrambling back.

Abner Doubleday understood that it was only the failure of the Confederate commanders to coordinate their efforts that allowed him to maintain his position on McPherson's Ridge. "It would of course have been impossible to hold the line if Hill attacked on the west and Ewell assailed me at the same time on the north," he later reflected.

Units of the Third Division of the Eleventh Corps continued to reach the open fields north of town and just east of Oak Ridge. Even as Dilger's gunners were beating up the Rebel batteries near Oak Hill, the rest of the First Brigade and all of the Second came panting onto the scene. Their passage through Gettysburg was swift but rewarding. "We were wet as cats, hungry as wolves," wrote a Wisconsin sergeant. "Our thirst was satisfied by the good citizens when we run in full gallop through the town." Colonel Wlodzimierz Krzyzanowski commanded the Second Brigade. The Polish-born officer, called Kriz by his men, nurtured a fierce determination. "The fate of the nation was at stake," he later declared. "I felt it, the leaders felt it, the army felt it, and we fought like lions." Krzyzanowski's men were now massed in support of Dilger's artillery—a bad strategic choice, for the sight of the nearly 1,300 men clustered in a compact formation drew Rebel cannon fire that killed and wounded several soldiers.

Ahead of them, on Oak Hill, Rodes' efforts to salvage his attack were meeting with no success. Long after it could have done some good, O'Neal's Brigade tried again to move toward the Mummasburg Road. Pounded by Dilger's cannon, pecked at by the Eleventh Corps skirmishers, and facing portions of two First Corps brigades, the Alabama boys faltered. The action did, however, beckon acting corps commander Carl Schurz toward his front, causing him to miss the arrival of the First Division, Brigadier General Francis C. Barlow commanding, accompanied by Oliver Otis Howard.

Howard himself came in the wake of a scouting report he had forwarded to Schurz warning of the imminent approach of a large Confederate force on the Heidlersburg Road. The new left-wing commander likely also shared this intelligence with Barlow, who was operating under Schurz's instructions to use the First Division to extend the right flank of the Third. Leaving Barlow to deploy his men, Howard undertook what would prove to be his one and only survey of the Federal positions north and west of Gettysburg.

In slanting in behind the skirmishers confronting Oak Hill and then moving up onto Oak Ridge, Howard somehow managed to pass by Carl Schurz, who would thus remain in the dark regarding his plans. Next,

Howard (by his own account) rode among the First Corps units that had savaged Iverson, "had a few words with Wadsworth, and stopped a short time with Doubleday farther to the west." Doubleday remembered Howard's examining the position on McPherson's Ridge, after which he "gave orders, in case I was forced to retreat, to fall back to Cemetery Hill. I think this was the first and only order I received from him during the day." For his part, Howard returned to Cemetery Hill "feeling exceedingly anxious about the left flank."

The passage of the Eleventh Corps through Gettysburg rekindled hope among its citizens that they would be saved. Albertus McCreary and some of his pals perched on a rail fence to cheer on the infantrymen. McCreary assured his companions that "there are enough soldiers here to whip all the Rebs in the south." Teenager Henry Jacobs marveled at the fortitude shown by these troops: "They kept the pace without breaking ranks," he recollected, "but they flowed through and out into the battle-field beyond, a human tide, at millrace speed." Many residents offered the men water, though sometimes their officers waved off the Good Samaritans, insisting, as Catherine Foster remembered it, that "there was no time to drink."

Even as spirits were raised, the hard hand of war revealed itself in the growing number of wounded soldiers being cared for in the town. Mary McAllister was one of many of Gettysburg's noncombatants who now had to confront an aspect of war not depicted by Currier and Ives. "I didn't know what in the world to do," she admitted. But she and others were nevertheless determined to do everything in their power to help these brave young men who had come from such a distance to protect them.

Richard Ewell was beginning to wonder if his decision to pitch into the Union army had been the right one. His sole offensive effort thus far had been repulsed, and the pressure on George Doles' isolated brigade was increasing as more and more Yankee soldiers poured through the town. Robert E. Lee had not wanted a battle, but Ewell had forced one anyway, thinking he could deliver a quick victory. Instead, he now faced the real possibility of having to withdraw.

Campbell Brown returned and reviewed his conversation with Robert E. Lee, reporting that there were no new orders save those concerning

Jeb Stuart. Not five minutes after he passed his information to Ewell, Brown later remembered, "Maj. Venable of Jeb Stuart's staff with one courier, rode up to let us know where Jeb was. . . . Gen'l E. sent him on to report to Gen'l Lee, advising him to send the courier back to hurry up the Cavalry. . . . Gen'l E. gave me but a few minutes rest, sending me to look for [Jubal] Early & hurry him up & tell him to attack at once." As Brown left, he could hear a crescendo of popping, a signal that more of Rodes' infantry was going into action.

The sounds Brown heard issued from Junius Daniel's second drive on the Chambersburg Pike. He had failed the first time using two regiments, so now he hit the area defended by Roy Stone's brigade with four, leaving one to watch his rear. After repulsing Daniel's previous effort, the 149th Pennsylvania's colonel had posted a portion of his regiment in an advanced position in the railroad cut. The cut itself provided a great advantage against an enemy force charging straight on, but it would be a terrible place to be if any enemy cannon got into the unfinished road bed.

At first things worked out according to the Federal script, with the leading waves of charging Tarheels obligingly falling to the Pennsylvania volleys. Then one of Pegram's alert gunners on Herr's Ridge saw what was happening, pushed his battery forward into the cut, and began shot-gunning canister along the pathway. The 149th's commander shouted orders for the detachment to retreat, but for many it was already too late. An officer with them recalled that "some were shot while climbing the steep side [of the cut]; others losing their hold slid back; some ran to the right to get out; and numbers on the left never got out except as prisoners, for the foe was upon them before they could clear it."

The railroad cut proved to be a double-edged sword for both sides, however, for it slowed the momentum of Daniel's men, providing enough time for Stone to shift most of two of his regiments and part of a third to face the pike. After that it became a brawl pure and simple, as clusters of soldiers fought one another for self-defense or momentary advantage. In short order Stone's brigade was no longer Stone's, as the colonel went down with bullet hits to his arm and hip; command devolved to Colonel Langhorne Wister, who was soon exercising it with orders spat out in blood from a mouth wound. Not until the Pennsylvanians launched a near-suicidal charge was the railroad cut again cleared of the enemy. The

Union position had been held, but at high cost.* This would have been the time for fresh troops to replace the three Pennsylvania regiments, but no reserves were on hand. As Langhorne Wister staggered off to an aid station in the rear, Colonel Edmund C. Dana took over what was left.

The absence of any controlling plan for the Eleventh Corps became further evident as Francis Barlow moved his division into place. It was not where Carl Schurz wanted it, nor did it conform to any ideas that Oliver Howard may have had, but it was where Barlow wished it to be. Marching with his men eastward across the rear of the Third Division's line, he had grown increasingly fixated on some high ground slightly less than half a mile forward from where he was supposed to connect with the right flank of Schimmelfennig's position. Some four hundred feet high, Blocher's Knoll offered a cleared crown suitable for artillery and a good line of sight up the Heidlersburg Road. Already, skirmishers from Doles' Brigade were using the woods on its northern and northwestern slopes for some long-range sniping at Barlow's units. Without consulting or even notifying his superiors, Barlow issued orders that got his division moving toward that point.

Francis Barlow may have commanded 2,477 men, but he did not necessarily believe in them. Soon after taking charge of this division, he had admitted that he had "always been down on the 'Dutch' & I do not abate my contempt now." A month after making that remark, he still considered his soldiers "miserable creatures." During this day's movement from Emmitsburg, he had arrested one of his brigade commanders for allowing his men to break marching ranks to fetch water. Just minutes before ordering the movement toward Blocher's Knoll, Barlow was persuaded to return the officer to command, but only after sternly advising him to "shoot down stragglers." How much his decision to advance was motivated by his military appreciation of the moment and how much by the desire to strengthen a weak blade in fire, Barlow never revealed.

A skirmish line made up of the 54th and 68th New York and a portion of the 153rd Pennsylvania skittered forward to drive the Georgia and

*There were two Medals of Honor given to members of the 150th Pennsylvania for service in this action: one to Lieutenant Colonel Henry S. Huidekoper for continuing to lead his men while severely wounded, and the other to Corporal J. Monroe Reisinger for his "brave and meritorious conduct in the face of the enemy."

Alabama riflemen from the knoll area. Behind these Yankees followed the rest of Barlow's division, even as another Union skirmish line, drawn from the 17th Connecticut, splashed across Rock Creek east of the road.

By taking the high ground, Barlow did check to some extent the actions of Doles' Georgians, but in so stretching forward he also outdistanced Schimmelfennig's ability to support him. Devin's cavalry was supposed to protect his right flank, but when those troopers were regrouping near the York Pike, they had come under friendly fire from Cemetery Hill and subsequently sought cover in the town, rather than the positions where they were needed. Barlow was thus very much on his own.

Carl Schurz saw this and immediately ordered the nearest Third Division units to extend eastward in order to maintain contact with Barlow's men. The net result, he grimly noted, was to make "still thinner a line already too thin."

Richard Ewell's aide Campbell Brown found Jubal Early in the midst of setting up his attack against Barlow's position. "I . . . formed my line across the Heidlersburg road," Early reported afterward,

> with [John B.] Gordon's brigade on the right, Hoke's brigade (under Colonel [Isaac E.] Avery) on the left, [Harry T.] Hays' brigade in the center, and, [William] Smith's brigade in the rear of Hoke's. [Lieutenant Colonel H. P.] Jones' battalion of artillery was posted in a field, immediately in front of Hoke's brigade, so as to fire on the enemy flank, and, as soon as these dispositions could be made, a fire was opened upon the enemy's infantry and artillery by my artillery with considerable effect.

Carl Schurz knew it was the beginning of the end: "I saw the enemy emerging from the belt of woods on my right with one battery after another and one column of infantry after another, threatening to envelop my right flank and to cut me off from the town and the position on Cemetery Hill behind. . . . Our situation became critical."

It was about this time that Lee was located by Andrew R. Venable, Jeb Stuart's assistant adjutant and inspector general, who had been sent along by Richard Ewell. Little of what Venable reported was good news. Stuart's riders were no less than thirty miles distant and (at least when Venable was last with them) moving away from Gettysburg, in what Lee knew would be a fruitless attempt to contact Ewell near Carlisle. No record of Venable's meeting with Lee was set down; its only artifact is Stuart's later summary of the message that Venable carried back with him. Wrote Stuart, "I received a dispatch from General Lee (in answer to one sent by Major Venable from Dover, on Early's trail), that the army was at Gettysburg, and had been engaged on this day (July 1) with the enemy's advance."

Lee could expect no help this day from Jeb Stuart.

Junius Daniel was a determined man. Although he had already been twice rebuffed in his efforts to drive off the Union flank posted along the Chambersburg Pike, he at once set to work reorganizing for yet another thrust. Abner Doubleday knew full well that it was only unaccountable luck that had kept Hill's infantry off his back when Daniel attacked, and knew, too, that only a fool would count on such good fortune a third time. He sent an officer to Howard to request either reinforcements or permission to withdraw. Neither was forthcoming. "General Wadsworth reported half of his men were killed or wounded, and Rowley's division suffered in the same proportion," Doubleday would later claim. "Stone reported two-thirds of his brigade had fallen. Hardly a field officer remained unhurt." Needing some sort of reserve, Doubleday had the 151st Pennsylvania, from Biddle's brigade (holding the southern part of McPherson's Ridge toward the Fairfield Road), sent back to the seminary, forcing the brigadier to rejigger his formations.

These actions caught the eye of Robert E. Lee, who had been observing the situation with growing concern. He had not been looking for a battle this day, and indeed, when one of his divisions had gotten itself embroiled in a serious firefight with the enemy, he had striven to quell the combat before it exploded into a major engagement. No sooner had he managed to rein in Hill and Heth, however, than Ewell had arrived to reignite the conflict, and now *he* was heavily engaged. Thanks to the inactivity of Heth's men, the Federals seemed to be shifting units from McPherson's Ridge to meet Ewell's threat. The fighting had slithered from Lee's grasp; no longer in control of events, he was instead being controlled by them. It was time for instinct and experience to replace tattered plans.

Henry Heth returned to give Lee and Hill an update. By his own recollection, he informed Lee that the Federals "were withdrawing troops
from my front and push[ing] them against Rhodes, and [I] again
requested permission to attack."* Lee's reply, again as remembered by
Heth, was, " 'Wait a while and I will send you word when to go in.' " Lee
had made his decision: there would be more fighting today at Gettysburg.

*Heth's misspelling of Robert Rodes' name has been intentionally preserved here.

(2:45 P.M.–5:45 P.M.)

Help was coming to the Union forces. Couriers had been galloping into Emmitsburg throughout the morning and into the early afternoon, bringing terse reports on the situation. Having been caught not long before in a collision of orders between George Meade and John Reynolds, Daniel E. Sickles made sure to follow his instructions to outpost Emmitsburg. That is, he did so until about 3:00 P.M., when a courier brought word from Oliver Howard that John Reynolds was dead, the enemy was pressing him hard "in front of Gettysburg," and help was needed. A fight was something Daniel Sickles understood. Taking care to leave behind sufficient forces to guard his post, Sickles set most of his Third Corps marching "toward Gettysburg immediately." It would be hours before the first of his men could reach that point.

Other Union troops closer to Gettysburg were also in motion at this time. The irony was that many of these men, along with their commander, had been listening for several hours to the sounds of gunfire not far distant from them.

Two Taverns was, as its name suggests, a small collection of buildings centered on a pair of wayside establishments, located some four miles southeast of Gettysburg on the Baltimore Pike. Travel time between the two places—for veteran troops without opposition—was perhaps two hours. Following the orders of march issued from Meade's headquarters for July 1, the Twelfth Corps had left its camps around Littlestown, Maryland, starting at daylight and thereafter taken its time covering the six miles to Two Taverns, with the head of the column reaching the place at about 11:00 A.M. "The people all along the road manifested great curiosity to see us and assembled at all road crossings," recalled the commander of the first division on the scene. The weather was uncomfortably muggy.

Major General Henry W. Slocum, accompanying his front units, arrived at Two Taverns around midday. Reports had already come to him that some of his men were hearing the distant crack of guns. To Slocum's practiced ear it sounded like a cavalry scrap with horse batteries engaged. "As we had heard that Buford with his cavalry had driven the rebel cavalry out of the town [of Gettysburg] the day before, this was supposed to be an affair of cavalry and attracted little attention," attested a staff officer in the corps' Second Division.

As time passed, though, Slocum began to reassess his conclusion. After learning from one civilian refugee that there was heavy fighting going on at Gettysburg, he sent one of his own staff to scout toward the town. The officer returned to report that he had ascended to some high ground and there heard significant cannonading. More Twelfth Corps soldiers also made out the sounds, which led one to deduce "that the action was more serious than we had supposed." A few men climbed atop barns, from which vantage "the bursting of shell and clouds of smoke could be . . . plainly perceived." And finally, dispatches were delivered attesting to the severity of the fighting.

Still, Henry Slocum waited until after 3:00 P.M. to order his corps forward. Part of his confusion was related to Meade's Pipe Creek circular, which keyed his course of action to eventualities involving those units actually engaged with the enemy—in this case John Reynolds' left wing. Slocum was late in finding out that Reynolds was dead, and while the circular made clear what he should do if the left wing fell back, it was silent regarding his obligation in the event that the same wing entered a large-scale engagement. Another part of the problem was Slocum himself. The New Yorker was a competent manager of military assets, but he lacked the spirit of a warrior. Writing nearly twenty-three years after the battle, Slocum would offer his only explanation for his absence of initiative this day: "My orders were to march to Two Taverns, and await orders from General Meade. The Twelfth Corps was in that position when we heard of the engagement at Gettysburg. We received no word from General Howard [asking us to come], but started as soon as we heard of the battle."

The batteries under H. P. Jones that Jubal Early had positioned on high ground just east of the Heidlersburg Road opened fire on the Eleventh Corps at about 3:00 P.M. The situation for the Union infantry and artillery* was becoming untenable. Hoping to offset this Confederate

---

*Hubert Dilger's smooth-bore battery had been reinforced by the four rifled guns of Lieutenant William Wheeler's 13th Battery, New York Light Artillery.

advantage, Francis Barlow pushed four guns from the 4th United States Light Artillery, Battery G, onto Blocher's Knoll. They promptly drew fire from two of Jones' units, with one of the Rebel shells hitting the mounted commander of the Regulars, Lieutenant Bayard Wilkeson. As the young officer, whose father reported on the war for the *New York Times*, went down with a mortal leg wound, his gunners stuck gamely to their weapons.

The covering fire provided by Jones' cannoneers allowed Jubal Early to launch his attack. After driving the Yankee skirmishers (17th Connecticut) back across Rock Creek, Brigadier General John B. Gordon's all-Georgia brigade powered forward to the stream. "We advanced with our accustomed yell," recollected Private George W. Nichols of the 61st Georgia, "but they stood firm until we got near them." The Union defenders, two New York regiments belonging to Colonel Leopold von Gilsa's brigade, held momentarily, then began backing up the slope to the knoll. A supporting Pennsylvania regiment was also shoved back.

With their infantry guardians gone or getting out, the four Yankee guns on the knoll also hitched up, followed soon after by the other two from the battery, which had been supporting them off to the western side of the rise. A Federal counterattack collapsed in blood and confusion. In

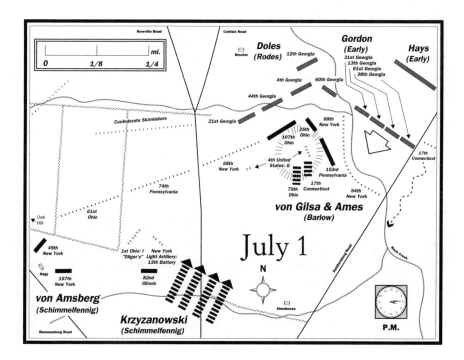

the chaos, Francis Barlow went down with a bullet hit in his left side. "Everybody was then running to the rear & the enemy were approaching rapidly," Barlow recollected.

Since moving into position along Herr's Ridge, the North Carolina regiments of Pettigrew's Brigade had been spectators to the punishment meted out by the Confederate artillery on the Union infantry standing along McPherson's Ridge. A minor crisis arose in the 26th North Carolina when John R. Lane, the regiment's second in command, told Henry King Burgwyn Jr. that he was feeling ill and asked for permission to leave the field. " 'Oh, Colonel, I can't, I can't,' " Burgwyn said. " 'I can't think of going into battle without you.' " He offered Lane some French brandy, which seemed to do the trick.

The two walked to the regiment's front to look across the long slope to Willoughby Run and the Federal positions behind it. " 'Colonel,' " Burgwyn asked Lane, " 'do you think that we will have to advance on the enemy as they are?' "

Henry Heth was not far away when Robert E. Lee's aide found him. Lee's orders were to attack.

What remained of the Iron Brigade was mostly tucked into the Herbst Woods, though its extreme ends stuck out into the open. After routing Archer's Brigade, Solomon Meredith had reset his line, putting the 7th Wisconsin and the 19th Indiana on his flanks.* In taking up the defensive position in the woods, Meredith had simply followed the contour of the ground, which resulted in his four regiments' being placed in a convex line that posed some problems. More than one officer pointed out to Meredith how the shape of the position inhibited the fields of fire and also how easily it could be enfiladed, but the Iron Brigade commander stuck with his decision.

From the cover of these woods the Western soldiers had heard Stone's brigade repel Daniel's two assaults, and from here they had watched the enemy artillery pound the ridge line south of them, as Biddle's men maneuvered extensively to avoid the worst of it. Now they saw

---

*Meredith was without the 6th Wisconsin, which was retained on detached service helping Cutler's brigade and supporting the artillery.

their own fate foretold as Pettigrew's Brigade, with Brockenbrough's Virginians moving along its left, began to come down off Herr's Ridge. One Indiana soldier could only marvel at how "the whole [Rebel] army in our front moved in magnificent lines across the intervening open fields." It did not take long for the remnants of the Iron Brigade to realize that the biggest regiment in the advancing line was coming straight toward them.

It took fifteen to twenty minutes of hard fighting for John Gordon's men, assisted by some of George Doles' regiments, to overrun Blocher's Knoll. The success was bittersweet for a member of the 13th Georgia who was mourning the loss of a friend: "When he was shot dow[n] he look[ed] up in my face and sed . . . I am hit take me [a]way, you cant tell how it made me feel to leave him there but I was a blige to do it [as] we wasn't al[l]owed to s[t]op to carry of[f] the wounded." "The Yankees . . . fought more stubborn than I ever saw them or ever want to see them again," swore one of Doles' soldiers. "I thought we would have to use the bayonet on them," recalled another 13th man, "but we got to them, their line gave way, and they retreated across the wheat field into town."

Gordon was awash in the adrenaline rush of combat. "There was no alternative for Howard's men except to break and fly," he exulted, "or to throw down their arms and surrender." He was right, up to a point: much of the First Division of the Eleventh Corps, forced to defend an exposed position against a determined and resourceful enemy, was in pieces, though frantic efforts were being made by officers to reorganize it near the town almshouse. But the rest of the Eleventh Corps was far from eliminated.

The first challenge to Gordon's euphoria came from Wlodzimierz Krzyzanowski, who deployed his brigade from column into line and drove toward the knoll. After the Pole's riflemen sent one of Doles' regiments scurrying for cover, the Yankee units strode into a stand-up shootout with two others, with neither side appearing willing to leave off the mutual destruction. The standoff ended when both Gordon and Doles managed to work some of their men around the flanks of Krzyzanowski's line. "So the horrible, screaming, hurtling messengers of death flew over us from both sides," recollected a New York soldier. "In such a storm it seemed a miracle that any were left alive." Even the combat-experienced brigade commander was shocked by the violence of this action: "The troops taking part were sweaty, blackened by the gunpowder, and they looked more like animals than human beings," recounted Wlodzimierz Krzyzanowski. "This portrait of battle was a portrait of hell." One by one, beginning with the 26th Wisconsin, the Georgia veterans chewed up the Federal ranks until every regiment in the brigade was streaming toward the town.*

Alexander Schimmelfennig could not just stand by helplessly and watch the Georgians methodically grind up his Second Brigade; he had to *do* something. He called up the 157th New York, from his First Brigade, and ordered it to charge toward the northeast, against the exposed flank of Doles' line. As the 409 officers and men of the 157th began to advance into the maelstrom, they could not help but notice that they were entering this fight alone and unsupported.

Their ranks carefully ordered and set, the regiments of Pettigrew's Brigade moved purposefully down the eastern side of Herr's Ridge toward the Yankee line on McPherson's Ridge. Forming the center of his imposing array were the eight hundred infantry of the 26th North Carolina, led by their boy colonel, Henry King Burgwyn Jr. A soldier in those ranks was awed and inspired by the way the Tarheels "stepped off, apparently as willingly and as proudly as if they were on review."

The long files of men breasted into a waist-high oat field that was already trampled down in places from this morning's actions. The leading ranks had covered about half the distance to the creek bed ahead of them when a soldier darted forward a few paces, set himself, and fired at the distantly visible Yankee formations. Whether prompted by this act or simply to acknowledge that the Rebels were within range, the Federals posted in the woods unleashed a volley that chipped a few Confederates from their places. On Henry Burgwyn's command, the 26th North Carolina returned the volley.

Colonel Henry A. Morrow of the 24th Michigan, the next-to-last unit on the Iron Brigade's left flank, later reported that Pettigrew's Brigade "advanced in two lines of battle, their right extending beyond and overlapping our left." "Their bearing was magnificent and their alignment seemed to be perfect," allowed a member of the 2nd Wisconsin. "In some instances their colors were advanced several paces in front of the line." A

---

*George Doles was almost captured in this action when his horse bolted toward the enemy. He saved himself by falling off the animal some fifty yards from the Yankee line.

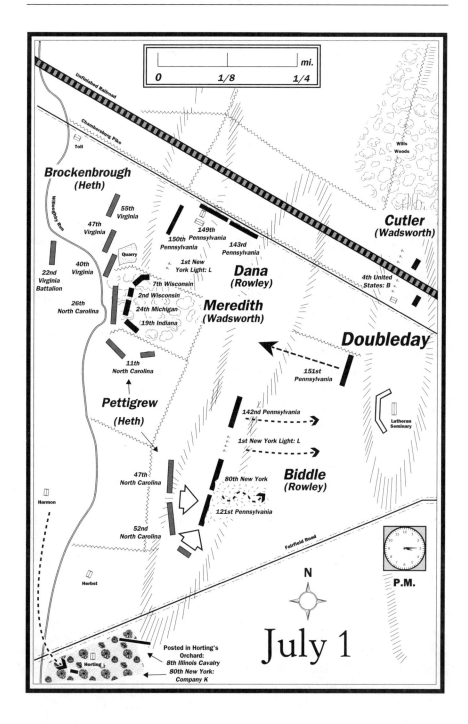

Unfinished Railroad

Chambersburg Pike

Toll

Brockenbrough
(Heth)

Wills
Woods

Willoughby Run

55th
Virginia

47th
Virginia

150th
Pennsylvania

149th
Pennsylvania

143rd
Pennsylvania

Cutler
(Wadsworth)

Quarry

40th
Virginia

1st New
York Light: L

Dana
(Rowley)

22nd
Virginia
Battalion

7th Wisconsin

2nd Wisconsin

24th Michigan

Meredith
(Wadsworth)

4th United
States: B

26th
North Carolina

19th Indiana

11th
North Carolina

Doubleday

151st
Pennsylvania

Pettigrew
(Heth)

142nd Pennsylvania

Lutheran
Seminary

1st New York Light: L

47th
North Carolina

80th New York

Biddle
(Rowley)

Harmon

121st Pennsylvania

52nd
North Carolina

Fairfield Road

N

P.M.

Herbst

July 1

Posted in Horting's
Orchard:
8th Illinois Cavalry
80th New York:
Company K

Horting

soldier in the 19th Indiana feared that "total annihilation stared us in the face." The Hoosiers could only look on in impotent anger as a skirmish line pushing ahead of the heavy Confederate formation flushed out their pickets, scattering some, killing some, and capturing others.

After absorbing a second volley in response to its own, the 26th North Carolina moved at the double quick until it reached the under-brush along Willoughby Run. Burgwyn's men were now in point-blank range, and the instant they slowed their advance to negotiate the briars and thorn bushes, the Iron Brigade loosed a carefully aimed massed fire. A dazed North Carolina sergeant could not even begin to estimate the number of "deadly missiles [that] were sent into our ranks, which mowed us down like wheat before the sickle." The few Federal cannon that had succeeded in holding on to positions along the southern portion of McPherson's Ridge found themselves with a clear shot at the Tarheel bat-tle lines. "The Yanks took advantage of that," another in the 26th's ranks recalled, "and began killing our men like forty."

For several long minutes, the resolute Iron Brigade veterans kept up a murderous fire on the creek crossings in their front. The officer com-manding the 19th Indiana later avowed that for some time following first contact, "no Rebel crossed the stream and lived." It was not for lack of trying: a young captain in the 2nd Wisconsin could not help but admire how the Rebels charged "with recklessness upon our walls of fire." Then, unbelievably, the tide turned, as the lack of flank support and the convex alignment that Solomon Meredith had stubbornly maintained conspired to end the Iron Brigade's stand. A portion of the 11th North Carolina (operating off the right of the 26th) worked its way around the exposed flank of the 19th Indiana and began raking the Union line. "The slaugh-ter in our ranks became frightful beyond description," a Hoosier recorded. Flesh and blood could endure only so much: dropping men at every step, the rank and file of the Iron Brigade backstepped a hundred yards to the position where their officers had established a second line of defense.

The advance by the 157th New York, intended to relieve the killing pres-sure on the Eleventh Corps, never stood a chance. The regiment moved north and then east to form along the Carlisle Road, targeting two Geor-gia units that had been decimating the barely organized remnants of Krzyzanowski's brigade. Alert Confederate officers saw the New Yorkers

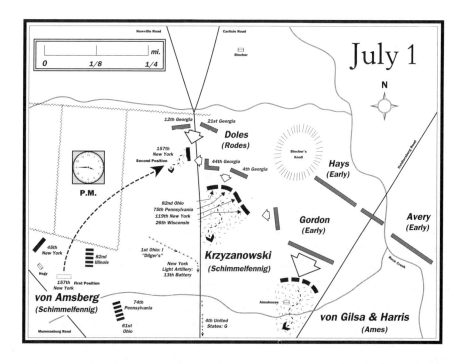

approaching, however, so by the time the men of the 157th reached the road, they were confronted by a Georgia regiment in their front, with two more moving to their left and rear. "The men were falling rapidly and the enemy's line was taking the form of a giant semi-circle . . . concentrating the fire of their whole brigade upon my rapidly diminishing numbers," reported the New York colonel. By the time the 157th finally fell back, it had lost more than 75 percent of the number engaged. Among the mortally wounded was the officer who had boasted that "the bullet is not molded which is to kill me."

Less than half a mile southeast of the site of the 157th's solitary ordeal, the defensive stand of the Eleventh Corps' First Division, near the almshouse, was collapsing. A private in the ranks of the 61st Georgia felt grudging admiration for his foe: "Their officers were cheering their men and behaving like heroes and commanders of the 'first water,'" he allowed. Nevertheless, the patchwork Union line could not hold against Gordon's men, already tipsy with victory. "We drove them on through Gettysburg and had them greatly confused," said the Georgia private. The officer who had assumed command after Francis Barlow was wounded later noted that the "whole division was falling back with little or no regularity, regimental organization had become destroyed."

The parallels to Chancellorsville were eerie. For the second time in two months, the unlucky Eleventh Corps had been poorly positioned on an exposed flank, allowing it to be struck by a sudden, well-handled enemy attack. Two full divisions of the corps had been ground into broken pieces. John B. Gordon later remembered that as "far down the line as my eye could reach the Union troops were in retreat."

Doubleday's line on McPherson's Ridge gave way slowly, sullenly, but inexorably. Pettigrew's Brigade was one of the best in Lee's army, and its men seemed especially determined to vanquish their foes this day. The first section of the Federal line to unravel was on the left, along the southern portion of the ridge, where three of Biddle's regiments had gamely held on throughout the Rebel artillery barrages, despite having very little to work with defensively. The two southernmost regiments of Pettigrew's line now took on Biddle's trio. After chasing off two companies from the 80th New York that were outposted west of Willoughby Run on the Harmon farm, the North Carolina units—the 47th and 52nd Regiments—splashed across the run, surged up the gentle slope, and delivered a devastating volley right into the faces of Biddle's men. The fire was returned by the approximately 900 Yankees defending against the 1,100-man Rebel force. A North Carolina officer in the 47th would later narrate the action in the present tense: "The struggle grows hotter and hotter, men are falling in all directions." Still Biddle's men held, until a portion of the 52nd North Carolina angled itself across the left flank of the southernmost Union unit, and enfilade fire began to peel the small Federal brigade off McPherson's Ridge, one regiment at a time.

The fighting in the Herbst Woods was ferocious. Too overwhelmed to hold and too proud to break, the Iron Brigade fought on, rear-stepping from the second defensive line to a third, always holding until just past the point of common sense. Solomon Meredith was badly wounded in one exchange, his head slammed by fragments of an exploding shell that also rolled his horse onto him, breaking bones. In the choking gunpowder fog enshrouding both sides, the color-bearers became clear and tempting targets. The 26th North Carolina lost several such in quick succession, but each time a new volunteer would grab the standard to keep the regiment pressing forward. "Lots of men near me were falling to the ground, throwing up their arms and clawing the earth," remembered one Tarheel. "The whole field was covered with gray suits soaked in blood."

Not everyone shared the suicidal thirst for glory. When someone told Lieutenant William W. Macy that the flag of the 19th Indiana was down, he shouted back, "Go and get it!" "Go to hell, I won't do it!" came the reply. Once Macy and another Hoosier officer had located the colors, they decided that their chances of making it out of the inferno alive would be improved if the standard was less visible, so they rolled it up and slipped its marching shuck over it. As the two men turned to go, Macy's companion was killed. Fighting back the shock of seeing his friend die, the young lieutenant clutched the furled flag and staggered off toward the northeast.

The hot and humid day, the insulating effect of the forest growth, and the sheer heat thrown off by men in combat all turned the Herbst Woods into a furnace. "[The] men had difficulty in ramming down their cartridges, so slick was the iron ram-rod in hands thoroughly wet with perspiration," said a North Carolinian. "All expedients were resorted to, but mainly jabbing the ram-rods against the ground and rocks." In the tumult, a fifth, sixth, and seventh color-bearer fell carrying the standard of the 26th North Carolina. "Although they knew it was certain death to pick it up, the flag was never allowed to remain down," swore a member of the regiment.

What was left of the Iron Brigade had by now backed up to the eastern edge of the Herbst Woods, beyond which open fields sloped down and then up to Seminary Ridge. Realizing that their next step back would put them out in the open, the Western soldiers drew on their last reserves of strength to ratchet up the firing rate.

The battered line of the 26th North Carolina shuddered under the impact of this desperate fusillade, seeming to stall. Henry Burgwyn was in the center of the holocaust, urging his men along. A courier arrived with an inspiring word from J. Johnston Pettigrew, who proclaimed that the 26th had already "covered itself with glory." Even as this message was being delivered, another flag carrier was spun to the ground nearby. Hardly skipping a beat, the young messenger ran over, caught up the standard, and had just begun waving it to advance the line when he was killed by a shot through the heart. Yet another Tarheel grabbed the colors next, managing only a few steps before he, too, was brought down.

A commanding figure now worked his way over to the flag and picked it up. " 'Dress on the colors,' " Henry Burgwyn shouted as he raised the standard for all to see. Slowly but surely, order began to reimpose itself as the ranks formed. Burgwyn called for someone to take the standard from him, and a young soldier stepped up to grasp the staff. Burgwyn's second in command, John R. Lane, came up to report that the regiment was ready to advance, and at that moment, a swarm of bullets pelted the group. The short-lived flag carrier was killed, and Henry Burgwyn was struck in the side. The bullet had drilled through the two journals he carried, ripped into his rib cage, and pierced both his lungs. Lane saw at once that there was nothing he could do for his friend, whose painful gestures made it clear that he wanted his second to perform a higher duty. Rising from the dying form of the boy colonel, Lane signaled for the line to move forward. His tenure was a matter of minutes: during the Iron Brigade's retrograde to Seminary Ridge, a noncommissioned officer in the 24th Michigan would shoot Lane in the head. Badly wounded, the stalwart Tarheel would survive to lead his regiment again.

Abner Doubleday may still have been hoping to salvage the failing situation on McPherson's Ridge when he committed his entire reserve—the 151st Pennsylvania—to the fighting in the Herbst Woods. The 467 soldiers moved from near Seminary Ridge to the eastern edge of the copse, where they suddenly encountered an enemy line of battle. For one amazed Pennsylvanian, it was "the first sight I had of the rebel Stars and Bars." The 151st prided itself on its marksmanship, so instead of being ordered to volley fire, the ranks were instructed to fire at will. The regiment's commander would afterward remark that his men "coolly waited until they saw an exposed enemy and then brought him to the ground."

The 151st's arrival on the scene was not enough to reverse the momentum, but it covered the Iron Brigade's withdrawal from the woods. Once they were clear, the obstinate Union regiments carried out a measured retirement to Seminary Ridge, pausing several times on the way to deliver volleys at their pursuing foe. The Pennsylvanians held their place long enough for the Westerners to disentangle themselves; then they joined in the rearward maneuver.

The loss of the Herbst Woods made it impossible for Rowley's Second Brigade (Third Division, First Corps) to continue defending the Chambersburg Pike near the McPherson stone barn and house. Colonel Stone and Wister had fallen for the cause, but now Edmund L. Dana realized that his troops could no longer remain in their exposed position. Rebel riflemen were chewing at his left flank from the cover of the Herbst Woods, while a full enemy brigade (Brockenbrough's) was pressing from the front. Then, to top off his catalog of misfortune, Dana had to contend again with Junius Daniel's determined North Carolina troops, coming at him from the north. If Dana saw the situation clearly, however, many of the others fighting did not. When a staff officer arrived from Seminary Ridge with orders to withdraw, one line officer was incredulous. " 'Adjutant, it is all damned cowardice,' " he exclaimed, " 'we have beaten them and will keep on beating them back!' "

The retreat off McPherson's Ridge was not easy for the three Pennsylvania regiments. In the confusion, the small party that had been set out to decoy enemy fire, after fending off several efforts to rush the standards, lost first the state flag, then the national colors. As the 149th and 150th Regiments stumbled eastward, small but cohesive groups made brief stands before continuing on their way. The 143rd Pennsylvania was the last to leave. Watching it from Herr's Ridge, even A. P. Hill had to admit that the Yankee unit "fought for some time with much obstinacy." He would never forget the sight of the 143rd's color-bearer "turning round every now and then to shake his fist at the advancing rebels." Before the battered regiment disappeared from view, Hill saw the defiant color-bearer fall.*

Following the devastating repulse of Iverson's Brigade, the Union troops on Oak Ridge near the Mummasburg Road had successfully repelled a second attacking wave from Stephen Ramseur's brigade. In turning back that assault, though, the First Brigade (Second Division, First Corps) had lost its commander, Gabriel Paul, who was shot in the head and blinded. Colonel Adrian R. Root now directed the regiments.

After throwing back Ramseur's effort, the Federals had watched as the world around them fell to pieces. They had seen the unraveling of the Eleventh Corps and the fury of Daniel's repeated drives toward the Chambersburg Pike, and had heard the terrible, never-ending tearing sound of constant musketry as Pettigrew's men locked horns with the

---

*Another heroic effort, this one made by Sergeant James M. Rutter in safely carrying his wounded captain off the field, would bring the Pennsylvanian a Medal of Honor.

Iron Brigade. Every Union soldier standing on that hillside knew that his own turn was coming.

The First Brigade held the extreme flank alone. Shortly after 1:00 P.M., Henry Baxter's brigade had been withdrawn to replenish its ammunition, as Cutler's had been pulled in from the Wills Woods. The collapse of the McPherson's Ridge line had left Root's men isolated, so it was with relief that their colonel greeted the courier from headquarters who brought orders for the unit to retire. It would be a difficult movement to accomplish. Inspired by the advance of Pettigrew's troops and the appearance of a fresh Confederate division (Pender's) along Herr's Ridge, a well-coordinated effort by three Rebel brigades was under way to drive the Yankees off Oak Ridge. Spearheaded by Ramseur's Brigade, the new push also included portions of Daniel's and O'Neal's commands.

If most of the First Brigade was to get off that ridge, one unit would have to buy time for the others. The division commander, John Robinson, rode out to the position, picked the outfit, and gave the orders. He had selected the 16th Maine. Its colonel, Charles W. Tilden, protested. He had not quite two hundred men with him, he said, so Robinson might as well "set a corporal's guard to stop the rebel army." But Robinson was not entertaining arguments. "Hold at any cost," he commanded.

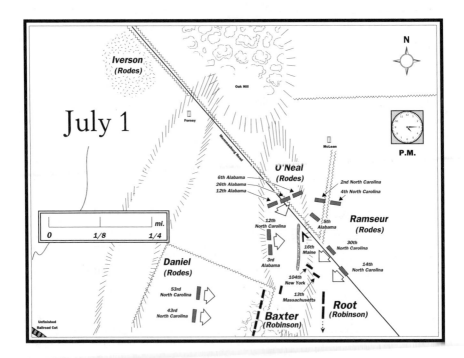

Tilden had in fact already begun shifting his regiment away from its exposed position in the sharp angle made by the brigade line as it met the Mummasburg Road and bent back toward the town. Now he led his men over to a spot where a stone wall angled up to the road, and there planted the unit's two flags. One by one, the brigade's six other regiments began moving off toward Gettysburg.

Also pulling back were Cutler's and Baxter's brigades, which had held different positions in the Wills Woods area. The boyish enigma who had been adopted by the 12th Massachusetts at Marsh Creek paid a high price for his enthusiasm: hit first in the arm, then in the thigh, he was left behind in the retreat and never seen again by the Bay State soldiers.*

Yet again, Ramseur's Brigade came at the Federal position, this time attacking from the north and northwest. Tilden's soldiers, receiving diminishing support as each of the other regiments peeled away, kept up a steady fire until their colonel determined that his boys were the only ones left on the ridge wearing blue uniforms: time to go. An effort was made to retire in order, but the pressure was too great. "They swarmed down upon us," declared the regiment's adjutant, "they engulfed us, and swept away the last semblance of organization which marked us as a separate command." A Maine lieutenant later confessed that "every man commenced to look after himself without further orders."

After Oliver O. Howard completed his circuit ride of the battlefield, he remained on Cemetery Hill, keeping in touch with the action through couriers and direct observation. Per his orders, one division of the Eleventh Corps, supported by one battery, had taken position on the hill. Almost from the moment of his arrival on the field, Howard had been convinced that Cemetery Hill must be held at all costs. So fixed was he in his purpose that he turned a deaf ear to requests from both Doubleday and Schurz for reinforcements, instead either offering obvious partial solutions (for example, instructing Buford to support Doubleday) or passing along impractical suggestions (asking Schurz if he could detach troops to help Doubleday).

Only when it became clear that the Eleventh Corps was disintegrating

---

*Years later, veteran George Kimball would launch a nationwide search that identified the "boy" (actually twenty-one years old) as J. W. Weakley. The mysterious recruit had survived his Gettysburg wounds to enlist officially in the 13th Pennsylvania Cavalry. He died of an epileptic seizure in late 1864.

north of town did Howard allow one of his two reserve brigades to go forward to help. "I feared the consequences of sparing another man from the cemetery," he later admitted. "It was not time to lose the nucleus for a new line that must soon be formed." In sum, rather than craft a flexible plan employing the resources he had on hand, Howard chose to fall back on a static defensive scheme. He was depending on the timely arrival of the Twelfth Corps to stabilize the situation.

None save Union dead, wounded, or captured now held McPherson's Ridge. It had not fallen without a terrible combat, one that had wrecked the victors almost as much as the defeated. Heth's Division had little punch left. Archer's and Davis' Brigades were minimally functional, Pettigrew's had fought itself to exhaustion, and Brockenbrough's was decidedly uninspired in its efforts this day. The man commanding them all was himself out of the action: while stationed with Pettigrew's men in the Herbst Woods, Henry Heth had been struck in the head by a piece of ordnance that ought to have killed him. He happened, however, to be wearing a loose-fitting hat lined with a wad of newspaper to keep it snug. Besides supporting the hat, the paper pads deflected enough of the blow that Heth was merely knocked unconscious, suffering from a painful but nonfatal wound. Command devolved to Pettigrew, who turned over his own battered brigade to Colonel James K. Marshall.

On the other side, despite its licking, Doubleday's command somehow held together. "What was left of the First Corps after all this slaughter rallied on Seminary Ridge," he recorded. The surviving fragments of Stone's, Biddle's, and Meredith's brigades gathered under their unit flags, still prepared to fight it out. Also in the mix were a couple of regiments from Cutler's brigade. What made this new line deadly was the cannon positioned here by the First Corps' artillery chief, Charles Wainwright.

The crusty colonel would later claim that his decision to hold this ridge had stemmed from the cultural divide between himself and one of Howard's aides who spoke English as a second language. Wainwright thought he heard the aide say that Howard intended to defend Seminary Hill at all hazards, when he actually said *Cemetery* Hill. "I thought it was the *Seminary Hill* we were to hold," Wainwright confided. "I had therefore strung my batteries out on it as well as I could. . . . Thus there were eighteen pieces on a frontage of not over two hundred yards."

In what would prove to be his final major contribution to the Battle of Gettysburg, A. P. Hill determined to sweep the enemy from the field. Pender's Division was on hand, and Hill, uncertain as to the condition of Heth's formations, ordered Pender's troops off Herr's Ridge to join them. Pender's instructions were to "pass Genl Heth's division, if found at a halt, and charge the enemy's position." He had a force of nearly 6,700 with which to do the job, but circumstances would remove more than 3,000 from his attack. One brigade (Brigadier General Edward L. Thomas') was held in reserve, while a second (Brigadier General James H. Lane's) was detailed to counter the Union cavalry still operating along the south side of the Fairfield Road. That left Brigadier General Alfred M. Scales' North Carolina brigade and Colonel Abner Perrin's South Carolina one to clear the enemy from Seminary Ridge.

Moving east off Herr's Ridge, Pender's battle lines encountered wounded and stragglers from Pettigrew's fight. A South Carolina soldier remembered that the fresh troops "did not halt, but opened ranks for them to pass to the rear." As they filtered through the determined files, a few bloody Tarheels told any of Pender's men who would listen that they "would all be killed if [they] went forward." Crossing Willoughby Run, portions of the formation passed over combat-weary soldiers of Pettigrew's Brigade, most of whom, Abner Perrin observed, "could scarcely raise a cheer for us." "The field was thick with wounded hurrying to the rear," remarked a company officer, "and the ground was grey with dead and disabled." Closer to the pike, Scales ordered his men to march over Brockenbrough's Virginians, who were "lying down."

The attack plan had no frills. The two brigades were to cross the swale between McPherson's and Seminary Ridges in a rush, without stopping to fire, and close with the enemy, who were expected to be in no better condition than Pettigrew's men. Like many plans this day, this one lasted only until the first soldier stepped forward. Perrin and Scales were supposed to move together, but no sooner had they started than Perrin's Brigade was retarded by a serious enfilade fire from the Yankee cavalry across the Fairfield Road. Lane's Brigade was assigned to handle this problem, but his North Carolina troops were late getting organized, so Perrin was slowed while Scales was not.

Scales' North Carolina battle line at once became the target for every Federal musket and cannon on Seminary Ridge. Charles Wainwright watched approvingly as one of his alert cannoneers obliqued half his battery so as partially to enfilade the Rebel line. "His round shot, together

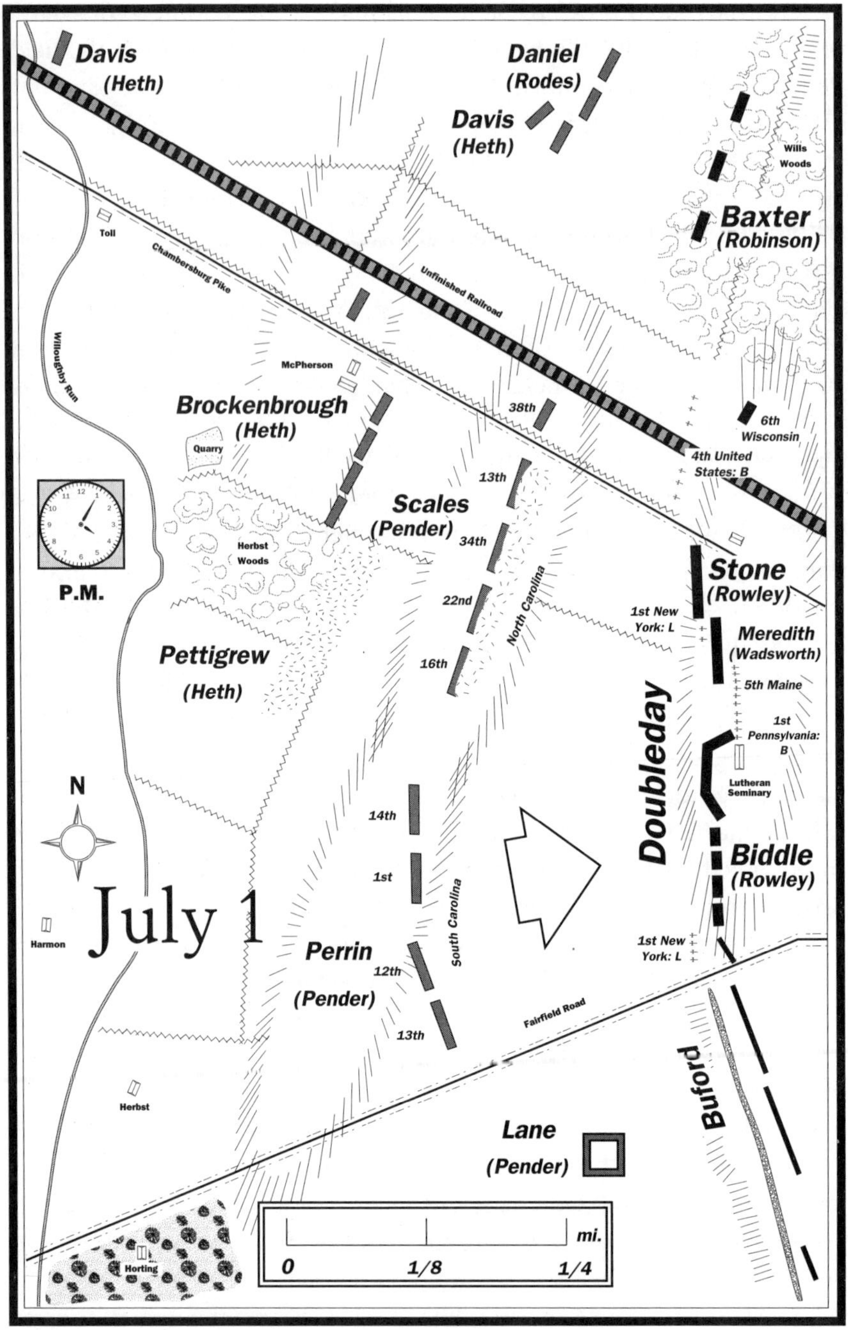
Davis
(Heth)
Daniel
(Rodes)
Davis
(Heth)
Wills
Woods
Baxter
(Robinson)
Toll
Chambersburg Pike
Unfinished Railroad
Willoughby Run
McPherson
Brockenbrough
(Heth)
Quarry
38th
6th
Wisconsin
4th United
States: B
13th
Scales
(Pender)
34th
Herbst
Woods
P.M.
Stone
(Rowley)
22nd
North Carolina
1st New
York: L
Meredith
(Wadsworth)
Pettigrew
(Heth)
16th
5th Maine
1st
Pennsylvania:
B
Doubleday
Lutheran
Seminary
N
14th
1st
Biddle
(Rowley)
South Carolina
July 1
Harmon
Perrin
12th
(Pender)
1st New
York: L
13th
Fairfield Road
Buford
Herbst
Lane
(Pender)
Horting
mi.
0
1/8
1/4

with the canister poured in from all the other guns, was cutting great gaps in the first line of the enemy," noted the colonel. "Never have I seen such a charge. Not a man seemed to falter." For a member of the 38th North Carolina, in contrast, "Every discharge made sad loss in the line." Rufus Dawes and his 6th Wisconsin, supporting three cannon posted just north of the railroad bed, had a good view of the field to their left. "The rebels came half-way down the opposite slope," Dawes recollected, "wavered, began to fire, then to scatter and then to run, and how our men did yell, 'come on Johnny, come on.' " The wall of fire was horrifying in its sudden attrition; Alfred Scales later observed that afterward, "only a squad here and there marked the place where regiments had rested." The adjutant of the 13th North Carolina would report, for example, that his tiny unit had lost 150 out of 180 men in advancing just 125 yards. A survivor of the 34th North Carolina would never forget having to face "this thunderous fire." "They threw shells, grape and canister as thick as hail," recorded another soldier in the regiment.

Although Abner Perrin's troops came forward later than expected, they were no less determined and initially enjoyed no more success than Scales' men. Like the maw of a living thing, the Yankee fire now turned away from the dazed and broken North Carolina regiments to seek out the South Carolinians. "We were met by a furious storm of musketry and shells," Perrin attested. His two left regiments, the 14th and 1st South Carolina, were rudely shoved together by the sheer force of the lead and iron blast that hit them, then, if by some force of physics, they were compressed into an inert mass that stalled before a rail-fence barricade. "We were fired upon from right, left, and centre, and to retreat would have been complete destruction," testified a member of the 14th.

As the two right regiments, the 12th and 13th South Carolina, drew near the ridge, they took hits from their right. The nettlesome Federal cavalrymen on the other side of the Fairfield Road had not been chased away by Lane's troops and were now maintaining a steady carbine fire into the flanks of Perrin's regiments. Perrin desperately ordered the 1st South Carolina to veer around the exposed southern side of the rail barricade, then directed his two rightmost units to oblique right toward the cavalry.

Perrin's men received little useful support from Lane's Brigade, which was supposed to be advancing parallel to them along the southern side of the Fairfield Road. Lane had marched his men across the road just east of Willoughby Run, then turned toward Seminary Ridge, only to become entangled with troopers from Gamble's brigade, in Buford's cavalry division, who were fighting dismounted from behind a stone wall. At the same time, the 8th Illinois Cavalry, by threatening charges against Lane's right flank, succeeded in drawing the 1,700-man force far enough south as to sever any practical connection between it and Perrin's regiments. Witnesses on the Union side attested that some of Lane's regiments were "forming against cavalry" while a few stragglers from the Eleventh Corps reported witnessing Lane's men "forming squares against some of our cavalry." In a private letter written not long after this battle, William Gamble proudly noted that his brigade had "fought the Rebels on the Seminary Ridge and saved a whole division of our infantry from being surrounded and captured—nothing of this . . . is mentioned in newspapers or dispatches." The net result of all of this, in any case, was that Perrin's troops advanced alone.

By chance and courage, Perrin's men struck at the weakest point in the Seminary Ridge line. After outflanking the barricade in front of the seminary, the 1st South Carolina began rolling up the line north of it. Simultaneously, the 12th and 13th South Carolina drove toward the Fairfield Road, shaking loose the few Federal units (cavalry and artillery) that were posted there.

The stubborn determination that had held the First Corps together throughout the bloody trials of this day was finally overcome by fatigue and Rebel opportunism. Abner Doubleday would recall that "the enemy were closing in upon us and crashes of musketry came from my right and left" as he gave the bitter command to all his units to retreat to Cemetery Hill.

The solitary brigade that Oliver Howard had detached from his reserve to delay the enemy advance north of Gettysburg was commanded by Charles R. Coster. It consisted of four regiments, two from New York (the 134th and 154th) and two from Pennsylvania (the 27th and 73rd)—perhaps 1,200 men altogether. Following Howard's orders, Coster's soldiers double-quicked down the Cemetery Hill slope to Baltimore Street, which they took toward the town square. Already the avenue was crowded with wounded and defeated men. Carl Schurz intercepted the relief force as it reached High Street. He sent the 73rd Pennsylvania (290 strong) straight into town to deploy near the railroad station, then led the rest along Stratton Street to Kuhn's brickyard, just north of Stevens Run.

While officers called out orders and the flood of blue-uniformed refugees around them swelled, the three regiments spread into a line of battle with the 27th on the left, the 154th in the middle, and the 134th on the right. The position was far from ideal, as there was high ground both to their left and in their front, the latter feature comprising a tall wheat field ready for harvesting. If the Rebels had become sufficiently disorganized thanks to their success, and if they advanced in loose enough formations, then Coster's small but tight line might turn them back. If, however, the enemy came forward in good order and in strength, the Union brigade would have no chance.

July 1 was proving to be one of Jubal Early's better days. He had been handling his units with a calm dexterity that made the most of his initial advantages of strength and position. Finding John Gordon's brigade winded by its effort at Blocher's Knoll and poorly positioned to confront the fresh Federal line that had suddenly appeared on the town's outskirts, he turned to the brigades of Hays and Avery. These two, he later recounted, "were then ordered forward, and advancing while exposed to a heavy artillery fire of shell and canister, encountered the . . . line and drove it back in great confusion into the town."

A New York soldier in the 154th would never be able to erase the image of the advancing Confederate brigades from his thoughts. "It seemed as though they had a battle flag every few rods," he remembered. In a pattern that had been repeated throughout this desperate afternoon, the Confederate lines overlapped the Federal ones, enabling Rebel units to rush around the Union flanks and shoot into the side and rear of the Yankee regiments. "I never imagined such a rain of bullets," exclaimed the 134th's commander. Both of Coster's flanks were turned, causing each of those regiments to fall back, which left the 154th on its own. A courier sent to coordinate their withdrawal never reached the New Yorkers, who fired another volley before realizing that the enemy had them nearly surrounded. They had no choice but to fight their way to safety, which they did as individuals or in small groups. One corporal later noted that the "few that did get away were the best runners and the most exposed to danger." In the utter confusion of the retreat, the flags of the 134th were saved by a member of the 154th, while a soldier of the 134th recovered the Stars and Stripes belonging to the 154th.

Sergeant Amos Humiston of the 154th, whose thoughts in quieter times were often of his three children, fled the brickyard, ran south along Stratton Street, crossed Stevens Run, and got over the railroad tracks

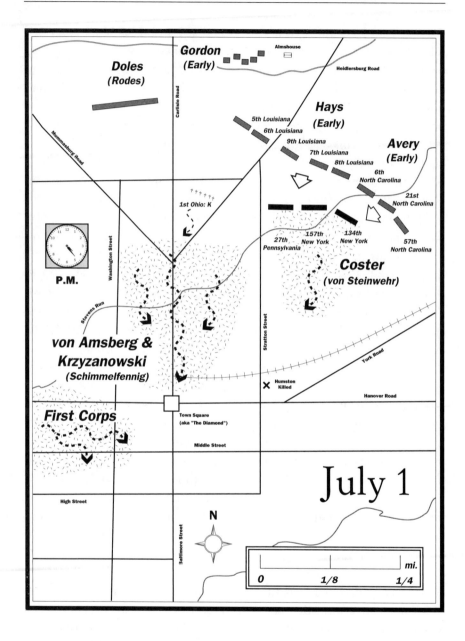

before a Rebel bullet brought him down. The wound was mortal. Humiston dragged an ambrotype from his pocket, a picture of his young ones. It was in his hand when he died, unseen and unnoticed by anyone nearby.

* * *

"Word was sent to the citizens to go to their cellars, as the enemy were driving our men and the fighting would probably be from house to house on our streets," remembered Mary Horner. While the combat never reached that scale, the town's streets were filled with soldiers from both sides, and violent incidents were without number. "Four of our men were carrying a wounded soldier on a stretcher down the street when a [cannon] ball came along and took the legs off the two front men," testified Jennie McCreary. Other shells caused casualties when they struck buildings, and Rebel musketry reaped even more lives. One of Cutler's regimental commanders noted that he "lost 8 or 10 men by falling bricks and infantry fire in the streets." Writing right after the battle, a member of the 2nd Wisconsin recalled that the Rebel shells "made drains & bricks fly around quite promiscuously."

Watching wide-eyed from his cellar window, Henry Jacobs "saw a Union soldier running, his breath coming in gasps, a group of Confederates almost upon him. He was in full flight, not turning or even thinking of resistance. But he was not surrendering, either. 'Shoot him! Shoot him!' yelled a pursuer. A rifle cracked, and the fugitive fell dead at our door." Looking back on the moment, Charles McCurdy, all of ten years old, would declare, "If there is a more thrilling spectacle than an army in frenzied retreat through the narrow streets of a town, I cannot imagine it."

Charles Wainwright never expected to get himself, much less most of the First Corps artillery, safely off Seminary Ridge. To his amazement, he did both. Even in the midst of the deteriorating situation that enveloped him, Wainwright maintained his professional aplomb. His stern orders to his gunners were to limber up and "move at a walk towards the town. I would not allow them to trot for fear of creating a panic among the infantry with which the road was now crowded." That same pride demanded that Wainwright himself be the last artillery officer to leave. "As I sat on the hill watching my pieces file past, and cautioning each one not to trot, there was not a doubt in my mind but that I should go to Richmond [as a prisoner]," he reminisced. Only when the last of his guns were moving off and he saw that the road was clear did Wainwright call out "Trot! Gallop!" and then put the spurs to his horse. Counting heads later, the astonished colonel found that he had lost just one gun. "The more I think of it, the more I wonder that we got off at all," he marveled.

Years after the fighting had ended, both Carl Schurz and Abner Doubleday would resolutely deny that their respective commands had succumbed to widespread panic. "That there were a good many stragglers
hurrying to the rear in a disorderly fashion as is always the case during
and after a hot fight, will not be denied," was Schurz's only concession.
"The First Corps was broken and defeated, but not dismayed," swore
Doubleday. "There were but few left, but they showed the true spirit of
soldiers." (One exemplar was Edward Fowler, commanding the 14th
Brooklyn, who gave the order, " 'Fall back, boys, but do not make a run
of it.' ") Schurz, for his part, proudly maintained that "in whatever shape
the troops issued from the town, they were promptly reorganized, each
was under the colors of his regiment, and in as good a fighting trim as
before, save that their ranks were fearfully thinned by the enormous losses
suffered during the day."

Winfield Scott Hancock reached Cemetery Hill somewhere between 4:00
and 4:30 P.M. He was on horseback, having transferred out of the ambulance after he finished studying all the available area maps. He would later
write that "owing to the peculiar formation of the country, or the direction of the wind at the time," he had not even heard the fighting until he
was a few miles from the town. Hancock had some experience with the
seeming chaos of a battlefield, and his instincts told him that while these
soldiers had been whipped, they were not yet ready to run. What they
needed was a demonstration of pure, physical leadership, something he
was better equipped than most to provide.

As Hancock told it, "I rode directly to the crest of the hill where
General Howard stood, and said to him that I had been sent by General
Meade to take command of all the forces present; that I had written
orders to that effect with me, and asked him if he wished to read them.
He replied that he did not, but acquiesced in my assumption of command." This exchange would become a point of controversy after the
battle, with the prideful Howard insisting that Hancock (below him in
rank) had not taken command from him but merely shared the responsibility. The evidence, from the wording of Meade's orders to Hancock's
careful recollections, does not support Howard's case, though he nevertheless assumed proprietary authority over the units reaching the northern face of Cemetery Hill, as did Doubleday over those (mostly First
Corps) reaching the western side.

Hancock was the right man in the right place at the right time. "I shall never forget the inspiration of his commanding, controlling presence or the fresh courage he imparted, his whole atmosphere strong and invigorating," remembered a Federal on that hill. Displaying "no excitement in voice or manner," observed a fellow officer, the general issued "only cool, concise, and positive directions, given in a steady voice and a conversational tone." Following his brief meeting with Howard, Hancock "at once rode away and bent myself to the pressing task of making such dispositions as would prevent the enemy from seizing that vital point [Cemetery Hill]." The real question was whether or not the triumphant Rebels would allow him time enough to do that.

Richard Ewell had barely begun to taste the heady wine of victory when the cold odds of combat nearly claimed him. He had watched his forces defeat the enemy on Oak Ridge and across the valley north of the town. Eager to be present at the finish, he rode down Oak Hill into the valley, in search of Jubal Early. He had made it as far as the McLean barn when a shell exploded nearby, letting fly a fragment that struck his sorrel mare in the head and caused her to throw her one-legged rider to the ground. Helping hands levered the slightly shaken corps commander onto another horse so he could continue his journey.

Ewell had knowingly ignored Lee's prime directive in initiating his attack against the two Union corps, and he had won big. But now, soberly aware of his transgression, and confronting a tactical situation that was neither as clear nor as obviously advantageous as that obtaining at midday, he could sense his tolerance for risk diminishing by the minute. Riding on, he encountered John Gordon, who was flushed with success and eager to press forward—so eager, in fact, that he did not even acknowledge the injuries and exhaustion suffered by his brigade in the fighting.

As Ewell and Gordon were talking, Edward Johnson's aide Major Henry Kyd Douglas appeared, heralding the imminent arrival of Ewell's only unengaged division. Johnson's men were just a few miles away, Douglas reported, adding that they would be ready for action as soon as they reached the battlefield. But Ewell was suddenly feeling less eager to press matters. " 'Gen. Lee is still at Cashtown, six miles in the rear,' " he told Douglas. " 'He directed me to come to Gettysburg, and I have done so. I do not feel like going further or making an attack without orders from him.' "*

*Lee was actually close at hand, but he had yet to establish communication with Ewell.

*   *   *

The Federals' retreat through Gettysburg was a kaleidoscopic blur of memories for all the soldiers involved. One of Ramseur's North Carolina soldiers recalled the clearing of Oak Ridge this way: "We had them fairly in a pen, with only one gap open—the turnpike that led into Gettysburg—and hither they fled twenty deep, we all the while popping into them as fast as we could load and fire." When Stephen Ramseur saw the crowd of Yankees on the Chambersburg Pike, he briefly lost his self-control. " 'Damn it! tell them to send me a battery! I have sent for one a half dozen times!' " he shouted. Then, catching himself, he raised his hand toward Heaven. " 'God almighty,' " he prayed, " 'forgive me for that oath.' "

Abner Perrin led a detail from the 1st South Carolina into town, in pursuit of the Federals fleeing Seminary Ridge. "Now when our line was reformed it was long enough to reach across the street with two or three files of men turned at one end," recalled a sergeant with the group. "At the command forward by Col. Perrin, we marched on up the street. . . . As we passed the cross streets there were great numbers of Federal troops on right and left but [they] had no arms . . . , and why we were not all captured has been a mystery to me."

Rufus Dawes still commanded the 6th Wisconsin, though it was now just a fragment of the regiment that had charged into the railroad cut. His men maintained a loose formation as they hustled east along the pike before making the turn south along Washington Street. "The first cross street was swept by the musketry fire of the enemy," Dawes would recollect. Glancing across the way, he saw a barnyard fence that had a couple of boards loose, making it possible for one man to slip through at a time. The lieutenant colonel grabbed one of his regiment's flags, dodged across the street, and positioned himself just inside the fence hole. "Officers and men followed rapidly," he noted. Dawes held his place by the opening, so that "when any man obstructed the passage-way through it, I jerked him away without ceremony or apology. . . . Two men were shot in this street crossing. The regiment was reformed in the barn-yard, and I marched back again to the street leading . . . to the Cemetery Hill."

After watching Pender's men drive Doubleday's off Seminary Ridge, and Rodes' perform a like service on Oak Ridge, Robert E. Lee rode toward the town. According to his aide, Charles Marshall, Lee "established his headquarters near where the Chambersburg pike crosses the ridge . . . , and from that position he observed the retreat of the enemy through Gettysburg before General Ewell's advance."

Lee's ride from Herr's Ridge to Seminary Ridge was a sobering experience. The dead and wounded of Pettigrew's Brigade filled the McPherson farm area, while Scales' North Carolina men lay in orderly rows where Wainwright's canister had found them. A. P. Hill was unfazed by the sight; he could see only the prospect of an even more complete victory as compensation for the heavy losses Heth's Division had suffered. But where Hill believed that "the rout of the enemy was complete," Lee's more analytical scrutiny revealed that many of the Federal units were maintaining some order as they fell back.

Lee had reluctantly allowed himself to be drawn into the fray only when it seemed that the advantage secured by Ewell's arrival would be lost if the enemy were free to maneuver against him. It had cost much to force the enemy corps off McPherson's Ridge—so much, Lee felt, that Hill's men now had no more fight left in them. But the job was not finished: Lee could see that the Federals were organizing a defense on high ground just south of the town. He summoned his staff officer Walter Taylor and directed him "to go to General Ewell and to say to him that, from the position which he occupied, he could see the enemy retreating over those hills . . . , that it was only necessary to press 'those people' in order to secure possession of the heights, and that, if possible, he wished him to do this."

Taylor rode off. Less than three miles west of Lee's position was a 7,000-man striking force of fresh troops, in camp on his orders. Major General Richard H. Anderson had marched his division forward from Cashtown, reaching Knoxlyn Ridge just after 4:00 P.M. According to Anderson's later recollection, as told to one of Heth's staff officers, he "was met by a messenger from General Lee with an order for him to halt and bivouac his brigade." After passing the word along to his subordinates, the puzzled division commander rode across the next two ridges to confirm that order, reaching Lee not long after Walter Taylor left with the message for Ewell. Lee told Anderson that there had been no mistake, "that he was in ignorance as to the force of the enemy in front, . . . and that a reserve in case of disaster, was necessary."

*   *   *

The first impression of many of those who managed to reach Cemetery Hill was chaos. "Panic was impending over the exhausted soldiers," remembered Rufus Dawes. "It was a confused rabble of disorganized regiments of infantry and crippled batteries." "Many of the troops . . . thought that it was an utter defeat of our forces, and they made an effort to get as far away from the enemy as possible," recollected a rather tactful Ohio man. Not every officer rose to the occasion. Third Division (First Corps) commander Thomas Rowley, for one, appeared so far out of control that he was arrested and later court-martialed for his erratic behavior this day. "Many brave, strong men of the regiment sobbed like children," recalled a member of the 94th New York, "thinking of the seemingly utter wreck of our noble corps."

If not every house in Gettysburg was harboring wounded men, a good many were. The stone barn on the McPherson farm was filled with First Corps casualties, including Roy Stone. On Seminary Ridge, the house of C. P. Krauth "was used for Hospital purposes . . . [the] first floor filled with wounded; the surgeon and wounded officers upstairs." At the Trinity German Reformed Church, just north of the square, one resident swore that the "wounded were carried into the lecture room . . . and there was so much amputating done there that the seats were covered with blood and they had to bore holes in the floor to let the blood run away."

There were as many battle stories this day as there were soldiers in the field. Crusty old John Burns, who had made his stand with the Iron Brigade in the Herbst Woods, had suffered three wounds before being left behind in the retreat; he would spend this night lying in a field, and find help the next morning at the Henry Dustman farm, not far from Lee's headquarters tent. Brigadier General Alexander Schimmelfennig had his own close call when he took a wrong turn into a dead-end alley, with Confederates hot behind him. His horse shot, the Third Division (Eleventh Corps) commander scrambled over a board fence and then hid in a covered drainage ditch, where he hoped to hide until dark.

The surgeon from John Robinson's command (Second Division, First Corps) had selected the Christ Lutheran Church on Chambersburg Street to serve as the divisional hospital. As Rebel riflemen were closing on the place, a Federal officer came out onto the church steps and seemingly ignored signals to surrender. One quick shot felled the officer, who proved to be Chaplain Horatio S. Howell of the 90th Pennsylvania, a tragic victim of misunderstanding and confusion.*

Prominent among the wounded left behind by the retreating Eleventh Corps was Francis Barlow, who had lain helpless in the fields north of town until sympathetic Confederate officers carried him to a field hospital.[†] There surgeons unsuccessfully probed his wound and then solemnly informed the young Yankee general that the bullet was imbedded in his pelvic cavity, and inoperable. Told to prepare himself for death, the fiercely ambitious Barlow was equally determined that he would not die.

Even as he struggled to stay alive, however, Barlow was racked by worry for the safety of his wife, who had traveled with the division to Gettysburg and had been waiting for him on Cemetery Hill. He finally persuaded a Rebel soldier to go looking for her, but the man returned empty-handed: he had roamed the streets asking, but no one had ever heard of Arabella Barlow.

Winfield Scott Hancock decided that the position chosen by Oliver Otis Howard on Cemetery Hill would be held, at least until nightfall. "Orders were at once given to establish a line of battle on Cemetery Hill," he later reported, "with skirmishers occupying that part of the town immediately in our front." The Eleventh Corps units were consolidated to cover that portion of the hill overlooking the southern edge of Gettysburg "and commanding the Emmitsburg and Taneytown roads and the Baltimore turnpike." Hancock then turned his attention to the First Corps, sending "General Wadsworth to the right to take possession of Culp's Hill with his division." Next, the "rest of the First Corps, under Major-General Doubleday, was [set] on the right and left of the Taneytown road, and connected with the left of the Eleventh Corps."

In forming the lines, Hancock "received material assistance from Major-General Howard, Brigadier Generals [Gouverneur K.] Warren and [John] Buford, and officers of General Howard's command." Although

---

*Unlike most chaplains, Howell followed army regulations to the letter, even going so far as to wear a straight dress sword, which likely contributed to the Confederates' failure to identify him as a noncombatant.
[†]One of those aiding Barlow *may* have been John B. Gordon. Long after the events of this day, Gordon would make a claim to that effect in print and public lectures. Unfortunately, his account remains the only source for this anecdote of the battle.

he usually respected formalities regarding the chain of command, Hancock had no such qualms on this occasion. "I made such disposition as I thought wise and proper," he later testified. Nor did he forget George Meade, starving for information at Taneytown: he dispatched a trusted aide to inform the army commander "of the state of affairs, and to say that I would hold the position until night." Not one for false modesty, he would always insist, "After I had arrived upon the field, assumed the command, and made my dispositions for defending that point . . . , I do not think the Confederate force then present could have carried it."

(5:45 P.M.–Midnight)

Richard Ewell, still shaky from the fall off his stricken horse, made his way into Gettysburg, likely following Carlisle Road. Hardly had one courier met him with word that Robert E. Lee was nearby, on Seminary Hill, when Walter Taylor found him and conveyed Lee's desire that he press on up Cemetery Hill. It was a good antidote to the Second Corps commander's anxiety over disregarding his superior's prime directive. Taylor saw the concern on Ewell's face turn to determination; he left convinced that Lee's suggestion would soon become action.

Ewell did want to act on Lee's advice, but not until he had heard from the two of his division commanders who had fought well this day, Robert Rodes and Jubal Early. Ewell set himself up at the center diamond, and sent riders looking for his subordinates. A staff officer with him recalled that the "square was filled with Confederate soldiers, and with them were mingled many prisoners, while scarcely a citizen was to be seen." The corps chief passed the time "receiving reports from all his command, giving directions as to the disposition of his troops, directing supplies of ammunition and making disposition of a large number of prisoners that had fallen into our hands." (Among this number was Henry A. Morrow of the 24th Michigan, who bristled when Ewell lectured him about his having kept his unit in action even after the situation became hopeless. " 'Genl Ewell, the 24th Mich. came here to fight, not surrender,' " the proud officer declared.)

At length Rodes and Early joined Ewell. "They desired General Lee to be informed that they could go forward and take Cemetery hill if they were supported on their right; that to the south of the Cemetery there was in sight a position commanding it which should be taken at once," recalled Ewell's aide Captain James Power Smith, who was promptly detailed to deliver that message. Not wishing to sit idle waiting for Lee's reply, the three officers rode south along Baltimore Street in hopes of ascertaining just how much of a problem Cemetery Hill might pose.

Despite the efforts of Yankee sharpshooters who soon drove them to seek cover, they learned a thing or two about the position—enough, that is, to convince them that it would not be a simple matter of walking up the hill to claim it.

Ewell had paid a price for his victory. Rodes' Division was battered, scattered, and not at all ready to undertake another serious offensive operation. Early's troops were less combat-worn, but their occupation of Gettysburg had so disorganized them that it would take some time to get them back under full control. Still, Ewell acknowledged that there was a chance here to finish this day's work—if only he could push the Yankees off that hill.

James Longstreet had ridden well ahead of his corps, which was just then moving through the Cashtown Pass. He put the time at a little after 5:00 P.M. when he reached Lee's headquarters, near the Chambersburg Pike on Seminary Ridge. There was a martial racket drumming in the town as the last organized Federal units elbowed their way south. Lee was busy when Longstreet arrived, so the First Corps commander took the opportunity to examine the situation, especially on Cemetery Hill. Lee was also interested in that point. He called up his staff officer Colonel Armistead L. Long and, as Long remembered it, "directed me to reconnoitre the position to which the enemy had retired."

To Longstreet's way of thinking, a frontal assault on an entrenched position was a tactic always best avoided. When Lee joined him he therefore suggested straight off that the Confederate forces disengage in order to "file around [the enemy's] left and secure good ground between here and his capital." Lee was surprised by Longstreet's proposal, particularly since he knew that his First Corps commander had not been briefed of the overall situation. " 'If the enemy is there tomorrow,' " Lee answered, pointing toward Cemetery Hill, " 'we must attack him.' " All of Longstreet's concerns about the current campaign now welled up in a rare burst of insubordinate testiness. " 'If he is there, it will be because he is anxious that we should attack him,' " Longstreet said, " 'a good reason, in my judgment[,] for not doing so.' " He himself could have pointed in another direction—at the orderly rows of bodies in a field just a few hundred yards away—to provide proof of the price paid for any direct effort. Reflecting back upon this moment, Longstreet would feel certain that "General Lee was impressed with the idea that, by attacking the Federals, he could whip them in detail,"

Ewell's aide James Power Smith found Lee and Longstreet together, still in discussion, and delivered his message. Lee passed the young officer his binoculars, pointing once again as he did so to Cemetery Hill, and said that he supposed that was the high ground that Ewell was referring to in his communication. Lee told Smith that "he had no force on the field with which to take that position," and then asked Longstreet how near his closest division was. Longstreet replied that it was six miles away—and even then "was indefinite and noncommittal," Smith observed. After Lee reiterated his desire that Ewell "take the Cemetery Hill if it were possible," the aide immediately set off on the return circuit to his corps commander.

Longstreet took Lee's reaction as a complete rejection of his idea. "The sharp battle fought by Hill and Ewell on that day had given him a taste of victory," he would reflect afterward. It was a brooding, doubting First Corps commander who rode back to his troops sometime after 5:30 P.M. "I believed that he had made up his mind to attack," Longstreet later stated, "but was confident that he had not yet determined as to when the attack should be made."

In fact, despite any impression he may have given to the contrary, Lee was *not* absolutely committed to continuing the offensive here. It would take more than Longstreet's scheme, however, to deflect him from that course. There would be great risk indeed involved in pulling Ewell's Corps back from Gettysburg during the night, as Longstreet advocated, and to try to do it in daylight would be to invite the enemy's revenge. Arguing against an advance, though, was the report delivered by the reconnoitering Armistead L. Long, who testified that Cemetery Hill was "occupied by a considerable force, . . . and . . . an attack at that time . . . would have been hazardous." Then Walter Taylor returned from his errand. He had conveyed Lee's suggestion regarding Cemetery Hill to Ewell, he said, and felt certain that the Second Corps commander would act on it. Lee now realized that a great deal was riding on conditions about which he knew very little. He called for his horse. He would ride over and speak with Ewell himself.

When kept apart, the separate elements of the Union retreat and the Confederate pursuit through Gettysburg were by and large inert, but mixed together they were volatile. Huddled with her family in the cellar of their house, Salome Myers recollected how they all "knelt shivering and prayed. The noise above our heads, the rattling of muskets, the unearthly cries mingled with the sobbing of children, shook our hearts." Daniel Skelly watched as a wounded Federal lieutenant was cornered by Confederates who still had the blood lust. His amazement at what happened next would stay with him for the rest of his life: "My mother intervened," he remembered, "offering to dress his wound first. The Confederates agreed and never came back for him. We hid him from capture the whole time." Watching similar scenes from her family's cellar, Liberty Hollinger reflected, "we were really in the midst of an awful reality."

Inspired by solid leaders such as Captain Francis Irsch, the 375-strong 45th New York had opened the fighting north of Gettysburg and held its own throughout the collapse of the Eleventh Corps. Only after it joined the retreating procession through the town did disaster strike the regiment, as nearly two thirds of the men were cut off near the Eagle Hotel. These soldiers, joined by stragglers from other commands, forted themselves in a row of houses, from the relative safety of which, wrote a member of the 45th, "several attempts of the enemy to dislodge us were repelled successfully."

The intrepid band held out until nearly sundown, when the offer of a parley was accepted by Irsch. During these negotiations, he observed that Confederate forces completely controlled the town. According to a regimental history, "Upon returning and reporting what he saw, Captain Irsch, with other officers, ordered their men to destroy their arms and ammunition and throw them into the wells, and then all formally surrendered."*

The closer he got to Gettysburg, the unhappier Henry Slocum became. The Union Twelfth Corps commander, as one of the most senior officers in Meade's army, could expect to assume control of all units on hand when he reached the battlefield. It was not a prospect he relished. With Meade's Pipe Creek circular by now old news, Slocum was heading into an unknown situation filled with ominous portents. Shortly after his column got under way, an orderly had come forward from Two Taverns carrying a note from Meade informing him of John Reynolds' death.

*For his leadership this day, Francis Irsch would receive a Medal of Honor.

Although he had not been instructed to do anything more than manage his own corps, Slocum had turned over temporary control of the Twelfth to his senior division commander, Brigadier General Alpheus Williams. He would never explain this curious action, but it seems likely that he anticipated being put in command of the right wing of Meade's forces.

Something of Slocum's state of mind may be gleaned from his response to a message delivered by one of Oliver Howard's aides, who had been dispatched to meet the general on the road and request that he ride forward to Gettysburg to take charge. " 'I'll be damned if I will take the responsibility of this fight,' " Slocum snapped in reply. Soon after this encounter, Slocum sent Meade a gloomy progress report: "A portion of our troops have fallen back to Gettysburg. Matters do not appear very well." Nevertheless, he directed his two divisions to continue toward the town. Again inexplicably, he instructed Alpheus Williams to march his division north from the Baltimore Pike just prior to crossing Rock Creek, on a route that would ultimately take it toward Gettysburg from the east, via the Hanover Road.

Williams would later relate that his men (some 5,000 or so) "turned off to the right on a narrow, winding path or country road, and after a couple of miles reached a dense wood, behind which was a high, bald hill on which a good position could be had in sight and rear of the town." The elevation in question was Benner's Hill, smack on the flank of those portions of Ewell's Corps that were then in Gettysburg. While Federal scouts reported that Rebels were holding the hill, a personal reconnaissance by Williams revealed some mounted personnel but no infantry. He made plans to storm the rise, but the action was aborted when a courier arrived with orders from Slocum, directing him to pull back and join the rest of the Union army on Cemetery Hill. The time was approaching 7:00 P.M.

Williams' advent provided welcome reinforcement for Hancock, who was still setting his defenses when this first Twelfth Corps division arrived. By his own account, Hancock placed Williams and his men "some distance to the right and rear of Wadsworth's division." The other Twelfth Corps division, under Brigadier General John W. Geary, came up from Two Taverns not long after. Although Hancock did not have direct control of this unit, he advised its commander "to take possession of the high ground" to the south, and thereby obtained some security for the left flank.

*   *   *

The message that James Power Smith brought back from Lee was unhelpful. Anything that happened on Cemetery Hill, Ewell saw, would have to
be his doing alone, as A. P. Hill could provide no assistance from the western side. Robert E. Lee, quoted Smith, "regretted that his people were not
up to support him on the right, but he wished him to take Cemetery Hill
if it were possible." The clear subtext was that he should do it *if* it could be
done without a significant fight. The defenses that Ewell had personally
observed already on the hill made such a scenario unlikely.

There might, however, be another way to gain some ground without
bringing on more serious fighting. Lying adjacent to Cemetery Hill on
an easterly tack was another rise, known as Culp's Hill. The Federals
appeared not to have covered that point, which also overlooked the Baltimore Pike. Ewell now decided to concentrate on taking *that* hill, using
his one unengaged division, Johnson's, which was expected at Gettysburg
momentarily. This decision did not suit Isaac Trimble, the unwelcome
supernumerary whom Lee had appended to Ewell's headquarters. After
loudly insinuating that Ewell lacked the nerve to assault Cemetery Hill,
Trimble stalked off.*

Ewell's caution was justified when a report arrived from one of Jubal
Early's brigade commanders. Brigadier General William "Extra Billy"
Smith's Virginia brigade had not participated in the fighting north of
Gettysburg but had instead been detailed to guard the flank and rear of
Early's deployment. By Early's recollection, the gist of Smith's sighting
report was that "the enemy was advancing a large force of infantry,
artillery, and cavalry on the York Road, menacing our left flank and rear."
Although he would later profess not to have put much stock in Smith's
credibility, Early nonetheless "thought it best to send General Gordon
with his brigade out on that road, to take command of both brigades, and
to stop all further alarms from that direction."

Ewell had to be sure, so he and Jubal Early followed Gordon's men
to a vantage point. He spotted some skirmishers in the distance; on further investigation, they proved to be Smith's Virginians, but the threat
was potentially so ruinous that Ewell thought it better to leave Gordon
out on the road. The reconnaissance had also brought him closer to
Culp's Hill, so he took advantage of the moment and detailed two staff

*Trimble would get his revenge through a series of postwar retellings of this incident,
with each iteration making Ewell sound more hesitant and indecisive than the one
before.

officers to scout the position while he returned to town to see Edward Johnson. When they met, his long-absent division commander informed Ewell that while his troops were no more than a mile away, they were stuck in a traffic jam with a wagon train that would take the better part of an hour to untangle.

Ewell turned to Jubal Early, whose troops were nearest to Culp's Hill, and wondered aloud if they could not make an effort to secure the place right away. Early replied testily that "his command had been doing all the hard marching and fighting and was not in condition to make the move." Johnson took this as a personal insult, and the two officers engaged in a sharp exchange that Ewell finally had to cut off. He would wait for Johnson's men to arrive.

Soldiers on both sides faced the setting sun with a wide range of emotions. Some were frustrated. "Why we failed to push on and occupy the heights around and beyond Gettysburg is one of the unsettled questions," griped a private in Archer's Brigade. "Our army expected to do so and were disappointed when we did not." Many were exhausted. "Tired soldiers mopped from their sweaty mouths the black powder smudge of bitter cartridges," wrote a soldier in the 43rd North Carolina. A musician-turned-medical-assistant in the 26th North Carolina recalled that "as our wounded men came in, we helped the surgeons with them until 11 o'clock at night, when I was so thoroly tired I could do no more, and lay down for a little rest." "We laid all night among the dead Yankees," noted a soldier camped along McPherson's Ridge, "but they did not disturb our peaceful slumbers."

Others were in shock. The 24th Michigan counted 102 present out of the nearly 500 who had marched this morning. "A sorrowful band, indeed, that night!" remembered one survivor. "Company officers called loudly for their men to fall in, not yet realizing that all but a few had fallen out forever," another declared.

There was a good deal of clean-up to be done. One such assignment went to the South Carolina troops who had broken Doubleday's line on Seminary Ridge. "Volunteers were called for, to go through Gettysburg and secure such of the enemy as might be lurking there," recorded an officer. "But so many offered themselves that details had finally to be made. . . . A goodly number of prisoners were brought in." "I think we dragged as many as 500 from the cellars," a Virginia officer boasted.

A different kind of tidying-up was going on across the fields west of the town, where Mississippi surgeon LeGrand Wilson presided over one of the details charged with burying the dead. "This forced me to go all over that horrid field," he recollected. "The poor, wounded Federals were crying piteously for water in every direction. . . . This was my first experience on the battlefield after the fighting, and it was horrible beyond description."

Confederate forces held all the areas that had witnessed fighting this day. As troops were pulled back in the evening to refit, they passed through the scenes of earlier combat. "Then it was we saw the sickening horrors of war," a lieutenant in Pettigrew's Brigade wrote. "A great many of our wounded had not yet been carried to the hospital. The enemy's dead . . . lay with their wounded—crying piteously for water. . . . Our dead were laying where they had fallen, but the 'Battlefield Robbers' had been there plundering the 'dead.' They seem to have respected neither the enemy's nor our own dead." Mulling over all he had seen this day, Rufus Dawes thought, "It is a troubled and dreamy sleep at best that comes to the soldier on the battlefield."

Sleep was the last thing on Arabella Barlow's mind. Francis Barlow's wife had been in town when her husband's troops, the Eleventh Corps' First Division, retreated through to Cemetery Hill. She had been swept along with the wave, searching all the while for her husband. Finally she had encountered an aide to one of Barlow's brigadiers, who told her that the commander lay " 'wounded outside of Gettysburg.' " The resourceful Arabella found an ambulance driver who was willing to take risks, and then, remembered an aide, "sitting next to the driver with a white flag in her hand, [she] drove quickly towards the town, although we could still hear firing."

July 1 proved to be a never-to-be-forgotten day for the English observer with Lee's army, Arthur Fremantle. He began and ended it appended to Longstreet's headquarters, and in between spent the entire morning on the western side of the Cashtown Pass waiting for the traffic to clear. It was well into the afternoon before Fremantle managed to get through the cut and close to Gettysburg. His introduction to the fighting came when he overtook a column of wounded men seeking aid. "This spectacle, so revolting to a person unaccustomed to such sights," he remarked, "produced no impression whatever upon the advancing troops, who certainly go under fire with the most perfect nonchalance."

Before coming into sight of Gettysburg, Fremantle also passed gangs of Union prisoners. He located A. P. Hill's field headquarters and was able to speak for a short while with·Lee's Third Corps commander, who confessed that "he had been very unwell all day." Hill reported the success won by two of his divisions but added without prompting "that the Yankees had fought with a determination unusual to them."

Dinner at Longstreet's headquarters was served after sundown. The resourceful Englishman found himself a place near the head of the table so he could converse with the man in charge of the First Corps. "General Longstreet spoke of the enemy's position as being 'very formidable,' " Fremantle quoted, appending Longstreet's cautionary note that the Federals "would doubtless intrench themselves strongly during the night."

Responding to a comment made by his medical director, Longstreet insisted that it would require the "whole army" to take Cemetery Hill, and even "then at a great sacrifice." Despite these forebodings at the top, the mood among the headquarters staff was upbeat. From these officers Fremantle learned that "the universal feeling in the army was one of profound contempt for an enemy whom they have beaten so constantly, and under so many disadvantages."

Richard Ewell could not get that hill out of his mind. Johnson's Division had finally navigated through the jammed roads and reached the body-strewn fields north of Gettysburg just before sunset. Meeting with all three of his division commanders, Ewell shared the report he had received from his two staff scouts, who had found Culp's Hill apparently unoccupied. He asked for opinions. Robert Rodes saw no urgent need to secure the position. Jubal Early, while adamant that *his* men could not be involved, nonetheless thought it vital that *somebody* be sent to claim the place. "If you do not go up there tonight, it will cost you 10,000 lives to get up there tomorrow," he warned. That was enough for Ewell, who instructed Johnson to take position on the eastern side of town and occupy Culp's Hill.

Members of the First and Eleventh Corps who had felt disappointed earlier this day about missing the action began to realize tonight, on reaching their commands, just how lucky they had been. The 41st New York came in past 10:00 P.M., after a day spent guarding wagons near Emmitsburg, to find that about half their brigade had been lost. Also arriving at Cemetery Hill before daybreak were the two hundred men detached from Coster's brigade. The fifty from the 154th New York were told, as one of them later recorded, "that our regiment had been engaged and that every man had been killed, wounded or taken prisoner."

Colonel Ira Grover had risked his military career by marching his regiment, the 7th Indiana, to Gettysburg. Part of Cutler's brigade, the unit had been left behind near Moritz Tavern with orders to guard the First Corps wagon train until such time as it was relieved. Through messages shouted by passing couriers, Grover had kept tabs on the fighting to the north until it became clear that his corps was being hard pressed. At that point he ignored his instructions and led his men up to the battle without being relieved.*

Traveling on the Baltimore Pike, the 434 Hoosiers reached Cemetery Hill not long after Hancock began organizing the defenses. Besides the dispiriting sight of a defeated army regrouping, the Indiana men encountered their division commander, James Wadsworth, who was in a mild state of shock over the mauling of his command. When Lysander Cutler greeted the new arrivals with the comment " 'If the Seventh had been with us we could have held our position,' " Wadsworth snapped back, " 'Yes, and all would now be dead or prisoners.' "

When Hancock gave Wadsworth the job of securing Culp's Hill, the weary general first sent in the Iron Brigade, which took up a painfully short line on the hill's western slope. The 6th Wisconsin was sent over last, taking station on the right of the brigade, nearest the crest. The much-diminished Western unit did not have the manpower to cover the hilltop, so Wadsworth tagged the fresh 7th Indiana for the task.

Ira Grover marched his men over to the hill in the gathering darkness, sent them filing in to the right of the 6th Wisconsin, and spread them out as far as he dared. The bulk of the regiment faced north, with a picket line covering the portion of the hill crest that dipped toward the east. It was far from a perfect deployment, but it was the best Grover could manage under the circumstances.

---

*Grover would later be court-martialed for this dereliction of duty, but the military tribunal would completely exonerate him.

* * *

In both capitals the information received today was of an encouraging nature. Confederate War Department clerk John Beauchamp Jones noted in his diary that the "intelligence of the capture of Harrisburg and York, Pa., is so far confirmed." At the same time, Abraham Lincoln's navy secretary, Gideon Welles, was recording in his own diary the receipt of reports "that the Rebels have fallen back from York." He was not sanguine that the marauding Confederates could be brought to bay, though he closed his entry with the words "We have rumors of hard fighting to-day."

Robert E. Lee met Richard Ewell at the Second Corps headquarters, located in a small house near the Carlisle Road. It was the first time the two had spoken since June 9. If Ewell feared that Lee had come to chastise him for fighting this day, he was soon relieved on that point. Lee was interested in just two things: the fighting condition of the Second Corps and the prospects of its renewing the attack in the morning. Only Generals Rodes and Early were present with Ewell, Edward Johnson then being occupied with getting his division aligned near Culp's Hill. While both of Ewell's subordinates were positive about their readiness, neither felt that the terrain the Confederates were facing was suitable for offensive operations.

Lee's disappointment was evident to Jubal Early, who could see that he was serious about attacking "the enemy as early as possible the next day." Was the area assigned to Johnson's Division a possibility? Lee asked. Early shook his head. In addition to his observation this day, he had surveyed the area when he passed through on June 26. He explained that the "ground over which we would have to advance on our flank was very rugged and steep," adding that since the town's narrow streets made it difficult to stage troops for an assault, any attacking force would have to "go on the left of the town right up against Cemetery Hill and the rugged hills on the left of it." Even if such an action were to succeed, Early concluded, it would "be at a very great loss."

Now that Early had managed to exempt his division from the mission handed to Johnson, he turned his attention to the entire Second Corps. He gestured toward the area south of Cemetery Hill, where high ground could be seen—ground that he argued "must evidently command the enemy's position and render it untenable." Ewell and Robert Rodes strongly endorsed this line of thinking.

" 'Then perhaps I had better draw you around toward my right, as the line will be very long and thin if you remain here, and the enemy may come down and break through it?' " Lee asked. Again Early begged to differ with his commander. Pulling the men back now, he argued, after they had fought so hard to take the town, would put a "damper . . . [on] their enthusiasm." There was also the question of moving the wounded, which was no quick process. Early "did not like the idea of leaving those brave fellows to the mercy of the enemy." Again Ewell and Rodes seconded him.

Frustrated though Lee may have been with this discussion, it likely never entered his mind to issue peremptory orders for Ewell to either attack or withdraw. The notion of imposing his will on a subordinate was simply too alien to Lee's nature for him even to admit as a possibility. Yet the situation would have been enough to tax the patience of Job. Hill's Corps had taken stiff casualties this day and was in no condition to carry the lead role in renewing the attack, and Ewell and his division commanders had firmly opted themselves out of playing a principal part. That left Longstreet, who had already crossed a tacit line into disrespectful behavior with his insubordinate outburst today. Thus burdened with a collection of poor options, Lee returned to his headquarters.

There was something decidedly funereal about the scene. In the near distance a horse battery was banging away in an irregular but steady cadence that suggested the firing of a minute gun, and the air was tanged with the incense of burned wood. Had he not been so overpoweringly tired, Jeb Stuart might well have registered how appropriate it all seemed, for his hopes of a triumphal and successful completion of his mission were as ashes in the dust.

The stop in Dover had accomplished little in the way of resting his troopers. An officer in the column later recollected that "the men were overcome and so tired and stupid as almost to be ignorant of what was taking place around them." It did not help that their route from Dover to Carlisle took them across the northernmost spur of the South Mountains, requiring extra exertion from the already exhausted men and animals. Then, to round off this thoroughly wretched day, Stuart's leading elements under Fitzhugh Lee reached Carlisle to find that not only had they missed contacting Ewell's column by a matter of hours, but the town itself was now occupied by Yankee militia who gave no signs of abandoning it.

Since it was only militia, after all, and lacking any better ideas, Stuart allowed Fitzhugh Lee permission to frighten the garrison into submission. Nimbly bypassing a mounted picket posted east of the town, Lee used his six-gun battery for a slow bombardment on Carlisle, punctuated by several parleys during which he offered the enemy commander his choice between an honorable surrender and total destruction. To everyone's surprise, the Federal officer (a regular army man with something to prove) refused to give up, so the desultory cannonade persisted, starting some small fires and knocking away pieces of a few buildings.

Stuart stubbornly and dully let the purposeless drama continue. According to one observer on the scene, "The men were falling asleep around the guns, and the present writer slept very soundly within ten feet of a battery hotly firing. . . . The best example, however, was the one which General Stuart mentioned. He saw a man climb a fence, put one leg over, and in that position drop asleep!" As midnight approached, a thoroughly irritated Fitzhugh Lee sent men forward to torch the Carlisle barracks and other town property. At least one Rebel trooper was alert enough to marvel at the way the firelight from the burning barracks "fell magnificently upon the spires of the city, presenting an exquisite spectacle."

The first news reports of the Gettysburg fighting left Taneytown for Frederick right around sunset. One bore the byline "Agate," the nom de plume of Whitelaw Reid; the second was penned by Lorenzo L. Crounse, covering the war for the *New York Times*. Reid got his story almost entirely from Crounse, who on his own meanderings in search of the army had crossed paths with several couriers, a bit of serendipity that enabled him to piece together a broadly accurate picture of what was happening at a place called Gettysburg.

Crounse's first brief dispatch to the *Times* reported a "heavy engagement" just outside the town, involving two Rebel and two Federal corps. Because his information string had run out by early afternoon, though, his scoop on John Reynolds' death was accompanied by the claim that the First and Eleventh Corps were "successfully" resisting all attacks against them.

Reid wrote up his own report, opportunistically incorporating Crounse's intelligence (while taking care to acknowledge his companion's role in obtaining the information), and the two entrusted their stories to a rider bound for the telegraph hub at Frederick. Then the newspaper-

men rode toward the fighting. They made their way past columns pressing northward, all the while hastily interrogating anyone who seemed to
be coming from the scene of the action. The Federals were either enjoying great success or on the brink of ruin, depending upon the source.

Hoping to make better time, they angled off the packed Taneytown
Road and traveled across country for a while before intersecting with the
Baltimore Pike, which led them into Two Taverns. There they learned
that a Union corps headquartered in the hamlet had moved toward Gettysburg some hours earlier. "That didn't look like a serious disaster," Reid
concluded. Other snatches of information made it clear that armies of
both sides were concentrating near Gettysburg, leading Reid to observe
that July 2 "must bring the battle that is to decide the invasion."

It would do the reporters no good to reach the action in a state of
exhaustion, so they prevailed on one of the two tavern keepers to put
them up for a few hours. The pair planned to reach Gettysburg by sunrise. "If the situation is as we hope, our army must attack by daybreak,"
Reid declared.

It was the waiting that was hardest on George Meade. He had accomplished nothing important since sending Hancock off to Gettysburg,
other than tracking the obviously worsening situation through the messages and testimony of the couriers arriving from the various commands.
At perhaps 4:45 P.M., cavalry commander Alfred Pleasonton brought
Meade a dispatch sent by John Buford about an hour earlier. After
reporting the presence of two Confederate corps pressing from the north
and west, Buford rated the morning's fighting as a "tremendous battle."
Moreover, "In my opinion," Buford declared (casting aspersions on both
Howard and Doubleday), "there seems to be no directing person " His
terse postscript spoke volumes: "We need help now."

Meade did everything he could within the limits of prudence and caution, because until he heard from Hancock, he was not going to commit
himself fully. Orders were sent to the other corps commanders, instructing
them to be prepared to march on short notice. Shortly before 6:00 P.M.,
Hancock's aide arrived and reported that the army at Gettysburg could
maintain itself until dark. Meade knew from the message traffic that the
First and Eleventh Corps were soon to be joined by the Twelfth, which
was likely just reaching the town, and later by the Third and Fifth Corps,
now on their way there. "It seems to me," Meade declared in a dispatch

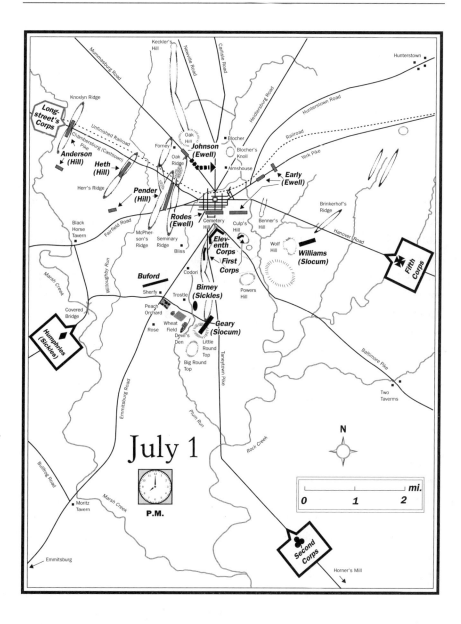

July 1

P.M.

sent at 6:00 P.M. to both Hancock and Doubleday, "we have so concentrated that a battle at Gettysburg is now forced on us."

At virtually the same moment, the army commander dictated a summary for Henry Halleck in Washington, relating all he knew. "I see no other course than to hazard a general battle," he conceded. He still did not commit himself irrevocably, however, adding, "Circumstances during the night may alter this decision, of which I will try to advise you." About an hour after this note left on its journey to the telegraph exchange at Frederick, Meade received another update from Hancock, who had written, "I think we can retire; if not, we can fight here, as the ground appears not unfavorable with good troops." While not exactly a ringing endorsement of the position, it was all the confirmation Meade needed. Starting at 7:00 P.M., orders began to issue from his headquarters directing all units not already moving toward Gettysburg to get on the march. The Pipe Creek plan became just another what-might-have-been.

Everything bustled as tents came down and matériel was packed up preparatory to moving army headquarters forward to Gettysburg. Meade was not expecting Hancock in person this night, but the Second Corps commander surprised him by appearing shortly before 10:00 P.M., followed soon after by the army's chief engineer, Gouverneur K. Warren. Henry Slocum had finally reached Cemetery Hill and assumed command by virtue of his seniority, making it possible for Hancock to return to Taneytown. There he briefed Meade personally on the day's actions, as well as the general situation as of sunset. Hancock was dead on his feet, so Meade allowed him to catch some much-needed sleep. For George Meade himself, there would be none for quite a while.

It was shortly after 10:00 P.M. when he and his staff set off for a place he had never seen, but where he expected to meet Robert E. Lee in battle.

Both sides had taken prisoners this day. Just from Archer's, Davis', and Iverson's Brigades, Union provosts corralled more than a thousand men, with other Rebel commands contributing a few hundred more. "I will never forget, & yet I can never describe my feelings & thoughts, just at that time, when I found I was a *prisoner*," reflected a Mississippi soldier snagged at the railroad cut. He and others were quick-marched through Gettysburg, some of whose citizens "jeered and laughed at us from their doors, tops of houses & other places of safety," he noted bitterly.

Many Confederate prisoners were accumulated in a field just south of Cemetery Hill; one of Archer's men thought they "remained in the vicinity of the town about three hours." That was about the time when Ewell's Corps was making its presence known on the field. "Started us at almost a 'double quick' toward Baltimore," recounted the Mississippi man. It was early evening when the first batches neared Taneytown, where the general army's provost units took them. Soon George Sharpe's officers were interviewing the POWs and rapidly adding detail to their picture of the size and composition of the enemy force at Gettysburg.

For their part, the victorious Confederates made little attempt at a systematic analysis of the approximately 3,655 officers and men they had captured. Many of the Federals were wounded and scattered about the area in makeshift aid stations and private houses. One of the ambulatory prisoners, a member of the 99th Pennsylvania, recalled marching "over back of Seminary Ridge, and [then they] rounded us up in a field, thru which a sluggish stream ran, Marsh Creek, I think." There the Yankee boys were herded together and guarded. Many of these July 1 prisoners would have nothing to eat for another two days.

The more Robert E. Lee considered it, the less sense it made to him to leave Ewell's Corps where it was. He had hardly returned to Seminary Ridge before he had his staff officer Charles Marshall heading back to Ewell's headquarters with orders for the Second Corps to slide around to the south. When Marshall reported in again, just after 10:30 P.M., he had Ewell with him. The situation had changed, Ewell explained. Johnson's men had moved up into line, and if they had not yet taken control of Culp's Hill, they should be doing so at any moment. The position was ideally suited for cutting Federal communication and supply along the Baltimore Pike, and it would constitute a critical springboard for taking Cemetery Hill. It would be foolhardy to pull back from it, Ewell argued.

Lee was not quite so ready to believe that the Federals would leave something as crucial as Culp's Hill uncovered, but if Ewell was right, it would be a blunder to relinquish it. He therefore reversed himself: the Second Corps would hold its position. He would find a role for it in the actions to come.

It was not yet midnight when Ewell, victorious once more this day, rode back toward his headquarters.

On one matter Lee had not changed his mind one iota. A battle had been begun today but not completed; he would finish it tomorrow. All the strategic points he had discussed so long ago with Jefferson Davis compelled him to give battle sometime during this campaign. Circumstances had chosen Gettysburg as the place. But there was another reason for his resolve: the Federals had fought well this day, and they must not be allowed the time to draw pride from that experience. As Lee later reported, "Encouraged by the successful issue of the engagement of the first day, and in view of the valuable results that would ensue from the defeat of the army of General Meade, it was thought advisable to renew the attack."

Private E. C. Culp of the 25th Ohio (Eleventh Corps) may well have been the most optimistic Yankee on the field this night. "We lay on our arms," he would later recollect, "happy in the thought that by morning our position would be re-enforced by the balance of the best army ever organized, and that for once we would 'have things our own way.' "

Nightfall found the citizens of Gettysburg in every mood possible: some frightened, some curious, some just plain excited. From a young boy's perspective, July 1 had been a time of terrible wonderment. Charles McCurdy would always remember it as a "day of excitement and strange adventure." Daniel Skelly, still aglow over having helped Oliver Howard find an observation post, "enjoyed a good night's rest after the feverish anxiety of the first day's battle."

Sleep was anything but welcome for Tillie Pierce. After the fighting ended, she had gone exploring with her friend Beckie Weikert. The pair had looked into a barn that was now being used as an aid station. "Nothing before in my experience had ever paralleled the sight we then and there beheld," Tillie would reminisce in later years. "There were the groaning and crying, the struggling and dying, crowded side by side." Sleeping was hard for her this night, for she was "surrounded with strange and appalling events, and [had] many new visions passing rapidly through my mind." "At night all was quiet," recalled another of Gettysburg's young women, "but the tramp of the guards reminded the town that its citizens were prisoners." Sarah Broadhead saw not only the present moment but also what was to come. "As I write all is quiet," she confided to her diary, "but O! how I dread to-morrow."

Even as Ewell was convincing Lee, the entire basis for their discussion was being eliminated by three Indiana soldiers endowed with a good deal of pluck and more than their share of luck. As he set his regiment in place on the crest of Culp's Hill, Ira Grover took a calculated gamble by covering the right and rear of his position with just a few picket posts, opting to mass his strength instead toward the north, the direction in which he knew the enemy lay. Unbeknownst to him, Johnson's Division of Ewell's Corps had extended the Confederate line until it stretched around the Hoosiers' right flank. Once his troops had settled into their positions, Johnson sent out his own scouting party, which moved up the hill's eastern face.

Indiana Sergeant William Hussey was manning a picket post just off the right of the main line. With him were Privates A. J. Harshbarger and W. S. Odell, two likewise steady and resourceful individuals. When they heard the "noise . . . as of men moving cautiously in the timber," the trio quietly headed toward the intruders to set up an ambush. The Rebel scouts eased into the trap with their officer out in front. Hussey let the first man pass, then jumped him from behind. At the same time, the two privates opened fire. This brought the picket reserve at a run, sweeping up more prisoners on the way and sending the others tumbling down the hill convinced they had blundered into a well-defended position.

Hussey turned over his captures to Ira Grover, who learned that they were from the 42nd Virginia. Save for a few alarms engendered by jittery survivors of the day's fight, the rest of the night passed without incident on Culp's Hill.

When his scouts returned to report, Edward Johnson decided that it would be risking too much to try to advance up Culp's Hill in the dark. By the time this information moved along the chain of command to Richard Ewell, there was no time for him to act on Lee's earlier desire to pull the Second Corps away from the town. "Day was now breaking," he reported later, "and it was too late for any change of place."

The Sixth Corps had done some hard marching to reach its assigned station in George Meade's broad frontage deployment. The more-than-13,000-strong corps (the Army of the Potomac's largest) had tramped into Manchester, Maryland, on the night of June 30. Sunrise, July 1, had brought unexpected news: "Were pleased to hear that we could rest today," noted one grateful diarist. Many soldiers took the opportunity to pen or pencil letters home. "I feel very tired from irregular hours, and I am footsore," wrote a member of the 37th Massachusetts. "A day or two of rest, *if we ever get it,* will make all right again." Not every motivation was so noble, however. Surgeon George T. Stevens observed with stern disapproval that Manchester appeared "well supplied with rye whiskey," and that many Sixth Corps soldiers seemed to "have a way of finding out the existence of that luxury."

The atmosphere began to change dramatically at around 7:30 P.M., when, according to a Wisconsin soldier, "some of us saw a mounted officer come galloping down the pike from the West." The rider spotted the men and approached them. " 'Where is Corps Headquarters?' " he demanded. A few in the group gestured to a knoll about sixty-five feet away, where the corps headquarters flag was visible. According to one of those present, the orderly "struck spurs to his horse and dashed in that direction, leaped from the saddle and rushed into the tent." Any hope of a full day's rest went by the boards as the headquarters erupted in a frenzy of "staff officers . . . rushing in all directions." Within minutes, bugle and drum calls signaling "Assemble" began to echo from the camps.

By this point in the war and this campaign, veteran units were proficient in the drill, so it was not long after 8:00 P.M. that the first regiments began marching. "None of us knew our destination," recorded a Pennsylvania soldier, "but we suspected something important would soon occur." According to John Sedgwick, commanding the Sixth Corps, "I received orders from General Meade to march for Taneytown, which at that time was his headquarters." To accomplish the movement, Sedgwick's staff led the various columns along a series of roughly parallel country roads, in the dark. "We would march a while then stop and stand until we had to sit down and rest," recollected a Pennsylvania man. "But scarcely would we get down until the order 'forward' would be given." "We go limping around with blistered feet and chafed limbs, and lame shoulders," added a Massachusetts comrade.

The columns had been moving for several hours when an unsettling rumor skittered over the army grapevine. "Head of the column seems to have lost its way," scribbled a diarist during one halt. After George Meade decided to relocate his headquarters to Gettysburg, it had taken a while for his staff officers to find the Sixth Corps and redirect its officers to turn their men onto the Baltimore Pike, instead of marching them across it to connect a few miles farther on with the route to Taneytown. The word came too late for the leading elements in Sedgwick's column. "By the time the right road was discovered," grumbled a Maine foot soldier, "the boys were mostly asleep; and the starting up and the turning of them around to retrace their steps, caused much strong language."

The action of July 1 was a battle of brigades and regiments, not of divisions and armies. Nowhere was it written in stone that the two sides would fight at Gettysburg, nor was the slow escalation inevitable once the combat began. The actions of this first day occurred because no one in a position to end the fighting ever saw the whole picture.

At a corps level, Confederate leadership covered the extremes, from A. P. Hill's distrait control to the opportunistic initiative of Richard Ewell (however false his impression that Hill's men were under threat), a cocky mood that faded by day's end into a wary caution. Both men looked to Robert E. Lee for some sign, but neither received clear guidance, nor did either successfully interpret the messages Lee *did* send. The army commander, for his part, was mentally unprepared for the scale of this day's encounter and poorly informed by his key subordinates. His unleashing of Hill's men late in the afternoon was less a considered action born of a comprehensive strategy and more a reflex to protect Ewell.

The Confederate brigade-level report card was decidedly mixed. Henry Heth failed to key on Archer's justified caution and ignored Davis' enthusiastic ignorance, both of which qualities led to tactical disasters. He was far better served by the hard-hitting Pettigrew, whose accomplishments might well have been less costly if Brockenbrough had carried out his assignment. In the closing phase on Seminary Ridge, Scales and Perrin showed what valor could and could not accomplish, while Thomas waited offstage and Lane played his own solitary, unhelpful game. To the north, Robert Rodes was extremely well served by Doles, Daniel, and Ramseur and badly underserved by Iverson and O'Neal. Jubal Early wisely relied on John Gordon to deliver the coup de main, which might not have shone with such luster had Avery and Hays not ably completed the job.

The lack of a well-thought-out follow-through at day's end was as much of Lee's making as of anyone else's. His failure to communicate his intentions, coupled with the restraining effect of his nonengagement order of the day and his decision to withhold Anderson's fresh division from the fray, made the questions faced by Richard Ewell difficult indeed. Lee's later capitulation, in allowing the Second Corps to remain tied up in Gettysburg, would offer its commander few advantages for July 2.

For the Union side, the death of John Reynolds meant more than the loss of an inspiring leader; it also removed from the equation the one person with enough vision and sense of purpose to manage this battle. Howard never came close to filling the leadership vacuum, leaving two corps to fend for themselves. Doubleday nailed the First Corps to McPherson's Ridge not because it offered great defensive strengths (it did not), but almost entirely because he feared countermanding Reynolds' last order even more than he feared the Rebels. The able Carl Schurz was handed a busted plan, forced to deploy in an impossible position, and undone by a subordinate's ill-conceived adventure; and more than that, he was just plain unlucky. Following his masterly delaying action of the morning, John Buford retired to a supporting role, which his men performed all out of proportion to their small numbers. There is no evidence that he was asked for or offered any advice once John Reynolds passed from the scene.

Of Doubleday's division commanders, only Rowley called it in; all the others did the jobs assigned them. On the brigade level, Meredith's lack of an open mind bound the crack Iron Brigade to a poor defensive position, while Baxter's and Paul's successors performed effectively in a very exposed one. Even though the rest of the army expected the Eleventh Corps to fail (which it did, after all), it was through no fault of its brigade commanders, who fought from their often hopeless positions with more tenacity and skill than they have been credited with.

For the Confederacy, Lee arrived on the field with no plan, tried halfheartedly to improvise one late in the day, and ultimately decided to defer exerting his full control until July 2. For the Union, beyond holding Cemetery Hill and waiting for the Twelfth Corps to come up, Howard appears to have had no scheme in mind, nor even any desire to influence events beyond his line of sight.

Although it would pale in comparison with the two days yet to come, July 1 was a hard-fought action. Of the approximately 23,500 Union soldiers engaged this day, almost 9,000 (38 percent) were casualties. On the Confederate side, out of 28,300 on the field, slightly more than 6,000 (22 percent) were killed, wounded, or captured.

NOCTURNE
Night, Wednesday, July 1

Coiled within and without the infantry camps on the roads feeding into Gettysburg were the artillery parks, harboring the most potent killing weapons in each army's arsenal. For the moment the tubes were cold and silent, but once heated by action they would spew out death in large measures and small. The men who tended them were a breed apart, bonded by specialized training that molded them into a single entity dedicated to the meticulously choreographed sequence of actions required to feed their beasts. For some of the gunners, this night brought rest, while for others there was movement toward Gettysburg.

Edward Porter Alexander was on the move. His artillery battalion, part of Longstreet's Corps, had begun marching from a bivouac near Greenwood, west of the Cashtown Gap, just after sunset. The gunners had waited throughout the day for the infantry and baggage trains to clear the pass—a prudent decision, as it turned out, for now they were enjoying, in Alexander's words, "a lovely march over a fairly good pike by a bright moon."

The Georgia-born officer, who had celebrated his twenty-eighth birthday on May 26, was considered one of the best artillerists in Lee's army. That recognition galled his immediate superior, Colonel John B. Walton, who resented the amount of responsibility conferred on his subordinate. Walton was riding with the head of the column this night, allowing Alexander and his six batteries the privilege of bringing up the rear. Alexander cared little for personal politics, for he knew that there would be more fighting soon, and it was in combat that he felt most at home. "All the accounts we had of the fighting [at Gettysburg] represented it as having been very hard & bloody on both sides," he later recollected, "& though we had finally gotten the ground & the town, we heard enough to assure us that the little dispute was not entirely settled."

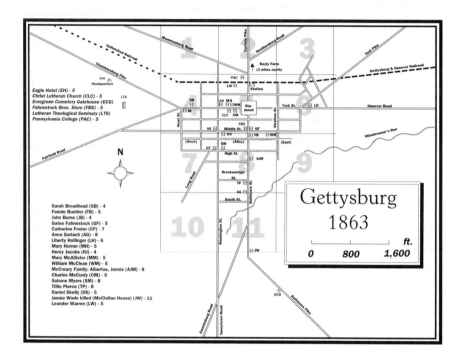

Eagle Hotel (EH) - 5
Christ Lutheran Church (CLC) - 5
Evergreen Cemetery Gatehouse (ECG)
Fahnestock Bros. Store (FBS) - 5
Lutheran Theological Seminary (LTS)
Pennsylvania College (PAC) - 5

Sarah Broadhead (SB) - 4
Fannie Buehler (FB) - 5
John Burns (JB) - 5
Gates Fahnestock (GF) - 5
Catherine Foster (CF) - 7
Anna Garlach (AG) - 8
Liberty Hollinger (LH) - 6
Mary Horner (MH) - 5
Henry Jacobs (HJ) - 4
Mary McAllister (MM) - 5
William McClean (WM) - 5
McCreary Family: Albertus, Jennie (AJM) - 8
Charles McCurdy (CM) - 5
Salome Myers (SM) - 8
Tillie Pierce (TP) - 8
Daniel Skelly (DS) - 5
Jennie Wade killed (McClellan House) (JW) - 11
Leander Warren (LW) - 5

**Gettysburg
1863**

ft.
0   800   1,600

Alexander's presumption was a matter of fact for another of the South's capable artillerymen, Major Joseph W. Latimer. A battalion commander like Alexander, Latimer commanded four batteries attached to Johnson's Division in Ewell's Corps. These gunners had trailed their infantry, not reaching Gettysburg until nightfall. After parking his cannon in a wheat field east of the town, the twenty-year-old Virginian rode to headquarters seeking orders.

People liked Latimer; Ewell's aide Campbell Brown described him as "one of those born soldiers whose promotion is recognized by all to be a consequence of their own merit." His gunners, many of whom were older than he, respected his intensity and skill and had fondly dubbed him the "Boy Major." This night, on reporting to Colonel John Thompson Brown, Ewell's artillery chief, Latimer was told to find firing positions on the left of the Second Corps line. Because it would be too dangerous to explore the area in the dark, Latimer snatched what sleep he could, determined to be up before dawn.

As Alexander marched and Latimer tossed restlessly, awaiting sunrise, John L. Marye left a party. A sergeant in the four-gun battery known as the Fredericksburg Artillery (in Pegram's Battalion, Hill's Corps), which had fired the opening cannon shot near Marsh Creek this morning, Marye had rested little since daybreak. He and his mates had found themselves at day's end "in the yard of a large country residence" that had been hastily abandoned by its owner, who had been thoughtful enough to leave behind a full larder and a well-stocked wine closet. Good news had a way of spreading, so before long the battery boys were joined by lots of new friends. Even as burial parties and stretcher bearers were prodding across the churned-up ridges west of the town, Marye and his comrades were having what he would later term "a universal romp."

Stepping outside for some fresh air, the sergeant and a companion decided to visit Gettysburg. "We found the streets dismal and deserted enough," Marye remembered. "Here and there a scared and pale-faced woman scurried along towards a . . . Federal hospital." It was a surreal scene. On one street, Marye recounted, "A few stragglers in Confederate uniforms were attempting to beat in the door of a store, but the provost guard, sent to patrol the town, appearing, they made off."

Captain John Bigelow's 9th Massachusetts Battery* had been garrisoning Washington when the Army of the Potomac passed by the capital, sweeping it and other units like it into Hooker's force for the emergency. The gunners were used to the easy routine of manning fixed entrenchments, so the transition into mobile artillery had not been accomplished without its share of blisters and aching muscles, but Bigelow, who had been assigned the battery in 1862 with orders to shape it up, had done his job. His men may have been sore and tired, but they were also confident of their skills and training.

The Harvard-educated Bigelow looked and acted older than his twenty-three years and was quietly proud of his "self-possession to stand alone." Camped near Taneytown this night, the 9th was one of twenty-one batteries forming the Army of the Potomac's powerful Artillery Reserve. It did not take a veteran to read the signs. One of Bigelow's artillerymen noted that "the body of Gen Reynolds and a large number of prisoners passed through," and the rumor mill was operating at full capacity. Some of the reserve had moved off toward Gettysburg before darkness put an end to all but urgent travel. Like thousands of other Union soldiers, John Bigelow and his men waited nervously for dawn, under orders to be ready to march at a moment's notice.

*Properly the Ninth Independent Battery, Massachusetts Light Artillery.

Much of Bigelow's anxiety stemmed from not knowing what lay ahead—something that was not a problem for Lieutenant Alonzo H. Cushing, commanding Battery A, 4th United States Light Artillery, part of Captain John G. Hazard's Second Corps artillery brigade. A confident and likable twenty-two-year-old West Point graduate, Cushing had found a place among the small gaggle of staff accompanying Winfield Hancock to Gettysburg this day. He had seen the situation on Cemetery Hill near dusk and helped George Meade's surrogate bring order out of chaos. Then he had rejoined his battery on its march from Taneytown, guiding it into camp for the night some three miles south of Gettysburg. Cushing was no novice when it came to combat, and his experience undoubtedly helped him this long night as he mentally prepared himself for what tomorrow morning would bring.

Captain James E. Smith, commanding the six guns of the 4th New York Independent Battery, had a nagging sense tonight that he was missing the show. His unit was one of those chosen by Daniel Sickles to keep watch over the Emmitsburg area while the bulk of the Third Corps marched on to Gettysburg. The newlywed captain was a prideful man who zealously protected his personal reputation and his battery's honor. He had organized the unit in New York City in 1861 and commanded it through a number of major Virginia campaigns. The march north into a region untouched by war had moved Smith, who would never forget the images of "great fields of yellow wheat, orchards loaded with fruit, green stretches of pasture and meadow-land, snug farmhouses and huge, red-roofed barns."

Ahead of Smith and his men lay an appointment with destiny on a rocky ridge soon to be immortalized as Devil's Den. The tramp from Virginia would take on a sad new gravity: "It was, indeed, a gay and jolly march, such as seldom fell to our lot," reflected Smith in 1888. "But to many brave boys it was a march to death."

THIRTEEN

July 2, 1863

(Midnight–Sunrise)

George Meade, accompanied by some key staff members, reached Cemetery Hill at approximately 1:00 A.M. The ride from Taneytown in the dark had not been without incident: at one point, after traffic congestion forced his party off the road, a collision with some low-hanging branches had cost the general his spectacles. Fortunately, he had a spare pair. On the way, Meade had paused for a short while at John Gibbon's headquarters, where after briefing the acting corps commander he had ordered him to move the Second Corps to Gettysburg at daybreak.

Approaching Gettysburg on the Taneytown Road, Meade rode up to the two-story, arched brick gatehouse of the Evergreen Cemetery, where he was met by Oliver Howard, still stewing about his reputation and the significance of Meade's having sent Hancock to assume control of the battlefield. "The first words he spoke to me were very kind," Howard remembered. "I believed that I had done my work well the preceding day; I desired his approval and so I frankly stated my earnest wish. Meade at once assured me that he imputed no blame."

The pair entered one of the gatehouse's lower rooms, where Meade found many of his generals engaged in a July 1 postmortem. Each offered his appraisal of the day's events and then expressed his opinion regarding the army's situation. " 'I am confident we can hold this position,' " Howard said. " 'It is good for defense,' " Henry Slocum agreed, doubtless happy that he was no longer responsible for the battlefield. Daniel Sickles was characteristically pugnacious: " 'It is a good place to fight from, general!' " he declared. Meade, for his part, was not given to stirring bromides. " 'I am glad to hear you say so, gentlemen,' " he responded, " 'for it is too late to leave it.' "

The conversation continued for a while longer before Slocum and Sickles left for their respective headquarters. Meade followed them out, then crossed the Baltimore Pike and stood contemplating the enemy's lines, delineated by campfires to the north and west. "There was a rumor that Lee's army was fully as strong as ours," Carl Schurz later wrote, ". . . and from what we saw before us, we guessed that it was nearly all up and ready for action."

Meade returned to the gatehouse. Then, accompanied by his artillery chief, Brigadier General Henry J. Hunt, Captain William H. Paine (an engineer on the headquarters staff), and Oliver Howard, the commander of the Army of the Potomac, set off on horseback to inspect the position fate had selected for this contest.

Finally, Jeb Stuart knew his destination. The report delivered to him by Andrew R. Venable at around 1:00 A.M. both pinpointed Lee's army and provided a route of approach. The pesky Yankee militia squatting in Carlisle were no longer of any importance. Orders went out to Fitzhugh Lee, directing him to leave off his cannonade and withdraw, while other couriers delivered marching instructions to the half of Stuart's column that had been halted ten miles to the southeast. By 2:00 A.M., the weary troopers and their exhausted animals were moving on roads toward Gettysburg.

Sunrise was at 4:37 A.M., but Robert E. Lee was up and about well before then. Between his late session with Richard Ewell and the duties of his position, he had managed perhaps two or three hours of rest this night. After a hasty breakfast, he strode off in the direction of the Lutheran seminary, bound for a point from which he could see not only the western face of Cemetery Hill but also activity as far east as Benner's Hill and south toward the Codori farm. In the predawn darkness, only campfires signaled the enemy's position. The flickering light revealed nothing of the nature of those troops—whether they were the same ones Lee had beaten yesterday or fresh units.

When James Longstreet joined Lee, he noted that "the stars were [still] shining brightly." The First Corps commander had also risen early, then headed over to Lee's headquarters with a retinue that included several of the foreign observers accompanying the army, Arthur Fremantle among them. While Longstreet conferred privately with Lee, the Englishman climbed a nearby tree with another guest, Justus Scheibert. A major in the Prussian Royal Engineers, Scheibert had been with this army at Chancellorsville and would later offer the opinion that Lee was "not at his ease" this early morning, appearing "care-worn." It may well have been around this time that Lee heard from Ewell, as later reported by a Second Corps aide, that "Culp's Hill [was] already occupied" by the enemy.

Longstreet wasted little time before restating his "views against making an attack." But Lee, as Longstreet recollected, "seemed resolved." If he was resolved *to* attack, however, he was not yet decided *where* he would do it. Soon there was sufficient light for the two to observe the Federal positions and get "a general idea of the nature of the ground." Lee needed eyes closer to the enemy, so he called forward a captain of engineers on his staff. "General Lee . . . said he wanted me to reconnoiter along the enemy's left and return as soon as possible," remembered Samuel R. Johnston. Likely as Johnston departed, Longstreet signaled for one of his own engineer officers, Major John J. Clarke, to accompany him. Lee was also thinking about the Second Corps, representing his army's left. Staff officer Charles Venable was dispatched to Ewell's headquarters in order to, in Longstreet's words, "make a reconnaissance of the ground in his front, with a view of making the main attack on his left."

Lee's well-intentioned and moderately capable artillery chief, Brigadier General William N. Pendleton, announced that he was going to scout Seminary Ridge southward for suitable battery placements. As Pendleton moved off, Lee had Armistead L. Long of his staff follow after him "to examine and verify the position of the Confederate artillery."

A. P. Hill now came over from his headquarters, bringing Henry Heth along. From up in his tree, Fremantle saw Heth's head wound and remarked the fact that the Third Corps division commander had insisted "upon coming to the field" even though he was obviously in no shape to take charge. A British correspondent for the *London Times,* Francis Lawley, stood a respectful distance away, eyeing Lee carefully. He noted that the Rebel chieftain appeared "more anxious and ruffled than I had ever seen him before, though it required close observation to detect it."

*   *   *

Nothing Daniel E. Sickles had seen thus far persuaded him that George Meade had come to Gettysburg looking for a fight. Unlike Reynolds or Howard, Sickles had received the Pipe Creek circular, which he had immediately interpreted as a blueprint for a retreat. Its very wording, he believed, provided Meade with all the cover he needed. By announcing that the enemy had ceased his advance to the Susquehanna, the army commander (as Sickles later testified) had planted the implicit suggestion that "he need not attack, but might fall back towards Washington, take up a defensive line, and wait until he was attacked in his works."

Nor was that the only evidence, to Sickles' way of thinking, of Meade's lack of resolve. He had not responded promptly to John Reynolds' predicament on July 1, though he could have done so by ordering Sickles forward from Emmitsburg; indeed, it was only Sickles' inspired insubordination in marching his men to Gettysburg that had sufficiently stiffened everyone's will to hold the high ground. Speaking later before a congressional committee, Sickles would proudly claim, "I . . . moved to Gettysburg on my own responsibility."

Sickles' brooding had so preoccupied him on the night of July 1 that he had paid scant attention to the actual disposition of his Third Corps. Major General David Birney's division had arrived via the Emmitsburg Road not long after dark, followed by Brigadier General Andrew A. Humphreys' men at about 2:00 A.M. Humphreys had been misdirected by the guide provided to him by Sickles, but the level-headed officer had discovered the error in time to avoid blundering into the Rebel lines. Each division (minus a brigade apiece left in Emmitsburg) had camped on low ground near water, just off the southwestern side of Cemetery Ridge. "The Third Corps had simply gone into bivouac," recorded Sickles' aide Henry Tremain, "pretty much of it in the gloom of evening. . . . Neither the batteries nor the infantry were occupying any special posts selected for defence or offence. That awaited the light." So, too, did Daniel Sickles, anxious that George Meade should not refuse the Rebel challenge.

George Meade's assessment of his lines began at Cemetery Hill and then headed west and south along Cemetery Ridge. His party moved slowly, passing behind the weary remnants of the Eleventh and First Corps, then the encampments of the Third. The talented William Paine had a good eye for terrain, which he put to use in making sketches of the various positions. One of his efforts depicted a sizable hill that the group halted to survey, which seemed to mark what Henry Hunt deemed "the natural termination of our lines." Variously called Sugar Loaf or Signal Hill, it would soon become fixed in the story of this battle by yet another name: Little Round Top. From there the party rode back toward Cemetery Hill, with a detour over to Culp's Hill and nearby areas. During this portion of the ride, Henry Slocum sought out Meade to report that there was a dangerous gap between the First Corps troops on Culp's Hill and his own Twelfth Corps division near Wolf Hill, almost a mile farther east.

George Meade made two quick decisions. In the hasty alignment of the previous evening, Winfield Hancock had posted one Twelfth Corps division near Little Round Top and the other on Wolf Hill. Now that Sickles' Third Corps was on hand, Meade would make the Twelfth Corps whole by using both divisions to extend the First Corps line. Until that could be accomplished, he told Henry Hunt to utilize any available artillery to cover the area. Hunt left on his assignment, inordinately pleased that Meade no longer considered him a technical adviser but instead regarded him as an officer with real authority. George Meade and William Paine returned to the gatehouse, where the engineer began producing map tracings on which Meade indicated the positions he wanted his arriving corps to occupy.

Their work was made easier by the fact that the sun was rising.

(Dawn–3:40 P.M.)

Dawn ended the spirit of live-and-let-live that had been nurtured by the darkness. Trouble brewed almost immediately, when Rebel soldiers posted in the southern part of Gettysburg realized that their foes on Cemetery Hill were within easy rifle range. "As soon as it was light on the morning of the 2nd of July, we could see the Johnnies moving along the fences in our front, keeping out of sight as much as possible," remembered an Eleventh Corps officer. "It was not long before 'zip' came the bullets from them, and our boys promptly returned their fire, although it was difficult to see them."* A Tarheel on the receiving end of this attention noted in his diary that "the enemies picket a firing on us all day."

Rifles were not the only weapons involved in this morning scrap. When the 41st New York was repositioned behind a stone wall facing the town, the action drew some shells from Confederate batteries. Federal cannon were not long silent, either. As the 153rd Pennsylvania deployed in skirmishing order, Rebel snipers in a brickyard behind the McCreary house on Baltimore Street began causing enough problems that the lieutenant commanding asked for heavy support. The willing artillerymen on Cemetery Hill solved the problem by throwing a few shells into the brickyard.

The steady popping of musketry backed by the sporadic bass crack of cannon discharges convinced George Meade that his right was especially vulnerable, and that shoring it up must be his first priority. The Twelfth Corps division moving from near Little Round Top would soon connect with the First Corps line along the southeastern slope of Culp's Hill. Even as these men were marching into place, the Twelfth's other division came off Wolf Hill across Rock Creek. Once linked, the two units would spread the Union defense unbroken over Culp's Hill's upper and lower summits.

*For his actions locating Confederate snipers along his regiment's front, Private Charles Stacey of the 55th Ohio was to receive a Medal of Honor.

The Second Corps (still under John Gibbon) began reaching the field by 6:00 A.M. Uncertain as to the nature of the firing coming from the direction of town, Meade held Gibbon's men in reserve about a mile south of the action until he was satisfied that nothing serious was developing. At around 7:00 A.M., he started placing the Second Corps along the northern part of Cemetery Ridge, extending the line southward from the Eleventh Corps toward the Third near Little Round Top.

While these actions were essentially defensive ones, Meade was also actively considering offensive possibilities on his right. As he would later testify before Congress, "Early in the morning it had been my intention, as soon as the 6th corps arrived on the ground . . . , to make a vigorous attack from our extreme right upon the enemy's left. . . . The attacking column was to be composed of the 12th, 5th and 6th corps."

Meade's headquarters were established some nine hundred yards south of Cemetery Hill, along the Taneytown Road, in a two-room wood-frame house belonging to Lydia Leister, a widow. It offered a sheltered location close to the battle lines, on the shoulder of one of the principal roads being used by the army. This modest structure now became the Army of the Potomac's nerve center.

The skirmishing on the southern edge of town posed its own dangers for Gettysburg's civilians. "Sharp shooters were stationed all through the town to do their deadly work," reported Nellie Aughinbaugh. "It was hot and sultry and the lines of battle were quiet with the exception of an occasional exchange of shots between pickets or sharpshooters," noted the now veteran Daniel Skelly. Catherine Garlach was determined to remain in her house, even though the safest place in it, the cellar, was a foot deep in water. She and her son hauled in some wood intended for furniture construction and used it to build a stilted platform strong enough to hold not only the four Garlachs but also eleven neighbors who came by in search of refuge.

Sarah Broadhead worried about her foolish husband, who insisted on dodging stray friendly fire to harvest their backyard-garden bean crop. "He persevered until he picked all," she remembered, "for he declared the Rebels should not have one." Liberty Hollinger's father was equally determined to feed his barn animals, even though his efforts drew Union sniping. When he took the matter up with a squad of Confederates who happened to be nearby, the officer in charge seemed amused. " 'Why, man, take off that gray suit,' " he said. " 'They think you are a "Johnny Reb." ' "

The skirmishing did not go unnoticed by Robert E. Lee. With his scouts out checking the Federal positions and due back at any time, he could not wander far, so he stalked about like a caged animal. The Prussian observer, Scheibert, recalled his "riding to and fro, frequently changing his position, making anxious inquiries here and there." It was quite possibly at this time that Richard Ewell, recognizing that Lee would be curious about the firing, sent his aide Campbell Brown to report and request instructions.

In a memoir penned not long after the war, Brown recounted his meeting with Lee on Ewell's behalf sometime between the night of July 1 and July 2. As Brown remembered it, Lee instructed him "to tell Genl E. to be sure not to become so much involved as to be unable readily to extricate his troops, 'for I have not decided to fight here, and may probably draw off by my right flank . . . , so as to get between the enemy & Washington & Baltimore, & force them to attack us in position.' "

Two brigades from Pender's Division began extending Lee's line southward from the McMillan Woods, bordering the Fairfield Road. One of these was Lane's unit, relatively unbloodied in yesterday's fighting; the other was Scales', whose ordeal before Wainwright's wall of cannon had left the survivors (in the words of the brigade's acting commander) "depressed, dilapidated and almost unorganized."

Even as the regiments spread down Seminary Ridge, each brigade commander sent forward selected companies to create a protective skirmish line perhaps five hundred feet east of the ridge crest. Settling into positions of convenience behind whatever cover they could find, the Rebel riflemen peered warily into the glare of the rising sun. Before them was a lone farmstead with a modest-sized orchard west of the buildings. A few bold skirmishers eased ahead to check out the structures.

The William Bliss family, owners of this sixty-acre farm lying west of the Emmitsburg Road, had fled the day before at the first sign of trouble. A Yankee soldier who was at the farm later this day could still observe that the householders had "evidently left in a hurry as they left the doors open, the table set, the beds made." Although not on a commanding

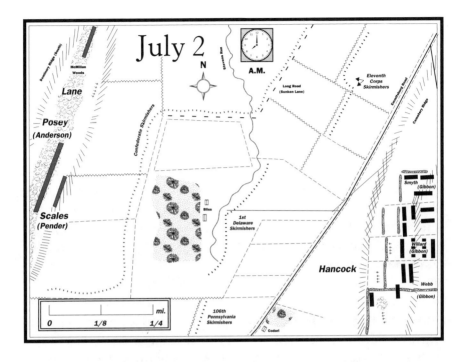

piece of ground, the Bliss farm land had the misfortune to be situated nearly midway between the principal lines that were taking shape on both sides.

Almost as soon as the Tarheels settled into watchful positions, they began to make out figures heading toward the farm buildings from Cemetery Ridge. As it moved into line, the Federal Second Corps was also screening its front, and responsibility for the forward sector encompassing the Bliss farm had fallen to the 251 members of the 1st Delaware, commanded by Lieutenant Colonel Edward P. Harris. Deploying in two wings, the regiment advanced in a line stretching from just south of the buildings into the peach orchard north of them. Hardly had these Yankee boys hustled into place when, as Lieutenant John L. Brady of the regiment recorded, they came under "a rattling fire from the enemy, which was repaid with interest."

Whitelaw Reid and Lorenzo L. Crounse left Two Taverns "a little after daybreak" to follow the irresistible flow of Yankee matériel toward Gettysburg. On the approach to Cemetery Hill, after passing several farms already pressed into hospital service, they at last spotted the headquarters of James Wadsworth. Perhaps in the knowledge that Crounse represented a home-state paper, New Yorker Wadsworth recounted yesterday's events to the pair, who scribbled notes as he talked. When the correspondents moved on to Cemetery Hill, Reid saw Oliver Howard walking alongside the "spare and somewhat stooped form" of George Meade.

Reid ventured far enough ahead to glimpse occupied Gettysburg. "No sound comes up from the deserted town," he wrote, "no ringing of bells, no voices of children, no hum of busy trade. Only now and then a blue curl of smoke rises and fades from some high window; a faint report comes up, and perhaps the hiss of a Minie [ball] is heard." Once he had determined that combat was not imminent, Reid spoke with generals and other officers who had fought on July 1. Out of their recollections he fashioned one of the first dispatches chronicling the scope of the previous day's fighting.

Among the first officers to find George Meade at the Leister house was Brigadier General John Newton, a division commander in Sedgwick's Sixth Corps. Based on reports from Oliver Howard and John Buford, Meade had decided against retaining Abner Doubleday as John Reynolds' successor. He now tapped Newton for the job of leading the First Corps, an action that the proud, vain Doubleday would never forget or forgive. Speaking to a congressional committee in March 1864, he would declare that "Meade thought a couple of scapegoats were necessary; in case the next day's battle turned out unfavorably, he wished to mark his disapprobation of the first day's fight."

The prospect of irritating Doubleday did not weigh heavily on Meade this morning. His inventory of military assets indicated that the First and Eleventh Corps had fired off much of their ready artillery stock the day before; moreover, as Meade now learned, the fact that Daniel Sickles had brought the Third Corps to Gettysburg without its ammunition train meant that those guns, too, had minimal supplies. The army commander discussed the matter with his artillery chief, Henry Hunt, who had the best of surprises for his boss: anticipating just such a contingency, Hunt had the Reserve Artillery train carrying twenty rounds more per gun than regulations required. He therefore had enough extra on hand to restock the three corps and then some. According to Hunt, upon hearing this, Meade "was much relieved, and expressed his satisfaction."

* * *

As the three brigades belonging to John W. Geary's Twelfth Corps division began ascending Culp's Hill, the key officers met to plan their defenses. Most passed along the west-facing First Corps line, where they saw the mix of breastworks and earthworks the soldiers had constructed during the night. One Twelfth Corps officer remembered hearing John Geary remark that he personally did not favor the use of entrenchments because he believed it "unfitted men for fighting without them"; still, he allowed each brigade commander to decide for himself. Brigadier General George S. Greene, the oldest Union general on the field, leading the 1,400-man Third Brigade, made it clear that his men would dig. He said that "so far as his men were concerned, they would have [entrenchments] if they had time to build them."

Greene's brigade drew as its position the crest of Culp's Hill. An officer recalled that the well-wooded slope provided plenty of raw material for defensive works: "Right and left the men felled the trees, and blocked them up into a close log fence. . . . Fortunate regiments, which had spades and picks, strengthened their work with earth." As Geary's Second Brigade extended Greene's line down the southeastern slope, its members imitated their comrades. Where picks and shovels were not available, "bayonets, tin pans, tin cups etc were improvised as implements in the construction of earthworks," noted one soldier.

Culp's Hill was actually a collective name for a pair of unequal summits, aligned northeast to southwest and linked by a ravinelike sag or saddle. Greene's men were to cover the eastern side of the upper or higher summit all the way down to the saddle, where the Second Brigade took over. Prudence compelled Greene to take the additional precaution of having his men construct a short traverse at the lower end of their sector, providing an emergency line facing the saddle. With a full brigade digging in on the right and another standing in close support, there was little likelihood that the line would be needed, but Greene ordered it built anyway.

Samuel R. Johnston, the engineer captain delegated by Lee to "reconnoiter along the enemy's left," returned at around 8:00 A.M. His had been a remarkable excursion. By his own account, upon leaving Lee, Johnston had ridden out with three others, heading west along the Fairfield Road and then turning south after crossing Willoughby Run. The foursome had trekked along the creek's western bank until they intersected with a lane leading in an easterly direction up the slope of Warfield Ridge, a southern continuation of Seminary Ridge. Passing to the edge of some woods, they had found themselves facing the Emmitsburg Road, opposite the Sherfy farm peach orchard. Ahead of him, Johnston had discerned the dark form of two hills, the southern elevation higher than the northern. His group had cautiously made its way to the foot of these hills and ascended partway up one, gaining what the officer would later term "a commanding view." On descending the hill, the party had moved south and then west, looping back toward Warfield Ridge.

"When I . . . again got in sight of the Emmitsburg road, I saw three or four troopers moving slowly and very cautiously in the direction of Gettysburg," Johnston remembered. "I had to let them get out of sight before crossing the road, as to see and not be seen is what was required of a reconnoitering officer. . . . They . . . got out of sight and I lost no time in getting back."

Johnston found Lee at his observation post with Generals Longstreet and Hill. "General Lee saw me and called me to him," the young officer recalled. "The three Generals were holding a map. I stood behind General Lee and traced on the map the route over which I had made the reconnaissance." When he came to the two eminences that had marked the climax of his journey, Johnston pointed to the smaller one, Little Round Top. He described his climb partway up the slope and noted that he had seen no Yankee troops save those on the road. Lee, wrote Johnston, "was surprised at my getting so far, but showed clearly that I had given him valuable information." The commander needed to be sure, however. " 'Did you get there?' " he pointedly asked Johnston, indicating Little Round Top on the map. "I assured him I did," Johnston testified.

Johnston's intelligence provided a key element for the plan Lee was formulating. He had been constructing a picture of the Federal position based on his own observations and on scouting reports—now, especially, Johnston's. Tragically, both the observations and the reports were flawed. As Lee viewed the southward extension of the enemy's Cemetery Hill line, it appeared to him that the Yankee force was holding "the high ground along the Emmitsburg road, with a steep ridge in rear, which was also occupied." In point of fact, Meade had placed none of his main strength along the Emmitsburg Road, but instead had followed the line of Cemetery Ridge, which diverged from the road. The angle from which Lee was looking at the position made it seem as if the road represented the Federal defensive line.

Had Johnston followed the course he claimed, he would have come upon the encampments of the Third Corps, located just north and west of Little Round Top. He would also have encountered trouble from John Buford's cavalry vedettes, some of whom were posted about Sherfy's peach orchard. Only if Johnston had bypassed the orchard farther south and gone up the slope of the *larger* hill—*Big* Round Top—would his story not strain credulity. He truly believed there were no Federals near Little Round Top, and though the reality was otherwise, his account helped confirm Lee's notion of the Union position.

Robert E. Lee pondered the tactical problem of July 2 with the intention of attacking if a suitable arena could be found. " 'The enemy is here, and if we do not whip him, he will whip us,' " the army chief remarked this morning to Brigadier General John B. Hood, one of Longstreet's division commanders. Richard Ewell and company had apparently ruled out the rugged Confederate left as the primary point, and Hill's position opposite the enemy's strong Cemetery Hill defenses took his sector out of serious consideration. Lee had been hoping to find an opening on the Rebel right, and all the evidence in hand suggested that he had succeeded.

Lee thanked Johnston and asked him to remain for another assignment. Longstreet's Corps would soon be marching to the area reconnoitered by the young officer, so he understood Lee to mean that he was to "aid [Longstreet] . . . in any way that I could." At some point in their early-morning discussions, Longstreet had expressed to Lee his preference that any attack be led by Major General Lafayette McLaws and his division. When the thickly bearded McLaws appeared at about 8:30 A.M., Lee was ready with instructions.

Lee's inner turmoil seems to have subsided once his basic decision had been made; McLaws found the army commander "as calm and cool as I ever saw him." Lee spread out a map of the vicinity and pointed to a line drawn perpendicular to the Emmitsburg Road, near Sherfy's peach orchard, where he believed the Federal position terminated. " 'General, I wish you to place your division across the road, and I wish you to get there if possible without being seen by the enemy,' " Lee said, looking hard at McLaws. " 'Can you get there?' " he asked.

In the admirable spirit of "can do," McLaws answered that he knew of no reason that he could not make the movement requested. He had not a clue as to the lay of the land, though, so when Lee mentioned a survey undertaken by Johnston, McLaws misunderstood the context and asked at once to accompany that officer. Longstreet stepped forward from where he had been standing. " 'No, sir, I do not wish you to leave your division,' " he said, not bothering to explain that Johnston's reconnaissance had already occurred.

While McLaws was digesting this, Longstreet surprised him by running his finger over the map to indicate an orientation at a right angle to the one designated by Lee. " 'I wish your division placed so,' " Longstreet said. Lee firmly corrected his First Corps commander before allowing McLaws to depart to prepare his division. Prior to leaving, McLaws once more asked permission to accompany Johnston, and again Longstreet turned him down without explanation. "General Longstreet appeared as if he was irritated and annoyed," noted McLaws, "but the cause I did not ask."

There remained one sizable loose end: Ewell's Corps. With no report yet from Charles Venable, Lee decided that the time was right for him to pay another visit. It was nearing 9:00 A.M. when he set out for the Second Corps headquarters.

Even as Lee was heading for Ewell's position, the rattle of musketry around the Bliss farm began to crescendo. Lee's decision to prolong his line south along Seminary Ridge had brought up Anderson's Division of Hill's Corps, which provided ready reinforcements for the Rebel skirmishers opposing the 1st Delaware.

Union Lieutenant John Brady suddenly realized that his skirmish line north of the farm buildings "was being slowly pressed back toward our regimental centre." An even bigger surprise awaited young Brady when he reported this development to the regiment's commander, Edward P. Harris, who had set up his command post in the basement of the barn. As soon as Brady had explained things, Harris, "after carefully venturing from this, his safe retreat, and taking a very hasty glance over the situation, turned and fled precipitately, towards our main lines." His rapid departure left a captain and a couple of lieutenants on their own to confront the increasingly intense pressure of a numerically superior enemy.

After making a valiant effort to rally the skirmishers on the right, Brady retreated with them toward Cemetery Ridge. Word of the withdrawal was slow in getting to the Delaware troops south of the buildings, who suddenly found themselves almost cut off. In the ensuing confusion, Captain Martin W. B. Ellegood was mortally wounded, The twenty-three-year-old's letters reveal that he was a patriot sensitive to the ironies

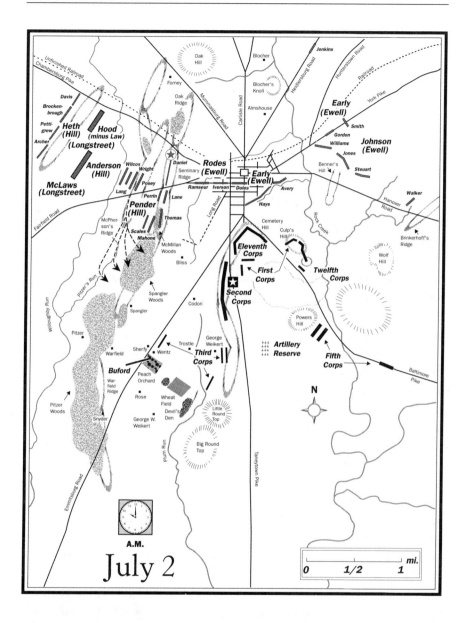

of war, as well as a serious scold when it came to his sister's constant over-spending. Ellegood would linger for four days before his wound finally claimed him, on July 6.

Watching the 1st Delaware tumble back from the Bliss farm, its Second Corps division commander, Alexander Hays, immediately began organizing a counterattack. As long as Rebel snipers held the place, he knew, it would be deadly difficult for Union troops to move along the crest of Cemetery Ridge. Between 9:30 and 10:00 A.M., Hays drew ten companies from one Ohio and two New York regiments and sent them forward to take the Bliss farm back.

With each passing hour, the Army of the Potomac was accomplishing something more important than bringing more men and arms to the field: it was finding its operational balance, setting in place the systems necessary for effective command and control. By 9:00 A.M., all corps present had established headquarters and reported their locations to Meade's staff. Signal officers had set up observation points on every Union-held piece of high ground; all were linked to Meade's nerve center by flag communication. The Reserve Artillery was in place, supply limbers of active guns were being serviced, and staff functions were being carried out.

Among those now on hand at headquarters was Meade's inherited chief-of-staff, Daniel Butterfield, who had requested an assignment upon his arrival. According to his own recollection, Meade told him, " 'General Butterfield, neither I nor any man can tell what the results of this day's operations may be. It is our duty to be prepared for every contingency, and I wish you to send out staff officers to learn all the roads that lead from this place, ascertain the positions of the corps—where their [supply] trains are; prepare to familiarize yourself with these details, so that in the event of any contingency, you can, without any order, be ready to meet it.' " Butterfield, whose loyalty to the dismissed Hooker had never wavered, took Meade's statement as a directive "to prepare an order to withdraw the army from that position," an interpretation he would discuss with other officers.

Also arriving from Taneytown around this time was Gouverneur K. Warren, who had already spent the evening hours of July 1 here, helping Hancock secure the position. Meade promptly entrusted Warren with the important task of examining the ground around Culp's Hill to assess the feasibility of an offensive. With his right flank settling down, Meade began to consider his left, where Daniel Sickles' Third Corps was positioned. On switching John Geary's division from Little Round Top to Culp's Hill, he had instructed Sickles to cover the position abandoned by the Twelfth Corps men. Now he asked his son George Meade Jr., who was serving with him as a staff aide, to ride over to the Third Corps headquarters and see how the deployment was going.

More eager than experienced, the younger Meade rode south along the Taneytown Road until he saw the diamond-emblemed headquarters flag flapping near a grove of trees just to the west. There he located Captain George E. Randolph, the Third Corps' artillery chief, and asked if the troop placement was going according to George Meade's wishes. By way of reply, Randolph reported that Sickles was resting, having been up most of the night. The artillerist entered the only tent that was pitched and remained inside for a few minutes. When he emerged, it was to announce that the corps had not taken up any position at all because Sickles was unclear as to where exactly his men were supposed to go.

This surprised young Meade, who was under the impression that his assignment was merely to confirm orders already given, not to explain the deployment. A more seasoned staff aide might have assumed enough of the commanding general's authority to insist that the orders be carried out as they were best understood, but George Junior was out of his depth. All he could do was tell Randolph that he would convey the situation to the general, his father, and ask what his wishes were.

When Robert E. Lee reached Richard Ewell's headquarters, he learned that the Second Corps commander was out reconnoitering his lines with Charles Venable. Present, however, was the unhappy supernumerary, Isaac Trimble, who said he knew just the place when Lee asked to be taken to a good vantage point. Trimble led Lee to the almshouse, which boasted a cupola with a view. From it Lee observed that the Federals on Cemetery Hill were not hopelessly disorganized, as he had hoped. According to Trimble, Lee declared, " 'The enemy have the advantage of us in a short and inside line, and we are too much extended.' "

They returned to Ewell's headquarters to find that the Second Corps leader had not yet returned. When Armistead L. Long, back from identifying artillery positions along Seminary Ridge, caught up with Lee here, he sensed that "the general had been waiting . . . for some time."

At last Ewell arrived with Venable, who was now fully convinced that conditions on this flank would seriously hamper any offensive effort. His earnest seconding of Ewell's previous arguments confirmed Lee's conclusion the Second Corps might at best support an assault. This provided the final piece of his attack plan: a flanking movement by Longstreet against the Federal left, accompanied by opportunistic advances in the center by Hill and on the Confederate left by Ewell. One of Ewell's staff officers, Jed Hotchkiss, recorded, "General Lee was at our quarters in the a.m. and there planned the movement, though not, in my opinion, very sanguine of its success. He feared we would only take it at a great sacrifice of life."

George Meade Jr. made a quick round trip between the respective headquarters of Daniel Sickles and his father. The message he brought back from the army commander contained little ambiguity. Sickles, as Meade *fils* recollected the instructions, was "to go into position on the left of the Second Corps [so] that his right was to connect with the left of the Second Corps, [and] he was to prolong with his line the line of that corps, occupying the position that General Geary had held the night before."

On his return, young Meade found the Third Corps headquarters all in motion. Sickles displayed no emotion as his superior's aide delivered the message, and commented only that his troops were deploying even as they spoke. Turning toward the front, Sickles offered the parting observation that Geary's troops had not held any real position at all but had merely been "massed in the vicinity."

Sickles rode first to his left, the sector assigned to David B. Birney's division. By now the corps commander had most likely made up his mind on two important points. First, he was convinced that George Meade's commitment to stand and fight at Gettysburg was far from resolute. Second, he had concluded that the lack of attention his flank had received from the commanding general made it his responsibility to act. Thus self-empowered, Sickles, with Birney's willing collaboration, began a deployment that paid a superficial obeisance to Meade's directives while actually constituting a stealthy repositioning of the Third Corps.

Almost from the instant he first traversed the area Meade had assigned him to defend, Sickles had deemed it "an unsatisfactory line because of its marked depression and the swampy character of the ground between Cemetery Ridge and Little Round Top." Nor was that his only complaint, for he believed that "to abandon the Emmitsburg road to the enemy would be unpardonable." Every subsequent action taken by Sickles stemmed from his conviction that the Federal left flank "was our assailable point." Although he would never explain why he thought so, he would later credit what he perceived to be "the enemy's movements on our left" with furnishing "conclusive indications of a design on [the Confederates'] part to attack there."

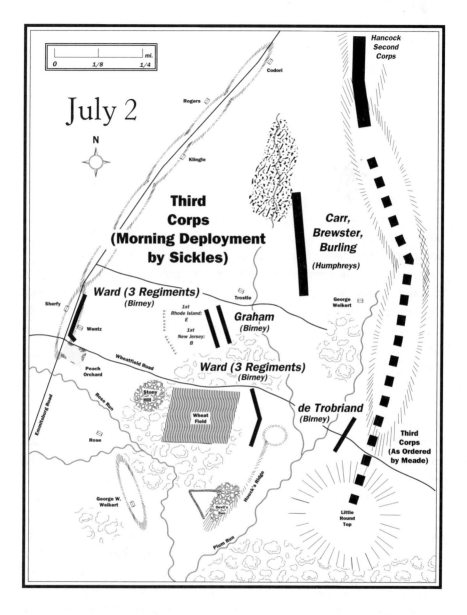

Birney's troop deployment provided scant protection for Little Round Top. Instead, the division commander set up a strong outpost line of three regiments along the Emmitsburg Road, near the Sherfy house. Three more regiments were posted northwest of Little Round Top, behind a stone wall fronting a large wheat field. Several batteries assigned to the corps were positioned between these two groups of regiments, aiming generally southward toward the John Rose farm. When Birney's absent brigade (Graham's) came up from Emmitsburg sometime before 10:00 A.M., it was massed to support the cannon. Slightly north of this activity, Sickles' other division, commanded by the no-nonsense Andrew Humphreys, remained in an armed bivouac, with pickets out but troops otherwise resting.

Among the Third Corps units arriving from Emmitsburg was the 4th New York Independent Battery, led by Captain James E. Smith. Smith later recounted, "As we approached the ground between the two armies in the vicinity of the 'peach orchard,' I noticed that the fences had been cleared away and all preparations made that usually precede a battle; even then the pickets and skirmishers were uneasy and kept up a desultory fire, little puffs of thin blue smoke dotting the plain before us." An aide to artillery chief George Randolph directed the battery to a modest road running east from the peach orchard, which it was to follow until it reached a wheat field,* and there park. While Smith's practiced eye would have taken in the excellent fields of fire near the peach orchard, it would likely not have missed the tumbled, rocky ground just southeast of where his guns halted. It was the kind of place no artilleryman would want to defend.

Following a course correction outside Westminster, Maryland, to get onto the road that would become the Baltimore Pike into Gettysburg, the Sixth Corps, representing nearly one fifth of Meade's army, trudged on. "Little is said by any one, for we are too weary to talk," reminisced a Rhode Island soldier, "only now and then an officer sharply orders the men to close up." Not long after dawn, halts were ordered to allow the men to make coffee, but in several instances, as recollected by a Massachusetts man, "before the coffee is made the bugle rings out its unwelcome call and the procession is resumed."

The leading elements began crossing the Pennsylvania border shortly before midday. "The bands all discoursed sweet music and you know the almost magical effect which national melodies would have upon the minds of our wearied but brave soldiers," wrote a member of the 49th Pennsylvania. The Sixth Corps reinforcements were some six miles from Gettysburg.

* * *

*This rough lane would later become known as the Wheatfield Road.

After departing Ewell's headquarters, Robert E. Lee rode back to his own, on the southern side of the Chambersburg Pike along Seminary Ridge. There he met with the cavalry brigadier, Albert Jenkins, who had been fetched by an aide sent out by Lee when he was still with the Second Corps. Ewell had complained that he had three good infantry brigades tied down watching after the army's left flank. On learning that Jenkins' horsemen had reached the battlefield late the previous day, Lee had decided to use them to relieve Ewell's units. Jenkins acknowledged the order and left to carry it out.

Lee next checked on Longstreet's progress. Riding along Seminary Ridge, he passed through an artillery position that he thought belonged with Longstreet's column. When the officer commanding gently corrected his superior, Lee apologized and asked, " 'Do you know where General Longstreet is?' " Colonel R. Lindsay Walker, A. P. Hill's artillery chief, spoke up to say that he knew where to find him, and offered himself as a guide. "As we rode together," Walker later recollected, "General Lee manifested more impatience than I ever saw him exhibit upon any other occasion."

Lee learned from Longstreet that all of McLaws' Division was on hand and ready to march, and that Hood's lacked only Law's Alabama brigade to be complete. Law's men were expected soon, so Longstreet asked to delay starting his flank march until they arrived. By Longstreet's account, "General Lee assented. We waited about forty minutes for these troops." At some point during the delay, Longstreet waved up Edward P. Alexander, who at his direction was operating with the authority of First Corps artillery chief. Alexander later wrote, "My recollection is that a lot of our infantry was halted not far off & some of their generals were around, & quite a lot of staff officers. In Gen. Lee's presence Longstreet pointed out the enemy's positions & said that we would attack his left flank. . . . He . . . suggested that I go at once . . . & get an idea of the ground, & then go & bring my own battalion up." Not needing to be told twice, the officer hurried away.

Few units had as hard a time waiting this day as Brigadier General Harry T. Hays' brigade, of Jubal Early's division. It was one of two all-Louisiana brigades in Lee's army, and of the pair it was Hays' men who reveled in their unsavory reputation as the "wharf rats from New Orleans." Fierce fighters in combat, verging on uncontrollable when not under fire, the twelve hundred or so soldiers, grouped into five regiments, were cocky and proud of being nicknamed the Louisiana Tigers.

They were very much caged tigers during most of the daylight hours of July 2. According to Captain William J. Seymour of Hays' staff, Richard Ewell had intended to press his entire line close to the enemy but had discovered soon after daylight that the topography prevented him from doing so. By then, however, the Louisiana Tigers had already been positioned, so they were stuck, strung out along a little ravine that followed the course of a creek called Winebrenner's Run. The open ground in their rear was commanded by Yankee cannon frowning on them from Cemetery Hill, rendering it impossible to withdraw the brigade "without an immense loss," noted Seymour. Federal sharpshooters made their situation miserable: it was, Seymour observed, "almost certain death for a man to stand upright" from the scant cover provided by the ravine.

Matters were even worse on the picket line. A Louisiana lieutenant posted behind a fence recalled that "if any one showed themselves or a hat was seen above the fence a volley was poured into us." Men dropped almost every hour as snipers harvested the unwary or unlucky. July 2 would turn out to be another hot, sticky day, making the ordeal of so many unwashed men cramped together in a muddy ravine even more wretched.

Sharing the experience of the Louisiana soldiers were the nine hundred North Carolinians of Hoke's Brigade, fighting at Gettysburg under the command of Colonel Isaac Avery. While his three regiments were not snugged quite as close to the enemy as Hays' men, they were posted along another inhospitable section of Winebrenner's Run. One officer would later recall only "lying all day under a July sun, suffering with intense heat, and continually [being] annoyed by the enemy's sharpshooters from the heights."

The acting brigade commander was a large and popular man who won praise for his "chivalrous bearing." Like his men, he spent this hot day crouching or lying along Winebrenner's Run, with "enemy . . . balls hissing all round us," in the words of an aide. When his nervous subordinate suggested moving somewhere less exposed, Avery laughed and pointed around them, saying that there was no such place.

Any hope George Meade had of staging an attack from his right flank vanished when Gouverneur K. Warren reported his reconnaissance, "I did not think that the ground was favorable for directing an attack with proper intelligence and vigor," Warren recalled. His assessment was that the area was "rough, being the valley of a considerable stream with dams upon it, that therefore it was favorable to the defense and not to the attack, and that artillery could only be moved with difficulty through woods and marshy places."

Hardly had Meade begun considering what to do next when an anxious-looking Daniel Sickles arrived. The Third Corps commander was more certain than ever that the Rebels were targeting his flank. "I found that my impression as to the intention of the enemy to attack in that direction was not concurred in at headquarters," Sickles later declared. According to another account, Meade dismissed his concerns with the comment, " 'O[h], generals are all apt to look for the attack to be made where they are.' " "I asked General Meade to go over the ground on the left and examine it," Sickles recorded. But the commander declined to leave his headquarters, and when Sickles requested that Warren be deputized for the task, Meade indicated that his engineer officer had other things to do. "I then asked him to send General [Henry] Hunt, his chief of artillery, and that was done," the Third Corps chief reported. Together the two men rode off to inspect the left flank of Meade's Gettysburg position.

Few Federal units came to Gettysburg with as much to prove as the Third Brigade of Alexander Hays' Second Corps division. Commanded by Colonel George L. Willard, its four regiments bore the stigma of having surrendered with the Union garrison at Harper's Ferry in September 1862. Although they had not then been brigaded together, the fifteen hundred men nonetheless felt the humiliation that had been heaped upon them for events over which they had had no control. One of the regiments, the 126th New York, had been especially singled out for failing to hold an exposed position.

Following a dreary stay in a U.S. parole camp awaiting proper exchange, the dispirited regiments had been joined into a brigade and assigned to Washington's defenses, where they were put under the stern leadership of Alexander Hays. Under him the men were rigorously prepared for their next combat experience, and they responded with a will. Soon even the hypercritical Hays was writing that the "Harper's Ferry boys have turned out trumps, and when we do get a chance look out for blood." The brigade had been appended so quickly as the Second Corps passed Washington that it arrived at Gettysburg lacking a corps battle flag and the proper corps insignia for the men's uniforms. Nevertheless, the Harper's Ferry brigade, in the words of one of its members, "panted to remove that stigma."

In joining the Army of the Potomac, Alexander Hays had been elevated to command the division, leaving the brigade to the colonel of the 125th New York. It was the first decent break Willard had gotten since the war began. He had transferred from the regular army to the volunteers seeking promotion, only to have his aspirations stalled by the Harper's Ferry debacle. Now, finally, he was leading his men into what everyone felt would be an important battle. It was a good match: four regiments yearning for vindication led by an officer desperate for validation.

Willard's brigade joined Hays' other two on Cemetery Ridge, connecting on their right with the Eleventh Corps and fronting the Bliss farm, some two thousand feet away. The Harper's Ferry boys, designated the division's reserve, were withheld from the first line, save for the 39th New York, which was drawn into the Bliss farm action.

In its hurried march to Gettysburg, the Second Corps had outpaced its supply wagons, so many foot soldiers went hungry today. One of them recollected that "by a diligent search of our pockets and haversacks we got coffee enough to give [us] a swallow or two apiece. . . . We gave our belts a hitch and all who smoked indulged vigorously while we awaited events."

The fighting around the Bliss farm fell into a grim pattern. After one side gained control, there would be a roiling lull as the other began increasing the pressure. Then things would erupt into brief violence that would dispossess the party holding the buildings, thereby starting the whole cycle again.

The ten companies that Alexander Hays had sent forward after the eviction of the 1st Delaware maintained control of the Bliss farm until about 11:00 A.M. Then Brigadier General Carnot Posey's all-Mississippi brigade took over the sector and promptly reinforced the Confederate voltigeurs. "The enemy occupy a very commanding position having their artillery planted on a high ridge, with their infantry in rear," observed one of them. A Yankee described "a lively skirmish" around the Bliss farm that again ousted the Union soldiers. Still determined to control the advanced post, Hays cobbled together a reaction force from the 125th New York, the 12th New Jersey, and even the 1st Delaware and sent it forward to regain the farm buildings.

Some of the artillery on Cemetery Ridge was now getting into the fray as well, with several batteries arrayed along the high ground opening fire on the farmhouse and barn. Among them was the 4th United States, Battery A, Lieutenant Alonzo Cushing commanding. The Yankee cannon were answered by Rebel guns posted in the vicinity of the McMillan Woods.

Henry Hunt would long remember his ride along the Third Corps line that July 2. As they left army headquarters, he told Sickles that he "did not know anything of the intentions of General Meade" and asked the Third Corps commander for his ideas. Sickles, Hunt recalled, "wished to throw forward his line from the position in which it was then placed, and where it was covered in its front by woods and rocks, with a view to cover the Emmitsburg road." Instead of moving south to follow Cemetery Ridge, Sickles led Hunt on a tangent that took them along the Emmitsburg Road.

At first Hunt assumed that Sickles' interest in covering the road was related to his absent artillery train, which might be using that route. By the time they reached the Sherfy peach orchard, however, he had realized that the general wanted to do more than push out a covering force: he wanted to reset his entire corps along the road's axis. Ever the professional, Hunt had to admit that a position starting at the peach orchard and continuing north along the Emmitsburg Road would have its advantages. Small ripples of ridges, he later remembered, "commanded all the ground behind, as well as in front of them, and together constituted a favorable position for the enemy to hold." Hunt also recognized that any line set on the peach orchard would have to bend sharply back toward Little Round Top, creating a difficult-to-defend salient angle that would be susceptible to enfilading fire; but he felt that the rolling ground offered enough protection to "reduce that evil to a minimum."

Sickles' scheme had a critical flaw, though, and the Army of the Potomac artillery chief put his finger on it, noting that "it would so greatly lengthen our line . . . as to require a larger force than the Third

Corps alone to hold it." Stopping at the orchard, Hunt pointed to a patch of woods across an open field to the west, lying along a ridge line. If the enemy got in there, he said, it would make it very difficult to hold the Emmitsburg Road. He suggested that Sickles send in some troops to check out the area, known as the Pitzer Woods.*

Off to the north, the Bliss farm was erupting in another skirmish cycle, again involving artillery on Cemetery Ridge. Upon hearing the cannon boom, Hunt decided that his place was with his gunners, not riding with Daniel Sickles. He offered a hasty explanation and made a quick exit, promising to swing around toward Little Round Top before stopping at Meade's headquarters to pass along what he had learned.

Before Hunt could break away, Sickles asked him "whether it would be proper to move forward his line." No, Hunt answered, adding that the Third Corps commander "should wait orders from General Meade." He then rode off, leaving Daniel Sickles convinced that he intended to obtain the necessary permission himself. Until those orders arrived, there was the reconnaissance to be conducted into the Pitzer Woods.

Of the fifty-one Union infantry brigades gathered at Gettysburg, few were more distinctive or more proudly conscious of their distinction than five regiments in Brigadier General John C. Caldwell's Second Corps division, self-styled the Irish Brigade. Organized in 1861 by the popular Erin émigré Thomas Francis Meagher, the little brigade was perhaps 530 strong this day. The three New York regiments representing its 1861 nucleus were still present, though barely at company strength; also shorthanded was the 116th Pennsylvania, which, with the 28th Massachusetts (224 strong), rounded out the command.

The Irish Brigade had reached Gettysburg this morning with the rest of the Second Corps, after a march of only a few miles. Following an hour's pause as a reserve while the threat to Cemetery Hill was being evaluated, the Second Corps had been positioned southward along Cemetery Ridge. Along with Caldwell's three other brigades, the Irishmen were "massed" near the George Weikert farm. "Here we stacked arms, and the men were ordered to rest," reported an officer in the 116th Pennsylvania. "Every movement of the enemy was watched with interest," remembered an officer, "and the hours seemed long on that bright summer day."

*Hunt was not alone in recommending that the Pitzer Woods be investigated.

The large number of men grouped in one place, coupled with the ominous portents of battle, suggested to the brigade's spiritual adviser, Chaplain William Corby, that his duties on this day included lifting the burden of sin from his flock through the act of conditional absolution. Although the most frequently cited account of this ceremony places it late in the afternoon, when combat was imminent, another, more contemporary source puts it at midmorning, when there would have been time for it.

"The brigade stood in a column of regiments, closed in mass," wrote an officer in attendance. "Father Corby . . . addressing the men, [said] . . . that each one could receive the benefit of the absolution by making a sincere Act of Contrition and firmly resolving to embrace the first opportunity of confessing his sins, . . . and remind[ed] them of the high and sacred nature of their trust as soldiers. . . . Then, stretching his right hand toward the brigade, Father Corby pronounced the words of the absolution. . . . The service was more than impressive, it was awe-inspiring."

Many of Gettysburg's residents tried their best to carry on with their normal routines. Sarah Broadhead, for one, made a point of preparing a solid dinner, including shortcake and ham (using the last of the meat she had). She remembered that "some neighbors coming in, joined us, and we had the first quiet meal since the contest began."

For others in town, there was a new activity to observe: the building of barricades. Henry Jacobs watched Rebel soldiers tear down a stone wall opposite his home to get material for a breastwork that they then spread across the street. "It lay there," he wrote, "a spectacle of ruin and a promise of destruction, all day." Near Charlie McCurdy's house, the Confederate soldiers piled up wagons, boxes, and barrels to create defensive choke points that were soon being put to a use their builders had not anticipated: "It only served as a source of entertainment for small boys who found a new game in climbing over the obstruction," McCurdy recollected. Daniel Skelly made friends with a Rebel major who said he was from Pittsburgh. "He was a fair minded man and reasonable in his opinions," Skelly allowed, "there being no rancor or bitterness evident in any of his observations on the progress of the conflict."

There was a domestic dispute of sorts being waged in Nellie Aughinbaugh's house. Her father hated the very idea of Rebels' occupying his town and would do "no more for them [than] he could help." But Nellie's mother felt sympathy for the young Southern boys, particularly after she saw them eating looted fish raw. "While Father would be gone with baskets full of provisions to the [Union] hospitals," Nellie reminisced, "Mother would tell the men to give her the fish to broil off for them, and would set one of us children to watch for Father's return. Mother would say those poor fellows were somebodies' sons. . . . When we would see Father approaching we would call, 'Mother here he comes!' and she would take the fish off the stove quickly and give them to the men."

"The greatest danger was from the sharpshooters," Jennie McCreary explained. Attorney William McClean found this out firsthand when he yielded to temptation and ascended from the cellar that was sheltering his family to take a peek from a second-story window of his house. He had just cracked open the shutter when some inner sense warned him to turn away. Almost at that instant, a sniper's bullet smashed through the thin wood and struck the bed where his sick wife had lain until he helped her down to the cellar. "I learned that the indulgence of curiosity at such a time was perilous," the attorney intoned.

Whether or not they admitted it, all in Gettysburg were holding their breath. "Comparative quiet along both lines this morning," noted diarist Jane Smith. "The day wears on; still only skirmishing."

Of the U.S. units reaching Gettysburg this day, the Fifth Corps perhaps most clearly reflected, in its minor odyssey, the progressive changes in George Meade's thinking. The corps had halted its march just after midnight, stretched along the Hanover Road west of that town. Like some other soldiers engaged in this campaign, Major General George Sykes' men had greeted with cheers the false rumor that George B. McClellan would be taking command of the Army of the Potomac a third time.

The two divisions leading the line of advance had broken camp to march early on July 2, turning south off the Hanover Road before reaching Brinkerhoff's Ridge, then massing near there as part of Meade's tentative plan to launch an offensive from his right. Shortly after 7:00 A.M., a few Fifth Corps skirmishers had even tangled with some of Ewell's outpost line. Three hours later, once Meade had abandoned his offensive dreams and filled the Cemetery Ridge line with the Second and Third Corps, the Fifth marched into a central reserve position, where it was joined by its late-arriving Third Division.

Little of the larger scheme was apparent to the men and officers marching under the symbol of the Maltese Cross. The four regiments constituting Colonel Strong Vincent's Third Brigade, in Brigadier General James Barnes' First Division, had no more insight than their comrades. A busy diarist in the 16th Michigan griped that the brigade had taken up "position several times and spent the whole forenoon maneuvering & marching around." All the back-and-forth imparted only confusion to the officer commanding the 20th Maine in Vincent's brigade, Joshua Chamberlain. "We knew the battle was to be fought, and a sharp one," he reflected, "but what most impressed our minds was the uncertainty of its plan. Indeed there seemed as yet to be none." When the men at last halted, around midday, they expected they would rest for a time.

In the 44th New York, of the same brigade, the halt allowed for personal business. "We cooked breakfast and rested until noon," wrote one soldier. "Then the most of us took our pants off and went for the graybacks for a while."* Adding up "the spiteful firing along the picket line, an occasional exchange of artillery shots, [and] the hurrying to and fro of staff officers," another New Yorker concluded "that a great battle was about to be fought." If so, a soldier in the 83rd Pennsylvania worried that their brigade commander would rush headlong into trouble. "Vincent had a peculiar penchant for being in the lead," he later observed. "Whenever or wherever his brigade might be in a position to 'get ahead' . . . , he was sure to be ahead."

"The men of our corps employed their time in rest and in making preparations for the work before them," held an officer in the 44th New York. In the 20th Maine, that work meant carrying a full combat munitions load. According to a line officer, "At this point twenty rounds of cartridges were issued to each man in addition to those already in the boxes, making a total of sixty rounds."

It was approaching noon when reporter Whitelaw Reid passed near the Leister house. "General Meade had finished his arrangement of the lines," Reid scribbled. "Reports of the skirmishing were coming in; the facts developed by certain reconnaissances were being presented[;] . . . aid[e]s and orderlies were galloping off and back; General Warren . . . was with

*Graybacks were lice, endemic in the ranks.

the General Commanding, poring over the maps of the field which the engineers had just finished; most of the staff were stretched beneath an apple tree, resting while they could."

One of the figures commanding Reid's attention was the "trim, well-tailored person of Major-General [Alfred] Pleasonton," Meade's cavalry chief. Only after the battle would Reid realize that at least one of the trips he had seen Pleasonton make in and out of army headquarters had had as its purpose to deal with a major tactical blunder. Whether due to exhaustion or to an imperfect understanding of the army's situation, late this morning, when John Buford requested permission to withdraw his division for refitting, Pleasonton agreed, then directed the experienced cavalry commander to take his troopers "back to Westminster, our depot, to protect it, and also to recruit." With this decision, one of the army's best combat leaders and his veteran command left the Gettysburg area, not to return until the fighting was over.

George Meade approved this action on the unspoken assumption that another mounted force would come up to protect the army's left flank. Pleasonton would later explain that Buford's division had been "severely handled" on July 1 (which was untrue) and assert that he had promptly moved up another cavalry unit to replace it (a bald lie). No one took over for Buford's men after they began pulling out, around midday. Not until Daniel Sickles complained about losing his flank protection did Meade realize that Pleasonton had not followed through. Dispatches demanding corrective action were forwarded to the cavalry chief at 12:50 and 12:55 P.M.; an hour later, Pleasonton sent instructions to a cavalry unit posted on the far Union right, directing it to move to the far left. The riders would not arrive in time to accomplish anything this day.

Following their long tramp to reach Gettysburg yesterday, and their active probing of Culp's Hill last night, the soldiers of Edward Johnson's division in Ewell's Corps expected to fight early. Instead of advancing into combat, though, save for the few companies dispersed as skirmishers, the men waited. "Greatly did officers and men marvel as morning, noon, and afternoon passed in inaction," noted Randolph McKim, a Maryland officer in Brigadier General George H. Steuart's brigade. The commander of the 10th Louisiana, in Nicholls' Brigade,* concurred, later report-

*Colonel J. M. Williams commanded the brigade at Gettysburg.

ing that there was "nothing doing along our line, men getting restless; the hour of noon had passed; we heard the chopping of trees on the hill; it [was] evident the enemy were building a line of entrenchments." Less exposed to enemy fire than most Southern units on the field, Johnson's three brigades (a fourth was watching the Hanover Road) spent the hot day wondering if they would ever fight.

Following his brief conference with Robert E. Lee, Albert Jenkins returned to his 1,300-man mounted brigade, encamped just a short distance north of Gettysburg along the Heidlersburg Road. Representing the largest cavalry force then available to Lee, Jenkins' men had been cast in an important role: they were to replace the Second Corps infantry now providing flank security east of town. "Boots and Saddles" sounded, regiments and battalions were formed, and Jenkins waved his troopers southward. Possibly because time was short, or maybe as was his wont, Jenkins shared little about the mission with his subordinates.

Just as the head of the column reached the spot where John B. Gordon had staged his July 1 assault, Jenkins signaled his riders to halt, then move off the road. One of his staff imagined that he was waiting for some signal. "We were wondering at the silence prevalent," the aide recalled. "Only in long intervals the report of a gun [was] heard." Jenkins remained quietly motionless for some long minutes before gathering about half a dozen of his staff and heading off toward the town. Immediately after crossing Rock Creek, he steered his gaggle to the right to ascend Blocher's Knoll, from atop which they could see Gettysburg and the high ground beyond.

An officer on Jenkins' staff rode out from town and joined them, bringing information about the army's position. The others naturally massed around him as he indicated troop locations on his map. Soon enough the mounted crowd attracted the attention of some sharp-eyed Federal artillery spotters on Cemetery Hill, two miles away, who promptly sent over some shells. It took them only a couple of rounds to get the range; before the Confederate party could react, a fuzed shell exploded almost directly over Jenkins, punching him and his mount to the ground. By the time his staff reached him, the general was unconscious and bleeding from a scalp wound.

Jenkins' Brigade was not an especially tightly run outfit, and the sudden incapacitation of its commander disrupted the chain of command.

While his staff carried the wounded cavalryman back to the house he had used the night before, his brigade was stalled. No further effort was made to carry out Jenkins' assignment, nor was any word sent to Robert E. Lee.

The deployment of Anderson's Division of A. P. Hill's corps, assigned to extend the Confederate right, added five brigades to those already arrayed along the southern sweep of Seminary Ridge. One of those five comprised the four Georgia units of Brigadier General Ambrose R. Wright's command, three regiments and a battalion. Wright took up an eastward-facing line just north of Spangler's Woods. His fourteen hundred men, who had seen no fighting yesterday, were positioned in "a narrow strip of oak woods, with an old grassfield in rear of our line, and fields of oats, young corn and wheat in our front." The 2nd Georgia Battalion deployed on the skirmish line, so close to the enemy that the Rebels, as one recollected, "could see our Federal brothers." The only noteworthy action through midday came when a Yankee artillery shell spooked a red fox, which was then chased north along the ridge by soldiers from Wright's and Thomas' Brigades until someone from Lane's Brigade "caught and killed it."

Wright held a middle position in Anderson's deployment, with Carnot Posey's Mississippi brigade on his left and Perry's Brigade of Florida troops, under Colonel David Lang, on his right. The honor of being Anderson's rightmost unit went to Brigadier General Cadmus M. Wilcox, whose brigade consisted of five Alabama regiments. Anderson's instructions to Wilcox suggest that as late as midday, the details of Lee's attack plan had not yet filtered through to the Third Corps. Wilcox was told to use part of his force to refuse his line—that is, bend it back— to front southeast and south, to guard against any enemy effort to get in behind Hill's position. Had Anderson known, when he set the formation, that Longstreet's Corps would be filling in farther south, he would not have bothered to give Wilcox that order.

Wilcox's Brigade marched off toward the Pitzer Woods, where Wilcox was to pivot his refused right flank. The 10th and 11th Regiments had been selected to cover that section. As the pair advanced, the 10th entered some woods, which slowed its progress, while the 11th, moving more quickly over open fields, pressed ahead, reaching its designated station well before its partner. Just as the men of the 11th attained their

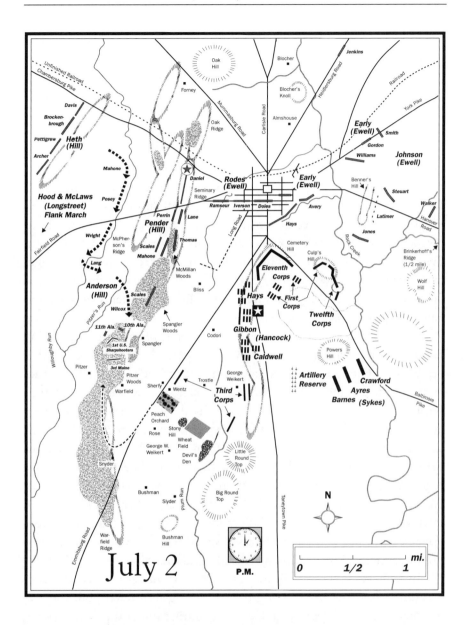

Unfinished Railroad
Chambersburg Pike
Oak Hill
Blocher
Jenkins
Forney
Blocher's Knoll
Hagerstown Road
Railroad
York Pike
Davis
Brocken-brough
Oak Ridge
Mummasburg Road
Almshouse
Early (Ewell)
Smith
Pettigrew
Heth (Hill)
Carlisle Road
Gordon
Johnson (Ewell)
Archer
Williams
Mahone
Daniel
Rodes (Ewell)
Early (Ewell)
Benner's Hill
Steuart
Walker
Hood & McLaws (Longstreet) Flank March
Posey
Seminary Ridge
Ramseur Iverson Doles
Avery
Latimer
Hanover Road
Perrin
Lane
Long Road
Hays
Jones
Pender (Hill)
Fairfield Road
Wright
McPher-son's Ridge
Scales
Thomas
Cemetery Hill
Culp's Hill
Brinkerhoff's Ridge (1/2 mile)
Lang
Mahone
McMillan Woods
Eleventh Corps
Wolf Hill
Anderson (Hill)
Scales
Bliss
Hays
First Corps
Wilcox
Pitzer's Run
11th Ala. 10th Ala.
Spangler Woods
Codori
Gibbon
Twelfth Corps
1st U.S. Sharpshooters
Spangler
(Hancock)
Powers Hill
Willoughby Run
3rd Maine
Caldwell
Pitzer
Pitzer Woods
Sherfy
Wentz
Trostle
George Weikert
Artillery Reserve
Crawford
Warfield
Third Corps
Ayres
Barnes (Sykes)
Baltimore Pike
Peach Orchard
Rose
Stony Hill
Wheat Field
George W. Weikert
Devil's Den
Little Round Top
Snyder
Emmitsburg Road
Bushman
Slyder
Plum Run
Big Round Top
Taneytown Pike
N
War-field Ridge
Bushman Hill
July 2
P.M.
0   1/2   1   mi.

position, the woods in which the 10th was supposed to be posted erupted in a burst of gunfire that ripped into their surprised ranks.

The Alabama soldiers had encountered the reconnaissance force dispatched from the Union Third Corps, at the suggestion of Henry Hunt and others, to investigate the Pitzer Woods. Two regiments had drawn the task: the 3rd Maine and one of the most coldly efficient combat units in the Army of the Potomac, the 1st United States Sharpshooters. This latter was an elite outfit that required prospective candidates to pass a tough marksmanship test. Clad in distinctive dark-green uniforms with leather leggings, and armed mostly with Sharp rifles, its members were men used to operating in small groups with little support, men used to showing initiative and nerve in carrying out their assignments, and, perhaps most important, men used to killing.

The U.S. Sharpshooters were the brainchild of Hiram Berdan, an unconventional and controversial soldier in his own right, who had obtained government approval to form two such regiments in the fall of 1861. They had proven their worth on more than one occasion, so for David Birney they were the obvious choice for this assignment. Lieutenant Colonel Casper Trepp led the 1st in this action, though Colonel Berdan was also present, and in overall command. To avoid being caught in the open fields west of Sherfy's peach orchard, the scouting force had first marched south along the Emmitsburg Road and then swung west to enter the Pitzer Woods from the south.

Skirmishers from the 10th Alabama were only just making contact with Berdan's men when the 11th unknowingly offered its flank to the Yankees' deadly rifles. Hit by a rapid series of well-aimed fusillades, the 11th fled back to the main column to be reformed. Several sharpshooters forgot their stealth training and raced into the open after the 11th, presenting easy targets for the 10th's skirmishers, who were now fully alerted to the danger. The 10th advanced through the woods from the north, slowly pressing the sharpshooters back until they reached the reserve line held by the 3rd Maine. For some twenty-five minutes, the combat was roughly even. "It was quite a spirited little fight . . . ," Wilcox would remember, "and brought to the front several staff officers, who inquired if we needed reinforcements." When the 8th Alabama arrived to assist the 10th by working its way around the Yankee flank, Hiram Berdan ordered a withdrawal.

In later years, Daniel Sickles and others would insist that Berdan's expedition had uncovered Longstreet's turning movement, but this was not the case. Longstreet's march was just getting under way at that point, and its forward elements were a good distance removed from the scene of this scrap. Still, for Sickles, Berdan's report served as confirmation that the enemy was extending across his front. Soon after digesting the colonel's tale, Sickles took another significant part-step toward the greatest insubordination of his military career, by ordering David Birney to shift his entire division into a line touching the Emmitsburg Road.

*   *   *

If any unit in the Army of the Potomac could be said to be operating under an unlucky star, it would have to be Colonel Leopold von Gilsa's First Brigade, in the Eleventh Corps' First Division (commanded on July 1 by Francis Barlow, and on July 2 by Adelbert Ames). At Chancellorsville on May 2, von Gilsa's four regiments had held the army's right flank, meaning that they were the first to be swamped under the human tide when half of Lee's army crashed over them. Nearly 300 out of the unit's approximately 1,500 members had been killed, wounded, or captured (the last category representing half the total) inside of ten terrible minutes. On July 1, three of the brigade's regiments,* about 900 men in all, had again been manning the army's rightmost outpost, and once more they had been engulfed by the violent Rebel tide of Gordon's Brigade. Slightly more than half had survived the fighting and the jumbled retreat to Cemetery Hill.

George Meade needed every hand and every gun, so as quickly as brigades could be reorganized, they were shoved into spaces along Cemetery Hill. Von Gilsa's men now found themselves aligned along a stone wall bordering a lane that connected with a brickyard at the northeastern base of eastern Cemetery Hill. Yesterday, when their commander had finally disentangled himself from the chaotic retreat, an aide had dolefully informed him that bugles and drums were no longer needed, as the brigade was now small enough to "command . . . with the voice."

During the night of July 1 and the early-morning hours of July 2, the absent 41st New York had rejoined the brigade, adding two hundred rifles to the count. That unit plus the 153rd Pennsylvania provided skirmishers for the small-scale actions undertaken throughout the morning and midafternoon. According to one of the few extant accounts by men in von Gilsa's command, several in the brigade "were wounded and others killed, while going for water to a spring in front of them, by a rebel sharpshooter hidden in a tree, who was finally brought down by a bullet from one of the Fifth-fourth [New York]." An officer of the 153rd Pennsylvania who was on the skirmish line spent much of the early afternoon warily watching "quite a body of men in a depression of the ground between us and the rebel battery on a hill back of them."

Many of von Gilsa's men were German by birth or heritage. They had endured cruel jeers and epithets after Chancellorsville and knew that

---

*The fourth regiment, the 41st New York, had been on detached duty at Emmitsburg, guarding the corps' trains.

their performance yesterday would only bring more of the same. Whether or not the scorn was justified, their morale was very low this day. Crouching behind the stone wall along Brickyard Lane, under the hot sun and subject to the sudden death visited by enemy snipers, von Gilsa's soldiers could look ahead to more fighting only with a mixture of wounded pride, anxiety, and dread.

The arrival of Brigadier General Evander M. Law's brigade, just before noon, was the signal for Longstreet to begin his flank march. Preceding the infantry columns were the guns commanded by Edward P. Alexander. The capable colonel had little problem picking a route that would bypass an open patch of ground being observed by Federal signal officers on Little Round Top. The fighting in the Pitzer Woods was over by the time Alexander halted his march, not far below the point where Pitzer's Run branched northward from Willoughby Run. After seeing to the parking of his guns, the artillery officer retraced his route until he found the infantry column, McLaws' Division leading, immobilized just shy of the exposed clearing.

If Longstreet's troops were to have the desired shock effect once they went into action, it was essential that they not be spotted moving into position. In an omission that would never be explained, neither Longstreet nor McLaws had detailed any officer of Alexander's caliber to scout the way. A partial explanation for Longstreet was that his failure to persuade Lee to attempt a much wider flanking move had left him visibly agitated and not sufficiently focused on the myriad of small details that a corps commander had to handle on such a march.

To the end of his days, Longstreet would remain convinced that Lee had appended Samuel Johnston to the expedition as its guide, while that young officer himself understood his duties as being solely advisory. Johnston's scout this morning had been undertaken not to locate a route sufficient for a corps, but to reconnoiter the enemy line, so he was as surprised as anyone when McLaws' column ground to a halt before the clearing.

Although he would later have some tart observations to make about Longstreet's management of this enterprise, McLaws would never offer a rationale for his own failure to follow the bypass already used successfully by Alexander. Instead, McLaws flew into a rage (a soldier would afterward recall his "saying things I would not like to teach my grandson   to repeat") and decided that nothing less than a reverse march to a different route would suffice. Hood's Division, following closely behind, was already intermingled with his, so time would be lost separating the two. When Longstreet was at last alerted to the situation, he suggested that the columns might simply about-face, but that maneuver would upset the plan calling for McLaws' Division to lead the attack, and its commander would not countenance that. Even as Lee was reluctant to intervene with his direct subordinates, so was Longstreet passive in his response to McLaws' obstinacy. It took even more time, then, to negotiate a path for McLaws' countermarch. As E. P. Alexander would later comment, "There is no telling the value of the hours which were lost by that division that morning."

Of all the tactical problems confronting Richard S. Ewell this day, the most vexing was how to deploy his artillery. Plainly stated, he had more guns available than places to put them. Joseph W. Latimer, responsible for the cannon assigned to Edward Johnson's division, knew that firsthand. After spending much of the morning scouting locations, he had to admit that there was only one viable site, Benner's Hill, and even that was far from ideal. Although it would afford a clean shot at the enemy guns on Cemetery Hill, only the southern tip of the position would bear on Culp's Hill; conversely, Yankee gunners from Culp's Hill to Cemetery Hill could target the Benner's Hill crest. Added to that was another problem: the space was limited, so Latimer could not employ all of his guns.

The moment his batteries moved into the open area, Latimer knew, they would come under fire; it therefore made no sense to commit them until they were needed. The artillerist was able to preposition six longer-range guns belonging to the Rockbridge Battery on the portion of the hill just north of the Hanover Road, but that was all. For the rest, there was nothing to do but wait in readiness to push out into the open on command. Latimer's cue would come from the other flank, with the sound of Longstreet's batteries opening fire serving as the signal for him to order his men forward. Until then, the gunners could only bide their time in the sultry heat.

David Birney's division occupied a defensive line unlike anything intended by George Meade. Brigadier General Charles K. Graham's all-Pennsylvania brigade took position partly along the Emmitsburg Road and partly in a line facing southwest, forming a forty-five-degree angle that pivoted on the corner of Sherfy's peach orchard. Brigadier General J. H. Hobart Ward's brigade took Houck's Ridge and Devil's Den, leaving Colonel Philippe Regis de Trobriand to fill in the space between the two with his brigade.

These officers would have had difficulty covering their sectors even with their full complement of troops, and that was a luxury they did not have. Ward's brigade, for instance, which had counted nearly 2,600 men on June 30, had two regiments dispersed on skirmish lines and a large number of men on the roster books who were not actually on hand (having been lost largely to straggling, illness, and detached duty), leaving Ward with barely 1,800 men to hold his position. The other brigade commanders faced similar problems.

Daniel Sickles now began to ease Andrew Humphreys' division out to match Birney's. The able Humphreys, having been kept in the dark throughout the day, had little sense of the overall scheme. He knew only that an advance toward the Emmitsburg Road from his position along Cemetery Ridge had broken his connection with Hancock's corps to his right. Sickles had one more surprise in store for Humphreys: even as he commenced moving his division, orders came detaching the smallest of his three brigades, Burling's, to serve as a reserve for Birney, whose command was now too thinly spread out to provide its own.

Once Birney's infantry were all in place, George Randolph began filling the gaps with his artillery. Several batteries were tightly packed into the salient angle, and three more were lined up to cover the space between the troops in the peach orchard and those near the wheat field. With one critical location remaining for Randolph's attention, James E. Smith got the call. As he later recollected, "Capt. G. E. Randolph, Chief of Third Corps Artillery, piloted the [4th New York Independent] Battery to 'Devil's Den,' pointing to a steep and rocky ridge running north and south, indicating that my guns were to find location thereon."

The spot indicated by Randolph lay at the southern end of Houck's Ridge, which itself formed the western wall of a valleylike area that was bounded on its eastern side by the more formidable Little Round Top and gently pierced by a slight, southward-flowing creek called Plum Run. The southern tip of Houck's Ridge offered the best field of fire toward the west, but there were formidable obstacles to placing cannon on its crest. A Pennsylvania soldier later wrote that Devil's Den seemed "as though nature in some wild freak had forgotten herself and piled great rocks in mad confusion together." A New York veteran observed that about "its base huge boulders, some of them as large as a small house, rest in an irregular, confused mass, forming nooks and cavernous recesses suggestive of its uncanny name."

There was no easy way to put Smith's cannon into this place. A soldier from the 124th New York, sent along as security, watched as the "guns were unlimbered at the foot of Rocky Ridge and hauled up the steep acclivity into position amid the rocks on its crest." "Here I could not place more than four guns on the crest," recorded Smith. "In rear of this ridge, the ground descended sharply to the east, leaving no room for the limbers on the crest, therefore they were posted as near to the guns as the nature of the declivity permitted. The remaining two guns were stationed in rear about seventy-five yards, where they would be used to advantage, covering the Plum Run Gorge passage, which lies to the south of and below the crest."

One thing Smith knew for sure: if the enemy came at him, he would be hard pressed to get any of his guns safely away from Devil's Den.

Robert E. Lee exercised his command over the Army of Northern Virginia through his corps commanders. Each was expected to understand both the overall plan and his specific role within it. Once he had conveyed his intentions, Lee assumed the role of observer. He is reported to have said once of his late and able lieutenant "Stonewall" Jackson, "I have but to show him my design, and I know that if it can be done it will be done. No need for me to send [instructions] or watch him." Applying this same principle to his three Gettysburg lieutenant generals, Lee ceded control of his plans and aspirations to them.

"General Lee rode with me a mile or more," James Longstreet later wrote of this afternoon's march toward the Federal left flank. In a different account he added, "I left General Lee only after the line had stretched out on the march." Certainly Lee was not present for the countermarch, when Longstreet's column folded back on itself before resuming a course to its destination. The division commanded by Lafayette McLaws was finally nearing Warfield Ridge, west of the Emmitsburg Road, when Longstreet intercepted his subordinate.

"How are you going in?" he asked. McLaws answered, "That will be determined when I can see what is in my front." "There is nothing in your front," Longstreet told him. "You will be entirely on the flank of the enemy." McLaws asserted that if such was the case, he would move his command forward in column until he was perpendicular to the enemy's position, then face left and attack. "That suits me," Longstreet said, and rode off.

On the opposite Confederate flank, Richard S. Ewell was playing wait-and-see. Anticipating that Albert Jenkins' brigade would relieve his units, as Lee had indicated, he allowed Jubal Early to march John B. Gordon's brigade from its position on the York Road to a point just in the rear of the two brigades he had waiting to attack Cemetery Hill. Ewell himself headed into town and there found a church with a tall steeple that would make a good observation post. He remained inside for a while, most likely taking advantage of the relative lull to catch some sleep.

After leaving James Longstreet, Robert E. Lee returned to his morning observation position. Watching him was the British observer Arthur Fremantle, once again up in his tree after prowling around Gettysburg. Another flare-up of skirmishing near the Bliss farm provided a sonic backdrop as Lee joined A. P. Hill, whose major task this day was to make certain that each of his division commanders knew his part in the scheme of things, since together they represented the critical junction between Longstreet and Ewell.

A wayward officer around whom many questions would soon swirl made his very belated appearance about this time: Jeb Stuart had finally completed his mission. His meeting with Lee on Seminary Ridge went unrecorded by anyone present and seems to have been remarkably anticlimactic. Perhaps the impending battle kept Lee from investing much personal capital in the moment. In any case, Stuart left as quickly as he had arrived. In his official report, he noted only that his new orders were to take position "on the left wing of the Army of Northern Virginia."

Stuart's visit was so short and uneventful, in fact, that the anxiously perceptive Fremantle missed seeing him entirely; he would not meet the cavalry chief until several days later. Fremantle's only recollection was that Lee stayed in one spot "nearly all the time; looking through his fieldglass—sometimes talking to Hill and sometimes to Colonel Long of his Staff. But generally he sat quite alone on the stump of a tree."

Lee himself would later describe his battle plan for today thus:

> It was determined to make the principal attack upon the enemy's left, and endeavor to gain a position from which it was thought that our artillery could be brought to bear with effect. Longstreet was directed

to place the divisions of McLaws and Hood on the right of Hill, partially enveloping the enemy's left, which he was to drive in. General Hill was ordered to threaten the enemy's center, to prevent reenforcements being drawn to either wing, and co-operate with his right division in Longstreet's attack. General Ewell was instructed to make a simultaneous demonstration upon the enemy's right, to be converted into a real attack should opportunity offer.

Even as large forces were moving into place for what would become a mighty contest, small groups of soldiers were setting their minds to the practical problems of killing one another. Hiding indoors at her family home on Baltimore Street, near the edge of the Rebel-controlled area, Anna Garlach watched with innocent fascination as a deadly game was played out across the street. "The [Weinbrenner] building along the alley was brick and the men there had thrown up a kind of barricade on the pavement," she later noted. From a protected position, some of the Rebels "put a hat on a stick over the barricade [to] . . . draw the fire of the Union sharpshooters." Whenever a Yankee rifleman on nearby Cemetery Hill took the bait, other Confederates hiding nearby would "jump up and fire out the street."

Slightly more than a mile to the south, Union officers along Cemetery Ridge looked on as some Massachusetts sharpshooters plied their trade. The two sides were in another intermission between acts of the continuing drama around the Bliss farm, this time with the Confederates controlling the buildings. Several Rebel snipers had taken station in the second story of the brick barn, not only "using rifles that had sufficient range, but also [using them] with remarkable precision," according to a New Jersey soldier.

At first the Yankee sharpshooters had enjoyed considerable success by shooting in pairs, the first shot causing the enemy snipers to duck, and the second, coming right after the first, catching them as they bobbed back up to retaliate. But when the Rebels adapted by faking a quick return, a new plan was needed. The Union riflemen were now operating in teams of three, with the third man delaying his shot long enough to let the enemy believe he had managed to dodge the whole series. The methodical nature of the Yankees' planning afforded the New Jersey soldier time for reflection. "Alas!" he later exclaimed. "How little we thought human life was the stake for which this game was being played."

*   *   *

Lafayette McLaws was experienced enough to handle the usual run of unforeseen situations arising from the uncertainties of a battlefield. What Longstreet's division commander encountered when he reached the departure point for his positioning march across the Union flank, however, was far beyond the bounds of the merely unexpected. He was supposed to be clear of the enemy flank, with room enough to pass a column across the Emmitsburg Road, but as he later wrote, "the view presented astonished me, as the enemy was massed in my front, and extended to my right and left as far as I could see." Daniel Sickles' unsanctioned act in advancing Birney's division had filled Sherfy's peach orchard with infantry and cannon. McLaws turned much of his anger on his commander: "General Longstreet is to blame for not reconnoitering the ground," he complained afterward, "and for persisting in ordering the assault when his errors were discovered."

There was nothing McLaws could do now but prepare to give battle along Warfield Ridge. Ironically, he was deploying his men as Longstreet had first envisaged, instead of as Lee had dictated. McLaws stacked his division in two lines of battle, two brigades to each line. The first had Brigadier General Joseph B. Kershaw's South Carolinians on the right, with Brigadier General William Barksdale's four Mississippi regiments to their left. Backing up Kershaw were the four Georgia regiments under Brigadier General Paul J. Semmes, while another all-Georgia outfit, Brigadier General William T. Wofford's brigade, was posted to Barksdale's rear. McLaws also called forward his artillery. With Yankee infantry and artillery in the peach orchard, there was work to be done.

The discovery of Federals in strength where they were not expected also meant that a new plan must be improvised for Hood's Division, originally slated to support McLaws' flank attack. It made no sense now for Hood to stage behind McLaws, so instead he directed his units to extend the line southward. Any pretense of concealing the movement was abandoned as Hood's troops swung off their covered line of approach in order to take station as quickly as possible. "This movement was accomplished by throwing out an advanced force to tear down fences and clear the way," Hood later reported. Anxious to forestall any more surprises, the Kentucky-born officer also "sent forward some of my picked Texas scouts to ascertain the position of the enemy's extreme left flank."

*   *   *

Shortly before 3:00 P.M., George Meade finished drafting a situation report for Henry Halleck, who would not receive it for another nineteen hours. "The army is fatigued," Meade stated, adding that he was presently maintaining "a strong position for [the] defensive," having suspended any decision to attack the enemy until Lee's "position is more developed" and all of his own troops (most notably the Sixth Corps) were on hand. If there was any pattern to Lee's troop placements this day, it was not evident to Meade. "He has been moving on both my flanks apparently, but it is difficult to tell exactly his movements," the Union commander admitted. If he was not attacked this day, he continued, he would make every effort to go on the offensive tomorrow. Meade also allowed for the possibility that Lee might bypass him, in which case the Army of the Potomac would fall back to Westminster. "I feel fully the responsibility resting on me," he concluded, "but will endeavor to act with caution."

Immediately after he sent this note on its way by courier to the nearest telegraphic connection, Meade began summoning his corps commanders to the Leister house, intent on bringing everyone up to date. Noticeable by his absence was Daniel Sickles, who declined several "invitations" before Meade finally issued a peremptory order for him to report. It was near the end of these briefings that Meade's chief engineer appeared. Gouverneur K. Warren looked apprehensive: an officer he had dispatched to investigate the left flank, he told Meade, was reporting that the Cemetery Ridge position assigned to the Third Corps "was not occupied." The shield of confidence that had been building for the army commander throughout the morning and early afternoon began to disintegrate.

Daniel Sickles now arrived with some aides and orderlies. William Paine of army headquarters staff would later recollect that he had "never [seen] General Meade so angry. . . . He ordered General Sickles to retire to the position he had been instructed to take. This was done in a few sharp words." It was Sickles' memory that Longstreet's batteries had just begun firing on the Third Corps as he was approaching the Leister place: "General Meade met me just outside of his headquarters and excused me from dismounting. . . . He said that I should return at once and that he would follow me very soon."

As Sickles departed, Meade and Warren checked some maps to confirm that the Third Corps "could hardly be said to be in position." From the regular tracking reports he had been receiving throughout the day, Meade understood that the Sixth Corps was close at hand, so without knowing precisely where Sickles' men were, Meade ordered the Fifth Corps, then representing his only reserve, to begin moving into the area that should have contained the Third Corps. Then he and his staff set off on their ride to the left flank. Cresting Cemetery Ridge, they could clearly see the empty spaces to their left and the advance posting taken by Sickles' troops. " 'Here is where our line should be,' " Gouverneur Warren said, indicating the unoccupied ridge. Meade replied grimly, " 'It is too late now.' "

While Meade focused all his attention on the problem caused by Daniel Sickles, Warren took in a larger view of the Union position. He had a bad feeling about "the condition of affairs" at the end of the Cemetery Ridge line. Such was Meade's trust in his opinion that it required only the merest hint to release him. " 'I wish you would ride over and if anything serious is going on, attend to it,' " Meade said, indicating the high ground to the south. Quickly gesturing for some aides to accompany him, Gouverneur K. Warren galloped off toward Little Round Top.

The firing Sickles had heard from Meade's headquarters was likely not Longstreet's opening guns but rather his own artillery in the peach orchard, reacting to the sighting of McLaws' Division in their front and Hood's moving to their left. This challenge did not go long unanswered, as Colonel Henry G. Cabell's eighteen-gun battalion soon began returning the compliment.

It was taking some time for a clear picture of the situation to pass up the Confederate chain of command. Lafayette McLaws discovered this when an officer on Longstreet's staff arrived to inquire why he had not marched his column forward as called for in the original plan. An increasingly exasperated McLaws told the emissary "that the enemy was so strong in my front that it required careful preparation for the assault." The aide made a hurried round trip, returning with the same message, though this time implying (or so McLaws thought) that Robert E. Lee had seconded Longstreet's directive. McLaws asked for five minutes and began to prepare for what every instinct told him would be a bloody disaster. A reprieve was quick in coming, however, as a courier galloped up with new orders: McLaws was to hold his position until Hood was ready, and then act in concert with him.

The professional equilibrium Longstreet had maintained in carrying out Lee's orders (despite his personal opposition to them) slipped mea surably as the situation unraveled. First there had been the misdirection of the flank march, and next came the realization that all the intelligence upon which the operation had been based was flawed. Longstreet now did something he should have done much earlier: he rode to the front to see things for himself. He arrived at the Pitzer Woods ridge line "very much disconcerted and annoyed," according to McLaws.

Right away, Longstreet demonstrated his sour mood by finding fault with McLaws' deployment and ordering a battery placed where the road he had followed crossed the ridge. He ignored McLaws' protest that with his infantry clustered along that road, putting cannon there would draw counterfire that could only hurt his soldiers.

Some of those soldiers were the 1,600 men of William Barksdale's all-Mississippi brigade, considered among the best fighters in McLaws' Division. Their Tennessee-born commander was a public figure of note, having represented his adopted state in the U.S. Congress for eight years. Following an action in 1862, Robert E. Lee had proclaimed that Barksdale possessed the "highest qualities of a soldier," while an infantryman who served under him deemed him "a brave and fearless leader."

During their early-morning march from Marsh Creek to McPherson's Ridge, the Mississippi veterans had viewed the morbid debris of the July 1 fighting—a cold reminder, if they needed it, of their own mortality. The message hit home for J. W. Duke of the 17th Mississippi, whose brother sought him out before daylight with a tearful prediction: " 'Something is going to happen to-day.' "

At the end of their wearying flank march, Barksdale's men were in the front, almost directly opposite Sherfy's peach orchard. "We formed our line under a ledge of rocks along a small branch, a small hill from the branch up to the edge of the field, enough hill and timber to hide us from the Yankees," remembered a soldier in the 13th Mississippi. Ahead of them was a wide-open field fronting the enemy position in the peach orchard, which appeared to be filled with infantry and bristling with cannon.

James Longstreet's other division commander was also causing him problems. An aide from Hood reported to Longstreet that since scouts* had found no Federal troops on the southern side of Big Round Top, the Ken-

---

*Evander Law, too, had scouts probing Big Round Top. He also interrogated several Union prisoners who mentioned lightly guarded wagons parked east of the large hill.

tuckian wanted to alter the plan further and swing around that point. Longstreet turned down the request. The movement Hood was proposing would not assist McLaws' assault, and it could dangerously isolate that division, well beyond Longstreet's ability to provide support. He offered no reasonable explanation for his rejection of Hood's plan, stating only that "General Lee's orders are to attack up the Emmitsburg Road." This was not sufficient for Hood, who tried twice more to get Longstreet to reconsider, only to have each appeal refused. His third messenger was followed back by one of Longstreet's staff officers, Major John Fairfax, who saw at once Hood's real difficulty. The key factor was not that the enemy was absent south of Big Round Top; it was that the eastward bend of the Yankee position at the peach orchard was not the terminus of the Federal line, which instead continued east for a short distance and then veered southward to the end of a ridge at the foot of Little Round Top.

A reporter for the *Savannah* (Georgia) *Republican* saw the situation with a clarity that somehow eluded the Confederate leaders this day. "It was well known that Meade had chosen a formidable position," he wrote, "but the extent and strength of his line, the disposition of his forces, as well as the nature of the ground, and especially the relation his line bore to the mountain spurs on the right, were but little understood." Hood, however, could see that any effort to move perpendicular to the Emmitsburg Road would subject his men to an enfilade fire from their right flank and rear. Fairfax brought this message back to Longstreet.

Any clear historical perspective on what happened next has been thoroughly obfuscated by several postwar personality clashes among the participants. It is probable that Longstreet had some exchange of views with Lee at this time. The military observer FitzGerald Ross recalled Longstreet's having "a long consultation with the Commander-in-Chief." By whatever means, Longstreet acquired a broader sense of Lee's objectives, which he now understood to be "to envelop the enemy's left, and begin the attack there, following up, as near as possible, the direction of the Emmitsburg road." This granted him greater flexibility in setting up Hood's attack, a latitude that he in turn conveyed to his subordinate.

The attack that Hood prepared was nothing like the supporting action originally proposed, nor was it a movement entirely oriented along the axis of the Emmitsburg Road. Hood, who like McLaws had deployed his men in two lines of two brigades each, intended his first wave to break up the enemy's concentration near Devil's Den and turn the Federals' flank there. If need be, the second wave would directly assist the first,

Lee's Initial Plan

Longstreet's Modification

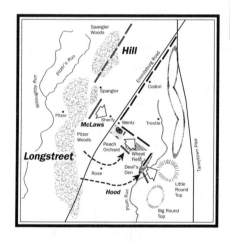

Hood's Digression

otherwise, it could also be redirected to carry out the initial mission of attacking along the Emmitsburg Road.

Although nowhere articulated in any account by Longstreet or Hood, this is the best explanation for the advance of Hood's first line, which occurred under Longstreet's and Hood's direct observation and yet bore little relation to the movement mapped out hours earlier by

Robert E. Lee. Longstreet would always insist that the order he had executed was the one to attack up the Emmitsburg Road, and within the liberal definition of enveloping the enemy's left, that was what he did.

John B. Hood's first attacking wave consisted of Brigadier General Jerome B. Robertson's Arkansas and Texas brigade on the left and Evander M. Law's Alabama brigade on the right. The pair represented a veteran shock force of perhaps 2,700 men. Robertson's soldiers had marched from the Chambersburg area the day before, halted for a while near Cashtown, then marched again to bivouac along Marsh Creek. After a few hours' rest, they had been moved to McPherson's Ridge, where they had again played the waiting game.

For one man in the 4th Texas, there was "a calm, as of death" that "seemed to rest upon the earth" that morning on McPherson's Ridge. Nevertheless, the sight of so many armed men and other weapons of war served as a sobering reminder "that the carnival was at hand." The consequences of that carnival were on display for any who cared to see them. Another 4th Texas veteran would never forget passing a field hospital today "where I saw a great many wounded soldiers, who were mangled and bruised in every possible way, some with their eyes shot out, some with their arms or hands, or fingers, or feet or legs shot off, and all seeming to suffer a great deal."

It would become fashionable to assert, in postwar accounts, that Robertson's men were eager for the fray. Not everyone agreed. "It is very true that these men were tried and seasoned soldiers, with powers of endurance equal to any, yet they were not made of iron, and there is a limit to all human endeavor," reflected a soldier in the 3rd Arkansas. That limit was very much on the mind of Evander Law, whose Alabamians had covered eighteen miles in eight hours just getting to Gettysburg this hot day. At least seven more miles were added to that total following the roundabout route before Law's men began moving into their jump-off positions.

Several of Longstreet's batteries were already engaging the enemy guns that were visible in the peach orchard. In preparation for Hood's forward movement, all the cannon that had been brought up to the line of battle prepared to open fire on the position held by the Federal Third Corps. It was approaching 3:30 P.M.

Gouverneur K. Warren's pensive survey of the Union left flank eventually led him to Little Round Top. He likely ascended its northern slope and from there made his way to the busy flag signal station on the hill's western side. "I saw that this was the key of the whole [Union] position," Warren later wrote. "The long line of woods on the west side of the Emmitsburg road . . . furnished an excellent place for the enemy to form out of sight." In a moment of pure inspiration, he sent an aide to Smith's battery in the Devil's Den, requesting that "the captain . . . fire a shot into these woods. He did so, and as the shot went whirling through the air the sound of it reached the enemy's troops and caused everyone to look in the direction of it. This motion revealed to me the glistening of gun barrels and bayonets of the enemy's line of battle, already formed and far outflanking the position of any of our troops." Warren's feelings at that moment were "intensely thrilling . . . and almost appalling."

This moment would become one of the cherished stories of Gettysburg, leading some to credit Warren with discovering Lee's flanking movement. Certainly by this time Daniel Sickles and any troops posted in Sherfy's peach orchard knew that the Rebels were opposite them in force. But Warren's important discovery went beyond the Third Corps, for it revealed that except for a small signal-corps unit, Little Round Top had no defenders. Meade's chief engineer immediately dispatched aides in different directions to find some.

George Meade and his entourage located Daniel Sickles and his entourage by the Wheatfield Road, at Sherfy's peach orchard. Several versions of their ensuing conversation would later be advanced. By his own account, Meade asked Sickles "to indicate to me his general position. When he had done so I told him it was not the position I had expected him to take." Sickles, for his part, would later recall that Meade had "expressed his doubts as to my being able to hold so extended a line." He even agreed with the West Pointer—to a degree. "I replied that I could not, with one corps, hold so extended a line against the rebel army," Sickles said, "but that, if supported, the line could be held; and, in my judgment, it was a strong line, and the best one."

Meade was not buying that. He informed his Third Corps commander "that he had advanced his line beyond the support of my army, and that I was very fearful he would be attacked and would lose the artillery, which he had put so far in front, before I could support it, or that if I undertook to support it I would have to abandon all the rest of the line which I had adopted—that is, that I would have to fight the battle out there where he was." Sickles told Meade that if he objected to the Third Corps' deployment, "it was not yet too late to take any position he might indicate." According to a Meade aide who was present, the army commander considered this possibility for a moment before answering, " 'You cannot hold this position, but the enemy will not let you get away without a fight, & it may begin now as at any time.' "

This exchange was observed by Meade's artillery chief, Henry Hunt, whose protective prowling of the army's battery positions had brought him back to the peach orchard. There the Third Corps' artillery commander, George Randolph, solicited his help in placing some guns. Taking Meade's presence as a sign that he had approved Sickles' move, Hunt sent back to the Reserve Artillery for more pieces, because even with every tube in line, there were not enough cannon in Randolph's arsenal to do the job.

The riders dispatched by Gouverneur K. Warren to bring troops to Little Round Top began delivering their messages. One of the first that Warren had sent reached George Meade just after he left Daniel Sickles. Recognizing the importance of the flank position, and believing that Andrew Humphreys' division was the closest available, Meade sent instructions directing that command to Little Round Top. Hardly had his staff officer sped away, though, when the army chief learned that a column from the Fifth Corps was already approaching the position in question. A second rider followed the first and countermanded his instructions, but not before Humphreys had already given orders redirecting his two brigades toward the hill. Scarcely blinking, though likely swearing a bit, Humphreys reoriented them back toward the Emmitsburg Road.

Warren's second messenger found Daniel Sickles, who, not surprisingly, had no troops to spare. Either with Sickles' blessing or on his own, the courier sought out Major General George Sykes, commanding the Fifth Corps, who consented to help. On meeting with George Meade at around 3:00 P.M., Sykes had understood that the Fifth Corps was now being tasked with supporting the left flank, so he unquestioningly agreed to the aide's request. An orderly was sent off with directions for James Barnes, whose First Division was already marching westward from its reserve position.

Strong Vincent's brigade was waiting near the George Weikert house on Cemetery Ridge, where it had halted pending new orders. Vincent spotted Sykes' aide and intercepted him, "Where is General Barnes?" the staff officer asked. The brigadier had his own agenda, and answered with a question of his own: "What are your orders?" he demanded. "Give me your orders." "General Sykes told me to direct General Barnes to send one of his brigades to occupy that hill yonder," the orderly replied, pointing toward Little Round Top. Protocol dictated that Vincent should direct the rider to Barnes and receive his approval, but the brigade commander did not intend to wait. "I will take the responsibility of taking my brigade there," he said.

Quickly assigning Colonel James C. Rice of the 44th New York to lead the unit to Little Round Top, Vincent rode ahead to scout the location with an aide. He decided to ascend the hill's eastern side, breaking out of the trees near its southern crest. Ironically, Gouverneur K. Warren, anxiously holding his place on the hill's northeastern face, never saw Vincent or his men as they began arriving not a hundred yards away, the first to respond to his call for help.*

George Meade's reluctant decision to support Sickles' advance line also brought an end to the charade of easing the remaining Third Corps units to the Emmitsburg Road. Relieved of that constraint, Andrew Humphreys moved his two brigades forward with style. "Soon the long lines of the Third Corps are seen advancing, and how splendidly they march," recalled an officer in Hancock's corps. "It looks like a dress parade, a review. On, on they go, out towards the peach orchard, but not a shot fired." Winfield Hancock, who had resumed command of the Second Corps shortly after it took position along Cemetery Ridge, was as surprised by this display as anyone: "I recollect looking on and admiring the spectacle," he later testified, "but I did not know the object of it." Standing near Hancock, John Gibbon worried about the way Sickles was exposing his left flank. "There was quite a thick wood away off to the left of Sickles's line," Gibbon remarked, indicating an area known as Biesecker's Woods, "and I asked General Hancock if he supposed there was anything in those woods."

Returning to his headquarters, Meade could hear the full-throated rumble of the enemy artillery pounding Sickles' position. There was no longer any question in his mind as to what Lee intended to do.

---

*Although the testimony is conflicting, it is very possible that Warren briefly left Little Round Top around the time Vincent's men came on the scene, to make a direct appeal to George Sykes.

(3:40 P.M.–4:10 P.M.)

The preassault artillery barrage organized by E. P. Alexander, coming from some fifty-four cannon, began at about 3:40 P.M. The young artillery chief had hoped to unleash his firepower in a single dramatic volley, but that kind of coordination was difficult to achieve under combat conditions. A few of his gunners had already exchanged shots after being goaded by the enemy, so as Hood's Division began coming into line, the general went ahead and ordered the two batteries with him to open on the Federals, hoping to get them to reveal their positions. This drew a concentrated return fire that left Alexander with little option but to let all his guns engage. "I had hoped, with my 54 guns & close range, to make it short, sharp & decisive," Alexander later wrote. "At close ranges there was less inequality in our guns, & especially in our ammunition, & I thought that if ever I could overwhelm & crush them I would do it now."

His gunners did him proud. High on their priority target list were Smith's four guns in the Devil's Den. "The accuracy of the enemy's aim was astonishing," Smith later admitted. Captain Charles A. Phillips' 5th Massachusetts Battery went into action right after the Rebel metal began flying. "As soon as the battery was in position the guidon took his position on the right," Phillips recollected, "and the first shot was apparently directed at the flag and killed two horses on the right piece." Lieutenant John K. Bucklyn held an especially exposed position with his Battery E, 1st Rhode Island Light Artillery, posted along the Emmitsburg Road just north of Sherfy's peach orchard. "I fired slow and carefully," Bucklyn remembered. "Men and horses fell around me." The "shrieking, hissing, [and] seething" were such that to a young gunner in the 9th Massachusetts Light Artillery, "it seemed as though it must be the work of the very devil himself."

Only a few minutes into his effort, Alexander had to admit that these Federals were good. "They really surprised me," he acknowledged, "both

with the number of guns they developed, & the way they stuck to them."
Captain O. B. Taylor of Virginia's Bath Artillery lost Corporal William P.
Ray under this return fire. "He was killed while in the act of sighting his
guns," Taylor reported. "He never spoke after receiving the shot, walked
a few steps from his piece, and fell dead." There was even a near miss for
the architect of the action: "I had . . . my right knee skinned by a bullet
which passed behind one leg & in front of the other as I was walking

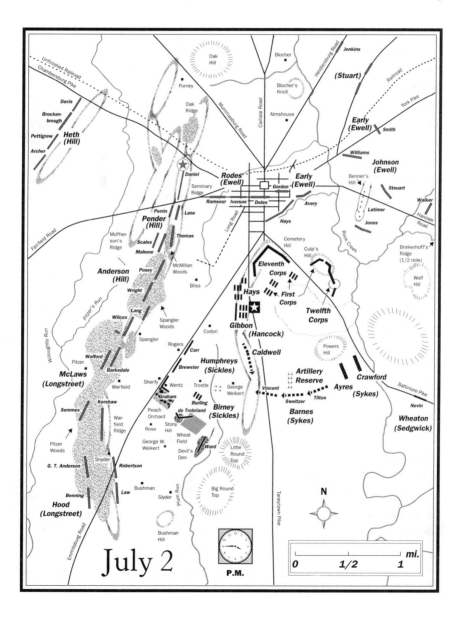

between Gilbert's guns,"* E. P. Alexander related. He also noted that one of his four gun batteries "had two [cannon] fairly struck by the enemy's shot & dismounted."

The artillery thundering on the southern end of the battlefield was barely audible seven miles to the northeast, near Hunterstown, through which Jeb Stuart's weary cavalry columns were passing on the final leg of their journey. The leading elements in the mounted procession had reached the outer picket line north of Gettysburg by the time the rear guard, under the immediate control of Brigadier General Wade Hampton, pulled out of the small Pennsylvania village. Hampton was already in a truculent mood, having been the target of an entire carbine magazine pumped at him by a Yankee scout—a remarkably inept Yankee scout, evidently, as he managed only to graze the formidable Rebel officer before escaping with a slight wound inflicted by Hampton's pistol. At about 4:00 P.M., Stuart learned that an outpost left by Hampton in Hunterstown had been driven out by an enemy force of unknown size. Hampton, getting the word to clear the town, was quick to respond.

The Federals in question were four Michigan cavalry regiments under the flamboyant Brigadier General George A. Custer. To buy time for his horse artillery to deploy, Custer launched a bold spoiling attack against Hampton's heavy columns. "I'll lead you this time, boys. Come on!" Custer yelled, directing fifty or so troopers in a wild charge. Such bravado nearly cost him his life when the first Rebel volley took down his horse, leaving its rider shaken but uninjured. A 1st Michigan trooper galloped over to his unhorsed leader and hauled him aboard, then raced to safety.

The combat just south of Hunterstown continued to intensify as both sides sent in reinforcements, each convinced that the other was attempting a major flanking move. While it remained modest in overall scale, the fighting was close in and bitter. A 6th Michigan trooper, sent forward dismounted to defend a battery, afterward wrote to his parents that "a few Rebels rode right over us on and up to our guns of the Battery and it was then that [occurred a] hand to hand encounter with the saber until every one that reached the guns was hewn down under the saber or shot to death with Revolvers."

*The guns belonged to the Brooks (South Carolina) Light Artillery, Lieutenant S. Capers Gilbert commanding.

The combat reached a point of exhaustion beyond which each side waited to see what the other intended to do. Since their common intent was defensive, the weary pause became a permanent end to this furious and violent action that cost the two sides not quite seventy casualties between them. Nothing had been accomplished, nothing gained, in what one Federal trooper would later term "a hard, bold and bloody fight."

Much closer to Gettysburg, the artillery rumbling on the southern end of the battlefield was the signal Joseph Latimer had been expecting. After confirming his orders with Edward Johnson, Latimer led his batteries to the limited open crest of Benner's Hill. A foot soldier who watched them go thought it "a splendid sight. Sixteen guns . . . streaming over the field in bustle and busy speed and enveloped in clouds of dust." As each tube swung into its place and dropped its stabilizing trail, cannoneers aimed the weapons and fired. Scarcely had the first ragged volley belched off the hill when the first rounds of Federal response began landing across the crest. One of Latimer's gunners felt "a continuous vibration like a severe storm raging in the elements."

There was no time for ranging shots, and the distance to their targets was some four thousand feet, but the Confederate gunners knew their business. Grading them from across the way was the First Corps' demanding artillery chief, Charles Wainwright, who judged the two sides evenly matched as to their number of cannon. However, "in every other respect the rebel guns had the advantage of us," he believed. Just how much of an advantage became gruesomely evident when an enemy shell burst under one gun of the 1st Pennsylvania Light Artillery, Battery B, killing one crewman and horribly wounding another. Wainwright, who had nothing but admiration for the way the survivors took up the slack, would retain a vivid image of the mortally wounded man, who "lost his right hand, his left arm at the shoulder, and [had] his ribs so broken open that you could see right into him."

Using Alexander's guns to soften the enemy positions on the southern portion of the line was a calculated risk, for it did not take long for some of the Yankee overshoots to begin landing amid the infantry concentrated for the attack. Hardest hit was Robertson's Texas Brigade. "We were standing in an open field, under the shot and shell of those batteries, for half an hour," recollected a member of the 4th Texas, "and a good many soldiers were killed all around me." "It is very trying upon men to remain still and in ranks under a severe cannonading," testified an officer in that regiment. "To avoid as much danger as possible, we were ordered to lie down until all were in readiness," recalled a 1st Texas private.

Throughout it all, John B. Hood kept hoping that James Longstreet would formally modify his orders. Spurred one more time by opposition to the plan expressed by his brigadier Evander Law, Hood sent his adjutant general, Major Harry Sellers, to make a final plea. Sellers returned with Longstreet's last word on the subject: "You will execute the orders you have received."

It was not what Hood wanted to hear. He had decided nevertheless to obey only the spirit, not the letter, of Lee's orders. He would secure his right flank from enfilde fire and then meet Lee's objectives by moving up the Emmitsburg Road. " 'Very well,' " Hood told Sellers. " 'When we get under fire I will have a digression.' "

Hood later wrote, "After this urgent protest against entering the battle of Gettysburg according to instructions—which protest is the first and only one I ever made during my entire military career—I ordered my line to advance and make the assault."

It was roughly 4:00 P.M. when the most forward files of the Sixth Corps reached Rock Creek, just two miles from the Union left flank. "Directly the familiar roar of battle began to be heard distinctly," reminisced a member of the 61st Pennsylvania, "then louder and more continuous." These sounds, plus the sight of wounded men from yesterday's fight, provided the necessary stimulus for the soldiers to complete their epic march. "There was much to inspire the men in their dogged resolution to push on," noted a Wisconsin officer.

Other troops were also approaching Gettysburg—troops that were just as tired from marching this hot day as the Sixth Corps, and just as ready to fight if they were needed. These soldiers, belonging to George E. Pickett's division of Longstreet's Corps, had been left behind at Chambersburg to guard the Confederate supply trains; on being relieved by late-arriving cavalry, they had been sent marching east before dawn. As they passed through the town, William Henry Cocke of the 9th Virginia had hoped to find the woman who had jeered the men for appearing to retreat just days earlier. Admittedly "anxious to see the young lady who spoke to me before to let her know that it was the same party returning," Cocke was disappointed to discover that "no one was stirring" at that early hour.

"The roads were hard and firm," recalled a soldier in the 7th Virginia, "and we made good time, but the day was terribly hot and clouds of dust stifling. Water was scarce and we suffered much." As the column entered the Cashtown Gap around midday, remembered another Virginian, "the vertical rays of the sun seemed like real lances of steel tipped with fire!" Lieutenant John Dooley of the 1st Virginia, in charge of the rear guard, was under orders to keep the troops moving. He heard every kind of excuse, some reasonable, others just a pretext for dropping out. Concluded Dooley, "It is a hard thing to keep these men upon the move."

As the division approached Gettysburg on the Chambersburg Pike, one Virginia soldier heard "the sullen 'Boom!' 'Boom!' 'Boom!' of artillery in the distance." Nearer the town, Pickett sent his adjutant and inspector general, Major Walter Harrison, to report their arrival to Robert E. Lee, while he himself went to check in with James Longstreet. Lee's instructions to Pickett were to let his men rest as they reached Marsh Creek; they would not be needed this day.

(4:10 P.M.–10:00 P.M.)

There was a conscious sense of time's standing still as John B. Hood rode before his division and halted in front of the Texas Brigade. Once his troops had engaged the enemy, Hood's ability to control events would rapidly diminish. That was the nature of Civil War combat: men communicated by words, gesture, or sound, all of which became increasingly obscured when the action began. Hood knew this and was well aware of the many hundreds of eyes that were fixed on him in that frozen moment.

He spoke some words that did not carry far. Soldiers watching him from a distance could only imagine the exhortation, and those who said they caught it recalled different things. The officer commanding the 1st Texas heard Hood exclaim, " 'Forward, my Texans, and win this battle or die in the effort!' " A private in the ranks of the 4th Texas swore that he said only, " 'Forward—Steady—forward.' " According to another, Hood's speech ended, " 'Fix bayonets, my brave Texans; forward and take those heights!' " As soon as the Texas Brigade began moving, Law's Alabama brigade, off its right, took its cue. Law's adjutant, Captain Leigh R. Terrell, spurred his horse to the brigade's front, where he shouted, " 'Attention! Shoulder—Arms. Right Shoulder Shift—[Arms]. Guide Center. Forward. March!' "

A member of the 1st Texas recollected, "We moved quietly forward down the steep decline, gaining impetus as we reached the more level ground below." "We could see the Federals on the hills to our left," wrote a comrade in the 4th Texas, "and the Stars and Stripes waving at us." Already there were problems. Some of the Alabamians, wound taut by the marching and waiting, began moving too rapidly and had to be slowed by their officers. The battle lines wriggled like prescient entities as portions navigated fences, bushes, trees, and marshy ground. To these obstacles was added the enemy fire, for once the leading waves emerged into the open, every Federal gun that could bear began targeting them.

* * *

Although the fighting here was on a much smaller scale than that breaking out to the south, the area around the Bliss farm, opposite the Federal center, heated up again now as well. The mixed force of companies taken from New York, New Jersey, and Delaware regiments had held on to the farm throughout the afternoon, until Carnot Posey, across from them, received and acted on two sets of orders. The first instructed him to watch the brigade of Ambrose Wright, just to his south, and to be prepared to match any advance it might attempt. The second seemed to contradict the first by detailing Posey "to advance but two of my regiments, and deploy them closely as skirmishers." One way to reconcile the contradiction would be to have the two regiments clear the pesky Yankees off his front; then, if Wright advanced, Posey would be free of any obligation and could follow. He therefore directed two of his regiments—the 19th and 48th Mississippi—to advance in skirmishing formation toward the Bliss farm and link up with elements of the 16th Mississippi already engaged there.

The combined force quickly scattered the Federals holding that position. Once again, Edward P. Harris was in charge, and once again he hastily cleared out. Sergeant George D. Bowen of the 12th New Jersey joined the hurried exodus, "soon catching up with Lieut. Col. Harris of the 1st Del. . . . [who] was getting to the rear as fast as he could. . . . [He] swung his sword around, called me a hard name, telling me to go back. . . . [This] I did not do but made a detour around him."

A counterattack by skirmishers from the 106th Pennsylvania, posted south of the farm, failed. The Bliss farm was once more in Rebel hands.

Accompanied by Private Oliver W. Norton, carrying the brigade flag, Strong Vincent stood on the vacant southern crest of Little Round Top and considered how to position his four regiments. No sooner had he begun his survey than a Rebel shell crashed into some nearby rocks and boulders. Vincent realized that the headquarters pendant that Norton was holding so proudly was giving some distant gunner a perfect aiming point. " 'Down with that flag, Norton!' " he yelled. " 'D—n it, go behind the rocks with it!' " The young private scrambled for cover as his grim-faced commander returned to a task made the more urgent by the long lines of Confederate infantry visible in the distance.

Some fifteen hundred feet almost due west, artilleryman James E. Smith was also eyeing the approaching enemy. "The four guns were now used to oppose and cripple this attack and check it as far as possible," he later wrote. "I never saw the men do better work; every shot told; the pieces were discharged as rapidly as they could be with regard to effectiveness, while the conduct of the men was superb." It was not easy. "Every round of ammunition had to be carried from the foot of the ridge," a watching infantryman marveled. "Man after man went down, but still the exhausting work went steadily on."

The Army of the Potomac's artillery chief, Henry Hunt, paid a brief visit to offer encouragement and advise Smith that he would likely lose his guns. Descending into the Plum Run valley, Hunt found the path to his horse blocked by a "herd of horned cattle" that had been driven into a frenzy by the shelling. "All were *stampeded*," Hunt recorded, "and were bellowing and rushing in their terror, first to one side and then to the other." Ignoring the ironic possibility that he might be gored to death, Hunt made it through the herd to his horse and rode off.

Smith was getting help from the other big guns posted west of him in the wheat field and peach orchard, as well as from the twelve score or so small guns being wielded in the fields to the southwest by more of the elite United States Sharpshooters, members of the 2nd Regiment under Major Homer Stoughton. Earlier this day, Stoughton had deployed six companies in a fairly traditional picket line screening the area southwest of the Third Corps. After Buford's cavalry withdrew, and some of his own scouts began reporting the enemy buildup behind Warfield Ridge, the major carefully deposed his sharpshooters in four-man cells along a paper-thin line stretching north from Bushman Hill (southwest of Big Round Top) to the area around the Slyder farm. Their assignment was not to hold any specific position but rather, by operating independently, to delay and harass the Rebels.

Already their stings were having an effect. A few marksmen infiltrated the Confederate picket lines to begin picking off gunners in Captain James Reilly's Rowan (North Carolina) Artillery. This in turn provoked Evander Law to detach three companies from the 47th Alabama to handle the threat. The three were soon followed by two companies from the 48th Alabama, which would be further reinforced from Hood's second line by 375 Georgians belonging to Anderson's Brigade. Each such subtraction weakened the assault power of the Rebel units.

As it happened, however, it was not sharpshooters but instead an unidentified artillery crew who dealt Longstreet's advance a crippling blow just minutes after it began. Having watched his beloved Texan and

Arkansas troops commence their movement, John B. Hood rode down the slope toward the center of his line. He had just reached an orchard on the grounds of the Bushman farm, from which point he probably intended to oversee the deployment of the supporting brigades of Benning and Anderson, when a sputtering fuse touched powder twenty feet over his head. The explosion of the Yankee spherical case rained iron fragments down onto Hood. "I . . . saw him sway to and fro in the saddle and then start to fall from his horse, when he was caught by one of his aides," observed the commander of the 1st Texas. Hood had received a bad wound in his left arm.

The division commander was out of the action. Gone with him was any prospect that the "digression" he had intended would be implemented, for he had shared his decision with no one. Instead of making a wide sweep around the Yankee flank (for the first wave) and then following that up on an inside track (for the second), Hood's units would be guided by the exigencies of the moment—exigencies that immediately began to assert themselves.

From the start of the advance, the Texas Brigade's commander, Jerome B. Robertson, believed that he was to keep the Emmitsburg Road close on his left, to provide a pivot point on which the two brigades would swing around to face north. He now observed that the road veered more northward than he had anticipated, and for some reason Law's Brigade was pushing almost due east, showing no sign of turning to the north. Even before he could react, his brigade began to pull apart. His two right regiments, the 4th and 5th Texas, angled more to the east to maintain contact with the Alabama men, while his left pair, the 3rd Arkansas and 1st Texas, tried to hold to a northeasterly course.

Faced with a choice between Law and the Emmitsburg Road, Robertson decided to abandon the latter. But even now he was losing his ability to manage events. His orders instructing the 3rd Arkansas and 1st Texas to rejoin the rest of the brigade were ignored, as the two units had settled on a more pressing objective: the guns of Smith's battery, now spitting death at them from Devil's Den.

Tillie Pierce could hardly believe the events of the past twenty-four hours. Terribly frightened by the July 1 fighting, she had fled her family's home on Baltimore Street, found temporary refuge in the Evergreen Cemetery gatehouse, then extended her odyssey as far as the Jacob Weikert farm, just off the Taneytown Pike on the eastern slopes of Big and Little Round Top.

The first part of this day kept her busy providing water and bread to the Federal soldiers as they marched past on their way to the front. All that changed, however, when "toward the middle of the afternoon heavy cannonading began on the two Round Tops just back of the [Weikert] house," she recorded. "This was so terrible and severe that it was with great difficulty we could hear ourselves speak. It began very unexpectedly; so much so, that we were all terror-stricken, and hardly knew what to do."

What had begun as an orderly row of nine regiments in one grand Confederate line of battle rapidly underwent a complicated reshuffling as the units moved eastward from the Emmitsburg Road. The two leftmost regiments in Hood's two-brigade front had veered to the northeast soon after leaving the point of departure, heading toward Devil's Den. Law's Brigade, along with the 4th and 5th Texas Regiments, continued more directly east, swatting at the 2nd U.S. Sharpshooters while trying to hold course through the gorge between Devil's Den and Big Round Top.

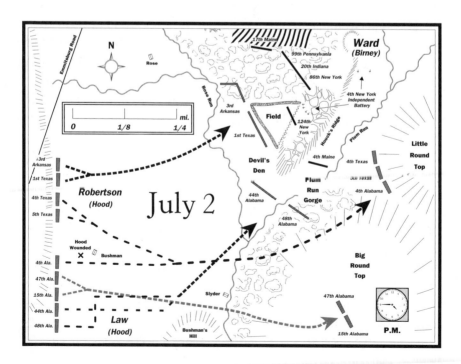

When this formation reached a tangled outcropping of woodland spilling off Bushman Hill, it became impossible for the 48th Alabama (the rightmost regiment) to advance farther, so it halted before sidestepping in behind the 15th Alabama.

The Bliss farm now changed hands yet again. It had been controlled by the two Mississippi regiments of Posey's Brigade for about thirty minutes, but Union Brigadier General Alexander Hays was not going to let that situation continue. Once more he organized a strike force, this one taken predominantly from the 12th New Jersey. There was no subtlety in his plan, just a straight dash right down the middle. A determining factor in the choice of this direct route was the guns carried by the New Jersey soldiers: sixty-nine-caliber smoothbore muskets. These weapons were useless at long range, but up close their "buck and ball" load made them the equivalent of shotguns. So the more quickly the men closed the range, the better.

The command to advance was given, and two hundred New Jersey soldiers raced toward the Bliss farm buildings. "When we were within a short distance of the barn, our column halted, delivered their fire, then charged with a cheer, surrounding first the barn and then the house," recollected a sergeant. "The Rebels [held] until we poured in through the doors and windows and almost [met] them face to face, [whereupon they cried] out for quarters: 'We surrender Yanks—don't, don't shoot!' "

The charge cost the New Jersey command almost 20 percent of its strength in killed and wounded. But the Bliss farm was once more in Union hands.

The will-o'-the-wisp U.S. sharpshooters were rarely in one place long enough for any of Law's Alabama troops to get a good bead on them. Only when the Rebel battle line approached the somewhat open area around the William Slyder farm did several sharpshooter companies spontaneously coalesce, behind a stone wall, into a momentarily firm line that chewed at the enemy. So fierce was this brief stand that the area would afterward become known as the Hornet's Nest. As Law's men, assisted by some of Robertson's Texans, flanked this line, the Yankee marksmen reverted to their more flexible four-man cells, some falling back toward Devil's Den while others backpedaled up the slope of Big Round Top.

When the moment arrived for Evander Law to wheel his composite strike force to the north to enter Plum Run Gorge, the sharpshooters made another significant contribution that mitigated the strength of the blow. The green-clad soldiers so bedeviled Colonel William Oates, commanding Law's two-regiment right wing, that he directed the 15th and 47th Alabama Regiments to continue pursuing them up Big Round Top. "I received an order from Brigadier General Law to left-wheel my regiment and move in the direction of the heights upon my left," Oates later reported, "which order I failed to obey, for the reason that when I received it I was rapidly advancing up the mountain."

Strong Vincent may not have been a warrior born, but at the moment of his greatest martial trial, he acted with a cool intelligence that any military professional would have envied. By the time James Rice brought the head of his quarter-mile-long brigade column to the southern end of Little Round Top, Vincent had decided to post his four regiments along the lower ledge of the southern and western slopes, thus allowing the enemy less room to maneuver than would have been the case if the Yankee line had been positioned closer to the crest.

The 44th New York took its place first, with its fellow regiments snapping into place successively to its left: the 83rd Pennsylvania, the 20th Maine, and the 16th Michigan. Skirmish lines eased forward from each regiment, filtering southward into the trees until they were lost from sight. After surveying his deployment, Vincent made up his mind to shift the 16th Michigan from his extreme left to his extreme right. He would never record his reasons, but his shrewd assessment of his brigade's situation may have suggested to him that the open western face of Little Round Top offered more advantages to the enemy than did the more wooded southern flank, meaning it would make sense to prolong his line in that direction.

Below Vincent and to his right, the southern crest of Houck's Ridge was wreathed in the smoke of Smith's cannon and the musketry of Ward's brigade. Vincent moved along his line, giving each regimental commander a hasty tactical briefing and offering encouragement. When he reached Colonel Joshua L. Chamberlain and his 20th Maine, he told the former Bowdoin College professor that, in Chamberlain's words, "this was the extreme left of our general line, and that a desperate attack was expected in order to turn that position, [and he] concluded by telling me I was to 'hold that ground at all hazards.' "

Like Vincent's other regiments, the 20th held a position that was hardly parade-ground-straight but instead wiggled back and forth so as to "best secure the advantage of the rough, rocky, and stragglingly wooded ground," as Chamberlain later related. Not subsequently recorded in the colonel's official report was his decision to detail his two brothers, Tom and John, both serving under him in the regiment, to opposite ends of his line. Chamberlain feared that if they fought side by side, a single Rebel shell "might make it hard for mother."

It was around this time that the 3rd Arkansas and 1st Texas closed on Devil's Den from the east, to find the Yankee boys of Ward's brigade waiting for them. The Federals held their fire until the two Rebel regiments came within two hundred yards, then loosed an aimed volley that staggered the Confederates so badly as to let Ward's men get off a second blast without a serious reply. While Smith's four cannon on the crest continued to hurl canister into the Texas ranks, Ward adroitly swung his two right regiments out to enfilade the Arkansas troops. More Union help came from the north, where de Trobriand's brigade was posted on the western edge of Rose's wheat field. The 17th Maine marched across and set itself along a wall bordering the field's southern side, thus gaining a clear shot into the flank of the 3rd Arkansas.

With his men being hit in front and flank, and no evident support coming from behind or to his left, Jerome Robertson called for reinforcements. His request reached Evander Law, who was as yet unaware that with Hood out of the action, command of the division had devolved to him. Concluding that the obstructions on his right would continue to constrict his movement there, Law pulled his rightmost regiment (the 44th Alabama) off the line and ordered it to wheel left and proceed north toward Devil's Den. Almost as soon as the 44th moved off, Law added the 48th to the assistance he was sending to Robertson.

The Federal line along Houck's Ridge was also shifting around. Artilleryman James Smith had realized that portions of the enemy line seemed to be heading toward the Plum Run Gorge, to his left and rear, a point not covered by his guns. Wanting infantry down there, he tried to persuade the officer commanding the 4th Maine, then directly supporting his battery, to move off the ridge into the valley. When he refused, Smith immediately went over his head to J. H. H. Ward, who agreed with the cannoneer.

Once the 4th Maine had begun to descend from the rocks, Smith's closest support became the 124th New York. On returning to his guns, the artillerist learned that the first wave of Rebels had already slipped through his net. A second line (Benning's Brigade) was appearing along the edge of Warfield Ridge, and it now became the priority target. When Smith called for spherical case, however, he was informed that the available supplies of long-distance munitions had been exhausted. He was beside himself with frustration. "Give them shell; give them solid shot," he screamed. "D—n them, give them anything!"

In planning his assault, John B. Hood had backed up Law's Brigade with the all-Georgia outfit of Brigadier General Henry L. Benning. According to Benning, Hood's orders specified that his "brigade would follow Law's brigade at the distance of about 400 yards." By the time Benning reached his jumping-off point, though, Hood was down, and there seemed to be no one in overall command of the operation. Catching sight of a line of battle ahead of him in the distance, he assumed it was Law's and so set his course by it.

Had what Benning saw actually been Law's Brigade, his four regiments (some 1,400 muskets) would have pushed into Plum Run Gorge, bringing their power to bear against Little Round Top. But Benning was *not* following Law; he had mistaken Robertson's line for the one he was to guide on, so his blow would land against Devil's Den and Rose's wheat field, leaving the troops already battling against Vincent's brigade without any support.

"As soon as we cleared the woods we were in full view of Round Top Hill, some half mile in our front," recalled one of Benning's Georgians. "We had not got out of the woods before the guns from the hill top were turned on us." "Down the plunging shot came," scribbled a reporter covering the battle for Georgia's *Savannah Republican,* "bursting before and around and everywhere tearing up the ground in a terrific rain of death. . . . [As Benning's Brigade] approached the [Yankee] guns, the rain of grape and canister began, mingling their sharp cries with the shrill whistle of the mad minnie balls which seemed to come in showers."

*   *   *

With some of the pressure off them due to Smith's having switched targets, the men of the 1st Texas managed to lurch forward in a semblance of a charge that brought them into the open just below the four guns in Devil's Den, at the southwestern edge of a three-acre triangular field. Their surging, screaming scramble up the hill scattered some of Smith's gunners and brought the battery's support at a run. The 124th New York advanced to a barrier marking the field's northeastern border and from there poured two volleys into the Texas troops, who fell back under cover. This in turn drew the New Yorkers into an impetuous charge down the hill, straight into a steady Rebel volley that ripped great rents in the Federal line, killing the regiment's major, twenty-two-year-old James Cromwell.

" 'My God! My God men!' " shouted Colonel Augustus van Horne Ellis, commanding the 124th. " 'Your Major's down; save him! save him!' " A second downhill charge that erupted spontaneously was no more successful than the first. When the shocked survivors pulled back this time, it was their colonel who lay dead on the Pennsylvania soil. For a terribly brief moment, the New Yorkers thought their sacrifice had won a respite, but they soon realized that was not the case. No sooner had the 1st Texas fallen back out of range than a second line appeared off to the left of the 124th. It was a portion of the 44th Alabama, one of the two regiments sent over from the right by Evander Law to help Robertson's men. A soldier in the 124th would always remember the enemy's appearing "not more than 150 yards from us, on our left flank, [who] . . . opened an enfilading fire. No troops could long stand such a storm."

The fourth brigade in Hood's Division was an all-Georgia unit commanded by Brigadier General George T. Anderson. Anderson, nicknamed Tige (from "Tiger") for his aggressiveness, believed that his men were the designated reserve, so he did not automatically advance when Benning's Brigade, to his right, did so. Only minutes after Benning's Georgians departed, however, Anderson received Jerome Robertson's call for help. Lacking any other orders, or even a sense of whom to turn to for direction, Anderson led his brigade to Robertson's aid. Thus, by chance and well-intentioned instinct, the full weight of Hood's second wave was moving toward the center of Sickles' position, leaving the units struggling against Little Round Top to fend for themselves.

The 44th and 48th Alabama Regiments of Law's Brigade had begun their advances on the extreme right of that line, but thanks to a series of position shifts, they were now moving on a tangent to the left flank, which brought them into the opening of the Plum Run Gorge. Colonel William F. Perry, commanding the 44th, was navigating by the sound of the fighting at Devil's Den. "The enemy were as invisible to us as we were to them," he later recollected. "The presence of a battery of artillery of course implied the presence of a strong supporting force of infantry. Of its strength, its position, and the nature of its defenses, we were in total ignorance." He knew only that with the 48th Alabama advancing parallel to him, on his right, he was not alone.

After a spate of individual shots alerted Perry's men to the proximity of the enemy, the veteran Rebel soldiers hugged the ground, allowing most of the first aimed volley to pass harmlessly overhead. The two Alabama regiments had come up against the 4th Maine, now positioned at the entrance to the gorge. While the 48th, more sheltered by virtue of being in the woods, maintained its regimental cohesion, the 44th, already thinned by straggling throughout the day's hot march, was further reduced when each wing focused on a different, divergent objective. The left wing slid along the eastern side of the triangular field to enfilade the 124th New York, even as the right tackled the 4th Maine.

Despite assistance provided by the 48th, the thin right wing of the 44th Alabama enjoyed scant success at first. When the time later came for the commander of the 4th Maine to write his report, Colonel Elijah Walker would term this formation "a strong skirmish line." Yet even as the left wing of the 4th Maine stopped the Alabama troops in the gorge, the left wing of the 44th was scattering the 124th New York and surging to the crest of Devil's Den, where the Alabamians got in among Smith's artillery. The New York cannoneers fled, taking their firing implements with them to deny the enemy the use of their tubes. Just as the Alabama soldiers were savoring their moment of victory, artillery shells began bursting among the captured guns, forcing them to seek cover.* The commotion was not enough to deter a few determined members of the 1st Texas, who slipped in among the abandoned guns and thereby laid

*Although some accounts credit this shelling to Hazlett's Battery, not yet on Little Round Top, a more likely candidate is the 1st Ohio Light Artillery, Battery L, then positioned at the northern end of the Plum Run valley.

the groundwork for a series of postwar arguments with 44th Alabama survivors over which regiment had actually taken possession of Smith's three cannons.*

A Federal counterattack boiled up almost at once, undertaken by the right wing of the 4th Maine, a portion of the 124th New York, and the 99th Pennsylvania, which had just been hustled over from its place on the extreme right of Ward's line. A corporal in the ranks of the Pennsylvania regiment would describe the moment when his unit entered the fray: "Above the crack of the rifle, the scream of shell and the cries of the wounded, could be heard the shout for 'Pennsylvania and our homes,' " he recalled. It took only minutes for the 99th Pennsylvania to regain control of Smith's guns. A member of the regiment later proudly recollected how the men stood "as firm as the rocks beneath their feet and poured volley after volley into the gorge below."

It was the nature of this close-in fighting that an advantage along one part of the line was often secured at the expense of another part. Dedicating its right wing to the effort to retake Smith's guns so diminished the 4th Maine's firepower that the 48th Alabama was able to press past its flank into the more open area of the Plum Run valley, whence it could sweep in behind the Federal line along Houck's Ridge. James Smith's decision to position his two extra guns about midway to the rear of the valley now paid a dividend, as the pair blasted the Alabama troops. "The enemy are taken by surprise," Smith noted. "Their battle flag drops three different times from the effect of our canister." The Alabama men, exhausted beyond measure, fell back into the woods.

The cost had been high, but Union arms still held Houck's Ridge. Sergeant Harvey May Munsell, the color-bearer for the 99th Pennsylvania, somehow made it through the tempest unhit, even though he had conspicuously borne the United States flag. Munsell put on a brave front, but inwardly he felt real fear. Only afterward did he learn that others in the ranks "thought I was the only man in the regiment not frightened half out of his senses."

Like small animals fleeing an approaching conflagration, the skirmishers sent out by Strong Vincent's right-side regiments came scrambling back out of the woods and up the slope to where the Union battle line girded

*One gun had broken down earlier in the action and been successfully hauled away.

lower Little Round Top. With them were some green-clad figures from the 2nd United States Sharpshooters, still busy dogging Longstreet's men. Any distraction provided by the fighting at Devil's Den was forgotten in an instant when the battle lines of the 4th Alabama and the 4th and 5th Texas Regiments appeared at the woods' edge. "We had to fight the Yankees on a Mountain," was how a soldier in the 4th Texas would remember it, "where it was very steep and [there were] rocks as large as a meeting house."

That these Confederate troops, after their long march and difficult advance in the heat, had any fight left in them at all was amazing; that they retained the discipline, courage, and drive to charge across the broken ground into a prepared defense was beyond understanding. In this first attack, the three Confederate regiments hit Vincent's right flank, with the 83rd Pennsylvania and the 44th New York taking the brunt of it.

"In an instant a sheet of smoke and flames burst from our whole line," recalled a Pennsylvania officer, "which made the enemy reel and stagger, and fall back in confusion." "For the first time in the history of the war, our men began to waver . . . ," noted a Texan in the 5th. "The balls [were] whizzing so thick around us that it [looked] like a man could hold out a hat and catch it full." The Confederate line stood the fire longer than the Yankee recollected, but not a great deal longer. Too many key officers were down, too many men on the verge of exhaustion. A number did not fall back but instead lay down at the farthermost point of advance. Many of these were captured by a handful of resolute New Yorkers who, after calling to their comrades to hold their fire, scampered forward to grab some of the shaken Rebels and propel them to the crest as prisoners. "Their dead and wounded were tumbled promiscuously together, so that it was difficult to cross the line where they fell without stepping on them," testified one of the New York soldiers. Another confronted a frightened Texan who "stood directly in front of me begging me not to shoot him, when a bullet, from the musket of a brother Texan, entered his back."

Along the tree line, the sweating, thirsty, bone-weary soldiers from Alabama and Texas showed the kind of mettle that made them the stuff of legend. "Now, it was to be expected that our men having tried it and seeing the impossibility of taking the place would have refused to go in again," wrote a member of the 5th Texas. "But no, they tried it a second time."

* * *

Partly because it had a shorter distance to march before making contact, and partly because its route brought it under a hurry-up fire from the Federal cannon posted near Sherfy's peach orchard, Tige Anderson's brigade closed quickly with the Yankee troops by Rose's wheat field. With McLaws having yet to advance, these Georgians were hammered on both flanks and from their front. "For nearly an hour the enemy were on three sides of us, and a battery of sixteen guns enfilading us with grape," an officer in the 8th Georgia remembered. "Grape, canister and musket balls fell in a shower like hail around us," asserted the commander of the 59th Georgia. "I could hear bones crash like glass in a hail storm." A young soldier in that regiment could only explain to his mother that "our Regiment got Cut all to Peaces."

By now the Third Corps units of de Trobriand's brigade were no longer alone, having been reinforced by portions of Andrew Humphreys' division and joined on their right by the brigades of Colonels William S. Tilton and Jacob B. Sweitzer, both part of Barnes' First Division of the Fifth Corps. Most of the fighting here was centered on the southwestern border of Rose's wheat field, where the combined elements of the two Federal corps were able to hold the line, at least for the moment.

The 17th Maine, in de Trobriand's command, held a key spot behind a stone wall that anchored the left flank of the position. As Anderson's battle lines approached, according to Private John Haley, "our fire began to tell on their ranks, which were more dense than usual. We peppered them well with musketry while Randolph's battery, which was on a gentle rise [in the middle of the wheat field] in rear of us, served a dose of grape and canister every few seconds."*

Somehow, William Oates, his 15th Alabama, and the accompanying 47th Alabama clawed their way toward the crest of Big Round Top. "In places the men had to climb up, catching to the rocks and bushes and crawling over the boulders in the face of the fire of the enemy [sharpshooters], who kept retreating, taking shelter and firing down on us from behind the rocks and crags which covered the side of the mountain thicker than gravestones in a city cemetery," Oates observed. A number finally reached the

---

*George E. Randolph commanded the Third Corps' artillery brigade. The guns in question made up Captain George B. Winslow's Battery D, 1st New York Light Artillery.

summit. "Some of my men fainted from heat, exhaustion, and thirst," their commander recorded.

Just minutes before the advance was ordered from Warfield Ridge, Oates had allowed a detail of twenty-two men to gather canteens to be filled at the Andrew Currens farm, a short distance south along the Emmitsburg Road. The detachment had not returned by the time the attack was set to begin. Oates' hope that these men would rejoin his command was not to be realized, for as they attempted to catch up, they encountered several cells of the 2nd U.S. Sharpshooters, who took them prisoner.

One who did reach Oates, though, was none other than Leigh R. Terrell, whose stentorian tones had launched the brigade's advance. The plucky aide to Evander Law made his way to the top on horseback. His instructions to Oates were "to press on, turn the Union left, and capture Little Round Top, if possible, and to lose no time." Oates tried to argue that there was an advantage to be had in his holding his present position, but Terrell's instructions were peremptory. Oates roused his regiment back into line in readiness to begin moving down the northern slope of Big Round Top.

More Federal firepower was bound for Little Round Top, in the form of Lieutenant Charles E. Hazlett's Battery D, 5th United States (Light) Artillery. The six ten-pounder parrott cannon had been attached to James Barnes' division while it began moving from its reserve position to the front. At first Hazlett's guns had seemed destined for a place near Rose's wheat field, but then the call had come for help on Little Round Top. There was no path visible through the jumble of trees and boulders that collared the cleared summit. Trying afterward to explain how they managed the ascent, one of Hazlett's officers wrote, "We went there at a trot, each man and horse trying to pull the whole battery by himself." "Our guns tipped over," recalled a cannoneer, "[but] we put them back and somehow got them on top of the hill." Any spare hands were put to use, including those belonging to stragglers from Vincent's brigade.

The man whose timely warning had brought these Federal troops to this threatened point remained on hand. Gouverneur K. Warren intercepted Charles Hazlett to make the obvious observation that the summit of Little Round Top was a poor position for artillery, as the steep slope rendered it impossible for the guns to bear on the ground directly in their front. "Never mind that," Hazlett told Warren. "The sound of my guns will be encouraging to our troops and disheartening to the others, and my battery's of no use if this hill is lost."*

As quickly as they could be set in place, Hazlett's guns began firing on targets below, in the Plum Run valley.

Responding to Strong Vincent's instructions to deploy skirmishers, Joshua Chamberlain detached the 20th Maine's Company B (forty-two men) and sent it forward under Captain Walter Morrill. The Maine men had just reached the foot of the northeastern slope of Big Round Top when they heard the tearing sounds of mass musketry to their right and rear, signaling the attack by the Texans and Arkansans against Vincent's right. Morrill wisely backed off to the east, finally settling on a position behind a stone wall some four hundred feet east of the regiment. Soon after Company B had hunkered into place, a dozen or so U.S. sharp-shooters slipped in among them to warn that there were Rebels coming down off Big Round Top. The riflemen offered to stick around, an offer that Morrill gratefully accepted.

Benning's Georgia brigade moved through the stalled elements of Robertson's and Law's Brigades to attack Devil's Den. It fell to the 20th Georgia to advance across the open slope marking the triangular field. As a resolute Private J. W. Lokey traversed the clearing, he passed by a prone comrade who called out, " 'You had better not go up there; you'll get shot.' " Lokey ignored the admonition, pressed on nearly to the summit, and got shot. Making his way to the rear he corralled an unwounded Yankee to help him. As the two stumbled out of range, the Federal asked, " 'If you and I had this matter to settle, we would soon settle it, wouldn't we?' "

The advance of the 20th halted just short of Smith's abandoned guns. To its right, two other Georgia regiments pushed into the Plum Run Gorge, only to be hit and stopped by counterattacks launched by two Federal regiments sent to help, one (the 40th New York) from de Trobriand's brigade, the other (the 6th New Jersey) from Burling's.

---

*Warren later wrote, "I was wounded [in the throat] with a musket ball while talking with Lieutenant Hazlett on the hill, but not seriously."

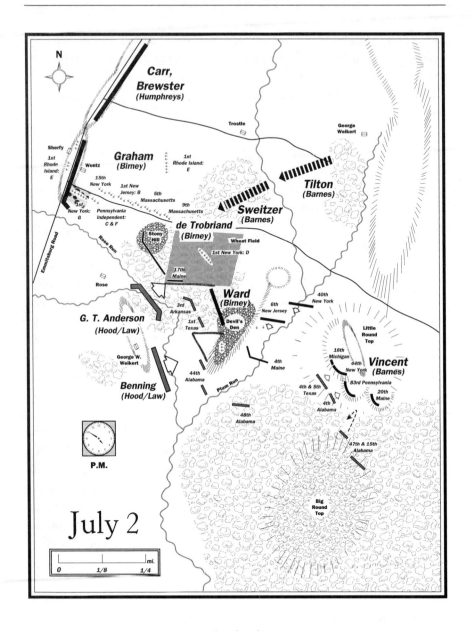

The first Confederate regiment to descend from Big Round Top was the 47th Alabama, commanded by Lieutenant Colonel Michael J. Bulger, who had taken over in midadvance after Colonel James Washington Jackson collapsed from illness and exhaustion. Bulger was leading his men toward the unseen enemy position when he was met by another of Evander Law's seemingly indefatigable staff officers, on horseback, who ordered, "Colonel Bulger, charge that line." "Tell General Law that I am charging to the best of my ability," Bulger responded. "For God's sake put in the Fifteenth [Alabama] upon my right, and my life for it, we'll drive them when we come to them."

The 15th had yet to complete its descent when the 47th made contact with Vincent's line, striking it on the left of the 83rd Pennsylvania and the right of the 20th Maine. Amply warned by their skirmishers, both regiments were ready and hit the 47th with a well-aimed volley that scythed men down, Bulger among them. According to a postwar interview, Bulger crawled for cover into a rocky crevice, where he sat "with the blood gushing from his mouth and nostrils." Its leadership decimated, its men bewildered, the 47th fell back, its offensive power spent.

Brigadier General Joseph B. Kershaw was a perceptive, determined leader. His brigade had been the first in McLaws' Division to take its place along Warfield Ridge, opposite Sherfy's peach orchard. In the time it took for the rest of McLaws' and all of Hood's brigades to deploy, Kershaw considered his tactical situation. His preparations were based on two pieces of information. The first was that Hood's men were "to sweep down the Federal lines in a direction perpendicular to our line of battle." The second was that once his own South Carolina units (five regiments and a battalion) began their advance, Barksdale's Mississippi brigade on his immediate left was to "move with me and conform to my movement." Kershaw planned his assault to target a stony hill located on the western edge of Rose's wheat field. He had also noted what appeared to be a gap between the hill and the Union cannon posted along the Wheatfield Road. He intended to exploit that gap.

Kershaw got his first unpleasant surprise when he observed Hood's brigades moving "independently against Round Top," a departure from plan that meant they would not "directly participate in the joint attack." With Hood off track, he could only hope that Barksdale would do his part, for without the Mississippians' striking the peach orchard in tandem with his advance, the Yankee cannon would scourge his flank with a terrible power.

Kershaw brought his battle lines forward to their jump-off point and waited. The signal to advance was received, and as Kershaw later recalled with pride, his "men . . . were promptly aligned, the word [to advance] was given, and the brigade moved off at the word, with great steadiness and precision. . . . General Longstreet accompanied me in this advance on foot, as far as the Emmitsburg road . . . ," he continued. "When we were about the Emmitsburg road, I heard Barksdale's drum beat the assembly, and knew *then* that I should have no immediate support on my left, about to be squarely presented to the heavy force of the infantry and artillery at and in rear of the Peach Orchard."

With plan A shot, Kershaw wasted no time in improvising a plan B. He divided his brigade into two wings: the left (two regiments and the battalion) wheeled north to face the peach orchard salient, while the right wing (the remaining three regiments) pressed toward the stony hill. Communicating this change to his subordinates and carrying it out under a killing shower of canister and spherical case constituted a supreme test of Kershaw's leadership.

His left wing took horrible losses as it pushed within rifle range of the cannon. "You could constantly see men falling on all sides and the terrible missiles of death were flying thick and fast everywhere," recollected a member of the 2nd South Carolina, "cutting off large trees and plowing up the ground everywhere." "Shells were cutting off the arms, legs and heads of our men, cutting them in two and exploding in their bodies, tearing them into mincemeat," shuddered another in that regiment.

Most of the left wing went to ground, opting to use their rifles to clear the artillery row of its gunners. A problem arose with the other wing as several units crowded together and the ranks became intermingled. To separate them, Kershaw gave the order, intended solely for the right wing, to "move to the right and open at the line." However, the order to "move by the right flank" was communicated by mistake to the officers of the left wing, who promptly pulled their men away from the cannon and turned their flank and rear to the eager Yankee gunners. "We were, in ten minutes' or less time, terribly butchered," declared a soldier in the left wing. "I saw half a dozen at a time knocked up and flung to the ground like trifles." A Rebel private in the midst of the storm would never forget "the awful deathly surging sounds of those little black [canister] balls as they flew by us, through us, between our legs and over us!" "Hundreds of the bravest and best men of Carolina fell," Kershaw noted, "victims of this fatal blunder."

Daniel Sickles' unauthorized move into a position that required more men than he had at his disposal immediately sucked in the reserve forces of the Fifth Corps and the batteries of the Reserve Artillery. The manpower drain would not end there—Hancock's Second Corps soon felt it imperative to support the struggling Third Corps. Andrew Humphreys, while advancing his division to the Emmitsburg Road, pulled his right flank away from its covering connection with the Second, leaving it, in military parlance, "in the air."

Humphreys appealed to John Gibbon, whose Second Corps division was close at hand, to "close the line by filling up the open space between them." Gibbon decided to send two of his regiments (the 15th Massachusetts and the 82nd New York) out to the Emmitsburg Road near the Codori farm. Once there, recalled a Massachusetts soldier, "we built a small breastwork of rails behind the fence [lining the road], during which time the enemy were engaged on our left, and there was a rapid picket firing in our front."

On Little Round Top, Strong Vincent's brigade had successfully withstood several attacks on its right flank by the 4th Alabama and 4th and 5th Texas Regiments. None of these later attempts had had the desperate, frenzied determination of the first one, exhaustion having exacted its toll on the Rebel assault force. For the moment, the fighting across the southwestern slope was being carried out in Indian fashion, with the men on both sides firing slowly from cover. An Alabama soldier noted that "Minie balls were falling through the leaves like hail in a thunderstorm."

Approaching the fray from the summit of Big Round Top, William Oates heard the disciplined volleys of the 83rd Pennsylvania and the 20th Maine shredding the 47th Alabama. The sound helped Oates fix the location of the Federal position in his front. Obeying his orders to flank the enemy's line, he instructed his 15th Alabama to "swing around, and drive the Federals from the ledge of rocks, . . . gain the enemy's rear, and drive him from the hill."

Along the sector held by the 20th Maine, Joshua Chamberlain was informed by one of his company captains, positioned near the center of the line, that "something queer was going on in his front." Chamberlain followed the officer back to his spot and climbed onto a boulder to get a better view. His second in command, Major Ellis Spear, came over from the regiment's left wing to recommend that the line be refused—that is, bent back—the better to protect that flank. From his perch, Chamberlain saw "thick groups in gray [who] were pushing . . . in a direction to gain our left flank."

Joshua Chamberlain was of that rare breed of citizen-soldiers whose métier was combat. Faced in the heat of battle with a tactical problem requiring a quick solution, he coolly came up with an unconventional riposte. Ordering his men to maintain a steady fire to their front, he simultaneously directed them to sidestep to their left, so the second rank merged with the first. By this means, the standard double-ranked lines of battle were transformed into a much longer single line, which Chamberlain then bent back at the place where his left flank had formerly ended. This enabled him to extend his refused flank along a larger perimeter than would have obtained if he had merely bent back the double lines, as Ellis Spear had proposed.

It was not a textbook maneuver, but Chamberlain knew he had to do *something*. "If a strong force should gain our rear," he later explained, "our brigade would be caught as by a mighty shears-blade, and be cut and crushed."

The 3,300 men of John C. Caldwell's Second Corps division had been watching the fight on their left with more than detached interest. "Smoke rises in dense clouds from Little Round Top," remembered one officer. "The rattle of musketry, the crash of . . . canister through the dense woodland tells the story of the conflict." Then the bugles and drums were sounding Assembly, summoning the men into ranks that soon enough began marching toward the maelstrom—or so they thought. Another column was seen cutting across the path of Caldwell's division: Barnes' Fifth Corps division, coming forward to buttress Little Round Top and the wheat field. With the advent of that unit, Winfield Hancock told Caldwell to return to his starting point, which he did, doubtless to ample grumbling in the ranks.

Hancock found a place along his sector from which he could observe a good deal of the fighting on his left. Then an aide appeared to request that Hancock send a division to help without reporting to Sickles. Calling for assistance was the Fifth Corps, then battling G. T. Anderson's and Benning's Brigades near Rose's wheat field. " 'Caldwell, you get your division ready,' " Hancock ordered.

It was not long before the four brigades were marching south past Hancock, led by Edward E. Cross' First Brigade. " 'Colonel Cross, this day will bring you a [general's] star,' " Hancock shouted. Cross looked anything but pleased. " 'No General,' " he replied, " 'this is my last battle.' " The Federal officer usually sported a red bandana when in action, but today the one he wore was black. Behind Cross came the brigades of Colonels Patrick Kelly and John R. Brooke and Brigadier General Samuel K. Zook. A member of Kelly's Irish Brigade recalled that the men "at once took arms and were marched by the left flank toward the scene of action."

Like many other aspects of Daniel Sickles' repositioning of the Third Corps, the line taken along Houck's Ridge both aided and endangered the Army of the Potomac. It threatened it by forcing Sickles to uncover the more strategically important Little Round Top; it helped it by absorbing the offensive energies of portions of three Confederate brigades, so draining them of power that they would contribute little to what remained of this day's combat. In accomplishing that, however, Brigadier General J. H. Hobart Ward's brigade would itself sacrifice some 781 soldiers out of perhaps 2,200 engaged.

Once Benning's Georgia brigade had added its full weight to the assault on Devil's Den, the ability of Ward's men to sustain their position rapidly eroded. Recognizing at last the impossibility of holding against such odds, and believing that the reinforcements Meade was committing to Rose's wheat field meant that his defense of the ridge had accomplished its purpose, Ward began pulling his units away from that deadly sector.

The regiments nearest the wheat field got the orders first, while those at Devil's Den received them last, if at all. The worst fate fell upon the 4th Maine, posted below and facing the gorge. Heavily assailed in its front and from Devil's Den, the regiment finally backed out of the Plum Run valley with losses approaching 50 percent of those engaged.

The last intact Federal unit to leave Devil's Den was the 99th Pennsylvania. Sergeant Harvey Munsell, still hiding his fear from the others, would never forget a final act of sacrifice performed by his decimated color guard. Some powerful emotion bound together three enlisted men in the group, Privates George Broadbent and Charles W. Herbster and Corporal George Setley. After Broadbent was killed, toward the end of the fighting, Herbster and Setley positioned themselves alongside their friend's body, grimly set on vengeance. Even orders to retreat did not deter them from their self-appointed destiny. "Nothing could move them," Munsell would remember. "There they were, riveted to the ground, avenging the lives of their comrades, and there we left them. Setley was frothing at the mouth with excitement and anger, and Herbster taking it as cool as a cucumber." Munsell knew he would never see the pair again alive.*

Once the Federals had relinquished Devil's Den, it became a favorite target for Union artillery at the northern end of the Plum Run valley. "The shell and shrapnel shot descended, exploding in the earth and hurling the rocks to an amazing height," recorded the *Savannah Republican*'s reporter, "but in spite of all, our [Confederate] men held their places firmly."

One unintended effect of the artillery duel on the southeastern side of Gettysburg was a multitude of close calls for the town's noncombatants. Still clucking over her husband's insistence on picking garden beans under sniper fire, Sarah Broadhead joined him in the cellar of a neighbor's house when the firing became so intense that it "seemed as though heaven and earth were being rolled together." There were some twenty-two townspeople crowded into the space. "Whilst there a shell struck the house," Broadhead noted, "but mercifully did not burst, but remained embedded in the wall, one half protruding."

Quite near the George Little house, which was providing sanctuary for ten (mostly women and children), two shells exploded. Asked by one girl present what they should do, Little answered gravely, "Pray." A third shell, this one exploding even closer, galvanized him into action: he quickly shepherded his flock from the house proper down into the cellar, through the outside door. Hardly had they settled into their new refuge when a fourth shell struck the home, careening into the room they had just left and exploding as it did so.

Henry Jacobs and his professor father, who should have known better, decided they would be safe enough experiencing events in their backyard, sitting on their "old-fashioned sloping cellar door." For a short while, they enjoyed the spectacle of bright-sounding explosions and whiffs of burned gunpowder. Then a shrapnel shell burst overhead, and the showering of small pieces, Henry reminisced, "made us retreat hastily to the refuge of the cellar." They were safely sheltered there when Henry

*Sergeant Munsell, carrying the national flag, was temporarily knocked unconscious but then successfully hid the flag, eluded capture, and returned the colors to his regiment, a feat that would earn him a Medal of Honor. Charles W. Herbster was killed on July 2; George Setley was taken prisoner and would die in Richmond in 1864.

saw a Rebel soldier slip into the spot they had just vacated. To the boy's lasting horror, the soldier "suddenly groaned, and we heard his body fall over and gently slide downward. He had been killed where he sat."

Ellis Spear commanded the left wing of the 20th Maine, which was now a long, thin line bent back at an angle to its original south-facing position. Those along the front line had already been engaged, first with the 47th Alabama on their right, then against a fair portion of the 15th Alabama that had come at them head-on. The Rebel commander, William Oates, was veteran enough to seek the enemy's most vulnerable point. "I advanced my right," he later recalled, "swinging it around, overlapping and turning their left." In doing so, Oates struck Spear's sector. "The fire on both sides was soon hot and men were falling," remembered the Yankee major.

These Maine men had not had time to fortify their position, so they spread out as each sought his own piece of cover. This allowed Oates' more compact formation to press in and among Spear's men, who bent further but did not break. "I ordered a charge, and the enemy in my front fled," Oates insisted, "but that portion of his line confronting the two companies on my left held their ground, and continued a most galling fire upon my left."

Joshua Chamberlain, commanding the 20th Maine, had a different perspective on the action: "We opened a brisk fire at close range, which was so sudden and effective they soon fell back among the rocks and low trees in the valley, only to burst forth again with a shout, and rapidly advance, firing as they came," he related. "They pushed up to within a dozen yards of us before the terrible effectiveness of our fire compelled them to break and take shelter."

Perhaps fifteen hundred feet north of the spot where Joshua Chamberlain was holding the flank, Gouverneur K. Warren was feeling the same chill of apprehension that had first motivated him to summon help to Little Round Top. "The full force of the enemy was now sweeping the 3d Army Corps from its untenable position and no troops nor any reinforcements could maintain it," he later wrote. Warren could see that the effort to sustain Sickles' line was drawing reinforcements from the Fifth and Second Corps, diverting or diluting any assistance that might otherwise have been intended for him.

Warren himself had lent what help he could to Hazlett's gunners as they wrestled their tubes and carriages into place. Now, spying a Fifth Corps column passing toward Rose's wheat field from the northern side of Little Round Top, he did not give it a second thought: he rode down the hill to intercept those troops.

There were times in battle when a commander required plain luck. George Meade's luck was riding high at this moment as one of his ablest subordinates, in search of desperately needed reinforcements, encountered a brigade that he had once commanded. The man now in charge of it, Brigadier General Stephen H. Weed, had ridden ahead to find out where his regiments were to go. Warren recognized the rider heading the column as Colonel Patrick O'Rorke, of the 140th New York. More luck: Warren knew him.

"Paddy, give me a regiment," Warren said.

O'Rorke hesitated. He was supposed to be guiding the brigade forward until Weed provided other instructions, and he told Warren as much. "Never mind that," Warren interjected. "Bring your regiment up here and I will take the responsibility." That was enough for O'Rorke, an Irish-born West Point graduate described by one observer as "a man of noble character." Directing that the rest of the brigade continue on its course toward the wheat field, O'Rorke led the 140th up Little Round Top.

At first, Philippe Regis de Trobriand had done the impossible, by maintaining a position at the wheat field in the center of the line held by David Birney's division. It had helped that the main thrust of the first Rebel wave had been focused on Devil's Den and Big and Little Round Top, and that reinforcements had been forthcoming in the form of two brigades from James Barnes' Fifth Corps division. But it had hurt that he had had to release some of his regiments to assist other sectors, and that some of the Georgia regiments belonging to G. T. Anderson's and George Benning's brigades had targeted Rose's wheat field. Still, de Trobriand's mixed force of Third and Fifth Corps units had stubbornly held its own, at least until the right wing of Joseph Kershaw's South Carolina brigade rammed into the stony hill that rose on the wheat field's western side.

As Kershaw remembered it, his men "advanced into a piece of wood beyond the ravine and to the top of a rocky knoll . . . and thus became heavily engaged." Their commander at once recognized the value of his objective, as it comprised "a point from which I could distinctly see the movement of troops in the wheat field." The pendulum of luck now took a swing in Lee's direction, for Kershaw was able to capture this important position with minimum resistance from the two brigades of Barnes' division. While Barnes himself would never satisfactorily explain why he had ordered his men off the stony hill, the move may have had to do with the threat posed by Kershaw's right wing, as well as a concern that the artillery line along the Wheatfield Road was in need of support. The lapse underscored another failing of Sickles' scheme: the lack of planning and coordination left a number of operational questions regarding tactical responsibility unresolved, leading to a confusion of authority that was made the more acute by the mixing of the different commands.

With the stony hill in Kershaw's hands, the few Third Corps units that remained in Rose's wheat field had to fall back midway across it to support the battery located there. Disaster seemed unavoidable unless help was on its way. Luck swung back to George Meade: help *was* on its way.

Taut as an arrow ready for flight, William Barksdale's Mississippi brigade was aimed at Sherfy's peach orchard, ready to go. The unit's fiery commander, a former U.S. congressman and champion of states' rights, sensed victory, though he knew it would take courage and maximum determination to secure it. Barksdale had both of those qualities in ample measure; his men, however, were rather more phlegmatic. "Some strolled down to the little stream in their rear, where canteens were filled," recalled one waiting soldier. "Others crossed over and broke off great branches from the numerous cherry trees which were in full bearing."

A few minutes earlier, before joining Kershaw near the Emmitsburg Road, James Longstreet had spoken with Barksdale. "I wish you would let me go in, General," the brigadier had pleaded, pointing east, toward the Federal cannon that were firing on his men. "I would take that battery in five minutes." Longstreet shook his head as he left to meet Kershaw. "Wait a little," he called out. "We are all going in presently."

A crisis loomed on Little Round Top. Pressure was building against the extreme left of the Union position, where the 15th Alabama and the 20th Maine were locked in a desperate struggle. While continuing to press the Federal line facing Big Round Top, William Oates was doggedly shifting strength against the thinned, refused left flank, knowing intuitively that a success at this point would mean victory at every other. Joshua Chamberlain had no difficulty gleaning his opponent's intent, but doing something about it was a different matter altogether. He tried moving his two right companies over to assist the left, but the effort created more confusion than he had anticipated, so he countermanded his order. They would have to hold with what they had. "The two lines met and broke and mingled in the shock," Chamberlain remembered. "The crash of musketry gave way to cuts and thrusts, grapplings and wrestlings."

The situation was even more desperate on Vincent's right flank, where the 16th Michigan held the critical position. These troops and the regiments to their left had already beaten back several assaults undertaken by the 4th Alabama and the 4th and 5th Texas. It spoke volumes about the fierce resiliency of these Southern units—worn as they were from long marches, lacking water, and already under fire for more than an hour—that they regrouped for another try. This time they had help from the 48th Alabama, one of the two regiments from Law's Brigade that had helped force entry into Plum Run Gorge.

The sight that met the Confederates as they left the cover of the woods around lower Big Round Top was enough to quail the most stalwart soul. To the daunting height of the Federal position was added the grim necessity of passage through a kill zone already littered with the dead, dying, and wounded casualties of the previous efforts. It proved to be too much for portions of the 5th Texas. "We forwarded without a murmur, until we struck the danger point," related Private William A. Fletcher. "The men about faced near as if ordered and marched back. The command 'Halt!' was not heeded." Enough nonetheless remained in these and other ranks to make it seem to the equally weary Federals that a human wave was about to break over them.

Command and control collapsed suddenly in the 16th Michigan. Some would later surmise that an order intended to tighten the defense had set off a chain of events that nearly ended in catastrophe. Perhaps in an effort to better control the maneuver, or out of a misunderstanding as to its context, a subordinate officer without authority ordered the regimental colors to the rear, which resulted in nearly a third of the 16th's falling back. The regimental commander, Lieutenant Colonel Norval E. Welch, was evidently quite overwhelmed by these events; he assumed that a general retreat had been ordered and proceeded to lead the one-third contingent off the hill. To the sweaty, powder-smeared Texas and

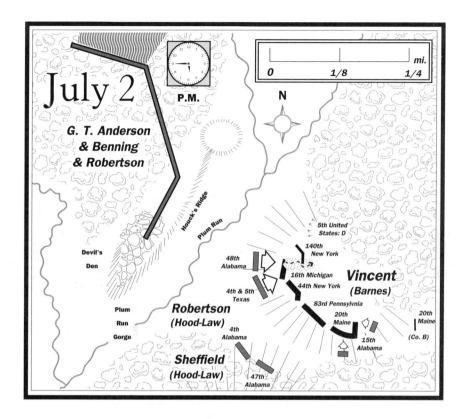

Alabama soldiers scrambling up the rugged southwestern slope of Little Round Top, it looked as if the entire Yankee line were giving way.

The Federal unit to the left of the 16th, the 44th New York, shifted some of its fire to the right. The danger drew the brigade commander, Strong Vincent, to the scene. According to a soldier on the hill, "Throwing himself in the breach he rallied his men, but gave up his own life." Mortally wounded by a rifle ball in his groin, Vincent was carried to the rear. " 'This is the fourth or fifth time they have shot at me,' " he gasped, " 'and they have hit me at last.' " Command devolved to James C. Rice of the 44th New York, who kept his nerve, impressing everyone who saw him with his determination to stay on Little Round Top.

All the courage in the world would not fill the empty space to the right of the reduced 16th Michigan, now being filled by squads of Rebels. Help did arrive, however, in the form of the 140th New York. The 526 Empire State men huffed up the hill and deployed in a line of battle split more or less into two wings. A soldier in the ranks recollected, "Our

Generals did not take the precaution to have our men load before we came into the contest, and so we were delayed a few moments in loading." Gouverneur K. Warren mistook their stopping to load for a halt preparatory to straightening their formation. "No time now, Paddy, for alignment," Warren shouted at O'Rorke. "Take your men immediately into action."

The 140th crested Little Round Top just to the right of the 16th Michigan. Seeing the confusion in the Yankee ranks, O'Rorke charged forward, followed by two companies from the 140th's right wing. "Here they are men," O'Rorke yelled. "Commence firing." The order ignited a fusillade from both sides, in the course of which O'Rorke fell with a mortal throat wound. The 140th had the initiative now. More and more men piled into a sloppy line, firing as fast as they could reload. Their dramatic appearance breathed renewed life into the other Union regiments on the hill, which now picked up their firing rates. It was all too much for the Alabama and Texas men, who began falling back. One embittered Texan in the 5th noted that the Federal position would have been "impossible to take had the enemy only been armed with rocks."

Timely Federal reinforcements were also reaching Rose's wheat field, where the abrupt departure of the two Fifth Corps brigades had allowed Kershaw's South Carolinians to secure the stony hill. Kershaw was well aware that his command was not in the best of shape and that he needed help, but the only lines of battle he saw approaching were Yankee ones.

These troops belonged to Caldwell's division of Hancock's Second Corps, which, due to the urgency of the situation, was being committed piecemeal, a brigade at a time. Hurried as they were, the brigades were also entering the fray inside out—that is, oriented in the wrong direction which meant that key individuals had to pass through shifting files to properly guide the combat advance. A member of the 148th Pennsylvania spoke for many in the brigade when he insisted that "this eccentricity of formation . . . did not, in the slightest manner, affect the conduct of our regiment. Previous drill and discipline had provided [for] just such condition."

The first to arrive was Edward E. Cross' First Brigade, which angled across the eastern edge of the wheat field to strike at a ragged battle line in the woods to the southwest. The Federals' objective was made up largely of "Tige" Anderson's Georgians, with a few of Jerome Robertson's Texans and even some of Kershaw's South Carolinians mingled in. Cross' men levered the right end of the Confederate line back a bit but ran out of offensive punch before they achieved any breakthrough. During this combat, their leader fell, gut-shot. He was carried off to a field hospital, knowing his wound was mortal. " 'I think the boys will miss me,' " Cross said before he died. " 'Say goodbye to all.' "

The next wave of Federals into the wheat field had been the last brigade in Caldwell's column as it wriggled across the landscape to this trouble spot. Daniel Sickles had sent his aides out to pull in all the reinforcements they could find, regardless of where they were headed. Time and again, units were intercepted by Third Corps aides who quickly got them marching in directions having little to do with their orders. Following this pattern, one of Sickles' staff had met the head of Caldwell's trailing brigade and voiced the usual urgings for its commander to follow him. Taking these for official orders, Samuel K. Zook swung his brigade out past the next pair in line, deployed near the Trostle farm, and advanced against Kershaw's men on the stony hill.

Fighting from the better cover afforded by the boulders and trees, Kershaw's men staggered Zook's brigade to a halt, mortally wounding Zook in the process. Kershaw's troubles were far from over, though, for another Federal battle line soon hove into view, this one heading toward his exposed right flank, which was nestled on the edge of an unoccupied ravine. The new threat came from Patrick Kelly's Irish Brigade. Watching it approach, a South Carolina officer was impressed. "Is that not a magnificent sight?" he remarked to a companion.

Kelly's men battered their way into the ravine, then scrambled up its side to close with the enemy. "The Confederates were on a crest while the regimental line was below them, their feet about on a level with the heads of the men," recalled a Pennsylvania officer. "When the Regiment charged and gained the ground on which the enemy stood, it was found covered with their dead, nearly every one of them being hit in the head or upper part of the body." A South Carolina officer remembered that the fighting here was "so desperate I took two shots with my pistol at men scarcely thirty steps from me."

Kershaw looked back for his support, Semmes' Georgia brigade, which was not yet engaged. As Semmes began rousing his men for the advance, he took a serious thigh wound that would eventually kill him. His men provided enough stiffening to halt the Irish Brigade but not enough to drive it back. A surly stalemate had fallen over Rose's wheat field.

* * *

On Little Round Top, it was all coming down to the combative wills of two opposing regimental commanders. The men fought as they had been trained; discipline, pride, and stubbornness kept them to their task, despite the horrors around them. In one sense they had it easy, for they had to focus only on the small areas before them and could shut out the bloody havoc wreaked by the soft lead bullets that both sides used.

It was different for the two commanders, who needed acute situational awareness and a readiness to take risks. Neither of those traits conferred immunity to bullets. Joshua Chamberlain endured two glancing hits; one cut his foot, and the other was deflected by his sword scabbard, leaving a painful thigh bruise. Anyone looking at him would have thought him a picture of calm, but his mind was racing with the possibilities. Several of his requests for assistance or extra ammunition had been met by regretful refusals: everyone was hard pressed and low on munitions. Chamberlain knew that the bloody stalemate could not last forever. Every minute meant more irreplaceable cartridges gone, so that soon there would be nothing left to shoot. While he might not have a solution, Chamberlain never lost his determination. "We were on the appointed and entrusted line," he later explained.

William Oates had already seen too much death this day. One of his best line officers, Captain Henry C. Brainard, had fallen with the cry " 'Oh God! that I could see my mother!' " And then there was the private who approached to advise him that the gunsmoke was too thick to see through. After Oates suggested that he duck under it, the boy did so, fired a round, and then fell with a head shot before he could reload. Oates sensed now that his men had one good effort left in them. He summoned every ounce of will for one more push against the Yankee left flank, positioned along a stone shelf. "Forward, men, to the ledge," he cried out.

To the end of his days, Oates would believe that this last lunge had come very near to breaking the 20th Maine. "I led this charge," he declared, "and sprang upon the ledge of rock, using my pistol within musket length, when the rest of my men drove the Maine men from their ledge." There was no time to be lost. Without stopping to regroup, Oates again led his men charging toward what he thought was the 20th Maine's principal line. "About forty steps up the slope there is a large boulder . . . , my regimental colors [were planted] just a step or two to the right of that boulder and I was within ten feet," he reported.

But the Maine soldiers remained solid. A fusillade ripped into the yelling Rebels, and Oates could only watch in shock as his beloved brother John crumpled under the weight of multiple bullet wounds. Angry enough to cry, Oates knew that he and his men had reached their limit. He led his regiment back down the slope to a point where the shelf provided some cover. He was not yet ready to pull back, still convinced that he could find some way to take this position.

Three of John C. Caldwell's four brigades had charged into Rose's wheat field and fought the advancing Confederates to a standstill. Now the Second Corps division commander committed his last brigade, Colonel John R. Brooke's, in hopes of tipping the balance toward victory. Brooke would later recollect that his line of battle "covered nearly the width of the field, [though] there was a small portion of the field on each flank, which was not covered by my line." When formation got to about midfield, the colonel ordered a halt and then "fire at will." "The men were firing as fast as they could load," noted a Union officer. "The din was almost deafening."

Brooke's advance became slightly entangled with the movements of Cross' brigade to the left and the composite Zook-Kelly command on the right. When Confederate riflemen began finding their range, Brooke realized he could not hold here. The choice was between forward and back. "Fix bayonets!" he shouted. It took some effort on the part of his officers to spread the word against the martial cacophony. A few flags finally began to move haltingly forward—one of them reportedly borne by Brooke himself. Soon the brigade began to pick up speed, charging toward the wheat field's southwestern corner.

The momentum of the battle now lay with the Union. Brooke's rush overran portions of Tige Anderson's brigade, forcing Kershaw to backpedal from the stony hill to an area near the Rose farm. Brooke recalled halting "on the edge of the wood, fronting the Rose farm buildings. The open country was now in our front."

Brooke's success prompted one of the two Fifth Corps brigades that had initially been posted to the stony hill (and that had subsequently withdrawn a short distance north) to advance again to cover his left flank. Three regiments of Colonel Jacob B. Sweitzer's brigade moved toward the southern side of the wheat field.

Also on hand to offer support were two brigades of regular United States Army troops, part of Brigadier General Romeyn B. Ayres' Fifth

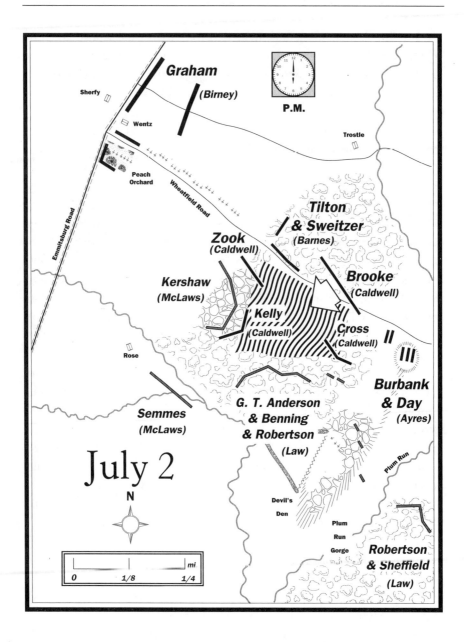

Graham (Birney)

Sherfy

Wentz

P.M.

Trostle

Peach Orchard

Wheatfield Road

Emmitsburg Road

Tilton & Sweitzer (Barnes)

Zook (Caldwell)

Kershaw (McLaws)

Kelly (Caldwell)

Brooke (Caldwell)

Cross (Caldwell)

Rose

II

III

Burbank & Day (Ayres)

Semmes (McLaws)

G. T. Anderson & Benning & Robertson (Law)

July 2

N

Devil's Den

Plum Run

Plum Run Gorge

Robertson & Sheffield (Law)

0   1/8   1/4   mi

Corps division. Having advanced to the northern end of Houck's Ridge, these units were blocked in their front by the melee in the wheat field and being harassed from their left by heavy sniping from the Rebels controlling Devil's Den. Absent any officer in overall charge, Ayres and Caldwell between them worked out a rough scheme by which the regulars could help stabilize the section held by remnants of Cross' brigade. Caldwell believed he had closed out the fighting here, noting that up to this point, "everything had progressed favorably."

It appeared that the Rebel effort to overwhelm the Federal flank had failed, save for Devil's Den. But the situation was changing quickly on this hot July day.

The entirely self-made Daniel Sickles had risen to the pinnacle of Civil War military status through a complex mixture of ambition, ruthlessness, cronyism, patriotism, personal magnetism, and luck. All of these things had compelled him to act as he had done this day, when he gambled with the fate of an army with no more concern than he would exhibit while squandering several fortunes over a colorful lifetime that would carry him into the twentieth century. Whether one of his possible prizes might be a place in the White House would depend to a great extent on how well his luck held today. If he could maintain his position even to a tactical draw, his cunning and connections would let him weave his tale of near disaster into a glowing paean to victory. At his headquarters near the Trostle farm, Sickles may have sensed that Meade's forthright efforts to bolster his line were apparently stemming the Rebel tide, and for a few moments he may even have allowed himself the sly pleasure of counting the payoff of a high-stakes risk.

Sickles' dreams began to fade, however, when William Barksdale rode to the front of his assembled brigade, about a mile to the west of the Trostle place. " 'Attention, Mississippians!' " he shouted. " 'Battalions, Forward!' " As the 1,400 men began to move, their throats swelled with the eerie "Rebel yell," purpose-designed to inspire and terrorize. With their commander in the lead, Barksdale's Mississippi troops advanced in close ranks across the open fields toward Sherfy's peach orchard, their formation's compact front no more than 350 yards wide. An Alabama soldier watching from farther north proclaimed the entire scene "grand beyond description."

In the years following the battle, many Mississippi veterans would claim that their charge to the Emmitsburg Road had been overpowering, suggesting that the Yankee infantry and artillery had had no effect. It was true that both Union branches were depleted after the long artillery exchanges and the heavy skirmishing preceding Barksdale's advance. Nevertheless, the Federals were stubborn. John K. Bucklyn's 1st Rhode Island Light Artillery, Battery E, located on the western side of the road,

blasted canister into the Mississippi ranks, even as several advanced Union
regiments maneuvered frantically to keep as many guns as possible trained
on the enemy force. "Our men began to drop as soon as they came to
attention, and were well peppered in covering the distance to the enemy,"
remembered a member of the 21st Mississippi. "All [regiments] met with
stiff resistance."

But William Barksdale was not to be denied. His men drove forward,
a living definition of unstoppable. Overwhelmed Federal units began to
scramble out of their way, batteries limbering to the rear, regiments
falling back in hasty disorder. "The shattered line was retreating in separated streams[,] artillerists heroically clinging to their still smoking guns,
and brave little infantry squads assisting them with their endangered cannon over the soft ground," wrote a Federal caught in the cauldron. A
member of the 17th Mississippi recollected that the stunned Yankees "ran
in crowds. You could not shoot without hitting two or three of them."
The final collapse of the Federal salient anchored in Sherfy's peach
orchard was not explicitly dramatic, but it was tactically decisive. Once
the angle had been breached, the lines connecting to it on the east and
north were doomed.*

Barksdale's regiments were just beginning to congregate throughout
the peach orchard when their commander was approached by one of his
officers. The man counseled a halt to correct the troops' alignment after
the inevitable confusion of the charge. Barksdale was emphatic: " 'No!
Crowd them—we have them on the run. Move your regiments.' " As one
of the battered Federal regiments retreated from the peach orchard
toward Cemetery Ridge, the officer in charge was met by Daniel Sickles.
" 'Colonel!' " Sickles exclaimed. " 'For God's sake can't you hold on?' "
The bleary-eyed officer looked at the pitiful soldierly remnants around his
regiment's flag. " 'Where are my men?' " he asked plaintively.

William Oates may have had a stubborn streak, but he was not foolhardy.
His maximum effort had nearly folded the 20th Maine in on itself, but
the attempt had failed. A soldier sent to scout for the next friendly unit to

---

*For quick thinking on his part that enabled his battery to escape from the peach
orchard, Lieutenant Edward M. Knox of the 15th New York Light Artillery would
receive a Medal of Honor. Also cited for this action was Private Casper R. Carlisle of
Company F, Independent Pennsylvania Light Artillery, who saved one of his battery's
guns while under fire.

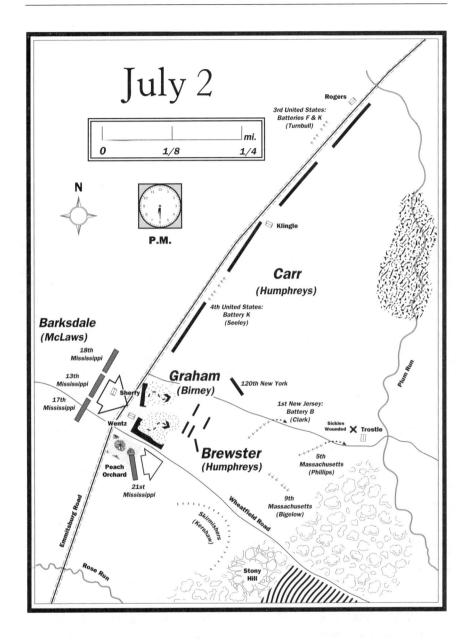

the west came back to report that there was none, so far as he could see—only Yankee troops were moving in that area. Then Oates' right wing began taking hits from the concealed skirmishing company that Joshua Chamberlain had sent out earlier.

For a few moments, sheer pride filled the Confederate colonel with a determination never to yield, but instead to "sell out as dearly as possible."

Then common sense asserted itself: it was time to get out. This withdrawal would not be a parade-ground maneuver, he knew: "I . . . advised [my officers] that when the signal was given every one should run in the direction from whence we came, and halt on the top of the [Big Round Top] mountain."

Oates' opposite number had come to a decision as well—one born of the same anger and desperation that gripped the Alabama officer, but leading in a totally different direction. "My thought was running deep," Joshua Chamberlain later admitted. What he did, and the events of the next minutes, have been filtered through the gauze of popular history into a single action executed in smooth unison. But what actually transpired was the result of a complicated combination of elements that left even its architect somewhat confused.

It began with a courageous resolution by Chamberlain. "Desperate as the chances were, there was nothing for it, but to take the offensive," he later wrote. He shouted, "Bayonet!," and the men nearest him passed along the command even as they began unshipping the weapons from their belts. Amid the noise and confusion, the word did not make it all the way down the line; left wing leader Ellis Spear, for one, never heard it.

As the Maine men along the right and center of the line readied themselves, the officer commanding the color guard embarked on a humanitarian mission. There were a number of wounded Maine men in front of the color company who Lieutenant Homer Melcher felt should be secured before the charge. Without first checking with Chamberlain, or even informing anyone else of his intention, he took a squad of men forward to bring in the casualties. Seeing him advance, the color-bearers assumed that the order had been given, and followed. The sight of the regiment's flags moving down the hill in turn triggered action on both flanks of the 20th Maine's line.

Ellis Spear saw the standards moving, concluded that he had missed hearing an order, and yelled to his men to move with the flag. "The left took up the shout and moved forward," he later related. Getting the men started was one thing, Spear discovered, and directing that movement was something else again. Spotting clusters of Rebels directly before them, some of Spear's men charged eastward, driving the enemy toward the Jacob Weikert farm, where they took a number of prisoners. Other Confederate squads running that way encountered Walter Morrill's skirmishing company. Several burst through the thin screen in their panic, while others were shot or captured.

Groups of Federals, some of them Spear's men and some from Morrill's command, pursued a pack of retreating Rebels southeastward, toward Big Round Top. From his position near the apex of his V-shaped line, Joshua Chamberlain saw the chase and, assuming that the bluecoats were all from Spear's wing, pronounced the action a "right wheel." While it may indeed have *seemed* to be a swinging movement by the left, no one on that flank knew anything about such an order. Nevertheless, Chamberlain would enshrine the memory of this imagined maneuver in his report and other subsequent recountings of the fight. For now, however, he waved the right wing forward in a charge that tumbled into the valley between Big and Little Round Top.

Aided in no small way by Oates' nearly simultaneous decision to retreat, the 20th Maine herded back most of the 15th Alabama, scooping up prisoners in the process. "The rebel front line, amazed at the sudden movement, thinking we had been reinforced . . . threw down their arms and [cried] out 'don't fire! we surrender!,' [while] the rest fled in wild disorder," recollected one of Chamberlain's troops. A portion of the 83rd Pennsylvania meanwhile pitched forward from the right, cutting off those of Oates' men who were trying to link up with units near Devil's Den.

Chamberlain managed to halt his Maine soldiers before they got too far up the slope of Big Round Top, and then, with some difficulty, to return them to the position they had so ably defended. As he later put it, "We disposed ourselves to meet any new assault that might come from the courage of exasperation."

There would be no such action today, at least not on Little Round Top.

"Brave Mississippians, one more charge and the day is ours." William Barksdale's declaration and resolve to press on without stopping after overrunning the Federal position in Sherfy's peach orchard had several repercussions, both positive and negative. It accomplished his avowed purpose of not allowing the enemy time to regroup, but at the same time, it diminished his command and control of his brigade, which broke into two unequal portions as a result. The three leftmost regiments—the 13th, 17th, and 18th Mississippi—angled toward the Emmitsburg Road to flank the Federal formation that was still trying to hold that line. The officer commanding the remaining regiment in Barksdale's Brigade, Colonel Benjamin G. Humphreys, saw that his 21st Mississippi was on the flank of a delectable row of Yankee cannon lined up along Wheatfield Road. So while the rest of the brigade pulled away to the northeast, Humphreys directed his 400 men almost due east to do a little battery busting.

"Benner's Hill was simply a hell inferno," according to a gunner in one of the four batteries that Joseph Latimer, the boy major, had crammed onto that elevation's limited crest. For about the first half of their ninety-minute-plus engagement here this day, the two sides had been fairly evenly matched. The Federal guns, however, were more widely dispersed between Culp's Hill and Cemetery Hill, so they could add to their total, whereas Latimer already had every tube he could fit in action. Shortly before 5:00 P.M., the scales of destruction had begun to turn on the Southern gunners stubbornly holding station on Benner's Hill.

As the cannoneers worked their weapons, they were completely exposed to the shards of exploding shells, and ever conscious that the munitions they were handling were potentially no less deadly to them than their foes. In Captain William F. Dement's 1st Maryland Battery, a gunner neglected to close the metal-shielded lid on an ammunition chest and paid for the lapse with his life when a nearby bursting shell threw sparks into the case. One of the first men on the scene after the fiery flash would long remember the sight: "Clothes scorched, smoking and burning, head divested of cap and exposing a bald surface where [there] use[d] to be a full suit of hair, whiskers singed off to the skin, eye-brows and eye-lids denuded of their fringes, and the eyes set with a popped gaze and facial expressions changed to a perfect disguise."

Things were not much better on the Federal side. The First Corps' artillery chief, Colonel Charles S. Wainwright, watched with clinical detachment as one of Latimer's shells arced in among a line of infantry who thought they were safe behind a stone wall. "Taking the line lengthways," Wainwright observed, "it literally ploughed up two or three yards of men, killing and wounding a dozen or more." On at least two occasions, the doughty colonel had himself only narrowly escaped being killed—once by a Rebel shell, and the second time by a friendly muzzle blast from one of his own guns, which he had absentmindedly masked.

Watching the bright flashes blossom across Cemetery Hill, and at the same time trying to gauge the progress of Longstreet's action to the south, were several members of Richard Ewell's command staff, who had made an observation post out of the cupola atop the Roman Catholic church. As best they could tell, Longstreet's men were advancing at every point, bringing their victorious wave closer and closer to the Confederate left. Perhaps regretting his earlier refusal to sanction an offensive movement from his flank, Ewell now decided to exercise the authority bestowed on him by Lee: he would eschew making any demonstration with his infantry and instead simply attack.

Ewell quickly worked up a scheme to assault Culp's Hill and Cemetery Hill. Since Edward Johnson's men had the most ground to cover, they would move first, followed by Jubal Early's troops and then those of Robert Rodes. As couriers carried word of the plan to the various division headquarters, another messenger sought out Brigadier General James H. Lane, of Hill's Corps, who was next in line on Rodes' right. Ewell's note explained what he planned to do and urged Lane to join him in the offensive. Invested with no direct authority over a brigade belonging to another corps, Ewell could only hope for the best.

On Benner's Hill, the only place along Ewell's front where combat action was then occurring, things began to go badly for the boy major. A match for their opponents in skill and courage, but eventually outgunned by them in numbers and position, Latimer's men were clearly getting the worst of the exchange by 5:45 P.M. No sooner had Edward Johnson received Ewell's instructions for an assault than a sergeant major of Latimer's command presented himself to explain on the major's behalf, as Johnson later reported, "that the exhausted condition of his horses and men, together with the terrible fire of the enemy's artillery, rendered his position untenable." Johnson allowed Latimer to withdraw, with the proviso that he leave four guns in action "to cover the advance of my infantry." By 6:00 P.M., all but that valiant quartet had been pulled under cover, some by hand.

Slightly more than a mile west of where Ewell's division commander was organizing his advance, a Pennsylvania cavalry captain was making a snap decision that would have a subtle but profound impact on Johnson's chances of success. Union and Confederate forces had been skirmishing all day across a slight north-south swell of land intersecting the Hanover Road, known as Brinkerhoff's Ridge. Because the road led directly into Ewell's left flank, the approach needed to be covered, and the veteran Stonewall Brigade (all-Virginians) of Johnson's Division had gotten the call. Brigadier General James Walker had detailed the 2nd Virginia to picket Brinkerhoff's Ridge; soon after the sun rose, the Virginia boys had begun scrapping with Yankees from the Twelfth Corps, whose parent body was posted just to the south.

The Twelfth Corps foot soldiers were replaced around midmorning by men with a similar mission from the Fifth Corps, then arriving from near Hanover. When George Meade shifted the Fifth from near his right to a more centralized reserve position, the Union infantry skirmishers were themselves relieved by cavalrymen, just reaching the scene as part of Brigadier General David McMurtrie Gregg's division. Ironically, the completion of Jeb Stuart's long circuit to connect with the Army of Northern Virginia also brought to Gettysburg the two Federal cavalry divisions that had been sent to intercept him—meaning that the addition to Lee's combat strength was countered by one to Meade's. The big difference on Brinkerhoff's Ridge was that there were no Confederate cavalry units on hand to take over the flank security. In itself, this suggests that Robert E. Lee was not informed of the failure of Jenkins' Brigade to picket his left, so sent no orders for Stuart's weary but available regiments to lend a hand.

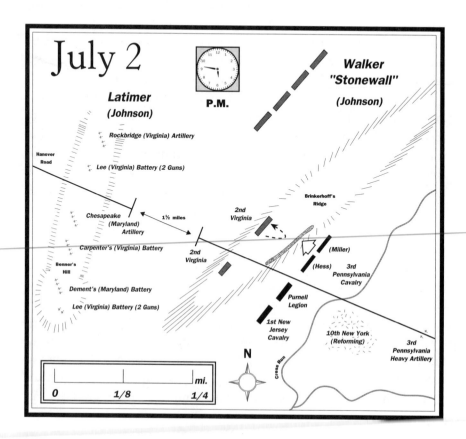

It was not long after the last Fifth Corps rifleman tramped off to the south that the Confederates, realizing that their opponents were now dismounted cavalry, began raising the ante. James Walker, eager to assess the nature of the force confronting him, ordered Colonel John Quincy Adams Nadenbousch to deploy all of his 2nd Virginia "to clear the field, and advance into the wood [beyond], and ascertain, if possible, what force the enemy had at that point." The determined advance of the Virginia soldiers shoved back four companies of the 10th New York Cavalry that had been spread out north of the Hanover Road, and so threatened four more companies from the 10th posted south of the lane that they, too, retreated. When an understrength counterattack attempted by the two remaining companies of the 10th failed to do anything more than slow the Rebel advance, more cavalry units were committed. The critical moment came north of the road, along a farm wall running perpendicular to the Hanover Road.

Captain William Miller of Company H, 3rd Pennsylvania Cavalry, led his dismounted squadron in tandem with another, under Captain Frank Watson Hess, up a slope toward the stone wall. "It was discovered . . . that some Confederate infantry were advancing from the opposite direction," Miller later wrote. "Double-quick was ordered, and a race for the fence ensued. The men seeing the importance of the position, quickened their steps and arrived at the wall about twenty paces in advance of the enemy." Levering their carbines for all they were worth, and aided by a two-gun battery firing over their heads from the road below, the Pennsylvanians threw up enough fire that the Rebels stopped, then eased back. The Yankee troopers would hold this place until a Confederate flanking force bent them back, after dark—but by then the damage would be done.

Nadenbousch was convinced that he was facing several cavalry and infantry regiments backed by artillery, and reported as much to Walker. When Edward Johnson began gathering his division for its lunge against Culp's Hill, he asked Walker if the situation along the Hanover Road was secure enough that the Stonewall Brigade could be released from flank duty. Walker was not sanguine about that prospect, as he believed it would be imprudent to leave the road uncovered, and he was wary as well of moving his brigade within the sight and range of the Federals he knew to be present. Accordingly, the Stonewall Brigade—comprising some 1,300 veteran soldiers—remained in place when Johnson's other three brigades began to move toward Culp's Hill.

* * *

Once Longstreet's assault was under way, there was little for Daniel E. Sickles to do but send for help. He made a few trips to Sherfy's peach orchard to observe the movement to the south and offer some inspiration to his boys, but otherwise he stayed close to his headquarters, located near the Abraham Trostle farm. There was no sign of panic in his demeanor or in his exchanges with subordinates, one of whom would recall that he spoke "in an easy, quiet tone without any excitement." A passing artillery officer remembered seeing "General Sickles . . . standing beneath a tree close by, staff officers and orderlies coming and going in all directions." By Sickles' own recollection, after George Meade departed from the peach orchard, he "received no communication from Gen. Meade, nor did I again see him on the field." He did meet with Samuel Zook before his Second Corps brigade engaged the enemy at the stony hill, but there is no record of what they discussed.

With most of his staff off seeking assistance or helping to place units where they were needed, Sickles often had no more than a few officers or orderlies aiding him. One who remained nearby was George E. Randolph, the Third Corps' artillery chief. Randolph later noted that at about the time Barksdale's men attacked the peach orchard salient, the area around the Trostle farm "became too hot for a corps headquarters; not so much from fire directed at that point as on account of high shots coming over the crest on both sides and centering there."

Sickles had just decided to move his operations behind the Trostle buildings, to take advantage of the extra cover they offered, when a round shot struck his right knee a glancing blow. There was something appropriately bizarre in the way the cannon ball managed to shatter his lower leg without even spooking his horse. Once Sickles had succeeded in dismounting, it became clear from the bleeding that his wound was severe. "We bound his leg first with handkerchiefs and finally with a strap from a saddle," Randolph recounted, "and sent for Surgeons and [an] ambulance."

The Third Corps commander asked to be moved behind a nearby boulder for protection and then, as the collapse of Graham's brigade in the peach orchard become more and more obviously inevitable, "repeatedly urged us not to allow him to be taken [prisoner]," according to his artillery chief. When Sickles' resourceful staff officer Henry Tremain returned from one of his many missions, Sickles instructed him to "tell General Birney he must take command." Birney himself arrived just as Tremain was leaving to find him. The aide's effort to brief the deputy about the situation was interrupted by Sickles, who announced loudly and clearly, " 'General Birney, you will take command, sir.' " Birney bent over his chief, exchanged a few words with him, and rode off. Before the ambulance appeared to transport him to the Third Corps field hospital, the wounded Sickles had himself propped up with cigar in mouth, jauntily urging the soldiers who passed to stand firm.

Lafayette McLaws had set up his assault force in two waves. Backing up Joseph Kershaw's South Carolina brigade were Paul Semmes' Georgians, both units engaged around the Rose farm. Behind Barksdale's Mississippians was Brigadier General William T. Wofford's all-Georgia brigade, which now came on. James Longstreet led the procession toward the Emmitsburg Road, until a courier who was riding with him pointed out "the danger of being shot down by our own troops." Thus cautioned, Longstreet "checked his horse and waited until Wofford's men had gotten in front of us."

Wofford apparently lacked specific orders to keep station with Barksdale, who in turn seems to have made no attempt to coordinate with him. Meanwhile, the hard-pressed Kershaw had been appealing for help at the stony hill. Once his battle line reached the debris-littered peach orchard, Wofford kept it heading east, toward Kershaw. The South Carolinian's report reflected the great relief he felt, on looking up from his efforts to rally his brigade near the Rose farm, at seeing "Wofford coming in splendid style."

George Meade did everything he could to make good on the position staked out for him by his Third Corps commander, appalled though he was by what Sickles had done. He seems never even to have considered using the reserves on hand to establish his preferred Cemetery Ridge line and then allowing the Third Corps to fight its way back to that point; instead he directed every available military asset into the cauldron, desperate to shore up what his professional judgment told him was an unacceptable position.

It was George Meade who began moving George Sykes' Fifth Corps toward Sickles even before Longstreet's assault took shape. It was Meade who instructed Hancock to release Caldwell's division to fight in Rose's wheat field. Immediately after leaving Sickles, Meade had returned to the

Leister house, where he found John Sedgwick, arriving well ahead of his Sixth Corps. "General Meade said that he had been out to the front; that General Sickles had not taken the position he had directed, but had moved out from a quarter to three-quarters of a mile in advance," Sedgwick related. "I asked General Meade why he had not ordered him back. He reported that it was then too late; that the enemy had opened the battle."

Meade instructed Sedgwick to bring his corps forward to support the beleaguered left flank. After Sedgwick departed, Meade turned to Henry Slocum for help. Except for the artillery duel, there was no real fighting going on in his sector, nor any visible evidence that Rebel infantry were being committed there. In his anxiety to salvage his left flank, Meade was willing to risk his right, but only with the agreement of the subordinate most responsible for that part of the line. In conversation with Slocum, Meade may have wished aloud that he could shift both Twelfth Corps divisions over to the left, and he expressed his desire for Slocum to release all the troops he could spare to assist Sickles.

Slocum at once ordered one of his two divisions to abandon Culp's Hill and head for the left flank. Tagged for this detail was Alpheus S. Williams, whose three brigades had been responsible for extending the Culp's Hill line southward and over to the Baltimore Pike. In short order Williams had his men out of their just-constructed earthworks, forming up, and marching toward the sound of the guns. For reasons he would never explain, Henry Slocum was convinced that Meade wanted the entire Twelfth Corps to shift over, if at all possible. His decisions would do as much to imperil the Union right as Daniel Sickles' had done to endanger the left.

He may have been a touch fastidious in his personal habits, and conversely, his reputation for swearing might be one of the most formidable in the Union Army, but if someone had to be nominated to command a forlorn hope in a tight spot, Andrew Atchinson Humphreys was the best possible choice. An army regular with extensive prewar engineering experience, the fifty-three-year-old officer seemed genuinely indifferent to whether or not his stern leadership style made him popular. In the year after Gettysburg, he would confess to one fondness appropriate for a warrior: "Ah," he said, "war is a very bad thing in the sequel, but before and during the battle it is a fine thing!"

The collapse of David Birney's position in the peach orchard meant real trouble for Humphreys, who faced an aggressive enemy flush with victory on his right and rear, with all the signs in his front indicating that a serious attack was coming there next. It did not help when Birney brought the news that Sickles was down and he was in charge, and then with his new authority proposed that Humphreys bend back his left flank, in order to connect with what remained of his division and form a new line back to Big and Little Round Top. It took just one southward glance for Humphreys to recognize the utter impossibility of the scheme, for there was, he noted, "nobody to form a new line but myself—Birney's troops [having] cleared out."

Nevertheless, the threat posed by Barksdale forced Humphreys to protect his left. He ordered the officer holding that section, Colonel William R. Brewster, to pivot his brigade eastward, changing its orientation from west to southwest. Brewster executed the directive, but not all of his regiments kept their nerve, and the new line threatened to collapse until the 120th New York made a forceful stand that stiffened the rest. Even as this repositioning was being carried out, there was an ominous movement to the west, where the next of Lee's troops began advancing to challenge what remained of the Third Corps' position. One of Humphreys' aides would never forget the moment: "The crash of artillery and the tearing rattle of our musketry was staggering, and added to the noise in our side, the advancing roar & cheer of the enemy's masses, coming on like devils incarnate."

William T. Wofford's decision to direct his Georgia brigade east toward the stony hill instead of following Barksdale had a dramatic effect on the fighting there. His approach reinvigorated the offensive spirit among the South Carolinians of Kershaw's Brigade and the Georgians under Semmes and Anderson, who renewed their efforts against the Union Second and Fifth Corps brigades spread across the hill and the wheat field.

Brooke's brigade, which had driven to the edge of the Rose farm fields, was flanked on its right, forcing it to backpedal, a regiment at a time. As Brooke's men began retreating, they were joined by the members of Zook's brigade and the Irish Brigade.* Because there was little

---

*Edward Cross' brigade had pulled back a short time earlier. During the retreat of Zook's brigade, Lieutenant James J. Purman and Sergeant James M. Pipes, both of the 140th Pennsylvania, each assisted a wounded comrade to cover and was himself seriously wounded in doing so. Both would receive Medals of Honor.

coordination among units of different corps, the three regiments of Sweitzer's Fifth Corps brigade, which had only just been repositioned forward, suddenly found themselves holding the southern end of Rose's wheat field all alone.

Fortunately, more help had come up from a different quarter, in the form of five small regiments of regular U.S. army troops, constituting Colonel Sidney Burbank's Fifth Corps brigade of Ayres' division. Making a sacrificial stand in the middle of the wheat field, Burbank's regulars provided enough cover to allow Sweitzer's men to exit. An admiring volunteer on the field later remarked that "for two years the U.S. Regulars taught us how to be soldiers[;] in the Wheatfield at Gettysburg, they taught us how to die like soldiers."

After breaking away from the rest of Barksdale's Brigade, Benjamin G. Humphreys and his 21st Mississippi embarked on one of the most memorable freelance odysseys of the entire battle. Passing through the peach orchard, the 21st engaged a Yankee regiment, the 2nd New Hampshire, one of whose members would recall this fighting as "close, stubborn and deadly work." Among those left in its wake when the New Hampshiremen reeled back toward Cemetery Ridge was Charles K. Graham, who had taken a musket ball through both shoulders and had a chunk of hip gouged by some shrapnel. Graham tried to ride to safety, "throwing myself forward on [my horse's] . . . neck to present as little surface as possible" as a target. The practical Rebels brought down Graham's horse, then pulled the bloody officer out from under his mount and took him prisoner.

While several of the Federal batteries that had been lining the Wheatfield Road had already limbered and left, one, Captain A. Judson Clark's 2nd Battery, New Jersey Light, was slow to go. A few of Benjamin Humphreys' Mississippians scrambled among the departing cannon. "Halt, you Yankee sons of ——; we want these guns," a Confederate yelled. "Go to h—l," came the rejoinder. "We want to use them yet awhile." Another retreating Union regiment paused long enough to supply a covering volley that shook the Rebels off the guns and let Clark's men escape. But the 21st Mississippi was not yet done for the day.

James Longstreet's acting artillery chief, Edward P. Alexander, could barely restrain himself. "When I saw their [peach orchard] line broken &

in retreat, I thought the battle was ours," he later reflected. A big factor in Longstreet's decision to give the young officer authority exceeding his rank and seniority had been his boldness, and now Alexander more than justified that trust. It was no time to rest on laurels. Mentally getting beyond the damage some of his batteries had sustained in their long exchange with the Yankee tubes, Alexander "rode along my guns, urging the men to limber to the front as rapidly as possible, telling them we would 'finish the whole war this afternoon.' " He led his cannoneers on a wild, bouncing ride across the body-cluttered fields, quickly deploying them along a rough line running from the peach orchard north along the Emmitsburg Road.

The sight that met his eyes was disappointing, even discouraging. Alexander had been under the impression that the Emmitsburg Road position was the hard shell of the Yankee defense, which, once cracked, would reveal nothing but softness inside. He now saw that such was not the case. The enemy's principal position "loomed up near 1000 yards beyond us," he realized, "a ridge giving good cover behind it & endless fine positions for batteries. And batteries in abundance were showing up & troops too seemed to be marching & fighting every where." Alexander's only solace was that there were "plenty [of targets] to shoot at." Grateful that he had no greater responsibility than his guns, he soon had his crews sweating and the cannon firing.

Even as Alexander was setting his guns into place, James Longstreet was making one of the hardest decisions of his life. Carefully evaluating the ebb and flow of the combat that engulfed his two divisions, Longstreet concluded that a victory was not possible. Every thrust forward had met with a riposte, or what Longstreet called "the sturdy regular blow that tells a soldier instantly that he has encountered [enemy] reserves or reinforcements. . . . To urge my men forward under these circumstances would have been madness." With the same determination he had shown after launching this day's action, James Longstreet now began to bring it to an end.

With the advance of Wofford's Brigade, the torch was passed from Longstreet's Corps to A. P. Hill's. Next in the Confederate line extending northward from Warfield Ridge to Seminary Ridge were units belonging to Richard H. Anderson's division, which had seen no action the previous day.

Earlier, when the Alabama regiments of Cadmus M. Wilcox's brigade were finished scrapping with Berdan's sharpshooters and had taken position on Hill's extreme right, orders had arrived from division headquarters describing the role they were to play. "My instructions were to advance when the troops on my right should advance, and to report this to the division commander in order that the other brigades should advance in proper time," Wilcox later recorded.

South to north, Anderson's brigades were lined up as follows: first Wilcox's Alabamians, then the brigade of three Florida regiments under David Lang (named Perry's Brigade for its absent regular commander), next the all-Georgia brigade of Ambrose R. Wright, the Mississippi brigade of Carnot Posey, and finally the Virginia brigade of Brigadier General William Mahone. One Floridian vividly recalled the tension as the men "caught the roar of the cannon and rattle of musketry, coming nearer and nearer, [and] we soon see brigade after brigade going in to charge the enemy's line of defenses." He further recollected that the "men who had been playing cards immediately tore them up and threw them away."

Little unfolded today as advertised. When the moment arrived to advance, Wilcox realized that he could not proceed straight on without entangling his men with some from McLaws' Division who had veered north in their charge; he thus had to shift his brigade four hundred yards to the north before turning it east to attack. Somehow the 8th Alabama missed getting the word, so when the advance sounded, it moved ahead with a gap of some two hundred yards between its left and the rest of the brigade.

Since Andrew Humphreys' division had yet to be pried from the Emmitsburg Road, there were still cannon positioned opposite Wilcox. They began slinging shells into the human lines as soon as they appeared. An Alabamian recorded that he could barely hear himself and his comrades cheering for "the sound of the shells that were bursting above and around us."

Cued by the forward movement of Wilcox's men, David Lang led his three Florida regiments up the slight slope that had sheltered them, only to be "met at the crest . . . with a murderous fire of grape, canister, and musketry." Wright's Georgians, next in line, stepped off soon after Lang's Floridians, but almost at once they were slowed by enemy fire and by numerous obstacles blocking their way.

*   *   *

The Union officer of superior rank who came closest to matching George Meade's activities this day was Winfield S. Hancock. Ever since Andrew Humphreys marched his division out to the Emmitsburg Road, Hancock had been closely monitoring events in his sector. Like most on the field, he had only the sketchiest idea of what was happening off to the left. When, at Meade's request, he dispatched Caldwell's division, he did so believing that it was a temporary measure to take up a part of the line until the Fifth Corps arrived. He expected that the division would return to him in good condition.

As the battle racket continued without pause, Hancock grew anxious. Still, he could take some comfort in the fact that with the exception of Caldwell's men and the two regiments Gibbon had sent forward to cover Humphreys' right flank, his Second Corps had not been drawn into the Third Corps' fight. Then a courier arrived with instructions from Meade, directing Hancock to send another brigade to assist Birney. He decided that his Third Division, Hays', would be the most capable of providing it. Hancock's aide found Alexander Hays on Cemetery Ridge, watching the fields to his front and left with George L. Willard, commander of the so-called Harper's Ferry Brigade. After the staffer delivered the message, Hays turned to Willard and said, " 'Take your Brigade over there and knock the H— out of the rebs.' "

No sooner had Willard begun marching than Hancock received news from another headquarters orderly: Daniel Sickles was wounded, and Meade wanted him to assume command of the Third Corps. It was not exactly the directive he had been expecting. As Hancock turned over the Second Corps to John Gibbon, Gibbon "was not surprised [to hear him] utter some expressions of discontent at being compelled at such a time to give up command of one corps in a sound condition to take command of another which, it was understood, had gone to pieces."

Hancock overtook Willard's brigade, which was advancing not in a standard linear formation but rather in a four-column spread, with the regiments marching abreast. In another unusual move, their commanding officer had ordered bayonets fixed, an action generally reserved for the moments just before close contact, since it was difficult to load and fire a rifle quickly with the long bayonet attached to the muzzle. On reaching the head of the columns, Hancock slowed down, and the men in turn set their pace on him. Near the George Weikert farm, they began to encounter fragments of the Third Corps, and then saw David Birney himself.

Birney, thinking only of the fate that had overcome his division, informed Hancock that "the 3d Corps had gone to pieces and fallen to the rear." His new corps commander allowed the discouraged officer to continue in that direction to help rally his shattered unit. "The enemy's advancing musketry shots were falling at that point," Hancock later recalled, "and their artillery shots as well." He turned to Willard and told him to prepare his brigade for battle.

Even now, a few Federal batteries were still scrambling to escape the collapsed peach orchard salient. If conditions were hard on the cannoneers, however, they were hell itself on the horses. The last tubes to go were those farthest east along the Wheatfield Road from Barksdale's breakthrough. Most left the field by prolonge—that is, jerked backward by manhandled ropes in synchrony with the recoil as the guns were fired. This technique was used when the enemy was so close that the gunners could not cease firing to limber up, or when there were not enough live horses left to do the job. In the case of a piece in Battery E, 5th Massachusetts Light Artillery, the crewmen brought the limber team in to help with the hauling, but by the time they got the horses turned and the tow attached, all five animals had been shot.

After the departure of the 5th Massachusetts, only the 9th Massachusetts Light Artillery, commanded by John Bigelow, remained. These gunners had drawn the interest of both the freelancing 21st Mississippi and some skirmishers from Kershaw's left wing, who targeted the exposed battery. Relying on a combination of manpower and horsepower, Bigelow hauled his six guns by prolonge in a northerly direction from the Wheatfield Road toward the Trostle farm.

"No friendly supports of any kind, were in sight," Bigelow remembered, "but Johnnie Rebs in great numbers. Bullets were coming into our midst from many directions and a Confederate battery added to our difficulties." Harassing him from his left front were Kershaw's South Carolinians; to his right front were the more compact formations of the 21st Mississippi. Bigelow kept both at bay by firing canister from his left section and solid shot from his right.

Somehow the battery survived this gauntlet, making it over the crest and into a natural amphitheater near the Trostle farm that provided enough cover for Bigelow to hook the guns to his surviving horse teams.

His men were frantically bent to this task when Lieutenant Colonel Free-man McGilvery arrived from Cemetery Ridge, his horse bleeding from four wounds received in the course of the short journey. McGilvery had discovered that the section of the Union line just to the east along Ceme-tery Ridge was devoid of organized troops. He had conceived a plan to plug the hole with cannon—any cannon he could grab out of those retreating or those arriving from the reserve. He would need time, how-ever, to accomplish this.

"'Captain Bigelow,'" McGilvery said, "'there is not an infantryman back of you along the whole line which Sickles moved out; you must remain where you are and hold your position at all hazards, and sacrifice your battery, if need be, until at least I can find some batteries to put in position and cover you.'" Bigelow promised McGilvery that he "would try to do so."

Bigelow's retreat had brought him to a point just south of the east-west-running Trostle Lane, almost directly opposite the farmhouse and barn. A stone wall extended southward behind him, from the road into a marshy area; the ground sloped down toward him from the south and west, the swell forming a crest line about a hundred yards distant. He had his caissons dump their munitions next to the cannon before clearing out. After sending a few solid shots bounding blindly over the bowl rim, Bigelow ordered his four right guns to load with double canister charges. With the grand battle still raging in the distance, Bigelow's battery and the 21st Mississippi were about to engage in a very private little war.

From the south to the north, Confederate units either were completing their victories or had run out of offensive power. All supports were in, so whether or not these efforts would prove decisive would depend in large measure on how much fight the enemy had left in him. In the area of Rose's wheat field, a composite force drawn from the brigades of Tige Anderson, Semmes, Kershaw, and Wofford drove out the U.S. regulars to take control of the sector. Directly east of them was the lower portion of Cemetery Ridge, ending on the northern slope of Little Round Top. Alone among the four brigadiers, Wofford believed that his men had enough strength remaining for one last thrust.

Farther north, Andrew Humphreys' Third Corps division had com-pleted its punishing withdrawal from the Emmitsburg Road to a section of Cemetery Ridge to the left and rear of the Second Corps.* As Winfield Hancock passed this command on his way to the left, he thought "there seemed nothing left of the division but a mass of regimental colors still waving defiantly." Except for some fragments of units and a few guns still struggling to find a way out, the area formerly held by Humphreys' division was now Confederate territory.

Through this arena William Barksdale now led three of his Mississippi regiments. Closing with him off his left rear was Cadmus Wilcox with four Alabama regiments. George W. Hosmer, covering the battle for the *New York Herald,* reported that the Rebels "came forward in their usual magnificent style. They had difficult ground to come over; but on they came, over rocks and through low wood, until within a fair distance, when they made a rush with all possible yells roared out in one. They did not keep their lines very even, but they were scarcely less impetuous as a mass than they would have been in line."

The combat between John Bigelow's cannon and the 21st Mississippi (with help from Kershaw's South Carolinians) lasted for almost thirty minutes. The veteran Rebels used the thin cover provided by the swell of the depression sheltering the gunners to snipe viciously at the Federal cannoneers and their animals. Bigelow would remember that "men and horses were falling like hail. . . . Sergeant after Sergt., was struck down, horses were plunging and laying all around." Yet whenever an organized body of Confederates tried a rush, it was scattered by canister blasts. With antipersonnel ammunition stock running low, Bigelow took a chance and ordered his men to fire case shot with its fuses cut so it would explode near the gun muzzle. Still the patient Rebels kept extending their perimeter, until shots began coming from the rear, near the Trostle farm.

Bigelow ordered his guns to get out. The first to leave overturned just beyond the narrow gate opening in the stone wall, blocking the only exit until the crew could right it again. In a panic, the crewmen assigned to the next gun simply drove at the wall, crashing their team and equip-

---

*In this retreat, Corporal Nathaniel M. Allen of the 1st Massachusetts saved the regiment's flag from capture, for which act he would be awarded a Medal of Honor. Sergeant George W. Roosevelt of the 26th Pennsylvania would also receive the medal, for his unsuccessful attempt to capture a Rebel color-bearer. A successful effort by Sergeant Thomas Horan of the 72nd New York would win him a medal as well.

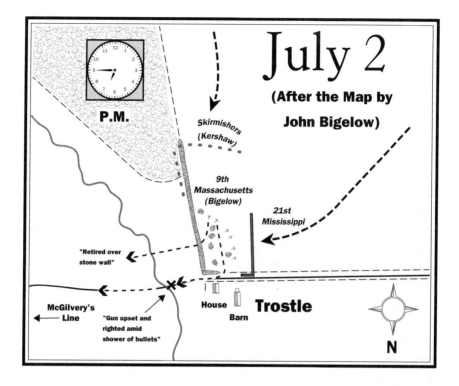

ment through it. These two were the only cannon saved, as exultant Mississippi troops swarmed the remaining four. "We fired with our guns until the rebs could put their hands on [them]," wrote a young artilleryman. "The bullets flew thick as hailstones." It was every man for himself. Bigelow had been wounded twice and would have been captured had not his bugler (and amateur artist), Charles Reed, helped him onto his horse and, mounted alongside, led it toward safety at a walk.*

Approaching the line of cannon that Freeman McGilvery had cobbled together along lower Cemetery Ridge, Reed and Bigelow were almost blown away by friendly fire, but by following a course that their experience told them would skirt the kill zone, they succeeded in passing through the smoking guns. Behind them, along McGilvery's line, Union cannon blasted at anything that moved, the gunners wholly conscious that they were the only line of defense for this portion of Cemetery Ridge.

*   *   *

*Reed would receive a Medal of Honor for his action.

William Barksdale's rough but effective loose formation was suddenly struck in its front and left flank by a fresh Union line, bayonets at the ready. This was the Harper's Ferry Brigade, led by George Willard. Willard had set up his attack using just the 125th and 126th New York, leaving two regiments in reserve, but as he advanced, it had become apparent that his right flank was imperiled by an approaching enemy column. Winfield Hancock had immediately sent one of Willard's two reserve regiments, the 111th New York, forward to cover the flank.

The Federal line that hit Barksdale's mass thus consisted of the 125th, 126th, and 111th New York Regiments, which advanced through a curtain of protective fire laid down by Alexander's forward battalions along the Emmitsburg Road. "On we rushed with loud cries!" recollected a member of the 125th. "With shells screaming and cannon balls tearing the air, like so many fiends bent on destruction; now bursting above and around us; now ploughing the ground at our feet . . . ; on, on, we rushed, through storm of fire and death, thundering above and darting around us like the thunder and lightning of Heaven."

When the two sides collided amid the broken ground, bushes, boulders, trees, and soggy earth of the Plum Run swale, the New Yorkers were at the peak of their frenzy, while the Mississippians had spent theirs. The Confederate lines began to disassemble, with portions falling back, portions turning to fight, portions surrendering, and everywhere men dropping dead or wounded. Their determination to advance rested solely on William Barksdale, who was frantic in his efforts to regain the initiative. A Union officer later would recollect that "Gen. Barksdale was trying to hold his men, cheering them and swearing, directly in front of the left of the 126th near the right of the 125th who both saw and heard him as they emerged from the bushes." Yankee guns swung toward the conspicuous figure, who fell after being hit several times. As its advance continued, the Federal line passed over the desperately wounded Confederate leader.*

Although no one present recognized it at the time, the moment had arrived on the left flank of the Federal line when the two sides had fought

*In the course of this action, Corporal Harrison Clark took up the colors of the 125th New York after its bearer fell; the act would earn him a Medal of Honor.

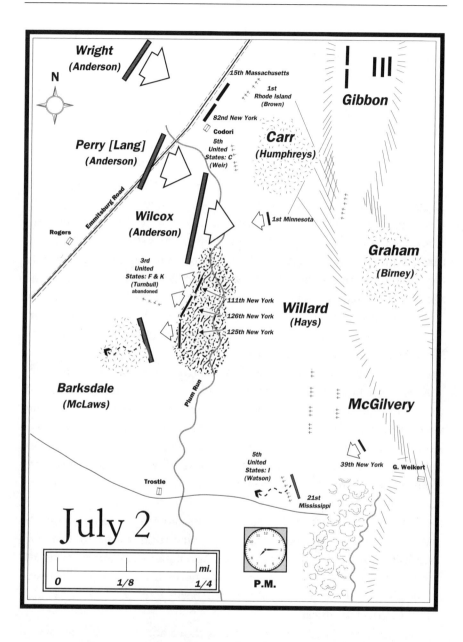

to a point of exhausted balance. Everywhere the Confederate soldiers felt that victory was near, but claiming it would require fresh troops that were not available. For their part, the Federals had taken a terrible licking; they had seen their comrades shot down by the score, their guns overrun, and their positions engulfed by human waves swelling under Rebel flags. But they had exacted a high price for their suffering. Arriving to join them were lines of reinforcements that would soon make all the difference. And most important, the Army of the Potomac had not lost its collective nerve.

At the southernmost edge of the battlefield, final efforts by the brigades of G. T. Anderson, Semmes, Kershaw, and Wofford to push across the northern neck of Little Round Top were stopped by counter-charges by the Pennsylvania Reserves, Fifth Corps, supported by a Sixth Corps brigade just arrived on the field.* Behind them stood more Sixth Corps brigades, insurance that this flank would hold.

One Confederate success remained to be registered, thanks to the still freelancing 21st Mississippi. After ending Bigelow's stand near the Trostle farm, the Mississippi men continued eastward and managed to envelop the exposed southern end of McGilvery's line of cannon. In almost no time, they took Battery I, 5th United States Light Artillery, commanded by Lieutenant Malbone F. Watson. "We charged and captured these guns before they fired," reported the 21st's commander, Benjamin Humphreys.

Once he had had an opportunity to survey his conquest, however, Humphreys pronounced himself less than happy with his situation. "I now saw we had advanced too far to the front for safety," he related, "though no gun was firing at us. I could see that Barksdale, several hundred yards to my left, was checked as well as Kershaw on my right in front of Little Round Top." The question of whether to stay or go was answered for Humphreys when he observed a line of battle approaching from his left front. "I saw my safety was in a hurried retreat," he later admitted.

The rapid withdrawal of the 21st Mississippi was speeded along by the arrival of the 39th New York, which had been part of the reserve established by George Willard before he charged Barksdale's Brigade. While Winfield Hancock had detached one of the reserve regiments to assist Willard, the other, the 39th, had been grabbed by a fast-talking Third Corps staff officer.

The aide to David Birney, acting without authority, had discovered the New Yorkers waiting patiently while their comrades were engaged to

*During this action, six members of the 6th Pennsylvania Reserves would collectively earn the Medal of Honor for rushing a cabin that sheltered Rebel sharpshooters and capturing the lot. The six were Sergeants John W. Hart, Wallace W. Johnson, and George W. Mears, and Corporals Chester S. Furman, J. Levin Roush, and Thaddeus S. Smith.

their front. His first attempt to direct the regiment to move toward Watson's battery was met with a curt refusal by the regimental commander, who added, " 'I am not in Birney's command.' " After learning that this regiment belonged to Hancock's Second Corps, the never-say-die aide repeated his request, this time substituting Hancock's name where he had previously used Birney's.* His sense of protocol thus satisfied, the 39th's commander led his men into a charge that repossessed Watson's battery. His proud soldiers would later claim the honor of having ejected the Mississippi troops, who would be equally adamant that the New Yorkers had simply hastened their leave-taking. In any case, the battery was back in Federal hands, and the 21st Mississippi finally finished for the day.

There was more that George Willard's brigade, those Harper's Ferry boys, had to accomplish. Their charge had first stopped and then repulsed Barksdale's Mississippi brigade, ending that threat to the Union center. They were not yet through, however. They regrouped, continued their advance, and suddenly found themselves retaking three guns of Lieutenant John Turnbull's 3rd United States Light Artillery, which had been abandoned during the Third Corps' retreat from the Emmitsburg Road.

The New Yorkers were by now the target of choice for Edward P. Alexander's batteries, as well as for the remnants of Barksdale's command. Soon enough they also began to be fired on by Cadmus Wilcox's brigade to their right, advancing along Barksdale's left. Willard's advance had brought his brigade to a point near the right and rear of Wilcox and the Florida brigade moving with him. This was enough for Willard, who ordered his men to fall back; they had done their job.

In fact, his brigade had done more than he would ever know. Its presence at this time and in this place had been reported to David Lang, commanding the three Florida regiments trailing Wilcox. Lang had taken this information to mean that enemy troops were working around his right and getting into his rear. "I immediately ordered my men back to the [Emmitsburg] road," he testified. This left Wilcox with no help on either flank.

The opportunity to savor the vindication of his men and the validation of his own leadership would be denied to George Willard. Hardly

---

*The aide, Captain John B. Fassitt of the 23rd Pennsylvania, would be given a Medal of Honor for his initiative.

had he led his brigade back into the rough cover of the Plum Run swale when a Confederate shell struck him, carrying "away part of his face and head." He was dead before he hit the ground.

Cadmus Wilcox continued to urge his men forward, only too aware that he had lost track of the units that were supposed to be on his flanks. His men, having fought through Andrew Humphreys' collapsing but still potent division, remained fixed on Cemetery Ridge, but every step was harder than the one before. From fully manned Yankee batteries in his front, "grape and canister were poured into our ranks," Wilcox recollected. And then just when the prize of Cemetery Ridge at last seemed to be within his grasp, he observed a "line of [enemy] infantry [that] descended the slope in our front at a double-quick."

That line of enemy infantry was a single regiment, the 1st Minnesota. Not an hour earlier, its 262 men had been shifted from their reserve position near Cemetery Hill to the area occupied by Caldwell's division before its departure for the wheat field. The Minnesotans had witnessed the drama on the Union left: the broken units in retreat, the cheering reinforcements charging into the cauldron, the gunshots and cannon discharges mixed in a grand cacophony. And then it had become obvious that a dark cloud of enemy soldiers was heading toward them, with nothing in its way.

Winfield Hancock had also seen it. He had enlisted the 1st Minnesota's commander, Colonel William Colvill, in a vain effort to corral enough Third Corps stragglers to form a line; he finally had to tell him to stop, for fear that the demoralization would spread. The acting Third Corps commander had then sent back a call for help, but he knew that unless something was done right away, the Rebels would reach Cemetery Ridge.

Hancock broke from his thoughts and looked at the 1st Minnesota, as if for the first time. "My God!" he exclaimed. "Are these all the men we have here?" He demanded to know, and was told, the regiment's name. "Colonel, do you see those colors?" he asked Colvill, pointing to some of the Rebel battle flags bobbing amid Wilcox's Brigade. When Colvill said he did, Hancock gave his orders: "Then take them," he said.

The 1st Minnesota moved down the gentle slope, bayonets fixed, a line of battle perhaps a hundred yards from end to end. The soldiers came under fire right away. "Men stumbled and fell," recalled an officer in those ranks. "Some stayed down but others got up and continued." The charging line of Minnesotans drove into the advance screen of Wilcox's Brigade and hustled it back to a second line, which fell back to the main body. This last, some 1,000 strong, was not going to be scattered by 250 or so Yankees. The men of the 1st Minnesota halted along the dry stream bed of Plum Run, firing for all they were worth. A torrent of Confederate rifle fire lashed into the Yankee regiment from Wilcox's men in their front and from some of Lang's Florida troops, who got an enfilade position. After enduring a few minutes of this, the Union survivors ran back to Cemetery Ridge. Between 170 and 178 Minnesota soldiers fell in this counterattack; it was not quite the 82 percent loss that has often been cited, but it was bad enough.

One more Union regiment added its weight to the blows against Anderson's two brigades. The 19th Maine of the Second Corps' Second Division, Colonel Francis E. Heath commanding, had maintained its cohesion despite lying down in the path of Andrew Humphreys' retreating division. A distraught Third Corps officer had tried ordering the Maine soldiers to stop his men with their bayonets, but his instructions had immediately been countermanded by Heath. The 19th now rose and delivered several volleys into Perry's Florida regiments—confirming Colonel Lang's decision to retreat—before falling back in an orderly fashion to Cemetery Ridge.

This was the final straw for Cadmus Wilcox. His requests for reinforcements had not been answered, and both his flanks were exposed. "Without support on either my right or left," he reported, "my men were withdrawn, to prevent their entire destruction or capture."

Three pieces had yet to be put into play in the chess game that was Richard Anderson's attack against the Union left: Wright's Georgia, Posey's Mississippi, and Mahone's Virginia brigades. One would succeed; one would find the distraction of the Bliss farm too much to overcome; and one would never make it into action.

Posey's men had been entangled for much of the day in the deadly rounds of take-away at the Bliss farm. Catching the rhythm rolling up from the south, the Mississippi skirmishers swept past the buildings, a few even aligning with the Georgians to their right. But when Posey sought to advance his entire brigade to support Wright, he found that two of his four regiments were so ensnared around the structures that they could not participate; even though they had driven away the New Jersey soldiers, they were not strong enough to force back the Federal skirmishers just north of them. As Posey's other two regiments advanced, they exposed their flank to an enemy skirmish line. They did the best they could, but the Emmitsburg Road marked the limit of their effort. The Mississippi riflemen would later claim to have briefly driven off some of the Union gun crews along Cemetery Ridge, but their contribution went unacknowledged by Ambrose Wright, whose report unfairly declared that Posey's men had provided no assistance at all.

When William Mahone was called upon to help, he declined on the ground that Anderson had designated him as the division's reserve. Mahone was convinced that A. P. Hill had seconded that selection, so even when a staff officer appeared to convey Anderson's personal directive that he move forward, the brigade commander refused.

In a heated print exchange after the battle, a Georgia reporter would accuse Posey and Mahone of failing in their duty. In reply, he would receive a note from Richard Anderson, who insisted that the pair "were acting under instructions from himself," and that "his own actions 'were in strict conformity with his orders' from his 'own immediate commander.' " The reporter concluded that "we are permitted to infer from the tenor of Gen. Anderson's card, . . . [that the movements of the two brigades were] arrested on orders from their military superiors."

Mahone himself also answered the charges in the papers, noting that Anderson's Division "was not the attacking party" but instead "a cooperating force." The only call for an advance, as Mahone understood it, came when the "successes of the attacking corps on the right became susceptible of assistance." Carnot Posey, who coauthored this response, asserted his own understanding that his brigade "was moved forward more to protect . . . [Anderson's] right brigades from any flank attack of the enemy" than to participate directly in the assault. Between them, the two officers ended by avowing that Confederate "success on the right had not yet arrived at that stage, which invited any advance from this part of the line."

George Meade was so preoccupied by his struggle to contain Longstreet's and Hill's efforts against his left flank that he permitted a potentially catastrophic misunderstanding to develop between him and Henry Slocum. Meade had already withdrawn one of the two Twelfth

Corps divisions covering Culp's Hill, but so concerned was he for his left, and so confident that his right flank was secure, that he began to press Slocum for even more troops.

Henry Slocum was in something of a fog in any case. He persisted in believing that his role was that of wing commander on Meade's right, an odd leftover from the marches to Gettysburg, when he had been assigned that task to ensure better control of the corps grouped at the distant ends of the deployment. His impression that he still retained that responsibility was Meade's doing to some extent. Early this day, when he was actively considering attacking from his right flank, Meade had counted on Slocum's coordinating three corps. After the plan became impracticable, he failed to apprise his subordinate that he was no longer to watch over that wing. Slocum accordingly chose to cast himself still in the more important role, leaving the tactical handling of the Twelfth Corps to Alpheus Williams.

When Meade, anxious about affairs on his left, asked Slocum for all the help he could spare, Slocum took it to mean he was to send everything he had. According to Slocum, an aide he dispatched to Meade to convey his opinion that at least a division should be kept on Culp's Hill returned with Meade's reluctant permission for him to retain a single brigade there. Slocum made no further effort to change his commander's mind; he simply passed along the directive pulling all but George S. Greene's brigade off Culp's Hill, leaving some 1,400 men to hold a sector previously occupied by almost 10,000. In his own defense, Slocum would later state that the "first duty of a subordinate is to obey the orders of his superior."

Compounding the confusion, the initial order received by Second Division commander John Geary detailed all three of his brigades for duty on the left. A hasty follow-up message instructed George Greene to remain and "to occupy the whole of the intrenchments previously occupied by the Twelfth Army Corps."

Greene had to make some quick decisions. Fortunately for the Union cause, most of them were also wise ones. Faced with the choice of either occupying the entire Twelfth Corps line by greatly thinning his own, or taking up a shorter section that would afford him a better concentration of firepower, Greene elected to do the latter. He filled the abandoned trenches for a distance of three regiments, kept two more back to cover his original position, and sent the fifth forward to stiffen the picket line. Greene's extreme right flank was held by the 137th New York, commanded by Colonel David Ireland, whose line barely reached the lower or lesser summit of Culp's Hill. Nearly four hundred yards of earthworks extending south from the 137th's right flank were left uncovered. Even to hold what he had selected, Greene had to take the risk of nearly doubling the front assigned to each regiment.

The uncoordinated and unsuccessful advances against Cemetery Ridge by Wilcox's and Perry's Brigades had left Ambrose Wright's alone. With one regiment detached as skirmishers, Wright had perhaps 1,000 men available. He was a determined man, and at his direction, his troops swept over a Union skirmish line, knocking down fences with their bodies as they came forward, and then swelled as a fierce human wave that crashed into the two regiments John Gibbon had pushed out to the Codori farm. The outnumbered Federals held for as long as honor required, then ran for Cemetery Ridge.* A Yankee in those ranks would report that they had "retired in some disorder, being pressed so closely that we lost quite a number of prisoners, captured by the enemy."

Gibbon had backed up these two regiments with a battery posted about halfway between Cemetery Ridge and the Codori house. For a few minutes, its six guns played havoc with Wright's line. According to a Georgia soldier who came under fire, "Shells around us tore our bleeding ranks with ghastly gaps . . . , [but] we pressed on, knowing that the front was safer now than to turn our backs, and with a mighty yell, we threw ourselves upon the batteries and passed them, still reeking hot." In fact, the Federal gunners managed to save four of the guns, abandoning just a pair to the enemy.

That he was on his own was rapidly becoming the least of Wright's problems. He could see the movement of troops gathering against him on the ridge ahead. His men surged up the slight slope of Cemetery Ridge, overtaking one of the four guns that had initially escaped their grasp. Some Georgia soldiers battled their way to the goal of the entire day's effort, reaching a stone wall just south of the soon-to-be-famous clump of trees on Cemetery Ridge. An officer in the 3rd Georgia recalled that "Wright's Brigade was driven into the Federal position like a wedge and was exposed on the right and on the left. The enemy quickly moved on both flanks to envelop this command."

*Hugh Carey of the 82nd New York would receive a Medal of Honor for capturing a Rebel flag in this fight.

How many of Wright's men got this far, and how far they actually did get, remain matters of dispute. Wright himself would be utterly convinced that all of his troops had made it, but in any case, the achievement was of little real consequence. With no help on the way, and Federal units rushing at him all across his front, Wright pulled back, so rapidly that the three guns his men had taken were left to be reclaimed by the enemy. The Georgians were hurried on their way by an impetuous charge carried out by five companies of the 13th Vermont. When the colonel leading the Vermont men got entangled with his stricken horse, he yelled to his battalion to continue forward: "Go on, boys, go on," he shouted. "I'll be at your head as soon as I get out of this damn saddle."*

In his after-action report, Ambrose Wright would declare, "I have not the slightest doubt but that I should have been able to have maintained my position on the heights, and secured the captured artillery, if there had been a protecting force on my left, or if the brigade on my right had not been forced to retire."

On Richard Ewell's orders, Edward Johnson sent his division—minus the Stonewall Brigade, which had been retained at Brinkerhoff's Ridge—southward to attack Culp's Hill. Brigadier General John M. Jones' Virginia brigade, already providing security for Joseph Latimer's guns, was positioned east and just south of Benner's Hill. The two brigades remaining—Nicholls' Louisiana unit[†] and George H. Steuart's mixed Maryland/North Carolina/Virginia force—advanced from their positions north of the Hanover Road to extend Jones' left flank. Once they had drawn abreast, the three headed south and west. Behind them, Latimer's four guns reopened in support, drawing concentrated Yankee counterbattery fire. The gunners lost their commander when a shell-burst tumbled the boy major and his horse, killing the latter and mortally wounding the former, who would linger until August 1.

The movement of Johnson's brigades conveyed an unintended piece of misinformation to the Federal officers watching from the eastern end of Cemetery Hill. Brigadier General Adelbert Ames, fretting about the

*In this action, Captain John Lonegran led a rush against the Codori house, where he and his company captured eighty-three prisoners. For this act, Lonegran would be awarded the Medal of Honor.
[†]Brigadier General Francis Nicholls had been badly wounded at Chancellorsville, leaving Colonel Jesse M. Williams in charge.

forces that might combine against his thin line along the base of the hill, sent two of his regiments forward about 1,500 feet to observe from a wooded hillock. The 700 men from the 33rd Massachusetts and 41st New York took their assigned station and from there watched Johnson's men moving well off to their right, toward the eastern side of Culp's Hill. While that meant trouble for the troops up there, Ames allowed himself to feel some relief, believing he would not be challenged this day.

A final bit of postcurtain theater was played out on the Union left as the first Twelfth Corps units, marched over from Culp's Hill, reached the area near the George Weikert farm. As the luck of the draw would have it, the regiments leading the way were some of the least experienced on the entire battlefield. The pair belonged to Brigadier General Henry H. Lockwood's brigade, only recently appended to the Army of the Potomac from the Baltimore district. One was the 150th New York, raised in Dutchess County; the other was the 1st Maryland (Regiment) Potomac Home Brigade, whose usual duty had it guarding railroads and various Federal properties.

Alpheus S. Williams, leading the column, was met by Freeman McGilvery, who had just one thing on his mind: putting some infantry in with his beleaguered cannon. Williams ordered Lockwood to take control of some woods in their front. With a confidence based solely on inexperience, the Marylanders never deployed into combat formation but merely marched in a column up the lane as far as the Trostle farm; the New Yorkers at least had enough sense to spread into lines of battle before scampering to catch up with the eager newbies. Both units secured postwar bragging rights when they came upon the guns John Bigelow had abandoned and happily reclaimed them for the Union.*

Behind these two regiments, along Cemetery Ridge, the two remaining brigades of the Twelfth Corps' First Division appeared and were deployed for battle, though there was no action for them. Something of a mystery surrounds the odyssey of the other two Twelfth Corps brigades dispatched from Culp's Hill to the left flank. Under the personal direction of the capable John W. Geary, the pair had departed from Culp's Hill about half an hour after Williams led away the First Division. They followed the Baltimore Pike south, but instead of picking up the crossroads

*Three of the four abandoned cannon were hauled back to Cemetery Ridge. The fourth, having been spiked, was left on the field.

that would have taken them west to Cemetery Ridge, they kept going straight on until they reached Rock Creek. There Geary stopped and sent a rider back to corps headquarters for instructions.

Adding to the enigma is the fact that in order to reach that point, Geary's column had to march past the Twelfth Corps' headquarters on Powers Hill, where none present seems to have noticed that he was going in the wrong direction. Given his belief that he was in charge of the right wing and Williams was the acting Twelfth Corps commander, Henry Slocum may have assumed that Geary was acting on independent instructions from Williams. Some hours would pass before everyone realized that Geary had marched off the game board and needed to be recalled to Culp's Hill. In the meantime, for several critical hours on the Union right, his two brigades had simply disappeared.

Of all the Confederate brigades attacking this day, none drew a worse assignment than the three units of Edward Johnson's Division that were

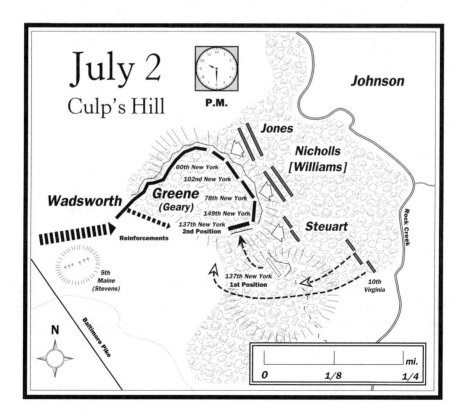

sent against Culp's Hill shortly before sunset. Once they had crossed the relatively open fields south of the Hanover Road, their situation swiftly began to deteriorate. Their first real obstacle was Rock Creek, which was not in itself especially formidable* but whose far bank was steep in places and infested with Yankee soldiers ready to contest any passage. For perhaps thirty minutes, Johnson's men battled the reinforced picket line thrown forward by George Greene. "We held this point with the briskest fire we could concentrate," the Federal officer directing the skirmishers reported. "I desired to . . . sweep them as they crossed the brook."

Having achieved its delaying purpose, Greene's skirmish line started to fall back, though it persisted in stubbornly slowing the enemy down. Johnson's three brigades pushed across the stream, with Jones' Virginians on the right, Steuart's mixed command on the left, and Nicholls' Brigade of Louisianans (under Williams) in the center. The Virginia troops faced a steeper climb, so the Louisiana regiments likely made first contact.

Tragically for Confederate arms, the approach route taken by Johnson's brigades had directed two of the three into the teeth of the Federal defenses. Once George Greene knew for sure that the enemy was coming his way, he had sent couriers looking for help. They had found some from James Wadsworth and Oliver Otis Howard, who promised three and four regiments, respectively. All would take some time to get there, however, so for the moment Greene was on his own.

The first Rebel attacks were bloody disasters. The steep pitch of the hill and the darkness of the hour, compounded by the rocks and brush that everywhere hindered movement, rendered any sort of coherent assault an impossibility. A private under Jones later recalled the Virginians' objective only as a "ditch filled with men firing down on our heads." In a grim understatement, Jesse Williams would allow that his brigade's efforts "were attended with more loss than success."

George Steuart's men at first fared no better. Two of his regiments got ahead of the rest of their command and hooked onto the right flank of the Louisiana troops. This had the effect of funneling them into a deadly cul de sac, with unfriendly fire in their front and on both flanks. A soldier in those suffering ranks remembered that the battle lines, such as they were, "reeled and staggered like a drunken man" in the killing cross fire.

---

*One Maryland soldier described it as being "nearly waist deep," and another noted that the water came "up to our own waists."

*   *   *

George Greene's call for help on Culp's Hill also alerted the Union troops on Cemetery Hill. In a move intended to stiffen the Brickyard Lane line held by von Gilsa's brigade, Adelbert Ames positioned the four-regiment brigade then commanded by Colonel Andrew L. Harris in such a way as to extend von Gilsa's left flank southward. This caused that line to run awkwardly up the slope from the lane toward the crest of eastern Cemetery Hill.

Like most Eleventh Corps units, Harris' brigade had taken serious losses the day before and lacked the manpower actually to link with von Gilsa's. Worried about that gap, Ames made one of those judgment calls that would be forever after analyzed and evaluated: instead of ordering Harris to spread his entire command out to make the connection, he had him pull one regiment, the 17th Connecticut, out of the line to plug the hole between the two brigades. This gave Harris no option but to instruct the regiments on either side to stretch toward each other to cover the Connecticut front. As he later reported, "This left my line very thin and weak. [Every man] could get to the stone wall, used by us as a breast-work, and have all the elbow room he wanted."

Ames took these defensive measures more out of prudence than in anticipation of an attack; he likely believed that the lateness of the hour and the Rebels' commitment against Culp's Hill meant that his line would go untested this day. Andrew Harris spoke for many of the officers on eastern Cemetery Hill when he recorded the "complete surprise" he felt on seeing several battle lines of enemy troops debouched from Gettysburg move "directly in front of my brigade. . . . We could not have been much more surprised if the moving column had raised up out of the ground amid the waving timothy grass of the meadow."

The formations observed by Harris comprised the brigades of Harry T. Hays and Isaac E. Avery. They had been sent forward by Jubal Early, who recalled that Richard Ewell's orders were "to advance upon Cemetery Hill . . . as soon as General Johnson's division, which was on my left, should become engaged at the wooded hill on the left." Because Early's two brigades had set out at roughly a right angle to the section of eastern Cemetery Hill that they were to attack, a precision maneuver was needed to coordinate their swing and ensure that they would strike the enemy line as directly as possible. Avery's Tarheels, who had the farthest to go, jumped off first, moving out from Winebrenner's Run into the open fields before them.

The three North Carolina regiments immediately came under fire from the 5th Maine Light Artillery, posted some one thousand yards southeast of them on McKnight's Knoll.* The astute Yankee gunners had spent part of the day carefully registering the distances in their front, so when the battle lines came into view, they were able to hit their targets with their first salvo. One of those cocky artillerymen would recollect that "at once there was the flash and roar of our six guns, the rush of the projectiles, and along the front of the enemy's charging line every case shot—'long range canister'—burst as if on measured ground, at the right time and in the right place above and in front of their advance."

The impact of this accurate barrage was horrific. A Federal POW, watching from the nearby German Reformed church, was both appalled and fascinated by the spectacle. "To see grape and canister cut gaps through the ranks looks rough," he remarked. "I could see hands, arms, and legs flying amidst the dust and smoke. . . . It reminded me much of a wagon load of pumpkins drawn up a hill, and the end gate coming out, and the pumpkins rolling and bounding down the hill."

Edward Johnson's three-brigade assault on the eastern side of Culp's Hill began with just two, as most of George H. Steuart's unit had been hung up getting across Rock Creek. Given the terrible field conditions, it was hardly surprising that both Jones and Williams should be having problems keeping their men under good tactical control. Jones would later admit that there had been some confusion in his ranks, resulting from "the mixing up of the files and the derangement of the general line, . . . [which was] perhaps, unavoidable from the lateness of the hour at which the advance was made, the darkness in the woods, and the nature of the hill."

John Gibbon would subsequently make light of Ambrose Wright's claim of having briefly held Cemetery Ridge, noting that by the time the Georgia soldiers reached his section, "their propulsive force was pretty well spent, and they made no sensible impression upon [my line]." When George Meade rode past, Gibbon assured him "that the fight on our front was over."

*Today known as Stevens Knoll.

Once the ringing in his ears had begun to subside, Gibbon became aware that the sporadic firing he had been hearing throughout the day from the right flank, on the other side of Cemetery Hill, was now growing "into the roar of a line of battle." Gibbon was still puzzling over what it all meant when Winfield Hancock came over. He listened with Gibbon to the sounds of combat just off to their north. " 'We ought to send some help over there,' " Hancock remarked at last. " 'Send a brigade, send Carroll.' "

There was alarm among the Union troops posted along the Brickyard Lane when their skirmishers scampered in, followed closely by the Louisiana troops of Hays' Brigade. The wide swing that Avery's men needed to make to maintain their position in the attack formation took time, allowing the two regiments sent forward as observers to return to the Brickyard Lane and extend the right flank. As the Tarheels did their midfield marching, the Louisiana Tigers engaged the regiments that Andrew Harris had lined up along the hill slope and in the lane. Federal artillerymen tried to help, but they had to so depress their muzzles to bear on the targets that some of their munitions struck the Union lines, causing fatalities and adding to the confusion.

Even in the midst of this cacophony, there were pockets of resolute calm. A soldier in the 17th Connecticut would never forget the demeanor of two members of his regiment, George Wood Jr. and William ("Bill") Curtis. The pair "were sitting down behind the stone wall, and you would have supposed they were shooting at a target. I saw George shoot from a dead rest, and heard him say, 'He won't come any farther, will he, Bill?' Then Bill shot and said, 'I got that fellow, George.' And they kept it up that way perfectly oblivious to danger themselves."

The section of Harris' line that followed the slope was struck by two of Hays' Louisiana regiments. "At that point, and soon along my whole line the fighting was obstinate and bloody," Harris reported. "The bayonet, club-musket, and anything in fact that could be made available was used, both by the assailants and their assailers." A sergeant in the 75th Ohio was confronted by a Confederate officer carrying a revolver and his regimental colors. "I had no pistol nothing but my sword," the noncom wrote a few days later. "Just as I was getting ready to strike him one of our boys run him through the body so saved me."

By now the three North Carolina regiments under Avery,* having executed their right pivot, were closing on the Brickyard Lane. The Tarheel commander, one of the few in the assault on horseback, was down: around the time the wheel maneuver was completed, Isaac Avery had been felled with a mortal throat wound. In the darkness and the frenzy of combat, no one had seen him tumble to the ground. As he lay dying, Avery fumbled out a pencil and paper to write his last words for his friend, Major Samuel McDowell Tate:

Major: Tell my father I died with my face to the enemy. I. E. Avery.

On lower Culp's Hill, George Steuart had finally managed to bring his three lagging regiments into a rough alignment with the two already battling the Federal earthworks in the woods. Unlike the other units of Johnson's Division engaged on the hill, Steuart's trio found the going fairly easy. Their course brought them into an area on the hill's lesser summit that had been abandoned by Slocum and left uncovered by George Greene. After a few outposts were sent packing, and they got over their surprised relief, Steuart's men began reorienting themselves to tackle the upper crest.

Their advance along the unmanned trenches brought them against the right flank of George Greene's end regiment, the 137th New York. The New Yorkers had been counting on some help from the 71st Pennsylvania, sent over from the Second Corps on Cemetery Ridge, but the darkness, confusion, and enemy presence had proved to be too much for the Pennsylvania colonel, who cited orders to return to his parent command as he pulled his soldiers off Culp's Hill. "The men and officers appeared plucky enough and much mortified at the conduct of the[ir] colonel," noted one of Greene's aides.

The situation for David Ireland and the 137th New York bore a number of remarkable parallels to that experienced earlier this day by Joshua Chamberlain and the 20th Maine. Each regiment held the end of the line for the Union army at Gettysburg, and each faced, with little direct assistance, a determined, resourceful, and numerically superior enemy; each commander had to make some rapid decisions under great stress. When he became aware of the Rebel infiltration into the empty entrenchments off his right, Ireland refused the threatened flank. In this case, the maneu-

*Called Hoke's Brigade after a former commander.

ver was a more conventional swinging back of a single company, rather than the sidestepping spread that Chamberlain had accomplished.

It took a while for the Confederates now in control of the lesser summit to get themselves organized. There had already been several friendly-fire casualties in the darkness, and no one wanted to move without being certain that the gun flashes were coming from Yankee weapons. The few squads probing along the captured works ran into the refused flank of the 137th New York; though they recoiled, their actions helped to fix the extent of Ireland's position. Sensing an opportunity, George Steuart sent one of his regiments, the 10th Virginia, on a flank march to get around the line blocking him.

Chaos reigned along the Brickyard Lane line held by Harris and von Gilsa. Both Hays' Louisiana regiments and Avery's North Carolinians were pressing all along the position. Although some postwar accounts would suggest that the Federal line collapsed completely at this point, it is more likely that while some segments did get swept away from the lane, others stood fast and fought. Like water flooding into a stream spotted with rocks, the Rebel units in some places piled up in front of the steadfast defenders and in others poured through the gaps to clamber up the hillside.

A member of the 8th Louisiana described the brief fight at the stone wall, "behind which the Yankees were, and here we had a hand to hand fight, the Yankees on one side and we on the other side of the wall—knocked each other down with clubbed guns and bayonets." Two of Harris' Ohio regiments were driven from the wall, while the third—the 75th Ohio—held on in the Brickyard Lane. Into the opening went increasingly disorganized portions of Hays' Louisiana regiments, which then swarmed toward the four guns of Captain Michael Weidrich's Battery I, 1st New York Light Artillery. Yet even as groups of Louisiana infantry raced in among their now cold tubes, Wiedrich's cannoneers did not abandon their weapons. The First Corps' artillery chief, Charles Wainwright, himself no friend of foreigners in Union blue, had to admit that these "Germans fought splendidly, sticking to their guns."

Loose gangs of North Carolina troops, having penetrated the porous Brickyard Lane line, combined with some Tigers to overrun sections of the battery adjacent to Wiedrich's right—the 1st Pennsylvania Light Artillery, under Captain R. Bruce Ricketts, who would never forgive the

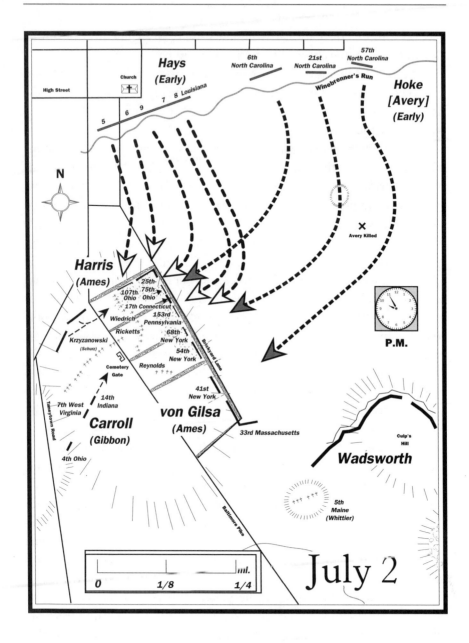

non-American troops assigned to guard his front. His harsh condemnation of the Eleventh Corps units, liberally spiced with his xenophobia,
presented a picture of utter cowardice not justified by the record. Portions of von Gilsa's line (the 33rd Massachusetts and 41st New York,
especially) were still holding as some of the enemy assailed Ricketts. The

fight for these cannon was close-in and brutal, with some using rocks to smash their opponents' heads.

The lack of any clear plan or controlling figure on the Confederate side now began to undercut the very real successes that had been achieved. The Louisiana and North Carolina soldiers had effectively silenced the Federal batteries along the eastern end of Cemetery Hill, making it possible for Rebel reinforcements to advance without running the gauntlet of their antipersonnel fire. Harry Hays was expecting help to arrive on his right from Robert Rodes' division, but every time he glanced in that direction, there was nothing stirring. Colonel A. C. Godwin, successor to the fallen Isaac Avery, looked for John B. Gordon's brigade, which had been moved to within supporting distance before the advance began, but Gordon had not moved. Jubal Early later reported that he had vetoed any effort on Gordon's part for fear that it would lead to a "useless sacrifice of life."

Robert Rodes had been under general instructions to support the attacks, which, given his central position, could have meant moving to bolster successes to his right or his left. Rodes had been very careful and cautious in marching his men out of Gettysburg and into line across from the northwestern corner of Cemetery Hill. The rolling attack coming from his right had died out before reaching his sector, so no action was automatically initiated. A belated effort by Rodes to coordinate with Pender's Division on his right came to naught when he learned that the capable and aggressive Pender was down with an ugly thigh wound, leaving a successor who had only a vague sense of any plan.*

Tactical control of Rodes' front was in the hands of Brigadier General Stephen D. Ramseur, another aggressive officer who nonetheless paled when he saw the strength of the enemy defenses. While some of his skirmishers scrapped with their opposite numbers, Ramseur enlisted the help of another of Rodes' brigadiers, George Dole, to persuade their division commander that the Federal position had not been weakened, and that the attacks by Ewell's Corps had not broken through the enemy's line. These arguments, plus the darkness, as Rodes later reported, "convinced me that it would be a useless sacrifice of life to go on, and a recall was ordered."

There would be no reinforcements this night for the Louisiana and North Carolina troops still battling on eastern Cemetery Hill.

---

*The well-liked Pender would die on July 18 from complications from this wound.

*   *   *

On the lower summit of Culp's Hill, David Ireland continued his high-stakes combat against several regiments from George Steuart's brigade. The Virginians sent by Steuart to flank the short refused segment of Ireland's line got in position and began firing into the flank and rear of the 137th New York. In response, Ireland took the bold step of pivoting his men on the right flank of the next regiment in line, the 149th New York, and occupying the emergency traverse, facing south. Carrying out this maneuver in the dark and under enemy fire required nerve and discipline, but the New Yorkers managed it. There were moments of confusion as portions of the 149th wondered if a general retreat was under way, but their colonel rallied his men with "a brief and patriotic speech."

Here and there, violent melees erupted as parties of Confederates worked in close to Ireland's line. To help relieve the pressure, Captain Joseph H. Gregg led a squad from the 137th in a bayonet charge against the 10th Virginia. The sudden thrust accomplished its purpose, but at the cost of the brave captain, who fell with a mortal wound. Then welcome help arrived in the form of several regiments that had already paid a high price at Gettysburg, including the 6th Wisconsin, 14th Brooklyn, and 157th New York. The steady cascade of musketry from the upper summit never slackened, and after the bloody collapse of several efforts to launch a coordinated attack, the units of Jones' and Nicholls' Brigades called it quits. Not so much under positive orders as out of pure exhaustion, the Virginia and Louisiana regiments sagged backward a short distance, their offensive energies spent. Farther out on Johnson's left, George Steuart broke contact with the enemy line but kept a careful hold on the trenches his men had occupied. The fighting on Culp's Hill was over—for the moment.

The combat on eastern Cemetery Hill continued because the Confederates who tenuously held several Federal batteries felt their best chance of survival lay in maintaining the fight. In the darkness, their modest numbers were magnified, leading some Federals to believe that a great force was in their midst—though many postbattle Confederate reports would veer the other way, suggesting that those gathered along the crest were a mere handful. Either way, they could not be allowed to remain.

The barely organized Rebel units were hit on both flanks by Federal counterattacks that managed to strike at almost the same time. A Tarheel on the hill recalled that "it was soon so dark and [there was] so much smoke that we couldent see what we was a doing." Several Eleventh Corps regiments, led in person by Carl Schurz, drove hard into the northern section holding Wiedrich's battery. "Our infantry made a vigorous rush upon the invaders," wrote an Eleventh Corps man, "and after a short but spirited hand-to-hand scuffle tumbled them down the embankment."

On the southern end of the artillery row, the Rebel soldiers were attacked by Samuel Carroll's brigade, sent over by Winfield Hancock on the presumption that it would be needed. Carroll was something of a reckless fighter, a good man to have on hand in a situation like this. An Ohio sergeant recollected the orders Carroll gave: " 'Halt! Front face! Charge bayonets! Forward, double-quick! March! Give them ———!' " The Second Corps ranks flooded into the contested gun pits. "At Rickett's Battery a tremendous struggle took place," remembered a West Virginia soldier. "It was a man to man, hand to hand fight."

Courage and determination could not offset superior numbers and fresh troops. With no help coming and enemy units swarming around them, all those Rebels who were still under some command and control began falling back. The various units, such as they were, retreated to the bottom of the hill, retaining places along portions of the Brickyard Lane's stone wall for long enough to round up stragglers before returning to Winebrenner's Run. Atop the contested hill, Andrew Harris and other officers now set their men to humanitarian tasks. "We gathered up the dead and cared for the wounded of both friend and foe," the Second Brigade's colonel would later report.

(10:00 P.M.–Midnight)

On the southern side of Little Round Top, Joshua Chamberlain returned from a meeting with James Rice, the acting brigade commander, not knowing what to say to his men. The day's news was bad enough already: in addition to Strong Vincent, the list of dead or mortally wounded officers included Patrick O'Rorke of the 140th New York, his brigade commander, Stephen Weed, and the artillery officer who had placed his battery atop the hill, Charles Hazlett. But that was not what was occupying Chamberlain's thoughts, because this was war, after all, and casualties were to be expected.

Instead, what Chamberlain was pondering was this: Rice had informed him that he had tried and failed to convince Colonel Joseph Fisher to use his brigade of Pennsylvania Reserves to occupy Big Round Top. Nobody knew how many Rebels were on the higher hill, but everyone realized that the Federals could not relax their guard until someone found out. Rice wanted Chamberlain to do it.

Ambition was a part of Chamberlain's personality, so he accepted the mission without hesitation. Walking back to his combat-weary regiment, now numbering perhaps 200 men, he wondered how he would break the news to his troops. He decided to tap their patriotism and pride by calling for the regimental colors and then announcing, "Boys, I am asked if we can carry that hill in front." It proved to be an effective approach: answering the call, the entire regiment formed quickly for the advance.

The thin line eased cautiously into the saddle between the hills, then began moving up the steep slope. The Maine soldiers met a scattering fire from nervous Confederate pickets, who fortunately fired high as they shot downhill. Finally, Chamberlain's line reached the top. The next minutes were filled with dry mouths and palpitating fear as the soldiers grouped into a defensive position, sent out patrols, and took some prisoners, fully expecting the darkness to explode with gunfire at any moment.

Hardly had the men of the 20th Maine settled uneasily into their position on Big Round Top when some of the reluctant Pennsylvania Reserves made a noisy effort to join them, only to be frightened off by unaimed enemy fire. Deciding that a little prudence was in order, Chamberlain set up a strong skirmish line on the crest, then pulled the rest of his regiment back toward Little Round Top pending the arrival of some more dependable support. Only after the 83rd Pennsylvania and 44th New York came up did Chamberlain return to Big Round Top.*

According to the British observer Arthur Fremantle, in all the hours of fighting along the whole Union line, Robert E. Lee "only sent one message, and only received one report." An artilleryman posted nearby observed that throughout the late afternoon, Lee's "countenance betrayed no more anxiety than upon the occasion of a general review." After the firing died down, Fremantle and newspaperman Francis Lawley headed back to Longstreet's headquarters. Lee likely returned to his own headquarters along the Chambersburg Pike, where information now began coming in.

To Lee's way of thinking, little of what he heard was bad news. It was true that his men had nowhere achieved the kind of breakthrough he was hoping for, but neither had they ended the day empty-handed. "Longstreet succeeded in getting possession of and holding the desired ground [along the Emmitsburg Road]," Lee later reported, adding that "Ewell also carried some of the strong positions which he assailed."

Ticking off the plus marks, Lee could now count on Stuart's cavalry, and he had a fresh infantry division on hand in the form of George E. Pickett's command. Apparently, very little was conveyed to him regarding the condition of the units engaged this day. While the names of prominent officers known to be missing, dead, or wounded were quickly passed along, details regarding the combat efficiency of the brigades fighting this day were not available. None of Lee's principal staff recorded any visits to the commands of Ewell or Longstreet this night. Given the nearly miraculous recuperative powers that Lee's soldiers had demonstrated on past

*For his "daring heroism and great tenacity in holding his position on the Little Round Top against repeated assaults, and carrying the advance position on the Big Round Top," Joshua L. Chamberlain would be given the Medal of Honor. Also earning the medal in this action was Sergeant Andrew J. Tozier of the 20th Maine.

occasions, he and his senior officers accepted it as fact that units heavily engaged this day would be ready, after a night's rest, to fight again.

Of his three corps commanders, only A. P. Hill reported in person to Lee this night. Both Longstreet and Ewell sent others with their summaries—an unusual measure for Longstreet, at least, who was not accustomed to absent himself. Reports of the damage done to the enemy were often exaggerated, but even allowing for a little reasonable skepticism, Lee knew that today's fighting had wreaked serious havoc on Meade's army.

"The result of this day's operations induced the belief that, with proper concert of action, and with the increased support that the positions gained on the right [by Longstreet] would enable the artillery to render the assaulting columns, we should ultimately succeed," Lee concluded, "and it was accordingly determined to continue the attack. The general plan was unchanged. Longstreet, re-enforced by Pickett's three brigades, . . . was ordered to attack the next morning, and General Ewell was directed to assail the enemy's right at the same time."*

Also receiving instructions was Jeb Stuart, though their content was not specified in either his report or Lee's. The only extant testimony regarding these orders was left by Stuart's adjutant general, Major Henry B. McClellan, who could be expected to know such things. According to McClellan, "Stuart's object was to gain position where he would protect the left of Ewell's corps, and would also be able to observe the enemy's rear and attack it in case the Confederate assault on the Federal lines [was] successful. He proposed, if opportunity offered, to make a diversion which might aid the Confederate infantry to carry the heights held by the Federal army."

A Confederate officer who visited Lee's headquarters late this night thought that the "commanding general looked well. He was all himself, and never appeared to better advantage." Lee emerged from his tent upon hearing the voice of A. P. Hill, and made a point of walking over and publicly shaking Hill's hand. " 'It is all well, General,' " Lee said. " 'Everything is well.' "

The fast pace of events over the last two days had made it difficult for the head of the Union Army's Bureau of Military Information to get his

*Pickett's Division contained five brigades, but one had been retained in Richmond to assist in defending the city, while a second was held back from joining its parent command until the threat to the capital had been fully assessed.

intelligence-gathering operation into action. Darkness provided the first real opportunity for George Sharpe's people properly to assess the enemy's situation. They concentrated on the several thousand Confederate prisoners held in the provost marshal's makeshift stockades; by simply noting each captured man's regiment, brigade, and division, Sharpe's staff learned much of importance.

Summoned to Meade's headquarters sometime before 9:00 P.M., Sharpe found Generals Meade, Hancock, and Slocum awaiting him. On the table before Meade were a plate of crackers and a half pint of whiskey that seemed silently to mock the tired and hungry officer. With one eye on the food, Sharpe reported that according to his organizational charts, the Rebel prisoners taken over the past two days represented every brigade in Lee's army except those in Pickett's Division. Sharpe's charts were less than perfect, as some units in Lee's army (most notably Junius Daniel's brigade) were not in fact represented, but on the whole, they made a convincing case for Lee's having committed virtually his entire strength to this battle.

Sharpe ducked out while the generals considered this information, then returned with some updates. As he spoke, he noticed that none of the men had touched the food. His people, he said, had also identified a small cavalry unit that had not yet been committed. And they had just learned, too, that "Pickett's division has come up and is now in bivouac, and will be ready to go into action fresh tomorrow morning."

This last news seemed to catch Hancock's fancy, for he exclaimed; "General, we have got them nicked!" Sharpe thought *nicked* an odd word, but he let it pass. Suddenly everyone seemed to be staring at those crackers and that whiskey. Again it was Hancock who spoke: "General Meade," he said, "don't you think Sharpe deserves a cracker and a drink?"

It was likely after Sharpe left that Meade sent a brief situation report to Washington. "I shall remain in my present position to-morrow," he indicated, "but am not prepared to say, until better advised of the condition of the army, whether my operation will be of a offensive or defensive nature." Writing later to his wife of this day's actions, Meade noted that their son had had two horses killed under him, and that his own favorite mount, "Old Baldy," had also been shot. "I had no time to think of either George [Jr.] or myself, for at one time things looked a little blue," Meade admitted, "but I managed to get up reinforcements in time to save the day. . . . The most difficult part of my work is acting without correct information on which to predicate action."

* * *

Night found Gettysburg's residents in the dark in every way. They dared not light too many lamps lest they draw friendly fire, and as to news, they were getting nil. "The Confederates maintained a clam-like silence on all matters concerning the battle," recalled Daniel Skelly. "We gain no information from the Rebels, and are shut off from all communication with our soldiers," seconded Sarah Broadhead. Attorney William McClean tried without success to find out how things were going: "I engaged in a little conversation with the Rebel soldiers in front of the house and was asked about the road and distance to Baltimore, which they seemed anxious to reach," he later recollected.

Somehow Tillie Pierce had mustered the inner strength to endure the experiences of this day on the Jacob Weikert farm, on the eastern side of Little Round Top. Its proximity to the fighting made it a natural collecting point for the wounded, who had begun flooding in. "They were laid in different parts of the house," Pierce would remember. "The orchard and space around the buildings were covered with the shattered and dying, and the barn became more and more crowded. The scene had become terrible beyond description." She did everything in her limited power to provide comfort. One patient in particular caught her attention, a badly wounded man who stared earnestly at her. " 'Will you promise me to come back in the morning to see me?' " he asked. Pierce could only answer, " 'Yes, indeed.' "

Back in town, Liberty Hollinger's father argued with some Confederate soldiers who were standing outside the family's house and demanding food. The Rebels' angry frustration vanished, however, when Hollinger's daughters came out onto the porch; suddenly polite, they asked if the girls would sing for them. Liberty's sister, Julia, was not intimidated. She would sing, she said, but not to please them; rather, she would sing Union songs in the hope that some of the boys in blue might hear her and be cheered. For each song the girls presented, the Confederates answered with one of their own, until finally an officer rode into the yard. " 'Cap,' " he said to the leader of the soldiers, " 'you'd better be careful about these songs.' " " 'Why that's all right,' " the one named Cap replied. " 'They sing their battle songs, and then we sing ours.' "

It was past 9:00 P.M. when, after being briefed by George Sharpe and sending his summary to Washington, George Meade brought all his senior officers together at the Leister house. Sometimes styled a war council, this was in fact more of an executive session, the most efficient way for Meade to learn his army's condition and gauge the fighting spirit of his key subordinates. Somehow they all managed to squeeze into the twelve-foot-square room: Meade, Warren, Butterfield, Slocum, Hancock, Gibbon, Williams, Birney, Sykes, Howard, Sedgwick, and Newton. The conversation ambled about for a while, during which time an exhausted Gouverneur Warren fell asleep.

Everyone wondered about the condition of the Third Corps. Had Sickles been present, he probably would have bluffed his way through with easy assurances, but the acting commander, David Birney, was no Daniel Sickles. His corps had been badly chewed up, and he doubted it was fit for much more. The generals next reviewed the supply situation, which, while tight, was not critical. The discussion moved on to events of the day, the merits of the present position, and the fate of a few officers. Then, for his own reasons, Daniel Butterfield decided to encapsulate the commentary into three questions, which he put to the group:

> Under existing circumstances, is it advisable for this army to remain in its present position, or retire to another nearer its base of supplies?

Everyone was for staying in place, though three (Gibbon, Newton, and Hancock) advocated some alterations in the line to improve the defenses.

> It being determined to remain in present position, shall the army attack or wait the attack of the enemy?

No one favored attacking Lee. The opinions ranged from Alpheus Williams' "Wait attack," to John Newton's "By all means not attack."

> If we wait attack, how long?

The consensus was that the Federals should wait for one more day. According to Meade's recollection, "The opinion of the council was unanimous, which agreed fully with my own views, that we should maintain our lines as they were then held, and that we should wait the movements of the enemy and see whether he made any further attack before we assumed the offensive. I felt satisfied that the enemy would attack again."

* * *

Among the thousands who suffered physical wounds after this day's fighting were many whose scars would be as much inner as outer. Certainly one of the most self-tortured was Lieutenant Gulian V. Weir, commanding the six-gun Battery C, 5th United States Light Artillery, part of Henry Hunt's Artillery Reserve. Weir's crew had seen extensive action, beginning the instant they were ordered to assist Humphreys' division along the Emmitsburg Road.

It started when Weir was intercepted by Winfield Hancock and given new orders: he was to place his cannon in the area vacated by Caldwell's division and from there fire on the Rebel formations approaching the Emmitsburg Road from the west. Not fifteen minutes later, Hancock reappeared and directed the lieutenant to move his battery closer to the road to help support the infantry and artillery units near the Codori farm. Weir did so under protest, pointing out that there were no friendly infantry units to support him. Once in this position, his six Napoleons fired across and south along the Emmitsburg Road.

Weir's gunners were there when Humphreys' line gave way to their left front, followed by Ambrose Wright's attack on the units near the Codori farm. A battery retreating from the Third Corps' sector passed through Weir's position in a near panic, disrupting some infantry coming up from the rear. Mistaking this outfit for Weir's, Hancock cursed the out-of-control unit and later filed a disparaging report based on his wrong identification.

Acting on his own authority, Weir pulled his battery out of its exposed position and reestablished it closer to Cemetery Ridge, about five hundred yards east of the Codori farm. From there he fired on the Florida brigade, lending some help to the 19th Maine in its counterattack. The place soon came under direct fire, however, so Weir ordered his guns pulled back to the ridge. It was then that his real troubles began. Some of Wright's Georgians were closing as the lieutenant rode off, having seen two of his guns away and feeling confident that the rest were out of danger. Glancing back to where the four cannon had been, Weir was horrified to see them still in place and now surrounded by the enemy. Just as he registered this dispiriting image, his horse went down. As Weir struggled to his feet, he was hit in the head by a spent bullet that knocked him senseless.

Bleeding, confused, and filled with shame, Weir somehow made it to his battery park, where he was unable to locate the two guns he had withdrawn. At this emotional nadir, he still managed to look after those of his battery who were still with him. "I saw that the men had something to eat and then I went to sleep," Weir recollected. He little realized that his saga would have more twists and turns before it was over.

The extension of the fighting to the southern portions of the battlefield also visited the consequences of combat on the homes and farmsteads in that area. The John Edward Plank farm, located along Willoughby Run on the afternoon route taken by Longstreet's Corps, became the central receiving station for Hood's casualties. According to a family member, Confederate medical staff commandeered the Plank home with the statement, " 'Now don't be frightened[;] this house will be a hospital and you can expect many wounded men here!' " It was said that the injured John B. Hood was first treated there.

Likewise pressed into emergency use was Francis Bream's Black Horse Tavern and farm, which became a triage area for McLaws' men. A surgeon attached to E. P. Alexander's battalion later recalled visiting the site. "The wounded appeared to be everywhere," he related. "They lay on blankets or on the bare ground; some were waiting their turn at the operating tables. A few screamed in their delirium, calling for their wives, sweethearts, or mothers. Others in shock were quiet and pale."

Union medical teams, too, claimed all suitable space. The Michael Frey farm, on the Taneytown Road near the turnoff for George Weikert's place, was used by the Third Corps. A Michigan soldier saw surgeons "busily at work probing for bullets and amputat[ing] Limbs. . . . [I]t requires a man with a steel nerve and a case-hardened heart to be an Army Sergeon." The nearby Jacob Hummelbaugh farm was appropriated by Second Corps' doctors. It was here that the captive William Barksdale was brought and where he died on July 3.

While the evidence is not conclusive, it seems likely that Daniel Sickles was transported by ambulance to the Daniel Sheaffer farm, off the Baltimore Pike about halfway to Two Taverns. Whether or not this was where his shattered leg was taken off will probably never be known for sure. One thing *is* known, however: after his leg was amputated, Sickles insisted on keeping it with him.*

---

*Packed in a small coffin, the amputated leg would eventually be turned over to, and later put on display at, the Army Medical Museum, where Sickles reportedly stopped in to visit his lost appendage whenever he was in Washington. He would receive a Medal of Honor for his "most conspicuous gallantry on the field."

* * *

The man who ran the military telegraph office in Washington would remember that Abraham Lincoln spent "hour after hour" there monitoring the news from Gettysburg. It was where Navy Secretary Gideon Welles found him this morning. The reports, noted Welles, indicated that there "was a smart fight, but without results, near Gettysburg yesterday." Returning in the evening, the cabinet member learned that John Reynolds was dead. Meade's July 1 dispatch from Taneytown, in which he declared that he could see "no other course than to hazard a general battle," was likely the most recent direct communication yet received in the Union capital. "The tone of Meade's dispatch is good," Welles pronounced.

There was a panic of modest proportions in Richmond this day, an indirect result of Lee's operations. In an effort to apply some "big picture" strategy to the eastern theater, military planners in Washington had instructed the man commanding the Federal enclaves along the Virginia and North Carolina coasts to concentrate his forces with a view to threatening the Confederate capital. This he had done, albeit reluctantly and cautiously, and already the expedition's first effort, a cavalry raid against railroad bridges north of Richmond, was having its effect. War clerk John Beauchamp Jones, while noting the enemy actions, felt certain that the Federal commander was wasting his time. "He cannot take Richmond," Jones wrote in his diary, "nor draw back Lee." From Lee himself there had been no recent report, only silence.

After two days of battle witnessed from inside the town of Gettysburg, there was little that could surprise Daniel Skelly, or so he thought. Skelly and a buddy were exploring when, as he recalled it, "we were halted by two Confederate soldiers who had a lady in their charge. She was on horseback and proved to be the wife of General Barlow who had come through Confederate lines under a flag of truce looking for her husband who had been severely wounded on July 1." The indefatigable Mrs. Barlow, having managed to cross the lines, was now riding around following up every lead she was given. Her husband, Francis Barlow, was in fact alive and being nursed in the home of Jane Smith, who lived near the almshouse on the northern side of town; none of the people Arabella Bar low spoke with knew this, though, and their attempts to be helpful just sent her from one wrong house to another. She was no more successful on July 2 than she had been on July 1.

Lorenzo Crounse of the *New York Times,* one of the first reporters to reach the battlefield, did not rest much after the fighting ended this night. "I visited some portions of the line by moonlight and can bear personal witness to the terrible ferocity of the battle," he would write. "In front of some of our brigades, who had good protection from stone walls or fences, the rebel dead laid piled in lines like windrows of hay." "Every one is exhausted," recorded G. W. Hosmer of the *New York Herald,* "and there is great misery for want of water."

Units that were positioned near where they had seen action did their best to take care of their own. A soldier in the 1st Minnesota later remembered how he and his unwounded comrades had "stumbled over the field in searching for our fallen companions, and when the living were cared for, laid ourselves down on the ground to gain a little rest . . . [,] the living sleeping side-by-side with the dead."*

Close by, Mississippi soldiers belonging to Posey's Brigade performed a similar duty. "Flitting forms a few feet off showed us our foe engaged in the same task," one of them recalled. "A whisper above the breath would call for a shot from our foe on picket, a shot called for a volley and a volley meant death. So in quietness, disturbed only by the groans of the stricken wretches, we finished our work."

Near the peach orchard, South Carolina soldiers "gathered the dead and wounded," recollected one of the lucky ones. "It was a melancholy task, for they were very numerous." A Georgian riding past the place this night remarked on the "groans of the wounded which the Enemy has not been able to remove." J. W. Duke, of Barksdale's Brigade, at last located his brother, whose presentiment that " 'something is going to happen today' " had been genuinely prophetic: he was lying, mortally wounded, in the peach orchard. " 'Thank God! my prayers are answered,' " he gasped at Duke. " 'I have asked him to take me in place of you, as I am prepared and you are not.' "

*This night, musician Richard Enderlin of the 73rd Ohio crossed into enemy lines and brought back Private George Nixon, for which action he would receive a Medal of Honor. The rescued private would become the great-grandfather of President Richard M. Nixon.

Taken solely on its own merits, the July 2 fight at Gettysburg was one of the Civil War's most intense battles. In retrospect, it was the day on which Robert E. Lee came closest to achieving the "concert of action" he believed to be necessary for victory, with more troops engaged according to an overall scheme than were employed on either July 1 or July 3. It was very much a soldier's battle, during which individual courage was commonplace and the level of personal effort, especially given the weather and the day's exhausting preliminary movements, was nearly fictional in its accountings.

July 2 laid bare the failings of Lee's command style and the dysfunctional nature of his army's operational culture. The broad front position Lee acceded to effectively isolated each corps, demanding even greater coordination on the part of his principal officers, few of whom rose to the occasion. There was no unity of purpose among Longstreet, Hill, and Ewell, only an ambiguous understanding of events that was replete with shades of interpretation. Lacking any clear direction from the top, division and brigade commanders were left on their own to determine how the overall assault was proceeding and what role they were meant to play in it.

From Hood's "digression" (which modified a modification of a busted plan) to Robert Rodes' inability to act with celerity or clarity, the contributions of Lee's division commanders were clouded by a fog of misunderstanding and miscommunication that muffed opportunities and needlessly squandered lives. Lee's responsibility for this miasma is painfully obvious. He did not impose his will upon his corps commanders, but neither did he convey a sufficient sense of purpose to enable them to operate according to any commonly understood objectives.

The breakdown of Confederate field intelligence this day was astounding. It resulted in an entire battle plan (such as it was) based on fatally incorrect information. Compounding the initial misinformation was an abject failure on the corps and divisional levels to confirm and refine the original data as events unfolded. The surprise expressed by James Longstreet when McLaws discovered the Union position in his front spoke volumes about the lack of adequate information gathering.

On this day of his greatest martial trial, George Gordon Meade operated more as a sort of supernumerary corps commander than as an army leader. Once Daniel Sickles' insubordination had derailed his defensive scheme, Meade began to behave like a fireman, always drawn to the flames and ignoring wisps of smoke portending danger elsewhere. He was courageous and forthright in his efforts to blunt the Rebel assaults against his left flank, but the situation he was trapped in compelled him to commit his forces in a piecemeal fashion that negated much of their value. He became so fixated on the crisis on his left that he knowingly stripped his right of troops who would prove to be largely unneeded where they were sent yet desperately missed in the positions they had abandoned. That he survived Lee's offensive was due as much to the compact nature of the Federal position, adroit leadership at the regimental, brigade, and divisional levels, failings on the enemy's part, and sheer luck as to any efforts of his own in shaping an overall response to the threat he was facing.

Ironically enough, had Meade and Sickles worked in tandem—that is, had the line taken by the Third Corps been shared with the Fifth, and had command matters been resolved and fallback plans established—Longstreet's troops would have been hard pressed to achieve any of their goals. Given the personalities involved, however, that kind of teamwork was impossible. Still, it was not what Daniel Sickles did that nearly destroyed the Army of the Potomac at Gettysburg; it was the manner in which he did it.

The roughly 9,000 Federal soldiers who had been killed, wounded, or captured on July 1 were joined by some 10,000 more on July 2, perhaps 1,200 of whom were in the prisoner category. Just as the first day of fighting had seriously damaged the First and Eleventh Corps, so the combat on July 2 marked the beginning of the end for the Third, which would never recover from its losses this day. With some 593 officers and enlisted men dead, 3,029 wounded, and 589 reported missing, Daniel Sickles' command suffered a casualty rate approaching 30 percent.

The Confederate toll for July 2 was estimated at 6,800, slightly more than that for July 1, even though the number of men engaged on this second day was much greater. The losses fell most heavily on Longstreet's Corps and Richard Anderson's division, with the former taking a loss of nearly 30 percent and the latter (at least in Wilcox's, Perry's, and Wright's Brigades) experiencing casualties of about 40 percent.

At day's end, the gains that would prompt Lee to renew his offensive on July 3 were largely illusory. The artillery platform provided by the peach orchard offered no significant advantages for E. P. Alexander's cannon, and the foothold gained by Johnson's men on Culp's Hill held more possibilities in the imagination than in reality. Yet it was on this basis that Lee committed his army to one more effort.

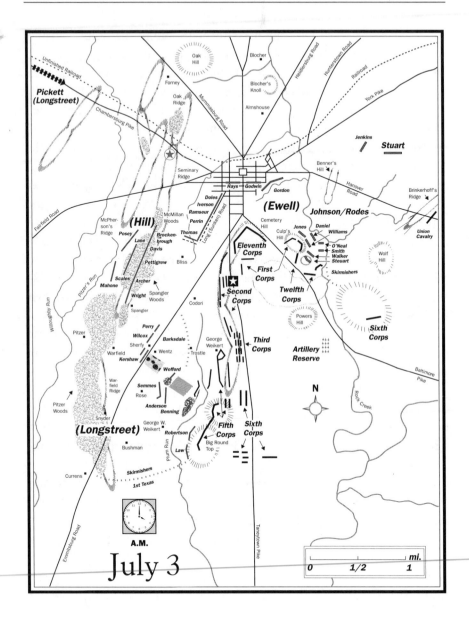

Pickett
(Longstreet)

(Hill)

(Ewell)

Johnson/Rodes

(Longstreet)

Stuart

Union
Cavalry

Eleventh
Corps

First
Corps

Second
Corps

Twelfth
Corps

Sixth
Corps

Third
Corps

Artillery
Reserve

Fifth
Corps

Sixth
Corps

A.M.

July 3

N

0   1/2   1   mi.

NOCTURNE
Night, Thursday, July 2

Franklin Aretas Haskell was a New England farm boy whose ticket out of the laboring, provincial life was his love of reading and thirst for knowledge. He followed his older brother, a lawyer, to the western frontier of Wisconsin, where he earned enough as a town clerk and school superintendent to pay his way through Dartmouth College in New Hampshire. There he drank deep of intellectual stimulation, determined to improve his lot. One astute professor evaluated him as being "ambitious as Lucifer and possibly mischievous and irregular." A career in law beckoned after Dartmouth, taking Haskell back to Wisconsin, where he was when the war began.

Frank Haskell marched off with the 6th Wisconsin as a lieutenant and adjutant. His administrative skills eventually elevated him to the brigade level, and when John Gibbon took command of what would soon be called the Iron Brigade, Haskell became his aide de camp. His ambition was to command a regiment, but a combination of state politics, personality issues, and bad luck conspired to keep him stalled on Gibbon's staff.

At thirty-four (he would turn thirty-five on July 18), Haskell was somewhat older than most aides, and downright elderly for a lieutenant. He had an air of authority about him that some admired and others found irritating. A wartime photograph of him shows a balding, officious-looking figure tending toward plumpness. His curiosity remained active at Gettysburg, and his eye for detail was excellent, as was his memory, but his willing acceptance of rumors and hearsay could mislead him.

Haskell had arrived at the battlefield with the Second Corps on the morning of July 2. His work with John Gibbon kept him busy but also in a position to see lots of things. At one point, while intently watching some of the fighting around the Bliss farm from horseback, he was targeted by a distant Rebel sniper, who let fly a bullet that, as Haskell recollected it, "hissed by my cheek so close that I felt the movement of the air distinctly." He was a witness to the terrible struggle of the Third Corps ("What a Hell is there down that valley!" he exclaimed), then a participant in another storm as the waves of Anderson's Division broke against the shore of the Second Corps on Cemetery Ridge.

"All senses for the time are dead but the one of sight," Haskell afterward wrote, trying to explain what it felt like to be in the midst of combat. "The roar of the discharges, and the yells of the enemy all pass unheeded; but the impassioned soul is all eyes, and sees all things, that the smoke does not hide." Then, reflecting on the battle's aftermath, he described the strange silence and the desolation of once-fertile fields that had been trampled underfoot by fighting men and were now littered with the castoffs of their contest. He found striking, too, the sharp contrast between the dead or wounded and the survivors, the former arranged in a thousand unnatural poses or bewildered by their fate, the latter "quite mad with joy."

His duties as a staff aide kept Haskell waiting outside the Leister house until Meade's nighttime conference with his key generals ended. From there he made his way back to Second Corps headquarters, leading his usually even-tempered horse, who seemed oddly agitated. Only after reaching the hitching line, where he could strike a light, did he realize that his favorite mount had been badly wounded in the course of the day's fighting. Dogged by that sad realization, Frank Haskell stretched out on a blanket tossed onto the ground and for the next four hours lost himself to the "delicious, dreamless oblivion of weariness and of battle."

Perhaps two miles west of where Frank Haskell slipped into an exhausted slumber, a twenty-five-year-old Mississippi farmer of equal rank was himself hoping that sleep would erase some of the images of this day. Lieutenant William Peel and his regiment, the 11th Mississippi, of Joseph R. Davis' brigade, not only had missed the July 1 fighting but had been little more than observers of the July 2 actions. Like Haskell, Peel had enlisted in 1861, and like that Yankee he was unmarried, dedicated to his cause, and hardworking. Unlike Haskell, he had never aspired to do anything more than farm his family's land, near Okolona, Mississippi, nor had he evidenced much of the pen-and-paper skill so amply demonstrated by the Wisconsin clerk and administrator. Yet something had moved Peel, at the outset of the present campaign, to begin a journal in which he faithfully chronicled his odyssey from Fredericksburg to Gettysburg.

Peel was sufficiently respected by the men of his company (who styled themselves "The Prairie Rifles") that they had elected him their lieutenant. At his place in the line of battle at Second Bull Run, he had taken a serious wound. He had been absent, recovering, when his regiment got chewed up at Antietam, losing nearly half of its number who entered the fight. He had rejoined the 11th in December in the North Carolina theater, which posting had kept the unit away from Chancellorsville.

The 11th had been held up watching supply wagons in Cashtown on July 1 and so had avoided the fighting along the railroad cut. Along with the much-reduced remnants of Davis' Brigade, William Peel and his regiment comprised the unused reserve on July 2. Even as Frank Haskell was drawn to the afterimages of battle, so was William Peel, whose own contemplation must have been nearly simultaneous with the Union lieutenant's. "Implements of war were scattered in every direction, while here & there lay horses & men in every conceivable degree of mutilation," Peel noted. "There are perhaps few stages of suffering of which the imagination may conceive, that were not here represented."

Unlike Haskell, whose exhaustion at least brought him some relief in sleep, Peel spent a restless night, "broken in upon occasionally by a report from the artillery of the wakeful enemy, & at one time by a sudden tremendous rattle of musketry." None of these noises registered on the consciousness of Lieutenant John Dooley, a proud member of the 1st Virginia in Brigadier General James Kemper's brigade of George Pickett's division, who had reached the western outskirts of the battlefield only a few hours earlier.

Dooley, named after his Irish father and devoted to his long-suffering Irish mother, had been born and raised in Richmond, where his family operated a successful clothing business. Young John was something of a prankster, though that roguery was offset by a love of books and a reflective turn. He had attended Georgetown College near Washington, D.C., but the call of his home state had proven to be too powerful to resist. Because he had had to wait until he was nineteen to enlist, he had not entered the Confederate service until mid-1862, when he signed on with a unit whose roots reached far back into his state's history. In the ranks of the 1st Virginia, Dooley (unlike William Peel) had made it through Second Bull Run without injury, and had also survived Antietam, though at the latter place he had learned firsthand that discretion was the better part of valor. "Oh, how I ran!" he recollected.

John Dooley had embarked on the Gettysburg campaign with a sober sense of the soldier's life and a refreshing ability not to take himself too seriously. Thanks to the genial nature of his personality, and, too, to the attritions of disease and military action, Dooley was now a lieutenant, "in charge of a company, although the newest and most ignorant officer in the Regt." He tried to comprehend the basic army manual but gave that up as a lost cause, instead trusting to "luck to hear that the Col. says and understand what he means."

Dooley and the 1st Virginia, like the rest of Pickett's Division, had spent July 1 in Chambersburg, guarding the army's supply train. Once word spread of the fighting at Gettysburg and the division began moving in that direction, Dooley observed a solemnity among the men, "as if some unforeseen danger was ever dropping darksome shadows over the road we unshrinkingly tread." As the lieutenant marched, he struggled with his own fears, which he freely admitted "grew not less as we advanced in the war." Even his duties commanding the rear guard while it passed through the Cashtown Gap did not displace the sense of apprehension that knotted his stomach.

John Dooley fell into a troubled sleep this night, with the sound of the July 2 fighting still ringing in his memory. To his veteran senses, the sounds denoted "a stubborn and bloody conflict and we are sure if we escape tonight, tomorrow we will have our full share."

FOURTEEN

July 3, 1863

(Midnight–Sunrise)

E dward P. Alexander was exhausted. As if it were not enough that the young acting artillery chief for Longstreet's Corps had directed his guns throughout the day's action, almost as soon as the last shot had been fired, he had to see to the tiring clean-up work. There were wounded to be tended to, and dead to be buried; horses to be fed, put out of their misery, or replaced; ammunition to be resupplied; scattered units to be reunited; and cannoneers to be provided with some food and rest. There would be little of the last for Alexander himself, who finished his immediate tasks and then reported to Longstreet's bivouac, where he was told "that we would renew the attack early in the morning. That Pickett's division would arrive and would assault the enemy's line. My impression is the exact point for it was not designated, but I was told it would be to our left of the Peach Orchard."

This meant more work for Alexander, whose efforts to locate firing positions for his guns would keep him moving until about 1:00 A.M. Sherfy's now thoroughly trashed peach orchard offered scant ground cover suitable for sleeping, but the artillerist was not too particular. He found two fence rails and fashioned them into a rough bed that at least propped him up off the spoiled ground. So, "with my saddle for a pillow & with the dead men & horses of the enemy all around, I got two hours of good sound & needed sleep."

*   *   *

Robert E. Lee would later report that his orders to Richard Ewell had directed him "to assail the enemy's right [the next morning]." Ewell himself interpreted these as instructions "to renew my attack at daylight Friday morning." To Ewell's way of thinking, there was nothing to be gained by again attacking Cemetery Hill, which left that portion of the Federal trenches held by George Steuart's men as the only point along the Second Corps' front "affording hopes of doing this to advantage."

Ewell expressed his intentions to his subordinates and was momentarily taken aback when some of them protested that such a move would be suicidal. According to a Federal POW who overheard him speaking with "one of his subordinate officers," Ewell "replied, with an oath, that he knew it could be done, and that it should be done, and that the assault should be renewed."

Once committed to renewing the assault against Culp's Hill, Ewell and Edward Johnson were determined to bring as many men as possible into the effort. Johnson ordered James Walker's Stonewall Brigade forward from where it had been guarding the flank near Brinkerhoff's Ridge. With the exception of two companies and a portion of a third from the 2nd Virginia left behind to picket the ridge, Walker's men made their way across the fields and forded Rock Creek to come into line behind Steuart's Brigade. Ewell also drew two brigades from Rodes' command—Edward O'Neal's Alabamians and Junius Daniel's North Carolinians—which sidled up behind the Louisiana regiments of Nicholls' Brigade and the Virginians of Jones' Brigade, respectively.* Where three brigades had attacked and scored a modest but potentially exploitable success the previous evening, Ewell was putting six brigades into action, with a seventh (William Smith's, of Early's Division) on the way.

Few of those who had battled in the dark on July 2 were sanguine about the chances for a renewed assault. "During the night . . . we could hear and see the arriving of the heavy reinforcements of the enemy in our front," remembered the officer commanding the 14th Louisiana. "We all realized what a large force we would have to contend against on the morrow." A soldier in the 23rd Virginia wished that Stonewall Jackson might rise from the dead to resume command, "for it was always his policy never to assault strongholds or storm positions as impregnable as these."

---

*With Jones now wounded, Lieutenant Colonel R. H. Dungan commanded the Virginia brigade.

* * *

Alone in her room, Gettysburg resident Jane Smith noted in her diary "a silence around us now that is ominous of to-morrow's struggle." It was just as keenly felt by Sarah Broadhead, who also described the fear that kept the civilians in the town in a high state of suspense. In contrast, young William Bayly was thinking about the sword and pistol that had been left hanging outside the door of the spare room in his family's house, commandeered for the night by several Rebel officers. Bayly "marveled that a man should be so careless when in the home of an enemy," but he decided not to liberate the items for fear of what might happen to the rest of his family "if I should confiscate the trappings."

After spending much of the night listening at their street window to catch what the Confederate soldiers were saying about the day's events, Daniel Skelly and his friends at last fell into "a sound sleep as boys do who have few cares and sound health." Sleep was more elusive for ten-year-old Charles M. McCurdy, whose dreams were invaded by images of what he had seen at the Lutheran church near the college, now being used as a hospital. "The church yard was strewn with arms and legs that had been amputated and thrown out of the windows and all around were wounded men for whom no place had yet been found," McCurdy recollected. Likewise haunted by troubling visions this night was Henry Jacobs, still reeling from the death of the young Johnny Reb on his family's back cellar door. Jacobs did take time to record that the "courteous, considerate Georgians" who had been posted in his neighborhood had since been replaced by "North Carolinians and Louisiana Tigers."

Diarist Jane Smith ended her early-morning entry with a prayer for all the young men who she knew were "girded for the conflict" coming with the sun: "Oh, make it, thou Almighty, to deliver down even to the eleventh hour, to them, the beginning of glory!"

As they had done countless times before, the 5,830 men of Brigadier Generals Robert B. Garnett's, James L. Kemper's, and Lewis A. Armistead's brigades filed into marching order, this day aligned along the Chambersburg Pike. "The usual jests and hilarity were indulged in . . . ," remembered one of Garnett's men, "and . . . no gloomy forebodings hovered over our ranks." The captain temporarily commanding one of Kemper's regiments had a personal contact at Lee's headquarters who had assured him that Pickett's men would be used merely to mop up an already broken Federal army.

The sun had not yet risen when Pickett's fifteen Virginia regiments began marching east along the pike toward Gettysburg. Kemper's Brigade led the way, followed by Garnett's and Armistead's, each comprising five regiments. About half a mile had gone by under their feet when the head of the column turned south off the pike onto a glorified trail that passed for a local road. Tramping along with the 1st Virginia, John Dooley spotted a mounted figure watching the column, whom he understood to be Robert E. Lee. "I must confess that the General's face does not look as bright as tho' he were certain of success," Dooley reflected. "But yet it is impossible for us to be any otherwise than victorious and we press forward with beating hearts."

Robert E. Lee's orders to James Longstreet were to "attack the next morning" according to the "general plan" of July 2. The army commander offered no further specifics in any of his post-Gettysburg reports, and Longstreet's various recollections are equally ambiguous regarding what was expected of him. Nevertheless, Edward P. Alexander's account suggests that Longstreet's thinking must have changed not long after he set his cannon to support an effort centered on Sherfy's peach orchard.

Longstreet's first response to Lee's directive was to begin preparations to renew the attack from the line of the Emmitsburg Road against Cemetery Ridge. Then, as he had done on July 2, the corps commander began pondering the possibilities offered by his superior's broader instruction to envelop the enemy's flank. That flank now rested on Big Round Top, whose western base was under Confederate control. In one memoir, Longstreet would declare, "I sent to our extreme right to make a little reconnaissance in that direction, thinking General Lee might yet conclude to move around the Federal left."

Alpheus S. Williams, still operating as acting commander of the Twelfth Corps, returned to his headquarters after the high-level discussion at the Leister house. He reckoned the time to be "near midnight" when he heard two pieces of information. First, he was told that the Yankees now held the trenches his men had dug on the lower summit of Culp's Hill. Williams received that intelligence "not with great surprise." What astonished him was the news that John Geary had marched off somewhere with two brigades, leaving only George Greene's men to hold Culp's

Hill. "The rebels, of course, walked in and took possession of the right of our deserted line, and began a severe attack upon Greene, who . . . manfully held the left, aided to some extent by reinforcements from Wadsworth . . . and [the] 11th Corps," he related.

Once he had determined that no one had a clue as to the whereabouts of Geary, Williams called on Henry Slocum, who was still presuming the authority of a right-wing commander, and explained what was happening on Culp's Hill. " 'Well!' " Slocum replied. " 'Drive them out at daylight.' " Williams came away muttering that Slocum's order "was more easily made than executed." After he thought matters through, he realized that his biggest advantage was his artillery: the Rebels had none, while he had a number of batteries on hand, and there were good positions for them along the Baltimore Pike and near Powers Hill.

Fortunately for Williams, by the time he returned from Slocum's headquarters, John Geary had reappeared with a sheepish story about being led astray by a group of stragglers. His troops were not far behind, so Williams could deploy them as well as his own three brigades. With all these pieces now in order, his plan quickly came together. He posted ten cannon along the pike with a clear shot at lower Culp's Hill, supporting them with Lockwood's brigade of his division. One of his two remaining brigades (Colonel Silas Colgrove's) was placed along Rock Creek just south of the occupied trenches, while the last (Colonel Archibald McDougall's) extended Colgrove's line to the Baltimore Pike. In like fashion, the two brigades with Geary were positioned to prolong Greene's line in a southwesterly direction toward the pike. This created a deadly gallery, whose sides were firm with infantry and whose end was a wall of cannon.

Come dawn, Williams intended to have the artillery soften up the enemy for fifteen minutes before Geary attacked. He did not dare underestimate the strength of the Rebels, who had "two lines of strong defenses against a frontal attack and the flank toward the creek [that] could not be turned, as a morass and impassable stream protected it; and across the creek they had filled the woods with sharp-shooters behind rocks and in a stone house near the bank." Nevertheless, his orders were to attack at first light.

Williams completed his preparations by about 3:30 A.M. That left him about thirty minutes in which to get some sleep, which he did "on a flat rock sheltered by an apple tree."

*   *   *

Edward P. Alexander was awake and about well before sunrise, moving his artillery units into a firing line that stretched northeastward from Sherfy's peach orchard. No sooner had he finished the task when the first light of dawn revealed to him a potentially disastrous error: he had mis-gauged the layout of the enemy's defenses, and set his row of batteries in a position that completely exposed them to deadly flanking fire. "But for-tunately they did not seem to be able to see us clearly," Alexander recalled, "& by quick work I got the line broken up, & thrown back in such a way as not to present a good target." The young artilleryman failed to share Robert E. Lee's positive assessment of possessing Sherfy's peach orchard. In Alexander's opinion, it was "very unfavorable ground for us, generally sloping toward the enemy."

The populations of most Northern cities were still unaware of the fight-ing at Gettysburg. It was not for lack of effort on the part of the corre-spondents on the scene, but there was no reliable telegraphic communi-cation within easy distance, and few were willing to leave the field for fear of missing the battle's conclusion. For two of the more resourceful reporters, however, the communication difficulties proved to be just one more obstacle to overcome. Uriah H. Painter of the *Philadelphia Inquirer* reached the battlefield on July 2 and stayed just long enough to get a full accounting of the first day's fight before heading back to West-minster, where he caught the government train to Baltimore. His suc-cinct summary of July 1 was approved by the censors that same evening and appeared on the streets of Philadelphia in his paper's July 3 issue.

Even more remarkable were the efforts of the *New York Tribune*'s Homer Byington, who, though something of an amateur compared to the veteran newspapermen on the scene, was not one whit less intrepid. He spent most of July 1 near Hanover, where he talked and bribed the local telegrapher and some workmen into helping him restring the sec-tions of the telegraph line east of town that had been torn down by Stu-art's cavalrymen. The gap turned out to be five miles long, but the expe-rienced workers had it bridged by late afternoon. Then, with the promise of much money forthcoming from his paper, the canny reporter got his crew to agree to reserve the repaired stretch exclusively for traffic from the *Tribune* or *Philadelphia Press*.

From there Byington rode to Gettysburg, arriving in time personally to witness some of the July 2 action and to pick up the story of July 1.

Turning around immediately, he telegraphed the news that night from Hanover to New York, enabling the *Tribune* to publish a Friday-morning extra that contained the most comprehensive account yet available of the two days' fighting.

Other reporters such as the *Boston Journal*'s Charles Coffin preferred to remain on the scene until the outcome of the battle was known. Along with a few kindred spirits from the correspondents' fraternity, Coffin settled down this morning "in an old farmhouse, near the Baltimore Pike." Against the backdrop of the steady rumble of wagons and cannon on the move, Coffin noted that "lights were gleaming in the hollows, beneath the shade of oaks and pines, where the surgeons were at work, and where, through the dreary hours, wailing and moanings rent the air." Notwithstanding the cacophony, he slipped into a refreshing slumber, "expecting that with the early morning there would be a renewal of the battle."

(Sunrise–1:07 P.M.)

By his own reckoning, Alpheus Williams slept for about half an hour. There was just enough daylight to see nearby objects when he turned to Lieutenant Edward D. Muhlenberg, commanding the Twelfth Corps' artillery, and gave him "the order to open fire." Between the cannon along the Baltimore Pike and those spread about Powers Hill, there were some twenty-six guns in all, going into action at ranges of eighteen hundred to twenty-four hundred feet. Williams watched approvingly for the next fifteen minutes as the "woods in front and rear and above the breastworks held by the rebels were filled with projectiles from our guns." A cannoneer on Powers Hill recalled that the Yankee batteries "poured shot & shell into the Rebel lines."

Given the relatively primitive nature of Civil War artillery ordnance, the effect on the Confederates nestled behind the Union-built earthworks was more nuisance than anything else. The trees overhead took a lot of punishment, recorded a Maryland Confederate, "and the balls could be heard to strike the breastworks like hailstones upon the roof tops." The way the shells exploding above made the leaves flutter brought comforting thoughts of autumn's pleasures to another hunkered-down Rebel.

Some units, finding themselves exposed to the firing, were able to shift position without great difficulty. The Federal shelling also failed to upset Confederate offensive plans, though it likely delayed them. When the artillery curtain lifted after the programmed fifteen minutes, John Geary's troops on the upper summit were supposed to spring into action. Instead, it was Edward Johnson's Rebels who moved first.

Johnson had no time for finesse. His plan, such as it was, called for the brigades on Culp's Hill to bludgeon through the enemy positions before them. The hope was that a weak point could be found and recognized as such, and that there would be troops enough on hand to exploit it. So almost the moment the Union barrage ended, the musketry crackled alive all along Johnson's front as his troops began pressing gamely

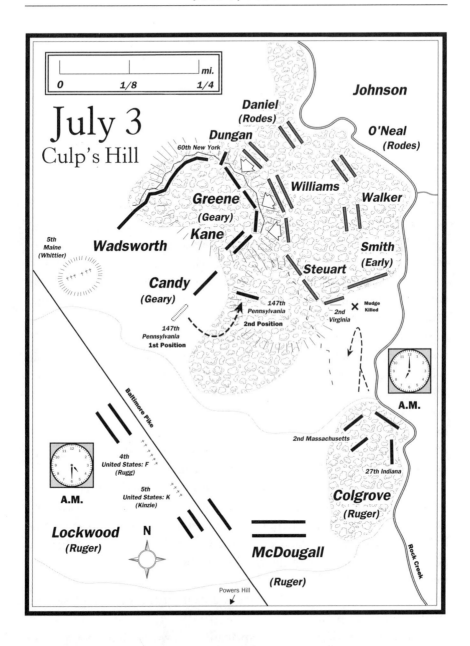

forward in search of a chink—any chink—in the enemy's wood-and-dirt armor.

The troubled look that John Dooley perceived on the face of Robert E. Lee was less the mark of any rumination on the coming day than it was a sign of Lee's concern over an even more immediate problem: Pickett's Division was running well behind the schedule he had projected when he sent out his broad directives a few hours earlier. After dispatching a courier to Richard Ewell to advise him of the delay, Lee hastened to Longstreet's headquarters, located in a schoolhouse adjacent to Willoughby Run, about nine hundred yards west of Warfield Ridge. On his way there, he passed a coffle of Federal prisoners, one of whom would remember seeing "General Lee and his staff making their way to the front."

Still believing that Lee's nonspecific orders for him to envelop the enemy's flank provided ample latitude, Longstreet greeted his chief with the words "General, I have had my scouts out all night, and I find that you still have an excellent opportunity to move around to the right of Meade's army and maneuver him into attacking us."

In his final report on the Gettysburg campaign, Robert E. Lee would limit his comments regarding this moment to the terse statement that "General Longstreet's dispositions were not completed as early as was expected." Longstreet would admit in his own report that his interpretation of Lee's broad directives had involved his passing "around the hill occupied by the enemy on his left, . . . [with a view] to gain it by flank and reverse attack." Realizing that he had been unclear as to his intentions, Lee pointed with his fist toward Cemetery Ridge. " 'The enemy is there, and I am going to strike him,' " he said. Lee was not interested in undertaking a flank move. He still anticipated that the two First Corps divisions already on the field would renew their attacks.

Now Longstreet comprehended that his understated summary of the night before had failed to convey the battered state of those two divisions. "I thought that would not do," Longstreet decided, and so he proceeded to give Lee the facts as he knew them, advising him "that the point had been fully tested the day before, by more men, when all were fresh; that the enemy was there looking for us . . . , [and that the enemy's units were well positioned to] strike the flank of the assaulting column, crush it, and get on our rear."

Lee listened to Longstreet's explanation, slowly coming to grips with the reality that his first plan was not going to be practicable. Yet he never wavered from his objective. " 'I am going to take them where they are on Cemetery Hill,' " he said, putting an end to that part of the discussion. A new plan would have to be drawn up, and, as the steady rumble of cannon and musketry fire coming from Culp's Hill reminded him, drawn up quickly. While Lee and Longstreet set out for a point where they could more clearly survey the enemy lines, aides went off to summon A. P. Hill to join them.

Edward Muhlenberg's bombardment was Gettysburg's wake-up call for day three. Sarah Broadhead remembered it as a "fierce cannonading" that sent families throughout the town hustling back into their cellars. "May I never again be roused to the consciousness of a new-born day by such fearful sounds!" wrote diarist Jane Smith. "It seemed almost like the crashing of worlds."

The firing also roused the snipers in town, who paid special attention to the artillerymen plying their trade from Cemetery Hill. Eugene Blackford, whose 5th Alabama Battalion had adroitly parried the advance of the Eleventh Corps north of town on July 1, now had his men assigned to suppressing, as far as they could, the Yankee cannon. Declared Blackford, "My orders were to fire incessantly, without regard to ammunition."

Jeb Stuart's cavalry column, perhaps 4,500 riders in all, uncoiled from near Rock Creek, north of Benner's Hill, and began a slow march to the northeast, following the York Pike. "We could only hear the battle, not see it," wrote one of Stuart's staff officers. Appended to the column was the independent brigade commanded until yesterday by Albert Jenkins. Colonel Milton J. Ferguson was supposed to be in charge, but he was likely guarding prisoners with the 17th Virginia Cavalry, leaving Lieutenant Colonel Vincent A. Witcher as the senior officer. Stuart's men moved at a slow pace, partly in deference to their worn-out animals but also in recognition of the fact that until the infantry made its move, they would have to watch and wait.

Ironically, the Federal cavalry force that had so nettled James Walker the day before had now been moved closer to the Baltimore Pike, leaving the Hanover Road wide open. Alfred Pleasonton, whose poor judgment had already allowed John Buford's division to depart the battlefield, had decided that keeping a closer watch over the infantry near Culp's Hill was more important than taking an advanced position to shield that flank along the Hanover Road. Brigadier General David McMurtrie Gregg, whose two brigades had been picketing that road, disagreed.

Even as he carried out his orders, Gregg protested to Pleasonton that the area where the Hanover Road was intersected by the Low Dutch

Road (about three miles east of Gettysburg) was strategically significant. According to one of his officers, Gregg argued that leaving this cross-roads uncovered "would invite an attack upon our rear with, possibly, disastrous results." Pleasonton relented to the extent that he authorized the posting of a brigade from Judson Kilpatrick's division in that position, but he would not budge from his insistence that Gregg's men stay closer to the Baltimore Pike. Convinced that leaving the back door wide open was a very bad idea, Gregg sent one of his aides to corral the allotted brigade while he directed his own pair south from the Hanover Road.

With George Steuart's brigade pinned in its earthworks by the slow but steady Twelfth Corps artillery fire, the Confederate effort on Culp's Hill shifted to the upper summit, where the Louisiana troops under Jesse Williams and James Walker's Stonewall Brigade tried to overwhelm George Greene's entrenched line. Little had changed from the previous evening, save that the Yankee boys had more light to aim by.

"I think it was the hardest battle we ever had," reflected a soldier in the 33rd Virginia. Another member of that regiment, named John Burner, was mortally wounded before he could get off a single shot. It would fall to Burner's brother-in-law to tell his sister that she was now a widow. Her husband was felled by a "ball entering his right side just below his arm, and pas[s]ing through near his heart to the left," her brother wrote. He "was conscious of his situation and wished to die that he might be relieved of his suffering. He told Lt. Buswell as soon as he was shot that he was killed, and said it seemed as if [there] were a dozen balls in his body."

With the entire Twelfth Corps now on hand, the Federals on Culp's Hill were able to mount an aggressive defense. Even as the Louisiana troops began pressing the lines in their front, a single Yankee regiment, the 66th Ohio, swung out from the summit to take a precarious position outside the trenches and at a right angle to them. Then, as later related by the regiment's commander, "protected behind stones logs trees &c we turned our fire down upon the enemy." A similar but more truncated movement on the opposite flank, by the 147th Pennsylvania, added to the killing crossfire that ripped into the broken waves of Rebels trying to force their way up the slope.

When the only Confederate reinforcements available, the regiments of William Smith's Virginia brigade, began reaching the scene in piecemeal fashion, they were posted on Steuart's left. Henry Kyd Douglas of Johnson's staff led the troops to their assigned place. He paid a price for the sense of an officer's dignity and propriety that kept him exposed on horseback: "There came little puffs of smoke, a rattle of small arms, the sensation of a tremendous blow and I sank forward on my horse, who ceased his prancing when my hold was loosened on his bridle reins," Douglas recalled. Friendly hands bore the wounded young aide to the rear, where he retained enough sensation to hear the rattle of musketry crescendo into tearing torrents as Smith's men entered the action.

Smith's men had hustled into a blocking position guarding the Confederate right flank just as a hastily organized Union threat manifested itself. The train of events on the Federal side began with the imagined right-wing commander, Henry Slocum, who at around 6:30 A.M. bypassed his own chain of authority by directly instructing Brigadier General Thomas Ruger, whose troops were holding the area just south of Culp's Hill, to attack what Slocum thought was a "shaky" Rebel flank, an assessment Ruger himself did not credit. It would be better, he argued, to probe the enemy strength before committing any large force. Slocum agreed.

Ruger decided that two regiments advancing with a skirmish line could do the job. If the widely dispersed voltigeurs provoked a strong response, the regiments could retire; if they discovered the enemy pulling out, the pair would be ready to take advantage of it. It was an eminently sensible plan. Unfortunately, however, Ruger was not familiar with the terrain, nor did he adequately brief the aide he sent to carry the orders to Silas Colgrove, whose troops were to be used for the operation. By the time the aide reached Colgrove, it seemed from the sounds to the north that some advance was already under way along the Union line, so the messenger urged a similar action on this front. The force deployed could still have been a regimental line screened by skirmishers, but after examining the ground, Colgrove concluded that there was not enough cover for the exposed advance line. The best option, as he saw it, would be a quick rush by two regiments.

From the five regiments in his brigade, Colgrove picked the 2nd Massachusetts and the 27th Indiana for the job. When the message reached Lieutenant Colonel Charles Mudge of the 2nd he was aghast. " 'Are you *sure* that is the order?' " he demanded. Assured that it was, he remarked, " 'Well, it is murder, but it's the order.' " Mudge formed his men quickly for the action and, without waiting for the Hoosiers to untangle themselves from portions of a New Jersey unit blocking their way, ordered the charge.

There was nothing shaky about this portion of the Confederate line, held mostly by Virginia troops of William Smith's brigade, who were anything but disorganized and only too eager for a little payback. For trained soldiers secure behind cover defending against an enemy advancing in the open, it was a turkey shoot. Massachusetts men fell every step of the way; color-bearer after color-bearer went down, either dead or wounded. A bullet ripped into Charles Mudge's throat, killing him. Isolated and getting further shredded by the second, the 2nd Massachusetts was saved only by the late-arriving 27th Indiana, which drew most of the fire, allowing the dazed Bay State soldiers to tumble back. The Indiana troops also suffered severely—also without gaining any advantage—before retreating on Silas Colgrove's orders.

The 2nd Massachusetts lost 45 killed and 90 wounded out of 316 men in the charge, while the 27th Indiana lost 111 killed and wounded out of 339.

Along Cemetery Ridge, opposite the Bliss farm buildings, the Confederate riflemen were again making life hell for the soldiers in the main Federal line. Once more, Alexander Hays gave orders for the farm to be retaken, and in response a party of about thirty men drawn from the 1st Delaware and 12th New Jersey tried a rush that failed. As they tumbled back, they were covered by several Federal batteries that in turn drew counterbattery fire from Rebel cannon along Seminary Ridge. The Bliss farm remained in Confederate hands.

This action spread as far south as Sherfy's peach orchard, where Parker's Virginia Battery was posted. Anticipating that they would soon become engaged, some of the gunners walked out into the fields in their front, which were dotted with Yankee dead and wounded. According to one Rebel artilleryman, "We told the wounded men to come into our lines as many as could walk as we would commence firing over them. A number of them came into our lines and we then commenced firing."

Still working out a new offensive battle plan for his right flank, Robert E. Lee conferred with James Longstreet and A. P. Hill in front of Heth's Division. Although not yet fit to resume command of his unit, Henry

Heth was present, as were several of Lee's staff, including Armistead Long, Walter Taylor, and Charles S. Venable. Because the aides kept a respectful distance, their recollections of this meeting would be fragmentary and incomplete, though few would recognize that fact. A courier standing even farther away than the favored aides would later note that a "consultation was held and the situation fully discussed."

It is likely that Lee was considering reversing himself on the use of McLaws' and Hood's Divisions. Staff officer Taylor clearly "understood the argument to be that General Longstreet should endeavor to force the enemy's lines in his front. That front was held by the divisions of Hood and McLaws." By the time Armistead Long patched into the conversation, "it was decided that General Pickett should lead the assaulting column, to be supported by the divisions of McLaws and Hood and such other force as A. P. Hill could spare from his command." Wearily, one suspects, Longstreet renewed his objections to employing those well-worn units. He later summarized his argument with the comment, "To have rushed forward my two divisions, then carrying bloody noses from their terrible conflict the day before, would have been madness."

No one would dare gainsay Longstreet regarding the condition of his own troops, though the silent challenge to Lee must have made for an awkward moment. Suddenly A. P. Hill, whose demeanor on July 2 had been less than assertive, spoke up with energy and enthusiasm, offering his entire corps for the effort. Lee graciously thanked Hill but pointed out that his troops now occupied an important central position, especially with regard to the Cashtown Gap in their rear. Nevertheless, the possibility of supplementing Pickett's fresh division with some of Hill's men was on the table.

Someone—most likely Henry Heth himself—volunteered Heth's Division for the task, and Lee quickly assented. Given his own shaky condition, it is improbable that Heth was current on the state of his command, but he may have felt that he needed to make up somehow for the coarse way he had managed affairs on July 1. The selection of Heth's Division also provided a focal point for the attack, since it was roughly opposite the Federal center; then, too, there was a concealed position to the right of Heth's line that offered room enough for Pickett's men.

With that, the question of the first assault wave was settled. Next on the agenda was the matter of close support. Hill's portion of the July 2 action had been noticeably lacking in that respect, so he may have been the one to suggest it here. Certainly only Hill could have recommended utilizing the two North Carolina brigades of Pender's Division to back up Heth. Similar help was needed for Pickett, and at this point all eyes must have turned to Longstreet, who remained unwilling, however, to consider using any part of McLaws' or Hood's Divisions. It does not require much imagination to picture Hill again stepping forward to add two of Richard Anderson's brigades to the mix. Due to their present position more than anything else, Wilcox's Alabama brigade and the Florida troops under Lang were tapped for the task.

With the players chosen, Longstreet and Hill conferred about some preliminary arrangements needed to mesh their two commands into one. One can only imagine Longstreet's surprise when they returned to Lee and learned that he expected his First Corps commander to direct the combined operation. Speaking with a bluntness that he perhaps hoped would recuse him once and for all, Longstreet declared, "General, I have been a soldier all my life. I have been with soldiers engaged in fights by couples, by squads, companies, regiments, divisions, and armies, and should know, as well as any one, what soldiers can do. It is my opinion that no fifteen thousand men ever arrayed for battle can take that position."

Lee was unmoved. What Longstreet did not know was that Lee had seen how abruptly and thoroughly Hill could be disabled by his affliction. Given the choice between a sickly general still unused to the mantle of corps command and a solid professional unhappy with his assignment, Lee did not hesitate in nominating the latter for this all-important task. "I said no more," Longstreet recalled.

According to Walter Taylor, "General Longstreet proceeded at once to make the dispositions for attack, and General Lee rode along the portion of the line held by A. P. Hill's Corps, and finally took position about the Confederate centre." It was most probably during or at the end of this ride that Lee briefed the army's artillery chief on what would be expected of him. In his report, William N. Pendleton noted that at the "direction of the commanding general, the artillery along our entire line was to be prepared for opening . . . a concentrated and destructive fire, consequent upon which a general advance was to be made."

Unable to sit on his heels, Lee rode out toward Sherfy's peach orchard, on the way encountering a skirmish line of Mississippi troops under Major George B. Gerald. The officer remembered Lee's pointing "to the crest of a hill some two hundred yards distant and slightly to the rear and [saying] he was going to place one hundred pieces of artillery there and for me to take a position so as to prevent the artillery from being harassed by federal infantry, which I did."

Another scrap began around the Bliss farm shortly after 7:30 A.M. This time there were about 200 Federals involved, largely from the 12th New Jersey, with a sprinkling from the 1st Delaware. The command formed into a compact column that raced down off Cemetery Ridge, punched through the thin Rebel skirmish line east of the buildings, and got among the enemy troops, though not without suffering some casualties in the process. There were just enough Yankees to clear the buildings but not a sufficient number to establish any effective perimeter, so the Confederates quickly rallied off to the west and began to encircle the farmstead once more.

Sergeant Frank Riley of the 12th had positioned himself at a barn loophole from which he was sniping at Rebels in nearby fields, firing as rapidly as possible with rifles handed to him by his comrades in assembly-line fashion. Then someone shouted, " 'Come down! come down quickly! They are trying to capture us!,' " and Riley ran out the back. Looking northward, he saw "what looked like a whole brigade" coming his way. As the raiding party fled back toward Cemetery Ridge, cannon on both sides filled the air around the Yankees with hissing projectiles. A well-aimed Confederate shot set off some limbers among the Federal batteries, throwing a spectacular column of smoke and flame up into the air. A head count showed that the failed effort had cost some twenty-eight more Second Corps men killed or wounded. The Rebels meanwhile reoccupied the farmstead, and the deadly game continued.

Something had convinced Richard Ewell and Edward Johnson that the Federal position on Culp's Hill could be taken, so even though their first efforts this day had been met with a savage massed firepower and repulsed with no advantages won, additional attacks were ordered. Between 8:00 and 8:30 A.M., Edward O'Neal's brigade of Alabama troops slogged up the slope, clambering over rocks slick with the blood and innards of Walker's Virginia men, to try to penetrate the wall of flame marking Culp's Hill's military crest. "The brigade moved forward in fine style," O'Neal reported, "under a terrific fire of grape and small-arms, and gained a hill near the enemy's works, which it held . . . exposed to a murderous fire."

By now the Federals defending Culp's Hill were operating in shifts. A soldier in the 7th Ohio later described the businesslike routine: "We lay behind our solid breastworks, obeying the command to reserve our fire until the first [enemy] line of battle was well up the slope and in easy range, when the command, 'Front rank—Ready—Aim low—Fire!' was given and executed, and immediately the rear rank the same, and kept up as long as the [enemy's] line remained unbroken." When the men had shot off the sixty or so rounds they carried, a reserve regiment would be drawn up under cover behind them, and at the word of command the reinforcements would rush forward to replace the first batch of troops, who would filter back a short distance one by one. There they would reform, clean their guns, replenish their cartridge boxes, and rest until it was their turn again. "This is the first time that our Regiment ever fought behind breastworks or fortifications, and all agree that it is a pretty good way to fight," wrote an Ohio officer.

Even as he monitored the Culp's Hill combat, George Meade kept abreast on events elsewhere on the battlefield. He was sufficiently sure of his conclusions that a little before 8:00 A.M., he dictated instructions for John Sedgwick's Sixth Corps to position itself so as better to reinforce Hancock's portion of the Federal line. As paraphrased by Meade's chief of staff, the message to Sedgwick indicated that "from information received . . . of the movements of the enemy, it is their intention to make an attempt to pierce our center."

Meade also found time, a little before 9:00 A.M., to pen a note to his wife. "We had a great fight yesterday," he wrote, "the enemy attacking and we completely repulsing them; both Armies shattered. . . Army in fine spirits and every one determined to do or die." Finally, Meade issued a pair of circulars, the first admonishing his corps commanders to keep their men under arms at all times, and the second directing that all stragglers be brought into the ranks and any loose weapons gathered in.

In preparation for Lee's assault, James Longstreet met with Edward P. Alexander, whom he had again designated to direct the First Corps' artillery. Alexander recollected his instructions as follows: "First, to give the enemy the most effective cannonade possible. It was not meant oim ply to make a noise, but to try & cripple him—to tear him limbless, as it were, if possible. . . . When the artillery had accomplished that, the infantry column of attack was to charge. And then, further, I was to 'advance such artillery as . . . can [be used] . . . in aiding the attack."

Alexander decided that in this case, more was better. Setting aside just two batteries to protect the extreme right of the First Corps' line, he deposed every other available gun—some seventy-six in all—along a four-

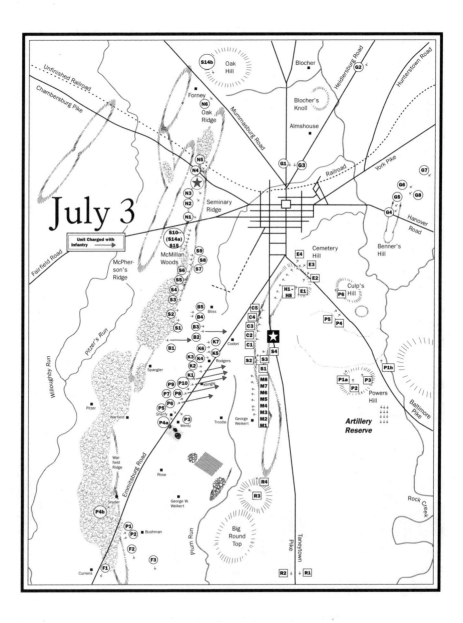

thousand-foot front between Sherfy's peach orchard and the northeast-ern end of Spangler's Woods. It was a daunting and challenging assignment, but there was at least one thing for which Alexander was grateful: the relative inactivity of the massed Federal batteries opposite him. "They had ammunition in abundance—literally to burn—& plenty more at close hand," Alexander observed. "We lay exposed to their guns, & getting ready at our leisure, & they let us do it."

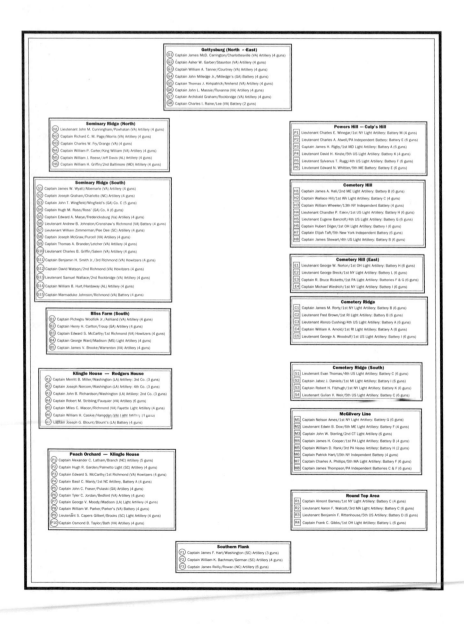

Gettysburg (North - East)
- G1 Captain James McD. Carrington/Charlottesville (VA) Artillery (4 guns)
- G2 Captain Asher W. Garber/Staunton (VA) Artillery (4 guns)
- G3 Captain William A. Tanner/Courtney (VA) Artillery (4 guns)
- G4 Captain John Milledge Jr./Milledge's (GA) Battery (4 guns)
- G5 Captain Thomas J. Kirkpatrick/Amherst (VA) Artillery (4 guns)
- G6 Captain John L. Massie/Fluvanna (VA) Artillery (4 guns)
- G7 Captain Archibald Graham/Rockbridge (VA) Artillery (4 guns)
- G8 Captain Charles I. Raine/Lee (VA) Battery (2 guns)

Seminary Ridge (North)
- N1 Lieutenant John M. Cunningham/Powhatan (VA) Artillery (4 guns)
- N2 Captain Richard C. M. Page/Morris (VA) Artillery (4 guns)
- N3 Captain Charles W. Fry/Orange (VA) (4 guns)
- N4 Captain William P. Carter/King William (VA) Artillery (4 guns)
- N5 Captain William J. Reese/Jeff Davis (AL) Artillery (4 guns)
- N6 Captain William H. Griffin/2nd Baltimore (MD) Artillery (4 guns)

Seminary Ridge (South)
- S1 Captain James W. Wyatt/Albemarle (VA) Artillery (4 guns)
- S2 Captain Joseph Graham/Charlotte (NC) Artillery (4 guns)
- S3 Captain John T. Wingfield/Wingfield's (GA) Co. C (5 guns)
- S4 Captain Hugh M. Ross/Ross' (GA) Co. A (6 guns)
- S5 Captain Edward A. Marye/Fredericksburg (Va) Artillery (4 guns)
- S6 Lieutenant Andrew B. Johnston/Crenshaw's Richmond (VA) Battery (4 guns)
- S7 Lieutenant William Zimmerman/Pee Dee (SC) Artillery (4 guns)
- S8 Captain Joseph McGraw/Purcell (VA) Artillery (4 guns)
- S9 Captain Thomas A. Brander/Letcher (VA) Artillery (4 guns)
- S10 Lieutenant Charles B. Griffin/Salem (VA) Artillery (4 guns)
- S11 Captain Benjamin H. Smith Jr./3rd Richmond (VA) Howitzers (4 guns)
- S12 Captain David Watson/2nd Richmond (VA) Howitzers (4 guns)
- S13 Lieutenant Samuel Wallace/2nd Rockbridge (VA) Artillery (4 guns)
- S14 Captain William B. Hurt/Hardaway (AL) Artillery (4 guns)
- S15 Captain Marmaduke Johnson/Richmond (VA) Battery (4 guns)

Bliss Farm (South)
- B1 Captain Pichegru Woolfolk Jr./Ashland (VA) Artillery (4 guns)
- B2 Captain Henry H. Carlton/Troup (GA) Artillery (4 guns)
- B3 Captain Edward S. McCarthy/1st Richmond (VA) Howitzers (4 guns)
- B4 Captain George Ward/Madison (MS) Light Artillery (4 guns)
- B5 Captain James V. Brooke/Warrenton (VA) Artillery (4 guns)

Klingle House — Rodgers House
- K1 Captain Merritt B. Miller/Washington (LA) Artillery: 3rd Co. (3 guns)
- K2 Captain Joseph Norcom/Washington (LA) Artillery: 4th Co. (3 guns)
- K3 Captain John B. Richardson/Washington (LA) Artillery: 2nd Co. (3 guns)
- K4 Captain Robert M. Stribling/Fauquier (VA) Artillery (4 guns)
- K5 Captain Miles C. Macon/Richmond (VA) Fayette Light Artillery (4 guns)
- K6 Captain William H. Caskie/Hampden (VA) Light Artillery (1 gun)
- K7 Captain Joseph G. Blount/Blount's (LA) Battery (4 guns)

Peach Orchard — Klingle House
- P1 Captain Alexander C. Latham/Branch (NC) Artillery (5 guns)
- P2 Captain Hugh R. Garden/Palmetto Light (SC) Artillery (4 guns)
- P3 Captain Edward S. McCarthy/1st Richmond (VA) Howitzers (4 guns)
- P4 Captain Basil C. Manly/1st NC Artillery, Battery A (4 guns)
- P5 Captain John C. Fraser/Pulaski (GA) Artillery (4 guns)
- P6 Captain Tyler C. Jordan/Bedford (VA) Artillery (4 guns)
- P7 Captain George V. Moody/Madison (LA) Artillery (4 guns)
- P8 Captain William W. Parker/Parker's (VA) Battery (4 guns)
- P9 Lieutenant S. Capers Gilbert/Brooks (SC) Light Artillery (4 guns)
- P10 Captain Osmond B. Taylor/Bath (VA) Artillery (4 guns)

Southern Flank
- F1 Captain James F. Hart/Washington (SC) Artillery (3 guns)
- F2 Captain William K. Bachman/German (SC) Artillery (4 guns)
- F3 Captain James Reilly/Rowan (NC) Artillery (6 guns)

Powers Hill -- Culp's Hill
- P1 Lieutenant Charles E. Winegar/1st NY Light Artillery: Battery M (4 guns)
- P2 Lieutenant Charles A. Atwell/PA Independent Battery: Battery E (6 guns)
- P3 Captain James H. Rigby/1st MD Light Artillery: Battery A (6 guns)
- P4 Lieutenant David H. Kinzie/5th US Light Artillery: Battery K (4 guns)
- P5 Lieutenant Sylvanus T. Rugg/1st US Light Artillery: Battery F (6 guns)
- P6 Lieutenant Edward N. Whittier/5th ME Battery: Battery E (6 guns)

Cemetery Hill
- H1 Captain James A. Hall/2nd ME Light Artillery: Battery B (6 guns)
- H2 Captain Wallace Hill/1st WV Light Artillery: Battery C (4 guns)
- H3 Captain William Wheeler/13th NY Independent Battery (4 guns)
- H4 Lieutenant Chandler P. Eakin/1st US Light Artillery: Battery H (6 guns)
- H5 Lieutenant Eugene Bancroft/4th US Light Artillery: Battery G (6 guns)
- H6 Captain Hubert Dilger/1st OH Light Artillery: Battery I (6 guns)
- H7 Captain Elijah Taft/5th New York Independent Battery (6 guns)
- H8 Captain James Stewart/4th US Light Artillery: Battery B (6 guns)

Cemetery Hill (East)
- E1 Lieutenant George W. Norton/1st OH Light Artillery: Battery H (6 guns)
- E2 Lieutenant George Breck/1st NY Light Artillery: Battery L (6 guns)
- E3 Lieutenant B. Bruce Ricketts/1st PA Light Artillery: Batteries F & G (6 guns)
- E4 Captain Michael Wiedrich/1st NY Light Artillery: Battery I (6 guns)

Cemetery Ridge
- C1 Captain James M. Rorty/1st NY Light Artillery: Battery B (6 guns)
- C2 Lieutenant Fred Brown/1st RI Light Artillery: Battery B (6 guns)
- C3 Lieutenant Alonzo Cushing/4th US Light Artillery: Battery A (6 guns)
- C4 Captain William A. Arnold/1st RI Light Artillery: Battery A (6 guns)
- C5 Lieutenant George A. Woodruff/1st US Light Artillery: Battery I (6 guns)

Cemetery Ridge (South)
- S1 Lieutenant Evan Thomas/4th US Light Artillery: Battery C (6 guns)
- S2 Captain Jabez J. Daniels/1st MI Light Artillery: Battery I (6 guns)
- S3 Captain Robert H. Fitzhugh/1st NY Light Artillery: Battery K (6 guns)
- S4 Lieutenant Gulian V. Weir/5th US Light Artillery: Battery C (6 guns)

McGilvery Line
- M1 Captain Nelson Ames/1st NY Light Artillery: Battery G (6 guns)
- M2 Lieutenant Edwin B. Dow/6th ME Light Artillery: Battery F (4 guns)
- M3 Captain John W. Sterling/2nd CT Light Artillery (6 guns)
- M4 Captain James H. Cooper/1st PA Light Artillery: Battery B (4 guns)
- M5 Captain William D. Rank/3rd PA Heavy Artillery: Battery H (2 guns)
- M6 Captain Patrick Hart/15th NY Independent Battery (4 guns)
- M7 Captain Charles A. Phillips/5th MA Light Artillery: Battery E (6 guns)
- M8 Captain James Thompson/PA Independent Batteries C & F (6 guns)

Round Top Area
- R1 Captain Almont Barnes/1st NY Light Artillery: Battery C (4 guns)
- R2 Lieutenant Aaron F. Walcott/3rd MA Light Artillery: Battery C (6 guns)
- R3 Lieutenant Benjamin F. Rittenhouse/5th US Artillery: Battery D (6 guns)
- R4 Captain Frank C. Gibbs/1st OH Light Artillery: Battery L (6 guns)

* * *

Cavalry officer David McMurtrie Gregg began breathing a little easier at around 10:00 A.M. His aide had found a brigade to screen the strategically important Hanover Road/Low Dutch Road intersection. It came from Judson Kilpatrick's division, which had been resting in Two Taverns before moving to Big Round Top. Kilpatrick himself had departed with Farnsworth's brigade before Gregg's man arrived, just in time to redirect the only remaining unit, consisting of four Michigan cavalry regiments under George A. Custer.

On reaching the crossroads, the Wolverines settled into a watchful mode, with skirmishers deployed and horse artillery set. The battery that accompanied the riders set up with its guns pointed in the direction from which trouble was expected, west along the Hanover Road toward Gettysburg.

Despite the repeated failure of his troops to achieve anything on the bloody slopes of Culp's Hill, Edward Johnson decided to mount a maximum effort. It was to be a three-brigade attack, with Steuart's mixed force swinging off the left of the line, Daniel's North Carolina troops moving up the center, and Walker's Stonewall Brigade on the right. Neither Steuart nor Daniel felt any enthusiasm for the plan; in fact, an aide present noted that both "strongly disapproved of making the assault." When Steuart's order reached the 1st Maryland Battalion, the officer commanding exclaimed that "it was nothing less than murder to send men into that slaughter pen."

Steuart's position required his men to form on the exposed side of the enemy's former earthworks before marching across an open field. "Our loss was frightful," a survivor would write to his family a few days later. "The men fell on my right and left and in front of me and I thought sure my time had come." Daniel's Tarheels, in the middle, fared no better: "It was truly awful how fast, how very fast, did our poor boys fall by our sides," remembered a North Carolina soldier. "You could see one with his head shot off, others cut in two, then one with his brains oozing out, one with his leg off, others shot through the heart. Then you would hear some poor friend or foe crying for water, or for 'God's sake' to kill him." On the right of the attacking line, the Stonewall Brigade charged; afterward a veteran officer in the ranks would avow that he had never "seen in all my fighting as bloody, or as hard contested [a] field, in my life."

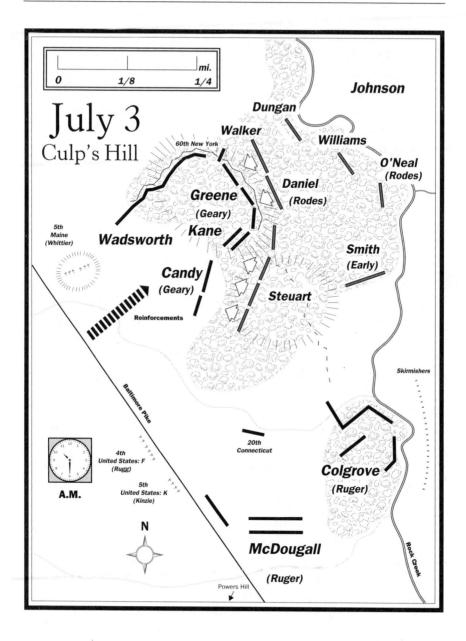

Some poignant vignettes would be enshrined in accounts of this large-scale carnage. The Yankee boys on one section of the line would never forget the pet dog that scampered out ahead of the Rebel charge, already limping on three legs. The iron fusillade showed no preference for man or animal, and the dog fell, later to be buried, it was said, "as the only Christian minded being on either side." In another sector, Federal soldiers watched with wary fascination as a badly wounded Confederate lying in their front painfully reloaded his gun, stuck the muzzle under his chin, and, using the ramrod to push the trigger, blew his brains out.

Edward Johnson finally conceded that the "enemy were too strongly intrenched and in too great numbers to be dislodged by the force at my command. . . . No further assault was made; all had been done that it was possible to do." George Steuart, whose brigade had done more than its share in the hopeless cause, was heard to cry repeatedly, " 'My poor boys! My poor boys!' "

The Culp's Hill fight was terribly one-sided when it came to counting the cost. On the Union side, the Twelfth Corps recorded losses of 1,082, with just 204 of those killed. On the Confederate side, Edward Johnson's division alone suffered some 2,002 casualties. Added to this were the losses taken by Smith's (213), O'Neal's (about 400), and Daniel's (also approximately 400) Brigades. The 2nd Virginia in the Stonewall Brigade counted itself very lucky in having just 16 wounded (3 mortally), 3 missing, and 1 killed. The dead man was John Wesley Culp, a native Pennsylvanian whose Gettysburg family had lent its name to the hill. Young Culp had died on the morning of July 2 while skirmishing east of Rock Creek, and contrary to some reports, did not meet his end on the land owned by his father's first cousin.

On Cemetery Ridge, Alexander Hays organized another attempt to take control of the Bliss farm. This time the attack force consisted of sixty men from the 14th Connecticut who happened to be carrying some of the most technologically advanced weapons on the battlefield: breech-loading Sharps rifles that gave them a firepower out of proportion to their numbers. Rather than moving in compact columns, the Connecticut men went at the barn in a wild rush that made them difficult to target.

These Federals, too, soon learned the bitter lesson of the Bliss farm—namely, that getting there was the least of the problem. Driven from the recaptured wooden house by heavy Rebel cannon fire and musketry, the Federals forted themselves in the stone-and-brick barn and, aided by some Yankee skirmish lines that had eased forward with them, grimly held the place as the sun heated the July air to near 80 degrees.

*   *   *

Tillie Pierce would remember that the "sun was high in the heavens" when she awoke from her exhausted slumber. Almost the moment she opened her eyes, she began thinking of the badly wounded soldier who had beseeched her to visit him this morning. She hurried to where she had seen him lying the previous evening, knowing in her heart what she would find: he had died during the night. Stricken, she made her way back slowly to the main house, where she learned that the Weikerts were evacuating and heading for Two Taverns. After packing up the few belongings she had brought along, Pierce headed for a waiting carriage, but before she could reach it, there was an artillery overshoot from the other side of the Round Tops that shattered her carefully constructed composure. "I was so frightened that I gave a shriek and sprang into the barn," she later recalled. Friendly hands helped her into the carriage, which was soon jouncing along the Taneytown Road, carrying her farther and farther away from the fighting.

In Gettysburg, the comparative lull following the end of the Rebel assault on Culp's Hill induced some townsfolk to venture out of their cellars for a deferred breakfast. There would be no such repast at Louis and Georgia McClellan's house on Baltimore Street, about midway up the slope of Cemetery Hill. Given their location inside the Union-controlled sector on the southern edge of town, the McClellans had thought it safe enough for them to remain at home, where they even made room for other family members, including Georgia's sister, Mary Virginia ("Jennie") Wade.

While Mrs. McClellan lay in bed upstairs nursing her newborn son, Jennie busied herself in the kitchen on the house's southern side, preparing dough for biscuits. Shortly after 8:00 A.M., a stray sharpshooter's bullet penetrated the door on the northern side of the house and passed through a small inner room, retaining enough force to pierce an inside door behind which Jennie was standing. The minié ball hit her in the back and blew out through her breast, piercing her heart on its way.

The young woman fell dead without a scream, never realizing what had happened to her. Gettysburg's only civilian fatality was a matter of record: Jennie Wade, twenty years old.

Following a line of march that for the most part concealed them, the columns constituting George Pickett's division began arriving at the southern end of Seminary Ridge between 9:00 and 10:00 A.M. There was some confusion as the brigades filled in a line running from south to north, with the leftmost brigade, Lewis Armistead's, jostling for space with troops of Hill's who had already occupied the area. It was decided that Armistead's men would form behind Garnett's and Kemper's.

Also advancing into place was Heth's Division, today led by J. Johnston Pettigrew. According to staff aide Louis Young, Pettigrew had at first been under the impression that his assignment was to support Pickett, but that misunderstanding was quickly corrected, and he was instructed that once the advance began, he was to keep "dressed to the right, and moving in line with Major-General Pickett's division."

As each Virginia regiment reached its designated area, the men went to ease, some flopping onto the ground to rest while others spread out to find water, shade from the hot sun, or both. One soldier found a well near a battery and took the opportunity to speak with the gunners about the Federal position on Cemetery Ridge. When he returned to the ranks, he remarked, "I would not give 25 cents for my life if the charge is made." Others had no apprehensions. "It was rumored that this division had been selected because they were Virginians, and that they were expected to be successful where others had failed," a member of the 9th Virginia proclaimed. An officer wandered near an apple tree under which Generals Longstreet, Lee, and Pickett were gathered. He distinctly recalled hearing Longstreet express doubts about the effort, and Pickett insist that his soldiers could do the job. Some in John Dooley's company came across a tree laden with small green apples, which they discovered were no good for eating but fine for pelting one another with. "So frivolous men can be even in the hour of death," Dooley reflected soberly.

Alexander Hays had had enough. For nearly an hour, the detachment of Connecticut troops he had sent out to the Bliss farm had held on to the advanced position, using the stone-and-brick barn as their stronghold. Far from accepting the situation, the Confederates had fed more and more men into the fight, until it began to look as if Hays would soon have a full-scale engagement on his hands. Enough was enough: Winfield Hancock had already given him discretionary authority to burn the buildings if he thought it prudent, and now he decided that the time had come to take that measure.

Two couriers raced forward with the orders, one a sergeant who went on foot, the other a mounted staff officer who drew more attention. That officer, Captain James Parke Postles, headed toward the barn at a gentle lope. He would afterward declare that "it was a constant wonder and surprise to me that none of the bullets, which I heard whistling around and so close to me, had hit me." Reaching the barn, Postles shouted as loud as he could, "Colonel Smyth orders you to burn the house and barn and retire." Then he wheeled about, not sparing the spur on his return ride. Once he felt he was out of easy range, he stopped, turned, and shook his hat defiantly at the Rebels who had tried so hard to kill him.

The officer commanding the Connecticut men in the barn wasted no time executing his new orders. A squad scrambled from the barn to the house, pulled out the wounded and the dead, and set fire to anything that would burn. Back at the barn, the hay was set ablaze, and then everyone hustled off toward Cemetery Ridge. A few of the most opportunistic Yankees had enough presence of mind to haul along the Bliss farm chickens as they fled. Behind them, the two buildings burned in the hot July air.

It was approaching 11:00 A.M. when Edward P. Alexander notified James Longstreet that the First Corps' artillery was positioned for the bombardment. Of the 86 artillery pieces under First Corps jurisdiction, Alexander had 76 aimed at positions from Little Round Top to Cemetery Hill. In addition, Robert E. Lee and his artillery chief, William Pendleton, had enlisted guns from the other two corps—55 from Hill's command, and 33 from Ewell's—for a total of 164 guns in all. All had been assigned targets and given careful instructions that once the cannonade began, they were to fire slowly and deliberately.

While satisfied with his work, Alexander fretted about things over which he had little control. He worried about having enough of the right kind of ammunition, especially after yesterday's fighting, which had made serious inroads on his store. He wondered how accurate his crews would be at the relatively long ranges they would face today. ("The great majority of the batteries took the field without having ever fired a round in practice [because of powder shortages], and passed through the war without aiming a gun at any target but the enemy," reflected Alexander.) And most of all, he was unhappy about the Bormann fuse, a feature common to all the munitions his gunners used, which had a very high failure rate. If the shells did not explode over their targets, the effectiveness of a bombardment on the scale anticipated for this day would be greatly diminished.

Alexander was extremely proud of having eased all his guns into their positions without drawing any significant counterbattery fire from the Yankees. The only casualty he would recall in the entire deployment was one of the horses in Captain Henry H. Carlton's Troup (Georgia) Artillery, which lost a buttock to a Union shell while making a controlled turn. "I never saw so much blood fly," Alexander declared, "or so much grass painted red before, & the pretty drill Carlton was wishing to show off was very much spoiled."

Now that they had been included among those scheduled to take part in Lee's grand assault, the troops of Joseph R. Davis' brigade were moved into position preparatory to advancing. In the 11th Mississippi, the only regiment in the brigade not engaged on July 1, Lieutenant William Peel and his men (still ignorant about their assignment) "distributed ourselves to the best advantage, behind trees, stumps, &c, some digging holes with spades that were scattered around . . . making ourselves as safe as possible."

From where he was resting, Lieutenant John Dooley of the 1st Virginia watched with interest as Generals Lee and Longstreet conferred with his division commander, George Pickett. Lee's decision to attack the Federal position in its center was but the beginning of a crash-planning phase that required the two key officers to draw heavily on their experience and knowledge. Critical to the success of the operation would be the principle of convergence. If the 15,000 or so troops merely advanced straight ahead, they would reach the enemy lines with little advantage in numbers, always a crucial factor for troops operating on the offensive. This meant that the advance needed to shrink its frontage during the action, so that by the time the men from the three different divisions reached the Yankee line, their formation would be as compact as possible.

There were other problems to be worked out as well. At the point of departure, the left of Pickett's Division was nearly fifteen hundred feet from the right of Heth's Division, a gap that would have to be closed through maneuver under fire. Also, the left of Heth's line was cramped by troops from Hill's and Ewell's Corps who were holding a sunken road in its front. Heth's left brigade would have to sidle around this obstacle with great care.

While later writers would refer knowingly to a small clump of trees amid the Federal line as the universal aiming point, it is unclear precisely how many units were actually navigating by that objective. For George

Pickett's troops, whose forward movement would also have to include several complicated slides to their left, the clearly visible roof of the Codori farm barn served as a far more useful guide. One immediate and practical outcome of the deliberation by Lee, Longstreet, and Pickett was a task given to the 1st Virginia: "Soon we are ordered to ascend the rising slope and pull down a fence in our front," recalled John Dooley, "and this begins to look like work."

Along Cemetery Ridge, the Federal soldiers took their ease. Staff officer and Lieutenant Frank Haskell was absorbing the impressions. "The men upon the crest lay snoring in their blankets," he observed, "even though some of the enemy's bullets dropped among them, as if bullets were harmless as the drops of dew around them. As the sun arose to-day the clouds became broken, and we had once more glimpses of sky, and fits of sunshine—a rarity, to cheer us."

The section of Cemetery Ridge held by Hancock's Second Corps covered about half a mile, into which were placed five infantry brigades and some twenty-eight cannon. Its northern end was situated in a small piece of woodland named Ziegler's Grove. Here, posted mainly behind a stone wall, were two of Alexander Hays' three brigades. Colonel Thomas A. Smyth's Second Brigade, which had been heavily tasked in the Bliss farm operations, held the wall, backed by the late George Willard's battered unit, now led by Colonel Eliakim Sherrill. The missing brigade was Samuel Carroll's, still detached to eastern Cemetery Hill, save for the 8th Ohio, performing skirmish duty near the Emmitsburg Road.

The stone wall ran southward a short distance toward a group of small trees—soon to be capitalized as the Copse of Trees—that had managed to grow in the rocky soil. It jogged sharply right (the "inner angle") before resuming its original southern course, creating a nearly 90-degree bend that the veterans would come to know as the Angle (the "outer angle"). This was the responsibility of Alexander Webb's brigade of John Gibbon's division, three Pennsylvania regiments providing close support for two batteries on either side of the copse. A fourth regiment was held in reserve. Except for the 71st Pennsylvania, which had seen brief and unhappy service on Culp's Hill on July 2, this brigade had been only lightly engaged thus far in the battle.

Next to the south were the brigades of Colonel Norman J. Hall and Brigadier General William Harrow. All of Harrow's regiments had seen action on July 2, as had some of Hall's. Prolonging the line below Harrow was a late-arriving portion of the First Corps, three Vermont regiments commanded by Brigadier General George J. Stannard. These volunteer units had been called up for just nine months' service, a term that was due to expire soon. One of the regiments, the 13th Vermont, had gotten in on the end of yesterday's action, but the other two had yet to see combat.

"I could not help wishing all the morning that this line of . . . the 2nd Corps were stronger," Frank Haskell worried. "But I was not Gnl. Meade, who alone had power to send other troops there; and he was satisfied, with that part of the line as it was." Since nothing seemed to be stirring on the Rebel side, the idea spread among Gibbon's staff that a picnic lunch would be in order. From various nooks came potatoes, bread, butter, coffee, tea, and some chickens, which Haskell pronounced "in good *running* orders." An invitation was extended to Winfield Hancock, who accepted with alacrity; when George Meade came by on an inspection tour, room was made for him as well, and then for several other officers whose noses brought them to the scene.

The food was consumed, cigars were lit, and the generals talked shop, with the small gaggle of aides hanging on their every word. According to Haskell, "Meade still thought that the enemy would attack his left again to day, towards evening. . . . Hancock [thought] that the attack would be upon the position of the 2nd Corps." Then, one by one, the officers departed for their commands, leaving only the original instigators, Gibbon and his staff. "We dozed in the heat," recollected Haskell, "and lolled upon the ground, with half open eyes."

Jeb Stuart's cavalry column, now heading in a southeasterly direction from the York Pike, began collecting in the woods on the northern end of Cress Ridge, about a mile and a half distant from the intersection of Low Dutch Road and the Hanover Road. Stuart's aide Henry B. McClellan deemed the position a good one: "The roads leading from the rear of the Federal line of battle were under . . . [Stuart's] eye and could be reached by . . . the road by which he had approached. Moreover, the open fields, although intersected by many fences, admitted of movement in any direction," he wrote. Although he did not expect it to last long, McClellan noted that for the moment, "the scene was as peaceful as if no war existed."

Missed in this pastoral survey was George Custer's brigade, now posted on low ground near the crossroads. David McMurtrie Gregg was with Custer, having been relieved of most of his picketing duties once the threat to Culp's Hill had faded. Gregg had brought along one of his brigades, an important piece of field intelligence, and some orders. The information had come through Oliver Otis Howard, on Cemetery Hill, whose signal officers had spotted "large columns of the enemy's cavalry . . . moving toward the right of our line." In response to the sighting, Alfred Pleasonton, in one of his rare sound decisions, had dispatched Gregg with a brigade back to the Hanover Road. He immediately negated the value of that action, however, by instructing Gregg to release Custer's brigade to rejoin its proper division, then on the Union left. Gregg was unhappy about the latter order but was nonetheless carrying it out when Jeb Stuart lent a hand.

Up until this moment in his flank march, Stuart had operated with circumspection; while he had not made any extraordinary effort to cloak his movements, he had undertaken them in such a way as to avoid any casual observation. Accordingly, he had two brigades concealed behind the woods on the northern side of Cress Ridge, within easy striking distance of the Hanover Road. Until now, Stuart's aide McClellan had thought he understood his chief's plan, but what Stuart did next would puzzle him to the end of his days. As McClellan watched, Stuart called up one of the four guns in Captain Thomas A. Jackson's Charlottesville Horse Battery* and had it fire "a number of random shots in different directions, himself giving orders to the gun." Almost with his next breath, Stuart instructed Vincent A. Witcher to advance a dismounted force to take control of the John Rummel farm, half a mile distant.

Responding to the cannon shots and the appearance of the Rebel skirmishers, George Custer had his horse battery return the compliments, and at the same time sent forward his own voltigeurs from the 5th and 6th Michigan Cavalry Regiments. When he met with Gregg, Custer expressed his feeling that there would be fighting here soon. Gregg replied "that if such was his opinion, I would like to have the assistance of his brigade." Although he was under orders to proceed to Big Round Top, Custer was not one to ride away from a fight. " 'If you will give me an order to remain I will only be too happy to do it,' " he said.

---

*In his writings, McClellan would consistently misidentify this unit as Captain William H. Griffin's 2nd Baltimore Maryland Artillery, which was back at Gettysburg by this time.

Gregg gave the order. Things were beginning to heat up along the Hanover Road.

Many of the correspondents on the scene took advantage of the relative lull to polish their notes, get something to eat, or simply rest. One exception was the reporter covering the action for the *Augusta* (Georgia) *Daily Constitutionalist,* who watched in amazement as battery after battery was eased into position in a continuous row stretching the length of the Confederate line. From his various sources, he learned of the impending attack against the Federals.

For many of the Northern newsmen, George Meade's headquarters was the best place to catch a whiff of what was happening. Sam Wilkeson of the *New York Times* was frantic with worry over unconfirmed reports that his son, Bayard, had been badly wounded on July 1 and was now in Confederate hands. He was particularly struck by the paradoxical peacefulness around the Leister house, a calm highlighted by "the singing of a bird, which had a nest in a peach tree within the tiny yard of the whitewashed cottage." Whitelaw Reid noted only the steady activity: "Meade was receiving reports in the little house, coming occasionally to the door to address a hasty inquiry to some one in the group of staff officers under the tree." "Aid[e]s were coming and going; a signal-officer in the yard was waving his flags in response to one on Round-top," added the *Boston Journal's* Charles Coffin. A reporter present for the *New York World* recorded the curious advent of a "flock of pigeons" in numbers large enough to darken "the sky above" over the battlefield.

Some important details regarding the assault ordered by Lee had yet to be ironed out. Critical to the proper coordination of the advance would be the joining of Heth's Division to Pickett's, or, more specifically, of Heth's rightmost brigade (Archer's) to Pickett's leftmost (Garnett's). With Archer now in a Federal POW stockade, Colonel Birkett D. Fry commanded the mixed force of Alabama and Tennessee regiments that had been so roughly handled on July 1. At the direction of Brigadier General J. Johnston Pettigrew (commanding the division while Heth convalesced), Fry went looking for George Pickett. The Virginia general "appeared in excellent spirits," Fry recollected, "and . . . expressed great confidence in the ability of our troops to drive the enemy when they had been 'demoralized by our artillery.' "

Some minutes later, Richard Garnett joined them. The forty-four-year-old West Point graduate was moving slowly, beset by constant leg pain from a kick by a horse. The trio agreed that Fry's would be the brigade of direction, meaning that all other units assigned to the first wave would orient themselves in relation to it.

As he made his way back to his command, Fry was unable to shake the memory of a meeting he had had the day before with A. P. Hill, during which the two had taken a careful survey of the Federal line on Cemetery Hill. Asked his opinion, Fry had conceded that the enemy position looked very strong. In reply, Hill had snapped shut his field glass and asserted that it was "entirely too strong to attack in front."

Once the Army of the Potomac's artillery chief, Henry Hunt, was satisfied that the situation on Culp's Hill was under control, he rode over to Cemetery Ridge. He was quite surprised by what he saw along the enemy's side: "Our whole front for two miles was covered by batteries already in line or going into position. . . . Never before had such a sight been witnessed on this continent, and rarely, if ever, abroad. What did it mean?" he wondered. His astonishment was of short duration; almost at once, he began moving several reserve units forward to within close supporting distance of Cemetery Ridge.

William Mahone was shocked when he learned of the assault plans that were taking shape. The brigadier general, whose command in Richard Anderson's division (Hill's Corps) would suffer fewer casualties in this battle than any other infantry brigade in Lee's army, "begged" his division commander to accompany him to a point of observation. "I said to him what was plain to my mind," Mahone later recounted. "That no troops ever formed a line of battle that could cross the plain of fire to which the attacking force would be subjected, and . . . that I could not believe General Lee would insist on such an assault after he had seen the ground." Anderson, however, refused to confront Lee on the matter, "saying, in substance, that we had nothing to do but to obey the order."

"Never was I so depressed as upon that day," James Longstreet would afterward admit. "With my knowledge of the situation, I could see the desperate and hopeless nature of the charge and the cruel slaughter it would cause." Nonetheless, he did everything he could to maximize the chances of success: "Division commanders were asked to go to the crest of the ridge and take a careful view of the field, and to have their officers there to tell their men of it, and to prepare them for the sight that was to burst upon them as they mounted the crest," he explained.

All necessary steps had been taken to synchronize the infantry advance and designate the artillery targets. It remained only to coordinate the artillery with the infantry. Longstreet had thus far shouldered the burden of this operation alone, but as he stood poised to act on his final orders, he sought to apportion some responsibility. "I was so much impressed with the hopelessness of the charge, that I wrote the following note to . . . [Edward P.] Alexander," he recalled.

> If the artillery fire does not have the effect to drive off the enemy or greatly demoralize him, so as to make our efforts pretty certain, I would prefer that you should not advise General Pickett to make the charge. I shall rely a great deal on your judgment to determine the matter, and shall expect you to let Pickett know when the moment comes.

Then, remembered Longstreet, "I rode to a woodland hard by, to lie down and study for some new thought that might aid the assaulting column."

The slow crescendo of carbine and rifle popping to the south along the Emmitsburg Road signaled a threat to Lee's extreme right flank that could not be ignored. Union Brigadier General Wesley Merritt's cavalry brigade, encamped this morning at Emmitsburg, had followed that road toward Gettysburg, making contact with Confederate pickets about a mile south of where Hood's Division had staged its attack the day before.

Merritt was moving his small brigade of mostly regular-army units* with no more serious purpose than to "annoy" the enemy's right and rear. Of course, no one on the Confederate side was privy to the Federal cavalryman's orders, so when news reached James Longstreet, whose flank it was, he had to react. "It was called a charge," he remembered,

---

*Minus the 6th United States Cavalry, which he had sent off toward Fairfield in search of a poorly guarded Rebel supply train that was reported to be there.

"but was probably a reconnaissance." Robert E. Lee had passed on to Longstreet a detachment of South Carolina cavalry under Colonel John L. Black, about a hundred troopers in all. These Longstreet sent along to assist Evander Law, who had taken over Hood's Division and was responsible for that sector.

By the time Black reached the infantry skirmish line, the Confederate pickets from the 9th Georgia were gamely trading shots with the Union troopers, who had dismounted once the action began. After adding his hundred to the screen, Black went looking for Evander Law, who was on his way with help: the divisional commander had pulled two more of G. T. Anderson's Georgia regiments off the area near the Round Tops and was bringing them himself. Law, knowing that the Yankee cavalryman was utilizing his greater mobility to stretch out the defenders, feared that his own "line beyond that road would soon become so weak that it might easily be broken by a bold cavalry attack."

Edward P. Alexander was standing near some of his guns, conversing idly with Ambrose Wright of Richard Anderson's division, when Longstreet's message was handed to him. "This note rather startled me," Alexander later recalled. "If that assault was to be made on General's Lee's judgment it was all right, but I did not want it on mine." He checked with Wright, who advised him to send Longstreet a reply stating his reservations. This Alexander did.

> General: I will only be able to judge the effect of our fire on the enemy by his return fire, as his infantry is little exposed to view and the smoke will obscure the field. If, as I infer from your note, there is any alternative to this attack, it should be carefully considered before opening our fire, for it will take all the artillery ammunition we have left to test this one, and if the result is unfavorable we will have none left for another effort. And even if this is entirely successful, it can only be so at a very bloody cost.

Throughout the morning of planning and preparations, Robert E. Lee had never wavered in his belief that the assault he had ordered against the enemy's center would succeed. "A careful examination was made of the ground secured [on July 2] by Longstreet," he later reported, "and his batteries placed in positions, which, it was believed, would enable them to silence those of the enemy. Hill's artillery and part of Ewell's [were] ordered to open simultaneously, and the assaulting column to advance under cover of the combined fire of the three. The batteries were directed to be pushed forward as the infantry progressed, protect their flanks, and support their attacks closely."

His own survey of the ground, supplemented by information regarding yesterday's advances by Wright's Brigade, convinced Lee that his men would not suffer serious losses covering the distance from Seminary Ridge to the Emmitsburg Road. There were ripples and folds in the land that would shield them from the worst, at least until they lost that cover crossing the Emmitsburg Road, with something like a thousand feet to go.

For that last stretch, Lee was counting on the aftereffects of his unprecedented artillery bombardment, which he assumed would have scoured the facing slope of enemy ordnance. Here his expectation was likely no different from that of his artillery chief, William Pendleton: "With the enemy, there was advantage of elevation and protection from earthworks; but his fire was unavoidably more or less divergent, while ours was convergent," Pendleton observed. "His troops were massed, ours diffused. We, therefore, [should suffer] . . . much less."

If the bombardment did its work, if the flanks were protected, and if enough of the artillery advanced with the infantry, Lee believed that his superb soldiers would cleave the Yankee army in twain. He hoped the Federal soldiers would lose their nerve and felt utterly confident that his own would press the attack all the way to Cemetery Ridge. He had planned carefully, brought the best elements together, and made clear to all what he had in mind. There was no more for him to do; it was all in God's hands now.

James Longstreet was not surprised by the tone or content of Edward P. Alexander's reply to his note. He was not yet prepared, however, to abandon this last possibility of postponing the effort. "I still desired to save my men," he later explained, "and felt that if the artillery did not produce the desired effect, I would be justified in holding Pickett off." So he sent a second message to Alexander:

Colonel: The intention is to advance the infantry if the artillery has the desired effect of driving the enemy's off, or having other effect such as

to warrant us in making the attack. When the moment arrives advise
Gen. Pickett and of course advance such artillery as you can use in aiding the attack.

Longstreet's follow-up did not lessen the unease Edward P. Alexander was feeling. "I hardly knew whether this left me discretion or not," he
reflected, "but at any rate it seemed decided that the artillery must
open." He passed the note on to Ambrose Wright. " 'He has put the
responsibility back upon you,' " Wright said after reading it. Alexander
later recalled, "I felt that if we went [as far as opening fire] . . . we could
not draw back, but the infantry must go too." He looked at Wright,
whose brigade had made it across those very fields not twenty-four hours
earlier. " 'What do you think of it?' " he asked. " 'Is it as hard to get there
as it looks?' "

    " 'Well, Alexander, it is mostly a question of supports,' " Wright
responded. " 'It is not as hard to get there as it looks,' " he said, then
added, " 'There is a place where you can get breath and re-form.' " Perhaps he paused here, thinking of the confusion of last night's fighting and
the frustration of standing at the threshold but having no one to help him
over. " 'The real difficulty is to stay there after you get there—for the
whole infernal Yankee army is up there in a bunch,' " he finished.

    Still uncertain, the artillerist rode over to George Pickett. He had no
intention of sharing the contents of Longstreet's communications with
him, but he needed to know if Pickett himself believed he could do it.
"He was in excellent spirits & sanguine of success," Alexander noted.
That settled it. He scribbled a last message to Longstreet:

> General: When our fire is at its best, I will advise Gen. Pickett to
> advance.

The temperature was passing 80 degrees, which, combined with the high
humidity, exacted a toll on the soldiers waiting behind the Confederate
guns. "The tension on our troops had become great," wrote a staff officer in Pickett's Division.

Alexander's concluding message to Longstreet had stated his position
with stark clarity. With all the burden back on him, Longstreet decided to

take one last survey of his options. "I rode once or twice along the ground between Pickett and the Federals, examining the positions and studying the matter over in all its phases so far as we could anticipate," he recollected. It was approaching 1:00 P.M. when Longstreet sent off the fateful message, this time directing it to the actual commander of the First Corps' artillery, James B. Walton.

> Colonel, Let the batteries open. Order great care and precision in firing. When the batteries at the Peach Orchard cannot be used against the point we intend to attack, let them open on the enemy's on the rocky hill.

George Pickett's inspector general, Walter Harrison, made a face that clearly conveyed his opinion of the cup of Gettysburg well water he had just been handed by Cadmus Wilcox. Harrison would later celebrate it as the "coldest, hardest water that ever sprung out of limestone rock." Harrison, Wilcox, and Richard Garnett were sitting near Sherfy's peach orchard, sharing a piece of cold mutton from Wilcox's larder. Harrison finally decided to mix a little Pennsylvania whiskey with the water—the only way, he suggested, to keep it from "freezing my whole internal economy, and petrifying my heart of hearts."

The three were enjoying the moment when, as Harrison remembered it, the "first signal-gun broke mysteriously upon the long tedium of the day."

Longstreet's courier found James B. Walton near Sherfy's peach orchard, where he was holding station with Major Benjamin F. Eshleman's Washington (Louisiana) Artillery. Walton gave the order to Eshleman, who had it carried out by two guns of the battalion's third company, commanded by Captain Merritt B. Miller. Eshleman would later report that the two signal guns had been fired "in quick succession," though some of the crew would remember that a bad friction primer had made for a pause between the shots. In any case, the interim likely felt longer than it was, but then the second shot sounded. According to Eshleman, this was "immediately followed by all the battalions along the line opening simultaneously upon the enemy behind his works."

(1:07 P.M.–2:40 P.M.)

Lieutenant William Peel and the 591 other members of the 11th Mississippi Regiment, in Joseph R. Davis' brigade, were crouched down on Seminary Ridge, just behind Captain Hugh M. Ross' six-gun battery, part of the Georgia "Sumter" Battalion. Peel had barely registered the sound of the signal guns when, almost "at the same instant, along the whole line, there burst a long loud peel of artificial thunder forth, that made the ground to tremble beneath its force." Lieutenant John Dooley's 1st Virginia (209 strong) was backing up the core of Edward P. Alexander's cannon row, perhaps a thousand feet west of the Klingle farm. "Never will I forget those scenes and sounds," Dooley later swore. "The earth seems unsteady beneath this furious cannonade, and the air might be said to be agitated by the wings of death."

On the receiving end of all this attention, Lieutenant Frank Haskell was lounging with John Gibbon and the rest of Gibbon's staff. At the sound of the signal guns, all present sprang to their feet. Then the first salvos of the Rebel barrage consumed the few seconds it took to cover the distance from ridge to ridge, Seminary to Cemetery. "The wildest confusion for a few minutes obtained among us," Haskell recorded. "The shells came bursting all about. . . . The horses, hitched to the trees or held by the slack hands of orderlies, neighed out in fright, and broke away and plunged riderless through the fields. The General at the first, had snatched his sword, and started on foot for the front. . . . I found [my horse] . . . tied to a tree near by, eating oats, with an air of the greatest composure, which under the circumstances, even then struck me as exceedingly ridiculous."

To Sarah Broadhead, again huddled in her home's cellar, it seemed "as if the heavens and earth were crashing together." Albertus McCreary noted that the "vibrations could be felt and the atmosphere was so full of smoke that we could taste the saltpeter." Charles McCurdy thought it "the most terrific cannonading that we had heard," while John Rupp declared it an "awful thunder." Henry Jacobs' cellar, from which he had seen the soldier killed on the sloping door, had been invaded by two maiden ladies who made a macabre game of the proceedings. "It was possible to distinguish the fire of the opposing sides," Jacobs remembered, "and as the cannonade made its thunderous calls and responses, they would exclaim: 'Their side—our side! Their side—our side!' "

It was Henry Hunt's intention that the Federal artillery should reply only sparingly, if at all, to the massive Rebel challenge. He recognized the effort for what it was: a well-planned barrage meant to "crush our batteries and shake our infantry." In such a situation, the greatest contribution his guns could make would be to smash the enemy's infantry when it appeared. That meant that his crews had to refrain from gun-to-gun fights that would use up their ready supplies of spherical case and shell.

But if Hunt's self-control and self-discipline were of the highest order, his subcommanders' restraint was often lacking. Perhaps most disappointing to Hunt in this regard was Major Thomas Osborn, the otherwise capable commander of the Eleventh Corps' artillery, which was under fire from the east (Benner's Hill), north (Oak Hill and along the Chambersburg Pike), and west (Seminary Ridge). Osborn's practiced eye saw that while the Rebels had the range down pat, their elevation was high, so most of their shells were passing some twenty feet overhead. Most, but not all: the Confederate cannon on Benner's Hill "raked the whole line of [the Eleventh Corps] batteries, killed and wounded the men and horses and blew up the caissons rapidly. I saw one shell go through six horses standing broadside." Osborn soon had his cannoneers actively returning the fire.

The enemy shelling was especially concentrated on the Second Corps batteries positioned along the center of Meade's Cemetery Ridge line. In this area were posted the six guns under Alonzo Cushing (4th United States, Battery A), the six under Captain William A. Arnold (1st Rhode Island, Battery A), and the six under Lieutenant George H. Woodruff (1st United States, Battery I). These guns, too, began to retaliate. A member of Cushing's crew later wrote that the "fire that we were under was something frightful, and such as we had never experienced before. . . . Every few seconds a shell would strike right in among our guns, but we could not stop for anything. We could not even close our eyes when death seemed to be coming." A cannoneer on Cemetery Hill would always remember the mixed sounds of the different shell types as they rushed overhead, "making discordant music that must have pleased the death angel." Another artilleryman retained a vivid memory of how the concussion from his battery's blasts sent "waves" rippling outward into the grass fields in his front "like gusts of wind." The experience was less poetic for the Union soldiers positioned in the cannon's blast zone, where the concussion "caused blood to flow from the ears and noses" of some men.

There was an ominous silence from one powerful row of Yankee guns. Building on the wall of cannon he had used to plug a hole in Meade's line the day before, Freeman McGilvery had packed eight batteries into a compact front of some fifteen hundred feet. Although the thirty-nine guns were aligned along the military crest of Cemetery Ridge, two slight swells of ground rising just to the west blocked easy viewing of them from Seminary and Warfield Ridges, so for the most part they were not targeted in the Confederate fire plan. That was just fine with McGilvery, who ordered his batteries not to return the shelling that was landing everywhere but on them.

There was no fixed time for the start of the Confederate bombardment, so just about everyone was surprised by it. Robert E. Lee was working at his headquarters when the guns opened. He crossed the Chambersburg Pike and made his way to a piece of high ground on the northern side of the railroad cut, from which he observed Captain William J. Reese's Jeff Davis (Alabama) Artillery in long-range operation. According to a letter to a hometown Alabama newspaper, Lee praised the sweating gunners for "their unsurpassed chivalry." A. P. Hill took station just south of Lee, near the Lutheran seminary, where he watched the crew of Captain David Watson's 2nd Richmond (Virginia) Howitzers go into action.

From his position just north of Sherfy's peach orchard, Edward P. Alexander could detect no moderation on the part of the Yankee batteries opposing him. As best he could tell, the "whole [enemy] line from Cemetery Hill to Round Top seemed in five minutes [from the commencement of the bombardment] to be emulating a volcano in eruption." Alexander also noted that his battalion was taking hits. A South Carolina infantryman near the peach orchard looked on as one Union gun got the range on a nearby Southern battery. The first three enemy shells "went high over our gun," he reported. "All the others struck the ground in front of our gun and then safely ricocheted over our gunners, but at the same time covering them with dirt and dust." The soldier thought that the "coolness of the officers and men was wonderful." A Florida man in Perry's Brigade "would look at the cannon around us, some of which were not over twenty feet away; could see the smoke and flame belch from their mouths, but could not distinguish a particular sound, it was one continuous and awful roar."

A gunner in Crenshaw's Richmond (Virginia) Battery would remember that "shell, [canister] and solid shot were hurled as thick as hail over our battalion." Seconding him was John L. Marye, whose Fredericksburg Artillery had fired that first shot at John Buford's troopers on July 1. Now, wrote Marye, "the uproar was terrific. Round shot whistled by and plowed the ground. The air was alive with screaming, bursting shells and flying fragments. . . . Cannoneers with jackets off and perspiration streaming down their faces, blackened with powder, kept the guns cool by plunging the spongeheads in buckets of water, and as fast as a man fell another took his place; guns were dismounted, limbers and caissons blown up and horses ripped open and disemboweled."

Located in a particularly exposed position in the open fields just north of the Rogers farm, Major James Dearing felt the need to inspire his men with exceptional bravado. One of his battery commanders described the spectacle Dearing presented when, "followed by his staff and his courier, waving the battalion flag, [he] rode from right to left of the battalion, backward and forward, decidedly the most conspicuous figures upon that field." John Dooley, too, remarked the young officer "out in front with his flag waving defiance at the Yankees." Finally, the horse ridden by Dearing's courier was killed, putting an end to the exhibition—much to the relief of the toiling artillerymen, who were convinced that it had accounted for the "special attention . . . they were then receiving from the enemy's guns."

For the second time in as many days, Edward P. Alexander began to suspect that his rosy assessment of the tactical situation might have been too optimistic. He had expected that a quarter hour of concentrated shelling would suffice to suppress most of the Yankee batteries, but once the scope of the enemy's position became evident, he realized "that I must wait longer than my proposed 15 minutes." And not only would it take more time to blast the enemy guns off Cemetery Ridge; it would also eat into the limited stock of ready ammunition. It was Lee's intention—an important part of his plan—that the batteries should advance with the infantry in order to lash the enemy's lines at close range. For the first time since he had blueprinted the action, Alexander worried that his gunners might run out of powder before they could do that.

The combination of the bad fuses common to the Confederate arsenal and the tendency of Civil War cannon to angle high with repeating firings soon had a lot of Rebel ordnance overshooting its targets. Along northern Cemetery Ridge, that brought much of the Rebel iron down onto the reverse (or eastern) slope and the Taneytown Road, placing many of the correspondents at ground zero. Whitelaw Reid and Sam Wilkeson were just discussing whether a stray bullet that had whizzed by them merited the phrase "muffled howl" when a shell arced over the ridge, passed within two feet of the Leister house, and buried itself in the road not four yards away. One of the newsmen present remarked that "those fellows on the left have the range of headquarters exactly." That shell, Wilkeson later wrote, was "instantly followed by another and another, and in a moment the air was full of the most complete artillery prelude to an infantry battle that was ever exhibited."

"The atmosphere was thick with shot and shell," scribbled the *New York World*'s man on the scene. "Horses fell, shrieking such awful cries . . . , and writhing themselves about in hopeless agony. The boards of fences, scattered by the explosions, flew in splinters through the air." Even as he was diving for cover, Sam Wilkeson made note of those unfortunate soldiers who were caught in the open and "torn to pieces . . . and died with the peculiar yells that blend the extorted cry of pain with horror and despair." Whitelaw Reid wasted little time in mounting his horse and beating a hasty retreat down the Taneytown Road, accompanied by "cries that ran the diapason of terror and despair."

Smack in the midst of the impact zone were a number of Federal field hospitals, whose suffering wounded now had to endure new torments. A surgeon at the medical post located on the Peter Frey farm could only watch helplessly as the "outbuildings, fences and fruit trees were completely torn to pieces." The bombardment caught a badly wounded soldier from the 125th New York in post-op, unable to be moved following an amputation. Someone later remembered how the man, after regaining consciousness "from the effects of the chloroform, and with a smile on his lips, remained uncomplainingly there all the terrible afternoon."

George Meade and his staff at first tried to tough it out. Then, when the cannonade showed no signs of ending and the number of near-fatal hits around the Leister house continued to increase, Meade decided to shift his flag to a more sheltered location. After initially moving to a nearby barn that provided no more protection than its predecessor, Meade went over to Henry Slocum's headquarters on Powers Hill. Other officers were less lucky: Daniel Butterfield, Abner Doubleday, James Barnes, and Thomas A. Smyth were all wounded in the shelling.

Conditions varied along the Federal line that wriggled across the forward slope of Cemetery Ridge. In Alexander Hays' sector, the artillerymen and infantry posted in Ziegler's Grove had to deal with falling branches, wood splinters, and oddly ricocheting cannon balls. The fiery, combative Hays was in his element, prowling his lines and offering his men inspiration and advice; time and again he instructed his soldiers to gather all the loose rifles they could see lying about them, so that many soon had two or more primed weapons at the ready. Along other segments of the Cemetery Ridge line, the troops succumbed to a stress-induced exhaustion, leading one officer to pronounce the sight of his men falling asleep under fire "the most astonishing thing I ever witnessed in any battle."

The visibility of the batteries on this part of the line invited especially heavy fire, which inflicted serious damage on all of them. In Arnold's battery, along the stone wall between Hays and Webb, a gunner complained of the "pitiless storm of shot and shell which burst and tore up the ground in all direction." Next to the south were Cushing's six guns. "The shot and shell," wrote one of the crew, "seemed to be tearing and plowing the hill to its very foundation around us." Brown's 1st Rhode Island (now commanded by Lieutenant Walter Perrin) completed the set; so many of its men were down that nearby infantry were drafted to keep the cannon firing. A Rebel shell struck the muzzle of one gun and exploded, killing some of the artillerymen. When the survivors tried to keep the tube in action, they discovered that the blow had dented it in such a way that the shot jammed, forcing them to withdraw it.

Whereas many of the Confederate overshoots fell on rear areas that were relatively free of massed troops, the Federal long rounds came down in the fields where Rebel troops were staged for the pending attack. In the 14th Virginia, a private named Erasmus Williams had endured the good-natured taunts of a lieutenant who mocked him for having dug a small foxhole, chiding, " 'Why Williams, you are a coward.' " Hardly had the Federal retaliation begun when Williams, in his hole, "was covered with the dirt from the shot and shell striking near me. Presently, indeed almost instantly, the defiant Lieutenant was swept away by a shot or shell, and his blood sprinkled all over me."

In John Dooley's 1st Virginia, "ever and anon some companion would raise his head disfigured and unrecognizable, streaming with blood, or would stretch his full length, his limbs quivering in the pangs of death." It was no different along the line taken by Heth's Division. Remembered William Peel:

> In the hot[t]est of the cannonading I heard a shell strike in the right of the reg't, & turning over, as I lay upon my back, I looked just in time to witness the most appal[l]ing scene that perhaps ever greeted the human eye. Lt. Daniel Featherstone, of Co. F from Noxubee County, was the unfortunate victim. He was a large man—would have weighed perhaps two hundred pounds. He was lying on his face, when the shell struck the ground near his head, &, in the ricochet, entered his breast, exploding about the same time & knocking him at least ten feet high & not less than twenty feet from where he was lying.

South of Gettysburg, less than a mile below where Hood's Division had launched its July 2 assault, Wesley Merritt's United States cavalry brigade continued to press northward, though the going was getting tougher. There were more and more Rebel infantry to contend with, and in addition to the shelling from the two-gun battery in front of them, the mostly dismounted troopers were drawing fire from two more batteries just east of the road. It was not a fight from fixed positions but rather an awkward give-and-take that swung back and forth with seemingly little purpose. In one rush, a section of mounted Federals threatened to overrun the two-gun battery, only to be dispersed by a Georgia regiment that arrived just in time to save the cannon.

Merritt's men pushed to the limit of their strength, finally drawing to them enough Rebel infantry to more than match their numbers. Then, in the face of a line of battle that, according to one report, "had that confident look of being there to stay," the Yankees ceased their forward motion. Once he was certain that there would be no more serious trouble from this sector, Confederate General Evander Law, by John Black's account, "took his Regiments and went back [toward the Round Tops,] saying he hoped I could hold the ground."*

The unexpected duration of the cannonade had completely upset Edward P. Alexander's calculations with regard to ammunition. After more than an hour of the slow but steady exchange, he was becoming quite anxious about having enough on hand for adequate close support of the infantry advance. He knew that even after he signaled that his guns had done their job—which condition had not yet been met—it would take George Pickett time to get moving, and "every minute now seemed an hour. . . . But instead of simply giving the single order 'charge,' I thought it due to Longstreet and to Pickett to let the exact situation be understood." So at about 2:20 P.M.,† Alexander sent a message to Pickett and a copy to J. Johnston Pettigrew.

> General: If you are to advance at all, you must come at once or we will not be able to support you as we ought. But the enemy's fire has not slackened materially and there are still 18 guns firing from the cemetery.

No sooner had Alexander dispatched this note than he noted a dramatic and amazing change in the rate of fire coming from Cemetery Ridge. He turned his glass in that direction to observe some of the battered Yankee guns being hauled off. He watched those positions carefully to see if the cannon were being replaced, but as far as he could tell, they were not. "Then I began to believe that we stood a good chance for the

*The regiment that Merritt had detached prior to this action to raid a reportedly unguarded Rebel wagon train to the west had found that train well guarded after all, but not until after the regiment (the 6th United States Cavalry) had become engaged and lost heavily. For their actions in this affair near Fairfield, Pennsylvania, troopers George C. Platt and Martin Schwenk would receive the Medal of Honor.
†Alexander's time estimates were perhaps his only failing as a chronicler. He guessed that the cannonade had lasted twenty-five minutes and put the time of the action here described at 1:25 P.M.

day," Alexander later reminisced. It was about 2:40 P.M. when the young gunner sent a follow-up note to George Pickett.

> For God's sake come quick. The 18 guns have gone. Come quick or my ammunition will not let me support you properly.

A sharp battle of wills was being waged along Cemetery Ridge between Winfield Hancock and Henry Hunt. The artillery chief did not want his gunners wasting precious ammunition on counterbattery fire, but Hancock was equally adamant that the need to maintain the morale of his foot soldiers required that the Yankee guns match the Confederate cannon shot for shot. This was one thing for the batteries under Captain John G. Hazard—which not only were clearly subject to Second Corps authority but also had come under a direct challenge that demanded a response—and something else entirely for guns that, so far as Henry Hunt was concerned, Hancock had no business commanding.

Anxious to keep up the pressure, Hancock had ridden south along Cemetery Ridge and soon begun encountering the batteries of McGilvery's hitherto undetected line. After McGilvery declined to implement Hancock's orders, the determined infantry officer rode among the cannon positions, instructing each crew to open fire. Captain Patrick Hart refused to do so absent a written order. The next officer Hancock addressed, Captain Charles Phillips, reluctantly agreed and had his guns open, but he ceased just as quickly when Freeman McGilvery arrived on Hancock's heels to countermand his command. Hancock also coerced Captain James Thompson to begin firing, an action that drew a Confederate response to McGilvery's line and brought on his only casualties stemming from the cannonade.

Not long after this playlet ran to its curtain, Henry Hunt had realized that if he could shut down all the Federal batteries, it might convince the Rebels that they had succeeded in suppressing the Yankee guns and induce them to bring their infantry into the open. Hunt conveyed the order to Thomas Osborn on Cemetery Hill, and Osborn started implementing it. As Hunt passed along the guns, moving south, he met a staff officer carrying orders to the same effect from George Meade. While he could not silence all the Federal guns, Hunt obtained enough cease that the volume of firing coming from Cemetery Ridge began noticeably to decrease.

*   *   *

The courier bearing Alexander's 2:20 P.M. note found George Pickett with his staff. After letting his aides know that action was imminent, Pickett rode to Longstreet and shared the message with him. "I have never seen him so grave and troubled," Pickett reflected later. He asked, " 'General, shall I advance?' " Longstreet froze, unwilling to speak lest he betray his feelings. "I bowed affirmation," Longstreet afterward wrote, "and turned to mount my horse." Behind him, Pickett called out, " 'I shall lead my division forward, sir.' "

On his way back to his command, Pickett received Alexander's second note, confirming his actions.

East of Gettysburg, the scrapping along Cress Ridge was becoming more and more contentious. The dismounted skirmishing between the Virginia troopers from Jenkins' Brigade, under Vincent Witcher, and the Michigan men under Custer lasted an hour or more, giving the lie to Jeb Stuart's later claim that these Virginians (not part of his regular command) had entered the action with only ten rounds apiece.

Stuart's plan, such as it was, called for his brigades to use the skirmish line as a screen behind which they would move southward to drive a wedge between the Federal cavalry along the Hanover Road and the Federal infantry over toward Culp's Hill. For his part, David McMurtrie Gregg had three brigades on the field, two representing his own division and one on reluctant loan from Judson Kilpatrick. Gregg's intentions were purely defensive. He formed a blocking position with Custer's regiments at the intersection of the Low Dutch Road and the Hanover Road, and placed Colonel J. Irvin Gregg's brigade west of that along the Hanover Road. Colonel John B. McIntosh's brigade meanwhile took station north of Custer, off the Low Dutch Road, with many of the men being posted in a patch of woods on the farm of one Jacob Lott.

Trouble brewed as each side sent reinforcements out to its skirmishers, first additional dismounted units, then mounted ones that flowed around the flanks. As each new force appeared, the other side would respond by sending forward one of its own. Reaction was the motivation, and initiative a hot potato flying from one side to the other. A mounted charge against the Michigan skirmishers by squadrons from two Virginia regiments of W. H. F. Lee's brigade, then commanded by Colonel John R. Chambliss, was answered by one from the 7th Michigan, with the long-haired Custer at its head. This in turn sparked a riposte by the 1st

North Carolina and the Jeff Davis Legion of Brigadier General Wade Hampton's brigade. Sorting out who had done what to whom would be virtually impossible in the years to come. "It is yelling, shooting, swearing, cutting, fight, fight—all fight," recalled a Michigan trooper.

Needing someplace to go, James Longstreet rode down to where Edward P. Alexander was stationed. Alexander had a mix of news for him, good and bad. The young artillery officer was encouraged by the fact that the guns had been either silenced or driven away from the center of the enemy's line; that was all to the good. On the debit side, the close support he was to provide for the attacking troops was in jeopardy.

Alexander had been counting on using some short-range howitzers from A. P. Hill's corps, passed to him by William Pendleton and subsequently sent by himself to a safe nearby position to the rear. He had just learned, however, that the guns had been moved—where to or by whom, no one seemed to know. While this story would loom large in Alexander's postwar thinking about the battle, either he or Pendleton had the facts wrong. The battery identified by Alexander—"Richardson's"—contained long-range rifles, not short-range howitzers. The guns' disappearance may have resulted from Pendleton's jumping the chain of command and speaking directly to the battery officer without informing his direct superiors. It was that officer's battalion commander, knowing nothing of Pendleton's "deal" with Alexander, who had shifted the battery's position.

Far more important than these details was Alexander's now-dour estimate of the number of rounds he had on hand for the direct support of Pickett's advance. It was an important aspect of Lee's plan that as many guns as possible move forward with the infantry, but they could not proceed without sufficient ammunition, and most did not have enough. This news startled Longstreet, who had never imagined that his cannon would run out of shells. " 'Go & halt Pickett right where he is,' " Longstreet said, " '& replenish your ammunition.' " Alexander shook his head. To avoid the enemy's counterfire, the reserve train had been moved well out of range. It would take more than an hour to bring it forward again to refill the nearly empty limbers, the artillerist explained, " '& meanwhile the enemy would recover from the pressure he is now under.' "

Longstreet rode ahead of Alexander a little way and looked through his glasses at the Union line along Cemetery Ridge " 'I don't want to make this attack,' " he said, pausing between sentences as if thinking aloud. " 'I believe it will fail—I do not see how it can succeed—I would not make it even now, but that Gen. Lee has ordered & expects it.' " There was nothing Alexander could say to ease Longstreet's pain. "So I stood by," he recalled, "& looked on, in silence almost embarrassing."

(2:40 P.M.–2:55 P.M.)

It was time for Lee's infantry to form for the assault. Mississippian William Peel felt the "momentary [lull], of men resuming their places in line, and silence—a silence as awful as the thunder of the minute before had been—settled itself around us. All ears were straining for the command we knew fulwell must follow soon." "I tell you there is no romance in making one of these charges . . . ," declared John Dooley of the 1st Virginia. "When you rise to your feet . . . , I tell you the enthusiasm of ardent breasts in many cases *ain't there,* and instead of burning to avenge the insults of our country, families and altars and firesides, the thought is most frequently, *Oh,* if I could just come out of this charge safely how thankful *would I be!*"

An aide to George Pickett described how the major general "rode along the long lines of his brave veterans and calmly bade them look at the heights they were ordered by Gen. Lee to take. He told them they could see the greatness of the undertaking and appreciate it as well as he could & that it *must* be done; he begged them to *remember they were Virginians,* and exhorted them to stand to the work." Halting alongside Richard Garnett, Pickett said, " 'I have no orders to give you, but I advise you to get across those fields as quick as you can, for in my opinion you are going to catch hell.' "

Frank Haskell, the lieutenant on John Gibbon's staff, was silently grateful to be alive. "The Artillery fight over, men began to breathe more freely, and to ask:—'What next I wonder?' The Battery men were among their guns, some leaning to rest, and wipe the sweat from their sooty faces,— some were handling ammunition boxes, and replenishing those that were empty. Some Batteries from the Artillery Reserve were moving up to take the places of the disabled ones:—the smoke was clearing from the crests."

Haskell found his commander, who said "he inclined to the belief that the enemy was falling back, and that the cannonade was only one of his noisy modes of covering the movement. I said that I thought that fifteen minutes would show that, by all his bowling, the Rebel did not mean retreat." Glancing up, Haskell saw Henry Hunt moving with much more haste than usual and gesticulating to his gunners with a sense of urgency. Gibbon called for horses. The staff officer who brought them forward looked pale but excited. " 'General,' " he confided, " 'they say the enemy's Infantry is advancing.' "

How many men rose from their various places of cover to form the companies that made up the regiments constituting the brigades of the divisions assigned to the assault remains a matter of speculation. A long-standing estimate of slightly more than 5,000 for Pickett's Division, based on a supposition by Pickett's assistant adjutant and inspector general, Walter Harrison, was challenged by a 1987 study (revised in 1993) that examined company-level muster rolls to conclude that the total number present on July 3 was 5,830.

A different problem is posed by the participation in the assault of Heth's Division and two brigades from Pender's Division, most of which had seen action on July 1. Working backward from the most reasonable determinations of strength available, the following estimates seem likely in Heth's Division: Archer's Brigade, 824; Pettigrew's Brigade, 1,205; Davis' Brigade, 1,605; and Brockenbrough's Brigade, 821, for a total of 4,455. Pender's Division contributed Scales' Brigade, at 951, and Lane's, at 1,355, for a grand total on the left wing of 6,761.

Two more brigades should also be accounted for: Wilcox's and Perry's were both selected to immediately support Pickett's advance. After serious losses on July 2, Wilcox probably counted about 1,036 in his ranks, while Perry's Brigade added another 444, for 1,480 in total.

All of this suggests that James Longstreet's much quoted figure of 15,000, which was scaled back by several twentieth-century studies to something around 12,000, was not that far off after all. However, if Wilcox's and Perry's men are subtracted in view of their very tardy advance, and another 500 are deducted to allow for overshoot casualties, then the number actually moving toward Cemetery Ridge at this time approaches 11,800.

*   *   *

The Union batteries within ground zero were affected to varying degrees by the Rebel barrage. George Woodruff's (1st United States Light Artillery, Battery I) was the least disrupted, sustaining only slight damage from falling tree limbs and the loss of a few horses; after some minor cleanup, the six cannon posted in Ziegler's Grove were ready for action. "Woodruff had his guns run to the crest of the hill, and gave the necessary orders to prepare for the struggle that was coming," wrote one of his crew. "He would not fire a shot until the enemy got in close range where our canister would be most effective."

William A. Arnold's six tubes (1st Rhode Island Light Artillery, Battery A), lacking the tree cover enjoyed by Woodruff's men, were badly battered. One of Arnold's crew would never forget that "awful, rushing sound of flying missiles, a sound that causes the firmest hearts to quail." Four of the guns were withdrawn, and a fifth disabled one was left in place; the last, with all the remaining ammunition, was pushed up close to the stone wall.

Alonzo Cushing's battery (4th United States Light Artillery, Battery A) had also taken a terrible beating. Several caissons had been exploded, numbers of Cushing's men had been mangled by shell fragments and explosions, two cannon had been hit and disabled, and the wheels of several others had been shattered, forcing the sweating cannoneers to swap in spares as deadly shells hissed around them. Even so, two more guns were lost. A hit so cruelly injured Private Arsenal H. Griffin that the agonized gunner put a pistol to his head, called out, " 'Good-by boys,' " and shot himself. Still the grimly determined Cushing remained undeterred; when Alexander Webb came over to offer his opinion that the Rebel infantry would be coming soon, Cushing replied, " 'I better run all the guns right up to the stone fence, and bring all my canister.' " " 'All right, do so,' " Webb replied.

The 1st Rhode Island Light Artillery, Battery B, next in line after Cushing's, was also in bad shape. The unit had lost its commander, Lieutenant T. Fred Brown, and twenty-two comrades on July 2. Today, two limbers had been exploded, thirty horses had fallen, and three of the six guns had been knocked out. Many crewmen were down as well. A dazed survivor recollected that the shells "came so thick and fast, there was no dodging them." A less lucky comrade had his shoulder ripped open by a shell fragment; as his life drained away with his blood, he died shouting, " 'Glory to God! I am happy! Hallelujah!' " The battery itself was almost as far gone, so a call went to the rear for a substitute to come forward and replace it.

The last in this set was Captain James M. Rorty's 1st New York Light Artillery, Battery B. It shared much of the fate of Cushing's and Brown's outfits. By the time the enemy fire lifted, young Rorty was dead, and his successor was down to one cannon operational out of four—and that only because he had managed to draft some nearby infantrymen to help his decimated crew. Despite the carnage, Rorty's battery showed no signs of pulling back.

The advance planned by Lee and Longstreet comprised two wings that would begin their movement with a gap of several hundred yards between them. Pickett's force, the right wing's principal element, was formed in two lines. On the left of the front line was Richard B. Garnett's brigade. Citing his horse-kick injury as an excuse, Garnett ignored the instructions calling for officers to advance on foot and instead was mounted. To the right and slightly to the rear of Garnett's Brigade was that of James Kemper, who was also on horseback. Behind those two, though primarily in back of Garnett, was Lewis Armistead's large command. Once the front formation had cleared out of the way, Armistead was to oblique slightly to his left and come up even with Garnett in order to form a continuous line connecting to Heth's Division, even as Garnett's men closed to their left.

Questions remain regarding the role to be played by the other two commands immediately associated with the right wing: Wilcox's and Perry's Brigades (the latter still led by David Lang), both from Richard Anderson's division of Hill's Corps. George Pickett thought they had been designated as reinforcements, to be called up should his advance stall. A. P. Hill, for his part, maintained that the pair were meant to be available to exploit any success realized by the assaulting force. And Robert E. Lee, in his report, indicated that he had intended for the two brigades to guard the vulnerable right flank of the advancing lines. Wilcox, meanwhile, made it clear in his own report that it had been his understanding that he was not to move until he received positive orders to do so. Such unnecessary confusion as to the goals and objectives of these important units marked another abandoned piece of Lee's careful plan for the attack.

Heth's Division, under J. Johnston Pettigrew, constituted the first line of the left wing. The only anomaly in its deployment was the decision of Colonel John M. Brockenbrough to subdivide his small brigade into halves, one (containing the 22nd Virginia Battalion and the 40th Virginia) under his direct control, and the other (consisting of the 47th and 55th Virginia Regiments) to be led by Colonel Robert Mayo. As the leftmost unit in the left wing, Brockenbrough had to squeeze past a battle line aligned along a sunken road and partially masking his front, so perhaps he reasoned that splitting his brigade would make it easier to maneuver in a tight spot.

Behind the right side of Heth's line were two brigades from Pender's Division. With Pender himself out of action, Lee had decided to appoint an outsider to command them, tapping the otherwise unattached brigadier Isaac Trimble for the job. Because the choice had been made only in the course of that morning's planning, it is unclear just how many in the ranks (officers or men) actually knew they were operating as a demidivision under Trimble. While he would later admit that these troops were "entire strangers to me," their new commander did address some of them, ordering that "no gun should be fired until the enemy's line was broken," and assuring them that he would "advance with them to the farthest point."

After this fight, Trimble would confide to a staff officer that he had been accompanied on his only review of his temporary command by Robert E. Lee, who had seemed surprised by the number of men in the ranks who sported bandages and other evidence of their hard fighting on July 1. " 'Many of these poor boys should go to the rear,' " Trimble remembered Lee's commenting. " 'They are not fit for duty.' " As they rode away from the lines of men, Trimble swore he heard Lee say, as if to himself, " 'The attack must succeed.' "

Seemingly lost amid the decades of dialogue about the events soon to transpire was the fact that Lee's planning had provided for a second assault group nearly as strong as the first. He hoped that all the elements he had brought together for this attack would make it possible for that first wave to penetrate the enemy's defenses, but he did not expect it to be able to exploit the breach. Longstreet would confirm this thinking: " 'We could not look for anything from Pickett except to break your line,' " he would later tell a Union officer. " 'The supports were to secure the fruit of that break.' "

Because there were so many variables that might trigger the advance of a second wave, Lee wisely resolved to forgo complicated instructions and instead settled on a simple plan. Likely working with Longstreet, he selected the brigades to be included in the second wave and directed their commanders to be alert to opportunities and to take advantage of them if they presented themselves. The after-action report filed by Richard Anderson makes this point most clearly: "I received orders to hold my division in readiness to move up in support, if it should become necessary. . . . Wilcox's and Perry's brigades had been moved forward, so as to be in position to render assistance, or to take advantage of any success gained by the assaulting column, and, at what I supposed to be the proper time, I was . . . to move forward [the other brigades]."

In addition to Anderson's five brigades, Lee had designated for this purpose Thomas' and Perrin's of Pender's Division, Ramseur's, Iverson's, and Doles' from Rodes' Division, and at least one more from McLaws' Division, possibly Wofford's.

These eleven brigades, numbering perhaps 11,000 men, represented the full extent of Lee's determined plan to smash the Federal center. Years after the war, veteran William Allen would speak with Lee about many subjects and then encapsulate some of their conversation in a letter to a Southern publication. "There was nothing 'foolish' in Pickett's attack had it been executed as designed," wrote Allen in echo of Lee. "Had [the supports been employed] . . . General Lee never doubted that the Federal army would have been ruined."

Most of Gettysburg's residents could not comprehend why the awful cannon firing seemed just to end at around 3:00 P.M. A few figured that something else was about to happen. Charles McCurdy and his father left their cellar and went up to the third floor of their house, where a dormer window offered a view of the fields to the south; to McCurdy's lasting disappointment, a "dense volume of smoke hid everything from view." Henry Jacobs' father had the good sense to take along a small telescope when he clambered up into the garret of his home, which overlooked Seminary Ridge. From this perspective he could make out some of the lines of Heth's Division as the men moved up to their departure point. " 'Quick!' " the elder Jacobs called down to this son. " 'Come! Come! You can see now what in all your life you will never see again.' "

* * *

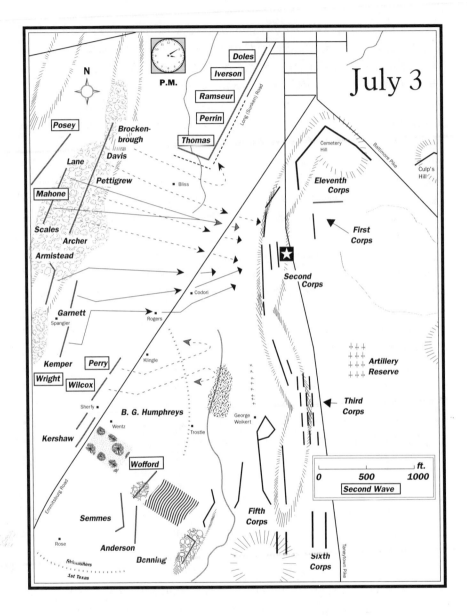

By agreement, Archer's Brigade, now led by Birkett D. Fry, was the unit upon which both wings were to orient themselves, so it most likely began moving first. "I never have known how or from whom Pettigrew received the order to advance," Fry would write, "but I received it from him." The brigadier was glad that the waiting was over. "After lying inactive under that deadly storm of hissing and exploding shells, it seemed a relief to go forward to the desperate assault," he recalled. That feeling must have been shared by his troops, for as he recollected it, "at the command the men sprang up with cheerful alacrity, and the long line advanced." Pettigrew also brought word to Colonel John K. Marshall, commanding his old brigade. " 'Now, Colonel,' " he exhorted, " 'for the honor of the good old North State, forward.' "

(2:55 p.m.–3:15 p.m.)

As Pettigrew's and Pickett's battle lines cleared the crests in their front, their formations opened to sift through the momentarily quiet batteries. Among the positions through which Pettigrew's men passed was that held by the Fredericksburg Artillery. "Many of us had friends in this command," John L. Marye remembered, "and we eagerly watched them as they swept by." One of Pickett's men noted that the cannoneers "raised their hats and cheered us on our way." Edward P. Alexander spotted his friend Richard Garnett and rode with him a short way, "wishing him good luck." In advancing, the long Virginia line spooked a rabbit that darted frantically through their ranks to the rear. " 'Run old hare,' " someone called. " 'If I were an old hare I would run too.' "

From atop his horse on Cemetery Ridge, Frank Haskell had a good perspective on the enemy force as it hauled into view. "Regiment after Regiment, and Brigade after Brigade, move from the woods, and rapidly take their places in the lines forming the assault," he observed. From the right flank of Pickett's Division to the left of Heth's, including the gap between the wings, the leading line of armed men stretched about six thousand feet. Some twenty-seven regiments, each centered on its battle flag, began to move forward at common time. At ninety steps a minute, each line covered approximately 225 feet every sixty seconds.

Richard S. Ewell, whose doggedly futile morning attacks on Culp's Hill had utterly wasted his corps' collaborative potential, was moved by the sight of the assault to try to do *something* to help. He sent a note to Jubal Early, whose troops held the town. "Longstreet, & A. P. Hill are advancing in splendid style," Ewell wrote. "If you see an opportunity, strike."

* * *

Like small fissures portending a larger earthquake, minor problems characterized the Cemetery Ridge assault from the outset. Kemper's Brigade, for example, emerged from the swale with its flank aligned along the lane leading from the Spangler farm to the Emmitsburg Road, which pointed it southeast and thus away from the axis of advance to the northeast. Although he had been cautioned to save his men's strength for the final rush, Kemper had no choice but to order a series of left obliques at quick-time to get his line closer to the right flank of Garnett's Brigade, which had begun to pull away.

The alignment was even more muddled on the opposite flank. Only half of Brockenbrough's subdivided brigade stepped off on cue; the other half, assigned to Robert H. Mayo, stood in line waiting for the word. Some minutes passed, but the two officers commanding the pair of regiments had yet to hear anything from Mayo; they watched unhappily as the distance between their half and that commanded by Brockenbrough increased. They finally decided it would be better to do *something* than nothing, so on their own authority they ordered their men forward. "We were a long ways behind and had to run to catch up with the rest of the Brigade," wrote one of the officers.

The concerns that Edward P. Alexander had expressed to James Longstreet were proving to be well founded. Lee wanted the batteries to advance with the infantry, but ammunition was in short supply: the longer-than-anticipated bombardment had emptied many of the caissons, and William Pendleton's poor judgment had sent the artillery reserve train too far to the rear to be of any use now. Unwilling to accept the situation, the combative James Dearing made a frantic effort to resupply his depleted battalion, whipping his empty caissons to the rear at breakneck speed. As they rattled past the marching files of the 8th Virginia, Dearing called out to the regiment's commander, " 'For God's sake, wait till I get some ammunition and I will drive every Yankee from the heights.' "

Alexander did his part as well, riding to each of his batteries to take a hurried inventory. "If it had enough long range projectiles left to give some 15 shots . . . , I ordered it to limber up & move forward after the storming column," he recalled. More often than not, he would select only the shorter-range weapons, leaving the others behind. Those cannon with fewer than fifteen rounds on hand were "ordered to wait until the infantry had gotten a good distance in front, then, aiming well over their heads, to fire at the enemy's batteries which were [then] firing at our infantry."

In this fashion, Alexander got perhaps eighteen cannon moving up behind the infantry. He hoped that his opposite number on the other flank, Colonel R. Lindsay Walker, the artillery chief for Hill's Corps, was having better luck. But in fact, Walker was not even aware of this part of Lee's scheme, either because the message had not been clear or because Pendleton had failed to deliver it. Whatever the reason, no guns attached to Hill's Corps advanced with his infantry. This important element in the assault plan would therefore be implemented not at all on the left wing and only symbolically on the right. Walker "advanced no guns," Alexander declared, "either before, during, or after the charge that I ever heard of, though the left half of the column was in Hill's front."

Hard-bitten and himself no stranger to combat, Henry Hunt was nevertheless in awe of Lee's audacity. "The Confederate approach was magnificent," Hunt admitted, "and excited our admiration." Hunt had a trick of equal daring up his own sleeve. Through a careful placement of guns along Cemetery Ridge and on Cemetery Hill, he had laid out a deadly latticework of crossfire lanes designed to scourge the fields in front of every living thing. Provided that each battery did its part, he was certain that no enemy force could make it across the Emmitsburg Road.

Almost as soon as the first distant lines of battle tramped into view, the batteries on the flank of Hunt's grid began targeting them with long-range fire. Once the full extent of Lee's line had revealed itself, Hunt, like a symphonic composer summoning forth the dramatic effect, looked toward the center of his artillery row for its contribution to the program. These guns, however, placed as they were among the Second Corps, remained mostly silent, thanks in large part to the earlier activity of Winfield Hancock. "They had unfortunately exhausted their long range projectiles during the cannonade, under the orders of their corps commander, and it was too late to replace them," Hunt would remark with some bitterness.

The Yankee gunners on the flanks would pen numerous testimonials to the havoc their munitions had wreaked in the Rebel ranks during this action. Thomas Osborn, directing the counterfire from Cemetery Hill, noted the difference in effect between solid and exploding shells: "Each solid shot or unexploded shell cut out at least two men," he recorded. "The exploding shells took out four, six, eight men, sometimes more than that." Battery commander Patrick Hart, on McGilvery's line, thought that the "gaps we made [in the Confederate lines] were simply terrible." The actual impact that the Union cannon had during this stage of the Rebel advance, however, was most likely much less destructive than its architects imagined.

In his after-action report, Joseph R. Davis, whose Mississippi/North Carolina brigade was somewhat shielded on its left by Brockenbrough's command, would insist that "not a gun was fired at us until we reached a [point] . . . about three-quarters of a mile from the enemy's position." An officer in the 11th Virginia (Kemper's Brigade) avowed that the men made it as close as the Union skirmish line before the artillery began really to chew at them, while another, in the 38th Virginia (Armistead's Brigade), recalled that the first six hundred feet of the Rebel advance went uncontested. An officer marching under Armistead conceded that some enfilade shots from Little Round Top did hit his brigade, but he maintained that the shells were "not striking the line often."

A few regiments, falling victim to the bad luck that always claims its share in military actions, did suffer. Because Kemper's Brigade was slow to take station off the right of Garnett, the latter became a target for McGilvery's now unmasked line. "The enemy's big guns . . . tore great gaps through our ranks," wrote a captain in the 18th Virginia. Another officer in Garnett's files would long remember how the "round-shot bounding along the plain tore through their ranks and ricocheted around them; shells exploded incessantly in blinding, dazzling flashes before them, behind them, overhead and among them."

Across the field, on the left flank, nothing was going right for Brock-enbrough's Brigade, which had begun this movement in halves as a consequence of inadequate communication and leadership. The two were now one again, thanks to a ravine that an officer remembered being about "half-way between our position and that of the enemy," which offered enough cover from the Federal long-range fire to allow the two regiments lagging behind to catch up with the others. Once they had cleared this ravine, though, Brockenbrough's men were on their own, no longer shielded by the line of friendly troops posted along the sunken road that stretched southwest from Gettysburg.

"The enemy's batteries soon opened upon our lines with canister, and the left seemed to stagger under it," recollected a soldier in the 22nd Virginia Battalion. Their advance east from behind the sunken road also brought Brockenbrough's Virginians within sight and range of Federal skirmishers. An Ohio officer along that line was appalled by the effect on the brigade of the cannon firing from Cemetery Hill: "They were at once enveloped in a dense cloud of smoke and dust," he remembered. "Arms, heads, blankets, guns, and knapsacks were thrown and tossed into the clear air."

It was all too much for these Confederate soldiers. "I feel no shame in recording that out of this corner the men without waiting for orders turned and fled, for the bravest soldiers cannot endure to be shot at simultaneously from the front and side," averred a member of the 40th Virginia. "They knew that to remain, or to advance, meant wholesale death or captivity. The Yankees had a fair opportunity to kill us all, and why they did not do it I cannot tell."

A handful pressed onward, but most shared the opinion of the sergeant in the 55th Virginia who explained, "We could see it was no use." A small group rallied back at the ravine under Colonel W. S. Christian and Robert Mayo, both of whom would vigorously assert that the portion of the brigade they commanded had "remained out in that field till all of the troops on our right had fallen back." Another important component of Lee's plan—the protection so necessary for the left flank of the advancing line—had collapsed.

While the lack of long-range munitions kept the Union artillerymen in the center of the Cemetery Ridge line relatively quiet, the batteries on the flanks did not have that concern. From the Cemetery Hill area, Thomas Osborn adroitly shifted his fire from Brockenbrough's broken brigade to the next in line, Joseph R. Davis'. By now Osborn's trained crews had all the ranges worked out. The gaps caused by their shells "could be distinctly seen from the hill as if we had been close to them," Osborn declared.

From Little Round Top, all six guns belonging to Hazlett's battery (now commanded by Lieutenant Benjamin F. Rittenhouse) at first bore on the southern Rebel lines, but as those lines veered northward, they moved out of the firing arc for all save the two rightmost tubes. The latter, however, were handled with deadly efficiency: "Many times a single percussion shell would cut out several files, and then explode in their ranks," remembered Rittenhouse. "Several times almost a company would disappear, as the shell would rip from the right to the left among them."

Along McGilvery's line, the infantry targets (initially Pickett's Division) were clearly visible, especially to the batteries on the northern end.

One of Captain James Thompson's gunners would recall that the enemy battle lines were some three hundred yards distant when the order was given to fire. "Their lines and columns staggered[,] reeled[,] and yelled like demons," he noted in his diary. "We mowed them down like ripe grain before the cradle."

With the exception of the infantrymen who had been posted out as skirmishers, and a few bands of sharpshooters still operating from various places of advantage, the Union infantry was biding its time. "All was orderly and still upon our crest,—no noise, and no confusion," Frank Haskell remarked.

> "The men had little need of commands, for the survivors of a dozen battles knew well enough what this array in front portended; and already in their places, they would be prepared to act when the right time should come. The click of the locks as each man raised the hammer, to feel with his finger that the cap was on the nipple; the sharp jar as a musket touched a stone upon the wall when thrust, in aiming, over it; and the clinking of the iron axles, as the guns were rolled up by hand a little further to the front, were quite all the sounds that could be heard. Cap-boxes were slid around to the front of the body;—cartridge boxes opened;—the officers opened their pistol holsters. Such preparation, little more, was needed.

Both wings of the Confederate assault were closing on the Emmitsburg Road. On the right, the plan for Pickett's three brigades to draw abreast of one another was not working out. Armistead's Brigade, which had begun the movement some two hundred yards behind Garnett's, had not closed the gap, and Kemper's men, who had been forced to perform several time-consuming maneuvers to remain in formation, likewise had yet to catch up. Lieutenant John Dooley, one of Kemper's boys, had to split his attention between a steady steam of orders and a clear view of the objective: "Onward—steady—dress to the right—give way to the left— steady, not too fast—don't press upon the center—how gentle the slope! steady—keep well in line—there is the line of guns we must take—right in front—but how far they appear! . . . Behind the guns are strong lines of [enemy] infantry. You may see them plainly and now they see us perhaps more plainly."

Although this advance was later to be immortalized as "Pickett's Charge," George Pickett at best controlled only his own three brigades and the two from Richard Anderson's division assigned to his support. The front line of troops on the left wing reported to J. Johnston Pettigrew, while the two supporting brigades answered to Isaac Trimble. As the first files of Pickett's men began to reach the Emmitsburg Road, their commander, who with his small staff had kept pace with them up to that point, rode south to find a vantage from which he could observe his entire division in action. Where he stopped to watch will likely remain one of Gettysburg's unsolved mysteries. Some postbattle accounts place him as close to the fighting as the Codori farm, while others suggest that he retired all the way to Spangler's. What is hardest to explain is how, in an engagement in which eight out of ten mounted men on the line were wounded or killed or had their animals shot out from under them, Pickett and his mounted staff (a total of six) could have emerged untouched. The most plausible explanation, given all the evidence, is that he set up his field post near the Rogers house, along the Emmitsburg Road.

From wherever he was, he dispatched his aides and orderlies to urge the artillery forward, to rally portions of his command that appeared to have broken, and to counter movements by the enemy. Although all three of his brigades were already leaving untidy bundles of dead and wounded behind them, the total loss, as Pickett must have been relieved to learn, was minimal. The chances seemed excellent that his men would be able to achieve the breakthrough sought by Lee. There was one worrisome threat, though, in the form of a small force of Yankee troops, just now in the process of projecting outward from the main line to catch his units in enfilade. Pickett scribbled a warning about it to Kemper and at the same time sent a note to James Longstreet asking for reinforcements.

The collapse of Brockenbrough's Brigade on the left wing sparked a disastrous chain of events. Fording the small flood of men spilling back toward Seminary Ridge, the brigade of Joseph R. Davis became the left flank of the first wave, subject to both artillery fire from Cemetery Hill and musketry from enemy skirmishers just to the north. Davis decided that getting through speedily was his best option, so he ordered his men to double-quick, which pace not only successfully pulled them away from the skirmishers but also brought them to the Emmitsburg Road well ahead of the rest of the left wing. Lieutenant William Peel, in the 11th Mississippi, positioned on the extreme left of Davis' Brigade, would be forever haunted by the memory of the "perfect tempest of maddened shells that ploughed our line & made sad havock in our ranks." Nevertheless, as the lines surged past the sunken road held by his brigade,

Brigadier General Edward L. Thomas impulsively ordered his men to advance. The command was heard only by a portion of the 35th Georgia, which briefly attached itself to Davis' formation.

If there is a fair supply of contradictory evidence regarding George Pickett's role in this charge, there is a comparable absence of information about the part played by the man commanding the left wing, J. Johnston Pettigrew. A North Carolinian who was something of a scholar and possessed of piercing black eyes, Pettigrew had, in the words of one of his aides, "taken every precaution to insure concert of action in the division." That aide's account suggests that Pettigrew and his staff, all mounted, held station a short distance in the rear of his three-brigade front, most likely tending to the right, where he expected to join hands with the left of Pickett's Division. Because his route was essentially straight ahead, there was little for Pettigrew to do—once he had taken account of the confusion caused by Brockenbrough's retreat—save urge any within the sound of his voice to press on.

What of Robert E. Lee? The prime mover and architect of the attack had also been an active participant in the preparations, but once matters were well in hand, he had returned to his headquarters to await the opening of the cannonade. His movements after he visited the Alabama battery near the railroad cut are obscure. As he had done on July 2, Lee allowed those entrusted with the responsibility freedom to operate. While the length of the bombardment must have surprised him, the fact that it drained the ready munitions supplies—thus rendering impotent the arm upon which so much of his plan depended—would not be reported to him until after the action.

None of Lee's key staff, all of whom wrote postwar memoirs, carried any message to the fighting troops. Around the time the first wave was crossing the Emmitsburg Road, the British observer Fremantle, moving from Gettysburg along Seminary Ridge in search of Longstreet, reported "passing General Lee and his Staff." That Fremantle made no further comment about the group suggests that there was little activity within it at this point. Immediately after seeing Lee, Fremantle witnessed "many wounded men retiring from the front." He also encountered members of Brockenbrough's spooked brigade, "flocking through the woods in numbers as great as the crowd in Oxford street in the middle of the day." It is difficult to believe that Lee would not have noted this phenomenon as well; he must also have observed batteries in place that by rights should have been moving forward.

Lee would write three reports on the Battle of Gettysburg. The first, composed on July 4, would be brief and very incomplete; the last, dated January 1864, would be the most comprehensive of the trio. The middle one, finished on July 31, offers more opinions and impressions than the others. It contains, among other things, hints as to the doubts Lee may have felt as he worked through, in his mind, the parts of his plan that had not been implemented, and searched for early signs of the disaster that had befallen the attacking force. Pondering the capabilities of his troops in that second report, Lee was to admit that "more may have been required of them than they were able to perform."

And George G. Meade? After shifting his headquarters to Powers Hill, away from the harassing enemy fire, Meade had checked in with both flanks and become ever more convinced that Lee's objective was an attack on his center. At almost the same instant that Henry Hunt concluded that a gradual cessation of artillery counterfire might lure out the Rebel infantry, Meade had the identical thought; his orders authorizing Hunt to take such action passed the courier from Hunt announcing that he had already done so. Meade simultaneously issued directives that would better position his infantry reserves to support the center, should it come to that.

It took a self-important civilian to lay bare some of the stress Meade was feeling. The local buttonholed the general to complain that his house

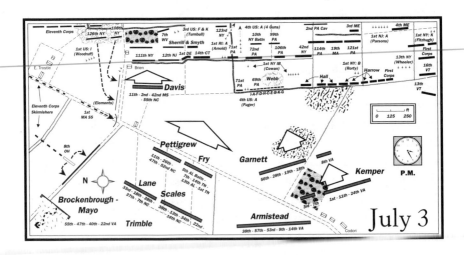

had been turned into a hospital and his property was being used as a graveyard. Who would pay for all this damage? he wanted to know. " 'Why, you craven fool,' " Meade snapped. " 'Until this battle is decided, you do not know, neither do I, if you will have a government to apply to. . . . If I hear any more from you, I will give you a gun and send you to the front line to defend your rights.' "

The termination of the Confederate bombardment signaled to Meade that the infantry assault was beginning, so he left Powers Hill to return to Cemetery Ridge. On the way, he met an aide from Alexander Hays, who reported that the enemy was indeed advancing. After ordering forward the closest reserve units, Meade rode toward where the Second Corps was defending his line.

(3:15 P.M.–3:40 P.M.)

Still pacing ahead of the rest of Pettigrew's left wing, the four regiments of Joseph R. Davis' brigade poured across the Emmitsburg
Road and surged up the slope toward the barn and house of Abraham
Brien. They were in a tight spot: from their left front, Woodruff's battery
was blasting canister at them; farther back on their left, several Yankee
regiments had taken up enfilade positions;* and ahead of them, the portion of the line held by the 12th New Jersey was vomiting bullets and pellets as the sixty-nine-caliber smoothbores spewed out their shotgun
blasts. "We opened on them and they fell like grain before the reaper,
which nearly annihilated them," recollected a New Jersey soldier. What
remained of the regiments quickly devolved into mobs fighting more for
survival than for cause or country. None penetrated the Federal positions
in an offensive capacity. "All that came as far as our line of battle came as
prisoners," boasted a New Jerseyman. Joseph Davis had seen enough:
convinced that "any further effort to carry the position was hopeless," he
spread the word "to retire to the position originally held."

Lieutenant William Peel and a few members of his company in the
11th Mississippi made it as far as the Brien barn, where they forted themselves and braced for the rest of the brigade to sweep over them. Glancing
anxiously to the rear, Peel could scarcely believe what he saw. "The state
of my feelings may be imagined, but not described," he wrote, "upon
seeing the line broken, & flying in full disorder, at the distance of about
one hundred & fifty yards from us." With enemy fire ripping across the
ground behind them, and every chance of success lost, Peel and the other
officer in the group decided to surrender. After showing a white flag, they

*During this portion of the action, Sergeant George H. Dore of the 126th New York
picked up his regimental flag after the color-bearer was killed, and held it for the rest
of the day, in the process earning himself a Medal of Honor. Another went to Corporal William H. Raymond of the 108th New York, who succeeded in resupplying his
regiment with ammunition while it was under a heavy fire.

were hustled to the rear, while behind them Cemetery Ridge shuddered with cannon and musket fire.

Captain Robert A. Bright was having a very busy afternoon. One of several aides to George Pickett, he had been sent to ask Longstreet for reinforcements. On the ride back to Seminary Ridge, he came across some soldiers in a category usually written out of postwar reminiscences. The aide recorded them as "small parties of [men] . . . going to the rear; presently I came to quite a large squad." Recognizing the stragglers for what they were—unwounded men not willing to face the enemy fire on Cemetery Ridge—Bright could not restrain himself: " 'What are you running for?' " he asked them hotly. One of the soldiers eyed the young officer and considered the direction from which he had come. " 'Why, good gracious, Captain,' " he said with a mix of amusement and accusation, " 'ain't you running yourself?' " Realizing that he had no good answer to that question, Bright continued on his mission.

He found the First Corps commander sitting alone on a fence. As he began delivering his message, Fremantle, the British observer, came up and interjected, " 'I would not have missed it for the world.' " " 'I would, Colonel Fremantle; the charge is over,' " Longstreet replied. Turning to the aide, he instructed, " 'Captain Bright, ride to General Pickett and tell him what you have heard me say to Colonel Fremantle.' " Bright started to reverse course but was checked by Longstreet. " 'Captain Bright!' " he called, pointing toward the Sherfy farm area. " 'Tell General Pickett that Wilcox's Brigade is in that peach orchard, and he can order him to his assistance.' "

By the time the mile-long files of the Rebel assault reached the Emmitsburg Road, the line had been compressed enough by maneuver and casualties that the soldiers of the Philadelphia Brigade knew they were going to be hit. It may not have occurred to many that they would be at the very focal point of the attack, but they certainly sensed that a life-and-death struggle was only minutes away.

At the moment the bombardment began, Cushing's six cannon had been covering the area of the outer angle, with the 69th Pennsylvania manning 250 feet of the stone wall fronting the Copse of Trees. Given the importance that this section of the front line would shortly assume, the company deployment was carefully recorded. From north (nearest the outer angle) to south, the order of companies was I-A-F-D-H-C-E-B-K-G. Lieutenant Colonel Martin Tshudy commanded the regiment's right wing, and Major James Duffy the left. Colonel Dennis O'Kane, in overall command of the regiment since Chancellorsville, was a fighter who, in the words of one of his officers, "above all despised a coward."

Two more of the brigade's regiments—the 71st and 72nd Pennsylvania—supported the first line from behind a second stone wall some 150 feet to the right and rear of the 69th. The final regiment in the outfit—the 106th Pennsylvania—had eight of its companies off on Cemetery Hill bolstering the Eleventh Corps, while the remaining two supplied men for the skirmish line near the Emmitsburg Road.

During the brief lull following the bombardment, Alexander Webb, to whose division the Philadelphia Brigade belonged, gave in to the wishes of the determined Alonzo Cushing by allowing him to push his two operational tubes down to the wall. Before the cannonade, the six guns had enjoyed the support of a regiment on either flank; now the surviving pair had more than a hundred feet of unoccupied wall to their right. To fill this gap, Webb ordered the 71st Pennsylvania forward and into it. The 71st's colonel, R. Penn Smith, doubted there was room enough for the whole regiment, however, and so sent only a portion of it out. The recollections of men and officers differ as to whether two companies manned the first wall and eight the second or vice versa, with many of the enlisted men recollecting the former deployment. In addition, some fifty men from the 71st replaced those from Cushing's crews who were too severely wounded to fight on. Welcome artillery reinforcement reached this sector in the form of Captain Andrew Cowan's 1st New York Independent Battery, which placed five guns just south of the copse and one north of it.

Events were unfolding quickly along the Confederate battle line. Even as Davis' Brigade retreated, its two companions pushed forward. The center brigade, Pettigrew's (under James K. Marshall), aimed for the open meadow just north of the outer angle, while the right, Archer's (under Birkett Fry), achieved one of its tactical objectives by linking with the left of Pickett's line. It was not Armistead's Brigade (still two hundred yards to the rear) but rather Garnett's that, following its orders to keep sidling to its left, made the connection. Fry saw Garnett giving orders to his men, "which amid the rattle of musketry I could not distinguish. Seeing my look or gesture inquiring he called out, 'I am dressing on you.' "

Making matters worse were visibility problems. "The smoke was dense," noted a Tarheel officer in Pettigrew's brigade, "and at times I could scarcely distinguish my own men." Getting across those sturdy railings was also murderous. "How like hail upon a roof sounded the patter of the enemy's bullets upon that fence!" a Tennessee man declared.

Fry had no sooner turned away than his luck ran out, and he fell, shot in the thigh. When a few of his men tried to carry him off, Fry waved them away, intent only on victory. "Go on," he urged through the pain, "it will not last five minutes longer!" Garnett's brigade, to the right of Fry's men, kept pressing ahead. Thus far, Garnett, who was mounted, had not been touched. He kept station in the rear of his line, cheering his men on. "Steady men! Close up! A little faster; not too fast! Save your strength!" Farther to the left, as Pettigrew's brigade charged up the slope from the Emmitsburg Road, their acting commander paused at the fence to wave them forward. Two Yankee bullets smashed into this head, killing him. Just minutes before, James Marshall had remarked to an aide: "We do not know which of us will be the next to fall."

As the Rebel lines maneuvered across the fenced fields west of the Emmitsburg Road, the Union skirmishers fell back. Once they crossed the road they really hustled, aware that they were in the primary kill zone for the riflemen along Cemetery Ridge. The soldiers on duty from the 106th Pennsylvania passed through the 69th Pennsylvania to rejoin their companions in the support line. Officers moved among the men, offering a mix of encouragement and threats. Dennis O'Kane told the soldiers of the 69th that he was confident their courage would win "the plaudits of our country," but just in case, he added that "should any man among us flinch in our duty," the soldier alongside was authorized to "kill him on the spot." O'Kane wanted his men to hold their fire until they "could distinguish the white of their eyes."

Straddling the Emmitsburg Road was a stretch of stout fencing that was too well seated to push over, leaving the Confederate soldiers the option of either squeezing through the rails or going over the top. For many, it proved to be a fatal impediment. An engineer observing from the north noted that as "soon as the top of the fence was lined with troops the whole line tumbled over, falling flat into the bed of the road, while

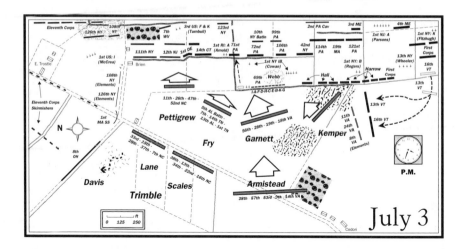

the enemy's bullets buried themselves into the bodies of the falling victims." A Union soldier would recollect that as the Rebels began climbing
the fence, "we opened fire on them with all the energy that each man
could put forth."

On crossing the road, Garnett's formation was thrown into some disorder after his right regiment, the 8th Virginia, had to divide to get around
the Codori farm. As the brigade pushed ahead, musketry blasts exploded
from its ranks, many of them aimed at the section of the wall harboring
Cushing's two guns. The young officer was struck twice, taking a terribly
painful wound to the genitals. Despite his pain, Cushing kept monitoring
the effect of each shot, calling out corrections all the while. A soldier in the
69th remembered hearing him declare, " 'That's excellent, keep that
range,' " just moments before an infantryman commented that "that
artillery officer has his legs knocked from under him." Cushing was yelling
another order or correction when a Rebel bullet entered his mouth, killing
him instantly.* Soon after this, his two guns exhausted their supplies, thus
creating an inviting chink in the Union line.

While some of Kemper's men went to cover in the rough ground just
south of the copse to begin sniping at Cowan's gunners, others headed
north to join those portions of Garnett's and Archer's commands that
were pressing into the gap marked by Cushing's silent guns. The increasingly disorganized formation was within fifty feet of the stone wall when

---

*Sergeant Frederick Fuger assumed command upon Cushing's death. His courageous
defense of what remained of his battery would win him a Medal of Honor.

most of the 69th, obedient to O'Kane's fire discipline, popped up on one knee to unleash a devastating volley. "The slaughter was terrible," testified a soldier in Company K. Frank Haskell would vividly recall how the opposing volleys blazed and rolled, "as thick the sound as when a summer hailstorm pelts the city roofs; as thick the fire as when the incessant lightning fringes a summer cloud."

The 71st Pennsylvania pitched in as well but soon found itself in trouble, as Archer's Brigade, driving hard toward the outer angle, began filling in the meadow just to its north. Under this pressure, the portion of the 71st along the front wall pulled back to its original position in the rear. Some of Garnett's men, along with a few of Archer's, quickly scrambled into the breach, taking control of the outer angle.

There was no doubt now in Winfield Hancock's mind as to where the main blow would fall. It said much about Robert E. Lee's perspicacity that the thousands of men who had debouched not twenty-five minutes ago from the woods to the west were converging on what Hancock knew to be the weakest part of his position. But there was no time for such reflections. Hancock had seen how thoroughly Alexander Hays had disrupted Davis' Brigade by flanking it. In the way the Rebel thrust at his center was taking shape, Hancock could see a similar opportunity emerging to the south. He had already sent an aide, Captain Henry H. Bingham, to find George Stannard and alert him to the possibility, but now he determined to go himself.

Riding south along his line, Hancock first encountered Colonel Arthur F. Devereux, whose regiment, part of Colonel Norman J. Hall's small brigade, fronted some rough ground that the Confederates appeared to be avoiding. Military courtesies fell by the wayside as Hancock pointed to the Copse of Trees and ordered Devereux to " 'get in God Damn quick.' " Hancock likely also spoke with the brigade commander, Norman Hall, before riding on toward the sector held by the Second Vermont Brigade, then attached to the First Corps.

Earlier this day, Stannard had disposed his regiments in such a way as to take advantage of the protection offered by the ground, which deployment had placed the 13th and 14th Vermont somewhat in advance of the rest of the Cemetery Ridge line. Skirmishers sent forward by him had been among the first to challenge Pickett's advance as his battle lines approached the Emmitsburg Road. When the Rebel forces veered across his front toward his right, Stannard saw a chance to rip into the enemy's right flank by directing the 13th Vermont to pivot to face north. By the time Hancock rode up, the brigadier general (possibly further encouraged by the Second Corps commander's suggestion through his aide Bingham) had decided to raise the ante by ordering the 16th Vermont forward to extend the left flank of the 13th.*

This repositioning seemed to open up a large hole in the Union line, even as it exposed the left flank of the 16th Vermont to an enfilade. Hancock, displeased about the risks Stannard was taking, complained as he arrived that the Vermont officer had "gone to hell." At first taken aback by the censure, Stannard retorted, " 'To hell it is then, as it is the only thing that can possibly save the day.' " One of Stannard's aides, Lieutenant George G. Benedict, observed the exchange but could not hear what was said over the din of the firing. He was just thinking that Hancock was "the most striking man I ever saw on horseback, and magnificent in the flush and excitement of battle," when, to his horror, he saw the corps chief start and then reel in the saddle.

A pair of nearby officers sprang toward the stricken general, catching him as he toppled from his horse. There was a frantic moment as the men searched for the wound before Hancock finally pointed to his thigh. Blood had begun flowing from it at an alarming rate. " 'Don't let me bleed to death,' " Hancock pleaded. " 'Get something around it quick.' " George Stannard produced a large handkerchief and with Benedict's assistance fashioned a tourniquet that stanched the flow. Someone went to fetch a doctor. Winfield Hancock lay dazed and in a mild state of shock, no longer a factor in the events that were roaring to a climax around him.

After Robert Bright brought him Longstreet's permission to call up Wilcox, an anxious George Pickett dispatched three orderlies in succession, in the hope that at least one might make it through the enemy fire. In the event, all three managed to get through, so that when the third

---

*For their contributions to this day's actions against Pickett and Wilcox, two Vermont officers would be awarded the Medal of Honor. Lieutenant George G. Benedict exposed himself to enemy fire while sorting out the 13th and 16th Vermont Regiments, which had become bunched up in their movement to enfilade Kemper's Brigade. Colonel Wheelock G. Veazy distinguished himself by his initiative in directing the flank movement of the 16th Vermont.

one, Bright, rode up, the exasperated brigadier could only throw up his hands and exclaim, " 'I know; I know.' " By Wilcox's account, "My brigade . . . then moved forward." To his left, David Lang also put the Florida brigade in motion, "in accordance with previous orders to conform to [Wilcox's] . . . movements." With Pickett's Division well out of sight and no one on hand to direct him, Wilcox struck off in the direction he believed Pickett had gone in, more due east than northeast. To the men in the ranks, it appeared as if they were going to take on the Federal army all by themselves. A soldier with Wilcox recalled that "one could hear frequent expressions from the men to the effect: 'What in the devil does this mean?' "

Due to the awkward way Pickett's Division had initially been deployed, Kemper's Brigade had had to execute a series of difficult maneuvers in order to take up its proper place on the right of the front line. After making that first sharp left oblique to close the gap with Garnett's Brigade, Kemper's men had marched toward the Rogers farm, seemingly on a collision course with the section of Cemetery Ridge held by George Stannard's Vermont Brigade. Once he was across the Emmitsburg Road, however, Kemper had stayed with the plan and again obliqued to the left to link with Garnett. This radical move would later allow some boastful Vermont soldiers to claim that their musket fire had turned the head of the Rebel column.

As Kemper's Brigade passed south of the Codori farm buildings, its commander took stock of the fact that he still had not caught up with Garnett. Spying Armistead's ranks coming up some two hundred yards behind Garnett's, James Kemper decided to coordinate with that brigade instead. Accordingly, he rode over to find Armistead, who, following orders, was on foot. " 'Armistead, hurry-up, my men can stand no more,' " Kemper said. " 'I am going to charge those heights and carry them, and I want you to support me.' " " 'I'll do it!' " Armistead declared, passing along the order to double-quick. As Kemper was turning to rejoin his command, Armistead pointed to his brigade with obvious pride. " 'Did you ever see a more perfect line than that on dress parade?' " he inquired.

On his way back to his men, Kemper rode by the Codori farm buildings, where he spotted a wounded officer from Garnett's Brigade. Kemper asked the officer if his wound was serious. The man replied that it was but explained that he expected to be captured soon. When Kemper expressed some surprise, the officer responded, " 'Don't you see those flanking columns the enemy are throwing out on our right to sweep the field?' " This reference to Stannard's maneuver brought Kemper up short; he had never even considered the possibility of such a threat to his flank but had simply assumed that the necessary flank protection for his brigade would be in place. Now recognizing that the danger was a very real one, he spurred on to reach his advancing columns, convinced that only a rush could save them from being chopped up by the enemy flankers. " 'There are the guns, boys,' " he shouted. " 'Go for them!' " His sentence was punctuated by a Yankee bullet that struck him in the groin before ranging upward on an agonizing course that Kemper would later describe as having been "excruciatingly painful." He tumbled to the ground, no longer capable of command. Through the red haze of his pain, he was conscious of enemy soldiers' attempting to carry him into captivity, only to be driven off by his own men, who hauled him a short distance to the rear. The first of George Pickett's division commanders had fallen.

Control of the brigade devolved to Colonel Joseph Mayo of the 3rd Virginia, but by the time he gave his first orders, Colonel William R. Terry of the 24th Virginia and Colonel William T. Fry of Kemper's staff had already addressed Stannard's threat by pivoting portions of two regiments to confront the flankers. All who remained of the 1,781 men who had begun the charge—Mayo later termed it a skirmish line—rushed toward the Copse of Trees. "Our men are falling faster now," recollected John Dooley, "for the deadly musket is at work." Thirty yards from the wall, Dooley himself went down, a bullet having pierced both of his thighs. As the yelling mob of men pressed past and over him, he had an odd thought: "Oh, how I long to know the result, the end of this fearful charge!"

The slaughterously efficient Alexander Hays was ready for all that Pettigrew and Trimble might bring on against him. "When within 100 yards of our line of infantry, the fire of our men could no longer be restrained," Hays later reported. "As soon as they got within range we poured into them and the cannon opened with grape and canister[, and] we mowed them down in heaps," wrote a member of the 125th New York. It was the recollection of John Brady of the 1st Delaware that the "grape, canis ter, minnie, buck and ball were simultaneously poured in one incessant stream, into the advancing column of the enemy." Some in the 14th Connecticut were firing their Sharps breech loaders so fast that they had to pour water "from their canteens . . . upon the overworked guns." The buck-and-ball charges spit out by the 12th New Jersey's Springfield smoothbores spread their own brand of devastation: "I doubt whether anywhere upon that field a more destructive fire was encountered," the regiment's commander bragged. Alexander Hays, given to taking occasional literary excursions in writing his reports, ventured to suggest that the "angel of death alone can produce such a field as was presented." Another Connecticut soldier would never forget how the "shrieks of the wounded and groans of the dying filled the air."

Pettigrew's Brigade was shredded by this fusillade. Lane's Brigade meanwhile drove in from the left, only to meet an all-too-familiar fate: like all the troops ahead of them, these North Carolinians had a difficult and deadly time getting over the stout fencing along the Emmitsburg Road. "Our loss in this vicinity was fearful," recorded an officer in the 7th North Carolina, "the dead and wounding lying in great numbers both in the field and road."

The vicious crossfire and sheeting musketry that swept the open meadow east of the road rendered patently suicidal any Confederate attempt to make it across to the stone wall shielding the enemy. Still, some brave souls tried. The single cannon from Arnold's Rhode Island battery that remained in action along that wall was loaded with canister when a group of Rebels tried to rush it. The crewman holding the lanyard

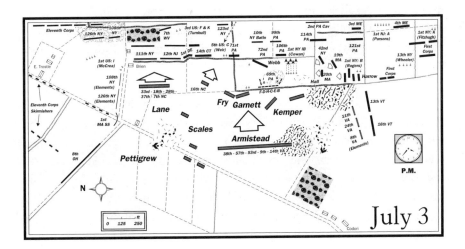

cord stared open-mouthed at the oncoming attackers until the battery's sergeant screamed, " '[W]hy the d——l don't you fire that gun! pull! pull!' " His words served as a bitter epitaph for the handful of soldiers blown away in the blast—who, though often afterward identified with the 26th North Carolina, were more likely members of the 16th.

Two days earlier, the 26th had marched into battle some 800 strong. Following the regiment's terrible struggle with the Iron Brigade in McPherson's Woods, fewer than 300 were left to make the assault against Cemetery Ridge. Another 100 or more were added this day to the rolls of the killed, wounded, and captured. Among those taken prisoner were Sergeant James M. Brooks and Private Daniel Boone Thomas, who together bore the proud flag of the 26th forward until they stood nearly alone, just feet from the stone wall. Then, instead of gun muzzles, hands were extended. " 'Come over on this side of the Lord!' " a Yankee called as the two were hauled over by members of the 12th New Jersey.

Back on the western side of the Emmitsburg Road, James Lane was trying to reorganize his brigade in response to a message from James Longstreet, who wanted him to clear the Yankee flankers away from the left of that deadly pocket fronting the stone wall. When he passed the word along to one of his regimental commanders, however, the man exploded, demanding, " 'My God, General, do you intend rushing your men into such a place unsupported, when the troops on the right are falling back[?]' " Lane thought for a moment and then, as he later wrote, "seeing it was useless to sacrifice my brave men, I ordered my brigade back."

It appears that the majority of Scales' Brigade, commanded here by Colonel W. Lee Lowrance, never crossed the Emmitsburg Road but instead took position along it to fire at the enemy on the hill. The soldiers from North Carolina who two days before had marched without flinching into the maw of Wainwright's cannon on Seminary Ridge could not repeat the performance; Lowrance would later report that "without orders, the brigade retreated." Isaac Trimble could only watch the suffering of Lane's men and the faltering of those under Lowrance. He shared the fate of many Southern officers this day when a bullet hit him, in the left leg. Lying on the ground, racked by pain, the otherwise combative commander was approached by an aide who asked if he should try to rally the demidivision. " 'It's all over! let the men go back,' " Trimble instructed before allowing himself to be helped to the rear.

Also heading back to Seminary Ridge was J. Johnston Pettigrew, whose horse had been killed and whose hand had been broken by a shell burst. With his aide Louis Young, Pettigrew began reforming his regiments as their members came stumbling back. Not long after reaching the ridge, Pettigrew encountered Robert E. Lee, who approved his efforts to rally his men. Before leaving him, Lee said one more thing: " 'General, I am sorry to see you wounded; go to the rear.' "

George Meade's ride to Cemetery Ridge brought him in through Ziegler's Grove, where Alexander Hays' men were tasting victory. An artillery officer in Woodruff's battery, having just watched Hays ride along his line dragging a captured Rebel standard behind him in the dirt, was a bit nonplussed when Meade rode up, addressed him by name, and asked if the enemy had turned. "I said yes, see General Hays has one of their flags," the cannoneer later recalled. To his surprise, Meade looked quite cross at hearing this reply. " 'I don't care for their flag,' " he snapped. " 'Have they turned[?]' " The officer said yes, adding, "They are just turning." At that, Meade set off toward the Copse of Trees, where the fighting was still raging.

Supported to their left by the Alabama and Tennessee regiments of what had been Archer's Brigade, and on their right by all that was left of Kemper's command, the soldiers of Garnett's Brigade were able to push into the section of the outer angle that had been abandoned by the 71st Pennsylvania. The rattle of musketry from both sides had crescendoed into a constant tearing. At some points along the wall, the Yankees had fled, and Garnett's men stood on the stones yelling triumphantly at their foes. Their commander sent word for Armistead to come forward right away, and then, anticipating the extra push that brigade would provide, ordered his own troops to fall back a little.

A Federal regiment now appeared ahead of Garnett on the crest, set itself, and fired a volley that swept through the Virginia files. Private Robert H. Irvine saw but could hardly comprehend what happened next: "Just as the General turned his horse's head slightly to the left he was struck in the head by a rifle or musket ball and fell dead from his horse." The image of Garnett's terrified bay galloping wildly to the rear was one that some would later regard as being emblematic of Confederate fortunes this day.

The last hope for a Southern victory on Cemetery Ridge emerged from the gunpowder fog, its ranks still holding enough shape to denote the regiments, its colorful battle flags defiantly marking the intervals. Lewis Armistead was marching toward his moment of destiny.

The situation was becoming desperate for the 69th Pennsylvania. On its left flank, friendly fire from Cowan's battery had killed two Company G privates and possibly two more in Company K. This added an unnerving extra element of risk to the hard fight in their front, mostly against Kemper's men positioned over the rough ground. A number of Pennsylvanians cracked and ran, some through Cowan's battery, others into the Copse of Trees.

A squad of Rebels made a desperate rush into the weakened flank, aiming for Cowan's guns. It cost Cowan two crewmen engaged in loading double canister charges. Behind the gunners appeared Henry Hunt, whose usual composure was another casualty of the moment: " 'See'em!' " he cried, and fired his revolver at the charging enemy squad. " 'See'em!' " Hunt's horse reared and fell, trapping him under its weight. The battery salvoed its shotgun blasts and obliterated the Confederate intruders, but with more Rebel infantry teeming nearby, it was time for Cowan's gunners to get out. They hauled their cannon back over the ridge, stopping on the way to free the Army of the Potomac's artillery chief from underneath his dead animal.

Like its predecessors, Armistead's Brigade had taken losses in covering the distance from the Emmitsburg Road to the Federal line along Cemetery Ridge. After carefully dressing the formation of his company in the 9th Virginia, which had been disordered in clambering over the fence along the road, Lieutenant John C. Niemeyer turned to a friend and exclaimed, " 'John, what a beautiful line.' " Minutes later, Niemeyer was dead. Another lieutenant, this one in the 53rd Virginia, thought it "awful the way the men dropped" as they approached the enemy position. The combination of Federal fire and the mobs of friendly troops near the stone wall caused Armistead's advance to lose steam. The brigadier general was with Lieutenant Colonel Rawley W. Martin as he reached the impasse. " 'Martin, we can't stay here; we must go over that wall,' " Armistead said. " 'Then we'll go forward,' " Martin responded. Armistead stuck his felt hat on the tip of his sword and raised it high for all to see, then dodged ahead to stand atop the stone wall. " 'Boys, give them the cold steel!' " he cried. " 'Who will follow me?' "

The 71st Pennsylvania, reunited in its support position, was holding its section of the stone wall, leading the brigade commander, Alexander Webb, to conclude that if only he could plug the gap at the angle, he might stand a good chance of ending the Confederate effort once and for all. The 72nd Pennsylvania was perfectly disposed to accomplish this, as its volleys had already told heavily on the enemy troops there. But conceiving a plan was one thing, and getting others to carry it out was something else again, as Webb soon discovered. In his frenzy to make things happen, he ignored the chain of command, bypassing the 72nd's colonel to call personally upon the men to charge. Most could not hear him amid the tumult, and those who could had little idea who he was; certainly none intended to follow him into a nest of deadly Rebels. To a man, the members of the 72nd stood their ground, deaf to Webb's pleas for them to advance. Driven by a mixture of irritation, frustration, and shame, Alexander Webb walked down the slope to the right flank of the 69th.

Sharing his frustration was Frank Haskell, whose pride and anger had been stirred by the sight of the "damned red flags of the rebellion" sprouting along the section of the wall conceded by the 71st. After trying without success to rally some stragglers (he thought they were from the 72nd, but more likely they were fragments of the 69th), he rode south along the ridge in search of help and found Norman Hall, pursuant to his conversation with Hancock, advancing his little brigade toward the copse of trees. Having confirmed Hall's intentions, Haskell continued on and observed some regiments from Harrow's brigade moving to the same purpose. Pointing toward the maelstrom, Haskell shouted, " 'See the gray-backs run!' "

The enemy's surge into the angle positioned Rebel soldiers to fire into the rear of the 69th. Someone in the regiment ordered the three right companies to change front to meet the new threat. Companies A and I, on the extreme end of the line, accordingly began wheeling east, backstepping south to face north. The captain in charge of Company F, however, was killed before he could issue the order, so his men remained facing west. Attracted by the opening, Rebel squads swarmed along the wall, coming up on Company F from behind and killing, wounding, or capturing every last man in its ranks. To an officer of the 69th, it seemed "as though our regiment would be annihilated, [as] the contest here became a hand to hand affair." At some point during this melee, the 69th's commander, Dennis O'Kane, was mortally wounded.

Sword still aloft, the pierced felt hat he had raised on its tip now resting on its hilt, Lewis Armistead pushed along with the surge that wiped out Company F. Inside the outer angle, there were at least 150 men, maybe more, representing both wings of the advance that had spread across more than a mile at its outset. Armistead had just reached the left gun of Cushing's abandoned pair when his luck ran out: hit in the chest and arm, he fell only a few yards inside the outer angle. The shock of his wounding was such that those around him thought he was dead. Armistead had been the driving force behind the last effort, and there was no one on hand to take up the initiative. Almost as quickly as it had come crashing in, the Rebel tide inside the outer angle ebbed back to the wall.

Little Round Top this day was more a point of observation than a place of danger, though Rebel snipers along Houck's Ridge made it deadly enough for the unwary. With a few precautions, the Federal signal station remained active throughout the day, affording its operators a bird's-eye view of the Cemetery Ridge assault. Signalman Norman H. Camp was not unused to the curiosities of combat situations, but even he was surprised by the reaction of the nearby infantry supports. As Camp recalled it, "When the gallant Virginians had pierced our first Artillery line, the men of a New York regiment . . . arose from their kneeling positions in a rifle pit running close to my signal station, and loudly applauded the rebel bravery by clapping their hands as if at a theater."

(3:40 P.M.–Midnight)

Armistead's fall roughly coincided with the arrival on the scene of Union reinforcements from the southern sector of the Cemetery Ridge line. Some of the units swung to the north of the Copse of Trees, while others angled around south of it.* In the thick of things, working to coordinate the counterstrokes, John Gibbon was shot in his left arm; the bullet fractured his shoulder blade on its way out. The fighting general was led from the field, "the sounds of the contest on the hill still ringing in my ears," as he later remembered. His men carried on without him: newly strengthened on both its flanks, the 69th Pennsylvania, whose center had never relinquished the front wall, restored its line. For the Confederates still within the perimeter, the options no longer included victory. "The final moment has come where there must be instant flight, instant surrender, or instant death," noted one of Pickett's officers.

Among the new arrivals was Battery C, 5th United States Light Artillery, Gulian Weir commanding. The young lieutenant had spent the worst night of his life convinced that he had lost almost all of his battery to the enemy. The morning light, however, had revealed the (to him) incredible sight of his missing guns in camp just a short distance away. Weir had reorganized his battery, gotten it resupplied, and then spent several frustrating hours trying to find something for it to do. Once the bombardment began, his short-range Napoleons were not in demand, as the call was for long-range rifled cannon; he and his gunners were actually on their way back to the artillery reserve when a frantic rider brought orders

---

*In this phase of the action, Corporal Henry D. O'Brien of the 1st Minnesota picked up his regiment's fallen flag and urged his men forward, despite being twice wounded. For this he would receive a Medal of Honor, as would Major Edmund Rice of the 19th Massachusetts, who, though wounded, led his men in their counter-charge.

for all guns to go to the front. After several more misadventures, Weir's six tubes rolled into position on Cemetery Hill, replacing Arnold's battered Rhode Island command.

Weir's gunners set up after the charge had reached its climax but while everything was still in a state of general confusion. Not knowing precisely where matters stood, Weir's well-drilled crews simply did as they had been trained, firing canister blasts into the Confederate troops mobbed in their front. Unfortunately, many of those men were at that moment trying to surrender. The young Yankee officer himself recollected that "numbers of the enemy came up in front of, and through the battery to give themselves up, throwing themselves on the ground, as my guns in their front were fired." Weir probably sensed that the situation was beyond anyone's control as his guns belched round after round into the enemy. When one frightened Rebel stumbled out of the maelstrom to ask him, " 'Where can I go to get out of this Hellish fire?,' " Weir pointed rearward and advised, " 'Go down there, I wish I could go with you.' "

The surviving officers of Pickett's and Archer's commands first tried to consolidate their units just a short distance from the stone wall, hoping to provide a base of fire that would bolster the next assault wave when it appeared. Among their number was Joseph Mayo, now commanding Kemper's Brigade. Mayo was looking to the rear—now bereft of men in gray, save for the knots of wounded men slowly heading back toward Seminary Ridge—when a private standing next to him voiced his very thought: " 'Oh! Colonel,' " he said, " 'why don't they support us?' "

There would be no support for them this day. James Longstreet, entrusted by Lee with responsibility for continuing the action if he believed it might succeed, had determined that it could not. According to Richard Anderson, who had already committed Wilcox's and Perry's Brigades to the effort, "I was about to move forward Wright's and Posey's brigades, when Lieutenant-General Longstreet directed me to stop the movement, advising that it was useless, and would only involve unnecessary loss, as the assault had failed."* Robert Rodes, whose division was in a similar position to support the left wing, also received notice "that the attack had already failed."

*The evidence is strong that in addition to Wright's and Posey's commands, Mahone's Brigade was also readied to advance at this time.

Waiting in Gettysburg on Ewell's orders to strike if the opportunity presented itself, Jubal Early was visited by a courier bringing news: "Longstreet & Hill have been driven back," he reported.

As the Confederates began retreating across the fields in groups or rough formations, some Federals chased after them, firing as they went. One defiant Rebel was shot dead after refusing to lower his gun when surrounded by members of the 13th Vermont. Most, however, were more resigned: a Second Corps staff officer saw many dispirited Rebels "holding up their handkerchiefs or a piece of white paper in token of surrender." Along the front held by the 69th Pennsylvania, the focus shifted from fighting to regrouping the various companies, tending to the wounded, and identifying the dead.*

"As soon as the smoke lifted sufficiently to permit us to see," recollected a member of the 1st Minnesota, "all that could be seen of the mighty force . . . was scattered and running to the rear." "It was a time of indescribable enthusiasm and excitement," added a New York officer. "Hats and caps and shouts filled the air. Sallies to the front were made, and battle-flags and trophies of our victory were gathered and brought in." A burst of gunfire from one portion of the line brought Alexander Hays riding over, still dragging the captured Confederate flag behind him. " 'Stop firing, you —— fools; don't you know enough to stop firing[?],' " he shouted. " 'It's all over—stop! stop! stop!' "

Several companies shook out from the main line and advanced cautiously as far as the Emmitsburg Road to round up prisoners and view the carnage. "We could have picked off many of them," a Federal rifleman reflected, "[but] somehow, we did not have much desire to kill someone." Such charity was not universal. A Yankee squad out gathering up prisoners faced off against a desperate Rebel who turned his gun on the

---

*A number of enemy regimental flags were captured in the course of this action, earning the Union soldiers involved Medals of Honor. Elijah W. Bacon, Christopher Flynn, and William B. Hincks of the 14th Connecticut; Morris Brown Jr. and Jerry Wall of the 126th New York; John E. Clopp of the 71st Pennsylvania; Joseph H. De Castro, Benjamin F. Falls, Benjamin H. Jellison, and John H. Robinson of the 19th Massachusetts; John B. Mayberry and Bernard McCarren of the 1st Delaware; John Miller and James Richmond of the 8th Ohio; Oliver P. Rood of the 20th Indiana; Marshall Sherman of the 1st Minnesota; and James Wiley of the 59th New York were all so honored. Also receiving the medal for his actions this day was Brigadier General Alexander S. Webb.

officer in charge, dropping it only when the Federal covered him with his own revolver. The officer recalled, "It was all I could do to keep the boys from killing him." "There were literally acres of dead lying in front of our line," wrote one of Hays' officers. "I counted 16 dead bodies on one rod square."

Second Corps staff officer Captain Henry Bingham saw a group of Union soldiers carrying a single Rebel; when he challenged them, he was informed that they were taking care of an important prisoner. Bingham dismounted, identified himself as an aide to Hancock, and asked the Confederate officer his name. It was Lewis Armistead. Observing the great suffering Armistead was experiencing, Bingham solicitously offered to protect his valuables. This led Armistead to confide that Hancock was "an old and valued friend of his" and to ask his aide to pass along a message: " 'Tell Gen. Hancock for me that I have done him and done you all an injury which I shall regret [until] . . . the longest day I live.' " Bingham secured the wounded officer's "spurs, watch, chain, seal and pocketbook," then saw that he was taken to a field hospital, where he died on July 5.

The ubiquitous Frank Haskell managed to meet up with George Meade as the latter reached the area near the breakthrough on Cemetery Ridge. Although he had already been told that the enemy was retreating, Meade needed to see it for himself. " 'How is it going here?' " he demanded of Haskell. " 'I believe, General, the enemy's attack is repulsed,' " came the answer. " '*What? is the assault entirely repulsed?*' " Meade asked. " 'It is, Sir,' " Haskell responded. Meade let this confirmation soak in for a moment. " '*Thank God,*' " he said.

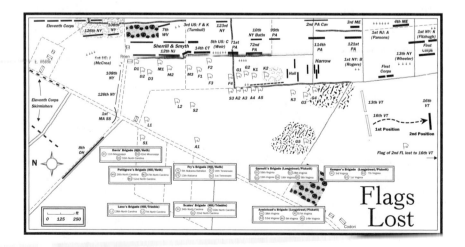

Collecting himself, Meade asked who commanded this section. Told by Haskell that John Caldwell was now in charge, the army chief relayed some orders to be passed on. The troops were to be reformed in case the enemy should try another attack, Meade instructed, and then he designated places for the reinforcements that would be arriving. Before moving along, he issued one more directive: " '*If the enemy does attack, charge him in the flank, and sweep him from the field, do you understand*[?]' " After indicating that he did understand, Haskell watched the general ride off.

Meade had not gone far before he encountered Major William G. Mitchell, another of Hancock's aides, carrying a message from the wounded general. As Mitchell later recollected it, he reported in Hancock's name that the " 'troops under my command have repulsed the enemy's assault and . . . we have gained a great victory. The enemy is now flying in all directions in my front.' " Mitchell also informed Meade of his commander's wounding, prompting the reply, " 'Say to General Hancock that I regret exceedingly that he is wounded and that I thank him for the Country and for myself for the service he has rendered today.' "

Lacking any field guide or brief regarding the objective of Pickett's attack, the two reinforcing brigades under Cadmus Wilcox, beginning from even farther south than Kemper's Brigade, had angled slightly left as they advanced, though not far enough left to connect with the Virginians. Instead, Wilcox and Lang marched straight into the sights of McGilvery's long line of cannon. Having enjoyed only a limited opportunity to pound Pickett's formations, the Yankee gunners lavished on the two small brigades that suddenly appeared before them their undivided and enthusiastic attention. An Alabama man soon to be struck down would recollect how "a storm of shot and shell was poured upon us." A Florida soldier, commenting on the wall of artillery ahead, declared with a touch of dry humor that given the Rebels' "weary and wasted forces, it was [thought] impolitic to storm." One of Lang's officers reported that his "men were falling all around me with brains blown out, arms off and wounded in every description."

The two Confederate brigades seemed to be targeting the 14th Vermont, in George Stannard's line. Observing their approach from Cemetery Ridge, alert Union officers turned the north-facing 16th Vermont completely about in order to add its musketry to the canister and shrapnel pummeling Wilcox's troops. The regiment's commander quickly secured permission from Standard to execute a short charge that snatched prisoners and some flags.*

There was brief respite from the punishment when Major John Cheeves Haskell arrived on the scene with five guns that Edward P. Alexander deemed suitable for close support. Haskell's men got in a few good shots against the Vermont troops before McGilvery's collection of batteries lashed out at them. "In a very few minutes these guns had disabled several of mine, killing and wounding quite a number of men and horses," Haskell wrote. In his after-action report, Wilcox would note that "seeing none of the troops that I was ordered to support, and knowing that my small force could do nothing save to make a useless sacrifice of themselves, I ordered them back." Added David Lang, "Owing to the noise and scattered condition of the men, it was impossible to have the order to retreat properly extended and I am afraid that many men, while firing from behind rocks and trees, did not hear the order, and remained there until captured."

East of Gettysburg, the largest cavalry-versus-cavalry fight of the three days was also coming to an end. Unlike the assault on Cemetery Ridge, the action here never reached a dramatic climax somehow worthy of the effort. Instead it unfolded as a seemingly purposeless series of actions and reactions that, when it was all over, left the participants feeling relieved, exhilarated, and generally confused.

There was no single controlling figure on the Confederate side. Although Jeb Stuart commanded all the Rebel units on the scene, he remained with the right wing near John Rummel's farm and appears to have exercised little actual direction over the left wing under Fitzhugh Lee. Stuart had the numerical edge in artillery, with fourteen guns to the Federals' ten, but he never massed them to advantage, whereas the Yankees' cannon worked in concert and thereby remained an effective factor throughout the engagement.

At one point, several thousand horsemen were either moving across

---

*Among those captured was a slightly wounded Lewis T. Powell of Company I, 2nd Florida. Powell would eventually escape his captors, link up with Confederate secret agents in Baltimore, and wind up playing a prominent role in John Wilkes Booth's 1865 assassination strike at the U.S. government leadership.

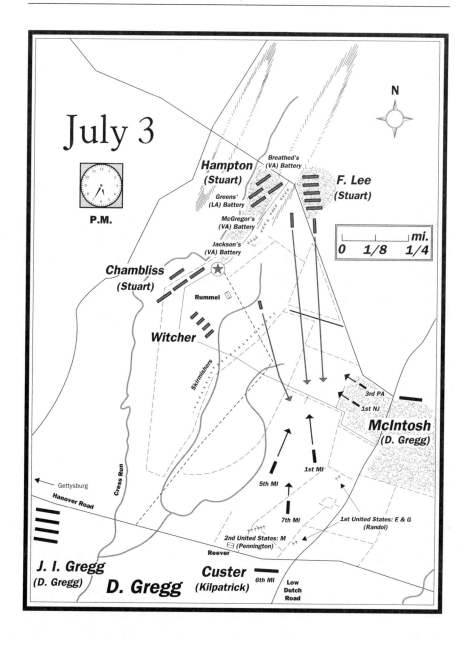

July 3

P.M.

Hampton
(Stuart)

Breathed's
(VA) Battery

F. Lee
(Stuart)

Greens'
(LA) Battery

McGregor's
(VA) Battery

Jackson's
(VA) Battery

N

mi.
0   1/8   1/4

Chambliss
(Stuart)

Rummel

Witcher

Skirmishers

3rd PA

1st NJ

McIntosh
(D. Gregg)

Cress Run

Gettysburg

Hanover Road

1st MI

5th MI

7th MI

1st United States: E & G
(Randol)

2nd United States: M
(Pennington)

Reever

J. I. Gregg
(D. Gregg)

D. Gregg

Custer
(Kilpatrick)

6th MI

Low
Dutch
Road

or fighting in the fields north of the Hanover Road and just west of the
Low Dutch Road. Although Confederate combat doctrine usually
favored the pistol over the sword, on this day, observed a Federal officer,
the Rebels advanced "with sabers drawn and glistening like silver in the
bright sunlight." A charging unit would drive back an enemy advance

that had reached the end of its tether, only to be struck either in front or in flank by a counterthrust that, more often than not, sent it reeling. It was likely one such countercharge by the 3rd Pennsylvania Cavalry* that knocked the props out from under the last major Rebel mounted effort, letting the combat subside into the dismounted skirmishing with which it had begun hours earlier. As darkness settled over the churned-up, bloody fields, the cannon on both sides closed the books on this day's fighting here.

Stuart's proper place this night was with the main army, so he withdrew to the York Pike, leaving behind a screen of pickets to cover the movement. The Federals remained on the scene in greater force and would later cite this fact as evidence of victory. In his postbattle report, Stuart would claim that his actions had rendered "Ewell's left [flank] entirely secure," inspired "some apprehension" on the part of the enemy infantry units near the Baltimore Pike, and maintained Confederate possession of a position that proffered an excellent "view of the routes leading to the enemy's rear." David Gregg had a simpler take on the entire affair, one that made it patently obvious which cavalry chief he believed had carried out his mission. Referring to Stuart, Gregg declared, "His was to do, ours to prevent."

Judson Kilpatrick was a doer. He was expected to get things done, to make things happen. Sadly for many of those fated to serve under the man they called "Kill-cavalry," no one responsible for supervising Kilpatrick looked very closely at how he obtained his results, or even considered whether they were really worth getting in the first place.

It was around midday when Kilpatrick brought Elon J. Farnsworth's brigade† of his division into a position southwest of Big Round Top, opposite the right flank of the Rebel infantry line that stretched from the Devil's Den around the western base of Big Round Top before swinging over toward the Emmitsburg Road. A detachment from Farnsworth's command chased Rebel pickets away from Bushman Hill, allowing Lieutenant Samuel S. Elder to set up his Battery E of the 4th United States

---

*For the courage he displayed in leading this countercharge, Captain William E. Miller of the 3rd Pennsylvania Cavalry would receive a Medal of Honor.
†Farnsworth was one of the three young cavalry officers who were promoted several ranks by Meade right after he took command. George Custer and Wesley Merritt were the other two.

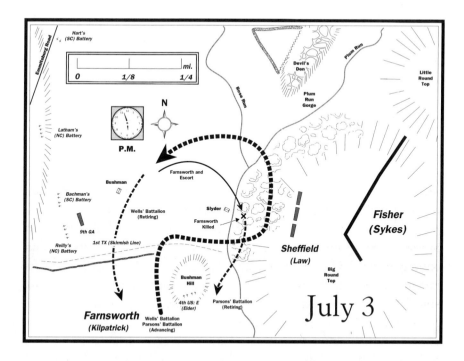

Light Artillery on that site. Not far away, a scouting squadron from the 1st Vermont Cavalry even poked along the dirt lane leading to the Bushman farm buildings without meeting a great deal of opposition.

At roughly the same time, Wesley Merritt was aggressively probing along the Emmitsburg Road, drawing to him all of the Confederate cavalry assigned to that flank, as well as portions of Tige Anderson's Georgia infantry brigade. Perhaps hoping to exploit the Confederate preoccupation with Merritt's effort, Kilpatrick hastily sent the 1st West Virginia Cavalry thrusting against the Rebels posted along Big Round Top's western base. The mounted charge, not preceded by any artillery fire to soften the defenses, got as far as a rail fence that no one had noticed, woven tight with withes. A few of the cavalrymen dismounted and tried to pull the fence apart, but they succeeded only in attracting the attention of a portion of the 1st Texas, which rushed into position to scythe the fence line with a killing volley. A second Mounted effort, by the 18th Pennsylvania and 5th New York, also foundered.

Kilpatrick, however, was not ready to quit. By the time he made up his mind, Merritt's reconnaissance up the Emmitsburg Road had lost its momentum, the Cemetery Ridge assault had collapsed, and the men of Hood's Division felt reasonably confident that the Yankee infantry on the

Round Tops posed no aggressive threat. Psychologically, the likelihood that even a sharp cavalry attack could incite panic among these Southern veterans was small indeed. Nor did the terrain aid Kilpatrick's cause: while not especially hilly, it featured a number of walled fields, narrow trails, and points of advantage that had already been secured by Rebel soldiers. Nonetheless, "Kill-cavalry" was determined to attack again.

The unit he selected for the mission was the 1st Vermont Cavalry. Elon Farnsworth conferred with Major John W. Benett, whose service on the regimental skirmish line earlier this day had provided him with a good sense of the ground. After listening to what Benett had to say, and seeing some of it for himself, Farnsworth concluded that there was not the "slightest chance for a successful charge." This was something that Judson Kilpatrick did not want to hear. " 'General Farnsworth, well, somebody can charge,' " Kilpatrick responded after his subordinate delivered his negative assessment. Getting the message, the younger, newly minted brigadier went off to organize the 1st Vermonters for the effort, though he told an officer that the prospect was "too awful to think of."

Two battalions of the 1st Vermont Cavalry undertook this attack, perhaps 300 men in all. Farnsworth accompanied Major William Wells' battalion, which was to be supported by the one led by Captain Henry Parsons. Since skirmish lines were never intended to hold ground, the charging Yankee column easily blew through the widely spaced screen maintained by the 1st Texas. Bursting out from around the western side of Bushman Hill, Wells' riders veered east to run along the rear of the Rebel picket line, toward the western slope of Big Round Top.

The portion of Hood's Division that held that sector was mostly posted up the slope a bit, so as the yelling, slashing cavalry column snaked over to their rear, the unpanicked Rebel infantrymen were able to turn and begin firing on the troopers from above. Evander Law now came hustling back from the Emmitsburg Road, having disposed of Merritt's threat, and ordered the regiment closest to the intruders to block the lane they were using. The nearest unit was the 4th Alabama, which threw its line across the lane too late to cut off Wells' men but just in time to be hit by Parsons' column. The first infantry section was still trying to form when the support group rode into its line, scattering many of the Alabamians.

Farnsworth and Wells crossed Plum Run and, after turning away from the boulder-strewn area around Devil's Den, headed toward the

Bushman farm, crossing Rose Run. On the crest of the ridge line west of the farm, they spotted the Rebel batteries that had dueled with Merritt's small column, all of them pointed toward the south. Even as Farnsworth paused to consider his next move, a double-quicking enemy infantry regiment, the 9th Georgia, moved among the guns and formed to confront the troopers. With them was Evander Law, who would later admit to having been " 'in hot water' for a few minutes, while watching to see what direction the cavalry would take." Around the same time, a portion of the 4th Alabama that had not been routed by Parsons' men began shooting into the rear of Wells' column.

Clearly, it was time to go. Most of the Yankee cavalrymen charged southward, broke through the rear of the 1st Texas skirmish line, and regained their starting point near Bushman's Hill. Not with them was Elon Farnsworth. Some of the Confederate cannon had been wheeled around to shell the intruders, and one of the first shots knocked him off his horse. With the 1st Texas rapidly closing that route, the 9th Georgia moving purposefully toward them, and the 4th Alabama still causing trouble, the only recourse for Farnsworth's small contingent seemed to be to return the way they had come in. An unlucky trooper on the lower end of the food chain surrendered his horse to the boy general, and he and the few riders with him pushed back toward Big Round Top, hoping to link up with Parsons' command.

Some did make it, but others, including Farnsworth himself, were felled by rifle fire from different Alabama troops, among them William Oates' 15th Regiment. Parsons and Wells, though badly wounded, escaped;* Farnsworth, shot several times, did not. Whether he was killed after refusing to surrender or shot himself when surrender became inevitable would be hotly debated after the battle. The testimony of two Federal surgeons who viewed his body and reported no head wounds tended to support the former scenario.

As for Kilpatrick, his hopes of disrupting the Confederate right flank or abetting a countermove by Meade were not to be realized this day. Drawn to the area by reports of the fight, James Longstreet found Evander Law and was informed by him that the danger was past. Law would proudly recollect how Longstreet "warmly congratulated me on the manner in which the situation had been handled."

*Wells would be awarded a Medal of Honor for his leadership in this action.

* * *

"As soon as the assault [against Cemetery Ridge] was repulsed," George Meade would afterward testify,

> I went immediately to the extreme left of my line, with the determination of advancing the left and making an assault upon the enemy's lines. So soon as I arrived at the left I gave the necessary orders for the pickets and skirmishers in front to be thrown forward to feel the enemy, and for all preparation to be made for the assault. The great length of the line, and the time required to carry these orders out to the front, and the movement subsequently made, before the report given to me of the condition of the forces in the front and left, caused it to be so late in the evening as to induce me to abandon the assault which I had contemplated.

Robert E. Lee's first tasks were to see that his troops were rallied and his officers prepared to meet any contingency. The English observer Fremantle pronounced Lee's comportment at this time "perfectly sublime. . . . His face . . . did not show signs of the slightest disappointment, care, or annoyance; and he was addressing to every soldier he met a few words of encouragement, such as, 'All this will come right in the end: we'll talk it over afterwards; but in the mean time, all good men must rally.' " A wounded officer being helped to the rear remembered passing "General Lee, who was forming a line of the slightly wounded," while another in retreat found strength in the army commander's composure, which he termed "ineffably grand." Noting how intently Fremantle was watching him, Lee commented to the foreign observer, " 'This has been a sad day for us, Colonel—a sad day; but we can't expect always to gain victories.' "

Generals Longstreet and Hill were kept busy as well. "I sent my staff officers to the rear to assist in rallying the troops," remembered Longstreet, "and hurried to our line of batteries, as the only support that I could give them, knowing that my presence would impress upon every one of them the necessity of holding the ground to the last extremity." He also tried to calm George Pickett, who exclaimed, " 'General, I am ruined. My division is gone; it is destroyed.' " A. P. Hill, for his part, went out to his skirmish line and ordered those troops to reform along Seminary Ridge. Another retreating soldier came across Joseph R. Davis, who seemed to be in shock; when asked where the brigade might be found, Davis "pointed his sword up to the skies, but did not say a word, and stood there for a moment knocking pebbles out of the path with the point of his sword," the soldier recalled. "He could not talk, and neither could I."

Lee, too, endured some personally painful moments. When he encountered George Pickett and began telling him where to regroup his division, a grief-stricken Pickett interjected, " 'General Lee, I have no division now, Armistead is down, Garnett is down, and Kemper is mortally wounded.' " " 'Come, General Pickett,' " Lee replied, " 'this has been my fight and upon my shoulders rests the blame. The men and officers of your command have written the name of Virginia as high today as it has ever been written before.' " He also met briefly with James Kemper, who was convinced (wrongly, as it developed) that he was dying from his wound, and Cadmus Wilcox, whose nerves had been badly shaken by two days of desperate combat. The former was the recipient of Lee's sympathy, and the latter of his best efforts at providing some comfort, as he claimed all responsibility and asked for Wilcox's help in setting things right.

One colorful thread of the Gettysburg legend has Lee apologizing to his soldiers and telling them that the whole debacle was his fault, and his alone. While such recollections may have been helpful in the postwar climate of factional healing, and while they may have promoted adulation of Lee, they must be docketed alongside Gettysburg's other myths. He had nothing to apologize for, as he had fully discharged his duties by crafting a well-considered plan and carefully weighing the odds. Nothing in life was certain, and unfortunate though the events of this day were, and however much it pained him to see his men suffer, he had no cause for self-recrimination.

Perhaps most important and significant was that Lee abandoned any further thought of offensive action at Gettysburg. All of his actions on July 2 and through the assault of July 3 had eschewed defensive concerns in favor of a single-minded focus on the offensive. Now, however, it was time for him to think of protecting his army. To ensure that there would be no misunderstandings, Lee met separately with each of his corps commanders.

His first conference was with James Longstreet, who recalled that his superior "remained with me for a long time." Together they decided to pull the First Corps back to its preassault positions of July 2. Lafayette McLaws received subsequent instructions to "retire to your position of yesterday," while Evander Law was told "to withdraw the division from the lines it had held since the evening of the 2d to the ridge near the

Emmitsburg Road, from which it had advanced to the attack on that day." Edward P. Alexander was also directed to return "to the position from which the attack began on the 2d."*

Lee spoke with Richard Ewell around sunset. No longer would Ewell's Corps hold its positions in and east of the town; the divisions under Rodes and Johnson were ordered to that part of Seminary Ridge where the Union First Corps had made its final stand on July 1, while Early's Division was posted to the low ground behind them, over which Scales' and Perrin's Brigades had attacked. Some of Johnson's men were misdirected in their march and did not find the way until early the next morning. Those who did reach the designated encampment on time were less than pleased with the conditions that greeted them there, as few of the dead Federal soldiers had been buried. The smell was horrendous in places.

It was well after dark when Lee met with A. P. Hill, whose corps was essentially to hold its positions along lower Seminary Ridge. A cavalry officer reporting to Lee for instructions found him and Hill "seated on camp-stools with a map spread upon their knees"; the two were very likely drawing up a plan for Hill's men to lead the army's withdrawal from Gettysburg, set to begin twenty-four hours later, unless the enemy attacked before that time.

Newsman Charles Coffin rode slowly along Cemetery Ridge. "The dead were everywhere thickly strewn," he observed. Such sights were not what the editors back home wanted their field men to dwell upon. Coffin and Whitelaw Reid were among those who found their way to Meade's head-quarters, moved near to but not back into the Leister house, which was now filled with wounded. Reid thought Meade looked "calm as ever," while Coffin described him as "stooping, weary, his slouched hat laid aside, so that the breeze might fan his brow."

At 8:35 P.M., Meade sent off a note to Henry Halleck reporting the repulse of the enemy assault. "The loss upon our side has been consider-able," he conceded. His efforts to determine whether Lee was retreating,

---

*In the midst of this withdrawal, several Federal regiments (mostly from Crawford's division) probed the area of the wheat field, where they scrapped with the 15th Georgia, serving as rear guard. In this, July 3rd's final combat action, Sergeant James B. Thompson of the 13th Pennsylvania Reserves captured the Rebel regiment's flag, for which action he would receive a Medal of Honor.

he noted, had led him to conclude that the enemy remained in force. "At the present hour all is quiet," he summarized, adding that the "army is in fine spirits."

This long day of combat made it impossible even for the indomitable Mrs. Barlow to cross the lines as she had done on July 2. The determined Arabella was thwarted but not discouraged. She would try again tomorrow to find her wounded husband, Francis. This time she would succeed.

When he went to bed this night, Navy Secretary Gideon Welles was as up to date on Gettysburg as anyone in Washington—meaning that he knew what the situation had been as of 3:00 P.M. the previous day, the time of the last dispatch received from Meade. Everything Welles had been hearing indicated that "there will be a battle in the neighborhood of Gettysburg." He had barely turned out the light when a courier arrived from the War Department to tell him that news was arriving via Hanover Station from a source using his name as a reference. Welles hurried over to the telegraph office, where he found Lincoln waiting. " 'Who is Byington?' " the president asked. Someone using that name was sending the latest Gettysburg news, and when instructed to identify himself had replied only, " 'Ask the Secretary of the Navy.' "

Welles thought for a moment, recalling the man. He confirmed that Homer Byington was a Connecticut newspaperman who also freelanced for the *New York Tribune*. With the bonafides established, those present read over Byington's reports, which conveyed the understanding, by Welles' account, that a "great and bloody battle was fought, and our army has the best of it, but the end is not yet." Even as Welles and Lincoln were digesting this news, rumors were trickling into the city by other means. The officer commanding Washington's defenses heard this evening that "we had a decided success near Gettysburg. The Rebel Generals Longstreet and Barksdale were killed and General Sickles lost a leg."

In Richmond, the prevailing mood this day was relief over the fact that the Yankee force that had been threatening the capital from the east was withdrawing. War Department clerk John B. Jones added his own optimistic spin, expressing the hope that the troops had been summoned to

Washington, "where they may be much needed." Although there was real concern about the health of President Jefferson Davis, Jones believed that affairs in Richmond would have very little impact on Lee's northern expedition. "Gen. Lee's course is right onward," Jones noted in his diary, "and cannot be affected by events here."

Army of the Potomac Provost Marshal Marsena Patrick had his hands full in the wake of the Cemetery Ridge assault. Making do with what he had, Patrick organized "a guard of Stragglers" to watch over the prisoners his mounted units were bringing in to a temporary stockade near Rock Creek. To a cavalryman who saw them, this crowd of POWs—Patrick put their number at around 2,000—"looked sorry." Mississippi officer William Peel was among those who were herded into an open field and subjected to a little speech designed both to reassure and to subdue them. After promising that they would be treated kindly, the provost marshal made it clear that any disturbances would be handled by his "splendid cavalry," under orders "to charge you, cutting & slashing, right & left, indiscriminately."

Returning toward the front, Patrick spotted a line of Rebel prisoners with a captured major in their midst. He rode over to the group and spoke with the officer, hoping to confirm a rumor he had heard that George Pickett had been killed in the attack. " 'No, sir,' " the Confederate officer replied. " 'Genl. Pickett is safe.' " Patrick looked up at the ridge line where so desperate a struggle had been fought, then ventured the opinion that with " 'a few more men Major, . . . you would have gained your independence right here.' " The captured officer thought for a moment. " 'Yes, General,' " he responded at last, " 'and right here we have lost it.' "

Because postbattle accountings of losses on the Federal side cover the entire period of the combat at Gettysburg, with no distinctions made among the three days, casualty counts are at best rough estimates. In its two days on the field, the Second Corps reported 4,369 killed, wounded, and missing, of which total approximately 2,800 fell on July 2, leaving losses of some 1,570 on July 3 (including casualties of the action at the Bliss farm). The addition of about 306 losses in the Second Vermont Brigade and perhaps 125 more in the artillery yields a presumed total of 2,001. Not surprisingly, the greatest sin-

gle loss was in the Philadelphia Brigade, which suffered 418 casualties in this day's action.

The fighting on July 3 took one corps commander (Hancock) and his first replacement (Gibbon) out of action; the man leading the principal division involved, Alexander Hays, emerged without serious injury. On a brigade level, Alexander Webb was struck in the groin—"but God preserved me," he noted. Equally unlucky were Hays' brigadiers Thomas Smyth (wounded) and Eliakim Sherrill (mortally wounded). The cadre of young artillery officers likewise paid a high price, with James Rorty and Alonzo Cushing dead and George Woodruff mortally wounded.

Ironically, the ambiguities that initially surrounded the Confederate losses would inspire generations of researchers to sift through the historical record, ultimately resulting in more accurate totals than are available for the Union side. George Pickett's division lost 2,640 men, or 45 percent of its roster, with the brigade losses at 1,057 for Armistead, 905 for Garnett, and 678 for Kemper. Of the 209 officers and men who began the advance in John Dooley's 1st Virginia, 113 would become casualties. Included in their number was the regiment's commander, Colonel Lewis B. Williams Jr., who, thanks to his insistence on riding, not marching, into this action, suffered a mortal wounding worthy of antiquity when he got shot off his horse and impaled himself on his own sword.

Heth's Division, under J. Johnston Pettigrew, lost 1,592 men (or 42 percent), with Marshall's command (Pettigrew's Brigade) hardest hit (610), followed by Fry's (Archer's 535), Davis' (440), and Brockenbrough's (7). William Peel's 11th Mississippi, in its first action in this battle, lost 312 out of 592 engaged. Trimble's supporting line added 570 casualties (30 percent of its strength) to the total, with Lane contributing 381 of those and Lowrance (vice Scales) 189. The already hard hit brigades of Wilcox and Lang (vice Perry) gave up 204 and 155 more, respectively, to the casualty rolls. Missing from this accounting are numbers for the artillery units, which faced only long-distance opposition, suggesting a figure of 75 as an estimated loss. This brings the total Confederate casualties for the units directly involved in the Cemetery Ridge assault to 5,236.

The toll was especially heavy at the command level. Divisional commanders Pettigrew and Trimble were wounded, with the latter requiring an amputation. Brigadiers Garnett, Armistead, and Marshall were either killed outright or mortally wounded, while Kemper and Fry were less seriously injured. The carnage was far worse on the line. Of the fifteen regimental commanders under Pickett, eight were killed or died from wounds suffered in the fighting, and five others were hurt; only two escaped without injury. Although the research undertaken on Pettigrew's and Trimble's divisions has been less exhaustive than that on Pickett's, it is clear that their losses were comparable. A lieutenant in the 11th Virginia summed it up for all when he declared, "We gained nothing but glory and lost our bravest men."

Sometime near midnight, along the line held by the 7th Ohio on Culp's Hill, the men were sleeping with their regimental flag propped upright against the life-saving earthworks. Suddenly a figure darted out of the darkness and made a a grab for the standard. The Ohio color sergeant awoke in time to shoot the intruder, who proved to be a Confederate sergeant bent on obtaining a trophy. As the Rebel crumpled dead to the ground, the Union line to either side crackled with pinpricks of flame as taut nerves snapped and scared young men fired at demons imagined in the night.

If July 1 was the battle of accidental encounters and July 2 the fight for dominant position, then the combat on July 3 was driven solely by Robert E. Lee's desire for a decisive victory. The information he was given persuaded him that he had cracked into the Federal position on his left and secured a commanding artillery platform on his right, making feasible a renewed effort against Cemetery Ridge. There were indications, for those who wanted to see it that way, that the Union army was tottering; but there were signs, too—again, for those who wished to think so— that it remained resilient and strong. Lee chose to join the former group.

The orders he issued to Ewell and Longstreet on the night of July 2 were open to—perhaps even begged—misinterpretation. Ewell perceived enough latitude in them to allow him to concentrate all his effort on Culp's Hill without even feinting against Cemetery Hill; the nature and timing of this ill-conceived undertaking ensured that he would have neither artillery support nor infantry assistance from the rest of his corps, and that the enemy need not weaken any other sector to repel him. Longstreet, for his part, exercised the same authority he had invoked on July 2 to envelop the enemy's flank, but this time he badly misread Lee's intentions. The difficulty of overseeing such a far-flung line of engagement was highlighted once again as Lee attempted in vain to coordinate the two corps. Why he did not direct Ewell to withhold the bulk of his blows until the Cemetery Ridge assault began will remain one of Gettysburg's mysteries. The repulse of Ewell's first attacks, initiated before he learned of Longstreet's delay, did not in and of itself compel him and Edward Johnson to sustain their effort until exhaustion finally set in, at 10:30 A.M. Either these two were seriously misinformed as to the situation on Culp's Hill, or they expected additional instructions that Lee never provided.

Once Lee's original intention to fight on July 3 according to the July 2 plan had been frustrated, the decisions that were to shape the climactic assault on Cemetery Ridge were incremental but unstoppable, given his determination. With a renewal on the right ruled out, and an attack through the town likewise impracticable, the Federal center was the only objective remaining.

It says much about Lee's depth as a military commander that the plans for the assault were as thorough as they were, especially considering the circumstances under which they were cobbled together. If all the parts had worked as they were designed to do, the grand attack might very well have succeeded. The rickety state of the Confederate command infrastructure, however, made perfect execution an impossibility. For all the confusion caused by small miscommunications, it was the large oversights that truly portended disaster. Pendleton's failure to manage the army's artillery situation in an effective manner not only resulted in the fatal supply shortage but also precluded Hill's cannon from advancing with his infantry. In turn, Hill's failure to recognize the severe damage suffered by Heth's Division on July 1, and his eagerness to volunteer it for the charge, cast that command in a key role that it was ill prepared to play. That it performed as well as it did is testament to the courage of individual Confederate soldiers and to the leadership of their line officers, who paid an excessively high price for their participation. Finally, knowing Longstreet's feelings about this attack, Lee should have reserved the decision to commit the second wave for himself. Barring a complete collapse of the Federal defense, it is hard to conceive of any condition that would have justified, in Longstreet's mind, the release of that force.

To imagine that George Meade could have followed up Lee's failed effort with an offensive of his own is to misunderstand both the situation and the man himself. The culture of the Army of the Potomac was very much defensively oriented; then, too, Meade was not a dominating personality, nor had he been in charge of the army long enough for his subordinates to be confident of what he expected of them. This was not a cohesive force operating as a single entity but rather a loose string of

component parts bound together only by a conservative tradition and a
prevailing tendency toward caution. Among the corps commanders on
the field, only Winfield Hancock had the mix of tactical acuity, situational
awareness, and determined aggressiveness that would have enabled a Federal counterpunch. His wounding and incapacitation at the height of the
assault must be counted among the greatest losses suffered by the Army
of the Potomac this day.

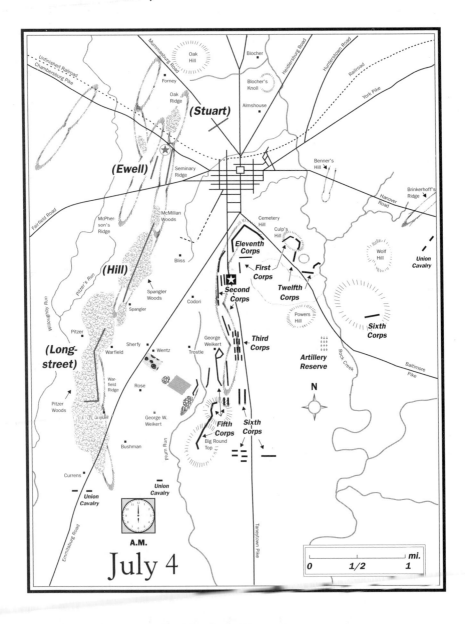

Fighting almost entirely from the relative safety of prepared defensive positions, and backed at almost every point by well-sited artillery, the Union army was comparatively unscathed on July 3, with just over 3,800 casualties. In bloody contrast, the Rebel advance, into the teeth of determined defenses on Culp's Hill and across the open fields fronting Cemetery Ridge, cost Lee's army its greatest number of losses, totaling more than 10,000.

Taking into account all actions of the three days, the price paid by the two sides was almost exactly, and terribly, even: 22,813 U.S., 22,874 C.S.

FIFTEEN

"I thought my men were invincible"

(Saturday, July 4)

The heavy rain that had showered earlier in the evening had hurried off as quickly as it came on, leaving the night sky scoured clean. The moon was high and the stars were bright (though more clouds were building along the skirt of the horizon) as Brigadier General John D. Imboden stood idle near Robert E. Lee's headquarters tent. The forty-year-old lawyer and businessman commanded a small, unattached cavalry brigade that was then on assignment to Lee. Imboden and his troopers, usually given higher marks for their foraging than for their fighting abilities, had taken over watching the army's supply trains in Chambersburg from George Pickett's men before moving up to Gettysburg on the afternoon of July 3. It was past 11:00 P.M. when the cavalryman received a summons to report to the army commander, learning on his arrival that Lee was in conference with A. P. Hill, Imboden had been instructed to wait.

He put the time at around 1:00 A.M. when Lee finally returned to his command post, weary beyond measure. The general seemed to have trouble dismounting, and once he had gotten down, he leaned against his horse and saddle, the very picture of exhaustion.

" 'General, this has been a hard day on you,' " Imboden said, feeling the need to say something.

" 'Yes,' " Lee replied at last, " 'it has been a sad, sad day to us.' " The usually reserved army commander followed up another minute or so of silence with a brief soliloquy in which he alternately praised Pickett's men and bemoaned the fact that his plan had not been properly implemented. With the anguish of a master designer who had seen one of his finest constructs fall victim to the failings of others, Lee allowed himself a rare venting: " 'Too bad! *Too bad!*' " he exclaimed. " 'Oh! Too Bad!' "

Almost as suddenly as it had roiled up, Lee's personal storm subsided, and he became all business. " 'We must return to Virginia,' " he told Imboden as they entered his headquarters tent. " 'As many of our poor wounded as possible must be taken home. I have sent for you because your men are fresh, to guard the trains back to Virginia. The duty will be arduous, responsible, and dangerous, for I am afraid you will be harassed by the enemy's cavalry. I can spare you as much artillery as you require, but no other troops, as I shall need all I have to return to the Potomac by a different route from yours.' " Lee outlined the course he wanted Imboden to take to Williamsport, where he was to cross the Potomac River into Virginia.

After they discussed a few small details, Lee summoned some of his staff to turn his intentions into written orders. When Imboden moved to depart, the commander made one additional request: " 'I will place in your hands [in the morning] . . . a sealed package for President Davis, which you will retain in your own possession till you are across the Potomac, when you will detail a trusty commissioned officer to take it to Richmond with all possible dispatch, and deliver it immediately to the President. . . . If you should unfortunately be captured, destroy it.' " Imboden nodded, suddenly aware that he was accepting the greatest professional challenge of his life.

Ever since the Rebels had first occupied Gettysburg, Mary McAllister had slept sitting in a chair pulled up beside an open window. She guessed it was around 2:00 A.M. when a distant sound awakened her: the low rumble of wagons moving out of the town to the west. Mary hurriedly woke her sleeping sister Martha and told her, "I believe the rebels are retreating." Martha dared not believe it until they both overheard a man outside speaking to the pair of Confederates guarding their house. "Get up, get," he told the soldiers. "We are retreating!" For a moment, Mary considered saying good-bye to her protectors, but then she decided "it would have seemed like mockery."

Others in Gettysburg likewise began gathering hints this night that the occupation's end was drawing near. Gates Fahnestock, for one, sensed that "there was movement among the Confederates." A wounded Federal POW noted with growing excitement that all the enemy columns in sight "were moving in the same direction—not *toward* our lines but *from* them." Daniel Skelly watched with dawning comprehension as Rebel officers passed noiselessly from post to post along the street below his window, "telling [their men] to get up quietly and fall back." Henry Jacobs had previously seen columns of soldiers being marched every which way, but the ones he saw now were different. Whereas those earlier formations had been ready to fight, these were "like some great current that had passed through innumerable scenes of wreck, bearing its jetsam with it."

Still others in town had not a clue as to what was happening. Sarah Broadhead drifted into an uninterrupted sleep, willing herself not to become hopeful. William Bayly recollected "nothing of special note during the evening and night."

Shortly before dawn, a 74th Pennsylvania sentinel posted to watch Baltimore Street saw several civilians in the town waving for him to come on. After a quick palaver with others on the picket post, a small patrol inched forward. "In every house we entered [there] were rebel soldiers sleeping," recalled a member of that group. Word swiftly spread along the outpost line, and soon a number of impromptu probes were poking into Gettysburg's southern outskirts. Two parties from the 58th New York laid claim to 280 prisoners. Several companies from the 106th Pennsylvania, on detached service with the Eleventh Corps, also took part in these initial explorations. Sarah Broadhead was awakened by the sound of Rebel officers herding their men out in a final sweep: "I looked up the street and saw our men in the public square, and it was a joyful sight, for I knew we were now safe," she declared. The commotion lured Alexander Schimmelfennig from his hiding place behind the Garlach residence. Catherine Garlach saw the Eleventh Corps officer walking "stiff and cramped like" toward the patrols, who welcomed the general as one returned from the dead.

Behind these first, improvised ventures, larger efforts were being organized. "This morning the enemy has withdrawn his pickets from the positions of yesterday," George Meade scribbled to Henry Halleck at 7:00 A.M. "My own pickets are moving out to ascertain the nature and extent of the enemy's movement." At 8:00 A.M., Wlodzimierz Krzyzanowski led the

119th New York and 26th Wisconsin of his brigade on a short reconnaissance along the town's southwestern outskirts and toward Seminary Ridge.

Shortly after 10:30 A.M., a full-scale mission was undertaken to fix the enemy's new position. Henry Slocum personally led a brigade-sized expeditionary force on a wide swing to the east that allowed it to enter the town via the Hanover Road. A soldier in those ranks would remember that he and his fellows "moved cautiously, every moment expecting to hear the rebel shells in their midst." When they at last reached Gettysburg, the Twelfth Corps men made quite an impression. "Ye gods!" exclaimed Daniel Skelly. "What a welcome sight for the imprisoned people of Gettysburg! The Boys in Blue marching down the street, fife and drum corps playing, the glorious Stars and Stripes fluttering at the head of the lines." The good spirits came to an abrupt end, however, on the western side of town, where Rebel riflemen had drawn a new dead line.

Especially dangerous was an area where Middle Street provided a clear line of sight on anyone crossing it using Washington Street. After seeing one unwary cavalryman be wounded in the intersection, sixteen-year-old Julia Jacobs positioned herself in the doorway of her family's home on the northwestern corner of the crossing and began shouting warnings to Federal soldiers approaching from the south along Washington Street. When the Rebel sharpshooters realized that someone was alerting the Yankees, they began targeting the doorway, forcing Jacobs deeper into the house, though she never abandoned her station. "We could see the leaves and twigs of our linden trees fly as they were snipped by the bullets," recollected Julia's brother Henry, "but none of them reached her." Finally, a determined squad of Federal soldiers threw a barricade across Middle Street and, after a furious exchange of gunfire, neutralized the threat.

Slocum's was not the only effort under way to locate Lee's new line. From the east, a patrol from the 4th Pennsylvania Cavalry moved north from the Hanover Road to the York Pike, which it then followed into town, capturing a picket post and several aid stations on the way. To the south, the United States Sharpshooters probed west from Little Round Top, while a force of U.S. Regulars supported by a brigade from the Sixth Corps pushed toward the Emmitsburg Road. "Found the Enemy in force about 1 mile in the rear of his old position," recorded a Pennsylvania soldier. "He opened up with shell on our advance."

This shelling was the product of an inspired bit of insubordination on the part of Captain William Parker's Virginia Battery. Lately posted in

Sherfy's peach orchard, Parker's men had been among the last to pull back, but their commander halted the movement when he spotted the approaching enemy recon force. Upon instructing his guns to open fire, Parker had the satisfaction of seeing the Yankee formation go to ground. He decided to hold his post for as long as he could, even begging some extra munitions from another battery retiring to his right. The firing brought out one of Longstreet's staff officers, come to investigate what all the noise was about; once he saw how effectively Parker's guns were fending off the inquisitive Federals, he ordered some infantry forward to support them. With this help, William Parker's men would calmly hold their advanced position throughout the day.

George Meade sent his second situation report to Henry Halleck at noon. "The enemy apparently has thrown back his left, and placed guns and troops in position in rear of Gettysburg, which we now hold," he wrote. He was careful not to raise expectations that he would be going over to an offensive posture. "I shall require some time to get up supplies, ammunition, &c., rest the army, worn out by long marches and three days' hard fighting," he explained.

As both sides became more and more convinced that there would be no large-scale conflict this day, concern grew about the need to deal with the battle's detritus. "Skirmishing today nothing else doing but both sides burying the dead," noted a diarist in the 6th Virginia. Many corpses, according to a North Carolina soldier in Daniel's Brigade, "have been lying on the field in the sun since the first day's fight; it being dusty and hot, the dead smell terribly." "There is no systematic work," admitted one of Longstreet's men, "time being too precious, and the dead are buried where they fell."

On Culp's Hill, an officer in the 147th Pennsylvania led a squad that moved across the gunfire-seared slope to bring in the Confederate wounded from Ewell's assault there. The Federal defense had itself been costly, he observed: "I saw a deep ditch or long excavated series of graves dug and a number of dead Union soldiers lying ready for interment," he recollected. "Each regiment selects a suitable place for its dead and puts a head-board on each individual grave," reported a member of the 8th

Ohio. "The unrecognized dead are left to the last, to be buried in long trenches."

Bodies were found in every conceivable position, with some even grouped in orderly formations where a fanning scythe of canister had cut them down. "The pen cannot perform its duties in describing the horrible, ghastly scenes there visible," avowed an infantryman from the 15th New Jersey. Trying to compare the horrid sights to something familiar, a soldier in the 136th New York suggested that the dead lay "as thick as we ever saw pumpkins in a cornfield."

There was other business to be attended to as well. Thousands of fallen soldiers meant thousands of abandoned weapons to be gathered in or destroyed, itself a wretched job under these conditions. "You can imagine what the field was like," wrote a Confederate engineer assigned to the task, "covered with dead men and horses which had lain in the hot July sun for three days." Not surprisingly, some saw opportunity amid the carnage. The men of the 15th New Jersey, for example, collected enough of the newer, more reliable Springfield model arms to replace the older Enfields they had originally been issued. Along another section of the line, soldiers designated the useful weapons by sticking them bayonets first into the ground. A member of the 64th New York would never forget the image of "acres of muskets standing as thick as trees in a nursery."

There was also the matter of prisoners, a more troublesome issue for Lee's army than for Meade's. Thanks to the open line of communication with Westminster, Union provosts had been moving captured Rebels toward that processing point since the very first evening. By contrast, Lee's officers had simply herded the Union POWs a short distance behind the Confederate lines, not wishing to spare any more manpower than necessary to guard them. Some would be released after accepting field paroles, while many more would be marched with the withdrawing Rebel army for eventual disposition in Richmond.

Robert E. Lee did send out a flag of truce this afternoon, hoping to convince George Meade to swap prisoners, but Meade rejected the proposal. There was a moment of light relief amid these dour events when a Federal in the truce party reassured a Confederate officer that the Union had the wounded James Longstreet in custody and was taking good care of him. According to the observer Arthur Fremantle, "Longstreet sent back word that he was extremely grateful, but that, being neither wounded nor a prisoner, he was quite able to take care of himself."

* * *

Everything was hampered by the weather. The heat of the previous days had now been replaced by precipitation and wind, beginning with a light rain at around 6:00 A.M. that grew more intense as the day wore on. A series of thunderstorms marched through in the early afternoon, accompanied by strong gusts that pushed the water into every orifice. Before long, the placid creeks and runs were flooded, forcing the relocation of several aid stations whose attendants had to frantically haul their helpless charges to higher ground. Someone in town took the measure of today's deluge and reckoned the rainfall at 1.33 inches.

The weather wreaked havoc on the efforts of John Imboden to move the long trains of wounded through the Cashtown Gap. "Canvas was no protection against its fury," the officer wrote, "and the wounded men lying upon the naked boards of the wagon-bodies were drenched. Horses and mules were blinded and maddened by the wind and water, and became almost unmanageable." Not until nearly 4:00 P.M. would the long, doleful caravan begin climbing into the pass.

Imboden was carrying Lee's first report of the battle, addressed to Jefferson Davis. Although necessarily brief, the document nonetheless made explicit Lee's understanding of some key points. At the end of July 1, he noted, the enemy "took up a strong position in rear of the town which he immediately began to fortify, and where his reinforcements joined him." The next day, July 2, found the Confederates attempting "to dislodge the enemy," but "though we gained some ground, we were unable to get possession of his position." Finally, on July 3, the "works on the enemy's extreme right & left were taken, but his numbers were so great and his position commanding, that our troops were compelled to relinquish their advantage and retired." Lee closed his brief by remarking that the Union army had "suffered severely," and appended a list of some of the prominent Confederate officers who had been killed or wounded. Since there was a real chance that this message might be intercepted, he offered no hint regarding his next move.

Reporter Whitelaw Reid caught a glimpse of Meade around midday, busily "dictating orders and receiving dispatches." Summaries of the situation were sent off to Darius Couch in Harrisburg and the officer commanding the Union forces at Frederick, Maryland. Circulars were distributed to the various corps headquarters on a variety of matters: status reports were requested regarding conditions and matériel; an inventory was ordered of captured Rebel flags; burial details were authorized; and a tally of on-hand ammunition supplies was demanded. In one of these memoranda, Meade stated his intention "not to make any present move, but to refit and rest for today." Explaining further in a letter to his wife, the army commander confided that he never even considered initiating offensive operations on July 4 because he was determined not to allow the Rebels to "play their old game of shooting us from behind breastworks."

Many of the energies expended by both sides today were directed not at taking lives but at saving them. Unlike their better armed and better trained comrades on the lines, those tending the wounded were desperately hampered by a lack of supplies and of adequate facilities, and overwhelmed by the excessive numbers in need of medical care. Just about anything large enough and with a roof overhead had been commandeered as a treatment center or operating area; there were stations in virtually every sector where men had fought.

Robert E. Lee's decision to reset his lines along the axis of Seminary Ridge had necessitated the abandonment of a dozen such setups east of Gettysburg, perhaps another half dozen north of it, and an additional number within the town proper. This in turn had placed an even heavier burden on the already packed Confederate infirmaries located west of the town. Among the busiest of these was the station on the Samuel Lohr farm, just past the point where the Chambersburg Pike crossed Marsh Creek. A chaplain in a Mississippi regiment described the sad spectacle of the wounded laid out "under open skies, on the bare ground, or a mere pile of straw . . . heroically suffering or unconsciously moaning their lives away." Surgeon LeGrand Wilson was one of those who were occupied here from morning to night "performing necessary operations, and redressing the wounds." Farther south along Marsh Creek, at the Fairfield Road crossing, was Bream's farm, another significant collecting point. The observer Fitzgerald Ross was especially moved by the sight there of "those fine young fellows, many of them probably crippled for life. . . . Many were to be left behind, too severely wounded to bear removal."

On the Union side, the medical crisis was particularly ironic because there was an effective system in place to deal with such emergencies, but it had been badly disrupted by the exigencies of the military campaign. Dr. Jonathan Letterman, the medical director of the Army of the Potomac, had designed a process whereby the battlefield wounded could be moved swiftly through several treatment stages behind the lines, with the most seriously afflicted being sent directly to the best-equipped and best-staffed infirmaries. The essential components of this system were a well-trained staff, adequate supplies, and viable temporary hospital facilities. Letterman's medical teams were present in good numbers at Gettysburg, but the rapid marches required to concentrate the army, combined with George Meade's uncertainty about holding his position, meant that the all-important medical supply trains remained in the rear. While Letterman himself was clear about what he considered the priority to be— "Lost supplies can be replenished," he declared, "but lives lost are gone forever"—Meade saw matters differently.

So as wagons filled with tenting stood immobile, parked between Union Mills and Westminster, thousands of wounded men lay outside aide stations, suffering from their wounds and exposed to the weather. The Eleventh Corps division commander Carl Schurz vividly recollected the results: "A heavy rain set in during the day. . . ." he wrote, "and large numbers had to remain unprotected in the open, there being no room left under roof. I saw long rows of men lying under the eaves of buildings, the water pouring down upon their bodies in streams." Because the Twelfth Corps' medical director had disobeyed orders by bringing his supply train forward, many of the soldiers wounded on Culp's Hill received prompt attention. For most of the other Union casualties, however, the immediate postbattle experience was horrific beyond description. Even the sober and serious Dr. Letterman called it "a field of Blood on which the Demon of Destruction reveled."

At age forty-four, the poet Walt Whitman was too old to soldier. Drawn to Washington to visit a younger brother reported wounded in action at Fredericksburg in 1862, Whitman had stayed on in the capital to nurse and comfort other stricken soldiers. Today he was making his way, around noon, along Pennsylvania Avenue when his attention was captured by "a big, flaring placard on the bulletin board of a newspaper office, announcing 'Glorious Victory for the Union Army!' " Moving along the street, Whitman encountered other displays, some reprinting George Meade's final message of the day before (which Whitman judged "very modest") and others presenting a proclamation by Abraham Lincoln, time-dated 10:30 A.M., July 4. The information received from the Army of the Potomac, Lincoln announced, "is such to cover that army with the highest honor." The president also gave thanks to God for this joyous news, a sentiment that struck Whitman as "a sort of order of the day . . . quite religious."

The poet cited the reports to cheer the wounded and sick soldiers he visited this day, supplementing the news with dollops of blackberry and cherry syrup that he mixed with ice water for them. In the background, as he ministered in his way, Whitman heard Independence Day being marked with "the usual fusillades of boys' pistols, crackers, and guns."

It was, after all, the birthday of the United States, but few on the battlefield were celebrating the occasion. A Rhode Island officer posted near Rose's wheat field would recollect that at about noon, "a National Salute with shotted guns was fired from several of our Batteries and the shells passed over our heads toward the Rebel lines." This commemoration appears to have been an isolated event, though numerous individual Federals undoubtedly reflected on the day's symbolic meaning. "Today is Independence Day," wrote a New Jersey soldier. "God grant it may be the restoration of the Union." Others merely noted its passing: "4th of July, while you were celebrating, we were busy burying the dead," a young New Yorker wrote to his mother. "Today is supposed to be a holiday," scribbled a diarist in town, "but it is a sad day for Gettysburg."

The significance was not lost on those along Seminary Ridge. "A heavy rain was falling," recalled an Alabama officer in Ewell's Corps, "and just then I remembered that it was the 4th of July, and that the villains would think more than ever of their wretched Independence Day." Some of those villains did just that. A Wisconsin soldier who had been captured on July 1 recorded in his diary, "We celebrated the Nation's birthday by singing patriotic songs and making ourselves jolly generally." Another group was huddled in the rain "with heavy hearts . . . when one of our officers, disregarding all possible consequences, gave vent to his feelings and in honor of the day began a patriotic song. We others took courage and all joined in the chorus." When their Confederate guards failed to intervene, one soldier found hope in their leniency. "Could it mean that they were beaten on July 3rd?" he wondered.

✦

Everything the English observer Fremantle saw convinced him that Lee's entire army was in denial. The soldiers he overheard "all were talking of [capturing] Washington and Baltimore with the greatest confidence." Officers passed on rumors "that the enemy was *retiring*, and had been doing so all day long." Yet from Fremantle's perspective, the signs of defeat were everywhere: long trains of Confederate wagons and herds of confiscated animals moved west along the Fairfield Road throughout the rainy day, James Longstreet had relocated his headquarters some three miles closer to Fairfield, and, perhaps most unsettling, incidents of pilferage and robbery were becoming common.

When evening arrived, Fremantle and the correspondent Francis Lawley were lucky enough to find space in a covered buggy assigned to a First Corps surgeon. Waiting in the dripping gloom for the withdrawal procession to get under way, Fremantle could not help contrasting the arrogance of the Rebel army with its actual situation. "It is impossible to avoid seeing that the cause of this check to the Confederates lies in the utter contempt felt for the enemy by all ranks," he asserted.

As he had done on the night of July 2, George Meade brought his corps commanders together this evening to share information and ideas. The changes in the cast of characters on hand were all the result of enemy action. In addition to Daniel Butterfield, present were John Newton, Henry Slocum, John Sedgwick, Oliver Howard, George Sykes, David Birney, Alfred Pleasonton, Brigadier General William Hays (replacing Hancock), and Gouverneur K. Warren.

Meade opened the discussion by reminding everyone that he was still operating under instructions to protect Washington and Baltimore. There were rumors, he noted, that reinforcements were heading toward them from the capital, but he had been unable to confirm that information. He looked to his officers for comments. There was no clear consensus of opinion, so following the model established on July 2, four questions were posed to the group.

Meade first asked if they believed the army should remain at Gettysburg on July 5. All but Slocum, Newton, and Pleasonton were in favor of holding fast. If they remained at Gettysburg, Meade asked as a follow-up, should they attack Lee? No one was ready to commit to that proposition. Meade's final two questions concerned the nature of any pursuit they might undertake. Here there was some agreement that just the cavalry should directly pursue, while the infantry marched south and then west to cut Lee off from the Potomac. Before the meeting broke up, Meade announced his intention to push out a strong reconnaissance force at dawn under Warren's direction.

At 10:00 P.M., George Meade sent his last situation report of this day to Henry Halleck. It contained nothing of particular significance, save for Meade's declaration that he meant to press Lee's new line on July 5, "to ascertain what the intention of the enemy is."

Although Robert E. Lee was kept busy all day with preparations for the army's return to Virginia, he made it a point to visit all parts of his line and to be seen by his men. The Texans cheered him as he passed their camps, a salute Lee acknowledged by raising his hat. He was spotted, too, by several Union POWs who were understandably interested in the mood of their enemy's leader. One Iron Brigade man reported that he "showed no signs of worry. His countenance was placid and he appeared as cool and collected as if nothing unusual had transpired." Another black-hatted soldier wrote in his diary that Lee "appears dignified and self-assured."

Times of great stress demanded even greater displays of self-control. When an aide of Ewell's pronounced his command ready for action and somewhat smugly hoped that " 'the other two corps are in as good condition for work as ours is,' " Lee put him in his place. " 'What reason have you, young man, to suppose they are not?' " he asked. Object lessons aside, Lee did have enough doubt about the combat efficiency of Pickett's Division that he assigned the shattered unit the undesirable task of guarding Federal prisoners. While this decision was understandable under the circumstances, it was a slight that George Pickett would never forgive or forget.

Lee pulled up stakes toward nightfall and joined Longstreet at his headquarters along the Fairfield Road. The pair were seen by the observer FitzGerald Ross, who recorded that they were "engaged in earnest conversation." (Lee would later tell Ross that he had been consid-ering halting the movement because of the atrocious weather, but that would have required turning the supply train around, an impossible maneuver in this context.) Another who was present heard Lee admit to a personal failing: " 'I thought my men were invincible,' " he said.

In the sanctuary of her room, Sarah Broadhead closed her diary entry for this "dreadfully long day. We know . . . the Rebels are retreating, and that our army has been victorious. I was anxious to help care for the wounded, but the day is ended and all is quiet, and for the first time in a week I shall go to bed, feeling safe."

One of Sarah's neighbors had opted to move out of her house for the latter part of the occupation, leaving just her father behind to watch over things. Upon returning to her home, she ran up to her room and was relieved to see that it remained much as she had left it. A second glance, however, revealed a "little pile of gray rags" that on closer inspection proved to be "the remnant of pants and a hat." Guessing what this meant, she pulled out the trunk in which her husband kept his best blue suit. The clothes were gone: "I suppose those gray rags were left in exchange," she reflected. Not caring for her end of the deal, she recalled, "I gathered them up on a stick and threw them out in the street."

SIXTEEN

Pursuit to a Personal Crossroads

August 8, 1863: Orange, Virginia

For the final time, Robert E. Lee reread the letter that he believed signaled the end of his professional career. It was a document so explosive in its contents that Lee had handwritten it himself instead of relying on his clerical staff to produce a first draft. Behind him now were the pressure-filled days following the Battle of Gettysburg, when it had seemed that God was bent on testing him to the utmost. The withdrawal that began early on July 5 had been difficult in every way. While the great wagon train of the wounded struggled on muddy roads leading it due west through the Cashtown Gap, then southward (avoiding Chambersburg) toward Williamsport, the infantry marched south along the eastern side of the mountains, passing through that barrier at Fairfield on the shortest route to Hagerstown. The rains that so dogged the ranks' efforts, desperately slowing their progress, also swelled the Potomac, with the result that crossing points that had been easily fordable on the march into Pennsylvania were now rendered impassable. A temporary pontoon bridge that Lee had maintained at Falling Waters had been destroyed by a Yankee raiding force on July 4, leaving the army commander with no other alternative than to knit his command, beginning on July 6, into a defensive line stretching from just below Hagerstown to Falling Waters, its back to the flooded Potomac. His engineers did a magnificent job of positioning the defenses and constructing earthworks at key points. Also magnificent was Jeb Stuart, whose cavalry effectively bought Lee sufficient time to get his infantry into this position.

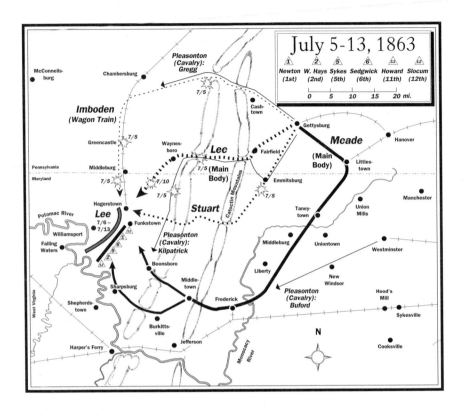

Despite some sharp attacks on his wagon train and several Yankee cavalry thrusts (which looked more threatening than they actually were), Lee held his position through the night of July 13. His men had managed to erect some emergency bridges, and starting late that night, the bulk of his army at last succeeded in crossing to the Virginia side. The final two divisions to reach the bridge approaches were caught unprepared by a pair of Union cavalry divisions across from Falling Waters, and before the confused fighting ended, the Confederates had lost some 700 prisoners. Ironically, the parting shots of this campaign were fired by the command that had opened the battle on July 1, Henry Heth's division.

Following this "success," there were the painful tasks of measuring the cost and assessing the great damage inflicted upon the army's command structure. And as if that were not an unpleasant enough prospect, Lee found himself under attack from another quarter, as segments of the Southern press railed against the entire operation. To cap it all off, news of his withdrawal from Gettysburg coincided with word that Vicksburg had fallen, surrendered on July 4.

Some two weeks after returning to Virginia, Lee submitted his report on the Gettysburg campaign. In it he noted the deaths of J. Johnston Pettigrew, mortally wounded in a last action covering the army's crossing, and Dorsey Pender, from wounds received on July 2. "The conduct of the troops was all that I could desire or expect, and they deserve success so far as it can be deserved by heroic valor and fortitude," Lee's report read. The personal letter he had written to Jefferson Davis would close out all accounts.

"We must expect reverses, even defeats," the letter allowed. "They are sent to teach us wisdom and prudence, to call forth greater energies, and to prevent our falling into greater disasters." Then Lee got to the point: "The general remedy for the want of success in a military commander is his removal. . . . I . . . propose to Your Excellency the propriety of selecting another commander for this army." Continuing in this vein, he cited the "growing failure of my bodily strength" and expressed his confidence "that a younger and abler man than myself can readily be attained." He signed his resignation note with "sentiments of great esteem."

The reply from the Confederate president was not long in coming. Writing on August 11, Jefferson Davis rejected Lee's request. "To ask me to substitute you by some one in my judgment more fit to command, or who would possess more of the confidence of the army, or of the reflecting men of the country, is to demand an impossibility," he declared. The matter of Robert E. Lee's resignation was closed. The war would continue.

March 5, 1864: Washington,
District of Columbia

By this point in the war, George Meade had confronted some of the best field officers in the Confederate army. As a corps commander, he had fought against Stonewall Jackson, and after his promotion to chief of the Army of the Potomac, his very first battle had pitted him against Robert E. Lee. At least on those occasions, Meade had known his ground and understood his foes. Now, sitting in a basement hearing room in Congress, Meade was clearly out of his element. Those facing him here were the antitheses of military display, though all the more powerful for their strength's concealment.

The two men questioning Meade this day represented the joint Congressional Committee on the Conduct of the War. Created in December 1861 and renewed in January 1864, it operated under a broad mandate to investigate every aspect of the conflict, from supply procurement to the management of individual campaigns. Although possessed of little actual authority, the committee could recommend action to its parent bodies and, perhaps even more important, throw the bright light of public scrutiny on the military's handling of the war. Motivated by a mixture of patriotic and highly politicized agendas, the committee served to expose corruption and poor administrative practices while at the same time providing a platform for politicians to pillory officers who were out of favor for one reason or another.

Benjamin Wade, who chaired the committee, was one of the two senators on hand to question Meade. The Massachusetts lawyer and judge was a vigorous advocate for women's rights, workers' rights, and abolition, a liberal who viewed the social conservatism of most West Point graduates as an impediment to victory. Sharing the bench with him today was Zachariah Chandler, a Michigan businessman and past mayor of Detroit. Like Wade, Chandler was a fervent enemy of disloyalty, which quality he attributed to those West Point generals who exhibited a reluctance to obliterate the slave powers.

The committee's interest in George Meade had begun with Lincoln's removal of Joseph Hooker, a favorite of several of its most powerful members. Its direct focus on Meade had a great deal to do with the ambitious lobbying done by former congressman Daniel Sickles during his long recuperation in Washington. Under the pretext of undertaking a general investigation into the Army of the Potomac's 1863 operations, the committee had summoned Sickles and others to testify in late February 1864. The list of those eventually called was decidedly stacked against Meade. Besides Sickles, it included Abner Doubleday, still smarting over Meade's decision to put John Newton in charge of the First Corps; Alfred Pleasonton, anxious to burnish a tarnished reputation ex post facto; and Daniel Butterfield, Meade's inherited chief of staff,* still intensely loyal to his former commander, Hooker.

Sickles and Doubleday had preceded Meade before the committee. Sickles was the more damning of the two, asserting that Meade's intention on July 2 had been "to fall back to Pipe creek, or to some place in that neighborhood"; only the combat initiated by the Third Corps' advance to the Emmitsburg Road had compelled him to stay and fight at Gettysburg, Sickles insisted. He was seconded on this point by Doubleday, whose bitterness had merely increased with time. Bolstered by this accusation and by the statement of a Sixth Corps divisional commander who had disapproved of his lackluster pursuit of Lee after Gettysburg, Wade and Chandler had met with Lincoln and Edwin Stanton on March 3 to press for Meade's removal. Their preferred candidate to replace him was the man *he* had replaced: Joe Hooker. The senators received no satisfaction from the president, however, so, upon learning that Meade himself would be in Washington on March 5, they issued a summons for him to appear before them and testify in his own behalf.

Much of Meade's testimony related to events that had occurred before and during the battle, but he was also pressed regarding decisions he had made following the repulse of the Cemetery Ridge assault on July 3. He recounted his efforts to locate Lee's new line on July 4 and expressed certainty that the heavy rains of that day would have "interrupt[ed] any very active operations if I had designed making them." On being informed on

---

*Meade had replaced Butterfield with Andrew Humphreys on July 8.

July 5 that Lee's army had withdrawn, he had ordered his cavalry toward Cashtown and detailed an infantry force from the Sixth Corps to the mountain pass at Fairfield. Not until July 6 had he concluded, based on John Sedgwick's reports, that any attempt to follow Lee could be readily frustrated by a small Rebel rear guard holding the passes. With his cavalry already assigned to pursue and harass the enemy, he therefore began to shift his infantry southward, establishing his new headquarters in Frederick, Maryland, on July 7.

There Meade had resolved to suspend all infantry operations for a day, as he explained to the committee, in order to "obtain the necessary supplies, and put my army in condition, and give them some rest." On July 8 and 9, the Army of the Potomac marched west through the South Mountain passes. Halts were interspersed with skirmishes as the army felt its way toward the enemy, finally fixing Lee's infantry in defensive lines below Hagerstown on July 12. "So soon as my troops were in line . . . and ready for offensive operations," Meade told Wade and Chandler, "although I had had no opportunity of examining critically and closely the enemy's position, . . . it was my desire to attack him in that position."

That night, he had convened his corps commanders and asked for their opinions ("I never called those meetings councils," Meade declared; "they were consultations"), which he summarized as being "very largely opposed to any attack without further examination." July 13 was accordingly spent scouting Lee's defenses, though the rain and mist meant that "not much information was obtained." Meade's orders for July 14 were nonetheless to attack, but then dawn brought the bitter news that "during the night of the 13th the enemy had retired across the river."

Questions put to Meade by the committee raised several issues that had been made much of by previous witnesses or in the press. He spoke to these one by one. He was convinced, he said, that Lee's army had been amply resupplied with ammunition by the time he caught up with it. Nor did he believe that the Army of Northern Virginia had dissolved into a disorganized rabble: "I doubt whether it was any more demoralized than we were when we fell back to Washington in 1862, after the second battle of [Bull Run]," he opined.

As to the reinforcements he had received in the course of his march to the Potomac, Meade discounted most of them as having been either "in a very unsuitable moral condition to bring to the front" or "totally undisciplined." With the exception of some more experienced units that had joined him from the Harper's Ferry garrison, he observed, he "was in front of the enemy at Williamsport with very much the same army that I moved from Gettysburg." Given that, an advance undertaken on either July 13 or July 14 would have replicated the Battle of Gettysburg, but in reverse—that is, with Lee on the defensive and Meade attacking.

After continuing his narrative through the end of 1863, Meade was asked if there was anything more that he wished to add to his testimony. "I would probably have a great deal to say if I knew what other people have said," he replied pointedly. Left unmentioned, either in direct testimony or in the questions posed by committee members, was the general's attempted resignation at the end of the campaign. Stung by a series of messages from Henry Halleck suggesting that the president had lost faith in him, Meade had stung back the only way he could. "Having performed my duty conscientiously and to the best of my ability, the censure of the President conveyed in your dispatch of 1 P.M. this day," Meade telegraphed at 2:30 P.M. on July 14, "is, in my judgment, so undeserved that I feel compelled most respectfully to ask to be immediately relieved from the command of this army."

The request was not granted by Henry Halleck. Although he had been deeply distressed by Lee's successful withdrawal across the Potomac, Abraham Lincoln rejected pressures to replace Meade. He, more than anyone, knew that the Spanish-born Pennsylvanian was as good as they got in the East, and that if he was not utterly irreplaceable, neither were the available alternatives so superior that Meade's ouster was even worth considering.

In a letter that he drafted but never sent to Meade, Lincoln admonished, "I do not believe you appreciate the magnitude of the misfortune involved in Lee's escape. He was within your easy grasp, and to have closed upon him would, in connection with our other late successes, have ended the war." To Gideon Welles, Lincoln said of the general, " 'He has made a great mistake, but we will try him farther.' "

In time, Lincoln was able to mask his disappointment behind the outward expression of simple humor that served him so well throughout his life. Conversing with Meade many weeks later, Lincoln asked, " 'Do you know, general, what your attitude toward Lee for a week after the battle reminded me of?' " Answered Meade (warily, one imagines), " 'No, Mr. President, what is it?' " Replied Lincoln, " 'I'll be hanged if I could think of anything else, than an old woman trying to shoo her geese across a creek.' "

SEVENTEEN

Judgments

The 50,000 or so men who returned with Lee into Virginia had differing opinions regarding their three days' fighting at Gettysburg. "You are aware the armies met at G.," a member of Ewell's staff wrote in a letter on July 12, "and after whipping and driving them many miles the first day, they secured so strong a natural position, which they strengthened by works, that after two days trial we found impracticable from the scarcity of artillery ammunition and the loss of many men to attempt a further assault and consequently withdrew our forces." "The army of Northern Virginia has not been, and will not be 'whipped' by yankees," insisted a defiant North Carolina soldier at the end of this campaign. "We simply failed to take a position which no amount of courage or endurance, nor any array of numbers, could storm." "We have voluntarily left the battle-field and abandoned a large number of wounded, but our falling back was slowly accomplished, and none followed in our rear," reported another. "The people where we['ve] been did not know anything of the war untill since wee came over," a Georgian declared on July 12. "They now feel the sting of it sure."

Others were less satisfied with the results. "There was a feeling among the *men* that *somebody* had blundered and had not done their duty," noted one of A. P. Hill's men. "We came here with the best army the Confederacy ever carried into the field but thousands of our brave boys are left upon the enemy's soil and in my opinion our Army will never be made up of such material again," a South Carolina soldier lamented. "Our army is badly whipped," summed up another of Hill's men. "I was sorry when it was begun," a Virginian in Mahone's Brigade attested on July 30. "I am glad it is over. I never expected to wage invasive warfare and I had enough of Maryland last year to satisfy me that we could never fight seccessfully upon that soil."

To every outward appearance, Robert E. Lee had lost none of his positive attitude. "Our noble men are cheerful and confident," he wrote to his wife while waiting at Williamsport for the river to subside. A day after crossing it, he wrapped up the campaign for her: "The army has returned to Virginia. Its return is rather sooner than I had originally contemplated, but, having accomplished much of what I proposed on leaving the Rappahannock—namely, relieving the [Shenandoah] Valley of the presence of the enemy, and drawing his army north of the Potomac—I determined to recross the latter river." Speaking soon afterward with a proxy sent by Jefferson Davis, he asserted, " 'Our loss was heavy at Gettysburg; but in my opinion no greater than it would have been from the series of battles I would have been compelled to fight had I remained in Virginia.' " In his final campaign report, submitted in January 1864, Lee pointed to the supplies he had confiscated and the enemy's subsequent failure to mount a fall invasion into northern Virginia as the effort's important results. Missing from his rhetoric was any mention of having diverted Union resources from the siege of Vicksburg.

Yet something *had* changed. Lee had staked everything—his splendid army, the fate of Richmond, and perhaps even the Confederacy itself—on a campaign aimed at destroying the Federal army. He had lost the bet, and now the prospect of an endlessly lingering war stretched before him like a dimly lit corridor lined with mirrors. Never again would his army be so powerful, or its spirit so untrammeled by weary resignation. His abrupt and very private decision to resign had manifested his deep doubt as to his usefulness to the Confederate cause. If a decisive victory, the battle of annihilation, could not be realized, what else could Lee do to satisfy his exacting personal sense of duty and honor? In time, he would fashion a new mission for himself. No longer would he and his army be the means to ultimate victory; instead they would be a thorn in the enemy's side, delaying and embarrassing Lincoln's generals' designs. In this way, Lee and his men might just buy Jefferson Davis enough time to work out a political settlement that would preserve the Confederacy. This new purpose would sustain Lee throughout the dark months ahead, until the spring of 1865, when it would become frighteningly apparent to him that

Davis had discarded the option of any such settlement in favor of a war to the knife. Then indeed would Robert E. Lee face the darkest moment of the soul.

But that was all in the unforeseeable future. For the present, Lee readied himself for the trials ahead. He acknowledged, "We must now prepare for harder blows and harder work."

Once again, Gettysburg was deluged with outsiders. This time, however, their mood was decidedly friendly, and the atmosphere, while solemn, was palpably celebratory. The date was November 19, 1863, and the occasion, the dedication of a national soldiers' cemetery located next to the town's burial plot on Cemetery Hill. Many notables had been invited to attend but had declined, among them Congressman Thaddeus Stevens, whose Caledonia Iron Works remained in ruins (he thought the whole affair a waste of his time), and George Meade, then busy directing the Army of the Potomac's operations along the Rappahannock River. To everyone's relief, the famous American orator Edward Everett had consented to address the crowd. To everyone's surprise, Abraham Lincoln had also agreed to come and say a few words.

Lincoln revealed how important this event was to him in a number of ways. More often than not, he declined such invitations, but this one he kept on his calendar, even though his son Tad was ill and he was feeling poorly himself. He had also rearranged his travel plans on learning that his visit had been set up as a one-day trip, because he knew that any delay could cause him to miss the ceremony. Instead of traveling on November 19, therefore, Lincoln arrived in Gettysburg shortly before dinnertime the evening before.

The few remarks he had been asked to make had assumed an importance in his own thinking well out of proportion to their length. Contrary to later legend that had him scribbling out his speech during the train ride to Gettysburg, Lincoln spent some time working on it in advance. He even spoke with the cemetery's designer beforehand, the better to understand its physical layout. It was *this* battle that he felt he must commemorate, for it had claimed a special place in his thinking about the war. Lincoln had waited fretfully at the War Department's telegraph office for news from the battle front before Gettysburg, and he would do so after it. Yet this dedication offered him a public opportunity to state clearly and plainly his feelings about the larger meaning of the war.

The town that Lincoln saw this morning could scarcely be said to have recovered from the unprecedented civic catastrophe visited upon its citizens by the great battle. The physical damage to Gettysburg was remarkably minor; there were many other places—in the North and South—that would endure far greater destruction in the course of the war. In human terms, though, the battle's impact beggared comprehension. In a span of three days, a municipality of some 2,500 residents had been confronted with more than 20,000 wounded, suffering men in need of comfort, care, and housing. And then, too, there were the bodies: some 7,000 soldiers killed, plus perhaps as many as 5,000 horses and mules. The armies did what they could to bury the human remains, but far too many corpses, and most of the dead animals, were left to decompose in the July sun when the opposing sides marched away.

Some outside help had arrived by then, and more was on its way, but an operation of this magnitude so far exceeded anyone's experience that the assistance was slow to get started and often horribly inefficient when it was in place. For weeks, recollected Albertus McCreary, "the stench was so bad . . . that everyone went around with a bottle of pennyroyal or peppermint oil." Chloride of lime was spread and respread to disinfect the streets and alleys and to discourage—or try to—the hordes of flies that feasted on the dead and the living.

Much that was good about Americans had shown itself. From Emmitsburg came the skilled nurses of the Sisters of Charity, and from the East representatives of the United States Sanitary Commission as well as the Christian Commission, bringing supplies and organizing skills. From cities, towns, and villages throughout the North, a steady procession of individuals converged on the crossroads, much as had the two armies before them. Many were seeking loved ones or at least confirmation of their fate. Some of those many hundreds came to help, among them a small brigade of women: Cornelia Hancock, Georgeanna Woolsey, Charlotte Elizabeth Johnson McKay, and many others. Often untrained in the tasks they were asked to perform, and unprepared for what they saw around them, they were nevertheless determined to do their part.

There had been conflicts among the different administrative groups, frustrations imposed upon family members desperate for news, problems with food and housing, and the inevitable presence of profiteers. Yet there was something healing, too, in the dull, comforting routines of the time before the battle, routines that slowly but inexorably began to reassert themselves after it. Almost all of those who had lived through

July's bloody days found ways to cope and even return to some semblance of normalcy.

Most of the wounded had been transferred to established medical facilities by early August, and even though bodies would continue to be discovered in out-of-the way locations for some while to come, the great majority were underground, either here or elsewhere, by the time Lincoln came. The battle would never leave the memory of Gettysburg's citizens. When Nellie Aughinbaugh's mother chided her grandmother for referring to the Battle of Gettysburg as the "war," she was told: "It is all the war *I* ever want to see."

Most of the battle veterans in Gettysburg when Lincoln arrived were civilians who had been present during those three days. Albertus McCreary, who had predicted that the Eleventh Corps would "whip all the 'Rebs' in the South" on July 1, got a good view of the president as he made his way to the ceremony. "He seemed very tall and gaunt to me, but his face was wonderful to look upon. It was such a sad face and so full of kindly feeling that one felt at home with him at once," McCreary recalled. Daniel Skelly, a ubiquitous presence the previous July, was everywhere in Gettysburg on November 19 as well. He later described how the procession formed in the town square, with feeder columns coming in from York and Carlisle Streets. The military-style formation headed south along Baltimore Street, covering about a mile before reaching the cemetery. There Skelly managed to wrangle a spot that let him see and hear all the speakers.

Everett went first. It was a fine speech, and a long one. The well-practiced orator had done his homework, consulting with several soldiers who had participated in the battle and whose accounts endowed his description of the action with the power of primary sources. When Everett was finished, the band played a number. Then it was Lincoln's turn.

Remembered Skelly, "He spoke in a quiet, forcible and earnest manner with no attempt at oratory." Also in the audience this day were representatives from many of the newspapers whose correspondents had covered the battle. Those invaluable combat reporters were elsewhere this day, as their particular skills were not needed here; rather, what was required was the ability to take accurate shorthand notes, especially important on this occasion because no advance copy of Lincoln's text had been released. Afterward, a slightly polished version of Lincoln's Gettysburg Address would be widely disseminated and become rightly famous

The nimble fingers of the ablest "phonographers" of the day, however, likely recorded the words actually spoken on this historic occasion:

> Fourscore and seven years ago our fathers brought forth upon this continent a new nation, conceived in Liberty and dedicated to the proposition that all men are created equal.
>
> Now we are engaged in a great civil war, testing whether that nation, or any nation so conceived and so dedicated, can long endure. We are met on a great battlefield of that war. We are met to dedicate a portion of it as a final resting place of those who here gave their lives that that nation might live. It is altogether fitting and proper that we should do this.
>
> But in a larger sense we cannot dedicate—we cannot consecrate—we cannot hallow this ground. The brave men, living and dead, who struggled here, have consecrated it far above our poor power to add or detract. The world will little note nor long remember what we say here; but it can never forget what they did here. It is for us, the living, rather to be dedicated here to the unfinished work that they have thus far so nobly carried on. It is rather for us to be here dedicated to the great task remaining before us—that from these honored dead we take increased devotion to that cause for which they here gave the last full measure of devotion—that we here highly resolve that these dead shall not have died in vain—that the nation shall, under God, have a new birth of freedom—and that government of the people, by the people, and for the people, shall not perish from the earth.

With these words, Abraham Lincoln transformed the three days of combat at Gettysburg, comprising one of the greatest battles of the Civil War, into a defining moment in American history.

THE PEOPLE: AFTERWARD

EDWARD P. ALEXANDER: Longstreet's premier artillerist served throughout the war, surrendering at Appomattox. Afterward he taught at a university, built railroads, and helped settle a border dispute between Costa Rica and Nicaragua. The author of several memoirs of great honesty and forthrightness, Alexander died in 1910.

RICHARD H. ANDERSON: A. P. Hill's underperforming divisional commander rose to corps level but was ultimately relieved on account of his lackluster results. He made a poor transition to the postwar milieu and died in near poverty in 1879.

FRANCIS BARLOW: Howard's overeager brigadier was nursed back to health by his loving Arabella and returned to serve until the end of the war. Worn out by her constant efforts as a nurse with her husband's army, Arabella died of disease in 1864. After the war, Barlow became a dynamic attorney general for New York whose efforts fatally weakened the Tweed ring. He died in 1896.

SARAH (SALLIE) BROADHEAD: Broadhead privately published her diary in 1864, intending it solely for "the kindred and nearest friends of the writer." She and her husband had a child after the war.

JOHN BUFORD: The hard-hitting, resourceful cavalry officer remained in active service until he was struck down by typhoid fever in the autumn of 1863. He died before the year was out and was buried at West Point.

DANIEL BUTTERFIELD: After briefly commanding a division in the Atlanta campaign under his mentor Joseph Hooker, Butterfield left active service. He became a consummate inside operator during U. S. Grant's presidency, with a reputation for profiting from his circumstances. He died in 1901.

JOSHUA CHAMBERLAIN: Wounded six times during the war, Chamberlain earned national prominence, first as postwar Maine's governor and later as president of Bowdoin College. He spoke and wrote extensively about his Civil War experiences, somewhat improving his performance in the retelling. Ironically, his indelibly heroic linkage to Little Round Top came through a fictionalized portrayal in Michael Shaara's 1975 Pulitzer Prize–winning novel, *The Killer Angels,* some sixty-one years after Chamberlain's death.

CHARLES C. COFFIN: The able war correspondent (nom de plume "Carleton") was less successful when there was no conflict to report. Coffin's postwar career consisted largely of refashioning his wartime dispatches into several books. He died in 1896.

RUFUS DAWES: The leader of the charge on the railroad cut enjoyed some business successes after the war, most of which were lost in the panic of 1873. He served a term in Congress and was a welcome fixture at countless Decoration Day parades until his death in 1899.

JOHN DOOLEY: The wounded survivor of the July 3 assault spent the remainder of the war as a Federal POW on Johnson's Island. He settled in Georgetown immediately after the war and there began preparing himself for the priesthood while also working on his *War Journal*. Dooley met his maker in 1873, nine months before his ordination.

ABNER DOUBLEDAY: The unhappy corps-commander-for-a-day saw no active service after Gettysburg. He began a writing campaign soon after his army retirement, aimed at rehabilitating his wartime reputation. Rather than receiving honors for his legitimate military service, however, Doubleday became enshrined in popular culture for inventing baseball, something he did not actually do. Plagued by a series of ailments, he died in 1893 and was buried in Arlington National Cemetery.

RICHARD S. EWELL: The chief of Lee's Second Corps retained his stewardship of that command until the summer of 1864, when his poor performance prompted Robert E. Lee to administratively banish him from the Army of Northern Virginia. After the war, he ran his wife's Tennessee plantation and kept out of the public eye. Ewell and his wife passed away within three days of each other in 1872.

ARTHUR J. L. FREMANTLE: The urbane English observer turned his experiences into a book that was published before the end of 1863 and subsequently widely reprinted in the paper-starved Confederacy. He died with many honors in 1901, having accomplished nothing else of such lasting significance.

JOHN GIBBON: Hancock's determined and dependable division commander remained in the regular army after the war, actively fighting Native Americans on the frontier. He commanded one of the infantry columns that were supposed to coordinate with George Custer's cavalry at the time of the Battle of the Little Big Horn. Gibbon lived five years beyond his 1891 army retirement. His memoirs were not published until 1928.

GEORGE SEARS GREENE: The doughty defender of Culp's Hill later commanded his brigade under Sherman and was severely wounded in the face during an action at Wauhatchie, Tennessee, in October 1863. Despite a difficult and painful recuperation period, he returned to command a division in 1865. He retired to civilian life and was a busy public figure despite suffering ongoing complications from his war wound. Greene's life ended some three months shy of his ninety-eighth birthday.

DAVID MCMURTRIE GREGG: One of the steadiest commanders in the Union cavalry service, Gregg continued to perform admirably until his resignation in 1865 for undisclosed personal reasons. He served President U. S. Grant briefly as the United

States consul to Prague and afterward settled in Reading, Pennsylvania, where he passed away in 1916.

HENRY W. HALLECK: Lincoln's general-in-chief was demoted to chief of staff when U. S. Grant took over the Union armies in 1864. His rise in the postwar army stopped abruptly when Grant reviewed War Department communications and discovered Halleck's intriguing against him. He died in 1872.

WINFIELD S. HANCOCK: Never quite the same after Gettysburg due to his wound, Hancock nonetheless returned to service in time to take part in the bloody Overland Campaign of 1864 before retiring from active field command at year's end. His popularity was such that he almost defeated James Garfield for president in 1880. Hancock was still in army service when he died in 1886.

HENRY T. HARRISON: Long misidentified as James Harrison, Longstreet's spy-scout lived a postwar life that can only be described as strange. Married in late 1863 and the father of two children, Harrison disappeared into the Montana Territory in 1866, not to reemerge until 1900, long after he had been declared dead. After trying unsuccessfully to visit his children, he again dropped from sight, this time forever.

FRANK HASKELL: Praise for his Gettysburg actions brought Haskell the promotion he craved: he was given command of a new regiment, the 36th Wisconsin. The unit's first action was in the disastrous Union charge at Cold Harbor, Virginia, on June 3, 1864, where Haskell was killed. His 1863 letter describing Gettysburg was first printed in 1881 and is considered a classic account of the battle.

HENRY HETH: A. P. Hill's division commander retained that position through the war's end in a career marked by an absence of dash or brilliance. His postwar life was a string of small failures that ended with his death from Bright's disease in 1899. He finished his memoirs shortly before succumbing, forever enshrining the shoe myth as the cause for the Battle of Gettysburg.

A. P. HILL: Lee's uneven corps commander remained in unpredictable control of the Third Corps through the siege of Petersburg. He was killed in action on April 2, 1865, trying to rally his forces after a decisive Union breakthrough.

JOHN B. HOOD: Despite the paralysis of his left hand from his Gettysburg wound, Hood returned to action in time to fight at Chickamauga, where he lost his right leg. He recovered to take part in the Atlanta campaign, during which he assumed command of the Army of Tennessee. He fought this army to pieces and was relieved in December 1864. Hood married in 1868, had several children, and made his living selling insurance. He fell in a Yellow Fever outbreak in 1879.

JOSEPH HOOKER: Returned to active service to command a corps under Sherman, Hooker resigned in late 1864 after a subordinate was promoted over him. A series of strokes disabled him after the war, though he remained in uniform until his death in 1878.

OLIVER OTIS HOWARD: After commanding a corps and then an army under Sherman, Howard put his abolitionist feelings to use as the first commissioner of the Freedman's Bureau. He helped establish Howard University in Washington and ineptly directed a brutal campaign against the Nez Perce in 1877. After retiring from the army, Howard lectured and wrote about his experiences, projecting an image that was often at variance with the facts. He died in 1909.

AMOS HUMISTON: This otherwise unnoticed Gettysburg fatality would have rested in a grave of unknowns save for the ambrotype of his children found clutched in his hand. Newspapers around the country carried a facsimile of the picture over the caption "Whose Father Was He?" Once identified, his family became wards of the nation and were resettled in the Homestead, a short-lived Gettysburg establishment for war orphans. Like many simple people thrust into notoriety, Humiston's kin struggled for normalcy, some succeeding, some failing.

HENRY HUNT: Meade's artillery chief never ceased pressing his case for a stronger artillery role in military strategy and hierarchy, straining several friendships in the process. He spent his last years governing the Soldiers' Home in Washington, where he died in 1889.

DAVID IRELAND: This unsung Union hero of Culp's Hill succeeded George Greene after the senior warrior fell wounded in 1863. Ireland led his brigade in the Atlanta campaign until he himself was wounded in combat on May 15, 1864. A microscopic enemy accomplished what the Confederates could not: Ireland died of dysentery on September 10, 1864.

ALFRED IVERSON: Robert Rodes' unlucky brigade commander left Lee's army under a cloud and returned to his native Georgia, where he redeemed himself in a brilliant action against raiding Union cavalry in 1864. After the war, he tended orange groves in Florida until his death, in 1911.

HENRY JACOBS: A teenager during the battle, Jacobs followed in his father's footsteps to become a reverend and dean of the Lutheran Theological Seminary.

EDWARD JOHNSON: The commander of the forces that vainly attacked Culp's Hill directed a division in Lee's army until his capture at Spotsylvania in 1864. He was imprisoned through the war's end and died in 1873.

JOHN BEAUCHAMP JONES: The observant Confederate War Department clerk lived just long enough after the war to publish his diary: its publication and his death both came in 1866.

JAMES KEMPER: Pickett's only surviving brigade commander was left behind in the retreat and spent three months imprisoned in Fort Delaware before being exchanged for the Union Commander at the Peach Orchard, Charles Graham. Kemper served the Confederacy in an administrative capacity through the war's end, entered politics, and became the governor of Virginia in 1874. He retired to farming and died in 1895, an invalid due to his Gettysburg wound.

JUDSON KILPATRICK: The headstrong cavalry commander ended the war under Sherman, who had specifically requested that the "damned fool" (Sherman's words) he assigned to him. After the war, Kilpatrick played politics unsuccessfully and eventually accepted a ministerial appointment to Chile, where he passed away in 1881.

ROBERT E. LEE: The South's premier general remained in command of the Army of Northern Virginia until he surrendered it to U. S. Grant at Appomattox in 1865. Grant's admiration prevented Lee from being tried for treason, though the vengeful U.S. government never restored his citizenship while he lived. Lee became the under-paid president of Washington College in Virginia until death claimed him in 1870. He gathered materials for a projected war history but never found time to begin the book.

JAMES LONGSTREET: Lee's outspoken subordinate retained command of the First Corps, led it brilliantly at Chicamauga and abysmally at Knoxville in late 1863, was badly wounded in the Wilderness (1864), and rejoined the army a few months before Appomattox. His criticism of Lee's generalship in numerous postwar print articles angered many Southerners and accounts for the scarcity of Longstreet statues. He died in 1904.

GEORGE G. MEADE: The unwilling commander of the Army of the Potomac remained, increasingly dissatisfied, in that position through Appomattox. After the war, he went where duty called him, though always noting with bitterness the promotion of better-regarded subordinates subordinates over him. He died, still unhappy, in 1872.

JOHN S. MOSBY: The officer whose advice launched Jeb Stuart on his ride around the Union army continued to direct guerrilla operations in the portion of northern Virginia that became known as Mosby's Confederacy. After the war, Mosby was a relent-less defender of Stuart's honor and the author of an extensive body of writing on Get-tysburg, which obscured as much as it illuminated. Mosby died in 1916.

WILLIAM OATES: Chamberlain's opposite number on July 2 continued to fight for the Confederacy until a battle wound in 1864 cost him an arm and took him out of active service. He served Alabama after the war, first as a congressman and then as governor, and donned an army uniform once more for the Spanish-American War. One of his few public failures was his inability to convince Gettysburg park commis-sioners to erect a marker for the 15th Alabama on Little Round Top. Oates died in 1910.

MARSENA PATRICK: Meade's crusty provost marshal retained his post through the war's end, though his lenient treatment of Richmond's citizens led to his being relieved from duty in that city. Fed up with radical Republicans, Patrick turned Democrat and was governing the Soldiers' Home in Dayton, Ohio, when he passed away in 1888.

WILLIAM PEEL: A slight wound Peel received at the time of his capture worsened and he died, a prisoner, in late 1863.

WILLIAM N. PENDLETON: Having remained in generally ineffective command of Lee's artillery through Appomattox, Pendleton after the war returned to his true vocation and ministered to the congregation at Lexington's Grace Church. His earthly service ended in 1883.

GEORGE E. PICKETT: Embittered by the repulse of his division, Pickett submitted a battle report so incendiary in its condemnation of supporting commands that Lee suppressed it. Pickett's post-Gettysburg career was wobbly, punctuated by his hanging of twenty-four Confederate deserters and by critical defeats at Five Forks and Sailor's Creek. After the war, he fled to Canada for a while before returning to the States to sell insurance. He died in 1875. His fame as a cavalier of the South was established when his child bride posthumously published his wartime letters, most of which she had either heavily doctored or created out of whole cloth.

TILLIE PIERCE: This Gettysburg girl returned to the Weikert farm after the fighting ended and continued to help nurse Union wounded. She married a Harrisburg man in 1871, had three children (two girls and a boy), and died in 1914.

ALFRED PLEASONTON: His limpid leadership of Meade's cavalry led to his reassignment to the Department of Missouri, where he performed more credibly. He left the army in 1888, angered by the promotion of some subordinates at his expense. He was plagued by illness until his death in 1897.

WHITELAW REID: Active as a reporter to the war's end, Reid joined the *New York Tribune* in 1868, improved its international coverage, and eventually became editor in chief. He received several government appointments, including the U.S. ambassadorship to England, and helped negotiate America's peace treaty with Spain. He died in 1912.

GEORGE H. SHARPE: The founding chief of the Bureau of Military Information remained active in intelligence operations through the war's end. Afterward he practiced law in Kingston, New York, and served as a U.S. marshal and surveyor of customs. He barely outlived the nineteenth century.

DANIEL E. SICKLES: Gettysburg's most determined revisionist outlasted most of his notable peers, assuring that his weighted perspective on the battle would gain widest circulation. He stirred up trouble as the U.S. minister to Spain just prior to the war of 1898, returned to Congress for a term, and participated in numerous memorial associations. He died in 1914, more certain than ever that he had won the Battle of Gettysburg.

DANIEL SKELLY: A teenager at the time of the battle, Skelly lived well into the twentieth century, finally penning his memoirs of those three July days in 1932.

HENRY W. SLOCUM: The stolid, steady officer later commanded a corps and a wing of Sherman's army, where he took part in the March to the Sea. Defeated by Francis Barlow in an election for the position of New York's secretary of state, Slocum entered Congress instead and served on the board of the Gettysburg Monument Commissioners. He died in 1894.

J. E. B. STUART: Although Lee never rebuked Stuart for his much-delayed link-up with his army, he neglected to promote the cavalry officer when the opportunity presented itself. Stuart remained in command of Lee's cavalry corps and was leading his men when he was mortally wounded in action outside Richmond in May 1864.

ISAAC TRIMBLE: His Gettysburg wound cost him a leg and resulted in his imprisonment until March 1865, when he was exchanged. Trimble was doggedly returning to Lee's army when he learned of its surrender. He settled in Baltimore, wrote about the Gettysburg campaign, and died in 1888.

GOUVERNEUR K. WARREN: Promoted to corps command after Gettysburg, Warren exercised a cautious leadership that smacked of timidity to more aggressive superiors. Relieved of command after Five Forks in 1865, Warren remained in the army and campaigned tirelessly to reclaim his reputation. He did not survive the review of a court of inquiry that essentially exonerated him in 1882.

GULIAN V. WEIR: The unlucky battery commander remained in the army and in the 1880s had to contradict the flawed memory of Winfield Hancock regarding the panicked artillery unit he had encountered on July 2. Plagued by a painful skin cancer, Weir committed suicide in 1886.

CADMUS WILCOX: Hill's brigade commander got a division after Gettysburg and commanded it through Appomattox. He lived after the war in Washington with his widowed sister-in-law. Wilcox died in 1890.

AMBROSE WRIGHT: The officer who briefly conquered Cemetery Ridge entered the Georgia legislature in late 1863 but returned to the army in time to surrender with Johnston in North Carolina. After the war, he practiced law, edited a newspaper, and was elected to Congress in 1872. He died before he could take office.

THE OPPOSING ARMIES

KEY: These augmented rosters, in addition to listing the units and commanders engaged at Gettysburg, provide several other types of data. The bracketed numbers following each unit designation represent, first, estimated strength on the battlefield, and second, estimated losses, a combined total of men killed, wounded, missing, and captured. (Losses to command field and staff are not cited separately but are included in corps/division/brigade totals.) The figures are based on the best information available, but where they are especially speculative, they appear in italics. (The principal reference source used for the casualty figures was the 1994 edition of *Regimental Strengths and Losses at Gettysburg,* by John W. Busey and David G. Martin.) The designations in parentheses following officers' names indicate that an individual was killed (k), wounded (w), or mortally wounded (mw) in the action. Finally, the first name listed is always that of the officer in charge at the beginning of the unit's combat action. A cross following a name (when there are multiples listed) denotes the officer who was in command when the fighting ended. In a few cases I was unable to determine who ended in charge of the unit and so have not designated anyone.

THE ARMY OF THE POTOMAC [93,534/22,813]

Maj. Gen. George G. Meade, commanding

ARMY HEADQUARTERS

Maj. Gen. Daniel Butterfield, chief of staff
Brig. Gen. Gouverneur K. Warren, chief of engineers (w)
Brig. Gen. Henry J. Hunt, chief of artillery
Brig. Gen. Marsena R. Patrick, provost marshal general
Brig. Gen. Rufus Ingalls, chief quartermaster
Dr. Jonathan Letterman, medical director
Capt. Lemuel B. Norton, chief signal officer
Col. G. H. Sharpe, Bureau of Military Information

FIRST ARMY CORPS [12,222/6,059]

Maj. Gen. John F. Reynolds (k)
Maj. Gen. Abner Doubleday
Maj. Gen. John Newton+

FIRST DIVISION [3,857/2,155]

Brig. Gen. James S. Wadsworth

FIRST BRIGADE ("Iron Brigade") [1,829/1,153]

Brig. Gen. Solomon Meredith (w)
Col. William W. Robinson+

19th Indiana [308/210]
   Col. Samuel J. Williams
24th Michigan [496/363]
   Col. Henry A. Morrow (w)
   Capt. Albert M. Edwards+
2nd Wisconsin [302/233]
   Col. Lucius Fairchild (w)
   Maj. John Mansfield (w)
   Capt. George H. Otis+
6th Wisconsin [344/168]
   Lieut. Col. Rufus R. Dawes
7th Wisconsin [364/178]
   Col. William W. Robinson
   Maj. Mark Finnicum+

SECOND BRIGADE [2,017/1,002]

Brig. Gen. Lysander Cutler

7th Indiana [434/10]
   Col. Ira G. Grover
76th New York [375/234]
   Maj. Andrew J. Grover (k)
   Capt. John E. Cook+
84th New York ("14th Brooklyn") [318/217]
   Col. Edward B. Fowler
95th New York [241/115]
   Col. George H. Biddle (w)
   Maj. Edward Pye+
147th New York [380/296]
   Lieut. Col. Francis C. Miller (w)
   Maj. George Harney+
56th Pennsylvania [252/130]
   Col. J. William Hofmann

SECOND DIVISION [2,997/1,690]

Brig. Gen. John C. Robinson

FIRST BRIGADE [1,537/1,026]

Brig. Gen. Gabriel R. Paul (w)
Col. Samuel H. Leonard (w)
Col. Adrian R. Root (w)
Col. Richard Coulter+
Col. Peter Lyle

16th Maine [298/232]
   Col. Charles W. Tilden
   Maj. A. D. Leavitt+
13th Massachusetts [284/185]
   Col. Samuel H. Leonard (w)
   Lieut. Col. N. Walter Batchelder+
94th New York [411/245]
   Col. Adrian R. Root (w)
   Maj. Samuel A. Moffett+
104th New York [286/194]
   Col. Golbert G. Prey

107th Pennsylvania [255/165]
   LC. James M. MacThompson (w)
   Capt. Emanuel D. Roath+

SECOND BRIGADE [1,452/649]

Brig. Gen. Henry Baxter

12th Massachusetts [261/119]
   Col. James L. Bates (w)
   Lieut. Col. David Allen Jr.+
83rd New York [199/82]
   Lieut. Col. Joseph A. Moesch
97th New York [236/126]
   Col. Charles Wheelock
   Maj. Charles Northrup+
11th Pennsylvania [270/127]
   Col. Richard Coulter (w)

Capt. Benjamin F. Haines
Capt. James B. Overmyer+
88th Pennsylvania [274/110]
  Maj. Benezet F. Foust (w)
  Capt. Henry Whiteside+

90th Pennsylvania [208/93]
  Col. Peter Lyle+
  Major. Alfred J. Sellers

THIRD DIVISION [4,701/2,103]

Brig. Gen. Thomas A. Rowley
Maj. Gen. Abner Doubleday+

FIRST BRIGADE [1,361/898]

Col. Chapman Biddle+
Brig. Gen. Thomas A. Rowley

80th New York [287/170]
  Col. Theodore B. Gates
121st Pennsylvania [263/179]
  Maj. Alexander Biddle+
  Col. Chapman Biddle
142nd Pennsylvania [336/211]
  Col. Robert P. Cummins (k)
  Lieut. Col. A. B. McCalmont+
151st Pennsylvania [467/337]
  Lt. Col. George F. McFarland (w)
  Capt. Walter F. Owens
  Col. Harrison Allen+

SECOND BRIGADE [1,317/853]

Col. Roy Stone (w)
Col. Langhorne Wister (w)
Col. Edmund L. Dana+

143rd Pennsylvania [465/253]
  Col. Edmund L. Dana
  Lieut. Col. John D. Musser+
149th Pennsylvania [450/336]
  Lieut. Col. Walton Dwight (w)
  Capt. James Glenn+
150th Pennsylvania [400/264]
  Col. Langhorne Wister (w)
  Lieut. Col. H. S. Huidekoper (w)
  Capt. Cornelius C. Widdis+

THIRD BRIGADE [1950/351]

Brig. Gen. George J. Stannard
Col. Francis V. Randall+

12th Vermont [700/0]
  Col. Asa P. Blunt
13th Vermont [636/123]
  Col. Francis V. Randall
  Maj. Joseph J. Boynton
  Lieut. Col. William D. Munson+
14th Vermont [647/107]
  Col. William T. Nichols
15th Vermont [621/0]
  Col. Redfield Proctor
16th Vermont [661/119]
  Col. Wheelock G. Veazey

ARTILLERY BRIGADE [596/106]

Col. Charles S. Wainwright

2nd Maine Light Artillery: Battery B [117/18]
  Capt. James A. Hall
5th Maine Light Artillery: Battery E [119/23]
  Capt. Greenleaf T. Stevens (w)
  Lieut. Edward N. Whittier+
1st New York Light Artillery: Batteries L & E [124/17]
  Capt. Gilbert H. Reynolds (w)
  Lieut. George Breck+
1st Pennsylvania Light Artillery: Battery B [106/12]
  Capt. James H. Cooper
4th United States Light Artillery: Battery B [123/36]
  Lieut. James Stewart

SECOND ARMY CORPS [11,347/4,369]

Maj. Gen. Winfield S. Hancock (w)
Brig. Gen. John Gibbon (w)
Brig. Gen. John C. Caldwell
Brig. Gen. William Hays+

FIRST DIVISION [3,320/1,275]

Brig. Gen. John C. Caldwell

FIRST BRIGADE [853/330]

Col. Edward E. Cross (k)
Col. H. Boyd McKeen+

5th New Hampshire [179/80]
  Lieut. Col. Charles E. Hapgood
61st New York [104/62]
  Col. K. Oscar Broady
81st Pennsylvania [175/62]
  Col. H. Boyd McKeen
  Lieut. Col. Amos Stroh+
148th Pennsylvania [392/125]
  Lieut. Col. Robert McFarlane

SECOND BRIGADE ("Irish Brigade") [532/198]

Col. Patrick Kelly

28th Massachusetts [224/100]
  Col. Richard Byrnes
63rd New York [75/23]
  Lieut. Col. Richard C. Bently (w)
  Capt. Thomas Touhy+
69th New York [75/25]
  Capt. Richard Moroney (w)
  Lieut. James J. Smith+
88th New York [90/28]
  Capt. Denis F. Burke
116th Pennsylvania [66/22]
  Maj. St. Clair A. Mulholland

THIRD BRIGADE [975/358]

Col. Samuel K. Zook (k)
Lieut. Col. John Fraser+

52nd New York [134/38]
  Lieut. Col. C. G. Freudenberg (w)
  Capt. William Scherrer+
57th New York [175/34]
  Lieut. Col. Alford B. Chapman
66th New York [147/44]
  Col. Orlando H. Morris (w)
  Lieut. Col. John S. Hammell (w)
  Maj. Peter Nelson+
140th Pennsylvania [515/241]
  Col. Richard P. Roberts (k)
  Lieut. Col. John Fraser+

FOURTH BRIGADE [851/389]

Col. John R. Brooke

27th Connecticut [75/37]
  Lieut. Col. Henry C. Merwin (k)
  Maj. James H. Coburn+
2nd Delaware [234/84]
  Col. William P. Baily
  Capt. Charles H. Christman+
64th New York [204/98]
  Col. Daniel G. Bingham (w)
  Maj. Leman W. Bradley+
53rd Pennsylvania [135/80]
  Lieut. Col. Richard McMichael
145th Pennsylvania [202/90]
  Col. Hiram L. Brown (w)
  Capt. John W. Reynolds (w)
  Capt. Moses W. Oliver+

SECOND DIVISION [3,608/1,647]

Brig. Gen. John Gibbon (w)
Brig. Gen. William Harrow+

UNATTACHED

Massachusetts Sharpshooters: 1st Company [42/0]
Capt. William Plumer
Lieut. Emerson L. Bicknell

FIRST BRIGADE [1,366/768]

Brig. Gen. William Harrow
Col. Francis E. Heath+

19th Maine [439/203]
    Col. Francis E. Heath
    Lt. Col. Henry W. Cunningham+
15th Massachusetts [239/148]
    Col. George H. Ward (k)
    Lieut. Col. George C. Joslin+
1st Minnesota/2nd Co. Minnesota
Sharpshooters [330/224]
    Col. William Colvill Jr. (w)
    Capt. Nathan S. Messick
    Capt. Henry C. Coates+
82nd New York [355/192]
    Lieut. Col. James Huston (k)
    Capt. John Darrow+

SECOND BRIGADE [1,244/491]

Brig. Gen. Alexander S. Webb

69th Pennsylvania [284/137]
    Col. Dennis O'Kane (mw)
    Capt. William Davis+

71st Pennsylvania [261/98]
    Col. Richard Penn Smith
72nd Pennsylvania [380/192]
    Col. De Witt C. Baxter (w)
    Lieut. Col. Theodore Hesser+
106th Pennsylvania [280/64]
    Lieut. Col. William L. Curry

THIRD BRIGADE [922/377]

Col. Norman J. Hall

19th Massachusetts [163/77]
    Col. Arthur F. Devereaux
20th Massachusetts [243/127]
    Col. Paul. J. Revere (mw)
    Lieut. Col. George N. Macy (w)
    Capt. Henry L. Abbott+
7th Michigan [165/65]
    Lieut. Col. Amos E. Steele Jr. (k)
    Maj. Sylvanus W. Curtis+
42nd New York [197/74]
    Col. James E. Mallon
59th New York [152/34]
    Lieut. Col. Max A. Thoman (k)
    Capt. William McFadden+

THIRD DIVISION [3,644/1,291]

Brig. Gen. Alexander Hays

FIRST BRIGADE [977/211]

Col. Samuel S. Carroll

14th Indiana [191/31]
    Col. John Coons

4th Ohio [299/31]
    Lieut. Col. Leonard W. Carpenter
8th Ohio [209/102]
    Lieut. Col. Franklin Sawyer
7th West Virginia [235/47]
    Lieut. Col. Jonathan H. Lockwood

SECOND BRIGADE [1,069/360]

Col. Thomas A. Smyth (w)
Lieut. Col. Francis E. Pierce+

14th Connecticut [172/66]
  Maj. Theodore G. Ellis
1st Delaware [251/77]
  Lieut. Col. Edward P. Harris
  Capt. Thomas B. Hizar (w)
  Lieut. William Smith (mw)
  Lieut. John D. Dent+
12th New Jersey [444/115]
  Maj. John T. Hill
10th New York Battalion [82/6]
  Maj. George F. Hopper
108th New York [200/102]
  Lieut. Col. Francis E. Pierce

THIRD BRIGADE [1,508/714]

Col. George L. Willard (k)
Col. Eliakim Sherrill (k)
Col. Clinton D. MacDougall (w)
Lieut. Col. James L. Bull+

39th New York [269/95]
  Maj. Hugo Hildebrandt (w)
111th New York [390/249]
  Col. Clinton D. MacDougall (w)
  Lieut. Col. Isaac M. Lusk (w)
  Capt. Aaron B. Seeley+
125th New York [392/139]
  Lieut. Col. Levin Crandell

126th New York [455/231]
  Col. Eliakim Sherrill (k)
  Lieut. Col. James L. Bull
  Capt. William A. Coleman+

ARTILLERY BRIGADE [605/149]

Capt. John G. Hazard

1st New York Light Artillery: Battery B
& 14th New York Light Artillery
[117/26]
  Lieut. Albert S. Sheldon (w)
  Capt. James M. Rorty (k)
  Lieut. Robert E. Rogers+
1st Rhode Island Light Artillery:
Battery A [117/32]
  Capt. William A. Arnold
1st Rhode Island Light Artillery:
Battery B [129/28]
  Lieut. T. Fred Brown (w)
  Lieut. Walter S. Perrin+
1st United States Light Artillery:
Battery I [112/25]
  Lieut. George A. Woodruff (mw)
  Lieut. Tully McCrea+
4th United States Light Artillery:
Battery A [126/38]
  Lieut. Alonzo H. Cushing (k)
  Sgt. Frederick Fuger+

THIRD ARMY CORPS [10,675/4,211]

Maj. Gen. Daniel E. Sickles (w)
Maj. Gen. David B. Birney+

FIRST DIVISION [5,095/2,011]

Maj. Gen. David B. Birney
Brig. Gen. J. H. Hobart Ward (w) +

FIRST BRIGADE [1,516/740]

Brig. Gen. Charles K. Graham
Col. Andrew H. Tippin+

57th Pennsylvania [207/115]
  Col. Peter Sides (w)
  Capt. Alanson H. Nelson+

63rd Pennsylvania [246/34]
　Maj. John A. Danks
68th Pennsylvania [320/152]
　Col. Andrew H. Tippin
　Capt. Milton S. Davis+
105th Pennsylvania [274/132]
　Col. Calvin A. Craig
114th Pennsylvania [259/155]
　Lieut. Col. Frederick F. Cavada
　Capt. Edward R. Bowen+
141st Pennsylvania [209/149]
　Col. Henry J. Madill

SECOND BRIGADE [2,188/781]

Brig. Gen. J. H. Hobart Ward (w)
Col. Hiram Berdan+

20th Indiana [401/156]
　Col. John Wheeler (k)
　Lieut. Col. William C. L. Taylor+
3rd Maine [210/122]
　Col. Moses B. Lakeman
4th Maine [287/144]
　Col. Elijah Walker (w)
　Capt. Edward Libby+
86th New York [287/66]
　Lieut. Col. Benjamin L. Higgins

124th New York [238/90]
　Col. A. Van Horne Ellis (k)
　Lieut. Col. Francis L. Cummins+
99th Pennsylvania [277/110]
　Maj. John W. Moore
1st U.S. Sharpshooters [313/49]
　Col. Hiram Berdan
　Lieut. Col. Casper Trepp+
2nd U.S. Sharpshooters [169/43]
　Maj. Homer R. Stoughton

THIRD BRIGADE [1,387/490]

Col. P. Regis de Trobriand

17th Maine [350/133]
　Lieut. Col. Charles B. Merrill
3rd Michigan [237/45]
　Col. Byron R. Pierce (w)
　Lieut. Col. Edward S. Pierce+
5th Michigan [216/109]
　Lieut. Col. John Pulford
40th New York [431/150]
　Col. Thomas W. Egan
110th Pennsylvania [152/53]
　Lieut. Col. David M. Jones (w)
　Maj. Isaac Rogers+

SECOND DIVISION [4,924/2,092]

Brig. Gen. Andrew A. Humphreys

FIRST BRIGADE [1,718/790]

Brig. Gen. Joseph B. Carr

1st Massachusetts [321/120]
Lieut. Col. Clark B. Baldwin
11th Massachusetts [286/129]
　Lieut. Col. Porter D. Tripp
16th Massachusetts [245/81]
　Lieut. Col. Waldo Merriam (w)
　Capt. Matthew Donovan+
12th New Hampshire [224/92]
　Capt. John F. Langley
11th New Jersey [275/153]
　Col. Robert McAllister (w)
　Capt. Luther Martin (w)
　Lieut. John Schoonover+

　Capt. William H. Lloyd (w)
　Capt. Samuel T. Sleeper
26th Pennsylvania [365/213]
　Maj. Robert L. Bodine

SECOND BRIGADE [1,837/778]

Col. William R. Brewster

70th New York [288/117]
　Col. J. Egbert Farnum
71st New York [243/91]
　Col. Henry L. Potter
72nd New York [305/114]
　Col. John S. Austin (w)
　Lieut. Col. John Leonard+

73rd New York [349/162]
  Maj. Michael W. Burns
74th New York [266/89]
  Lieut. Col. Thomas Holt
120th New York [383/203]
  Lt. Col. Cornelius D. Westbrook (w)
  Maj. John R. Tappen+

THIRD BRIGADE [1,365/513]

Col. George C. Burling

2nd New Hampshire [354/193]
  Col. Edward L. Bailey
5th New Jersey [206/94]
  Col. William J. Sewell (w)
  Capt. Thomas C. Godfrey
  Capt. Henry H. Woolsey+
6th New Jersey [207/41]
  Lieut. Col. Stephen R. Gilkyson
7th New Jersey [275/114]
  Col. Louis R. Francine (mw)
  Maj. Frederick Cooper+
8th New Jersey [170/47]
  Col. John Ramsey (w)
  Capt. John G. Langston+
115th Pennsylvania [151/24]
  Maj. John P. Dunne

ARTILLERY BRIGADE [596/106]

Capt. George E. Randolph
Capt. A. Judson Clark+

1st New Jersey Light Artillery: 2nd
Battery B [131/20]
  Capt. A. Judson Clark
  Lieut. Robert Sims+
1st New York Light Artillery: Battery D [116/18]
  Capt. George B. Winslow
New York Light Artillery: 4th Battery [126/13]
  Capt. James E. Smith
1st Rhode Island Light Artillery:
Battery E [108/30]
  Lieut. John K. Bucklyn (w)
  Lieut. Benjamin Freeborn+
4th United States Light Artillery:
Battery K [113/25]
  Lieut. Frances W. Sealey (w)
  Lieut. Robert James+

FIFTH ARMY CORPS [11,019/2,187]

Maj. Gen. George Sykes

FIRST DIVISION [3,418/904]

Brig. Gen. James Barnes

FIRST BRIGADE [655/125]

Col. William S. Tilton

18th Massachusetts [139/27]
  Col. Joseph Hayes
22nd Massachusetts [137/31]
  Lieut. Col. Thomas Sherwin Jr.
1st Michigan [145/42]
  Col. Ira C. Abbot (w)
  Lieut. Col. William A. Throop+
118th Pennsylvania [233/25]
  Lieut. Col. James Gwyn

SECOND BRIGADE [1,423/427]

Col. Jacob B. Sweitzer

9th Massachusetts [412/7]
  Col. Patrick R. Guiney
32nd Massachusetts [242/80]
  Col. George L. Prescott
4th Michigan [342/165]
  Col. Harrison H. Jeffords (k)
  Lieut. Col. George W. Lumbard+
62nd Pennsylvania [426/175]
  Lieut. Col. James C. Hull

THIRD BRIGADE [1,336/352]

Col. Strong Vincent (mw)
Col. James C. Rice+

20th Maine [386/125]
  Col. Joshua L. Chamberlain

16th Michigan [263/60]
  Lieut. Col. Norval E. Welch
44th New York [391/111]
  Col. James C. Rice
  Lieut. Col. Freeman Conner+
83rd Pennsylvania [295/55]
  Capt. Orpheus S. Woodward

SECOND DIVISION [4,013/1,029]

Brig. Gen. Romeyn B. Ayres

FIRST BRIGADE [1,553/382]

Col. Hannibal Day

3rd United States [300/73]
  Capt. Henry W. Freedley (w)
  Capt. Richard G. Lay+
4th United States [173/40]
  Capt. Julius W. Adams Jr.
6th United States [150/44]
  Capt. Levi C. Bootes
12th United States [415/92]
  Capt. Thomas S. Dunn
14th United States [513/132]
  Maj. Grotius R. Giddings

SECOND BRIGADE [954/447]

Col. Sidney Burbank

2nd United States [197/67]
  Maj. Arthur T. Lee (w)
  Capt. Samuel A. McKee+
7th United States [116/59]
  Capt. David P. Hancock

10th United States [93/51]
  Capt. William Clinton
11th United States [286/120]
  Maj. DeLancey Floyd-Jones
17th United States [260/150]
  Lieut. Col. J. Durell Greene

THIRD BRIGADE [1,491/200]

Brig. Gen. Stephen H. Weed (k)
Col. Kenner Garrard+

140th New York [449/133]
  Col. Patrick O'Rorke (k)
  Lieut. Col. Louis Ernst+
146th New York [456/28]
  Col. Kenner Garrard
  Lieut. Col. David T. Jenkins+
91st Pennsylvania [220/19]
  Lieut. Col. Joseph H. Sinex
155th Pennsylvania [362/19]
  Lieut. Col. John H. Cain

THIRD DIVISION [2,862/210]

Brig. Gen. Samuel H. Crawford

FIRST BRIGADE [1,248/155]

Col. William McCandless

1st Pennsylvania Reserve [379/46]
  Col. William C. Talley
2nd Pennsylvania Reserve [233/37]
  Lieut. Col. George A. Woodward

6th Pennsylvania Reserve [324/24]
  Lieut. Col. Wellington H. Ent
13th Pennsylvania Reserve [298/48]
  Col. Charles F. Taylor (k)
  Maj. William R. Hartshorne+

THIRD BRIGADE [1,609/55]

Col. Joseph W. Fisher

5th Pennsylvania Reserve [285/2]
    Lieut. Col. George Dare
9th Pennsylvania Reserve [322/5]
    Lieut. James McK. Snodgrass
10th Pennsylvania Reserve [401/5]
    Col. Adoniram J. Warner
11th Pennsylvania Reserve [327/41]
    Col. Samuel M. Jackson
12th Pennsylvania Reserve [273/2]
    Col. Martin D. Hardin

ARTILLERY BRIGADE [432/43]

Capt. Augustus P. Martin

Massachusetts Light Artillery: 3rd
Battery C [115/6]
    Lieut. Aaron F. Walcott
1st New York Light Artillery: Battery C
[62/0]
    Capt. Almont Barnes
1st Ohio Light Artillery: Battery L
[113/2]
    Capt. Frank C. Gibbs
5th United States Light Artillery:
Battery D [68/13]
    Lieut. Charles E. Hazlett (k)
    Lieut. Benjamin F. Rittenhouse+
5th United States Light Artillery:
Battery I [71/22]
    Lieut. Malbone F. Watson (w)
    Lieut. Charles C. MacConnell+

SIXTH ARMY CORPS [13,601/242]

Maj. Gen. John Sedgwick

FIRST DIVISION [4,215/18]

Brig. Gen. Horatio G. Wright

FIRST BRIGADE [1,320/11]

Brig. Gen. Alfred T. A. Torbert

1st New Jersey [253/0]
    Lieut. Col. William Henry Jr.
2nd New Jersey [357/6]
    Lieut. Col. Charles Wiebecke
3rd New Jersey [282/2]
    Lieut. Col. Edward L. Campbell
15th New Jersey [410/3]
    Col. William H. Penrose

SECOND BRIGADE [1,325/5]

Brig. Gen. Joseph J. Bartlett

5th Maine [293/0]
    Col. Clark S. Edwards

121st New York [410/2]
    Col. Emory Upton
95th Pennsylvania [309/2]
    Lieut. Col. Edward Carroll
96th Pennsylvania [309/1]
    Maj. William H. Lessig

THIRD BRIGADE [1,484/2]

Brig. Gen. David A. Russell

6th Maine [378/0]
    Col. Hiram Burnham
49th Pennsylvania [276/0]
    Lieut. Col. Thomas L. Hulings
119th Pennsylvania [404/2]
    Col. Peter S. Ellmaker
5th Wisconsin [420/0]
    Col. Thomas S. Allen

SECOND DIVISION [3,610/16]

Brig. Gen. Albion P. Howe

SECOND BRIGADE [1,832/1]

Col. Lewis A. Grant

2nd Vermont [444/0]
  Col. James H. Walbridge
3rd Vermont [365/0]
  Col. Thomas O. Seaver
4th Vermont [381/1]
  Col. Charles B. Stoughton
5th Vermont [295/0]
  Lieut. Col. John R. Lewis
6th Vermont [331/0]
  Col. Elisha L. Barney

THIRD BRIGADE [1,775/15]

Brig. Gen. Thomas H. Neill

7th Maine [216/6]
  Lieut. Col. Selden Connor
33rd New York [60/0]
  Capt. Henry J. Gifford
43rd New York [370/5]
  Lieut. Col. John Wilson
49th New York [359/2]
  Col. Daniel D. Bidwell
77th New York [368/0]
  Lieut. Col. Winsor B. French
61st Pennsylvania [386/2]
  Lieut. Col. George F. Smith

THIRD DIVISION [4,740/196]

Maj. Gen. John Newton
Brig. Gen. Frank Wheaton+

FIRST BRIGADE [1,770/74]

Brig. Gen. Alexander Shaler

65th New York [277/9]
  Col. Joseph E. Hamblin
67th New York [349/1]
  Col. Nelson Cross
122nd New York [396/44]
  Col. Silas Titus
23rd Pennsylvania [467/14]
  Lieut. Col. John F. Glenn
82nd Pennsylvania [278/6]
  Col. Isaac C. Bassett

SECOND BRIGADE [1,595/69]

Col. Henry L. Eustis

7th Massachusetts [320/6]
  Lieut. Col. Franklin P. Harlow
10th Massachusetts [361/9]
  Lieut. Col. Joseph B. Parsons

37th Massachusetts [565/47]
  Col. Oliver Edwards
2nd Rhode Island [348/7]
  Col. Horatio Rogers Jr.

THIRD BRIGADE [1,369/53]

Brig. Gen. Frank Wheaton
Col. David J. Niven+

62nd New York [237/12]
  Col. David J. Niven
  Lieut. Col. T. B. Hamilton+
93rd Pennsylvania [234/10]
  Maj. John I. Nevin
98th Pennsylvania [351/11]
  Maj. John B. Kohler
102nd Pennsylvania [103/0]
  Col. John W. Patterson
139th Pennsylvania [443/20]
  Col. Frederick H. Collier (w)
  Lieut. Col. William H. Moody+

ARTILLERY BRIGADE [937/12]

Col. Charles H. Tompkins

Massachusetts Light Artillery: 1st
Battery A [135/0]
    Capt. William H. McCartney
New York Light Artillery: 1st Battery
[103/12]
    Capt. Andrew Cowan
New York Light Artillery: 3rd Battery
[111/0]
    Capt. William A. Harn
1st Rhode Island Light Artillery:
Battery C [116/0]
    Capt. Richard Waterman

1st Rhode Island Light Artillery:
Battery G [126/0]
    Capt. George A. Adams
2nd United States Light Artillery:
Battery D [126/0]
    Lieut. Edward B. Williston
2nd United States Light Artillery:
Battery G [101/0]
    Lieut. John H. Butler
5th United States Light Artillery:
Battery F [116/0]
    Lieut. Leonard Martin

ELEVENTH ARMY CORPS [9,221/3,807]

Maj. Gen. Oliver O. Howard+
Maj. Gen. Carl Schurz

FIRST DIVISION [2,477/1,306]

Brig. Gen. Francis C. Barlow (w)
Brig. Gen. Adelbert Ames+

FIRST BRIGADE [1,136/527]

Col. Leopold von Gilsa

41st New York [218/75]
    Lieut. Col. Detleo von Einsiedal
54th New York [189/102]
    Maj. Stephen Kovacs
    Lieut. Ernst Both+
68th New York [230/138]
    Col. Gotthilf Bourry
153rd Pennsylvania [497/211]
    Maj. John F. Frueauff

SECOND BRIGADE [1,337/778]

Brig. Gen. Adelbert Ames
Col. Andrew L. Harris+

17th Connecticut [386/197]
    Lieut. Col. Douglas Fowler (k)
    Maj. Allen G. Brady+
25th Ohio [220/184]
    Lieut. Col. Jeremiah Williams
    Capt. Nathaniel J. Manning (w)
    Lieut. William Maloney (w)
    Lieut. Israel White+
75th Ohio [269/186]
    Col. Andrew L. Harris
    Capt. George B. Fox+
107th Ohio [458/211]
    Col. Seraphim Meyer (w)
    Capt. John M. Lutz+

SECOND DIVISION [2,894/952]

Brig. Gen. Adolph von Steinwehr

FIRST BRIGADE [1,217/597]

Col. Charles R. Coster

134th New York [400/252]
    Lieut. Col. Allan H. Jackson
154th New York [239/200]
    Lieut. Col. Daniel B. Allen
27th Pennsylvania [283/111]
    Lieut. Col. Lorenz Cantador
73rd Pennsylvania [290/34]
    Capt. Daniel F. Kelly

SECOND BRIGADE [1,639/348]

Col. Orland Smith

33rd Massachusetts [491/45]
    Col. Adin B. Underwood
136th New York [482/109]
    Col. James Wood Jr.
55th Ohio [327/49]
    Col. Charles B. Gambee
73rd Ohio [338/145]
    Lieut. Col. Richard Long

THIRD DIVISION [3,109/1,476]

Maj. Gen. Carl Schurz+
Brig. Gen. Alexander Schimmelfennig

FIRST BRIGADE [1,683/807]

Brig. Gen. Alexander Schimmelfennig
Col. George von Amsberg+

82nd Illinois [316/112]
    Col. Edward S. Salomon
45th New York [375/224]
    Col. George von Amsberg
    Lieut. Col. Adolphus Dobke+
157th New York [409/307]
    Col. Philip B. Brown Jr.
61st Ohio [247/54]
    Col. Stephen J. McGroarty
74th Pennsylvania [333/110]
    Col. Adolph von Hartung (w)
    Lieut. Col. Alexander von Mitzel
    Capt. Gustav Schleiter
    Capt. Henry Krauseneck+

SECOND BRIGADE [1,420/669]

Col. Wlodzimierz Krzyzanowski

58th New York [194/20]
    Lieut. Col. August Otto
    Capt. Emil Koenig+

119th New York [262/140]
    Col. John T. Lockman (w)
    Lieut. Col. Edward F. Lloyd+
82nd Ohio [312/181]
    Col. James S. Robinson (w)
    Lieut. Col. David Thomson+
75th Pennsylvania [208/111]
    Col. Francis Mahler (k)
    Maj. August Ledig+
26th Wisconsin [443/217]
    Lieut. Col. Hans Boebel (w)
    Capt. John W. Fuchs+

ARTILLERY BRIGADE [604/69]

Maj. Thomas W. Osborn

1st New York Light Artillery: Battery I
[141/13]
    Capt. Michael Wiedrich
New York Light Artillery: 13th Battery
[110/11]
    Lieut. William Wheeler
1st Ohio Light Artillery: Battery I
[127/13]
    Capt. Hubert Dilger

1st Ohio Light Artillery: Battery K
[110/15]
    Capt. Lewis Heckman

4th United States Light Artillery:
Battery G [115/17]
    Lieut. Bayard Wilkeson (k)
    Lieut. Eugene A. Bancroft+

TWELFTH ARMY CORPS [9,788/1,082]

Maj. Gen. Henry W. Slocum
Brig. Gen. Alpheus S. Williams+

FIRST DIVISION [5,256/533]

Brig. Gen. Alpheus S. Williams
Brig Gen. Thomas H. Ruger+

FIRST BRIGADE [1,835/80]

Col. Archibald L. McDougall

5th Connecticut [221/7]
    Col. Warren W. Packer
20th Connecticut [321/28]
    Lieut. Col. William B. Wooster
3rd Maryland [290/8]
    Col. Joseph Sudsburg
123rd New York [495/14]
    Lieut. Col. James C. Rogers
145th New York [245/10]
    Col. Edward J. Price
46th Pennsylvania [262/13]
    Col. James L. Selfridge

SECOND BRIGADE [1,818/174]

Brig. Gen. Henry H. Lockwood

1st Maryland Eastern Shore [532/25]
    Col. James Wallace

1st Maryland Potomac Home Brigade
[674/104]
    Col. William P. Maulsby
150th New York [609/45]
    Col. John H. Ketcham

THIRD BRIGADE [1,598/279]

Brig. Gen. Thomas H. Ruger
Col. Silas Colgrove+

27th Indiana [339/110]
    Col. Silas Colgrove
    Lieut. Col. John R. Fesler+
2nd Massachusetts [316/136]
    Lieut. Col. Charles R. Mudge (k)
    Maj. Charles F. Morse+
13th New Jersey [347/21]
    Col. Ezra A. Carman
107th New York [319/2]
    Col. Nirom N. Crane
3rd Wisconsin [260/10]
    Col. William Hawley

SECOND DIVISION [3,964/540]

Brig. Gen. John W. Geary

FIRST BRIGADE [1,798/139]

Col. Charles Candy

5th Ohio [302/18]
    Col. John H. Patrick

7th Ohio [282/18]
    Col. William R. Creighton
29th Ohio [308/38]
    Capt. Wilbur F. Stevens (w)
    Capt. Edward Hayes+

66th Ohio [303/17]
Lieut. Col. Eugene Powell
28th Pennsylvania [303/28]
Capt. John H. Flynn
147th Pennsylvania [298/20]
Lieut. Col. Ario Pardee Jr.

SECOND BRIGADE [700/98]

Col. George A. Cobham Jr.+
Brig. Gen. Thomas L. Kane

29th Pennsylvania [357/66]
Col. William Rickards Jr.
109th Pennsylvania [149/10]
Capt. Frederick L. Gimber
111th Pennsylvania [191/22]
Lieut. Col. Thomas L. Walker
Col. George A. Cobham Jr.+

THIRD BRIGADE [1,424/303]

Brig. Gen. George S. Greene

60th New York [273/52]
Col. Abel Godard
78th New York [198/30]
Lieut. Col. H. von Hammerstein

102nd New York [230/29]
Col. James C. Lane (w)
Capt. Lewis R. Stegman+
137th New York [423/137]
Col. David Ireland
149th New York [297/55]
Col. Henry A. Barnum+
Lieut. Col. Charles B. Randall (w)

ARTILLERY BRIGADE [391/9]

Lieut. Edward D. Muhlenberg

1st New York Light Artillery: Battery M
[90/0]
Lieut. Charles E. Winegar
Pennsylvania Light Artillery: Battery E
[139/3]
Lieut. Charles A. Atwell
4th United States Light Artillery:
Battery F [89/1]
Lieut. Sylvanus T. Rugg
5th United States Light Artillery:
Battery K [72/5]
Lieut. David H. Kinzie

ARTILLERY RESERVE [2,376/242]

Brig. Gen. Robert O. Tyler
Capt. James M. Robertson+

FIRST REGULAR BRIGADE [445/68]

Capt. Dunbar R. Ransom

1st United States Light Artillery:
Battery H [129/10]
Lieut. Chandler P. Eakin (w)
Lieut. Philip D. Mason+
3rd United States Light Artillery:
Batteries F & K [115/24]
Lieut. John G. Turnbull
4th United States Light Artillery:
Battery C [95/18]
Lieut. Evan Thomas

5th United States Light Artillery:
Battery C [104/16]
Lieut. Gulian V. Weir (w)

FIRST VOLUNTEER BRIGADE [385/93]

Lieut. Col. Freeman McGilvery

Massachusetts Light Artillery: 5th
Battery E [104/21]
Capt. Charles A. Phillips
Massachusetts Light Artillery: 9th
Battery [104/28]
Capt. John Bigelow (w)

Lieut. Richard S. Milton+
New York Light Artillery: 15th Battery
[70/16]
    Capt. Patrick Hart
Pennsylvania Light Artillery: Batteries C
& F [105/28]
    Capt. James Thompson

SECOND VOLUNTEER BRIGADE [241/8]

Capt. Elijah D. Taft

1st Connecticut Heavy Artillery:
Battery B [110/0]
    Capt. Albert F. Brooker
1st Connecticut Heavy Artillery:
Battery M [110/0]
    Capt. Franklin A. Pratt
Connecticut Light Artillery: 2nd Battery
[93/5]
    Capt. John W. Sterling
New York Light Artillery: 5th Battery
[146/3]
    Capt. Elijah D. Taft

THIRD VOLUNTEER BRIGADE [431/37]

Capt. James F. Huntington

New Hampshire Light Artillery: 1st
Battery [86/3]
    Capt. Frederick M. Edgell

1st Ohio Light Artillery: Battery H
[99/7]
    Lieut. George W. Norton
1st Pennsylvania Light Artillery:
Batteries F & G [144/23]
    Capt. R. Bruce Ricketts
West Virginia Light Artillery: Battery C
[100/4]
    Capt. Wallace Hill

FOURTH VOLUNTEER BRIGADE [499/36]

Capt. Robert H. Fitzhugh

Maine Light Artillery: 6th Battery F
[87/13]
    Lieut. Edwin B. Dow
Maryland Light Artillery: Battery A
[106/0]
    Capt. James H. Rigby
1st New Jersey Light Artillery: Battery A
[98/9]
    Lieut. Augustin N. Parsons
1st New York Light Artillery: Battery G
[84/7]
    Capt. Nelson Ames
1st New York Light Artillery: Battery K
/ 11th Battery [122/7]
    Capt. Robert H. Fitzhugh

CAVALRY CORPS [11,856/610]

Maj. Gen. Alfred Pleasonton

FIRST DIVISION [4,073/176]

Brig. Gen. John Buford

FIRST BRIGADE [1,600/99]

Col. William Gamble

8th Illinois Cavalry [470/7]
    Maj. John L. Beveridge

12th Illinois Cavalry [233/20]
    Col. George H. Chapman
3rd Indiana Cavalry [313/32]
    Col. George H. Chapman
8th New York Cavalry [580/40]
    Lieut. Col. William L. Markell

SECOND BRIGADE [1,148/28]

Col. Thomas C. Devin

6th New York Cavalry [218/9]
 Maj. William E. Beardsley
9th New York Cavalry [367/11]
 Col. William Sackett
17th Pennsylvania Cavalry [464/4]
 Col. Josiah H. Kellogg
3rd West Virginia Cavalry [59/4]
 Capt. Seymour B. Conger

RESERVE (THIRD) BRIGADE
[1,321/49]

Brig. Gen. Wesley Merritt

6th Pennsylvania Cavalry [242/12]
 Maj. James H. Haseltine
1st United States Cavalry [362/15]
 Capt. Richard S. C. Lord
2nd United States Cavalry [407/17]
 Capt. Theophilus F. Rodenbough
5th United States Cavalry [306/5]
 Capt. Julius W. Mason
6th United States Cavalry [471/242]
 Maj. Samuel H. Starr (w)
 Lieut. Louis H. Carpenter
 Lieut. Nicholas Nolan
 Capt. Ira W. Claflin+

SECOND DIVISION [2,614/56]

Brig. Gen. David McM. Gregg

FIRST BRIGADE [1,311/35]

Col. John B. McIntosh

1st Maryland Cavalry [285/3]
 Lieut. Col. James L. Deems
Purnell (Maryland) Legion: Company A
[66/0]
 Capt. Robert E. Duvall
1st Massachusetts Cavalry [250/0]
 Lieut. Col. Greely S. Curtis
1st New Jersey Cavalry [199/9]
 Maj. Myron H. Beaumont
1st Pennsylvania Cavalry [355/2]
 Col. John P. Taylor
3rd Pennsylvania Cavalry [335/21]
 Lieut. Col. Edward S. Jones

3rd Pennsylvania Heavy Artillery:
Battery H [52/0]
 Capt. William D. Rank

THIRD BRIGADE [1,263/21]

Col. J. Irvin Gregg

1st Maine Cavalry [315/5]
 Lieut. Col. Charles H. Smith
10th New York Cavalry [333/9]
 Maj. M. Henry Avery
4th Pennsylvania Cavalry [258/1]
 Lieut. Col. William E. Doster
16th Pennsylvania Cavalry [349/6]
 Lieut. Col. John K. Robison

THIRD DIVISION [3,902/355]

Brig. Gen. Judson Kilpatrick

FIRST BRIGADE [1,925/98]

Brig. Gen. Elon J. Farnsworth (k)
Col. Nathaniel P. Richmond+

5th New York Cavalry [420/6]
 Maj. John Hammond

18th Pennsylvania Cavalry [509/14]
 Lieut. Col. William P. Brinton
1st Vermont Cavalry [600/65]
 Lieut. Col. Addison W. Preston
1st West Virginia Cavalry [395/12]
 Col. Nathaniel P. Richmond
 Maj. Charles E. Capehart+

SECOND BRIGADE [1,934/257]

Brig. Gen. George A. Custer

1st Michigan Cavalry [427/73]
  Col. Charles H. Town
5th Michigan Cavalry [646/56]
  Col. Russell A. Alger
6th Michigan Cavalry [477/28]
  Col. George Gray
7th Michigan Cavalry [383/100]
  Col. William D. Mann

FIRST HORSE ARTILLERY
BRIGADE [493/8]

Capt. James M. Robertson

9th Michigan Light Artillery [111/5]
  Capt. Jabez J. Daniels
6th New York Light Artillery [103/1]
  Capt. Joseph W. Martin
2nd United States Light Artillery:
Batteries B & L [99/0]
  Lieut. Edward Heaton

2nd United States Light Artillery:
Battery M [117/1]
  Lieut. A. C. M. Pennington Jr.
4th United States Light Artillery:
Battery E [61/1]
  Lieut. Samuel S. Elder

SECOND HORSE ARTILLERY
BRIGADE [276/15]

Capt. John C. Tidball

1st United States Light Artillery:
Batteries E & G [85/0]
  Capt. Alanson M. Randol
1st United States Light Artillery:
Battery K [114/3]
  Capt. William M. Graham
2nd United States Light Artillery:
Battery A [75/12]
  Lieut. John H. Calef
3rd United States Light Artillery:
Battery C [142/0]
  Lieut. William D. Fuller

THE ARMY OF NORTHERN VIRGINIA
[70,226/22,874]

Gen. Robert E. Lee, commanding

ARMY HEADQUARTERS

Col. R. H. Chilton, chief of staff and inspector general
Brig. Gen. William Nelson Pendleton, chief of artillery
Dr. Lafayette Guild, medical director
Lt. Col. Briscoe G. Baldwin, chief of ordnance
Lt. Col. Robert C. Cole, chief of commissary
Lt. Col. James L. Corley, chief quartermaster
Maj. H. E. Young, judge advocate general
Col. A. L. Long, military secretary and acting assistant chief of artillery
Maj. Walter H. Taylor, aide de camp and assistant advocate general
Maj. Charles Marshall, aide de camp and assistant military secretary
Maj. Charles Venable, aide de camp and assistant inspector general
Capt. Samuel R. Johnston, engineer

FIRST ARMY CORPS [20,935/7,739]

Lieut. Gen. James Longstreet

MCLAWS' DIVISION [7,153/2,294]

Maj. Gen. Lafayette McLaws

KERSHAW'S BRIGADE [2,183/649]

Brig. Gen. Joseph B. Kershaw

2nd South Carolina [412/170]
  Col. John D. Kennedy (w)
  Lieut. Col. F. Gaillard+
3rd South Carolina [406/87]
  Maj. Robert C. Maffett
  Col. J. D. Nance+
3rd South Carolina Battalion [203/48]
  Lieut. Col. William G. Rice
7th South Carolina [408/115]
  Col. D. Wyatt Aiken+
  Lieut. Col. Elbert Bland (w)
8th South Carolina [300/105]
  Col. John W. Henagan
15th South Carolina [448/144]
  Col. William DeSaussure (k)
  Maj. William M. Gist+

SEMMES' BRIGADE [1,334/432]

Brig. Gen. Paul J. Semmes (mw)
Col. Goode Bryan+

10th Georgia [303/101]
  Col. John B. Weems
50th Georgia [302/96]
  Col. William R. Manning
51st Georgia [303/95]
  Col. Edward Ball
53rd Georgia [422/99]
  Col. James P. Simms

BARKSDALE'S BRIGADE [1,620/804]

Brig. Gen. William Barksdale (k)
Col. Benjamin G. Humphreys+

13th Mississippi [481/243]
  Col. John W. Carter (k)
  Lieut. Col. Kennon McElroy (w)

17th Mississippi [469/270]
  Col. William D. Holder (w)
  Lieut. Col. John C. Fiser+
18th Mississippi [242/137]
  Col. Thomas M. Griffin
  Lieut. Col. W. H. Luse
21st Mississippi [424/139]
  Col. Benjamin G. Humphreys

WOFFORD'S BRIGADE [1,627/370]

Brig. Gen. William T. Wofford

3rd Georgia Battalion Sharpshooters [229/13]
  Lieut. Col. Nathan L. Hutchins
16th Georgia [303/104]
  Col. Goode Bryan
18th Georgia [302/36]
  Lieut. Col. Solon Z. Ruff
24th Georgia [303/85]
  Col. Robert McMillan
Cobb's (Georgia) Legion [213/22]
  Lieut. Col. Luther J. Glenn
Phillips' (Georgia) Legion [273/66]
  Lieut. Col. Elihu S. Barclay Jr.

ARTILLERY BRIGADE [378/52]

Col. Henry Coalter Cabell

1st North Carolina Light Artillery:
Battery A [131/13]
  Capt. Basil C. Manly
Pulaski (Georgia) Artillery [63/19]
  Capt. John C. Fraser (mw)
  Lieut. W. J. Furlong+
1st Richmond Howitzers [90/13]
  Capt. Edward S. McCarthy
Troup (Georgia) Artillery [90/7]
  Capt. Henry H. Carlton (w)
  Lieut. C. W. Motes+

PICKETT'S DIVISION [5,473/2,904]

Maj. Gen. George E. Pickett

GARNETT'S BRIGADE [1,851/905]

Brig. Gen. Robert B. Garnett (k)
Maj. Charles S. Peyton+

8th Virginia [242/168]
   Col. Eppa Hunton (w)
   Lieut. Col. Norbonne Berkeley (w)
   Lieut. John Gray+
18th Virginia [371/231]
   Lieut. Col. Henry A. Carrington (w)
19th Virginia [426/168]
   Col. Henry Gantt (w)
   Lieut. Col. John T. Ellis (mw)
   Maj. Charles S. Peyton+
28th Virginia [376/171]
   Col. Robert C. Allen (k)
   Lieut. Col. William Watts+
56th Virginia [430/163]
   Col. William D. Stuart (mw)
   Lieut. Col. P. P. Slaughter+

KEMPER'S BRIGADE [1,781/678]

Brig. Gen. James L. Kemper (w)
Col. Joseph Mayo Jr.+

1st Virginia [218/136]
   Col. Lewis B. Williams Jr. (k)
   Lieut. Col. F. G. Skinner+
3rd Virginia [351/106]
   Col. Joseph Mayo Jr.
   Lieut. Col. A. D. Callcote (k)
   Maj. William H. Pryor+
7th Virginia [359/118]
   Col. Waller T. Patton (mw)
   Capt. Alphonso N. Jones+
11th Virginia [405/155]
   Maj. Kirkwood Otey (w)
   Capt. James R. Hutter (w)
   Capt. John Holmes Smith+

24th Virginia [442/160]
   Col. William R. Terry

ARMISTEAD'S BRIGADE [2,188/1,057]

Brig. Gen. Lewis A. Armistead (k)
Col. William R. Aylett+

9th Virginia [266/150]
   Maj. John C. Owens (mw)
   Capt. James J. Phillips+
14th Virginia [472/248]
   Col. James G. Hodges (k)
   Lieut. Col. William White+
38th Virginia [481/194]
   Col. Edward C. Edmonds (k)
   Lieut. Col. P. B. Whittle (w)
   Lieut. Col. Joseph R. Cabell+
53rd Virginia [463/213]
   Col. William R. Aylett (w)
   Lieut. Col. Rawley W. Martin (w)
57th Virginia [502/249]
   Col. John Bowie Magruder (mw)
   Lieut. Col. B. H. Wade (mw)
   Maj. Clement R. Fontaine+

ARTILLERY BRIGADE [419/29]

Maj. James Dearing

Fauquier (Virginia) Artillery [134/5]
   Capt. Robert M. Stribling
Hampden (Virginia) Artillery [90/4]
   Capt. William H. Caskie
Richmond Fayette Artillery [90/5]
   Capt. Miles C. Macon
Lynchburg (Virginia) Artillery [96/10]
   Capt. Joseph G. Blount

HOOD'S DIVISION [7,375/2,372]

Maj. Gen. John B. Hood
Brig. Gen. Evander M. Law+

LAW'S BRIGADE [1,933/500]

Brig. Gen. Evander M. Law
Col. James L. Sheffield+

4th Alabama [346/87]
    Col. Lawrence H. Scruggs+
    Maj. Thomas K. Coleman
15th Alabama [499/171]
    Col. William C. Oates
    Capt. Blanton A. Hill+
44th Alabama [363/94]
    Col. William F. Perry
47th Alabama [347/44]
    Col. James W. Jackson (w)
    Lieut. Col. J. M. Bulger (w)
    Maj. J. M. Campbell+
48th Alabama [374/102]
    Col. James L. Sheffield
    Capt. Thomas J. Eubanks+

ROBERTSON'S BRIGADE [1,734/603]

Brig. Gen. Jerome B. Robertson

3rd Arkansas [479/182]
    Col. Van H. Manning (w)
    Lieut. Col. Robert S. Taylor+
1st Texas [426/97]
    Lieut. Col. Phillip A. Work
4th Texas [415/112]
    Col. John C. G. Key (w)
    Maj. J. P. Bane+
5th Texas [409/211]
    Col. Robert M. Powell (w)
    Lieut. Col. King Bryan (w)
    Maj. J. C. Rogers+

G. T. ANDERSON'S BRIGADE [1,874/722]

Brig. Gen. George T. Anderson (w)
Lieut. Col. William Luffman (w)+

7th Georgia [377/21]
    Col. William W. White
8th Georgia [312/168]
    Col. John R. Towers
9th Georgia [340/189]
    Lieut. Col. John C. Mounger (k)
    Maj. W. M. Jones (w)
    Capt. George Hillyer+
11th Georgia [310/201]
    Col. Francis H. Little (w)
    Lieut. Col. William Luffman (w)
    Maj. Henry D. McDaniel+
59th Georgia [525/142]
    Col. Jack Brown (w)
    Maj. Bolivar Hopkins Gee
    Capt. M. G. Bass+

BENNING'S BRIGADE [1,420/519]

Brig. Gen. Henry L. Benning

2nd Georgia [348/102]
    Lieut. Col. William T. Harris (k)
    Maj. William S. Shepherd+
15th Georgia [368/171]
    Col. Dudley M. DuBose
17th Georgia [350/108]
    Col. Wesley C. Hodges
20th Georgia [350/137]
    Col. John A. Jones (k)
    Lieut. Col. J. D. Waddell+

ARTILLERY BRIGADE [403/27]

Maj. Mathis W. Henry

Branch (North Carolina) Artillery [112/3]
    Capt. Alexander C. Latham
German (South Carolina) Artillery [71/*11*]
    Capt. William K. Bachman

Palmetto (South Carolina) Artillery [63/7]
  Capt. Hugh R. Garden

Rowan (North Carolina) Artillery [148/6]
  Capt. James Reilly

ARTILLERY RESERVE (LONGSTREET'S CORPS) [918/169]

Col. James B. Walton

ALEXANDER'S BATTALION [576/139]

Col. Edward P. Alexander

Ashland (Virginia) Artillery [103/28]
  Capt. Pichegru Woolfolk Jr. (w)
  Lieut. James Woolfolk
Bedford (Virginia) Artillery [78/9]
  Capt. Tyler C. Jordan
Brooks (South Carolina) Artillery [71/36]
  Lieut. S. C. Gilbert
Madison (Louisiana) Artillery [135/33]
  Capt. George V. Moody
Virginia (Richmond) Battery [90/18]
  Capt. William W. Parker

Virginia (Bath) Artillery [90/13]
  Capt. Osmond B. Taylor

WASHINGTON (LOUISIANA) ARTILLERY [338/30]

Maj. Benjamin F. Eshleman

1st Company [77/4]
  Capt. Charles W. Squires
2nd Company [80/6]
  Capt. John B. Richardson
3rd Company [92/10]
  Capt. Merritt B. Miller
4th Company [80/10]
  Capt. Joe Norcom
  Lieut. H. A. Battles+

EWELL'S CORPS [20,503/6,777]

Lieut. Gen. Richard S. Ewell

EARLY'S DIVISION [5,460/1,508]

Maj. Gen. Jubal A. Early

HAYS' BRIGADE [1,295/334]

Brig. Gen. Harry T. Hays

5th Louisiana [196/67]
  Maj. Alexander Hart
  Capt. T. H. Briscoe+
6th Louisiana [218/61]
  Lieut. Col. Joseph Hanlon
7th Louisiana [235/58]
  Col. Davidson B. Penn
8th Louisiana [296/75]
  Col. Trevanion D. Lewis (k)
  Lieut. Col. A. de Blanc
  Maj. G. A. Lester+

9th Louisiana [347/73]
  Col. Leroy A. Stafford

SMITH'S BRIGADE [806/213]

Brig. Gen. William Smith

31st Virginia [267/59]
  Col. John S. Hoffman
49th Virginia [281/100]
  Lieut. Col. J. Catlett Gibson
52nd Virginia [254/54]
  Lieut. Col. James H. Skinner (w)
  Maj. John DeHart Ross+

HOKE'S BRIGADE [1,244/412]

Col. Isaac E. Avery (k)
Col. Archibald C. Godwin+

6th North Carolina [509/208]
  Maj. Samuel McDowell Tate
21st North Carolina [436/139]
  Col. William W. Kirkland
57th North Carolina [297/65]
  Col. Archibald C. Godwin

GORDON'S BRIGADE [1,813/537]

Brig. Gen. John B. Gordon

13th Georgia [312/137]
  Col. James M. Smith
26th Georgia [315/32]
  Col. Edmund N. Atkinson
31st Georgia [252/65]
  Col. Clement A. Evans

38th Georgia [341/133]
  Capt. William L. McLeod
60th Georgia [299/59]
  Capt. Walter B. Jones
61st Georgia [288/111]
  Col. John H. Lamar

ARTILLERY BRIGADE [290/12]

Lieut. Col. Hilary P. Jones

Charlottesville (Virginia) Artillery [71/2]
  Capt. James McD. Carrington
Courtney (Virginia) Artillery [90/2]
  Capt. William A. Tanner
Louisiana Guard Artillery [60/7]
  Capt. Charles A. Green
Staunton (Virginia) Artillery [60/1]
  Capt. Asher W. Garber

RODES' DIVISION [7,873/3,092]

Maj. Gen. Robert E. Rodes

DANIEL'S BRIGADE [2,052/926]

Brig. Gen. Junius Daniel

2nd North Carolina Battalion [240/199]
  Lt. Col. Hezekiah L. Andrews (k)
  Capt. Van Brown+
32nd North Carolina [454/181]
  Col. Edmind C. Brabble
43rd North Carolina [572/187]
  Col. Thomas S. Kenan (w)
  Lieut. Col. W. G. Lewis+
45th North Carolina [460/219]
  Lieut. Col. Samuel H. Boyd (w)
  Major. John R. Winston (w)
  Capt. A. H. Gallaway (w)
  Capt. J. A. Hopkins+
53rd North Carolina [322/117]
  Col. William A. Owens

IVERSON'S BRIGADE [1,384/903]

Brig. Gen. Alfred Iverson

5th North Carolina [473/289]
  Capt. Speight B. West
  Capt. Benjamin Robinson+
12th North Carolina [219/79]
  Lieut. Col. William S. Davis
20th North Carolina [372/253]
  Lieut. Col. Nelson Slough (w)
  Capt. Lewis T. Hicks+
23rd North Carolina [316/282]
  Col. Daniel H. Christie (mw)
  Capt. William H. Johnston+

DOLES' BRIGADE [1,323/219]

Brig. Gen. George Doles

4th Georgia [341/53]
  Lieut. Col. David R. E. Winn (k)
  Maj. W. H. Willis+
12th Georgia [327/53]
  Col. Edward Willis
21st Georgia [287/38]
  Col. John T. Mercer
44th Georgia [364/75]
  Col. Samuel P. Lumpkin (mw)
  Maj. W. H. Peebles+

RAMSEUR'S BRIGADE [1,027/275]

Brig. Gen. Stephen D. Ramseur

2nd North Carolina [243/67]
  Maj. Daniel W. Hurtt (w)
  Capt. James T. Scales+
4th North Carolina [196/69]
  Col. Bryan Grimes
14th North Carolina [306/64]
  Col. R. Tyler Bennett (w)
  Maj. Joseph H. Lambeth+
30th North Carolina [278/75]
  Col. Francis M. Parker (w)
  Maj. W. W. Sillers+

O'NEAL'S BRIGADE [1,688/696]

Col. Edward A. O'Neal

3rd Alabama [350/91]
  Col. Cullen A. Battle (w)
5th Alabama [317/209]
  Col. Josephus M. Hall
6th Alabama [382/165]
  Col. James N. Lightfoot (w)
  Capt. M. L. Bowie+
12th Alabama [317/83]
  Col. Samuel B. Pickens
26th Alabama [319/130]
  Lieut. Col. John C. Goodgame

ARTILLERY BATTALION [385/77]

Lieut. Col. Thomas H. Carter

Jeff Davis (Alabama) Artillery [79/8]
  Capt. William J. Reese
King William (Virginia) Artillery [103/23]
  Capt. William P. Carter
Morris (Virginia) Artillery [114/39]
  Capt. Richard C. M. Page (w)
Orange (Virginia) Artillery [80/7]
  Capt. Charles W. Fry

JOHNSON'S DIVISION [6,433/2,002]

Maj. Gen. Edward Johnson

STEUART'S BRIGADE [2,121/769]

Brig. Gen. George H. Steuart

1st Maryland Battalion [400/189]
  Lieut. Col. James R. Herbert (w)
  Maj. W. W. Goldsborough (w)
  Capt. J. P. Crane+
1st North Carolina [377/151]
  Lieut. Col. Hamilton Allen Brown
3rd North Carolina [548/218]
  Maj. William M. Parsley
10th Virginia [276/77]
  Col. Edward T. H. Warren

23rd Virginia [251/36]
  Lieut. Col. Simeon T. Walton
37th Virginia [264/98]
  Maj. Henry C. Wood

NICHOLLS' BRIGADE [1,104/389]

Col. Jesse M. Williams

1st Louisiana [172/39]
  Col. Michael Nolan (k)
  Capt. E. D. Willett
  Capt. Thomas Rice+

2nd Louisiana [236/62]
  Lieut. Col. Ross E. Burke (w)
10th Louisiana [226/110]
  Lieut. Col. Henry Monier
14th Louisiana [281/65]
  Col. Zebulon York
15th Louisiana [186/38]
  Col. Edmund Pendleton

STONEWALL BRIGADE
[1,323/338]

Brig. Gen. James Walker

2nd Virginia [333/25]
  Col. John Q. A. Nadenbousch
4th Virginia [257/137]
  Maj. William Terry
5th Virginia [345/58]
  Col. John H. S. Funk
17th Virginia [148/48]
  Lieut. Col. Daniel M. Shriver
33rd Virginia [236/70]
  Capt. James B. Golladay

JONES' BRIGADE [1,520/453]

Brig. Gen. John M. Jones (w)
Lieut. Col. Robert H. Dungan+

21st Virginia [236/50]
  Capt. William P. Moseley

25th Virginia [280/70]
  Col. John C. Higginbotham (w)
  Lieut. Col. J. A. Robinson+
42nd Virginia [265/80]
  Col. Robert Withers (w)
  Capt. S. H. Saunders+
44th Virginia [227/56]
  Maj. Norval Cobb (w)
  Capt. T. R. Buckner+
48th Virginia [265/87]
  Lieut. Col. Robert H. Dungan
  Maj. Oscar White+
50th Virginia [240/99]
  Lieut. Col. Logan H. N. Salyer

ARTILLERY BRIGADE [356/51]

Maj. James W. Latimer (k)
Capt. Charles I. Raine+

1st Maryland Battery [90/5]
  Capt. William F. Dement
Alleghany (Virginia) Artillery [91/24]
  Capt. John C. Carpenter
Chesapeake (Maryland) Artillery
[76/17]
  Capt. William D. Brown
Lee (Virginia) Battery [90/4]
  Capt. Charles I. Raine
  Lieut. William M. Hardwicke+

ARTILLERY RESERVE (EWELL'S CORPS) [648/74]

Col. J. Thompson Brown

FIRST VIRGINIA ARTILLERY
[367/50]

Capt. Willis J. Dance

2nd Richmond (Virginia) Howitzers
[64/3]
  Capt. David Watson
3rd Richmond (Virginia) Howitzers [62/4]
  Capt. Benjamin H. Smith Jr.
Powhatan (Virginia) Artillery [78/15]
  Lieut. John M. Cunningham
Rockbridge (Virginia) Artillery [85/21]
  Capt. Archibald Graham

Salem (Virginia) Artillery [69/7]
  Lieut. Charles B. Griffin

NELSON'S BATTALION [277/24]

Lieut. Col. William Nelson

Amherst (Virgina) Artillery [105/13]
  Capt. Thomas J. Kirkpatrick
Fluvanna (Virginia) Artillery [90/11]
  Capt. John L. Massie
Georgia Battery [73/0]
  Capt. John Milledge Jr.

HILL'S CORPS [22,026/8,049]

Lieut. Gen. Ambrose P. Hill

ANDERSON'S DIVISION [7,136/2,185]

Maj. Gen. Richard H. Anderson

WILCOX'S BRIGADE [1,726/778]

Brig. Gen. Cadmus M. Wilcox

8th Alabama [477/266]
   Lieut. Col. Hilary A. Herbert
9th Alabama [306/116]
   Capt. J. Horace King (w)
10th Alabama [311/104]
   Col. William H. Forney (w)
   Lieut. Col. James E. Shelley+
11th Alabama [311/75]
   Col. John C. C. Sanders (w)
   Lieut. Col. George E. Tayloe+
14th Alabama [316/48]
   Col. Lucius Pinckard (w)
   Lieut. Col. James A. Broome+

WRIGHT'S BRIGADE [1,413/696]

Brig. Gen. Ambrose R. Wright

2nd Georgia Battalion [173/82]
   Maj. George W. Ross (w)
   Capt. Charles J. Moffett
3rd Georgia [441/219]
   Col. Edward J. Walker
22nd Georgia [400/171]
   Col. Joseph A. Wasden (k)
   Capt. B. C. McCurry+
48th Georgia [395/224]
   Col. William Gibson (w)
   Capt. M. R. Hall+

MAHONE'S BRIGADE [1,542/102]

Brig. Gen. William Mahone

6th Virginia [288/10]
   Col. George T. Rogers
12th Virginia [348/22]
   Col. David A. Weisiger
16th Virginia [270/22]
   Col. Joseph H. Ham
41st Virginia [276/12]
   Col. William A. Parham
61st Virginia [356/25]
   Col. Virginius D. Groner

PERRY'S BRIGADE [742/455]

Col. David Lang

2nd Florida [242/106]
   Maj. Walter R. Moore (w)
   Capt. William D. Ballantine (w)
   Capt. Alexander Mosely (w)
   Capt. C. Seton Fleming+
5th Florida [321/129]
   Capt. Richmond N. Gardner (w)
   Capt. Council A. Bryan
   Capt. John W. Hollyman+
8th Florida [176/108]
   Lieut. Col. William Baya

POSEY'S BRIGADE [1,322/112]

Brig. Gen. Carnot Posey

12th Mississippi [305/13]
   Col. William H. Taylor
16th Mississippi [385/26]
   Col. Samuel E. Baker
19th Mississippi [372/34]
   Col. Nathaniel H. Harris
48th Mississippi [256/39]
   Col. Joseph M. Jayne

ARTILLERY BRIGADE (SUMTER
BATTALION) [384/42]

Maj. John Lane

Company A [130/13]
    Capt. Hugh M. Ross

Company B [124/9]
    Capt. George M. Patterson
Company C [121/20]
    Capt. John T. Wingfield

HETH'S DIVISION [7,458/3,358]

Maj. Gen. Henry Heth (w)
Brig. Gen. J. Johnston Pettigrew (w)

FIRST BRIGADE [2,581/1,450]

Brig. Gen. J. Johnston Pettigrew (w)
Col. James K. Marshall (k)
Maj. John T. Jones+

11th North Carolina [617/366]
    Col. Collett Leventhorpe (w)
    Maj. Egbert A. Ross (k)
    Capt. Francis W. Bird+
26th North Carolina [840/687]
    Col. Henry K. Burgwyn Jr. (k)
    Lieut. Col. John R. Lane (w)
    Maj. John T. Jones
    Capt. H. C. Albright+
47th North Carolina [567/217]
    Col. George H. Faribault (w)
    Lieut. Col. John A. Graves+
52nd North Carolina [553/177]
    Col. James K. Marshall (k)
    Lieut. Col. Marcus A. Parks (w)
    Maj. John Q. Richardson (mw)
    Capt. Nathaniel A. Foster+

SECOND BRIGADE [971/186]

Col. John M. Brockenbrough

22nd Virginia Battalion [237/24]
    Maj. John S. Bowles
40th Virginia [253/65]
    Capt. T. Edwin Betts
    Capt. R. B. Davis+
47th Virginia [209/48]
    Col. Robert M. Mayo
    Lieut. Col. John W. Lyell+
55th Virginia [268/49]
    Col. William S. Christian

THIRD BRIGADE [1,197/684]

Brig. Gen. James J. Archer
Col. Birkett D. Fry (w)
Lieut. Col. Samuel G. Shepard+

5th Alabama Battalion [135/48]
    Maj. Albert S. Van de Graaf
13th Alabama [308/214]
    Col. Birkett D. Fry (w)
1st Tennessee (Provisional Army)
[281/178]
    Lieut. Col. Newton J. George (w)
    Maj. Felix G. Buchanan+
7th Tennessee [249/116]
    Colonel John Fite
    Lieut. Col. Samuel G. Shepherd+
14th Tennessee [220/127]
    Capt. Bruce L. Phillips

FOURTH BRIGADE
[2,305/1,030]

Brig. Gen. Joseph R. Davis

2nd Mississippi [492/232]
    Col. John M. Stone (w)
    Maj. John A. Blair
    Lieut. Col. David W. Humphries (k)
    Senior Officer Present+
11th Mississippi [592/312]
    Col. Francis M. Green (w)
42nd Mississippi [575/265]
    Col. Hugh R. Miller (w)
    Capt. Andrew M. Nelson+
55th North Carolina [640/220]
    Col. John Kerr Connally (w)
    Maj. Alfred H. Belo (w)

Capt. George Gilreath
Lieut. M. C. Stevens+

ARTILLERY BRIGADE [396/22]

Lieut. Col. John Garnett

Donaldsville (Louisiana) Artillery
[114/6]
   Capt. Victor Maurin

Huger (Virginia) Artillery [77/11]
   Capt. Joseph D. Moore
Lewis (Virginia) Artillery [90/11]
   Capt. John W. Lewis
Norfolk (Virginia) Light Artillery Blues
[106/2]
   Capt. Charles R. Grandy

PENDER'S DIVISION [6,681/2,392]

Maj. Gen. William D. Pender (mw)
Brig. Gen. James H. Lane+
Maj. Gen. Isaac R. Trimble (w)

FIRST BRIGADE [1,882/593]

Col. Abner Perrin

1st South Carolina (Provisional Army)
[328/111]
   Maj. Charles W. McCreary
1st South Carolina Rifles [366/11]
   Capt. William M. Hadden
12th South Carolina [366/132]
   Col. John L. Miller
13th South Carolina [390/130]
   Lieut. Col. Benjamin T. Brockman
14th South Carolina [428/209]
   Lieut. Col. Joseph N. Brown (w)
   Maj. Edward Croft (w)

SECOND BRIGADE [1,734/792]

Brig. Gen. James H. Lane
Col. Clark M. Avery+

7th North Carolina [291/159]
   Capt. J. Mcleod Turner (w)
   Capt. James G. Harris+
18th North Carolina [346/88]
   Col. John D. Barry
28th North Carolina [346/237]
   Col. Samuel D. Lowe (w)
   Lieut. Col. W. H. A. Speer+
33rd North Carolina [368/132]
   Col. Clark M. Avery (w)

37th North Carolina [379/176]
   Col. William M. Barbour

THIRD BRIGADE [1,326/264]

Brig. Gen. Edward L. Thomas

14th Georgia [331/44]
   Col. Robert W. Folsom
35th Georgia [331/90]
   Col. Bolling H. Holt
45th Georgia [331/45]
   Col. Thomas J. Simmons
49th Georgia [329/85]
   Capt. O. H. Cooke

FOURTH BRIGADE [1,351/704]

Brig. Gen. Alfred M. Scales
Lieut. Col. G. T. Gordon
Col. W. Lee J. Lowrance+

13th North Carolina [232/179]
   Col. Joseph H. Hyman
   Lieut. Col. H. A. Rogers
   Lieut. R. L. Moir (w)
   Lieut. N. S. Smith+
16th North Carolina [321/123]
   Capt. Abel S. Cloud
22nd North Carolina [267/166]
   Lieut. Col. J. Ashford

34th North Carolina [311/104]
  Col. W. Lee J. Lowrance
  Lieut. Col. G. T. Gordon+
38th North Carolina [216/130]
  Col. William J. Hoke (w)
  Lieut. A. J. Brown
  Capt. William L. Thornburg (w)
  Lieut. John M. Robinson+

ARTILLERY BRIGADE [377/34]

Maj. William T. Poague

Albemarle (Virginia) Artillery [94/13]
  Capt. James W. Wyatt
Charlotte (North Carolina) Artillery
[125/5]
  Capt. Joseph Graham
Madison (Mississippi) Light Artillery
[91/0]
  Capt. George Ward
Virginia (Warrington) Battery [58/5]
  Capt. James V. Brooke

ARTILLERY RESERVE (HILL'S CORPS) [736/99]

Col. R. Lindsay Walker

McINTOSH'S BATTALION [357/48]

Maj. D. G. McIntosh

Danville (Virginia) Artillery [114/2]
  Capt. R. Sidney Rice
Hardaway (Alabama) Artillery [71/8]
  Capt. William B. Hurt
2nd Rockbridge (Virginia) Artillery
[67/6]
  Lieut. Samuel Wallace
Virginia (Richmond) Battery [96/10]
  Capt. Marmaduke Johnson

PEGRAM'S BATTALION [375/51]

Maj. William J. Pegram
Capt. E. B. Brunson

Crenshaw (Virginia) Battery [76/15]
  Capt. William G. Crenshaw
Fredericksburg (Virginia) Artillery
[71/2]
  Capt. Edward A. Marye
Letcher (Virginia) Artillery [65/17]
  Capt. Thomas A. Brander
Pee Dee (South Carolina) Artillery
[65/unknown]
  Lieut. William E. Zimmerman
Purcell (Virginia) Artillery [89/6]
  Capt. Joseph McGraw

CAVALRY DIVISION [6,702/285]

Maj. Gen. James E. B. Stuart

HAMPTON'S BRIGADE [1,751/112]

Brig. Gen. Wade Hampton (w)
Col. Laurence S. Baker+

1st North Carolina Cavalry [407/44]
  Col. Laurence S. Baker

1st South Carolina Cavalry [339/14]
  Col. John L. Black
2nd South Carolina Cavalry [186/7]
  Col. Matthew C. Butler
Cobb's (Georgia) Legion Cavalry
[330/21]
  Col. Pierce B. L. Young

Jeff Davis (Mississippi) Legion Cavalry [246/15]
    Col. Joseph F. Waring
Phillips' (Georgia) Legion Cavalry [238/10]
    Lieut. Col. Jefferson C. Phillips

FITZHUGH LEE'S BRIGADE [1,913/95]

Brig. Gen. W. Fitzhugh Lee

1st Maryland Battalion Cavalry [310/17]
    Maj. Harry Gilmore
    Maj. Ridgely Brown+
1st Virginia Cavalry [310/23]
    Col. James H. Drake
2nd Virginia Cavalry [385/16]
    Col. Thomas T. Munford
3rd Virginia Cavalry [210/6]
    Col. Thomas H. Owen
4th Virginia Cavalry [544/33]
    Col. William Carter Wickham
5th Virginia Cavalry [150/0]
    Col. Thomas L. Rosser

JENKINS' BRIGADE [1,179/18]

Brig. Gen. Albert G. Jenkins (w)
Col. Milton J. Ferguson+

14th Virginia Cavalry [265/6]
    Maj. Benjamin F. Eakle
16th Virginia Cavalry [265/6]
    Col. Milton J. Ferguson
17th Virginia Cavalry [241/8]
    Col. William H. French
34th Virginia Battalion Cavalry [172/0]
    Lieut. Col. Vincent A. Witcher

35th Virginia Battalion Cavalry [232/8]
    Lieut. Col. Elijah V. White
36th Virginia Battalion Cavalry [125/1]
    Capt. Cornelius T. Smith
Jackson's (Virginia) Battery [107/1]
    Capt. Thomas E. Jackson

W. H. F. LEE'S BRIGADE [1,173/56]

Col. John R. Chambliss Jr.

2nd North Carolina Cavalry [145/9]
    Col. Solomon Williams
9th Virginia Cavalry [490/18]
    Col. Richard L. T. Beale
10th Virginia Cavalry [236/12]
    Col. J. Lucius Davis
13th Virginia Cavalry [298/17]
    Capt. Benjamin F. Winfield

STUART HORSE ARTILLERY [628/4]

Maj. Robert F. Beckham

Breathed's (Virginia) Battery [106/1]
    Capt. James Breathed
Chew's (Virginia) Battery [99/0]
    Capt. R. Preston Chew
Griffin's (Maryland) Battery [106/0]
    Capt. William H. Griffin
Hart's (South Carolina) Battery [107/1]
    Capt. James F. Hart
McGregor's (Virginia) Battery [106/2]
    Capt. William M. McGregor
Moorman's (Virginia) Battery [*104/0*]
    Capt. Marcellus M. Moorman

CAVALRY UNITS NOT PRESENT AT GETTYSBURG ON JULY 1–3, 1863

IMBODEN'S COMMAND [2,250/0]

Brig. Gen. John D. Imboden

18th Virginia Cavalry [914/0]
    Col. George W. Imboden

62nd Virginia Mounted Infantry
[1,095/0]
   Col. George H. Smith
Virginia Partisan Rangers [90/0]
   Capt. John H. McNeill
Virginia (Staunton) Battery [142/0]
   Capt. John H. McClanahan

ROBERTSON'S BRIGADE [966/0]

Brig. Gen. Beverly H. Robertson

4th North Carolina Cavalry [504/0]
   Col. Dennis D. Ferebee

5th North Carolina Cavalry [458/0]
   Col. Peter G. Evans

JONES' BRIGADE [1,743/0]

Brig. Gen. William E. Jones

6th Virginia Cavalry [625/0]
   Maj. Cabel E. Flourney
7th Virginia Cavalry [428/0]
   Lieut. Col. Thomas Marshall
11th Virginia Cavalry [424/0]
   Col. Lunsford L. Lomax

CHAPTER NOTES

Note: Complete information for material cited in the chapter notes can be found in the bibliography. All references to the *The War of the Rebellion: A Compilation of the Official Records of the Union and Confederate Armies* are here designated *OR*, followed by the volume and number of the series. Similarly, all references to *Supplement to the Official Records of the Union and Confederate Armies* are abbreviated *ORS*. In a like fashion, references to *Report of the Joint Committee on the Conduct of the War* (volume 4) are *CCW*. Other frequently used source abbreviations appearing herein are as follows: ACHS (Adams Country Historical Society), CRC (Confederate Research Center), FNP (Fredericksburg National Military Park), GNP (Gettysburg National Military Park), HSP (Historical Society of Pennsylvania), ISL (Indiana State Library), LMS (Library of Memphis State University), LOC (Library of Congress), LVA (Library of Virginia), MHI (United States Military History Institute), MHS (Minnesota Historical Society), MOC (Museum of the Confederacy), NA (National Archives), NCDHA (North Carolina Department of History and Archives), NYSL (New York State Library), PHMC (Pennsylvania Historical and Museum Commission), SHC (Southern Historical Collection), SHSWI (State Historical Society of Wisconsin), TSL (Tennessee State Library), UVA (University of Virginia Library), VHS (Virginia Historical Society).

PROLOGUE

Page:

1 "volumes of sparks": *Richmond Whig,* May 16, 1863.

1 "gaunt form of wretched famine" (and all subsequent Jones quotations): Miers, ed., *Rebel War Clerk's Diary,* 182, 202, 207–10.

2 "one of the great military masters": *Columbus Daily Enquirer,* July 24, 1862.

4 "an encouraging re-enforcement": *OR,* 25/2: 708–9.

5 "An invasion of the enemy's country": Heth, "Letter to J. William Jones," 153.

5 Lee quotations: Gallagher, ed., *Lee the Soldier,* 17.

5 "realized the grave character"/"assembled early": Reagan, *Memoirs,* 151.

6 "superb figure": Quoted in Strode, *Jefferson Davis,* 405.

6 "I believe General Lee expected": Moore, ed., *Rebellion Record,* 6: 597.

6 "you have again let": Quoted in Hotchkiss, *Virginia,* 392.

6 "loss was severe": Heth, "Letter to Jones," 154.

7 "knew oftentimes that he was playing": Gallagher, ed., *Lee the Soldier,* 17.

7 "very glad to see": "A Lady," *Diary of a Southern Refugee*, 214.

7 "The complicated injuries": ORS, 4: 608.

7 "more than one poor fellow": Collins, *Memoirs of the 149th New York*, 116.

8 "legitimate property": Quoted in Swinton, *Campaigns*, 275.

8 "he is overconfident": Brooks, *Washington, D.C.*, 52.

8 "when the nation required": *CCW*, 144.

8 "Army of the Potomac did not fight": Humphreys, *Address of Maj. Gen. A. A. Humphreys*.

9 "would be more serious and injurious": George Gordon Meade, *Life and Letters*, 372.

9 Lincoln-Hooker exchange: OR, 25/2: 438.

CHAPTER ONE

11 "fearful shock": Garrish, *Army Life*, 94.

11 "in a comatose state": Quoted in Thomson, *From Philippi*, 158.

11 All Beecham quotations: Stevens, ed., *As If It Were Glory*, 56, 57.

11 "The army is neither disorganized": *Norwich Morning Bulletin*, June 5, 1863.

11 "There has been a big battle": Quoted in Longacre, *Joshua Chamberlain*, 113–14.

12 "The talk about demoralization": *Pittsburgh Evening Chronicle*, June 8, 1863.

12 "again buoyant and ready": Silliker, ed., *Rebel Yell*, 88.

12 "turned their minds and hands": Ripley, *Vermont Riflemen*, 106.

12 "the prospect of seeing an enemy": Rosenblatt, ed., *Anti-Rebel*, 96.

12 "He combines in one the song": Norton, *Army Letters*, 155.

12 "the whole 11th Army Corps": Beer, ed., *Boys from Rockville*, 124.

12 "Dutchmen . . . ran": Quoted in Byrne and Weaver, eds., *Haskell of Gettysburg*, 80.

13 "As for the last defeat": Church, *Civil War Letters*, 34.

13 "if such be the reward": Quoted in Raphelson, "Alexander Schimmelfennig," 172.

13 "It is only the miserable setup": Winkler, ed., *Letters of Frederick C. Winkler*.

13 "It was all General Howard's fault": Quoted in Pula, *For Liberty and Justice*, 89.

13 "secured reverence": Quoted in Longacre, "John F. Reynolds, General," 35.

14 Reynolds remarks: Quoted in Keller, "Soldier General," 124–25.

14 "possessed of the very decided confidence": Gibbon, *Personal Recollections of the Civil War*, 122.

14 "and that the idea prevails": OR, 25/2: 595.

14 "has been weakened": OR, 27/3: 3.

15 "campaign of long marches": Quoted in Fishel, *Secret War*, 417.

16 "nor its commander expected justice": *CCW*, 80.

16 "bad blood": Quoted in Locke, *Story of the Regiment*, 223.

16 "worked against": Butts, ed., *Gallant Captain*, 72.

16 "the rebellion rested": *CCW*, 112.

16 Huckaby letter: Reynolds, ed., "A Mississippian," 279.

37 "firmness, composure and naturalness": Samuel Eaton Papers (SHSWI).
37 sat patiently waiting: Cheek and Pointon, *History of the Sauk County Rifle-men*, 69.
37 "We left the men digging": Reid-Green, ed., *Letters Home*, 58.
 "very hot and dusty": Runge, *Four Years in the Confederate Horse Artillery*, 46.
38 "We had but few stragglers": Nichols, *A Soldier's Story*, 113.
38 "all quiet": Douglass, Diary (Internet).
39 "sufficient vacancies": Quoted in Davis, *Boy Colonel*, 266.
39 "growing weak"/"give all the encouragement we can"/"I wish": Dowdey and Manarin, eds., *Wartime Papers*, 508, 509.
39 "pritty and kind ladies": Pierson, ed., "Diary of Bartlett Yancey Malone," 34.
39 "I grieve I fear": Dowdey and Manarin, eds., *Wartime Papers*, 511.
39 Seddon-Lee exchange: Ibid., 513–14.

CHAPTER FOUR

41 "tedious and toilsome": Best, *History of the 121st New York*, 85.
41 "shameful waste"/"if the surgeons": *OR*, 27/3: 101.
41 "We marched Sunday morning": Dawson, *Service with the Sixth Wisconsin*, 149.
41 "We passed over farms": Winkler, ed., *Letters of Frederick C. Winkler*.
42 "too strong to be attacked": Gallagher, ed., *Lee*, 11.
42 Lincoln-Hooker exchange: *OR*, 27/1: 38–39.
43 "hot day"/"many were stricken": Zachry, "Fighting with the 3d Georgia," 74.
43 "when the common enemy": Miers, ed., *Rebel War Clerk's Diary*, 225.
43 "rapid and well directed"/"some of the shells": William J. Seymour Diary-Memoir (MHI).
45 "The day was very hot": Banes, *History of the Philadelphia Brigade*, 172.
45 "They came verry near Marched us to death": Benjamin Hough Letters, Town of Minisink Archives.
45 "The men carried heavy loads": Fox, ed., *New York at Gettysburg*, 2: 854.
45 "Here the court house was in flames": Holcombe, *History of the First Minnesota*, 312.
45 "I wondered at this act of vandalism": Muffley, *Story of Our Regiment*, 455.
45 "The destruction of such relics": Elon Brown Diary-Memoir (MHI).
45 "The call is made from outside pressure": Beale, ed., *Diary of Gideon Welles*, vol. 1, 331.
45 Lincoln to Hooker: *OR*, 27/1: 43.
45 "murderous trap": Kesses, Diary (MHI).
46 "spirits disembodied": Alexander S. Pendleton Letters (SHC).
46 "knee-deep"/"mixed in their sympathies": Leon, *Diary of a Tar Heel*, 32.
46 "The usual work"/"Horses, wagons, and cattle": *Great Invasion*, 34.
48 "destroying the railroad depot": Schuricht, "Jenkins' Brigade," 340.
48 "the greatest excitement": Hoke, *Great Invasion*, 97.
48 "When we appeared": Love, "Mississippi at Gettysburg," 125.
48 "Thus far Gen. Lee's plans": Hassler, ed., *One of Lee's Best*, 247–48.

49 "My corps left Culpeper": Longstreet, "Lee in Pennsylvania," 418.

49 "The heat is frightful": Durkin, ed., *John Dooley Journal*, 95.

49 "A good many of the men fainted": Oates, *War between the Union and the Confederacy*, 198.

49 Lee's report: Dowdey and Manarin, eds., *Wartime Papers*, 514–15.

49 "Longstreet started today": *Lee's Telegraph Book* (VHS).

CHAPTER FIVE

50 Marsena Patrick quotations: Sparks, ed., *Inside Lincoln's Army*, 260.

50 "News that the 'Rebs' are": Jacob W. Haas Diary (MHI).

50 "Reported rebels in Md.": Owen, "Diary."

50 "The Rebels are in Pennsylvania": H. C. Christiancy Diary and Letters (LOC).

50 "We seem to be completely isolated": Quoted in Dunkelman, *Gettysburg's Unknown Soldier*, 112.

52 Hooker-Lincoln-Halleck exchange: *OR*, 27/1: 45–47.

53 "better that we should lose men": *OR*, 27/3: 172.

53 "a cover to Lee's re-enforcing Bragg": *OR*, 27/1: 47.

53 "Halleck is running the Marching": Sparks, 260.

54 "The weather is very hot"/"Dust [is] shoe mouth deep": Unknown Soldier Letters (MHI).

54 "We seemed to be suffocating at each step": Bee, ed., *Boys from Rockville*, 137.

54 "They look very nice": Silliker, ed., *Rebel Yell*, 93.

54 "Well, if you're sick": Quoted in Smith, *Twenty-Fourth Michigan*, 115.

54 "The boys went out and killed them": Priest, ed., *John T. McMahon's Diary*, 50.

54 "They fear nothing so much": Silliker, ed., *Rebel Yell*, 93.

55 "large supplies": *OR*, 27/2: 550.

55 "an old soldier is ever happy": Hoole, ed., *Reminiscences of the Autauga Rifles*, 22.

55 "just out of winter-quarters": Hamilton, ed., *Papers of Randolph Shotwell*, 479.

55 "Everything thus far has worked admirably": Hassler, ed., *One of Lee's Best*, 249.

55 "is admirably organized": Quoted in Davis, *Boy Colonel*, 272.

56 "I very much regret": *OR*, 27/3: 905.

57 "a right jolly time": Quoted in Fishel, *Secret War*, 458.

58 "must whip us": Quoted in Fishel, *Secret War*, 465.

58 "Have we seen some sights": William Penn Oberlin Letters (MHI).

58 "We found Plenty of signs": Britton and Reed, eds., *To My Beloved*, 180.

58 "several grinning skeletons": Muffley, *Story of Our Regiment*, 457.

59 "While the Regiment": Smith, *History of the Nineteenth Maine*, 57.

59 "Wounded men lay": Smith, *History of the 118th Pennsylvania*, 224.

59 "I hope it will have a good effect": Rufus Meade Diary (LOC).

59 "It is really affecting": William Penn Oberlin Letters (MHI).

59 "Yes, he's in his chariot": Small, ed., *Road to Richmond*, 113.

59 Hooker to newspapers: *OR*, 27/3: 192.
60 "There is very large reason for doubt"/"himself dug the grave": *New York Herald*, June 19–25, 1863.
61 Jones quotations: Miers, ed., *Rebel War Clerk's Diary*, 228–29.
61 "I do not suppose any army": Bonham, "A Little More Light," 521.
61 "Our army is very large now": Welch, *Confederate Surgeon's Letters*, 56.
61 "We will march to Philadelphia": Jeffries, "Letter to His Sister," 253.
61 "I could never get over": Douglas, *I Rode with Stonewall*, 235.
61 Pender to his wife: Hassler, ed., *One of Lee's Best*, 249.
61 "Yankee papers say": Owen, "Diary."
62 "Several are immersed": Betts, *Experience of a Confederate Chaplain*, 38.
62 "up to our hips": Quoted in Hale and Phillips, *History of the Forty-Ninth Virginia*, 72.
62 "It was amusing": Quoted in Jones, *Lee's Tigers*, 163.
62 "flags fluttering": Hudgins, "With the 38th Georgia Regiment," 162.
62 "She said she felt very sorry": Runge, ed., *Four Years in the Confederate Horse Artillery*, 48.
62 "I need and must have": Basler, ed., *Collected Works of Abraham Lincoln*, 6: 281–82.
62 "sad and careworn": Beale, ed., *Diary of Gideon Welles*, vol. 1, 340.
63 "What disgust there is": *ORS*, 5: 31–32.
63 Hooker to Halleck: *OR*, 27/1: 55–56.
63 Lee communications: Dowdey and Manarin, eds., *Wartime Papers*, 524–25.
64 "We have again out-maneuvered": Trimble, "Battle and Campaign of Gettysburg," 121.
64 "If Harrisburg comes": Dowdey and Manarin, eds., *Wartime Papers*, 524.
64 "spread out like a fan"/"with the approval of General Lee": Mosby, "Confederate Cavalry in the Gettysburg Campaign," 251.
65 "Rebels were crossing": Broadhead, *Diary*, 5.
65 "it grew to be an old story": Buehler, *Recollections of the Great Rebel Invasion*.
65 "We do not feel much safer": Broadhead, *Diary*, 5.
66 "the last of Lee's entire army": Quoted in Fishel, *Secret War*, 478.

CHAPTER SIX

67 "Ho! for the Valley": Cooke, *Wearing of the Gray*, 237.
68 Lee-Stuart-Longstreet exchange: *OR*, 27/3: 913, 915, 923.
69 "The letter suggested": McClellan, *I Rode with Jeb Stuart*, 317–18.
70 "My advices": *OR*, 27/3: 306.
70 "Genl. Hooker intends": Sparks, ed., *Inside Lincoln's Army*, 264.
70 "about one-fourth of a mile": Smith, *Camps and Campaigns of the 107th Ohio*, 83.
70 "The women cheered us": Priest, ed., *John T. McMahon's Diary*, 51.
70 "We stopped and got good things to eat": Mesnard Reminiscence (MHI).
70 "First, boats": Bloodgood, *Personal Reminiscences of the War*, 121–22.
70 "No man who participated": Nicholson, ed., *Pennsylvania at Gettysburg*, 1: 196.

71 "We slipped back": Silliker, ed., *Rebel Yell,* 96.

71 "As the General commanding": *Norfolk County Journal,* August 29, 1863.

71 Lee communications: *OR, 27/3:* 931–32.

72 Francis Dawson quotations: Dawson, *Reminiscences of Confederate Service,* 90–91.

72 "the inspiriting strains": Hood, *Advance and Retreat,* 54.

72 "were bound to form squads": Johnston, ed., *Civil War Letters of Battle and Battle,* 15.

72 "command was frequently fired on": *Richmond Daily Dispatch,* October 21, 1900.

72 "seems to be full of 'bushwhackers' ": Schuricht, "Jenkins' Brigade," 342.

72 "were simply led out and shot": Quoted in Kross, "Attack from the West," 8.

73 "insignificant hamlet": Smith, *History of the Nineteenth Maine,* 58.

73 "After marching 2 miles": Stephen E. Martin Diary (GNP).

73 "At 12 m": Wolf, ed., "Campaigning with the First Minnesota," 358.

73 "There were several casualties": Lochren, "First Minnesota at Gettysburg," 44.

73 "The exploding shells": Holcombe, *History of the First Minnesota,* 314.

73 "In less than ten minutes": Smith, *History of the Nineteenth Maine,* 58.

73 "The forming of Harrow's brigade": Holcombe, *History of the First Minnesota,* 34.

74 "long lines of wagons": Cooke, *Wearing of the Gray,* 240.

74 Stuart's report: *OR, 27/2:* 692–93.

74 "was continued until the enemy moved"/"He consulted with no one": McClellan, *I Rode with Jeb Stuart,* 321–22.

74 "Since Hooker's appearance"/"I learn also": *ORS,* 5: 32.

75 "Where, in the mean time": Beale, ed., *Diary of Gordon Welles,* vol. 1, 343.

75 Soldier's account of execution: *Richmond Daily Dispatch,* March 6, 1914.

75 "four like executions": Blackford, ed., *Letters from Lee's Army,* 183.

75 "beneficial to other substitutes": Robertson Jr., *18th Virginia Infantry,* 20.

75 "Every one is asking": Broadhead, *Diary,* 8.

CHAPTER SEVEN

77 Stuart's report: *OR, 27/2:* 693.

77 "Had very poor grazing": William R. Carter Letters (LVA).

77 "hold the Gaps": *OR, 27/3:* 927–28.

77 "there were no skirmishes": Coltrane, *Memoirs,* 15.

77 "The men upon whom": Nicholson, ed., *Pennsylvania at Gettysburg,* 2: 777.

77 "They, of course": Fastnacht, *Memories of the Battle of Gettysburg,* 3.

77 "many 'contrabands' ": *Richmond Enquirer,* June 30, 1863.

77 "arrested . . . as a contraband": Zachry, "Fighting with the 3d Georgia," 75.

77 "We took a lot of negroes": Moore, ed., *Rebellion Record,* 6: 325.

80 "The free negroes are all gone": Welch, *Confederate Surgeon's Letters,* 58.

80 "Ben, the negro cook": Smith, *Anson Guards,* 199.

80 "entire line of march I saw only two negroes": Loyd, "Second Louisiana at Gettysburg," 417.

80 "A steady and continuous rain": *Detroit Free Press,* July 10, 1863.

80 "We had our knapsacks": George P. Metcalf, "Recollection of Boyhood Days" (MHI).

80 "We cannot help beating them": Beale, ed., *Diary of Gideon Welles*, vol. 1, 344.

80 "betrayed doubts of Hooker": Ibid.

81 "He was at that time about fifty-two"/Hoke's prediction: Hoke, *Great Invasion*, 167.

81 "testing the qualities of Pennsylvania poultry": *Atlanta Journal*, August 31, 1901.

81 "jolly set": Thomas L. Ware Diary (SHC).

81 "marched in four states that day": Robert T. Coles, "History of the 4th Regiment Alabama Volunteer Infantry" (Alabama Department of Archives and History).

82 "He did so": Cummings, "Chancellorsville, May 2, 1863," 406.

82 "60 head of cattle": McKim, "Gettysburg Campaign," 292.

82 "Our camp was in a wheat field": Smith, *Anson Guards*, 200–1.

83 "various deeds of barbarity": Jubal A. Early Papers (LOC).

84 "It has always seemed to me": Nicholson, ed., *Pennsylvania at Gettysburg*, 2:777–78.

84 "Our colonel": Richards, "Citizens of Gettysburg," 289.

84 "It was well": Early, *Autobiographical Sketch*, 257.

84 "I never thought I could bear": Quoted in Nye, *Here Come the Rebels!*, 278.

84 "It seemed as if Pandemonium": Clare, "A Gettysburg Girl's Story of the Great Battle" (ACHS).

84 "enough to frighten us all to death": Broadhead, *Diary*, 8.

84 "We were all scared": *Gettysburg Compiler*, July 26, 1905.

84 "boys looking through the slatted shutters": Fahnestock, "Recollections of the Battle of Gettysburg" (ACHS).

85 "ransacking the barns": *Gettysburg Compiler*, July 4, 1906.

85 "I began to plead for the horse": Alleman, *At Gettysburg*, 25.

85 Leander Warren's story: Warren, "Recollections of the Battle of Gettysburg" (ACHS).

85 "These Confederates were very firm": Jacobs, "How an Eye-Witness Watched."

85 "I never saw a more unsightly"/"dirty, . . . hatless": Buehler, *Recollections of the Great Rebel Invasion*.

85 "He suggested the propriety": *Philadelphia Weekly Press*, November 16, 1887.

86 "to furnish whatever they can": Hoke, *Great Invasion*, 171–72.

86 "exasperating"/"through the night": McCreary, "Gettysburg: A Boy's Experience."

86 Hooker-Halleck-Lincoln communications: *OR*, 27/1: 58.

CHAPTER EIGHT

88 "a most gallant officer": McClellan, *I Rode with Jeb Stuart*, 323.

88 "wild and desolate locality"/"What would Stuart do": Cooke, *Wearing of the Gray*, 242.

90   "The orders left with me": Robertson, "Confederate Cavalry in the Gettysburg Campaign," 253.

90   Testimony of Hagerstown refugees: *OR*, 27/3: 351–52.

90   General Orders number 73: *OR*, 27/3: 942–43.

90   "Our orders are very strict here": *The Index*, March 9, 1895.

90   "People of Pennsylvania were as safe": Hillyer, *Battle of Gettysburg*.

91   "no depredations": Cadmus M. Wilcox Papers (LOC).

91   "The greater part of the supplies": Polley, *Hood's Texas Brigade*, 147.

91   "The infantry did not have much chance": Robertson Jr., ed., *Four Years in the Stonewall Brigade*, 168.

91   "morning. Went out a foraging": Samuel Angus Firebaugh Diary (MHI).

91   "The people are scared into fits": Quoted in Hale and Phillips, *History of the Forty-Ninth Virginia*, 74.

91   "quartermasters and the small cavalry force": Bradwell, "Crossing the Potomac," 370.

91   "Our army is pressing in provision": George W. Hall Diary (LOC).

91   "We have provisions in abundance": Haynes, *Field Diary of a Confederate Soldier*, 31.

91   "I heard one man say": Stevens, *Reminiscences of the Civil War*, 109.

91   "Confederate 'conscript law' ": Quoted in *History of Clarke County*, 145.

91   "I hope the officers": William B. Taylor Letters (GNP).

91   "The wrath of southern vengeance": William H. Routt Papers (MOC).

92   "the people in this state": Daniel H. Sheetz Letters (Harper's Ferry National Park).

92   "Our men did very bad": Taylor, ed., *The Cry Is War*, 148.

92   "We are now in the enemy country": Watson, "Letter," 61.

92   "The most of our Virginia boys": Quoted in Gregory, *38th Virginia Infantry*, 36.

92   "I treated everybody": Henry L. Figures Letters (FNP).

92   "We started": Sparks, ed., *Inside Lincoln's Army*, 265.

92   Hooker-Halleck communications: *OR*, 27/1: 59; ibid., 27/3: 349.

93   " 'Halleck's dispatch Severs my connection' ": *Grand Rapids Democrat*, November 1879.

93   "expected of my by the country": *CCW*, 173.

93   "offusticated, muddy, uncertain and stupid": Beale, ed., *Diary of Gideon Welles*, vol. 1, 331.

94   " 'I did my share' ": Henry Lane Kendrick Papers (New-York Historical Society).

94   Lee's remarks to Trimble: Trimble, "Battle and Campaign of Gettysburg," 121–22.

95   Alexander quotations: Gallagher, ed., *Fighting for the Confederacy*, 228–29.

95   "For miles in every direction": Macnamara, *History of the Ninth Massachusetts*, 312.

95   "Passed through the finest part": Alfred Melancthon Apted Diary (FNP).

95   "about two hundred feet wide": Graham, "On to Gettysburg," 471.

95   "in a gale of good spirits": John W. Ames Papers (MHI).

95   "got thoroughly wet": Phillips and Parsegian, eds., *Richard and Rhoda*, 29.

95   Donaldson quotations: Acken ed., *Inside the Army of the Potomac*, 289–290.

96   Meade to his wife: Meade, *Life and Letters*, 389.

97 "in a talkative mood": Douglas, *I Rode with Stonewall*, 237.
97 "I have nothing of interest": J. H. S. Funk Letters (FNP).
97 "The war had not hurt them": J. A. Stikeleather, "Recollections" (SHC).
97 "Many of them were drunk"/"where they had a rough and disagreeable ride": William J. Seymour Diary-Memoir (MHI).
97 Early quotations: Early, *Autobiographical Sketch*, 259.
98 "Certainly not": Douglas, *I Rode with Stonewall*, 237.
99 "We were up bright and early": *Gettysburg Compiler*, July 4, 1906.
99 "report a large force": Broadhead, *Diary*, 10.
99 "paroled and allowed to go home": *Gettysburg Compiler*, July 4, 1906.
100 "By three o'clock": Blackford, *War Years with Jeb Stuart*, 225.
100 "He said that . . . it was a very . . . critical period": *CCW*, 82.

CHAPTER NINE

102 "3 A.M., I was aroused": Meade, *Life and Letters*, 11.
102 Hardie's account: Benjamin, "Hooker's Appointment and Removal," 243.
104 "The sun was several hours high": McClellan, *I Rode with Jeb Stuart*, 324.
104 "if I am able to move": *OR*, 25/2: 848–49.
104 "Move directly upon Harrisburg": Maurice, ed., *Aide-de-Camp of Lee*, 218.
105 "No intimation of any plan": *CCW*, 355.
105 "As a soldier, I obey it": *OR*, 27/1: 61.
105 "Your army is free to act": *OR*, 27/1: 61.
105 "grumpy, stern, severe and admirable": John W. Ames Papers (MHI).
105 "I was taken by surprise": A. P. Morrison Letters (FNP).
105 "received with a kind of apathetic indifference": S. H. Gay Collection (Columbia University Library).
106 "What Meade will do": Sparks, ed., *Inside Lincoln's Army*, 265.
106 "about 110,000 men": *CCW*, 329.
106 "The 28th and 29th were exciting days": Skelly, *A Boy's Experiences*, 10.
106 "a large body of our cavalry": Broadhead, *Diary*, 10.
106 "We were delighted": Barr, "Account of the Battle of Gettysburg" (ACHS).
106 "Lines of men": Quoted in *Michigan at Gettysburg*, 137.
107 "How well do I remember": Clare, "A Gettysburg Girl's Story of the Great Battle" (ACHS).
107 "We now felt assured": *Gettysburg Compiler*, June 6, 1906.
107 "listening to the very unusual sound": Mulholland, *Story of the 116th Pennsylvania*, 118.
107 "vibrating upon the calm morning": Marbaker, *History of the Eleventh New Jersey*, 88.
107 "Did you notice Col. Burgwyn": Quoted in Davis, *Boy Colonel*, 288.
108 "There is plenty of grass": Ephraim Bowman Correspondence (UVA).
108 "Did you ever see anything": Cooke, *Wearing of the Gray*, 248.
108 "It was as exciting as a fox chase": Blackford, *War Years with Jeb Stuart*, 226.
108 "Marching through a land of beauty": *Rochester Daily Democrat*, July 3, 1863.
108 "campaign of the war": Fulcher, ed., *Family Letters*, 100.

108   Reminiscence of Cross's aide: Hale, "With Colonel Cross," 32.

109   "I should always regard it": *CCW,* 303.

109   "Sickles is a great favorite": Silliker, ed., *Rebel Yell,* 102.

110   "in delicate health": *New York Herald,* July 2, 1863.

110   "dating from several incidents"/" 'You cannot ask to be relieved' ": Sickles, "Further Recollections," 259.

110   "Deep gorge or ravine"/"labored as earnestly": Gordon, *Reminiscences of the Civil War,* 147–48.

111   "I regretted this": Early, *Autobiographical Sketch,* 260.

111   "This week, it would seem": Smart, ed., *Radical View,* 4–5.

112   Coffin quotations: Coffin, *Boys of '61,* 286.

112   "I determined": *CCW,* 330.

112   Fremantle quotations: Fremantle, *Three Months in the Southern States,* 242–43.

113   "There are two reports": Miers, ed., *Rebel War Clerk's Diary,* 233.

113   "Such . . . was the universal belief": DeLeon, *Four Years in Rebel Capitals,* 285.

113   "This is the first intimation"/"Do not understand me": OR, 27/1: 75–77.

114   "We were consulted after the fact"/"He is not great": Beale, ed., *Diary of Gideon Welles,* 348–49.

114   "questioned me": John Walter Fairfax Papers (VHS).

114   "with great composure": Sorrel, *Recollections of a Confederate Staff Officer,* 164.

114   "I found [Lee] . . . sitting in his tent"/Lee's new orders: Maurice, ed., *Aide-de-Camp of Lee,* 218–19.

CHAPTER TEN

116   Stuart quotations: OR, 27/2: 695.

118   "Stuart had ridden around": Mosby, "Confederate Cavalry in the Gettysburg Campaign," 252.

118   "literally and promptly": *Memphis Weekly Appeal,* December 26, 1877.

118   "George A. Custer was, as all agree"/"acted like a man": Kidd, *Cavalryman with Custer,* 67, 127.

118   "This was taking morning exercise": Bicknell, *History of the Fifth Maine,* 238.

118   "carrying rifle, knapsack and contents": Fuller, *Battles of the Seventy-Seventh New York,* 13.

119   "The several divisions are stretched": Acken, ed., *Inside the Army of the Potomac,* 294.

119   "hard, hard march": Wilson N. Paxton Diary (MHI).

119   "as far as the eye could reach": Cook and Benton, eds., *"Dutchess County Regiment,"* 23.

119   "General Sickles . . . was welcomed": Ladd and Ladd, eds., *Bachelder Papers,* 1:191.

119   "a considerable number of the men": Craft, *History of the One Hundred Forty-First Pennsylvania,* 111–12.

119   "Meade is not liked": Levi Bird Duff Letters (MHI).

120   "Marched all day": Quoted in Hamblen, *Connecticut Yankees,* 4.

120 "they only exhibited curiosity": Hurst, *Journal-History of the Seventy-Third Ohio,* 65.

120 "The beauty and tranquillity": Lee, "Reminiscences of the Gettysburg Battle," 54.

120 "Marched us too fast": Robert S. Coburn Diary (MHI).

120 "It rained all day": Davis Jr., *Three Years in the Army,* 221.

120 "learn what they can": *OR,* 27/3: 397.

120 "Oh, boys"/"Bread and tears": Davis Jr., *Three Years in the Army,* 221.

121 "move in the direction": *OR,* 27/3: 943–44.

121 "faces thinking we were retreating"/"I told her to keep quiet": Cocke Family Papers (VHS).

121 "offspring of an education": *Savannah Republican,* July 14, 1863.

121 "On June the 29th": Morrison, ed., "Memoirs of Henry Heth, Part II," 303.

121 "in splendid condition": Clark, ed., *Histories of the Several Regiments and Battalions,* 3:296.

121 "You are marching mighty proudly"/"Because you put your trust": Dawson, *Reminiscences of Confederate Service,* 93.

122 "The General was evidently surprised"/"that General Lee expected": James Power Smith, "General Lee at Gettysburg," 139.

123 "General Meade will commit no blunder": Quoted in Freeman, *Lee's Lieutenants,* vol. 3, 64.

123 "Ah, General, the enemy": Hood, *Advance and Retreat,* 55.

123 "living upon the fat of Pennsylvania": Taylor, "Report of Captain O. B. Taylor," 214.

123 "great quantities of horses": Fremantle, *Three Months in the Southern States,* 244–45.

123 "thousands . . . enough to feed our army": Welch, *Confederate Surgeon's Letters,* 60.

123 "You can form no idea": *Richmond Whig,* July 6, 1863.

123 "Quiet has prevailed": Broadhead, *Diary,* 10.

123 "It is annoying"/"The news flew through the town": Quoted in Bennett, *Days of "Uncertainty and Dread,"* 16–17.

124 "on Monday morning, June 29": Schuricht, "Jenkins' Brigade," 343–45.

124 "About 9 A.M. received orders": McKim, "Gettysburg Campaign," 292.

124 "The people seemed delighted": John Samuel Apperson Diary (LVA).

124 "all of them [were] barefooted": Moore, *Story of a Cannoneer,* 191.

124 "I would let you'ins go": John Samuel Apperson Diary (LVA).

124 "disappointment and chagrin": Goldsborough, *Maryland Line,* 127–30.

124 "The General was quite testy": McDonald, ed., *Make Me a Map,* 156.

125 "We are marching as fast": Meade, *Life and Letters,* 13–14.

125 "full supply of forage": *OR,* 27/2: 695.

125 "We left that town": Cooke, *Wearing of the Gray,* 249–50.

126 "Traveled near forty miles": Samuel J. V. B. Gilpin Diary (LOC).

126 "to be mostly occupied": *Rochester Daily Union,* July 4, 1863.

126 "heard of the movements": *Rochester Daily Union,* July 4, 1863.

126 "responsive and ringing cheers": Nicholson, ed., *Pennsylvania at Gettysburg,* 2:875.

126   "The citizens were overjoyed"/"one of life's grandest days": Samuel J. V. B. Gilpin Diary (LOC).

CHAPTER ELEVEN

127   Buford quotations: OR 27/1, 926.

128   Heth's orders to Pettigrew: Young, "Pettigrew's Brigade at Gettysburg," 115.

129   "she couldn't be paid": Fastnacht, *Memories of the Battle of Gettysburg*, 3.

129   "Rebels [who] came to the top": Broadhead, *Diary*, 11.

130   "details were immediately sent out"/"We stirred up the Hornets": Cooke, *Wearing of the Gray*, 250.

130   "were peremptory, not to precipitate": Young, "Pettigrew's Brigade at Gettysburg," 115.

130   "brave, injudicious boy": Ford, ed., *Cycle of Adams Letters*, 79.

131   "We are as concentrated": *OR*, 27/3: 420.

131   "If [Lee] . . . could get off": *CCW*, 376.

132   "perfectly accoutered troops"/"a strong contrast": McCurdy, *Gettysburg: A Memoir*, 15.

132   "a novel and grand sight": Alleman, *At Gettysburg*, 28.

132   "receiving the most enthusiastic welcome": *Rochester Daily Union*, July 9, 1863.

133   "As some of us did not know": Alleman, *At Gettysburg*, 29.

133   "with General Lee": Longstreet, "Lee's Invasion," 419.

133   "unusually careless": Gallagher, ed., *Fighting for the Confederacy*, 230.

133   "blocked by [Anderson's Division]": Longstreet, "Lee's Invasion," 419.

133   "very pleasantly": Harwell, ed., *Cities and Camps*, 44.

133   "He is a perfect gentleman": Fremantle, *Three Months in the Southern States*, 248–49.

134   "I shall never forget": Blackford, *War Years with Jeb Stuart*, 227.

134   "enemy entering the town": *OR*, 27/1: 926.

134   "perfect view of the movements": Young, "Pettigrew's Brigade at Gettysburg," 116.

135   "in coming in contact with the enemy": *Winston-Salem Sentinel*, June 13, 1914.

136   Meade quotations: *OR*, 27/1: 69, *OR*, 27/3: 416.

~~136   " 'We'll give you all we have' "/"nine cheers": Smedley, *Life in Southern Prisons*, 54.~~

136   "After an extended search": Kimball, "Young Hero of Gettysburg," 133.

136   "The sisters gave us": Winkler, ed., *Letters of Frederick C. Winkler*.

136   "to the edification of all": Schurz, *Reminiscences of Carl Schurz*, 3.

137   "Lee's troops cannot be far off": Newell Burch Diary (MHS).

137   "told this evening": Smith, *Camps and Campaigns of the 107th Ohio*, 87.

137   Meade proclamation: *OR*, 27/3: 415.

137   "sat down . . . to study the maps": Howard, "Campaign and Battle of Gettysburg," 52.

137   "General Reynolds was a tall"/"Probably he was anxious": Howard, "First Day at Gettysburg," 241.

137 "Kilpatrick showed no disposition": McClellan, *I Rode with Jeb Stuart*, 329.
137 "was now a subject of serious": *OR*, 27/2: 696.
138 "cars crowded to overflowing": Smart, ed., *Radical View*, 12.
138 "dead horses and dead soldiers": Coffin, *Boys of '61*, 287.
138 "Frederick is Pandemonium": Smart, ed., *Radical View*, 12.
139 "Cashtown, near Gettysburg": *OR*, 27/2: 443.
139 "This explanation did not satisfy"/" 'Why can't a commanding General' ": Ladd and Ladd, eds., *Bachelder Papers*, 2: 927.
140 "A small band of Yankee cavalry": *OR*, 27/1: 938.
140 "that he had not gone to Gettysburg": Morrison, ed., *Memoirs of Henry Heth*, 173.
140 "cavalry, probably a detachment": Heth, "Letter to J. William Jones," 157.
140 "well-trained troops": Young, "Pettigrew's Brigade at Gettysburg," 116.
140 Hill-Heth exchange: Heth, "Letter to J. William Jones," 157.
141 Buford report: *OR*, 27/1: 927.
141 "calm demeanor": Skelly, *Boy's Experiences*, 10.
141 "had never seen him so apprehensive"/"anxious": Quoted in Kross, "Fight like the Devil," 10.
142 "massed back of Cashtown"/"coming over the mountains": *OR*, 27/1: 927.
143 "with a sense of security": Skelly, *Boy's Experiences*, 10.
143 "cavalry between us and the enemy": Quoted in Bennett, *Days of "Uncertainty and Dread,"* 18.
143 "some great military event": Alleman, *At Gettysburg*, 29.
143 "It begins to look as though": Broadhead, *Diary*, 11.

NOCTURNE: JUNE 30

144 "the Confederate soldier did not make war"/"Cherries were ripe": Clark, ed., *Histories of the Several Regiments and Battalions*, 2: 342, 234.
145 "Gen Lee expected to concentrate": Quoted in Bonham, "A Little More Light," 521.
145 "But for the firm mountain pike": Caldwell, *History of a Brigade of South Carolinians*, 133.
146 "None but a soldier": Welch, *Confederate Surgeon's Letters*, 62–63.
146 "That night whiskey was again issued": Caldwell, *History of a Brigade of South Carolinians*, 133.
146 "at once aroused our suspicions": Welch, *Confederate Surgeon's Letters*, 63.
146 "Even when our men awoke": Bradwell, "Crossing the Potomac," 371.
146 "I expressed to my staff": Gordon, *Reminiscences of the Civil War*, 140.
147 Buford communications: *OR*, 27/1: 924.
148 " 'You will have to fight' ": Hall, et al., eds., *History of the Sixth New York Cavalry*, 136.
149 "We lived high here": George Edward Finney Diary (ISL).
149 "I am kept full of business": Dawes, *Service with the Sixth Wisconsin*, 158.
149 "[We] shall soon be engaged": *New Haven Journal and Courier*, July 10, 1863.
149 "much needed rest": Bisbee, "Three Years a Volunteer Soldier," 120.
149 "If we had any lingering doubts": Small, *Sixteenth Maine Regiment*, 115.

149 "I have come to feel": Applegate, ed., *Reminiscences and Letters of George Arrowsmith*, 211.
150 "We are within two miles": Quoted in Dunkelman and Winey, "The Hard-tack Regiment in the Brickyard Fight," 19.
150 Messages to Meade: Quoted in Fishel, *Secret War*, 516–17.

CHAPTER TWELVE

(PREDAWN–7:30 A.M.)

152 Meade's orders: *OR*, 27/3: 416.
153 "a courier came and ordered": Fite Memoir (TSL).
153 "very delicate": Fremantle: *Three Months*, 254
153 "A courier came from Gen. Lee": Quoted in Kempster, "The Cavalry," 402.
153 "General Lee's . . . intention": Heth, "Letter to Jones," 157.
154 "The members of our household": Ziegler, "A Gettysburg Girl's" (ACHS).
154 "I got up early": Broadhead, *Diary of a Lady,* 11.
154 "Gettysburg awoke": Jacobs, "How an Eye-Witness."
154 "the camp was astir": Beveridge, "The First Gun," 90.
154 "riding the cavalry horses": Warren, "Recollections" (ACHS).
155 Reid quotations: Smart, ed., *Radical View*, 13–14.
156 "We moved forward leisurely": Marye, "First Gun," 62.
156 "He rode up to my headquarters": *CCW,* 413.
156 "General Reynolds read"/"He told me that he had already": *CCW,* 305.
156 "was . . . to fight the enemy": Doubleday, *Chancellorsville and Gettysburg,* 125.
157 "it is still cloudy": Heller Diary (MHI).
157 "Rainy": Jones Diary (NYSL).
157 "Whole regiments slept": *OR*, 27/2: 696.
158 Meade dispatch: *OR*, 27/1: 70.
158 "told General Archer": Young, "Pettigrew's Brigade," 117.
158 "That decided the question": Marye, "First Gun," 62–63.
159 "rode back to the color bearer": Boland, "Beginning," 308.
159 "he did not expect": Nevins, ed., *Diary of Battle*, 232.
159 "You have all the information": *CCW,* 355.
160 Jones material: "First Shot" (GNP).

(7:30 A.M.–10:45 A.M.)

161 "My God": Marye, "First Gun," 31.
161 "Reveille at 5": Buswell Diary (FNP).
161 "The weary miles": Goldsborough, *Maryland Line,* 102.
161 "We left camp at 6": Leon, *Diary of a Tar Heel,* 34.
161 "without thinking any danger": Wellman, *Rebel Boast,* 121.
162 "the prophecy of a hot July day": Tevis, *History of the Fighting 14th,* 81.
162 Dana quotations: *Philadelphia Weekly Times*, February 2, 1878.

163 "General Heth is ordered"/"We must fight them": Meredith, "First Day," 184.

163 "During Chaplain [W. C.] Way's invocation": Curtis, *History of the 24th Michigan*, 155.

163 "in the highest spirits": Dawes, *Service with the 6th Wisconsin*, 164.

163 "soul stirring song"/"odd for men to march": *Milwaukee (Sunday) Telegraph*, December 20, 1884.

163 "a hundred rumors circulated": J. D. S. Cook, "Reminiscences," 322.

163 "traveled very hard": Burch Diary (MHS).

164 "from the hurried & confused manner": Bonham, "A Little More Light," 521.

164 "warm"/"some rain": Hall Diary (LOC).

164 "The true character": *Philadelphia Weekly Times*, February 2, 1878.

165 "fought with the enemy overwhelming us": *National Tribune*, December 31, 1891.

165 "was looking in perfect health": Myers, "Campaign" (MOC).

165 "was in his usual cheerful spirits"/"General Lee proposed": Longstreet, *From Manassas*, 351.

165 "the enemy was advancing": Beveridge, "The First Gun," 91.

166 "Our orders were to hold": *National Tribune*, July 30, 1903.

167 "a good one for artillery"/"It was part of General Buford's plan": Calef, "Regular Artillery," 47.

168 Bayly material: Bayly, "Mrs. Joseph Bayly's Story" (GNP).

168 5th Alabama and the farmer: Fulton, *Family Record*, 79.

168 "the enemy's skirmishers open upon our pickets": Calef, "Regular Artillery," 48.

168 "an army corps advancing": Ladd, ed., *Bachelder Papers*, 1: 201.

169 "Buford and Reynolds were soldiers": Rosengarten, "General Reynolds' Last Battle," 62.

169 "they were probably after cattle": Ladd, ed., *Bachelder Papers*, 2: 891.

169 "It was a matter of momentary consultation": CCW, 413.

169 "that the enemy was advancing"/"The Genl sent an aid[e]": Veil Letter (PHMC).

170 "Presently the boys": Beveridge, "The First Gun," 91.

170 "to fire at the woods in his front": Morrison, ed.: *Memoirs*, 173.

170 " 'Devin, this is the key' ": Fox, ed., *New York at Gettysburg*, 2: 1153.

171 "steady and well aimed": Quoted in Krick, *Fredericksburg Artillery*, 59.

171 "Seeing the battery so greatly outnumbered": Calef, "Regular Artillery," 48.

171 "People were running": Broadhead, *Diary of a Lady*, 11.

171 "Many of us sat on our doorsteps": Quoted in Bennett, *Days of "Uncertainty and Dread,"* 21.

171 "there was then a general stampede": Skelly, *Boy's Experiences*, 11.

172 "did not climb down": Leander Warren, "Recollections" (ACHS).

172 "had the effect of utterly removing": *Gettysburg Compiler*, June 1, 1898.

172 "stated that our cavalry was fighting": Veil Letter (PHMC).

172 "The rebels are driving in": Weld, *War Diary*, 229.

172 "there was considerable excitement": Veil Letter (PHMC).

172 Reynolds-Buford exchange: Quoted in DePeyster, *Decisive Conflicts*, 153.

172 "The enemy's force (A. P. Hill's)": *OR*, 27/1: 924

172 "The Genl ordered Genl Buford": Veil Letter (PHMC).

173 "all his remarks and appearance": Rosengarten, *Reynolds Memorial Address.*

173 "to say that the enemy was coming on"/"and told me to ride": Weld, *War Diary,* 229–30.

173 "the sound of artillery firing": Tevis, *History of the Fighting 14th,* 82.

173 "shells burst[ing] a little to the left": *Brooklyn Daily Eagle,* July 11, 1863.

173 "gray-haired old men": Smith, *History of the 76th,* 236.

173 "Pennsylvanians have made a mistake": *Milwaukee (Sunday) Telegraph,* February 15, 1885.

174 "Our fellows cheered like mad": *Mauston Star,* February 13, 1883.

174 "conferring . . . as to the lay of the land": Calef, "Regular Artillery," 47.

174 "I . . . received instructions to hurry": Halstead, "First Day," 4.

174 " 'Gen. Reynolds desires' ": *National Tribune,* October 6, 1910.

174 "obliged to remove fences": Smith, *History of the 76th,* 236.

175 "Then was heard the wild rattle": Fox, ed., *New York at Gettysburg,* 3: 990.

175 "firing was heard": Long, *Memoirs,* 275.

175 "much older and somewhat careworn": Harris Diary (FNP).

175 "he is instructed"/"to move in such direction": Meade, *Life and Letters,* 31.

175 " 'Oh, they have been throwing dirt' ": Quoted in Edward J. Nichols, *Toward Gettysburg,* 203.

176 "that the enemy was in the vicinity"/"I . . . supposed it consisted": *OR,* 27/2: 637.

176 "I did some lively work": Kempster, "The Cavalry," 403.

176 "thick underbrush and briars": *OR,* 27/2: 649.

178 "a railroad which had been graded": Clark, ed., *Histories,* 3: 297.

178 "Is that the enemy?": Hofmann, *Military Record,* 15.

178 "Two men of the color guard": Clark, ed., *Histories,* 3: 297.

179 "just before [we reached]": Boland, "Beginning," 308.

179 "battle-flags looked redder": Calef, "Regular Artillery," 48.

179 "moved somewhat faster": Boland, "Beginning," 308.

179 "the sweetest music"/"We halted to reform": Moon, "Beginning," 449.

179 "suggested that his brigade"/"strength and line of battle": Turney, "First Tennessee," 535.

180 "not a man showed": Woollard, "Journals of Events" (LMS).

180 "After we got into the musketry": McLean, *Cutler's Brigade,* 69.

180 "no body of men ever withstood": *National Tribune,* July 21, 1887.

180 " 'Yes, but do not pay any attention' ": Clark, ed., *Histories,* 3: 297.

181 "heavy firing"/" 'Come quite up to Gettysburg' ": Hall Letter.

181 Howard quotations/exchange with Meysenburg: Howard, *Autobiography,* 409–10.

181 "nearly at the extreme advance"/"told me to inform you": Hall Letter.

182 " 'Tell General Sickles I think' ": Tremain, "Two Days," 14.

182 "I . . . received instructions to hurry forward": Halstead, "First Day," 4.

182 " 'Tell Doubleday' ": Doubleday, *Chancellorsville and Gettysburg,* 130.

182 "to charge as fast as they arrived": Rosengarten, "Admiral and General Reynolds," 629.

183 "You have not a second"/"form his regiment"/"in his immediate front": *Missouri Republican,* December 4, 1886.

212 "and became unfit for further command": Quoted in Martin, *Gettysburg July 1*, 238.

212 Brown quotations: Brown Papers (TSL).

212 Heth-Lee exchange: Heth, "Letter to Jones," 158.

213 "It would of course": Doubleday, *Chancellorsville and Gettysburg*, 139.

214 "We were wet as cats": Quoted in Pula, *Sigel Regiment*, 161.

214 "The fate of the nation": Pula, ed., *Memoirs*, 36.

215 "had a few words with Wadsworth": Howard, *Autobiography*, 414.

215 "gave orders, in case I was forced": Doubleday, *Chancellorsville and Gettysburg*, 141.

215 "feeling exceedingly anxious": Howard, *Autobiography*, 414.

215 "there are enough soldiers here": McCreary, "Gettysburg."

215 "They kept the pace": Jacobs, "How an Eye-Witness."

215 "there was no time to drink": Quoted in Bennett, *Days of "Uncertainty and Dread,"* 28.

215 "I didn't know what in the world": *Philadelphia Inquirer*, June 26, 1930.

216 "Maj. Venable of Jeb Stuart's staff": Brown Papers (TSL).

216 "some were shot": Ladd, ed., *Bachelder Papers*, 2: 830.

217 "always been down on the 'Dutch' "/"miserable creatures": Barlow Papers.

217 "shoot down stragglers": Butts, ed., *Gallant Captain*, 79.

218 "still thinner a line already too thin": Schurz, *Reminiscences*, 9.

218 "I . . . formed my line": OR, 27/2: 468.

218 "I saw the enemy": Schurz, *Reminiscences*, 9.

219 "I received a dispatch": OR, 27/2: 697.

219 "General Wadsworth reported half his men": Doubleday, *Chancellorsville and Gettysburg*, 146.

220 "were withdrawing troops"/" 'Wait a while' ": Morrison, ed., *Memoirs*, 175.

(2:45 P.M.–5:45 P.M.)

221 Sickles communications: OR, 27/3: 464.

221 "The people all along the road": Quaife, ed., *From the Cannon's Mouth*, 224.

222 "As we had heard that Buford"/"that the action was more serious": Ladd, ed., *Bachelder Papers*, 1:290.

222 "My orders were to march": Cooke, "First Day," 286.

223 "We advanced with our accustomed yell": Nichols, *Soldier's Story*, 116.

224 "Everybody was then running": Barlow Papers.

224 Lane-Burgwyn exchange: Quoted in Gragg, *Covered with Glory*, 97–98.

225 "the whole [Rebel] army in our front": Dudley, *Iron Brigade*, 11.

225 "when he was shot": Hodnett Family Collection (Duke).

225 "The Yankees . . . fought": William S. Evans, "Letter."

225 "I thought we would have to use the bayonet": Shivers, "An Account."

225 "There was no alternative": Gordon, *Reminiscences*, 151.

225 "So the horrible, screaming": *National Tribune*, August 19, 1897.

225 "The troops taking part": Pula, ed., *Memoirs*, 37.

226 "stepped off": Clark, ed., *Histories*, 2: 351.

226 "advanced in two lines": OR, 27/1: 268.

226 "Their bearing was magnificent": Otis, *Second Wisconsin*, 277.

228 "total annihilation stared": *Winchester Journal*, July 13, 1863.

228 "deadly missiles [that] were sent": *Lenoir News Topic,* April 8, 1896.
228 "The Yanks took advantage of that": Dorsett, "Fourteenth Color-Bearer," 5.
228 "no Rebel crossed the stream": Gaff, *On Many a Bloody Field,* 260.
228 "with recklessness upon our walls": Otis, *Second Wisconsin,* 85.
228 "The slaughter in our ranks": Orr Family Papers (ISL).
229 "The men were falling rapidly": Applegate, ed., *Reminiscences,* 211.
229 "Their officers were cheering"/"We drove them": Nichols, *Soldier's Story,* 116.
229 "whole division was falling back": *OR,* 27/1: 712.
230 "far down the line": Gordon, *Reminiscences,* 153.
230 "The struggle grows hotter": Clark, ed., *Histories,* 2: 106.
231 "Lots of men near me": Dorsett, "Fourteenth Color-Bearer," 5.
231 "Go and get it"/"Go to hell": *Richmond Palladium,* September 11, 1863.
231 "[The] men had difficulty": Clark, ed., *Histories,* 3: 84.
231 "Although they knew it was certain death": *Charlotte Observer,* December 22, 1895.
231 "covered itself with glory": Burgwyn Papers (NCDHA).
231 " 'Dress on the colors' ": Quoted in Gragg, *Covered with Glory,* 129.
232 "the first sight I had": *National Tribune,* April 13, 1899.
232 "coolly waited until they saw": Nicholson, ed., *Pennsylvania at Gettysburg,* 2: 762.
233 " 'Adjutant, it is all damned cowardice' ": Chamberlin, *History of the 150th Pennsylvania,* 134.
233 "fought for some time"/"turning round every now and then": Fremantle, *Three Months,* 204.
234 "set a corporal's guard"/"Hold at any cost": Small, ed., *Road to Richmond,* 101.
235 "They swarmed down upon us": *Maine at Gettysburg,* 47.
235 "every man commenced": Bisbee, "Three Years," 9.
236 "I feared the consequences": Howard, *Autobiography,* 416.
236 "What was left of the First Corps": Doubleday, *Chancellorsville and Gettysburg,* 147.
236 "I thought it was the *Seminary* Hill": Nevins, ed., *Diary of Battle,* 235.
237 "pass Genl Heth's division": *OR,* 27/2: 657.
237 "did not halt"/"would all be killed": Littlejohn, "Recollections."
237 "could scarcely raise": Bonham, "A Little More Light," 521.
237 "The field was thick": Caldwell, *History of . . . "McGowan's Brigade,"* 138.
237 "lying down": Ladd, ed., *Bachelder Papers,* 3: 1697.
237 "His round shot": Nevins, ed., *Diary of Battle,* 235–36.
239 "Every discharge made sad loss": Clark, ed., *Histories,* 2: 693.
239 "The rebels came half-way": Dawes, *Service with the 6th Wisconsin,* 175.
239 "only a squad here and there": *OR,* 27/2: 669–70.
239 "this thunderous fire": Clark, ed., *Histories,* 2: 587.
239 "They threw shells": Quoted in Taylor, ed., *Cry Is War,* 147.
239 "We were met by a furious storm": *OR,* 27/2: 660.
239 "We were fired upon from right": Harling, "At Gettysburg."
240 "forming against cavalry": Doubleday, *Chancellorsville and Gettysburg,* 149.
240 "Forming squares against": Fox, ed., *New York at Gettysburg,* 1: 380.
240 "fought the Rebels on the Seminary Ridge": Church Papers.

240 "the enemy were closing in": Doubleday, *Chancellorsville and Gettysburg*, 149.

241 "were then ordered forward": Early, *Autobiographical Sketch*, 268.

241 "It seemed as though they had": Quoted in Dunkelman and Winey, *Hardtack Regiment*, 75.

241 "I never imagined such a rain": *Schenectady Evening Star and Times*, July 13, 1863.

241 "few that did get away": Quoted in Dunkelman and Winey, *Hardtack Regiment*, 77.

243 "Word was sent to the citizens": *Philadelphia Weekly Press*, November 16, 1887.

243 "Four of our men were carrying": *Philadelphia Evening Bulletin*, July 2, 1938.

243 "lost 8 or 10 men": *OR*, 27/1: 286.

243 "made drains & bricks fly": Wheeler Letters (SHSWI).

243 "saw a Union soldier running": Jacobs, "How an Eye-Witness."

243 "If there is a more thrilling spectacle": McCurdy, *Gettysburg*, 18.

243 Wainwright quotations: Nevins, ed., *Diary of Battle*, 236.

244 "That there were a good many stragglers": Schurz, *Reminiscences*, 12.

244 "The First Corps was broken": Doubleday, *Chancellorsville and Gettysburg*, 150.

244 " 'Fall back, boys' ": Tevis, *History of the Fighting 14th*, 86.

244 "in whatever shape the troops issued": Schurz, *Reminiscences*, 12.

244 Hancock quotations: Hancock, "Gettysburg."

245 "I shall never forget": Walker, *General Hancock*, 112.

245 "no excitement in voice or manner": Cooke, "First Day," 285.

245 " 'Gen. Lee is still at Cashtown' ": Douglas, *I Rode with Stonewall*, 239.

246 "We had them fairly in a pen": *Semi-Weekly Standard*, August 4, 1863.

246 " 'Damn it' "/" 'God almighty' ": Quoted in Martin, *Gettysburg July 1*, 448.

246 "Now when our line was reformed": Ladd, ed., *Bachelder Papers*, 2: 1047.

246 Dawes quotations: Dawes, *Service with the 6th Wisconsin*, 176–77.

247 "established his headquarters": Maurice, ed., *Aide-de-Camp of Lee*, 227–28.

247 "the rout of the enemy": Robertson Jr., *General A. P. Hill*, 213.

247 "to go to General Ewell": Taylor, *Four Years*, 190.

247 "was met by a messenger"/"that he was in ignorance": Clark, ed., *Histories*, 5: 121.

248 "Panic was impending": *Milwaukee (Sunday) Telegraph*, February 3, 1884.

248 "Many of the troops": Smith, *Camps and Campaigns*, 89.

248 "Many brave, strong men": *Rochester Daily Democrat*, July 14, 1863.

248 "was used for Hospital purposes"/"wounded were carried into the lecture room": Coco, *Vast Sea*, 9, 11, 13.

249 Hancock on Cemetery Hill: *OR*, 27/1: 368; *CCW*, 404–5.

(5:45 P.M.–MIDNIGHT)

251 "square was filled with Confederate soldiers": Smith, "General Lee at Gettysburg," 144.

251 "receiving reports from all his command": Smith, "With Stonewell Jackson," 56.

251 " 'Genl Ewell, the 24th Mich.' ": Quoted in Pfanz, *Richard S. Ewell*, 309.

251 "They desired General Lee to be informed": Smith, "General Lee at Gettysburg," 144.

252 "directed me to reconnoitre" A. L. Long, "Letter to General Early," 66.

252 Longstreet-Lee exchange/Longstreet quotation: Longstreet, "Lee in Pennsylvania," 420–22.

253 Smith quotations: Smith, "General Lee at Gettysburg," 144.

253 Longstreet quotations: Longstreet, "Lee in Pennsylvania," 422.

253 "occupied by a considerable force": Long, "Letter," 66.

253 "knelt shivering": Salome Myers Stewart, "Recollections."

254 "My mother intervened": Skelly, *Boy's Experiences*, 11.

254 "we were really in the midst": Hollinger, *Some Personal Recollections*, 3.

254 Irsch incidents: Fox, ed., *New York at Gettysburg*, 1: 380.

255 " 'I'll be damned' ": Howard, "First Day," 238.

255 "A portion of our troops": *OR*, 27/3: 466.

255 "turned off to the right": Quaife, ed., *From the Cannon's Mouth*, 223.

255 "some distance to the right"/"to take possession": *OR*, 27/1: 368.

256 "regretted that his people": Smith, "General Lee at Gettysburg," 145.

256 "the enemy was advancing"/"thought it best to send General Gordon": Early, *Autobiographical Sketch*, 270.

257 "his command had been doing all the hard marching": *Charlottesville Progress*, March 22, 1904.

257 "Why we failed to push on": Fulton, *Family Record*, 77.

257 "Tired soldiers mopped": Wellman, *Rebel Boast*, 123.

257 "as our wounded men came in": *Winston-Salem Sentinel*, June 13, 1914.

257 "We laid all night": Leon, *Diary of a Tar Heel*, 35.

257 "A sorrowful band, indeed": Curtis, *History of the 24th Michigan*, 163.

257 "Company officers called loudly": Cooke, "First Day," 84.

257 "Volunteers were called for": Caldwell, *History of . . . "McGowan's Brigade*," 140.

257 "I think we dragged": Wilkes Letters (LOC).

258 "This forced me to go all over": Silver, ed., *Confederate Soldier*, 118.

258 "Then it was we saw the sickening horrors": Cureton Letter (SHC).

258 "It is a troubled and dreamy sleep": Dawes, *Service with the 6th Wisconsin*, 180.

258 " 'wounded outside of Gettysburg' "/"sitting next to the driver": Butts, ed., *Gallant Captain*, 79–80.

258 Fremantle quotations/account of conversations with Hill and Longstreet: Fremantle, *Three Months*, 253–56.

259 "If you do not go up there": Early Papers (LOC).

260 "that our regiment had been engaged": Quoted in Dunkelman and Winey, *Hardtack Regiment*, 77–78.

260 Cutler-Wadworth exchange: Thomson, *From Philippi*, 162–63.

261 "intelligence of the capture of Harrisburg": Miers, ed., *Rebel War Clerk's Diary*, 234.

261 Welles quotations: Beale, ed., *Diary of Gideon Wells*, vol. 1, 354.

261 Early-Lee exchange: Early, "A Review," 272–73.

262 "the men were overcome": Beale, *A Lieutenant*, 114.

263 "The men were falling asleep"/"fell magnificently": Cooke, *Wearing of the Gray*, 255.

264 Crounse and Reid quotations: Smart, ed., *Radical View,* 170.

264 Buford quotations: *OR,* 27/1: 924–25.

264 "It seems to me": *OR,* 27/3: 466.

265 Meade summary/Hancock update: *OR,* 27/1: 72.

266 "I will never forget"/"jeered and laughed at us": Woollard, "Journals of Events" (LMS).

266 "remained in the vicinity": Moon, "Beginning," 450.

266 "Started us at almost a 'double quick' ": Woollard, "Journals of Events" (LMS).

267 "over back of Seminary Ridge": *National Tribune,* March 23, 1911.

267 "Encouraged by the successful issue": *OR,* 27/2: 308.

268 "We lay on our arms": *National Tribune,* March 19, 1895.

268 "day of excitement": McCurdy, *Gettysburg,* 18.

268 "enjoyed a good night's rest": Skelly, *Boy's Experiences,* 16.

268 Pierce quotations: Alleman, *At Gettysburg,* 44–45.

268 "At night all was quiet": Quoted in Bennett, *Days of "Uncertainty and Dread,"* 42.

268 "As I write all is quiet": Broadhead, *Diary of a Lady,* 13.

269 "noise . . . as of men moving": *National Tribune,* February 11, 1886.

269 "Day was now breaking": Quoted in Pfanz, *Richard S. Ewell,* 314.

269 "Were pleased to hear": Keiser Diary (MHI).

269 "I feel very tired": Wentworth Papers (LOC).

269 "well supplied with rye whiskey": Stevens, *Three Years,* 239.

270 Mounted officer's arrival: Anderson, "March," 78.

270 "None of us knew our destination": Brewer, *History 61st Pennsylvania,* 62.

270 "I received orders from General Meade": *CCW,* 460.

270 "We would march a while": *National Tribune,* August 2, 1928.

270 "We go limping around": Murphy, ed., *Civil War Letters,* 134.

270 "Head of the column seems to have lost": Latta Diary (LOC).

270 "By the time the right road was discovered": Bicknell, *History of the 5th Maine,* 242.

NOCTURNE: JULY 1

273 Alexander quotations: Gallagher, ed., *Fighting for the Confederacy,* 235.

274 "one of those born soldiers": Brown Papers (TSL).

275 Marye quotations: Marye, "First Gun," 32.

275 "self-possession to stand alone": Quoted in Campbell, " 'We Saved the Line,' " 44.

275 "the body of Gen Reynolds": Reed Letters (Princeton).

276 Smith quotations: Fox, ed., *New York at Gettysburg,* 3: 1289–94.

CHAPTER THIRTEEN

(MIDNIGHT–SUNRISE)

277 Meade-Howard Slocum-Sickles exchange: Howard, *Autobiography,* 423.

278 "There was a rumor": Schurz, "Battle of Gettysburg," 278.

278 "the stars were [still] shining": Longstreet, *From Manassas,* 362.

279 "not at his ease"/"care-worn": Scheibert, *Seven Months,* 113.
279 "Culp's Hill [was] already occupied": Smith, "General Lee at Gettysburg," 148.
279 "views against making an attack"/"a general idea of the nature": Longstreet, "Lee in Pennsylvania," 422.
279 "General Lee . . . said he wanted me to reconnoiter": Freeman Papers (LOC).
279 "make a reconnaissance": Longstreet, "Lee in Pennsylvania," 422.
279 "to examine and verify the position": Long, *Memoirs,* 280–81.
279 "upon coming to the field": Fremantle, *Three Months,* 257.
279 "more anxious and ruffled": Hoole, ed., *Lawley,* 206.
280 "he need not attack"/". . . moved to Gettysburg": CCW, 297, 302.
280 "The Third Corps had simply gone": Tremain, *Two Days,* 37.
281 "the natural termination of our lines": Hunt, "Second Day," 295.

(DAWN–3:40 P.M.)

282 "As soon as it was light": Quoted in Archer, "*The Hour,*" 15.
282 "the enemies picket a firing": Pierson, ed., "Diary," 37.
283 "Early in the morning it had been my intention": CCW, 331.
283 "Sharp shooters were stationed": Aughinbaugh, *Personal Experiences,* 8.
283 "It was hot and sultry": Skelly, *Boy's Experiences,* 16.
283 "He persevered until he picked all": Broadhead, *Diary of a Lady,* 13.
284 " 'Why, man, take off that gray suit' ": Hollinger, *Some Personal Recollections.*
284 "riding to and fro": Scheibert, *Seven Months,* 113.
284 "to tell Genl E.": Brown Papers (TSL).
284 "depressed, dilapidated and almost unorganized": *OR,* 27/2: 671.
284 "evidently left in a hurry": George D. Bowen, "Diary."
285 "a rattling fire": Ladd, ed., *Bachelder Papers,* 3: 1388.
286 Reid quotations: Smart, ed., *Radical View,* 22–24.
286 "Meade thought a couple of scapegoats": CCW, 311.
286 "was much relieved, and expressed": Hunt, "Second Day," 297–300.
287 Geary-Greene comments: Collins, *Memoirs of the 149th New York,* 137.
287 "Right and left the men felled": Jones, "Breastworks," 316.
287 "bayonets, tin pans": Quoted in Pfanz, *Culp's Hill,* 115.
287 Johnston testimony: Freeman Papers (LOC).
288 "the high ground along the Emmitsburg road": *OR,* 27/2: 318.
289 " 'The enemy is here' ": Hood, *Advance and Retreat,* 57.
289 Johnston quotation: Freeman Papers (LOC).
290 McLaws quotations and exchanges with Lee and Longstreet: McLaws, "Gettysburg," 68–69.
290 Brady quotations: Ladd, ed., *Bachelder Papers,* 3: 1388.
292 Meade-Butterfield exchange: CCW, 424, 436.
293 " 'The enemy have the advantage' ": Trimble, "Battle and Campaign," 125.
293 "the general had been waiting": Long, *Memoirs,* 281.
294 "General Lee was at our quarters": McDonald, ed., *Make Me a Map,* 157.
294 "to go into position on the left: Meade Jr., *With Meade,* 101–2.
294 Sickles quotations: CCW, 297.

296 "As we approached the ground": Smith, *Famous Battery*, 101.

296 "Little is said by any one": Rhodes, ed., *All for the Union*, 115.

296 "before the coffee is made": Bowen, *History of the 37th Massachusetts*, 172–73.

296 "The bands all discoursed sweet music": Westbrook, *History of the 49th Pennsylvania*, 153.

297 " 'Do you know where' "/"As we rode together": Walker, "Letter," 181.

297 "General Lee assented": Longstreet, "Lee in Pennsylvania," 422.

297 "My recollection is that a lot of our infantry": Gallagher, ed., *Fighting for the Confederacy*, 235.

298 Seymour quotations: Seymour Diary-Memoir (MHI).

298 "if any one showed themselves": J. Warren Jackson Letters, 90.

298 "lying all day under a hot July sun": Clark, ed., *Histories*, 2: 136.

298 "enemy . . . balls hissing": McPherson Letter (SHC).

298 "I did not think that the ground"/"rough, being the valley": Quoted in Emerson G. Taylor, *Gouverneur Kemble Warren*, 122.

299 "I found that my impression": *CCW*, 298.

299 " 'O[h], generals are all apt' ": *OR*, 27/1: 130.

299 Sickles quotations: *CCW*, 298.

299 "Harper's Ferry boys have turned out trumps": Fleming, ed., *Life and Letters*, 296.

300 "panted to remove that stigma": Willson, *Disaster*, 176.

300 "by a dilgent search of our pockets": Thompson, "This Hell," 18.

300 "The enemy occupy a very commanding position": Ott, ed., *Civil War Diary*, 118.

300 "a lively skirmish": Quoted in Christ, *Struggle*, 22.

301 Hunt-Sickles material: *CCW*, 449; Hunt, "Second Day," 301.

302 "Here we stacked arms": *Irish American*, August 29, 1863.

302 "Every movement of the enemy was watched": Mulholland, *Story of the 116th Pennsylvania*, 123.

303 "The brigade stood in a column": Kohl, ed., *Memoirs of Chaplain Life*, 182–84.

303 "some neighbors coming in": Broadhead, *Diary of a Lady*, 13.

303 "It lay there": Jacobs, "How an Eye-Witness."

303 "It only served as a source": McCurdy, *Gettysburg*, 21.

303 "He was a fair minded man": Skelly, *Boy's Experiences*, 17.

304 Aughinbaugh quotations: Aughinbaugh, *Personal Experiences*, 8–9.

304 "The greatest danger was from the sharpshooters": Quoted in Bennett, *Days of "Uncertainty and Dread,"* 51.

304 "I learned that the indulgence": *Gettysburg Compiler*, June 1, 1908.

304 "Comparative quiet along both lines": *Star and Sentinel*, July 2, 1913.

305 "position several times and spent": Berry Diary (MHI).

305 "We knew the battle was to be fought": Quoted in Golay, *To Gettysburg*, 150.

305 "We cooked breakfast": Phillips and Parsegian, eds., *Richard and Rhoda*, 30.

305 "the spiteful firing along the picket line": Nash, *History of the 44th New York*, 141.

305 "Vincent had a peculiar penchant": *National Tribune*, February 25, 1892.

305 "The men of our corps": Nash, *History of the 44th New York*, 142.

305 "At this point twenty rounds": Styple, ed., *With a Flash,* 97.

305 Reid quotations: Smart, ed., *Radical View,* 25.

306 Pleasonton quotations: *CCW,* 359.

306 "Greatly did officers and men marvel": McKim, *Soldier's Recollections,* 194.

307 "nothing doing along our line": Zable Papers.

307 "We were wondering at the silence": Schuricht, "Jenkins' Brigade," 344.

308 "a narrow strip of oak woods": *Atlanta Journal,* March 9, 1901.

308 "could see our Federal brothers": *National Tribune,* March 20, 1929.

308 "caught and killed it": Zachry, "Fighting with the 3rd Georgia," 75–76.

310 "It was quite a spirited little fight": *National Tribune,* May 16, 1885.

311 "command . . . with the voice": Butts, ed., *Gallant Captain,* 80.

311 "were wounded and others killed": Fox, ed., *New York at Gettysburg,* 1: 404.

311 "quite a body of men": Ladd, ed., *Bachelder Papers,* 2: 1027.

312 "saying things I would not like to teach my grandson": Abernathy, *Our Mess,* 31.

313 "There is no telling the value": Gallagher, ed., *Fighting for the Confederacy,* 236.

314 "Capt. G. E. Randolph, Chief of Third Corps Artillery": Smith, *Famous Battery,* 101.

314 "as though nature in some wild freak": Stoke Letters (Gettysburg).

315 "its base huge boulders": Fox, ed., *New York at Gettysburg,* 1: 37.

315 "guns were unlimbered": *National Tribune,* February 4, 1886.

315 "Here I could not place more": Smith, *Famous Battery,* 102.

315 "I have but to show him my design": Quoted in Palmer, *Lee Moves North,* 115.

315 "General Lee rode with me": Longstreet, *From Manassas,* 367.

315 "I left General Lee": Longstreet, "Lee in Pennsylvania," 423.

315 Longstreet-McLaws exchange: *Savannah Morning News,* January 8, 1878.

316 "on the left wing": OR, 27/2: 697.

316 "nearly all the time": Fremantle, *Three Months,* 259–60.

316 "It was determined to make the principal attack": OR, 27/2: 318

317 Garlach quotations: Quoted in Bennett, *Days of "Uncertainty and Dread,"* 49.

317 "using rifles that had sufficient range"/"Alas!": Thompson, "A Scrap," 98.

318 McLaws quotations: McLaws, "Gettysburg," 69–70.

318 Hood quotations: Hood, *Advance and Retreat,* 57.

319 Meade dispatch to Halleck: *CCW,* 488.

319 "was not occupied": *CCW,* 377.

319 "never [seen] General Meade so angry": Paine Letter (HSP).

319 "General Meade met me": *CCW,* 299.

319 "could hardly be said": *CCW,* 377.

320 " 'Here is where our line' "/" 'It is too late now' ": Quoted in Taylor, *Gouverneur Kemble Warren,* 122.

320 " 'I wish you would ride' ": Quoted in Roebling, *Wash Roebling's,* 21.

320 "that the enemy was so strong": McLaws, "Gettysburg," 72.

321 "very much disconcerted": *Savannah Morning News,* January 8, 1878.

321 "a brave and fearless leader": Love, "Experience," 221.

321 " 'Something is going to happen today' ": Quoted in Duke, "Mississippians," 216.

321 "We formed our line": Love, "Experience," 221.
322 "General Lee's orders are to attack": Hood, *Advance and Retreat,* 58
322 "It was well known": *Savannah Republican,* July 22, 1863.
322 "a long consultation": Harwell, ed., *Cities and Camps,* 51.
322 "to envelop the enemy's left": Longstreet, "Lee in Pennsylvania," 424.
324 "a calm, as of death"/"that the carnival was at hand": Shuffler, ed., *Decimus,* 44.
324 "where I saw a great many wounded soldiers": West, *Texan,* 84.
324 "It is very true that the men": Jones, "Longstreet at Gettysburg," 551.
325 Warren quotations: Norton, *Attack and Defense,* 130–31.
325 Meade-Sickles exchange: *CCW,* 299, 332.
326 " 'You cannot hold this position' ": Meade Jr., *With Meade,* 114.
326 Vincent exchange with Sykes aide: Nicholson, ed., *Pennsylvania at Gettysburg,* 1: 461.
327 "Soon the long lines": Ibid., 1: 622.
327 "I recollect looking on": *CCW,* 406.
327 "There was quite a thick wood": *CCW,* 440.

<h1 style="text-align:center">(3:40 P.M.–4:10 P.M.)</h1>

328 Alexander quotations: Gallagher, ed., *Fighting for the Confederacy,* 239–40, 244.
328 "The accuracy of the enemy's aim": Smith, *Famous Battery,* 101–3.
328 "As soon as the battery": Ladd, ed., *Bachelder Papers,* 3: 1632.
328 "I fired slow": Ibid., 1: 72.
328 "shrieking, hissing, [and] seething": Reed Letters.
328 "They really surprised me": Gallagher, ed., *Fighting for the Confederacy,* 239.
329 "He was killed while in the act": *OR,* 27/2: 432.
329 Alexander quotations: Gallagher, ed., *Fighting for the Confederacy,* 244.
329 "I'll lead you this time": Quoted in Whittaker, *Popular Life,* 173.
329 "a few Rebels rode right over us": Baird Letters.
331 "a hard, bold and bloody fight": Fox, ed., *New York at Gettysburg,* 3: 1129–30.
331 "a splendid sight": Pfanz, *Culp's Hill,* 179.
331 "a continuous vibration": Hatton Memoir (LC).
331 Wainwright quotations: Nevins, ed., *Diary of Battle,* 242–43.
331 "We were standing in an open field": West, *Texan,* 85.
332 "It is very trying": Shuffler, ed., *Decimus,* 44.
332 "To avoid as much danger as possible": Sims Recollections (CRC).
332 "You will execute"/" 'Very well' ": Chilton, ed., *Unveiling,* 339.
332 "After this urgent protest": Hood, *Advance and Retreat,* 59.
332 "Directly the familiar roar": Nicholson, ed., *Pennsylvania at Gettysburg,* 1: 378.
332 "There was much to inspire": Anderson, "March," 641.
332 "anxious to see the young lady": Cocke Family Letters (VHS).
333 "The roads were hard and firm": *Atlanta Journal,* December 7, 1901.
333 "the vertical rays of the sun": Hamilton, ed., *Papers,* 498–501.
333 "it is a hard thing to keep these men": Durkin, ed., *John Dooley,* 100.
333 "the sullen 'Boom!' ": Hamilton, ed., *Papers,* 516.

(4:10 P.M.–10:00 P.M.)

334 " 'Forward, my Texans": Chilton, ed., *Unveiling,* 350.

334 " 'Forward—Steady—forward' ": West, *Texan,* 94.

334 " 'Fix bayonets, my brave Texans' ": Quoted in Pfanz, *Gettysburg: The Second Day,* 167.

334 " 'Attention!' ": Ward, "Incidents," 346.

334 "We moved quietly": Polley, *Hood's Texas Brigade,* 168.

334 "We could see the Federals": West, *Texan,* 94.

335 "to advance but two": OR, 27/2: 633.

335 "soon catching up with Lieut. Col. Harris": George D. Bowen, "Diary."

335 " 'Down with that flag' ": Norton, *Attack and Defense,* 167.

335 "The four guns were now used": Smith, *Famous Battery,* 103.

336 "Every round of ammunition": *National Tribune,* February 4, 1886.

336 Hunt quotations: Hunt, "Second Day," 305–6.

337 "I . . . saw him sway": Scott, "Texans."

338 "toward the middle of the afternoon": Alleman, *At Gettysburg,* 53.

339 "When we were within a short distance": *Final Report,* 112.

340 "I received an order": OR, 27/2: 392.

340 "this was the extreme left"/"best secure the advantage": OR, 27/1: 623.

341 "might make it hard for mother": Chamberlain, "Through Blood," 48.

342 "Give them shell": *National Tribune,* January 21, 1886.

342 "brigade would follow Law's brigade": OR, 27/2: 414.

342 "As soon as we cleared the woods": Fluker, "Graphic Account" (GNP).

342 "Down the plunging shot came": *Savannah Republican,* July 22, 1863.

343 " 'My God!' ": Weygant, *History of the 124th New York,* 176.

343 "not more than 150 yards from us": *National Tribune,* January 21, 1886.

344 "The enemy were as invisible to us": Perry, "Devil's Den," 161.

344 "a strong skirmish line": Ladd, ed., *Bachelder Papers,* 2: 1095.

345 "Above the crack of the rifle": *National Tribune,* February 4, 1886.

345 "as firm as the rocks": Fasnacht, *Speech,* 10.

345 "The enemy are taken by surprise": Smith, *Famous Battery,* 104.

345 "thought I was the only man": Rodenbough, *Bravest,* 186–87.

346 "We had to fight the Yankees": Landrum Letters (MHI).

346 "In an instant a sheet of smoke": Judson, *History of the 83rd Pennsylvania,* 127.

346 "For the first time in the history of the war": Stevens, *Reminiscences,* 114.

346 "Their dead and wounded were tumbled"/"stood directly in front of me": Nash, *History of the 44th New York,* 153, 300.

346 "Now, it was to be expected": Stevens, *Reminiscences,* 114.

347 "For nearly an hour": *Southern Banner,* July 29, 1863.

347 "Grape, canister and musket balls": Bass Letter (FNP).

347 "our Regiment got Cut all to Peaces": Everett Collection (Emory).

347 "our fire began to tell": Silliker, ed., *Rebel Yell,* 101.

348 Oates quotations/Terrell instructions: Oates, *War,* 211.

348 "We went there at a trot": Rittenhouse, "Battle," 37.

348 "Our guns tipped over": *National Tribune,* August 2, 1884.

349 "Never mind that": Quoted in Taylor, *Gouverneur Kemble Warren,* 129.

349 " 'You had better not go' "/" 'If you and I had' ": Lokey, "Wounded at Gettysburg," 400.

351 Bulger-aide exchange/"with the blood gushing": *New Orleans Picayune,* September 18, 1898.

351 Kershaw quotations these pages: Kershaw, "Kershaw's Brigade," 333–35; Ladd, ed., *Bachelder Papers,* 1: 454.

352 "You could constantly see men falling": Neill Letters (GNP).

352 "Shells were cutting off the arms": *Atlanta Journal,* July 27, 1901.

352 "We were, in ten minutes' ": Gaillard Collection (SHC).

352 "the awful deathly surging": Coxe, "Battle," 434.

353 "close the line": Gibbon, *Personal Recollections,* 137.

353 "we built a small breastwork": Ford, *Story of the 15th Massachusetts,* 267.

353 "Minie balls were falling": Ward, "Incidents," 348.

353 "swing around, and drive the Federals": Oates, *War,* 218.

354 Chamberlain quotations: Chamberlain, "Through Blood," 50.

354 "Smoke rises in dense clouds": Nicholson, ed., *Pennsylvania at Gettysburg,* 2: 683.

354 " 'Caldwell, you get your division read' ": Quoted ibid., 623.

354 " 'Colonel Cross' "/" 'No General' ": Hale, "With Colonel Cross," 35.

355 "at once took arms": *Irish American,* August 29, 1863.

355 "Nothing could move them": Rodenbough, *Bravest,* 189–92.

356 "The shell and shrapnel shot descended": *Savannah Republican,* July 22, 1863.

356 Broadhead quotations: Broadhead, *Diary of a Lady,* 14.

356 "Pray": Quoted in Bennett, *Days of "Uncertainty and Dread,"* 55.

356 Jacobs quotes: Jacobs, "How an Eye-Witness."

357 "I advanced my right": Oates, *War,* 214.

357 "The fire on both sides": *National Tribune,* June 12, 1913.

357 "I ordered a charge": OR, 27/2: 393.

357 "We opened a brisk fire": Chamberlain, "Through Blood," 51.

357 "The full force of the enemy": Warren Letters (NYSL).

358 "Paddy, give me a regiment"/"Never mind that": Quoted in Pfanz, *Second Day,* 225.

358 "a man of noble character": Norton, *Attack and Defense,* 320.

358 "advanced into a piece of wood"/"a point from which I could distinctly see": Ladd, ed., *Bachelder Papers,* 1: 456, 471.

359 "Some strolled"/Kershaw-Longstreet exchange: McNeily, "Barksdale's," 235.

360 "The two lines met and broke": Chamberlain, "Through Blood," 51.

360 "We forwarded without a murmur": Fletcher, *Rebel Private,* 80.

361 "Throwing himself in the breach": Nicholson, ed., *Pennsylvania at Gettysburg,* 1: 462.

361 " 'This is the fourth or fifth time' ": Quoted in Judson, *History of the 83rd Pennsylvania,* 67.

361 "Our Generals did not take the precaution": *Rochester Evening Express,* July 11, 1863.

362 "No time now, Paddy": *National Tribune,* April 30, 1885.

362 "Here they are men": Ladd, ed., *Bachelder Papers,* 1: 547.

362 "impossible to take": Felder Letters (CRC).

362 "this eccentricity of formation": Muffley, ed., *Story of Our Regiment,* 734.

363 " 'I think the boys will miss me' ": Child, *History of the 5th New Hampshire,* 208.

363 "Is that not a magnificent sight?": *Charleston News and Courier*, June 21, 1882.
363 "The Confederates were on a crest": Mulholland, *Story of the 116th Pennsylvania*, 126.
363 "so desperate I took two shots": Gaillard Collection (SHC).
364 "We were on the appointed and entrusted line": Chamberlain, "Through Blood," 51.
364 " 'Oh God!' ": Oates, "Battle on the Right," 176–77.
364 "Forward, men, to the ledge"/Oates quotations: Oates, *War*, 218.
365 Brooke quotations: Ladd, ed., *Bachelder Papers*, 2: 1140–41.
365 "The men were firing": *Cattaraugus Freeman*, July 30, 1863.
367 "everything had progressed": *OR*, 27/1: 634.
367 " 'Attention, Mississippians!' ": Claiborne Papers (SHC).
367 "grand beyond description": Clark, "Wilcox's Alabama Brigade," 229.
368 "Our men began to drop": Andrews, "Gallantry" (MHI).
368 "The shattered line was retreating": *National Tribune*, November 6, 1890.
368 "ran in crowds": Henley Letter (MHI).
368 " 'No! Crowd them' ": Love, "Missisippi," 32.
368 " 'Colonel!' "/" 'Where are my men?' ": Craft, *History of the 141st Pennsylvania*, 122.
369 "sell out as dearly": Oates, "Battle on the Right," 178.
370 Chamberlain quotations: Chamberlain, "Through Blood," 55–56.
370 "The left took up the shout": Quoted in Desjardin, *Stand Firm*, 70.
371 "The rebel front line, amazed": Coan Papers.
371 "we disposed ourselves": Chamberlain, "Through Blood," 56.
371 "Brave Mississippians": Love, "Missisippi," 32.
372 "Benner's Hill was simply a hell inferno"/"clothes scorched": Hatton Memoir (LC).
372 "Taking the line lengthways": Nevins, ed., *Diary of Battle*, 243.
373 "that the exhausted condition"/"to cover the advance": *OR*, 27/2: 504.
375 "to clear the field": *OR*, 27/2: 518.
375 "It was discovered": Ladd, ed., *Bachelder Papers*, 2: 818.
376 "in an easy, quiet tone": Quoted in Swanberg, *Sickles*, 177.
376 "General Sickles . . . standing beneath a tree": Bigelow, *Peach Orchard*, 52.
376 "received no communication from Gen. Meade": *National Tribune*, July 22, 1886.
376 "became too hot"/"We bound his leg"/"repeatedly urged us": Ladd, ed., *Bachelder Papers*, 1: 240.
376 "tell General Birney"/" 'General Birney' ": Tremain, *Two Days*, 88–89.
377 "the danger of being shot down"/"checked his horse and waited": Youngblood, "Personal Observations," 287.
377 "Wofford coming in splendid style": *OR*, 27/2: 369.
378 "General Meade said": *CCW*, 460.
378 " 'Ah, war is a very bad thing' ": Agassiz, ed., *Meade's Headquarters*, 243.
379 "nobody to form a new line": Humphreys Papers (HSP).
379 "The crash of artillery": Cavada Diary (HSP).
380 "for two years the U.S. Regulars": Quoted in Kross, " 'To Die like Soldiers,' " 23.

380 "close, stubborn and deadly work": Haynes, *History of the 2nd New Hampshire*, 180.
380 "throwing myself forward": Quoted in Kross, " 'To Die like Soldiers,' " 50.
380 "Halt, you Yankee"/"Go to h—l": Hanifen, *History of Battery B, 1st New Jersey*, 76–77.
380 Alexander quotations: Gallagher, ed., *Fighting for the Confederacy*, 240.
381 "the sturdy regular blow," Longstreet, "Lee in Pennsylvania," 425.
382 "My instructions were to advance": *OR*, 27/2: 618.
382 "caught the roar of the cannon"/"men who had been playing cards": Johnson Letter (FNP).
382 "the sound of the shells": Ladd, ed., *Bachelder Papers*, 2: 1056.
382 "met at the crest": *OR*, 27/2: 631.
383 " 'Take your Brigade' ": Richardson Papers.
383 "was not surprised": Gibbon, *Personal Recollections*, 137.
384 "the 3d Corps had gone to pieces": Humphreys Papers (HSP).
384 "The enemy's advancing musketry shots": Ladd, ed., *Bachelder Papers*, 2: 1134.
384 "No friendly supports"/Bigelow-McGilvery exchange: Bigelow, *Peach Orchard*, 55–56.
386 "there seemed nothing left": Humphreys Papers (HSP).
386 "came forward in their usual magnificent style": *New York Herald*, July 4, 1863.
386 "men and horses were falling like hail": Quoted in Campbell, " 'We Saved the Line,' " 56.
387 "We fired with our guns": Deane, ed., *"My Dear Wife,"* 63.
388 "On we rushed with loud cries!": Fox, ed., *New York at Gettysburg*, 2:886.
388 "Gen. Barksdale was trying": Richardson Papers.
390 Humphreys quotations: Ladd, ed., *Bachelder Papers*, 1: 481.
391 " 'I am not in Birney's command' ": Quoted in Pfanz, *Second Day*, 407.
391 "I immediately ordered my men": *OR*, 27/2: 618.
392 "away part of his face and head": Simons, *Regimental History 125th New York*, 112–13.
392 "grape and canister were poured into our ranks": *OR*, 27/2: 618.
392 Hancock quotations: Quoted in Moe, *Last Full Measure*, 268.
392 "Men stumbled and fell": *St. Paul Pioneer*, August 9, 1863.
393 "Without support on either my right or left": *OR*, 27/2: 618.
393 Anderson-Mahone-Posey exchange with reporter: *Richmond Enquirer*, August 5–7, 1863.
395 "first duty of a subordinate": Bates Papers (PHMC).
395 "to occupy the whole of the intrenchments": *OR*, 27/1: 856.
396 "retired in some disorder": Fox, ed., *New York at Gettysburg*, 1: 664.
396 "Shells around us tore our bleeding ranks": *Philadelphia Weekly Times*, October 8, 1881.
396 "Wright's Brigade was driven into the Federal position": Andrews, *Condensed History* (GNP).
397 "Go on, boys, go on": Quoted in Sturtevant, *Pictorial History 13th Vermont*, 499.
397 "I have not the slightest doubt": *OR*, 27/2: 623–25.

400 "We held this point": *OR*, 27/1: 862.
400 "ditch filled with men firing down": "Memoirs of Benjamin Anderson Jones" (VHS).
400 "were attended with more loss than success": *OR*, 27/2: 513.
400 "reeled and staggered like a drunken man": Quoted in Pfanz, *Culp's Hill*, 217.
401 "This left my line very thin"/"complete surprise": Ladd, ed., *Bachelder Papers*, 2: 745–46.
401 "to advance upon Cemetery Hill": *OR*, 27/2: 556.
402 "at once there was the flash": *Maine at Gettysburg*, 95.
402 "To see grape and canister cut gaps": Kiefer, *History of the 153rd Regiment*, 219–20.
402 "the mixing up of the files": *OR*, 27/2: 532.
403 Gibbon quotations/Hancock orders: Gibbon, *Personal Recollections*, 138.
403 "were sitting down behind the stone wall": Quoted in Archer, "*The Hour*," 48.
403 "At that point": Ladd, ed., *Bachelder Papers*, 2: 746.
403 "I had no pistol": Quoted in Archer, "*The Hour*," 52.
404 "Major: Tell my father I died": Avery Papers (NCDAH).
404 "The men and officers appeared plucky": Ladd, ed., *Bachelder Papers*, 1: 295.
405 "behind which the Yankees were": *Richmond Whig*, July 23, 1863.
405 "Germans fought splendidly": Nevins, ed., *Diary of Battle*, 245.
407 "useless sacrifice of life": Early, "A Review," 280–81.
407 "convinced me that it would be": *OR*, 27/2: 556.
408 "a brief and patriotic speech": *Syracuse Standard*, July 9, 1863.
409 "it was soon so dark": Pierson, ed., "Diary," 37.
409 "Our infantry made a vigorous rush": *National Tribune*, December 12, 1909.
409 " 'Halt! Front face!' ": *National Tribune*, December 10, 1908.
409 "At Rickett's Battery": *National Tribune*, July 29, 1909.
409 "We gathered up the dead": Ladd, ed., *Bachelder Papers*, 2: 747.

(10:00 P.M.–MIDNIGHT)

410 "Boys, I am asked": Quoted in Desjardin, *Stand Firm*, 84.
411 "only sent one message": Fremantle, *Three Months*, 260.
412 Lee summaries: *OR*, 27/2: 320.
412 "Stuart's object was to gain position": McClellan, *I Rode with Jeb Stuart*, 337.
412 "commanding general looked well"/" 'It is all well' ": Hoke, *Great Invasion*, 355.
413 Sharpe and Hancock quotations: Quoted in Fishel, *Secret War*, 527–28.
413 "I shall remain in my present position": *OR*, 27/1: 72.
413 "I had no time": Meade, *Life and Letters*, 125.
414 "The Confederates maintained a clam-like silence": Skelly, *Boy's Experiences*, 17.
414 "We gain no information": Broadhead, *Diary of a Lady*, 14.
414 "I engaged in a little conversation": *Gettysburg Compiler*, June 1, 1898.

414 "They were laid in different parts"/Pierce-soldier exchange: Alleman, *At Gettysburg*, 58.

414 " 'Cap, you'd better be careful' "/" 'Why that's all right' ": Hollinger, *Some Personal Recollections*, 172.

415 Meade council: *OR*, 27/1: 73; *CCW*, 350.

417 "I saw that the men had something to eat": Ladd, ed., *Bachelder Papers*, 2: 1152.

417 " 'Now don't be frightened' ": Plank (Beard) Memoir (GNP).

417 "The wounded appeared to be everywhere": Monteiro, *Confederate Surgeon.* "busily at work probing for bullets"/"it requires a man with a steel nerve": Houghton Diary.

418 Welles incidents: Beale, ed., *Diary*, 354.

418 "He cannot take Richmond": Miers, ed., *Rebel War Clerk's Diary*, 235.

418 "we were halted by two Confederate soldiers": Skelly, *Boy's Experiences*, 17–18.

419 "I visited some portions of the line": *New York Times*, July 4, 1863.

419 "Every one is exhausted": *New York Herald*, July 4, 1863.

419 "stumbled over the field": Carpenter Letters (MHS).

419 "Flitting forms a few feet off": *Philadelphia Weekly Times*, October 8, 1881.

419 "gathered the dead": *National Tribune*, January 21, 1926.

419 "groans of the wounded": Clifton Diary (NCDHA).

419 " 'Thank God!' ": Duke, "Mississippians," 216.

NOCTURNE (JULY 2)

423 Haskell material: Byrne and Weaver, eds., *Haskell.*

424 Peel material: Winschel, ed., "Gettysburg Diary."

425 Dooley material: Durkin, ed., *John Dooley.*

CHAPTER FOURTEEN

(MIDNIGHT–SUNRISE)

427 Alexander quotations: Gallagher, ed., *Fighting for the Confederacy*, 243–44.

428 Lee orders: *OR*, 27/2: 320.

428 Ewell quotations: *OR*, 27/2: 447.

428 "one of his subordinate officers": *CCW*, 416–17.

428 "During the night . . . we could hear": Zable Papers.

428 "for it was always his policy": *Richmond Times Dispatch*, October 4, 1908.

429 "a silence around us now": *Star and Sentinel*, July 2, 1913.

429 "marveled that a man should be so careless"/"if I should confiscate": *Gettysburg Compiler*, 1903.

429 "a sound sleep as boys do": Skelly, *Boy's Experiences*, 18.

429 "the church yard was strewn": McCurdy, *Gettysburg*, 22.

429 "courteous, considerate Georgians": Jacobs, "How an Eye-witness," n.p.

429 "girdled for the conflict"/"Oh, make it, thou Almighty": *Star and Sentinel*, July 2, 1913.

429 "The usual jests and hilarity were indulged in": Wiley, ed., *Reminiscences*, 43–48.

430 "I must confess that the General's face": Durkin, ed., *John Dooley*, 101.

430 Lee's orders: *OR*, 27/2: 320.

430 "I sent to our extreme right": Longstreet, "Lee's Invasion," 342.

431 Williams quotations/exchange with Slocum: Quaife, ed., *From the Cannon's Mouth*, 230.

431 Alexander quotations: Gallagher, ed., *Fighting for the Confederacy*, 244–45.

432 Coffin quotations: Coffin, *Boys of '61*, 309.

(SUNRISE–1:07 P.M.)

434 "the order to open fire"/"woods in front and rear": Ladd, ed., *Bachelder Papers*, 1: 220.

434 "poured shot & shell into": Nichol Diary (MHI).

434 "and the balls could be heard": *Philadelphia Record*, July 8, 1900.

436 "General Lee and his staff": Cavada, *Libby Life*, 2.

436 Longstreet-Lee exchange: *OR*, 27/2: 320, 359; Longstreet, "Lee in Pennsylvania," 429; idem, *From Manassas*, 386; idem, "Lee's Invasion," 342.

437 "fierce cannonading": Broadhead, *Diary of a Lady*, 15.

437 "May I never again": *Star and Sentinel*, July 2, 1913.

437 "My orders were to fire incessantly": Blackford Memoir (MHI).

437 "We could only hear the battle": Cooke, *Wearing of the Gray*, 257.

438 "would invite an attack upon our rear": Kempster, "The Cavalry," 416.

438 "I think it was the hardest battle": Coffman Letter (MHI).

438 "ball entering his right side"/"was conscious of his situation": Jessup, ed., *Painful News*, 148.

438 "protected behind stones logs trees &c": Ladd, ed., *Bachelder Papers*, 2: 1248.

439 "There came little puffs of smoke": Douglas, *I Rode with Stonewall*, 241.

439 Mudge quotations: Quint, *Record of the 2nd Massachusetts*, 180.

440 "We told the wounded men": Duffy Diary (VHS).

441 Conference (Lee-Longstreet-Hill): Longstreet, *From Manassas*, 288; idem, "Lee in Pennsylvania," 429; (aides/staff present): *Atlanta Journal*, July 13, 1901; Walter H. Taylor, *Four Years*, 103–4; Maurice, ed., *Aide-de-Camp of Lee*, 237–39.

442 "direction of the commanding general": *OR*, 27/2: 351.

443 "to the crest of a hill": *Waco Daily Times-Herald*, n.d.

443 " 'Come down!' "/"what looked like a whole brigade": *Final Report*, 111–12.

444 "The brigade moved forward in fine style": *OR*, 27/2: 593.

444 "We lay behind our solid breastworks": *National Tribune*, June 9, 1897.

444 "This is the first time that our Regiment": *Portage County Newspaper*, July 15, 1863.

444 "from information received": *OR*, 51/1: 1068.

444 "We had a great fight yesterday": Meade, *Life and Letters*, 103.

446 Alexander quotations: Gallagher, ed., *Fighting for the Confederacy*, 245–46.

447 "strongly disapproved of making the assault": McKim, "Steuart's Brigade," 297.

447 "it was nothing less than murder": Goldsborough, *Maryland Line*, 106.

447 "Our loss was frightful": Thomas, "Maryland Confederate Monument," 444–46.

447 "It was truly awful how fast": Leon, *Diary of a Tar Heel,* 36–37.

447 "seen in all my fighting as bloody": Funk Letters (FNP).

448 "as the only Christian minded being": Rothermel Papers (PHMC).

449 "enemy were too strongly intrenched": *OR,* 27/2: 504.

449 " 'My poor boys!' ": Goldsborough, *Maryland Line,* 109.

450 Pierce quotations: Alleman, *At Gettysburg,* 64.

451 "dressed to the right": Young, "Pettigrew's Brigade," 124.

451 "I would not give 25 cents": Loehr, "First Virginia Infantry," 33, 40.

451 "It was rumored that this division": Walker, "Survivor of Pickett's Division."

451 "So frivolous men can be": Durkin, ed., *John Dooley,* 102.

452 Postles quotations: Beyer and Keydel, eds., *Deeds of Valor,* 228–29.

452 "The great majority of the batteries": Alexander, "Confederate Artillery Service," 104.

453 "I never saw so much blood fly": Gallagher, ed., *Fighting for the Confederacy,* 253.

453 "distributed ourselves to the best advantage": Winschel, ed., "Gettysburg Diary," 104.

454 "Soon we are ordered to ascend": Durkin, ed., *John Dooley,* 102.

454 Haskell quotations: Byrne and Weaver, eds., *Haskell,* 139–47.

455 McClellan quotations: McClellan, *I Rode with Jeb Stuart,* 338.

456 "large columns of the enemy's cavalry": *OR,* 27/1: 956.

456 "a number of random shots": McClellan, *I Rode with Jeb Stuart,* 338.

456 Custer-Gregg exchange: Gregg, "Second Cavalry Division," 124.

457 "the singing of a bird": *New York Times,* July 6, 1863.

457 "Meade was receiving reports": Smart, ed., *Radical View,* 52.

457 "Aid[e]s were coming and going": Coffin, *Boys of '61,* 313.

457 "flock of pigeons"/"the sky above": *New York World,* July 8, 1863.

457 "appeared in excellent spirits" "entirely too strong to attack in front": Ladd, ed., *Bachelder Papers,* 1: 518.

458 "Our whole front for two miles": Hunt, "Third Day," 371–72.

458 "I said to him what was plain to my mind"/"saying, in substance": Mahone, "Gen. Mahone at Gettysburg."

458 Longstreet quotations: Longstreet, *From Manassas,* 390; idem, "Lee in Pennsylvania," 430; idem, "Lee's Invasion," 343.

459 "It was called a charge": Longstreet, *From Manassas,* 390.

460 "line beyond that road would soon become so weak": Law, "Struggle," 327.

460 Alexander quotations: Alexander, "Great Charge," 362; Gallagher, ed., *Fighting for the Confederacy,* 254–55; Edward P. Alexander, *Military Memoirs,* 421.

460 "A careful examination was made of the ground": OR, 27/2, 320.

461 "With the enemy, there was advantage of elevation": OR, 27/2, 352.

461 "I still desired to save my men"/message to Alexander: Longstreet, "Lee in Pennsylvania," 430.

462 Alexander quotations/exchange with Wright/note to Longstreet: Gallagher, ed., *Fighting for the Confederacy,* 255; Alexander, *Military Memoirs,* 421–22.

462 "The tension on our troops had become great": Crocker, *Gettysburg:* Pickett's Charge, 37.

462 "I rode once or twice": Longstreet, "Lee's Invasion," 343.

463 "Colonel, Let the batteries open": Longstreet, *From Manassas to Appomattox,* 390.

463 Harrison quotations: Walter Harrison, *Pickett's Men,* 91–107.

463 "in quick succession": *OR,* 27/2: 434; Wise, *Long Arm,* 677.

463 "immediately followed by all the battalions": OR, 27/2, 434.

(1:07 P.M.–2:40 P.M.)

464 "at the same instant, along the whole line": Winschel, ed., "Gettysburg Diary," 104.

464 "Never will I forget those scenes and sounds": Durkin, ed., *John Dooley,* 103.

464 "The wildest confusion for a few minutes obtained": Byrne and Weaver, eds., *Haskell,* 148.

464 "as if the heavens and earth were crashing": Broadhead, *Diary of a Lady,* 15.

464 "vibrations could be felt": McCreary, "Gettysburg."

465 "the most terrific cannonading": McCurdy, *Gettysburg,* 23.

465 "awful thunder": Rupp Letter (ACHS).

465 "It was possible to distinguish the fire": Jacobs, "How an Eye-Witness."

465 "crush our batteries": Quoted in Kross, "Pickett's Charge," 21.

465 "raked the whole line": Crumb, ed., *Eleventh Corps Artillery,* 72.

465 "fire that we were under": *Buffalo Evening News,* May 29, 1894.

466 "making discordant music": *National Tribune,* September 2, 1886.

466 "waves"/"like gusts of wind": *Buffalo Evening News,* May 29, 1894.

466 "caused blood to flow": Muffley, ed., *Story of Our Regiment,* 439.

466 "their unsurpassed chivalry": Quoted in Kross, "Pickett's Charge," 40.

466 "whole [enemy] line": Gallagher, ed., *Fighting for the Confederacy,* 257.

466 "went high over our gun"/"coolness of the officers and men": Coxe, "Battle," 435.

467 "would look at the cannon around us": Rollins, ed., *Pickett's Charge!,* 177.

467 "shell, [canister] and solid shot": *Richmond Enquirer,* July 15, 1863.

467 "the uproar was terrific": Marye, "First Gun," 33.

467 "followed by his staff and his courier": "Gen. James Dearing," 215.

467 "out in front with his flag waving defiance": Durkin, ed., *John Dooley,* 104.

467 "special attention . . . they were then receiving": "Gen. James Dearing," 216.

467 "that I must wait longer": Gallagher, ed., *Fighting for the Confederacy,* 258.

468 "those fellows on the left have the range": Smart, ed., *Radical View,* 53.

468 "instantly followed by another and another": *New York Times,* July 6, 1863.

468 "The atmosphere was thick with shot and shell": *New York World,* July 7, 1863.

468 "torn to pieces . . . and died": *New York Times,* July 6, 1863.

468 "cries that ran the diapason": Smart, ed., *Radical View,* 54.

468 "outbuildings, fences and fruit trees": Wafer Diary.

469 "from the effects of the chloroform": Maust, "Union Second Corps Hospital."

469 "the most astonishing thing": Benedict, *Vermont at Gettysburg,* 12–13.

469 "pitiless storm of shot and shell": Aldrich, *History of Battery A,* 211.

469 "The shot and shell seemed to be tearing": *Buffalo Evening News*, May 29, 1894.

470 Erasmus Williams story: Williams Letter (UVA).

470 "ever and anon some companion would raise": Durkin, ed., *John Dooley*, 103.

470 "In the hot[t]est of the cannonading": Winschel, ed., "Gettysburg Diary," 105.

471 "had that confident look": Newhall, "Address," 21.

471 "took his Regiments and went back": Black, *Crumbling Defenses*, 42.

471 Alexander quotations/messages to Pickett: Gallagher, ed., *Fighting for the Confederacy*, 258; Alexander, *Military Memoirs*, 423.

473 Longstreet-Picket quotations: Longstreet, *From Manassas*, 392; idem, "Lee in Pennsylvania," 431; Sorrel, *Recollections*, 162; Gallagher, ed., *Fighting for the Confederacy*, 260–61; Inman, *Soldier*, 60.

474 "It is yelling, shooting, swearing": *National Tribune*, May 27, 1886.

474 Longstreet-Alexander quotations: Longstreet, "Lee in Pennsylvania, 420–31;" Gallagher, ed., *Fighting for the Confederacy*, 261; Alexander, *Military Memoirs*, 424.

(2:40 P.M.–2:55 P.M.)

476 "momentary [lull], of men resuming their places": Winschel, ed., "Gettysburg Diary," 105.

476 "I tell you there is no romance": Durkin, ed., *John Dooley*, 104–5.

476 "rode along the long lines": Blackford Letter (UVA).

476 " 'I have no orders to give you' ": Berkeley, "Rode with Pickett," 175.

477 Haskell quotations: Byrne and Weaver, eds., *Haskell*, 157.

478 "Woodruff had his guns": Rollins, ed., *Pickett's Charge!*, 291.

478 "awful, rushing sound": Child, "From Fredericksburg," 183.

478 "Good-by boys": *Buffalo Evening News*, May 29, 1894.

478 Cushing-Webb exchange: Brown, *Cushing*, 241.

478 "came so thick and fast"/" 'Glory to God!' ": Rhodes, ed., *History*, 209–10.

480 "entire strangers to me"/"no gun should be fired": Quoted in Wert, *Gettysburg Day Three*, 128.

480 " 'Many of these poor boys' "/" 'The attack must succeed' ": Swallow, "The Third Day," 564–65.

480 " 'We could not look for anything from Pickett' ": Ladd, ed., *Bachelder Papers*, 2: 985.

481 "I received orders to hold my division": *OR*, 27/2: 614–15.

481 "There was nothing 'foolish' in Pickett's attack": Allen, "Letter," 79.

481 "dense volume of smoke": McCurdy, *Gettysburg*, 23.

481 " 'Quick!' ": Jacobs, "How an Eye-Witness."

482 "I never have known": Ladd, ed., *Bachelder Papers*, 1: 522.

483 " 'Now, Colonel, for the honor' ": Cureton Letter (SHC).

(2:55 P.M.–3:15 P.M.)

484 "Many of us had friends in this command": Marye, "First Gun," 33.

484 "raised their hats": Walker, "The Charge" (LVA).

484 "wishing him good luck": Alexander, *Military Memoirs,* 261.

484 " 'Run old hare' ": Dawson, *Reminiscences,* 96.

484 "Regiment after Regiment": Byrne and Weaver, eds., *Haskell,* 158.

484 "Longstreet & A. P. Hill are advancing": Daniel Memoir (VHS).

485 "We were a long ways behind": Quoted in Kross, "Pickett's Charge," 41.

485 " 'For God's sake, wait' ": *ORS,* 5: 310.

485 Alexander quotations: Gallagher, ed., *Fighting for the Confederacy,* 249–50, 262.

486 "The Confederate approach was magnificent"/"They had unfortunately exhausted": Hunt, "Third Day," 374–75.

486 "Each solid shot or unexploded shell": *Philadelphia Weekly Times,* May 10, 1879.

487 "gaps we made [in the Confederate lines]": Dow Letter (GNP).

487 "not a gun was fired at us": *OR,* 27/2: 651.

487 "not striking the line often": Quoted in Long, "Over the Wall," 70.

487 "The enemy's big guns": *Richmond Times Dispatch,* September 31, 1913.

487 "round-shot bounding along": *National Tribune,* December 31, 1891.

487 "half-way between our position"/"The enemy's batteries soon opened": *Richmond Times Dispatch,* May 21, 1916.

488 "They were at once enveloped": Sawyer, *Military History,* 131.

488 "I feel no shame in recording": Dunaway, *Reminiscences,* 93.

488 "We could see it was no use": O'Sullivan, *55th Virginia,* 55.

488 "remained out in that field": Christian Letter (UVA).

488 "could be distinctly seen": Crumb, *Eleventh Corps Artillery,* 77.

488 "Many times a single percussion shell": Rittenhouse, "Battle," 43.

489 "Their lines and columns staggered": Todd Diary (MHI).

489 "All was orderly and still": Byrne and Weaver, eds., *Haskell,* 158–59.

489 "Onward—steady": Durkin, ed., *John Dooley,* 105.

490 "perfect tempest of maddened shells": Winschel, ed., "Gettysburg Diary," 105.

491 "taken every precaution to insure": Clark, ed., *Histories,* 5: 124.

491 Fremantle quotations: Fremantle, *Three Months,* 264–65.

492 "more may have been required of them": *OR,* 27/2: 309.

493 " 'Why, you craven fool' ": Storrs, *20th Connecticut,* 104–5.

(3:15 P.M.–3:40 P.M.)

494 "We opened on them"/"All that came as far": Mead Letter (GNP).

494 "any further effort to carry the position": *OR,* 27/2: 650–51.

494 "The state of my feelings": Winschel, ed., "Gettysburg Diary," 106.

495 Bright encounter with stragglers/Lee-Fremantle exchange: Bright, "Pickett's Charge," 264–65.

496 "above all despised a coward": Ladd, ed., *Bachelder Papers,* 3: 1414.

497 "which amid the rattle of musketry/Go on": Ibid., 1: 519.

497 "The smoke was dense": *ORS,* 5: 411.

497 "How like hail upon a roof": Turney, "First Tennessee," 535–37.

497 " 'Go on, it will not last' ": Ladd, ed., *Bachelder Papers,* 1: 519.

497 " 'Steady men! Close up!' ": Irvine, "Brig. Gen. Richard B. Garnett," 391.

497 " 'We do not know' ": Letter (Virginia Military Institute).

497 O'Kane remarks: Ladd, ed., *Bachelder Papers*, 3: 1410.

497 "soon as the top of the fence": Swallow, "The Third Day," 567.

498 "we opened fire on them": *ORS*, 5: 168.

498 " 'That's excellent' "/"that artillery officer has his legs knocked from under him": Ladd, ed., *Bachelder Papers*, 3: 1410.

499 "The slaughter was terrible": Ibid., 3: 1403.

499 "as thick the sound as when a summer hailstorm": Byrne and Weaver, eds., *Haskell*, 161.

499 " 'get in God Damn quick' ": Quoted in Wert, *Gettysburg: Day Three*, 229.

500 Hancock-Stannard exchange/"the most striking man I ever saw"/Hancock wounding: Stannard Letter (Baseball); Benedict, *Army Life*, 182–83.

501 " 'I know; I know' ": Bright, "Pickett's Charge," 265.

501 "My brigade . . . then moved forward": *OR*, 27/2: 620.

501 "in accordance with previous orders": *OR*, 27/2: 632.

501 "one could hear frequent expressions": Clark, "Wilcox's Alabama Brigade," 230–31.

501 Kemper-Armistead exchange: Clement, ed., *History of Pittsylvania*, 248; Martin, "Armistead," 186.

501 " 'Did you ever see' ": Martin and Smith, "Battle," 188.

502 " 'Don't you see' ": *ORS*, 5: 312–13.

502 " 'There are the guns, boys' ": Quoted in George R. Stewart, *Pickett's Charge*, 205.

502 "excruciatingly painful": Quoted in Harrison and Busey, *Nothing but Glory*, 65–66.

502 Dooley quotations: Durkin, ed., *John Dooley*, 107.

502 "When within 100 yards of our line": *OR*, 27/1: 454.

502 "As soon as they got within range": Haynes Letters (NYSL).

502 "grape, canister, minnie, buck and ball": Ladd, ed., *Bachelder Papers*, 3: 1398.

503 "from their canteens": Page, *History of the 14th Connecticut*, 151.

503 "I doubt whether anywhere": Toombs, *New Jersey Troops*, 284–304.

503 "angel of death alone can produce": *OR*, 27/1: 454.

503 "shrieks of the wounded": Page, *History of the 14th Connecticut*, 151.

503 "Our loss in this vicinity was fearful": *Raleigh Observer*, October 10, 1877.

504 " 'Why the d——l don't you fire' ": Aldrich, *History of Battery A, First Rhode Island Light Artillery*, 216.

504 " 'Come over on this side of the Lord!' ": Gragg, *Covered with Glory*, 200.

504 " 'My God General' "/"Seeing it was useless": *Raleigh Observer*, October 10, 1877.

504 "without orders, the brigade retreated": *OR*, 27/2, 672.

504 " 'It's all over!' ": Ladd, ed., *Bachelder Papers*, 2: 933–34.

505 " 'General, I am sorry' ": Quoted in Stewart, *Pickett's Charge*, 256.

505 Meade-gunner exchange: Ladd, ed., *Bachelder Papers*, 1: 389–90.

505 "Just as the General turned": Irvine, "Brig. Gen. Richard B. Garnett," 391.

506 " 'See'em!' ": Quoted in Stewart, *Pickett's Charge*, 222–23.

506 " 'John, what a beautiful line' ": Walker, ed., *Memorial*, 407.

506 "awful the way the men dropped": *Philadelphia Weekly Press*, July 4, 1887.

506 Armistead-Martin exchange/Armistead's rallying cry: Harrison and Busey, *Nothing but Glory*, 91.

507 "damned red flags"/" 'See the gray-backs run!' ": Byrne and Weaver, eds., *Haskell*, 162–67.

508 "as though our regiment": Ladd, ed., *Bachelder Papers*, 3: 1411.

508 "When the gallant Virginians": Ibid., 3:1683.

(3:40 P.M.–MIDNIGHT)

509 "the sounds of the contest": Gibbon, *Personal Recollections*, 153.

509 "The final moment has come": Crocker, *Pickett's Charge*, 37–44.

510 Weir quotations: Ladd, ed., *Bachelder Papers*, 2: 1152–53; Weir Notes (GNP).

510 " 'Oh! Colonel' ": Mayo, "Pickett's Charge," 335.

510 "I was about to move forward": *OR*, 27/2: 614–15.

510 "that the attack had already failed": *OR*, 27/2, 556–57.

511 "Longstreet & Hill have been driven": Daniel Memoir (VHS).

511 "holding up their handkerchiefs": Ladd, ed., *Bachelder Papers*, 3: 1364.

511 "As soon as the smoke lifted": Wright, "Story" (MHS).

511 "It was a time of indescribable enthusiasm": Scott, "Pickett's Charge," 14.

511 " 'Stop firing, you —— fools' ": *Minneapolis Journal*, June 30, 1897.

511 "We could have picked off": *National Tribune*, February 18, 1909.

512 "It was all I could do": *Minneapolis Journal*, June 30, 1897.

512 "There were literally acres of dead": Scott, "Pickett's Charge," 14.

512 Bingham-Armistead exchange: Ladd, ed., *Bachelder Papers*, 1: 352.

512 Meade-Haskell exchange: Byrne and Weaver, eds., *Haskell*, 169–76.

513 " 'troops under my command' "/" 'Say to General Hancock' ": Rothermel Papers (PHMC).

513 "a storm of shot and shell": Clark, "Wilcox's Alabama Brigade," 230–31.

513 "weary and wasted forces": *Advertiser and Register*, July 27, 1863.

513 "men were falling all around me": Wentworth Diary (GNP).

515 "In a very few minutes these guns": Alexander, *Military Memoirs*, 429.

515 "seeing none of the troops": *OR*, 27/2: 620.

515 "Owing to the noise": *OR*, 27/2: 632.

515 "with sabers drawn and glistening": Brooke-Rawle, "Gregg's Cavalry," 163.

516 Stuart report: *OR*, 27/2: 699.

516 "His was to do": Gregg, "Second Cavalry Division," 126.

518 "slightest chance"/" 'General Farnsworth, well' ": Quoted in Kross, "Farnsworth's Charge," 47.

518 "too awful to think of": Quoted in Longacre, *Cavalry*, 242.

519 " 'in hot water' "/"warmly congratulated me": Law, "Struggle," 328–30.

520 "As soon as the assault [against Cemetery Ridge]": *CCW*, 333.

520 "perfectly sublime": Fremantle, *Three Months*, 267.

520 "General Lee, who was forming": *ORS*, 5: 315.

520 "ineffably grand": *Richmond Times Dispatch*, May 6, 1906.

520 " 'This has been a sad day' ": Fremantle, *Three Months*, 268.

520 "I sent my staff officers": Longstreet, "Lee in Pennsylvania," 431.

520 " 'General, I am ruined' ": Youngblood, "Personal Observations," 317.

520 "pointed his sword up to the skies": Cockrell and Ballerd, eds., *Mississippi Rebel*, 198.

521 " 'General Lee, I have no division now' "/" 'Come, General Pickett' ": Quoted in Freeman, *R. E. Lee,* 129.

521 "remained with me for a long time": Longstreet, "Lee's Invasion," 366.

521 "retire to your position of yesterday": McLaws, "Gettysburg," 87.

521 "to withdraw the division": Law, "Struggle," 330.

522 "to the position from which the attack began": Alexander, *Military Memoirs,* 426.

522 "seated on camp-stools with a map": Imboden, "Confederate Retreat," 420.

522 "The dead were everywhere thickly strewn": Coffin, *Boys of '61,* 319.

522 "calm as ever": Smart, ed., *Radical View,* 62.

522 "stooping, weary, his slouched hat": Coffin, *Boys of '61,* 320.

522 Meade to Halleck: *OR,* 27/1: 75.

523 Welles quotations: Beale, ed., *Diary,* 356–57.

523 "we had a decided success": *ORS,* 5: 37.

524 Jones quotations: Miers, ed., *Rebel War Clerk's Diary,* 235.

524 "a guard of Stragglers": Sparks, ed., *Inside Lincoln's Army,* 267.

524 "looked sorry": Beaudry, ed., *War Journal,* 50.

524 "splendid cavalry"/"to charge you": Winschel, ed., "Gettysburg Diary," 106.

524 Patrick-POW exchange: Timberlake Papers (VHS).

CHAPTER FIFTEEN

530 Imboden-Lee exchange: Imboden, "Confederate Retreat," 508–10.

531 McAllister quotations: *Philadelphia Inquirer,* June 29, 1938.

532 "there was movement": Fahnestock, "Recollections" (ACHS).

532 "were moving in the same direction": Locke, *Story of a Regiment,* 239.

532 "telling [their men] to get up": Skelly, *Boy's Experiences,* 19.

532 "like some great current": Jacobs, "How an Eye-Witness."

532 "nothing of special note": *Gettysburg Compiler,* 1903.

532 "In every house we entered": *National Tribune,* March 22, 1906.

532 "I looked up the street": Broadhead, *Diary of a Lady,* 16.

532 "stiff and cramped like": Quoted in Bennett, *Days of "Uncertainty and Dread,"* 70.

532 "This morning the enemy has withdrawn": *OR,* 27/1: 78.

533 "moved cautiously": Morhous, *Reminiscences of the 123rd New York,* 52.

533 "Ye gods!": Skelly, *Boy's Experiences,* 19.

533 "We could see the leaves": Jacobs, "How an Eye-Witness."

533 "Found the Enemy in force": Haas Diary (MHI).

534 Meade to Halleck: *OR,* 27/1:78.

534 "Skirmishing today": Mosely Diary (GNP).

534 "have been lying on the field": Leon, *Diary of a Tar Heel,* 37.

534 "There is no systematic work": Dickert, *History of Kershaw's Brigade,* 248–49.

534 "I saw a deep ditch": *National Tribune,* December 7, 1899.

534 "Each regiment selects a suitable place": Galwey, *Valiant Hours,* 121.

535 "The pen cannot perform its duties": *Hunterdon Republican,* July 20, 1863.

535 "as thick as we ever saw pumpkins": Metcalf "Recollection" (MHI).

535 "You can imagine what the field was like": Bolton, "With General Lee's," 299.
535 "acres of muskets": *Report of the Ninth.*
535 "Longstreet sent back word": Fremantle, *Three Months,* 272–73.
536 "Canvas was no protection": Imboden, "Confederate Retreat," 423.
536 Lee report: *OR,* 27/2: 298.
536 "dictating orders and receiving dispatches": Smart, ed., *Radical View,* 62–63.
537 "not to make any present move": Meade Jr., *With Meade,* 157–60.
537 "play their old game": Meade, *Life and Letters,* 125.
537 "under open skies": Quoted in Coco, *Vast Sea,* 136.
537 "performing necessary operations": Silver, ed., *Confederate Soldier,* 125.
537 "those fine young fellows": Harwell, ed., *Cities and Camps,* 64.
538 "Lost supplies can be replenished": Letterman, *Medical Recollections,* 156.
538 "A heavy rain set in": Schurz, *Reminiscences,* 39.
538 "a field of Blood": Letterman, *Medical Recollections,* 156.
538 Whitman quotations: Lowenfels, ed., *Walt Whitman's Civil War,* 70.
539 "a National Salute": Rhodes, ed., *All for the Union,* 117.
539 "Today is Independence Day": Evans Letters (MHI).
539 "4th of July, while you were celebrating": McLean Letters (NYSL).
539 "Today is supposed to be a holiday": *Daily Intelligencer.*
539 "A heavy rain was falling": Blackford Memoir (MHI).
539 "We celebrated the Nation's birthday": Rollins Diary (SHSWI).
539 "with heavy hearts"/"Could it mean": Wallber, "From Gettysburg," 195.
540 Fremantle quotations: Fremantle, *Three Months,* 272–76.
541 "to ascertain what the intention": *OR,* 27/1, 78.
541 "showed no signs of worry": Wallber, "From Gettysburg," 196.
541 "appears dignified and self-assured": Rollins Diary (SHSWI).
541 " 'the other two corps' "/" 'What reason have you' ": Quoted in Freeman, *R. E. Lee,* 136.
541 "engaged in earnest conversation": Harwell, ed., *Cities and Camps,* 65.
542 " 'I thought my men were invincible' ": Quoted in Freeman, *R. E. Lee,* 136.
542 "dreadfully long day": Broadhead, *Diary of a Lady,* 16.
542 Neighbor's story: *Gettysburg Compiler,* July 4, 1906.

CHAPTER SIXTEEN

543 Lee material: *OR,* 27/2: 309; Dowdey and Manarin, eds., *Wartime Papers,* 589–90.
545 Davis reply: *OR,* 29/2: 640.
546 Meade material: *CCW,* 334–47, 519; Basler, ed., *Collected Works,* 6: 327–28; Williams, *Lincoln and His Generals,* 270–71.

CHAPTER SEVENTEEN

550 "You are aware the armies met": Figgat Letter (MHI).
550 "The army of Northern Virginia": "To Pennsylvania and Back."
550 "We have voluntarily left": Shaffner Papers (NCDHA).

550 "The people where we['ve] been": Pryor, "Letters."

550 "There was a feeling": Ladd, ed., *Bachelder Papers*, 3: 1775.

550 "We came here with the best army": Neill Letters (MHI).

551 "Our army is badly whipped": Taylor, ed., *Cry Is War*, 148.

551 "I was sorry when it was begun": Quoted in Henderson, *12th Virginia Infantry*, 57.

551 "Our noble men are cheerful"/"The army has returned to Virginia": Fitzhugh Lee, *General Lee*, 294.

551 " 'Our loss was heavy' ": Heth, "Letter to Jones," 154–55.

552 "We must now prepare": Dowdey and Manarin, eds., *Wartime Papers*, 560–61.

552 Lincoln at Gettysburg: Starr, *Reporting*, 189–90; Wills, *Lincoln at Gettysburg*, 191–203.

553 "the stench was so bad": McCreary, "Gettysburg," 253.

554 "It is all the war *I* ever want to see": Aughinbaugh, *Personal Experiences*, 14.

554 "He seemed very tall and gaunt": McCreary, "Gettysburg," 253.

554 "He spoke in a quiet, forcible and earnest manner": Skelly, *Boy's Experiences*, 25–27.

BIBLIOGRAPHY

MANUSCRIPTS

ADAMS COUNTY HISTORICAL SOCIETY
Agnes Barr, "Account of the Battle of Gettysburg"
Lydia Catherine Ziegler Clare, "A Gettysburg Girl's Story of the Great Battle"
Gates D. Fahnestock, "Recollections of the Battle of Gettysburg"
John Rupp Letter
Leander H. Warren, "Recollections of the Battle of Gettysburg"

ALABAMA DEPARTMENT OF ARCHIVES AND HISTORY
Robert T. Coles, "History of the 4th Regiment Alabama Volunteer Infantry"

BASEBALL HALL OF FAME
Abner Doubleday Papers (George Stannard Letter)

BOWDOIN COLLEGE: HAWTHORNE-LONGFELLOW LIBRARY SPECIAL COLLECTIONS
Elisha Coan Papers
O. O. Howard Collection (Daniel Hall Letter)

CHICAGO HISTORICAL SOCIETY
W. S. Church Papers

COLUMBIA UNIVERSITY LIBRARY
S. H. Gay Collection

CONFEDERATE RESEARCH CENTER
(*HILL JUNIOR COLLEGE, HILLSBORO, TEXAS*)
Rufus K. Felder Letters
A. C. Sims Recollections

DOUGLAS LIBRARY: QUEEN'S UNIVERSITY AT KINGSTON (CANADA)

Francis M. Wafer Diary

DUKE UNIVERSITY

(Perkins Library Manuscript and Special Collections)
Hodnett Family Collection

EMORY UNIVERSITY

John A. Everett Collection

FREDERICKSBURG/SPOTSYLVANIA NATIONAL MILITARY PARK

Alfred Melancthon Apted Diary
M. G. Bass Letter
George D. Buswell Diary
Henry L. Figures Letters
J. H. S. Funk Letters
Henry Herbert Harris Diary
James Barbour Johnson Letter
A. P. Morrison Letters
James William Thomas Diary

GETTYSBURG COLLEGE

F. M. Stoke Letters

GETTYSBURG NATIONAL MILITARY PARK

Charles M. Andrews, *Condensed History of the Campaigns of the Third Regiment of Georgia Volunteer Infantry, Confederate States of America* (mss., n.p., n.d.)
Harriet Bayly, "Mrs. Joseph Bayly's Story of the Battle"
Elizabeth Plank Beard Memoir
Charles W. Belknap Diary
Edwin Dow Letter
William B. Floyd Papers
    William B. Taylor Letters
"First Shot" (anonymous manuscript)
William T. Fluker, "A Graphic Account of the Battle of Little Round Top Hill at Gettysburg"
Thomas A. Littlejohn, "Recollections of a Confederate Soldier"
Stephen E. Martin Diary
Christopher Meade Letter
Josiah (John) Mosley Diary
Alex M. Neill Letters
Gulian Weir, Notes on Gettysburg
James Wentworth Diary (article)

HARPER'S FERRY NATIONAL PARK

Daniel H. Sheetz Letters

HISTORICAL SOCIETY OF PENNSYLVANIA

Adolfo Fernandez-Cavada Diary
Gettysburg Letterbook (William H. Paine Letter)
Andrew Humphreys Papers
Letter to John Watts DePeyster

INDIANA STATE LIBRARY

George Edward Finney Diary
Henry C. Marsh Papers
Orr Family Papers

THE LIBRARY OF CONGRESS, MANUSCRIPTS DIVISION

Theodore A. Dodge Papers
Jubal A. Early Papers
Douglas Southall Freeman Papers
    Samuel R. Johnston Letters
Samuel J. B. V. Gilpin Diary
George W. Hall Diary
John William Ford Hatton Memoir
Jedediah Hotchkiss Papers
Hotchkiss-McCullough Manuscripts
    Samuel Thomas McCullough Diary
James William Latta Diary
Rufus Meade Diary
Pickett-Christiancy Papers
    H. C. Christiancy Diary and Letters
James M. Cline Letter
Ward Family Papers
    Jas. H. Wilkes Letters
Edwin D. Wentworth Letters
Cadmus M. Wilcox Papers

LIBRARY OF MEMPHIS STATE UNIVERSITY

Leander G. Woollard, "Journals of Events and Incidents as They Came to the Observation of the 'Senatobia Invincibles"

THE LIBRARY OF VIRGINIA (FORMERLY THE STATE LIBRARY OF VIRGINIA)

John Samuel Apperson Diary
William R. Carter Letters
John O. Donohoe Diary
James H. Walker, "The Charge of Pickett's Division by a Participant"

LOUISIANA STATE UNIVERSITY

Louisiana and Lower Mississippi Valley Collection
    J. Warren Jackson Letters

MASSACHUSETTS HISTORICAL SOCIETY

Francis C. Barlow Papers

MINNESOTA HISTORICAL SOCIETY

Newell Burch Diary
Alfred P. Carpenter Letters
James A. Wright, "Story of Company F"

MUSEUM OF THE CONFEDERACY, ELEANOR S. BROCKENBROUGH LIBRARY

Thaddeus Fitzhugh Memoir
Robert Pooler Myers, "Campaign from Culpeper C.H. Va. to Gettysburg, Pennsylvania"
William H. Routt Papers

NEW-YORK HISTORICAL SOCIETY

Henry Lane Kendrick Papers

NEW YORK STATE LIBRARY

Harriette Calkins Papers
　　James M. Jones Diary
Calvin A. Haynes Letters
William Clark McLean Letters and Diary
Gouverneur K. Warren Letters

NORTH CAROLINA DEPARTMENT OF ARCHIVES AND HISTORY

Isaac Erwin Avery Papers
W. H. S. Burgwyn Papers
J. B. Clifton Diary
John Francis Shaffner Diary and Papers
Francis D. Winston Papers

ONTARIO COUNTY (NEW YORK) HISTORICAL SOCIETY

Charles A. Richardson Papers

PENNSYLVANIA HISTORICAL AND MUSEUM COMMISSION

Samuel Penniman Bates Papers
Peter F. Rothermel Papers
Charles H. Veil, Letter to D. McConaughy

PRINCETON UNIVERSITY LIBRARY

Charles W. Reed Letters

SOUTHERN HISTORICAL COLLECTION
(UNIVERSITY OF NORTH CAROLINA, CHAPEL HILL)

William Beavans Diary

J. F. H. Claiborne Papers
Franklin Gaillard Collection
J. Bryan Grimes Papers
   J. A. Stikeleather "Recollections"
Robert F. Hoke Papers
   John A. McPherson Letter
John R. Lane Papers
   T. J. Cureton Letter
Lafayette McLaws Papers
Alexander S. Pendleton Letters
Thomas L. Ware Diary

STATE HISTORICAL SOCIETY OF WISCONSIN

Samuel Eaton Papers
Lucius Fairchild Papers
George Fairfield Diaries
Robert B. Hughes Journal
Nathaniel Rollins Diary
Jerome A. Watrous Papers
   Earl A. Rogers Letter
Cornelius Wheeler Letters

TENNESSEE STATE LIBRARY AND ARCHIVES, MANUSCRIPT DIVISION

Campbell Brown and Richard S. Ewell Papers
John A. Fite Memoir

TOWN OF MINISINK ARCHIVES (WESTTOWN, NEW YORK)

Benjamin Hough Letters

TULANE UNIVERSITY LIBRARY, MANUSCRIPT DIVISION

Louisiana Historical Association Collection, Civil War Collection
   Charles Moore Diary
   David Zable Papers

THE UNITED STATES MILITARY HISTORY INSTITUTE

U.S. Army Research Collection
   John W. Ames Papers
   Robert L. Brake Collection
   Levi Bird Duff Letters
   Charles Figgat Letter
   John S. Henley Letter
   Zack Landrum Letters
Civil War Miscellaneous Collection
   A. P. Andrews, "Gallantry at Gettysburg"
   Eugene Blackford Memoir
   Elon Brown Diary-Memoir

Orrel Brown Diary
B. H. Coffman Letter
Samuel Angus Firebaugh Diary
Calvin S. Heller Diary
Luther B. Mesnard Reminiscence
William Penn Oberlin Letters
Wilson N. Paxton Diary
Joseph Todd Diary
Civil War Times Illustrated Collection
   John Berry Diary
   Robert S. Coburn Diary
   John C. Kesses Diary
Harrisburg Civil War Roundtable Collection
   Jacob W. Haas Diary
   Henry Keiser Diary
   David Nichol Diary and Letters
   Gregory A. Coco Collection
   William J. Evans Letters
   George P. Metcalf, "Recollection of Boyhood Days"
   William J. Seymour Diary-Memoir
Timothy Brooks Collection
   Unknown Soldier Letters (140th Pennsylvania)

UNIVERSITY OF MICHIGAN, BENTLEY HISTORICAL LIBRARY

Michigan Historical Collections
   William Baird Letters
   James Houghton Diary

UNIVERSITY OF VIRGINIA LIBRARY

Blackford Family Papers
   Lancelot M. Blackford Letter
Ephraim Bowman Correspondence
John Daniels Papers
   Erasmus Williams/W. S. Christian Letters

THE VIRGINIA HISTORICAL SOCIETY

Cocke Family Papers
Confederate Military Manuscripts
   Edward Samuel Duffy Diary
   John Walter Fairfax Papers
John Warwick Daniel Memoir
Lee's Telegraph Book
"Memoirs of Benjamin Anderson Jones, Virginian, Civil War Experiences"
John Timberlake Papers

VIRGINIA MILITARY INSTITUTE

   Letter to "My Dear Uncle"

ELECTRONIC SOURCES: INTERNET

http://home.sprynet.com/sprynet/carlreed/GRA0005D.html. (Letters written by Capt. Samuel R. Johnston concerning his reconnaissance in the morning of 2 July 1863 on the far right of the Confederate position at Gettysburg)

www.snymor.edu/pages/library/local_history/sites/letters/owen.htmlx. (1863 diary of Robert T. Douglass)

www.snymor.edu/pages/library/local_history/sites/letters/owen17.htmlx. (1863 diary of William Owen)

STATE AND UNIT HISTORIES

Adelman, Garry E. "Hazlett's Battery at Gettysburg." *Gettysburg Magazine* 21 (July 1999): 64–73.

———. "Benning's Georgia Brigade at Gettysburg." *Gettysburg Magazine* 18 (January 1998): 57–66.

Aldrich, Thomas M. *History of Battery A, First Regiment Rhode Island Light Artillery in the War to Preserve the Union, 1861–1865.* Providence: Snow & Farnham, Printers, 1904.

Baker, Levi W. *History of the Ninth Mass. Battery.* South Framingham, Mass.: J. C. Clark Printing Co., 1888.

Banes, Charles H. *History of the Philadelphia Brigade.* Philadelphia: J. B. Lippincott & Co., 1876.

Best, Isaac. *History of the 121st New York State Infantry.* Chicago: Lieut. Jas. H. Smith, 1921.

Bicknell, George W. *History of the Fifth Regiment Maine Volunteers.* Portland, Maine: Hall L. Davis, 1871.

Bilby, Joseph G. *Three Rousing Cheers: A History of the Fifteenth New Jersey from Flemington to Appomattox.* Hightstown, N.J.: Longstreet House, 1993.

Bowen, James. *History of the Thirty-Seventh Regiment Massachusetts Volunteers in the Civil War of 1861–1865.* Holyoke, Mass.: Clark W. Bryan & Co., 1884.

Brewer, A. T. *History Sixty-First Regiment Pennsylvania Volunteers 1861–1865.* Pittsburgh: Art Engraving & Printing Co., 1911.

Bruner, Gary P. "Up over Big Round Top: The Forgotten 47th Alabama." *Gettysburg Magazine* 22 (January 2000): 6–22.

Caldwell, J. F. J. *The History of a Brigade of South Carolinians, Known First as "Gregg's," and Subsequently as "McGowan's Brigade."* 1866. Reprint, Dayton, Ohio: Press of Morningside Bookshop, 1984.

Campbell, Eric. "Baptism of Fire: The Ninth Massachusetts Battery at Gettysburg, July 2, 1863." *Gettysburg Magazine* 5 (July 1991): 47–78.

Chamberlin, Thomas. *History of the One Hundred and Fiftieth Regiment Pennsylvania Volunteers, Second Regiment, Bucktail Brigade.* Philadelphia: F. McManus Jr. & Co., Printers, 1905.

Chapman, Craig S. *More Terrible Than Victory: North Carolina's Bloody Bethel Regiment, 1861–65.* Dulles, Va.: Brassey's, 1998.

Cheek, Philip, and Mair Pointon. *History of the Sauk County Riflemen Known as Company "A," Sixth Wisconsin Veteran Volunteer Infantry 1861–1865.* Madison, Wisc.: Democrat Printing Company, 1909.

Cheney, Newel. *History of the Ninth Regiment New York Volunteer Cavalry.* Poland Center, N.Y.: Martin Merz and Son, 1901.

Child, William A. *A History of the Fifth Regiment, New Hampshire Volunteers in the American Civil War.* Bristol, N.H.: R. W. Musgrove, Printer, 1893.

Clark, George. "Wilcox's Alabama Brigade at Gettysburg." *Confederate Veteran* 17, no. 5 (May 1909): 229–30.

Clark, Walter, ed. *Histories of the Several Regiments and Battalions from North Carolina in the Great War 1861–65.* 5 vols. Raleigh, N.C.: E. M. Uzzell Printer and Binder, 1901.

Coffin, Howard. *Nine Months to Gettysburg: Stannard's Vermonters and the Repulse of Pickett's Charge.* Woodstock, Vt.: The Countryman Press, 1997.

Cook, S. G., and Charles E. Benton, eds. *The "Dutchess County Regiment" (150th Regiment of New York State Volunteer Infantry).* Danbury, Conn.: Danbury Medical Printing Co., Inc., 1907.

Craft, David. *History of the One Hundred Forty-First Regiment, Pennsylvania Volunteers, 1862–1865.* Towanda, Pa.: Reporter-Journal Printing Company, 1885.

Curtis, O. B. *History of the Twenty-Fourth Michigan of the Iron Brigade.* Detroit: Winn & Hammond, 1891.

Davis, Charles E., Jr. *Three Years in the Army: The Story of the Thirteenth Massachusetts Volunteers, from July 16, 1861, to August 1, 1864.* Boston: Estes and Lauriat, 1894.

Desjardin, Thomas A. *Stand Firm Ye Boys from Maine.* Gettysburg: Thomas Publications, 1995.

Dickert, D. Augustus. *History of Kershaw's Brigade.* 1899. Reprint, Dayton, Ohio: Press of Morningside Bookshop, 1976.

Divine, John E. *35th Battalion Virginia Cavalry.* Lynchburg, Va.: H. E. Howard, Inc., 1985.

Doster, William E. *A Brief History of the Fourth Pennsylvania Veteran Cavalry.* 1891. Reprint, Hightstown, N.J.: Longstreet House, 1997.

Dreese, Michael A. "The 151st Pennsylvania Volunteers at Gettysburg: July 1, 1863." *Gettysburg Magazine* 23 (July 2000): 51–65.

Dudley, William W. *The Iron Brigade at Gettysburg.* Cincinnati: Privately printed, 1879.

Dunkelman, Mark H., and Michael J. Winey. *The Hardtack Regiment: An Illustrated History of the 154th Regiment, New York State Infantry Volunteers.* East Brunswick, N.J.: Associated University Presses, Inc., 1981.

———. "The Hardtack Regiment in the Brickyard Fight." *Gettysburg Magazine* 8 (January 1993): 17–30.

Final Report of the Gettysburg Battle-field Commission of New Jersey. Trenton: John L. Murphy Publishing Company, 1891.

Ford, Andrew E. *The Story of the Fifteenth Regiment Massachusetts Volunteer Infantry in the Civil War 1861–1864.* Clinton, Mass.: Press of W. J. Coulter, 1898.

Fox, William F., ed. *New York at Gettysburg: Final Report on the Battlefield of Gettysburg.* 3 vols. Albany: J. B. Lyon Company Printers, 1900–1902.

Frye, Dennis E. *2nd Virginia Infantry.* Lynchburg, Va.: H. E. Howard, Inc., 1984.

Fuller, Edward H. *Battles of the Seventy-Seventh New York State Foot Volunteers.* Gloversville, N.Y.: N.p., 1901.

Gaff, Alan D. *On Many a Bloody Field: Four Years in the Iron Brigade.* Bloomington: Indiana University Press, 1996.

Gannon, James P. *Irish Rebels, Confederate Tigers: The 6th Louisiana Volunteers, 1861–1865.* Campbell, Calif.: Savas Publishing Company, 1998.

Goldsborough, William W. *The Maryland Line in the Confederate Army: 1861–1865.*

1869. Reprint with an introduction by Jean Baker, New York: Kennikat Press, 1972.

Gottfried, Bradley M. *Stopping Pickett: The History of the Philadelphia Brigade*. Shippensburg, Pa.: White Mane Publishing Co., Inc., 1999.

———. "To Fail Twice: Brockenbrough's Brigade at Gettysburg." *Gettysburg Magazine* 23 (July 2000): 66–75.

Gragg, Rod. *Covered with Glory: The 26th North Carolina Infantry at Gettysburg*. New York: HarperCollins Publishers, 2000.

Gregory, G. Howard. *38th Virginia Infantry*. Lynchburg, Va.: H. E. Howard, Inc., 1988.

Hadden, R. Lee. "Granite Glory: The 19th Maine at Gettysburg." *Gettysburg Magazine* 13 (July 1995): 50–63.

Haines, Alanson A. *History of the Fifteenth Regiment New Jersey Volunteers*. New York: Jenkins & Thomas, Printers, 1883.

Hale, Laura Virginia, and Stanley S. Phillips. *History of the Forty-Ninth Virginia Infantry C.S.A., "Extra Billy Smith's Boys."* Lanham, Md.: S. S. Phillips and Assc., 1981.

Hall, Hillman A., W. B. Besley, and Gilbert G. Wood, eds. *History of the Sixth New York Cavalry*. Worcester, Mass.: Blanchard Press, 1908.

Hanifen, Michael. *History of Battery B, First New Jersey Artillery*. Ottawa, Ill.: Republican Times Printers, 1905.

Harrison, Kathy Georg, and John W. Busey. *Nothing but Glory: Pickett's Division at Gettysburg*. Gettysburg: Thomas Publications, 1987.

Haynes, Martin A. *History of the Second Regiment, New Hampshire Volunteers*. Lakeport, N.H.: Privately printed, 1896.

Henderson, William D. *12th Virginia Infantry*. Lynchburg, Va.: H. E. Howard, Inc., 1984.

Holcombe, Return I. *History of the First Regiment Minnesota Volunteer Infantry*. Stillwater, Minn.: Easton & Masterman Printers, 1916.

Hurst, Samuel H. *Journal-History of the Seventy-Third Ohio Volunteer Infantry*. Chillicothe, Ohio: N.p., 1866.

Imholte, John Quinn. *The First Volunteers. History of the First Minnesota Volunteer Regiment 1861–1865*. Minneapolis: Ross & Haines, Inc., 1963.

Jones, Terry L. *Lee's Tigers: The Louisiana Infantry in the Army of Northern Virginia*. Baton Rouge: Louisiana State University Press, 1987.

———. "Twice Lost: The 8th Louisiana Volunteers' Battle Flag at Gettysburg." *Civil War Regiments* 6, no. 3 (1999): 89–105.

Jorgensen, Jay. "Holding the Right: The 137th New York Regiment at Gettysburg." *Gettysburg Magazine* 15 (July 1996): 60–67.

Joslyn, Mauriel P. " 'For Ninety Nine Years or the War': The Story of the 3rd Arkansas at Gettysburg." *Gettysburg Magazine* 14 (January 1996): 52–63.

Judson, Amos M. *History of the Eighty-Third Regiment Pennsylvania Volunteers*. Erie, Pa.: B. F. H. Lynn, Publisher, 1865.

Kepf, Kenneth M. "Dilger's Battery at Gettysburg." *Gettysburg Magazine* 4 (January 1991): 49–64.

Kepler, William. *History of the Three Months and Three Years' Service from April 16th, 1861, to June 22d, 1864, of the Fourth Regiment Ohio Volunteer Infantry in the War for the Union*. Cleveland: Leader Printing Company, 1886.

Krick, Robert K. *The Fredericksburg Artillery*. Lynchburg, Va.: H. E. Howard, Inc., 1986.

Laine, J. Gary, and Morris M. Penny. *Law's Alabama Brigade in the War between the Union and the Confederacy.* Shippensburg, Pa.: White Mane Publishing Co., Inc., 1996.

Laney, Daniel M. "Wasted Gallantry: Hood's Texas Brigade at Gettysburg." *Gettysburg Magazine* 16 (January 1997): 27–45.

Lochren, William. "The First Minnesota at Gettysburg." In *Glimpses of the Nation's Struggle: A Series of Papers Read before the Minnesota Commandery of the Military Order of the Loyal Legion of the United States, 1889–1892.* 1893. Reprint, Wilmington, N.C.: Broadfoot Publishing Company, 1992.

Locke, William Henry. *The Story of the Regiment.* Philadelphia: J. B. Lippincott & Co., 1868.

Loehr, Charles T. "The First Virginia Infantry at the Battle of Gettysburg, and the Charge of Pickett's Division." *Southern Historical Society Papers* 32 (January–December 1904): 33–43.

Loyd, W. G. "Second Louisiana at Gettysburg." *Confederate Veteran* 6, no. 9 (September 1898): 417.

Macnamara, Daniel George. *The History of the Ninth Regiment Massachusetts Volunteer Infantry.* Boston: E. B. Stallings & Co., Printers, 1899.

Maine at Gettysburg: Report of the Commissioners. Portland, Maine: The Lakeside Press, 1898.

Marbaker, Thomas D. *History of the Eleventh New Jersey Volunteers.* Trenton: MacCrellish & Quigley, Book and Job Printers, 1898.

Meinhard, Robert W. "The First Minnesota at Gettysburg." *Gettysburg Magazine* 5 (July 1991): 79–88.

Michigan at Gettysburg: July 1st, 2nd and 3rd, 1863. Proceedings Incident to the Dedication of the Michigan Monuments upon the Battlefield of Gettysburg, June 12th, 1889. Detroit: Winn & Hammond, Printers and Binders, 1889.

Moe, Richard. *The Last Full Measure: The Life and Death of the First Minnesota Volunteers.* New York: Avon Books, 1993.

Moyer, H. P. *History of the Seventeenth Regiment Pennsylvania Volunteer Cavalry.* Lebanon, Pa.: Sowers Printing Company, 1911.

Muffley, J. W., ed. *The Story of Our Regiment: A History of the 148th Pennsylvania Vols.* Des Moines: Kenyon Printing & Mfg. Co., 1904.

Mulholland, St. Clair A. *The Story of the 116th Regiment, Pennsylvania Volunteers in the War of the Rebellion.* 1903. Reprint, New York: Fordham University Press, 1996.

Murphy, T. L. *Kelly's Heroes: The Irish Brigade at Gettysburg.* Published by the author, 1997.

Nash, Eugene Arus. *A History of the Forty-Fourth Regiment New York Volunteer Infantry in the Civil War, 1861–1865.* 1910. Reprint, Dayton, Ohio: Press of Morningside Bookshop, 1988.

Nicholson, John P., ed. *Pennsylvania at Gettysburg: Ceremonies at the Dedication of the Monuments Erected by the Commonwealth of Pennsylvania.* 2 vols. Harrisburg: William Stanley Ray, State Printer, 1904.

Nolan, Alan T. *The Iron Brigade: A Military History.* Bloomington: Indiana University Press, 1961.

O'Brien, Kevin E. " 'Give Them Another Volley, Boys': Biddle's Brigade Defends the Union Left on July 1, 1863." *Gettysburg Magazine* 19 (July 1998): 37–52.

———. " 'Stubborn Bravery': The Forgotten 44th New York at Little Round Top." *Gettysburg Magazine* 15 (July 1996): 31–44.

O'Sullivan, Richard. *55th Virginia Infantry*. Lynchburg, Va.: H. E. Howard, Inc., 1989.

Otis, George H. *The Second Wisconsin Infantry*. Dayton, Ohio: Press of Morningside Bookshop, 1984.

Page, Charles D. *History of the Fourteenth Regiment, Connecticut Vol. Infantry*. Meriden, Conn.: Horton Printing Co., 1906.

Polley, John B. *Hood's Texas Brigade: Its Marches, Its Battles, Its Achievements*. 1910. Reprint, Dayton, Ohio: Press of Morningside Bookshop, 1976.

Proceedings of the 76th New York Infantry, at the Dedication of Their Battle Monument, at Gettysburg, Pa., July 1, 1888. Cortland, N.Y.: Daily Message Print., 1889.

Pula, James S. *The History of a German-Polish Civil War Brigade*. San Francisco: Rande Research Associates, 1976.

———. *The Sigel Regiment: A History of the 26th Wisconsin Volunteer Infantry, 1862–1865*. Campbell, Calif.: Savas Publishing Company, 1998.

Quint, Alonzo H. *The Record of the Second Massachusetts Infantry, 1861–1865*. Boston: James P. Walker, 1867.

Report of the Ninth Annual Reunion of the 64th N.Y. Regimental Association at Buffalo, New York, August 24, 1897. N.p., n.d.

Report of the Seventh Annual Reunion of the 64th N.Y. Regimental Association at Salamanca, New York, August 21 and 22, 1895. Salmanca, N.Y.: Randolph Publishing Co., 1895.

Rhodes, John H. *The History of Battery B, First Regiment Rhode Island Light Artillery, in the War to Preserve the Union, 1861–1865*. Providence: Snow & Farnham, Printers, 1894.

Ripley, William Y. W. *Vermont Riflemen in the War for the Union, 1861 to 1865: A History of Company F, First United States Sharp Shooters*. Rutland, Vt.: Tuttle & Co., Printers, 1883.

Robertson, James I., Jr. *18th Virginia Infantry*. Lynchburg, Va.: H. E. Howard, Inc., 1984.

Sauers, Richard A. "The 16th Maine Volunteer Infantry at Gettysburg." *Gettysburg Magazine* 13 (July 1995): 33–42.

Sawyer, Franklin. *A Military History of the 8th Regiment Ohio Volunteer Infantry, Its Battles, Marches and Army Movements*. Cleveland: Fairbanks and Co., 1881.

Shultz, David. "Gulian V. Weir's 5th U.S. Artillery, Battery C." *Gettysburg Magazine* 18 (January 1998): 77–95.

Simons, Ezra D. *A Regimental History: The One Hundred and Twenty-Fifth New York State Volunteers*. New York: Judson Print. Co., 1888.

Small, Abner R. *The Sixteenth Maine Regiment in the War of the Rebellion, 1861–1865*. Portland, Maine: B. Thurston & Company, 1886.

Smith, A. P. *History of the Seventy-Sixth Regiment New York Volunteers*. Syracuse, N.Y.: Truair, Smith & Miles, Printers, 1866.

Smith, Donald L. *The Twenty-Fourth Michigan of the Iron Brigade*. Harrisburg, Pa.: Stackpole Company, 1962.

Smith, J. L. *History of the 118th Pennsylvania Volunteers Corn Exchange Regiment*. Philadelphia: J. L. Smith Publisher, 1905.

Smith, Jacob. *Camps and Campaigns of the 107th Regiment Ohio Volunteer Infantry from August, 1862, to July, 1865*. N.p., 1910.

Smith, James E. *A Famous Battery and Its Campaigns*. 1892. Reprint, Benedum Books, 1999.

Smith, John Day. *The History of the Nineteenth Regiment of Maine Volunteer Infantry 1862–1865*. Minneapolis: Great Western Printing Company, 1909.

Smith, L. A. "Recollections of Gettysburg." In *War Papers: Being Papers Read before the Commandery of the State of Michigan, Military Order of the Loyal Legion of the United States*. 1898. Reprint, Wilmington, N.C.: Broadfoot Publishing Company, 1993.

Smith, W. A. *The Anson Guards: Company C, Fourteenth Regiment North Carolina Volunteers 1861–1865*. Charlotte, N.C.: Stone Publishing Co., 1914.

Storrs, John Whiting. *The Twentieth Connecticut, A Regimental History*. Naugatuck, Conn.: Press of the Naugatuck Valley Sentinel, 1886.

Sturtevant, Ralph O. *Pictorial History Thirteenth Regiment Vermont Volunteers War of 1861–1865*. N.p., 1910.

Tevis, C. V. *The History of the Fighting Fourteenth*. New York: Brooklyn Eagle Press, 1911.

Thomas, Howard. *Boys in Blue from the Adirondack Foothills*. Prospect, N.Y.: Prospect Books, 1960.

Thomson, Orville. *From Philippi to Appomatox: A Narrative of the Service of the Seventh Indiana Infantry in the War for the Union*. Reprint, Baltimore, Md.: Butternut and Blue, 1993.

Topps, David. "The Dutchess County Regiment." *Gettysburg Magazine* 12 (January 1995): 42–60.

Trimble, Tony L. "Paper Collars: Stannard's Brigade at Gettysburg." *Gettysburg Magazine* (January 1990): 75–80.

Venner, William Thomas. *The 19th Indiana Infantry at Gettysburg: Hoosier's Courage*. Shippensburg, Pa.: Burd Street Press, 1998.

Walker, Francis A. *History of the Second Army Corps in the Army of the Potomac*. New York: Charles Scribner's Sons, 1887.

Ward, Joseph R. C. *History of the One Hundred and Sixth Regiment Pennsylvania Volunteers 2d Brigade, 2d Division, 2d Corps, 1861–1865*. Philadelphia: F. McManus Jr. & Co., 1906.

Westbrook, Robert S. *History of the 49th Pennsylvania Volunteers*. Altoona, Pa.: Altoona Times, 1898.

Weygant, Charles H. *History of the One Hundred and Twenty-Fourth Regiment, N.Y.S.V.* Newburgh, N.Y.: Journal Printing House, 1877.

Willson, Arabella M. *Disaster, Struggle, Triumph: The Adventures of 1000 "Boys in Blue."* Albany: The Argus Company, Printers, 1870.

Winschel, Terrence J. "Posey's Brigade at Gettysburg, Part 2." *Gettysburg Magazine* 5 (July 1991): 89–102.

———. "Heavy Was Their Loss: Joe Davis's Brigade at Gettysburg, Part 2." *Gettysburg Magazine* 3 (July 1990): 77–86.

———. "Heavy Was Their Loss: Joe Davis's Brigade at Gettysburg, Part 1." *Gettysburg Magazine* 2 (January 1990): 5–14.

———. "Their Supreme Moment: Barksdale's Brigade at Gettysburg." *Gettysburg Magazine* 1 (July 1989): 70–77.

Wyckoff, Mac. "Kershaw's Brigade at Gettysburg." *Gettysburg Magazine* 5 (July 1991): 35–46.

Young, Louis. "Pettigrew's Brigade at Gettysburg." In Walter Clark, ed., *Histories of the Several Regiments and Battalions from North Carolina in the Great War 1861–'65*. 5 vols. Raleigh: E. M. Uzzell Printer and Binder, 1901.

BIOGRAPHIES, DIARIES, LETTERS, MEMOIRS, PERSONAL NARRATIVES, SPEECHES

Abernathy, William. *Our Mess: Southern Gallantry and Privations*. McKinney, Tex.: McKintex Press, 1977.

Acken, J. Gregory, ed. *Inside the Army of the Potomac: The Civil War Experience of Captain Francis Adams Donaldson*. Mechanicsburg, Pa.: Stackpole Books, 1998.

Agassiz, George R., ed. *Meade's Headquarters 1863–1865: Letters of Colonel Theodore Lyman from the Wilderness to Appomattox*. Boston: Atlantic Monthly Press, 1922.

Alexander, Edward Porter. *Military Memoirs of a Confederate: A Critical Narrative*. 1907. Reprint, New York: Da Capo Press, 1993.

———. "Confederate Artillery Service." *Southern Historical Society Papers* 11, no. 1 (January 1883): 98–113.

———. "The Great Charge and Artillery Fighting at Gettysburg." In Clarence C. Buel and Robert U. Johnson, eds., *Battles and Leaders of the Civil War*. 4 vols. New York: Century Company, 1884–1889.

Alleman, Tillie (Pierce). *At Gettysburg, or What a Girl Saw and Heard of the Battle*. New York: W. Lake Borland, 1889.

Allen, William. "Letter to J. William Jones." *Southern Historical Society Papers* 4, no. 2 (August 1877): 76–80.

Ambrose, Stephen E. *Halleck: Lincoln's Chief of Staff*. Baton Rouge: Louisiana State University Press, 1962.

Anderson, James S. "The March of the Sixth Corps to Gettysburg." In *War Papers: Being Papers Read before the Commandery of the State of Wisconsin, Military Order of the Loyal Legion of the United States*. 1914. Reprint, Wilmington, N.C.: Broadfoot Publishing Company, 1993.

Applegate, John S., ed. *Reminiscences and Letters of George Arrowsmith*. Red Bank, N.J.: John H. Cook, 1893.

Aschmann, Rudolf. *Memoirs of a Swiss Officer in the American Civil War*. Edited by Heinz K. Meier; translated by Hedwig D. Rappolt. Bern: Herbert Lang, 1972.

Aughinbaugh, Nellie E. *Personal Experiences of a Young Girl during the Battle of Gettysburg*. Privately printed, 1941.

Basler, Roy, ed. *The Collected Works of Abraham Lincoln*. 9 vols. New Brunswick, N.J.: Rutgers University Press, 1953–1955.

Beale, George W. *A Lieutenant of Cavalry in Lee's Army*. Boston: Gorham Press, 1918.

Beale, Howard K., ed. *Diary of Gideon Welles*. 3 vols. New York: W. W. Norton & Company, Inc., 1960.

Beaudot, William J. K. "Francis Ashbury Wallar: A Medal of Honor at Gettysburg." *Gettysburg Magazine* 4 (January 1991): 16–21.

Beaudry, Richard E., ed. *War Journal of Louis N. Beaudry, Fifth New York Cavalry*. Jefferson, N.C.: McFarland & Company, Inc., 1996.

Bee, Robert L., ed. *The Boys from Rockville: Civil War Narratives of Sgt. Benjamin Hirst, Company D, 14th Connecticut Volunteers*. Knoxville: University of Tennessee Press, 1998.

Benedict, George G. *Army Life in Virginia: Letters from the Twelfth Vermont Regiment and Personal Experiences of Volunteer Service in the War for the Union, 1862–1863*. Burlington: Free Press Association, 1895.

Benjamin, Charles F. "Hooker's Appointment and Removal." In Clarence C. Buel and Robert U. Johnson, eds., *Battles and Leaders of the Civil War*. 4 vols. New York: Century Company, 1884–1889.

Berkeley, Edmund. "Rode with Pickett." *Confederate Veteran* 38, no. 5 (May 1930): 175.

Betts, A. D. *Experience of a Confederate Chaplain 1861–1864*. N.p., n.d.

Beveridge, John L. "The First Gun at Gettysburg." In *Military Essays and Recollections: Papers Read before the Commandery of the State of Illinois, Military Order of the Loyal Legion of the United States*. 1894. Reprint, Wilmington, N.C.: Broadfoot Publishing Company, 1992.

Bigelow, John. *The Peach Orchard, Gettysburg: An Appeal*. 1910. Reprint, Baltimore, Md.: Butternut and Blue, 1984.

Bisbee, George D. "Three Years a Volunteer Soldier in the Civil War: Antietam to Appomattox." In *War Papers: Read before the Commandery of the State of Maine, Military Order of the Loyal Legion of the United States*. 1915. Reprint, Wilmington, N.C.: Broadfoot Publishing Company, 1992.

Black, John L. *Crumbling Defenses; or, Memoirs and Reminiscences of John Logan Black, C.S.A.* Macon, Ga.: J. W. Burke Co., 1960.

Blackford, Susan Leigh, ed. *Letters from Lee's Army*. New York: A. S. Barnes & Company, Inc., 1962.

Blackford, William Willis. *War Years with Jeb Stuart*. New York: Charles Scribner's Sons, 1945.

Blake, Henry N. *Three Years in the Army of the Potomac*. Boston: Lee and Shepard, 1865.

Bloodgood, J. D. *Personal Reminiscences of the War*. New York: Hunt & Eaton, 1893.

Boland, E. T. "Beginning of the Battle of Gettysburg." *Confederate Veteran* 14, no. 7 (July 1906): 308–9.

Bolton, Channing M. "With General Lee's Engineers." *Confederate Veteran* 30, no. 8 (August 1922): 298–302.

Bonham, Milledge Louis. "A Little More Light on Gettysburg." *Mississippi Valley Historical Review* 24, no. 4 (March 1938): 519–25.

Bowen, George D. "Diary of Captain George D. Bowen." *Valley Forge Journal* 11, no. 5 (June 1984).

Bowmaster, Patrick A., ed. "Confederate Brig. Gen. B. H. 'Bev' Robertson Interviewed on the Gettysburg Campaign." *Gettysburg Magazine* 20 (January 1999): 19–26.

Bradwell, Isaac G. "Crossing the Potomac." *Confederate Veteran* 30, no. 10 (October 1922): 370–73.

Bright, Robert A. "Pickett's Charge at Gettysburg." *Confederate Veteran* 38, no. 7 (July 1930): 263–66.

Britton, Ann H., and Thomas J. Reed, eds. *To My Beloved Wife & Boy at Home: The Diaries and Letters of John F. L. Hartwell, 121st New York Volunteer Infantry, 1862–65*. 2 vols. N.p., 1993.

Broadhead, Sarah M. *The Diary of a Lady of Gettysburg, Pennsylvania*. N.p., n.d.

Brooke-Rawle, William. "Gregg's Cavalry in the Gettysburg Campaign." In *Military Essays and Recollections of the Pennsylvania Commandery, Military Order of the Loyal Legion of the United States*. 2 vols. Wilmington, N.C.: Broadfoot Publishing Company, 1995.

Brooks, Noah. *Washington, D.C., in Lincoln's Time*. Edited by Herbert Mitgang. Athens, Ga.: University of Georgia Press, 1989.

Brown, Kent Masterson. *Cushing of Gettysburg*. Lexington, Ky.: The University Press of Kentucky, 1993.

Buehler, Fannie. *Recollections of the Great Rebel Invasion and One Woman's Experiences during the Battle of Gettysburg*. 1896, N.p.

Butts, Joseph Tyler, ed. *A Gallant Captain of the Civil War: Being the Record of the Extraordinary Adventures of Frederick Otto Baron von Fritsch*. New York: F. Tennyson Neely, 1902.

Byrne, Frank L., and Andrew T. Weaver, eds. *Haskell of Gettysburg*. Kent, Ohio: Kent State University Press, 1989.

Calef, J. H. "The Regular Artillery in the Gettysburg Campaign." *Journal of the Military Service Institution of the United States* 45 (July–August 1909): 32–38.

Cavada, F. F. *Libby Life: Experiences of a Prisoner of War in Richmond, Va., 1863–64*. Philadelphia: J. B. Lippincott & Co., 1865.

Chamberlain, Joshua L. "Through Blood and Fire at Gettysburg." *Gettysburg Magazine* 6 (January 1992): 43–58.

Child, Benjamin H. "From Fredericksburg to Gettysburg." In *Personal Narratives of Events in the War of the Rebellion, Being Papers Read before the Rhode Island Soldiers and Sailors Historical Society*. 1894–1899. Reprint, Wilmington, N.C.: Broadfoot Publishing Company, 1993.

Chilton, F. B., ed. *Unveiling and Dedication of Monument to Hood's Texas Brigade*. Houston: Press of Rein and Sons, 1911.

Church, Charles H. *Civil War Letters*. Rose City, Mich.: Rose City Area Historical Society, 1987.

Cleaves, Freeman. *Meade of Gettysburg*. Norman, Okla.: University of Oklahoma Press, 1960.

Cockrell, Thomas D., and Michael B. Ballerd, eds. *A Mississippi Rebel in the Army of Northern Virginia: The Civil War Memoirs of Private David Holt*. Baton Rouge: Louisiana State University Press, 1995.

Coffin, Charles Carlteon. *The Boys of '61; or, Four Years of Fighting*. Boston: Estes and Lauriat, 1896.

Collins, George K. *Memoirs of the 149th Regt. N.Y. Vol. Inft.* 1891. Reprint, Hamilton, N.Y.: Edmonston Publishing, Inc., 1995.

Coltrane, Daniel Branson. *The Memoirs of Daniel Branson Coltrane*. Raleigh, N.C.: Edwards & Broughton Company, 1956.

Cooke, John Esten. *Wearing of the Gray; Being Personal Portraits, Scenes and Adventures of the War*. New York: E. B. Treat & Co., 1867.

Cook, J. D. S. "Reminiscences of Gettysburg." In *War Talks in Kansas: A Series of Papers Read before the Kansas Commandery of the Military Order of the Loyal Legion of the United States*. 1906. Reprint, Wilmington, N.C.: Broadfoot Publishing Company, 1992.

Cooke, Sidney G. "The First Day at Gettysburg." In *War Talks in Kansas: A Series of Papers Read before the Kansas Commandery of the Military Order of the Loyal Legion of the United States*. 1906. Reprint, Wilmington, N.C.: Broadfoot Publishing Company, 1992.

Crocker, J. F. *Pickett's Charge and Other War Addresses*. Portsmouth, Va.: 1915, N.p.

Crumb, Herb S., ed. *The Eleventh Corps Artillery at Gettysburg: The Papers of Major Thomas Ward Osborn, Chief of Artillery*. Hamilton, N.Y.: Edmonston Publishing, Inc., 1991.

Cummings, C. C. "Chancellorsville, May 2, 1863." *Confederate Veteran* 23, no. 9 (September 1915): 405–7.

Davis, Archie K. *Boy Colonel of the Confederacy: The Life and Times of Henry King Burgwyn, Jr.* Chapel Hill: University of North Carolina Press, 1985.

Davis, Stephen. "The Death and Burials of General Richard Brooke Garnett." *Gettysburg Magazine* 5 (July 1991): 107–16.

Dawes, Rufus R. *Service with the Sixth Wisconsin Volunteers.* 1890. Reprint, Dayton, Ohio: Press of Morningside Bookshop, 1984.

———. "With the Sixth Wisconsin at Gettysburg." In *Sketches of War History 1861–1865: Papers Read before the Ohio Commandery of the Military Order of the Loyal Legion of the United States, 1888–1890.* 1890. Reprint, Wilmington, N.C.: Broadfoot Publishing Company, 1991.

Dawson, Francis W. *Reminiscences of Confederate Service.* 1882. Reprint, edited by Bell I. Wiley, Baton Rouge: Louisiana State University Press, 1980.

Deane, Frank Putnam, ed. *"My Dear Wife": The Civil War Letters of David Brett, 9th Massachusetts Battery, Union Cannoneer.* Little Rock, Ark.: Pioneer Press, 1964.

DeLeon, Thomas Cooper. *Four Years in Rebel Capitals.* New York: Collier Books, 1962.

Dorsett, Wilbur. "The Fourteenth Color-Bearer." *The Carolina Magazine,* 1932.

Doubleday, Abner. *Chancellorsville and Gettysburg.* New York: Charles Scribner's Sons, 1882.

Douglas, Henry Kyd. *I Rode with Stonewall.* St. Simons Island, Ga.: Mockingbird Books, 1979.

Dowdey, Clifford, and Louis H. Manarin, eds. *The Wartime Papers of R. E. Lee.* New York: Bramhall House, 1961.

Duke, J. W. "Mississippians at Gettysburg." *Confederate Veteran* 14, no. 5 (May 1906): 216.

Dunaway, Wayland Fuller. *Reminiscences of a Rebel.* New York: Neale Publishing Company, 1913.

Dunkelman, Mark H. *Gettysburg's Unknown Soldier: The Life, Death, and Celebrity of Amos Humiston.* Westport, Conn.: Praeger Publishers, 1999.

Durkin, Joseph T., ed. *John Dooley, Confederate Soldier: His War Journal.* South Bend, Ind.: University of Notre Dame Press, 1963.

Early, Jubal Anderson. *Autobiographical Sketch and Narrative of the War between the States.* 1912. Reprint, New York: Smithmark Publishers Inc., 1994.

———. "A Review by General Early." *Southern Historical Society Papers* 4, no. 6 (December 1877): 241–302.

Eckert, Ralph Lowell. *John Brown Gordon: Soldier, Southerner, American.* Baton Rouge: Louisiana State University Press, 1989.

Evans, William McKendree. "Parker's Boy Battery." *Confederate Veteran* 30, no. 7 (July 1922): 250.

Evans, William S. "Letter to His Sister." In *Recollections and Reminiscences 1861–1865.* United Daughters of the Confederacy, Georgia Division, 1996.

Fasnacht, Charles H. *Speech Delivered at Dedication of 99th Pennsylvania Monument, Gettysburg, Pa. July 2, 1886.* Lancaster, Pa.: Examiner Steam Book & Job Print, 1886.

Fastnacht, Mary Warren. *Memories of the Battle of Gettysburg.* New York: Princely Press, 1941.

Flanagan, Vincent J. "The Life of General Gouverneur Kemble Warren." Ph.D. diss., City University of New York, 1969.

Fleming, George Thornton, ed. *Life and Letters of Alexander Hays.* Pittsburgh: Privately printed, 1919.

Fletcher, William A. *Rebel Private: Front and Rear.* 1908. Reprint, New York: Dutton Books, 1995.

Ford, Worthington Chauncey, ed. *A Cycle of Adams Letters, 1861–1865.* New York: Houghton Mifflin Company, 1920.

Freeman, Douglas Southall. *R. E. Lee.* 4 vols. New York: Charles Scribner's Sons, 1935.

Fremantle, Arthur J. L. *Three Months in the Southern States.* 1864. Reprint, Lincoln, Nebr.: University of Nebraska Press, 1991.

Fulcher, Jane M., ed. *Family Letters in a Civil War Century.* Avella, Pa.: Privately printed, 1986.

Fulton, William Frierson II. *Family Record and War Reminiscences.* 191?, N.p.

———. "The Fifth Alabama Battalion at Gettysburg." *Confederate Veteran* 31, no. 10 (October 1923): 379–80.

Gaff, Alan D. "The Kid." *Civil War Times Illustrated* 37, no. 4 (August 1998): 38–43.

Gallagher, Gary W. *Stephen Dodson Ramseur: Lee's Gallant General.* Chapel Hill, N.C.: University of North Carolina Press, 1985.

———, ed. *Fighting for the Confederacy.* Chapel Hill, N.C.: University of North Carolina Press, 1989.

———, ed. *Lee the Soldier.* Lincoln, Nebr.: University of Nebraska Press, 1996.

Galwey, Thomas Francis. *The Valiant Hours.* Edited by Wilbur S. Nye. Harrisburg, Pa.: Stackpole Company, 1961.

Gambone, A. M. *Hancock at Gettysburg and Beyond.* Baltimore, Md.: Butternut and Blue, 1997.

Garrish, Theodore. *Army Life: A Private's Reminiscences of the Civil War.* Portland, Maine: Hoyt, Fogg & Donham, 1882.

"Gen. James Dearing." *Confederate Veteran* 9, no. 5 (May 1901): 215–16.

"Gettysburg, 1863–1893: Stories of Survivors as Told by Themselves." *Blue and Gray,* (July 1893): 19–36. (Cunnington, W. H., "Lincoln's Dedication Speech"; Diembach, Andrew, "An Incident at Cemetery Hill"; Hodam, James H., "From Potomac to Susquehanna"; Jones, Meredith L., "The First Day's Fight"; Mahone, William, "Gen. Mahone at Gettysburg"; Shepherd, Henry E., "Wounded and Captured"; Stewart, W. H., "The Grandeur of Battle"; Walker, James H., "A Survivor of Pickett's Division")

Gibbon, John. *Personal Recollections of the Civil War.* New York: G. P. Putnam's Sons, 1928.

Golay, Michael. *To Gettysburg and Beyond: The Parallel Lives of Joshua Lawrence Chamberlain and Edward Porter Alexander.* New York: Crown Publishers, Inc., 1994.

Gordon, John B. *Reminiscences of the Civil War.* New York: Charles Scribner's Sons, 1904.

Gorham, George C. *Life and Public Services of Edwin M. Stanton.* New York: Houghton Mifflin & Co., 1899.

Gorman, George, ed. "Memoirs of a Rebel." *Military Images Magazine* 3, no. 6 (May–June 1982): 21–26.

Graham, Ziba B. "On to Gettysburg." In *War Papers: Being Papers Read before the Commandery of the State of Michigan, Military Order of the Loyal Legion of the United States.* 1886–1893. Reprint, Wilmington, N.C.: Broadfoot Publishing Company, 1993.

Greene, George S. "The Breastworks at Culp's Hill." In Clarence C. Buel and Robert

U. Johnson, eds., *Battles and Leaders of the Civil War*. 4 vols. New York: Century Company, 1884–1889.

Gregg, David McMurtrie. "The Second Cavalry Division of the Army of the Potomac in the Gettysburg Campaign." In *Military Essays and Recollections of the Pennsylvania Commandery, Military Order of the Loyal Legion of the United States*. 2 vols. Wilmington, N.C.: Broadfoot Publishing Company, 1995.

———. "The Cavalry at Gettysburg." *Philadelphia North American*, June 29, 1913.

———. "The Union Cavalry at Gettysburg." In *The Annals of the War Written by Leading Participants North and South*. 1876. Reprint, Dayton, Ohio: Press of Morningside Bookshop, 1988.

Hale, Charles A. "With Colonel Cross at the Wheatfield." *Civil War Times Illustrated* 13, no. 5 (August 1974): 31–38.

Halstead, E. P. "The First Day of the Battle of Gettysburg." In *War Papers: Being Papers Read before the Commandery of the District of Columbia, Military Order of the Loyal Legion of the United States*. 1887–1897. Reprint, Wilmington, N.C.: Broadfoot Publishing Company, 1993.

Hamilton, J. G. Roulhac, ed. *The Papers of Randolph Shotwell*. 3 vols. Raleigh, N.C.: North Carolina Historical Commission, 1929–1936.

Hancock, Winfield S. "Gettysburg: Reply to General Howard." *Galaxy* 22, no. 6 (December 1876): 821–31.

———. "A Letter from General Hancock." *Southern Historical Society Papers* 5, no. 4 (April 1878): 168–72.

Harling, Rufus. "At Gettysburg." In *Recollections and Reminiscences 1861–1865*. United Daughters of the Confederacy, South Carolina Division, 1990.

Harrison, Walter. *Pickett's Men: A Fragment of War History*. New York: D. Van Norstrand, 1870.

Harwell, Richard Barksdale, ed. *Cities and Camps of the Confederate States*. Chicago: University of Illinois Press, 1997.

Hassler, William W. *A. P. Hill: Lee's Forgotten General*. Chapel Hill, N.C.: University of North Carolina Press, 1957.

———, ed. *One of Lee's Best Men: The Civil War Letters of General William Dorsey Pender*. Chapel Hill, N.C.: University of North Carolina Press, 1965.

Haynes, Draughton Stith. *The Field Diary of a Confederate Soldier*. Darien, Ga.: Ashantilly Press, 1963.

Hebert, Walter H. *Fighting Joe Hooker*. Indianapolis: Bobbs-Merrill Company, 1944.

Herdegen, Lance J. "The Lieutenant Who Arrested a General." *Gettysburg Magazine* 4 (January 1991): 25–32.

Herdegen, Lance J., and William J. K. Beaudot, eds. "With the Iron Brigade Guard at Gettysburg." *Gettysburg Magazine* 1 (July 1989): 29–34.

Heth, Henry. "Letter to J. William Jones." *Southern Historical Society Papers* 4, no. 4 (October 1877): 151–60.

Hillyer, George. *Battle of Gettysburg*. Walton, Ga.: Walton Tribune, 1904.

Hofmann, John William. *Military Record of Brevet Brigadier General John William Hofmann, United States Volunteers*. Philadelphia: A. W. Auner, Printer, 1884.

Hoke, Jacob. *Reminiscences of the War; or, Incidents Which Transpired in and about Chambersburg, during the War of the Rebellion*. Chambersburg, Pa.: M. A. Foltz, Printer and Publisher, 1884.

———. *The Great Invasion*. 1887. Reprint, New York: Thomas Yoseloff, 1959.

Hollinger, Liberty [Mrs. Jacob Glutz]. *Some Personal Recollections of the Battle of Gettysburg.* Privately printed, 1925.

Hood, John Bell. *Advance and Retreat.* 1880. Reprint, Secaucus, N.J.: Blue and Grey Press, 1985.

———. "Letter to Longstreet." *Southern Historical Society Papers* 4, no. 4 (October 1877): 145–50.

Hoole, William Stanley, ed. *Lawley Covers the Confederacy.* Tuscaloosa, Ala.: Confederate Publishing Co., 1964.

———, ed. *Reminiscences of the Autauga Rifles (Co. G, Sixth Alabama Volunteer Regiment, C.S.A.).* Prattville, Ala.: Privately published, 1879.

Hotchkiss, Jed. *Confederate Military History: Virginia.* Atlanta: Confederate Publishing Company, 1899.

Howard, Charles H. "First Day at Gettysburg." In *Military Essays and Recollections: Papers Read before the Commandery of the State of Illinois, Military Order of the Loyal Legion of the United States.* 1907. Reprint, Wilmington, N.C.: Broadfoot Publishing Company, 1992.

Howard, Oliver Otis. *Autobiography of Oliver Otis Howard.* 2 vols. New York: Baker & Taylor Company, 1907.

———. "Campaign and Battle of Gettysburg, June and July, 1863." *Atlantic Monthly* 38 (July 1876): 48–71.

Hudgins, F. L. "With the 38th Georgia Regiment." *Confederate Veteran* 26, no. 4 (April 1918): 161–63.

Humphreys, Andrew A. *From Gettysburg to the Rapidan: The Army of the Potomac, July, 1863, to April, 1864.* New York: Charles Scribner's Sons, 1883.

———. *Address of Maj. Gen. A. A. Humphreys on the Military Services of the Late Maj. Gen. George Gordon Meade, United States Army, Made at the Meade Memorial Meeting of the Citizens of Philadelphia, November 18, 1872.* Washington, D.C.: Gibson Brothers, Printers, 1872.

Hunt, Henry J. "The Second Day at Gettysburg." In Clarence C. Buel and Robert U. Johnson, eds., *Battles and Leaders of the Civil War.* 4 vols. New York: Century Company, 1884–1889.

———. "The Third Day at Gettysburg." In Clarence C. Buel and Robert U. Johnson, eds., *Battles and Leaders of the Civil War.* 4 vols. New York: Century Company, 1884–1889.

Imboden, John D., "The Confederate Retreat from Gettysburg." In Clarence C. Buel and Robert U. Johnson, eds., *Battles and Leaders of the Civil War.* 4 vols. New York: Century Company, 1884–1889.

———. "Lee at Gettysburg." *Galaxy* 11, no. 4 (April 1871): 507–13.

Inman, Arthur Crew, ed. *Soldier of the South: General Pickett's War Letters to His Wife.* Boston: Houghton Mifflin Co., 1928.

Irvine, R. M. "Brig. Gen. Richard B. Garnett." *Confederate Veteran* 23, no. 9 (September 1915): 391.

Jackson, Huntington W. "The Battle of Gettysburg." In *Military Essays and Recollections: Papers Read before the Commandery of the State of Illinois, Military Order of the Loyal Legion of the United States.* 1892. Reprint, Wilmington, N.C.: Broadfoot Publishing Company, 1992.

Jacobs, Henry E. "How an Eye-Witness Watched the Great Battle." *Philadelphia North American,* June 29, 1913.

Jeffries, John. "Letter to His Sister." In *Recollections and Reminiscences 1861–1865*. United Daughters of the Confederacy, South Carolina Division, 1991.

Jessup, Harlan R., ed. *The Painful News I Have to Write*. Baltimore, Md.: Butternut & Blue, 1998.

Johnston, David E. *Story of a Confederate Boy in the Civil War*. 1914. Reprint, Radford, Va.: Commonwealth Press, Inc., 1980.

Johnston, Hugh Buckner, ed. *The Civil War Letters of George Boardman Battle and of Walter Raleigh Battle of Wilson, North Carolina*. Wilson, N.C.: Wilson County Public Library, 1953.

Jones, A. C. "Longstreet at Gettysburg." *Confederate Veteran* 23, no. 12 (December 1915): 551–52.

Jones, Jesse H. "The Breastworks at Culp's Hill." In Clarence C. Buel and Robert U. Johnson, eds., *Battles and Leaders of the Civil War*. 4 vols. New York: Century Company, 1884–1889.

Jordan, David M. *"Happiness Is Not My Companion": The Life of General G. K. Warren*. Bloomington: Indiana University Press, 2001.

———. *Winfield Scott Hancock: A Soldier's Life*. Bloomington: Indiana University Press, 1988.

Keller, Oliver J. "Soldier General of the Army: John Fulton Reynolds." *Civil War History* 4, no. 2 (June 1958): 119–28.

Kempster, Walter. "The Cavalry at Gettysburg." In *War Papers: Being Papers Read before the Commandery of the State of Wisconsin, Military Order of the Loyal Legion of the United States*. 1914. Reprint, Wilmington, N.C.: Broadfoot Publishing Company, 1993.

Kershaw, J. B. "Kershaw's Brigade at Gettysburg." In Clarence C. Buel and Robert U. Johnson, eds., *Battles and Leaders of the Civil War*. 4 vols. New York: Century Company, 1884–1889.

Kidd, J. H. *A Cavalryman with Custer*. New York: Bantam Books, 1991.

Kimball, George. "A Young Hero of Gettysburg." *Century Magazine* 33, no. 1 (November 1886): 133–34.

Kohl, Lawrence Frederick, ed. *Memoirs of Chaplain Life: Three Years with the Irish Brigade in the Army of the Potomac*. 1894. Reprint, New York: Fordham University Press, 1992.

Ladd, David L., and Audrey J. Ladd, eds. *The Bachelder Papers: Gettysburg in Their Own Words*. 3 vols. Dayton, Ohio: Press of Morningside Bookshop, 1994.

"A Lady of Virginia." *Diary of a Southern Refugee*. New York: E. J. Hale & Son, 1868.

Law, E. M. "The Struggle for 'Round Top.' " In Clarence C. Buel and Robert U. Johnson, eds., *Battles and Leaders of the Civil War*. 4 vols. New York: Century Company, 1884–1889.

Lee, Alfred. "Reminiscences of the Gettysburg Battle." *Lippincott's Magazine* 6 (July 1883): 54–60.

Lee, Fitzhugh. *General Lee*. Greenwich, Conn.: Premiere Books, 1961.

Leon, Louis. *Diary of a Tar Heel Confederate Soldier*. Charlotte, N.C.: Stone Publishing Company, 1913.

Letterman, Jonathan. *Medical Recollections of the Army of the Potomac*. New York: D. Appleton and Company, 1866.

Lokey, J. W. "Wounded at Gettysburg." *Confederate Veteran* 22, no. 9 (September 1914): 400.

Long, A. L. *Memoirs of Robert E. Lee*. 1886. Reprint, Secaucus, N.J.: Blue and Grey Press, 1983.

———. "Letter to General Early." *Southern Historical Society Papers* 4, no. 2 (August 1877): 66–68.

Long, Roger. "A Mississippian in the Railroad Cut." *Gettysburg Magazine* 4 (January 1991): 22–24.

Longacre, Edward G. *Joshua Chamberlain: The Soldier and the Man*. Conshohocken, Pa.: Combined Books, 1999.

———. *General John Buford*. Conshohocken, Pa.: Combined Books, 1995.

———. "John F. Reynolds, General." *Civil War Times Illustrated* 11, no. 5 (August 1972): 26–43.

Longstreet, James. *From Manassas to Appomattox*. 1896. Reprint, Secaucus, N.J.: Blue and Grey Press, 1984.

———. "Lee in Pennsylvania." In *The Annals of the War Written by Leading Participants North and South*. 1876. Reprint, Dayton, Ohio: Press of Morningside Bookshop, 1988.

———. "Lee's Invasion of Pennsylvania." In Clarence C. Buel and Robert U. Johnson, eds., *Battles and Leaders of the Civil War*. 4 vols. New York: Century Company, 1884–1889.

———. "Lee's Left Wing at Gettysburg." In Clarence C. Buel and Robert U. Johnson, eds., *Battles and Leaders of the Civil War*. 4 vols. New York: Century Company, 1884–1889.

———. "Letter to Henry Heth." *Southern Historical Society Papers* 44 (1923): 240.

———. "The Mistakes of Gettysburg." In *The Annals of the War Written by Leading Participants North and South*. 1876. Reprint, Dayton, Ohio: Press of Morningside Bookshop, 1988.

Love, William A. "Experience in Battle." *Confederate Veteran* 33, no. 6 (January 1925): 221–22.

Marcus, Edward, ed. *A New Canaan Private in the Civil War: The Letters of Justus M. Silliman*. New Canaan, Conn.: New Canaan Historical Society, 1994.

Martin, Rawley W. "Armistead at the Battle of Gettysburg." *Southern Historical Society Papers* 39 (1914): 186–87.

Martin, Samuel J. *The Road to Glory: Confederate General Richard S. Ewell*. Indianapolis: Guild Press of Indiana, 1991.

Marye, John L. "The First Gun at Gettysburg: 'With the Confederate Advance Guard.' " *Civil War Regiments* 1, no. 1 (1990): 26–34.

Maurice, Frederick, ed. *An Aide-de-Camp of Lee: Being the Papers of Colonel Charles Marshall, Sometime Aide-de-Camp, Military Secretary, and Assistant Adjutant General on the Staff of Robert E. Lee, 1862–1865*. Boston: Little, Brown and Company, 1927.

Mayo, Joseph C. "Pickett's Charge at Gettysburg." *Southern Historical Society Papers* 34 (1906): 327–35.

McClellan, Henry B. *I Rode with Jeb Stuart: The Life and Campaigns of Major-General J. E. B. Stuart, Commander of the Cavalry of the Army of Northern Virginia*. 1958. Reprint, New York: Da Capo Press, 1994.

McCreary, Albertus. "Gettysburg: A Boy's Experience of the Battle." *McClure's Magazine* 33 (July 1909): 243–53.

McCurdy, Charles M. *Gettysburg: A Memoir*. Pittsburgh: Reed & Witting Company, 1929.

McDonald, Archie P., ed. *Make Me a Map of the Valley: The Civil War Journal of Stonewall Jackson's Topographer.* Dallas, Tex.: Southern Methodist University Press, 1973.

McKim, Randolph H. "The Gettysburg Campaign." *Southern Historical Society Papers* 40 (1912): 253–300.

———. *Soldier's Recollections.* 1910. Reprint, Washington, D.C.: Zenger Publishing Co., 1983.

———. "Steuart's Brigade at the Battle of Gettysburg." *Southern Historical Society Papers* 5, no. 6 (June 1878): 291–300.

McLaws, Lafayette. "Gettysburg." *Southern Historical Society Papers* 7, no. 2 (February 1879): 64–90.

McLean, James L., Jr., and Judy W. McLean, eds. *Gettysburg Sources.* 3 vols. Baltimore, Md.: Butternut and Blue, 1986, 1987, 1990.

Meade, George Gordon. *Life and Letters of George Gordon Meade.* 2 vols. New York: Charles Scribner's Sons, 1913.

Meade, George Gordon (son). *With Meade at Gettysburg.* Philadelphia: War Library and Museum, 1930.

Meredith, Jaquelin Marshall. "The First Day at Gettysburg." *Southern Historical Society Papers* 24 (1896): 182–87.

Miers, Earl Schenck, ed. *A Rebel War Clerk's Diary.* New York: A. S. Barnes & Company, Inc., 1961.

Monteiro, Aristides. *Confederate Surgeon.* Edited by S. G. L. Dannett and R. H. Burkart. New York: Dodd, Meade & Company, 1969.

Moon, W. H. "Beginning of the Battle of Gettysburg." *Confederate Veteran* 33, no. 12 (December 1925): 449–50.

Moore, Edward A. *The Story of a Cannoneer under Stonewall Jackson.* New York: Neale Publishing Company, 1907.

Morhous, Henry C. *Reminiscences of the 123rd Regiment, N.Y.S.V.* Greenwich, N.Y.: People's Journal Book and Job Office, 1879.

Morrison, James L., Jr., ed. *The Memoirs of Henry Heth.* Westport, Conn.: Greenwood Press, 1974.

———, ed. "The Memoirs of Henry Heth, Part 2." *Civil War History* 8, no. 3 (September 1962): 300–9.

Mosby, John S. "The Confederate Cavalry in the Gettysburg Campaign." In Clarence C. Buel and Robert U. Johnson, eds., *Battles and Leaders of the Civil War.* 4 vols. New York: Century Company, 1884–1889.

Motts, Wayne E. "Fighting Alex' Hays at Gettysburg." *Gettysburg Magazine* 24 (January 2001): 104–11.

——— "To Gain a Second Star: The Forgotten George S. Greene." *Gettysburg Magazine* 3 (July 1990): 65–76.

Murphy, Kevin C., ed. *The Civil War Letters of Joseph K. Taylor of the Thirty-Seventh Massachusetts Volunteer Infantry.* Lewiston, N.Y.: Edwin Mellen Press, 1998.

Nevins, Allan, ed. *A Diary of Battle: The Personal Journals of Colonel Charles S. Wainwright, 1861–1865.* 1922. Reprint, Gettysburg: Stan Clark Military Books, n.d.

Newhall, Frederick C. "Address." In *Dedication of the Monument to the Sixth Penna. Cavalry on the Battlefield of Gettysburg.* Philadelphia: Privately printed, 1868.

Nichols, Edward J. *Toward Gettysburg: A Biography of General John F. Reynolds.* University Park, Pa.: Pennsylvania State University Press, 1958.

Nichols, G. W. *A Soldier's Story of His Regiment.* Kennesaw, Ga.: Continental Book Company, 1898.

North, Edward. *Memorial of Henry Hastings Curran, Lieutenant-Colonel of the One Hundred and Forty-Sixth Regiment of the New York State Volunteers.* Albany: Joel Munsell, 1867.

Norton, Oliver Willcox. *Army Letters, 1861–1865.* 1903. Reprint, Dayton, Ohio: Press of Morningside Bookshop, 1990.

Oates, Stephen B. *With Malice toward None: The Life of Abraham Lincoln.* New York: Harper & Row, 1977.

Oates, William C. *The War between the Union and the Confederacy and Its Lost Opportunities.* 1905. Reprint, Dayton, Ohio: Press of Morningside Bookshop, 1985.

———. "Gettysburg—The Battle on the Right." *Southern Historical Society Papers* 6, no. 4 (October 1878): 172–82.

Osborne, Charles C. *Jubal: The Life and Times of General Jubal A. Early, CSA, Defender of the Lost Cause.* Baton Rouge: Louisiana State University Press, 1992.

Ott, Eugene Matthew, Jr., ed. "The Civil War Diary of James J. Kirkpatrick, Sixteenth Mississippi Infantry, C.S.A." Master's thesis, Texas A&M University, 1984.

Owen, Edward. "Diary." *Civil War Regiments* 5, no. 1 (1996): 120–35.

Pennypacker, Isaac. *General Meade.* New York: D. Appleton and Company, 1901.

Perry, Mark. *Conceived in Liberty: Joshua Chamberlain, William Oates, and the American Civil War.* New York: Viking, 1997.

Perry, W. F. "The Devil's Den." *Confederate Veteran* 9, no. 4 (April 1901): 161–63.

Pfanz, Donald C. *Richard S. Ewell: A Soldier's Life.* Chapel Hill, N.C.: University of North Carolina Press, 1998.

Phillips, Marion G., and Valerie Phillips Parsegian, eds. *Richard and Rhoda: Letters from the Civil War.* Washington, D.C.: Legation Press, 1981.

Pierson, William Whatley, Jr., ed. "The Diary of Bartlett Yancey Malone." *James Sprunt Historical Publications* 16 (1919): 3–59.

Pleasonton, Alfred. "The Campaign of Gettysburg." In *The Annals of the War Written by Leading Participants North and South.* 1876. Reprint, Dayton, Ohio: Press of Morningside Bookshop, 1988.

Priest, John Michael, ed. *John T. McMahon's Diary of the 136th New York 1861–1864.* Shippensburg, Pa.: White Mane Publishing Co., Inc., 1993.

Pryor, Shepard Green. "Letters." In *Recollections and Reminiscences 1861–1865.* United Daughters of the Confederacy, Georgia Division, 1996.

Pula, James S. *For Liberty and Justice: The Life and Times of Wladimir Krzyzanowski.* Chicago: Polish American Congress Charitable Foundation, 1978.

———, ed. *The Memoirs of Wladimir Krzyzanowski.* Translated by Stanley J. Pula. San Francisco: Rande Research Associates, 1978.

Quaife, Milo M., ed. *From the Cannon's Mouth: The Civil War Letters of General Alpheus S. Williams.* Detroit: Wayne State University Press, 1959.

Raphelson, Alfred C. "Alexander Schimmelfennig: A German-American Campaigner in the Civil War." *Pennsylvania Magazine of History and Biography* 87 (April 1963): 156–81.

Reagan, John H. *Memoirs.* New York: Neale Publishing Company, 1906.

Reid-Green, Marcia, ed. *Letters Home: Henry Matrau of the Iron Brigade.* Lincoln: University of Nebraska Press, 1994.

Reynolds, Donald E., ed. "A Mississippian in Lee's Army: The Letters of Leander Huckaby." *Journal of Mississippi History* 36, no. 3 (August 1974): 273–88.

Rhodes, Robert Hunt, ed. *All for the Union: A History of the 2nd Rhode Island Volunteer Infantry in the War of the Great Rebellion as Told by the Diary and Letters of*

Elisha Hunt Rhodes, Who Enlisted as a Private in '61 and Rose to the Command of His Regiment. Lincoln, R.I.: Andrew Mowbray Incorporated, 1985.

Richards, H. M. M. "Citizens of Gettysburg in the Union Army." In Clarence C. Buel and Robert U. Johnson, eds., *Battles and Leaders of the Civil War.* 4 vols. New York: Century Company, 1884–1889.

Rittenhouse, B. F. "The Battle of Gettysburg as Seen from Little Round Top." In *War Papers: Being Papers Read before the Commandery of the District of Columbia, Military Order of the Loyal Legion of the United States.* 1887–1897. Reprint, Wilmington, N.C.: Broadfoot Publishing Company, 1993.

Robertson, Beverly H. "The Confederate Cavalry in the Gettysburg Campaign." In Clarence C. Buel and Robert U. Johnson, eds., *Battles and Leaders of the Civil War.* 4 vols. New York: Century Company, 1884–1889.

Robertson, James I., Jr. *General A. P. Hill: The Story of a Confederate Warrior.* New York: Random House, 1987.

———, ed. *Four Years in the Stonewall Brigade.* Dayton, Ohio: Press of Morningside Bookshop, 1981.

Roebling, Washington A. *Wash Roebling's War.* Newark, Del.: Spiral Press, 1961.

Rollins, Richard, ed. *Pickett's Charge! Eyewitness Accounts.* Redondo Beach, Calif.: Rank and File Publications, 1994.

Rosenblatt, Emil, ed. *Anti-Rebel: The Civil War Letters of Wilbur Fisk.* Croton-on-Hudson, N.Y.: Published by the editor, 1983.

Rosengarten, Joseph G. "Admiral and General Reynolds." *The United Service* 2, no. 5 (July 1880): 613–34.

———. *Reynolds Memorial Address, March 8th, 1880.* Philadelphia: Historical Society of Pennsylvania, 1880.

———. "General Reynolds' Last Battle." In *The Annals of the War Written by Leading Participants North and South.* 1876. Reprint, Dayton, Ohio: Press of Morningside Bookshop, 1988.

Runge, William H., ed. *Four Years in the Confederate Horse Artillery: The Diary of Private Henry Robinson Berkeley.* Chapel Hill, N.C.: University of North Carolina Press, 1961.

Sauers, Richard A., ed. *Fighting Them Over: How the Veterans Remembered Gettysburg in the Pages of the National Tribune.* Baltimore: Butternut and Blue, 1998.

Scheibert, Justus. *Seven Months in Rebel States during the North American War, 1863.* Edited by William Stanley Hoole. Tuscaloosa, Ala.: Confederate Publishing Company, 1958.

Schuricht, Hermann. "Jenkins' Brigade in the Gettysburg Campaign." *Southern Historical Society Papers* 24 (1896): 339–50.

Schurz, Carl. *The Reminiscences of Carl Schurz.* 3 vols. New York: McClure Company, 1908.

———. "The Battle of Gettysburg." *McClure's Magazine* 29 (September 1907): 272–85.

Scott, Winfield. "Pickett's Charge as Seen from the Front Line." In *Civil War Papers of the California Commandery, Military Order of the Loyal Legion of the United States.* Wilmington, N.C.: Broadfoot Publishing Company, 1995.

Shivers, John Wilson. "An Account of Some of the Battles in Which I Fought." In *Recollections and Reminiscences 1861–1865.* United Daughters of the Confederacy, Georgia Division, 1997.

Shotwell, Randolph A. "Virginia and North Carolina in the Battle of Gettysburg." *Our Living and Our Dead* 4, no. 1 (March 1876): 80–97.

Shuffler, R. Henderson, ed. *Decimus et Ultimus Barziza: The Adventures of a Prisoner of War, 1863–1864.* Austin: University of Texas Press, 1964.

Sickles, Daniel E. "A Letter by General Daniel E. Sickles." In Clarence C. Buel and Robert U. Johnson, eds., *Battles and Leaders of the Civil War.* 4 vols. New York: Century Company, 1884–1889.

———. "Further Recollections of Gettysburg." *North American Review* 152, no. 3 (March 1891): 257–71.

Silliker, Ruth L., ed. *The Rebel Yell & the Yankee Hurrah.* Camden, Maine: Down East Books, 1985.

Silver, James W., ed. *The Confederate Soldier.* Memphis, Tenn.: Memphis State University Press, 1973.

Skelly, Daniel Alexander. *A Boy's Experiences during the Battles of Gettysburg.* Gettysburg: Published by the author, 1932.

Small, Harry Adams, ed. *The Road to Richmond: The Civil War Memoirs of Major Abner R. Small of the Sixteenth Maine Volunteers.* Berkeley, Calif.: University of California Press, 1939.

Smart, James G., ed. *A Radical View: The "Agate" Dispatches of Whitelaw Reid, 1861–1865.* Memphis, Tenn.: Memphis State University Press, 1976.

Smedley, Charles. *Life in Southern Prisons.* Lancaster, Pa.: Pearsol & Geist, Printers, *Daily Express* Office, 1865.

Smith, James Power. "General Lee at Gettysburg." *Southern Historical Society Papers* 33 (1905): 135–60.

———. "With Stonewall Jackson in the Army of Northern Virginia." *Southern Historical Society Papers* 43 (1920): 1–294.

Sorrel, G. Moxley. *Recollections of a Confederate Staff Officer.* 1905. Reprint, Dayton, Ohio: Press of Morningside Bookshop, 1978.

Sparks, David S., ed. *Inside Lincoln's Army: The Diary of Marsena Rudolph Patrick, Provost Marshal General, Army of the Potomac.* New York: Thomas Yoseloff, 1964.

Stevens, George T. *Three Years in the Sixth Corps.* Albany: S. R. Gray, Publisher, 1866.

Stevens, John W. *Reminiscences of the Civil War.* Hillsboro, Tex.: Mirror Print, 1902.

Stevens, Michael E., ed. *As If It Were Glory.* Madison: Madison House, Inc., 1998.

Stewart, Salome Myers. "Recollections of the Battle of Gettysburg." *Philadelphia North American,* July 7, 1900.

Stewart, William H. "Our March to Gettysburg." *Blue and Gray,* December 1893, pp. 300–301.

Strode, Hudson. *Jefferson Davis: Confederate President.* New York: Harcourt, Brace and Company, 1959.

Styple, William B., ed. *With a Flash of His Sword. The Writings of Major Holman S. Melcher 20th Maine Infantry.* Kearny, N.J.: Belle Grove Publishing Company, 1994.

Swanberg, W. A. *Sickles the Incredible.* New York: Ace Books, 1956.

Taylor, Emerson Gifford. *Gouverneur Kemble Warren: The Life and Letters of an American Soldier, 1830–1882.* New York: Houghton Mifflin Company, 1932.

Taylor, Michael W., ed. *The Cry Is War, War, War: The Civil War Correspondence of Lts. Burwell Thomas Cotton and George Job Huntley, 34th Regiment North Carolina Troops.* Dayton, Ohio: Press of Morningside Books, 1994.

———. "Col. James Keith Marshall: One of the Three Brigade Commanders Killed in the Pickett-Pettgrew-Trimble Charge." *Gettysburg Magazine* 15 (July 1996): 78–90.

———. "Ramseur's Brigade in the Gettysburg Campaign: A Newly Discovered Account by Capt. James I. Harris, Co. I, 30th Regt. N.C.T." *Gettysburg Magazine* 17 (July 1997): 26–40.

Taylor, Osmond B. "Report of Captain O. B. Taylor, Alexander's Battalion Artillery." *Southern Historical Society Papers* 13 (1885): 213–16.

Taylor, Walter H. *General Lee: His Campaigns in Virginia 1861–1865, with Personal Reminiscences.* 1906. Reprint, Dayton, Ohio: Press of Morningside Bookshop, 1975.

———. *Four Years with General Lee.* 1877. Reprint, with an Introduction by James I. Robertson, Jr., New York: Bonanza Books, 1962.

———. "The Campaign in Pennsylvania." In *The Annals of the War Written by Leading Participants North and South.* 1876. Reprint, Dayton, Ohio: Press of Morningside Bookshop, 1988.

Thomas, Emory M. *Robert E. Lee.* New York: W. W. Norton & Company, 1995.

Thomas, George. "The Maryland Confederate Monument at Gettysburg." *Southern Historical Society Papers* 14 (January–December 1886): 439–46.

Thompson, Benjamin W. "This Hell of Destruction." *Civil War Times Illustrated* 12, no. 6 (October 1973): 12–23.

Thompson, Richard S. "A Scrap of Gettysburg." In *Military Essays and Recollections: Papers Read before the Commandery of the State of Illinois, Military Order of the Loyal Legion of the United States.* 1899. Reprint, Wilmington, N.C.: Broadfoot Publishing Company, 1992.

"To Pennsylvania and Back." *Our Living and Our Dead,* April 22, 1874.

Tremain, Henry Edwin. *Two Days of War: A Gettysburg Narrative and Other Excursions.* New York: Bonnell, Silver & Co., 1905.

Trimble, Isaac R. "The Battle and Campaign of Gettysburg." *Southern Historical Society Papers* 26 (January–December 1898): 116–28.

Tucker, Glenn. *Hancock the Superb.* Indianapolis: Bobbs-Merrill Company, Inc., 1960.

Turney, J. B. "The First Tennessee at Gettysburg." *Confederate Veteran* 8, no. 12 (December 1900): 535–37.

Walker, Charles D., ed. *Memorial, Virginia Military Institute: Biographical Sketches of the Graduates and Elves of the Virginia Military Institute Who Fell during the War between the States.* Philadelphia: J. B. Lippincott & Co., 1875.

Walker, Francis A. *General Hancock.* New York: D. Appleton and Company, 1894.

Walker, R. Lindsay. "A Letter from General R. Lindsay Walker." *Southern Historical Society Papers* 5, no. 4 (April 1878): 180–81.

Wallber, Albert. "From Gettysburg to Libby Prison." In *War Papers: Being Papers Read before the Commandery of the State of Wisconsin, Military Order of the Loyal Legion of the United States.* 1914. Reprint, Wilmington, N.C.: Broadfoot Publishing Company, 1993.

Walters, Sara Gould. *Inscription at Gettysburg.* Gettysburg: Thomas Publications, 1991.

Ward, W. C. "Incidents and Personal Experiences on the Battlefield of Gettysburg." *Confederate Veteran* 8, no. 8 (August 1900): 345–49.

Watson, John W. "Letter." *Virginia Country's Civil War* 5: 61.

Welch, Spencer G. *A Confederate Surgeon's Letters to His Wife.* New York: Neale Publishing Company, 1911.

Weld, Stephen Minot. *War Diary and Letters of Stephen Minot Weld.* Cambridge, Mass.: Riverside Press, 1912.

Wellman, Manly Wade. *Rebel Boast: First at Bethel—Last at Appomattox.* New York: Henry Holt and Company, 1956.

Wert, Jeffry D. *General James Longstreet: The Confederacy's Most Controversial Soldier.* New York: Touchstone, 1993.

West, John C. *A Texan in Search of a Fight.* Waco, Tex.: Press of J. S. Hill & Co., 1901.

Whittaker, Frederick. *A Popular Life of Gen. George A. Custer.* New York: Sheldon & Co., 1876.

Wiley, Bell Irvin, ed. *Reminiscences of Big I.* Jackson, Tenn.: McCowat-Mercer Press, 1956.

Winkler, William K., ed. *Letters of Frederick C. Winkler 1862 to 1865.* Privately printed, 1963.

Winschel, Terrence, ed. "The Gettysburg Diary of Lieutenant William Peel." *Gettysburg Magazine* 9 (July 1993): 98–108.

Wolf, Hazel C., ed. "Campaigning with the First Minnesota: A Civil War Diary." *Minnesota History* 25, no. 4 (December 1944): 342–61.

Youngblood, William. "Personal Observations at Gettysburg." *Confederate Veteran* 19, no. 6 (June 1911): 286–87.

Zachry, Alfred. "Fighting with the 3d Georgia." *Civil War Times Illustrated* 33, no. 4 (September–October 1994): 26, 66–77.

OFFICIAL DOCUMENTS, REPORTS, AND MILITARY PAPERS

Hewett, Janet B., Noah Andre Trudeau, and Bryce A. Suderow. *Supplement to the Official Records of the Union and Confederate Armies.* Wilmington, N.C.: Broadfoot Publishing Company, 1994.

Report of the Joint Committee on the Conduct of the War. Washington, D.C.: Government Printing Office, 1863–1866.

The War of the Rebellion: A Compilation of the Official Records of the Union and Confederate Armies. Washington, D.C.: Government Printing Office, 1880–1901.

GETTYSBURG CAMPAIGN AND BATTLE STUDIES

Adams, William G., Jr. "Spencers at Gettysburg Fact or Fiction." *Military Affairs* 29 (spring 1965): 41–56.

Adelman, Garry E. *Little Round Top: A Detailed Tour Guide.* Gettysburg: Thomas Publications, 2000.

Adelman, Garry E., and Timothy H. Smith. *Devil's Den: A History and Guide.* Gettysburg: Thomas Publications, 1997.

Alexander, Ted. "Gettysburg Cavalry Operations, June 27–July 3, 1863." *Blue & Gray Magazine* 6, no. 1 (October 1988): 8–32, 36–41.

———. "Ten Days in July: The Pursuit to the Potomac." *North & South* 2, no. 6 (August 1999): 10–34.

Archer, John M. *"The Hour Was One of Horror": East Cemetery Hill at Gettysburg.* Gettysburg: Thomas Publications, 1997.

Arrington, B. T. *The Medal of Honor at Gettysburg*. Gettysburg: Thomas Publications, 1996.

Barnett, Bert. "Union Artillery on July 3." In *Mr. Lincoln's Army: The Army of the Potomac in the Gettysburg Campaign, Programs of the Sixth Annual Gettysburg Seminar*. Gettysburg: Gettysburg National Military Park, 1997.

Beecham, R. K. *Gettysburg: The Pivotal Battle of the Civil War*. Chicago: A. C. McClurg & Co., 1911.

Benedict, George G. *Vermont at Gettysburg*. Burlington, Vt.: Free Press Association, 1870.

Bennett, Gerald R. *Days of "Uncertainty and Dread."* Camp Hill, Pa.: Plank's Suburban Press, Inc., 1997.

Bertera, Martin, and Ken Oberholtzer. *The 4th Michigan Volunteer Infantry at Gettysburg: The Battle for the Wheatfield*. Dayton, Ohio: Press of Morningside Bookshop, 1997.

Black, Linda J. "Gettysburg's Preview of War: Early's June 26, 1864, Raid." *Gettysburg Magazine* 3 (July 1990): 3–8.

Boritt, Gabor S., ed. *The Gettysburg Nobody Knows*. New York: Oxford University Press, 1997.

Brown, Kent Masterson. "A Golden Bridge." *North & South* 2, no. 6 (August 1999): 56–65.

Busey, John W., and David G. Martin. *Regimental Strengths and Losses at Gettysburg*. Hightstown, N.J.: Longstreet House, 1994.

Campbell, Eric A. "Sacrificed to the Bad Management . . . of Others': Richard H. Anderson's Division at the Battle of Gettysburg." In *High Water Mark: The Army of Northern Virginia in the Gettysburg Campaign, Programs of the Seventh Annual Gettysburg Seminar*. Gettysburg: Gettysburg National Military Park, 1999.

———. " 'The Army Has Never Before Done So Much': The Army of the Potomac vs Public Opinion." In *Mr. Lincoln's Army: The Army of the Potomac in the Gettysburg Campaign, Programs of the Sixth Annual Gettysburg Seminar*. Gettysburg: Gettysburg National Military Park, 1997.

———. " 'We Saved the Line from Being Broken': Freeman McGilvery, John Bigelow, Charles Reed, and the Battle of Gettysburg." In *Unsung Heroes of Gettysburg, Programs of the Fifth Annual Gettysburg Seminar*. Gettysburg: Gettysburg National Military Park, 1996.

———. " 'Remember Harper's Ferry': The Degradation, Humiliation, and Redemption of Col. George L. Willard's Brigade." *Gettysburg Magazine* 7 (July 1992): 51–76.

———. "Caldwell Clears the Wheatfield." *Gettysburg Magazine* 3 (July 1990): 27–50.

Christ, Elwood. *The Struggle for the Bliss Farm at Gettysburg: July 2nd and 3rd 1863*. Baltimore: Butternut and Blue, 1994.

Coco, Gregory A. *A Concise Guide to the Artillery at Gettysburg*. Gettysburg: Thomas Publications, 1998.

———. *A Vast Sea of Misery: A History and Guide to the Union and Confederate Field Hospitals at Gettysburg, July 1–November 20, 1863*. Gettysburg: Thomas Publications, 1988.

Coddington, Edwin B. *The Gettysburg Campaign: A Study in Command*. New York: Charles Scribner's Sons, 1968.

Cooksey, Paul Clark. "The Plan for Pickett's Charge." *Gettysburg Magazine* 22 (January 2000): 66–79.

Coughenour, Kavin. " 'Andrew Atkinson Humphreys: Divisional Command in the Army of the Potomac.' " In *Mr. Lincoln's Army: The Army of the Potomac in the Gettysburg Campaign, Programs of the Sixth Annual Gettysburg Seminar.* Gettysburg: Gettysburg National Military Park, 1997.

Coxe, John. "The Battle of Gettysburg." *Confederate Veteran* 21, no. 9 (September 1913): 433–36.

Dickson, Christopher C. "Col. Francis Voltaire Randall and the 13th Vermont Infantry." *Gettysburg Magazine* 17 (July 1997): 83–102.

Downey, Fairfax. *The Guns at Gettysburg.* New York: Collier Books, 1962.

Durkin, James. "Never Shirking a Duty or Betraying a Trust." *Gettysburg Magazine* 14 (January 1996): 37–45.

Elmore, Thomas L. "The Grand Cannonade: A Confederate Perspective." *Gettysburg Magazine* 19 (July 1998): 100–12.

———. "Torrid Heat and Blinding Rain: A Meteorological and Astronomical Chronology of the Gettysburg Campaign." *Gettysburg Magazine* 13 (July 1995): 7–21.

———. "Courage against the Trenches: The Attack and Repulse of Steuart's Brigade on Culp's Hill." *Gettysburg Magazine* 7 (July 1992): 83–96.

Frassanito, William A. *Gettysburg: A Journey in Time.* New York: Charles Scribner's Sons, 1975.

French, Steve. "Hurry Was the Order of the Day." *North & South* 2, no. 6 (August 1999): 35–43.

Frey, Donald J. *Longstreet's Assault—Pickett's Charge: The Lost Record of Pickett's Wounded.* Shippensburg, Pa.: Burd Street Press, 2000.

Gallagher, Gary. "In the Shadow of Stonewall Jackson: Richard S. Ewell in the Gettysburg Campaign." *Virginia Country's Civil War* 5: 54–59.

———. "Brandy Station: The Civil War's Bloodiest Arena of Mounted Combat." *Blue & Gray Magazine* (October 1990): 9–22, 44–56.

———, ed. *The First Day at Gettysburg.* Kent, Ohio: Kent State University Press, 1992.

———, ed. *The Second Day at Gettysburg.* Kent, Ohio: Kent State University Press, 1993.

———, ed. *The Third Day at Gettysburg and Beyond.* Chapel Hill, N.C.: University of North Carolina Press, 1994.

Gottfried, Bradley M. "Wright's Charge on July 2, 1863: Piercing the Union Line or Inflated Glory?" *Gettysburg Magazine* 17 (July 1997): 70–82.

Hadden, R. Lee. "The Deadly Embrace: The Meeting of the Twenty-Fourth Regiment, Michigan Infantry and the Twenty-Sixth Regiment of North Carolina Troops at McPherson's Woods, Gettysburg, Pennsylvania, July 1, 1863." *Gettysburg Magazine* 5 (July 1991): 19–34.

Haines, Douglas C. "R. S. Ewell's Command, June 29–July 1, 1863." *Gettysburg Magazine* 9 (July 1993): 17–32.

Hamblen, Charles P. *Connecticut Yankees at Gettysburg.* Kent, Ohio: Kent State University Press, 1993.

Hanna, William. "A Gettysburg Myth Exploded: The Fabled Barlow-Goron Incident." *Civil War Times Illustrated* 24, no. 3 (May 1985): 42–47.

Hartwig, D. Scott. "It Struck Horror to Us All." *Gettysburg Magazine* 4 (January 1991): 89–100.

———. "The 11th Army Corps on July 1, 1863—'The Unlucky 11th.' " *Gettysburg Magazine* 2 (January 1990): 33–50.

———. "The Defense of McPherson's Ridge." *Gettysburg Magazine* 1 (July 1989): 15–24.

———. " 'Never Have I Seen Such a Charge': Pender's Light Division at Gettysburg, July 1." In *High Water Mark: The Army of Northern Virginia in the Gettysburg Campaign, Programs of the Seventh Annual Gettysburg Seminar.* Gettysburg: Gettysburg National Military Park, 1999.

Hassler, Warren W., Jr. *Crisis at the Crossroads: The First Day at Gettysburg.* 1970. Reprint, Gettysburg: Stan Clark Military Books, 1991.

Herdegen, Lance J., and William J. K. Beaudot. *In the Bloody Railroad Cut at Gettysburg.* Dayton, Ohio: Press of Morningside Bookshop, 1990.

Historical Publication Committee of the Hanover Chamber of Commerce. *Prelude to Gettysburg: Encounter at Hanover.* 1962. Reprint, Shippensburg, Pa.: Burd Street Press, 1994.

Jorgensen, Jay. "Confederate Artillery at Gettysburg." *Gettysburg Magazine* 24 (January 2001): 19–37.

Kegel, James A. *North with Lee and Jackson: The Lost Story of Gettysburg.* Mechanicsburg, Pa.: Stackpole Books, 1996.

Kross, Gary. "Gettysburg Vignettes: Attack from the West, Action on June 26." *Blue & Gray Magazine* 17, no. 5 (campaign 2000): 7–10.

———. "Gettysburg Vignettes: Pickett's Charge! Including Supporting Actions on Culp's Hill." *Blue & Gray Magazine* 16, no. 5 (campaign 1999): 6–64.

———. "Gettysburg Vignettes: 'To Die like Soldiers': The Retreat from Sickles' Front, July 2, 1863." *Blue & Gray Magazine* 15, no. 5 (campaign 1998): 6–65.

———. "Gettysburg Vignettes: Action on the Eastern Flank." *Blue & Gray Magazine* 14, no. 5 (campaign 1997): 6–65.

———. "Gettysburg Vignettes: The Confederate Approach to Little Round Top: A March of Attrition." *Blue & Gray Magazine* 13, no. 3 (winter 1996): 7–24.

———. "Gettysburg Vignettes: Farnsworth's Charge: "Cavalry Could Fight Anywhere, Except at Sea." *Blue & Gray Magazine* 13, no. 3 (winter 1996): 44–53.

———. "Gettysburg Vignettes: The Alabamians' Attack on Little Round Top: 'A Cheeky Piece of Work on Both Sides.' " *Blue & Gray Magazine* 13, no. 3 (winter 1996): 54–61.

———. "Gettysburg Vignettes: Fight like the Devil to Hold Your Own: General John Buford's Cavalry at Gettysburg on July 1, 1863." *Blue & Gray Magazine* 12, no. 3 (February 1995): 9–22.

———. "Gettysburg Vignettes: That One Error Fills Him with Faults: Gen. Alfred Iverson and His Brigade at Gettysburg." *Blue & Gray Magazine* 12, no. 3 (February 1995): 22–24, 48–53.

———. "Gettysburg Vignettes: At the Time Impracticable: Dick Ewell's Decision on the First Day at Gettysburg." *Blue & Gray Magazine* 12, no. 3 (February 1995): 53–59.

Lash, Gary. *The Gibralter Brigade on East Cemetery Hill.* Baltimore, Md.: Butternut and Blue, 1995.

Long, Roger. "Over the Wall." *Gettysburg Magazine* 13 (July 1995): 64–74.

Longacre, Edward G. *The Cavalry at Gettysburg*. Lincoln, Nebr.: University of Nebraska Press, 1986.

Love, William A. "Mississippi at Gettysburg." *Publications of the Mississippi Historical Society* 9 (1906): 25–51.

Martin, David G. *Gettysburg July 1*. Conshohocken, Pa.: Combined Books, 1996.

Martin, Rawley W., and John H. Smith. "The Battle of Gettysburg and the Charge of Pickett's Division." *Southern Historical Society Papers* 32 (1904): 183–95.

Maust, Roland R. "The Union Second Corps Hospital at Gettysburg, July 2 to August 8, 1863." *Gettysburg Magazine* 10 (January 1994): 53–101.

McLean, James L., Jr. *Cutler's Brigade at Gettysburg*. Baltimore: Butternut and Blue, 1994.

McNeily, J. S. "Barksdale's Mississippi Brigade at Gettysburg." *Publications of the Mississippi Historical Society* 14 (1914): 231–65.

Miers, Earl Schenck, and Richard A. Brown, eds. *Gettysburg*. New Brunswick, N.J.: Rutgers University Press, 1948.

Murray, R. L. *The Redemption of the "Harper's Ferry Cowards."* Published by the author, 1994.

———. *A Perfect Storm of Lead*. Wolcott, N.Y.: Benedum Books, 2000.

Nesbitt, Mark. *Saber and Scapegoat: J. E. B. Stuart and the Gettysburg Controversy*. Mechanicsburg, Pa.: Stackpole Books, 1994.

Norton, Oliver Willcox. *The Attack and Defense of Little Round Top, Gettysburg, July 2, 1863*. 1913. Reprint, Dayton, Ohio: Press of Morningside Bookshop, 1978.

Nye, Wilbur Sturtevant. *Here Come the Rebels!* 1965. Reprint, Dayton, Ohio: Press of Morningside Bookshop, 1984.

O'Brien, Kevin E. " 'A Perfect Roar of Musketry': Candy's Brigade in the Fight for Culp's Hill." *Gettysburg Magazine* 9 (July 1993): 81–97.

O'Neill, Robert F., Jr. *The Cavalry Battles of Aldie, Middleburg and Upperville*. Lynchburg, Va.: H. E. Howard, Inc., 1993.

Patterson, Gerard A. *Debris of Battle: The Wounded of Gettysburg*. Mechanicsburg, Pa.: Stackpole Books, 1997.

———. "The Death of 'Iverson's Brigade.' " *Gettysburg Magazine* 5 (July 1991): 13–18.

Penny, Morris M., and J. Gary Laine. *Struggle for the Round Tops*. Shippensburg, Pa.: Burd Street Press, 1999.

Pfanz, Harry W. *Gettysburg: The First Day*. Chapel Hill, N.C.: University of North Carolina Press, 2001.

———. *Gettysburg: Culp's Hill & Cemetery Hill*. Chapel Hill, N.C.: University of North Carolina Press, 1993.

———. *Gettysburg: The Second Day*. Chapel Hill, N.C.: University of North Carolina Press, 1987.

Powell, David A. "A Reconnaissance Gone Awry: Capt. Samuel R. Johnston's Fateful Trip to Little Round Top." *Gettysburg Magazine* 23 (July 2000): 88–99.

Priest, John Michael. *Into the Fight: Pickett's Charge at Gettysburg*. Shippensburg, Pa.: White Mane Publishing Co., Inc., 1998.

Reardon, Carol. *Pickett's Charge in History & Memory*. Chapel Hill, N.C.: University of North Carolina Press, 1997.

Rollins, Richard. "The Second Wave of Pickett's Charge." *Gettysburg Magazine* 18 (January 1998): 96–113.

———. "Pickett's Charge and the Principles of War." *North & South* 4, no. 5 (June 2001): 12–25.

———. "The Failure of the Confederate Artillery in Pickett's Charge." *North & South* 3, no. 4 (April 2000): 26–42.

———. "Confederate Artillery Prepares for Pickett's Charge." *North & South* 2, no. 7 (September 1999): 41–55.

Rollins, Richard, and Dave L. Shulz. "A Combined and Concentrated Fire: The Federal Artillery at Gettysburg, July 3, 1863." *North & South* 2, no. 3 (March 1999): 39–60.

Scott, John O. "The Texans at Gettysburg." *Sherman Register,* March 31, 1897.

Shevchuk, Paul M. "The Wounding of Albert Jenkins, July 2, 1863." *Gettysburg Magazine* 3 (July 1990): 51–64.

———. "The Fight for Brinkerhoff's Ridge, July 2, 1863." *Gettysburg Magazine* 2 (January 1990): 61–74.

———. "The Battle of Hunterstown, Pennsylvania, July 2, 1863." *Gettysburg Magazine* 1 (July 1989): 93–104.

Shue, Richard S. *Morning at Willoughby Run: The Opening Battle at Gettysburg, July 1, 1863.* Gettysburg: Thomas Publications, 1998.

Shultz, David L. *"Double Canister at Ten Yards!" The Federal Artillery and the Repulse of Pickett's Charge.* Redondo Beach, Calif.: Rank and File Publications, 1995.

Smith, Karlton. "Pettigrew and Trimble: The Other Half of the Story." In *Unsung Heroes of Gettysburg, Programs of the Fifth Annual Gettysburg Seminar.* Gettysburg: Gettysburg National Military Park, 1996.

Stewart, George R. *Pickett's Charge.* New York: Premier Books, 1963.

Storch, Marc, and Beth Storch. " 'What a Deadly Trap We Were In': Archer's Brigade on July 1, 1863." *Gettysburg Magazine* 6 (January 1992): 13–28.

———. "Unpublished Gettysburg Reports by the 2nd and 7th Wisconsin Infantry Regimental Commanders." *Gettysburg Magazine* 17 (July 1997): 20–25.

Swallow, William H. "From Fredericksburg to Gettysburg." *Southern Bivouac,* n.s., 1, no. 6 (November 1885): 352–366.

———. "The First Day at Gettysburg." *Southern Bivouac,* n.s., 1, no. 7 (December 1885): 436–44.

———. "The Second Day at Gettysburg." *Southern Bivouac,* n.s., 1, no. 8 (January 1886): 490–99.

———. "The Third Day at Gettysburg." *Southern Bivouac,* n.s., 1, no. 9 (February 1886): 562–72.

Taylor, Michael W. "The Unmerited Censure of Two Maryland Staff Officers, Maj. Osmun Latrobe and First Lt. W. Stuart Symington." *Gettysburg Magazine* 13 (July 1995): 75–88.

Toombs, Samuel. *New Jersey Troops in the Gettysburg Campaign.* Orange, N.J.: Evening Mail Publishing House, 1898.

Trinque, Bruce A. "Arnold's Battery and the 26th North Carolina." *Gettysburg Magazine* 12 (January 1995): 61–67.

Tucker, Glenn. *Lee and Longstreet at Gettysburg.* New York: Bobbs-Merrill Company, Inc., 1968.

———. *High Tide at Gettysburg.* 1958. Reprint, Dayton, Ohio: Press of Morningside Bookshop, 1980.

Vanderslice, John M. *Gettysburg: A History of the Gettysburg Battle-field Memorial Association with an Account of the Battle.* Philadelphia: J. B. Lippincott Company, 1897.

Ward, David A. " 'Sedgwick's Foot Cavalry': The March of the Sixth Corps to Gettysburg." *Gettysburg Magazine* 22 (January 2000): 42–65.

Wert, Jeffry D. *Gettysburg: Day Three.* New York: Simon & Schuster, 2001.

Williams, Frank J. " 'We Had Only to Stretch Forth Our Hands.' " *North & South* 2, no. 6 (August 1999): 66–73.

Wittenberg, Eric J. *Gettysburg's Forgotten Cavalry Actions.* Gettysburg: Thomas Publications, 1998.

———. "Merritt's Regulars on South Cavalry Field: Oh, What Could Have Been." *Gettysburg Magazine* 16 (January 1997): 111–23.

———. "John Buford and the Gettysburg Campaign." *Gettysburg Magazine* 11 (July 1994): 19–55.

———. " 'This Was a Night Never to Be Forgotten.' " *North & South* 2, no. 6 (August 1999): 44–55.

Wright, Steven J. " 'Don't Let Me Bleed to Death': The Wounding of Maj. Gen. Winfield Scott Hancock." *Gettysburg Magazine* 6 (January 1992): 87–93.

SECONDARY SOURCES

Adams, Michael C. C. *Our Masters the Rebels: A Speculation on Union Military Failure in the East, 1861–1865.* Cambridge, Mass.: Harvard University Press, 1978.

Andrews, J. Cutler. *The North Reports the Civil War.* Pittsburgh: University of Pittsburgh Press, 1955; rev. ed., 1983.

———. *The South Reports the Civil War.* Pittsburgh: University of Pittsburgh Press, 1970.

Beckett, Ian F. W. *The War Correspondents: The American Civil War.* London: Alan Sutton, 1993.

Beyer, W. F., and O. F. Keydel, eds. *Deeds of Valor: From the Records on File in the Archives of the United States Government: How American Heroes Won the Medal of Honor.* 2 vols. Detroit: Perrien-Keydel Co., 1907.

Buell, Thomas B. *The Warrior Generals: Combat Leadership in the Civil War.* New York: Three Rivers Press, 1997.

Chapman, John A. *History of Edgefield County from the Earliest Settlements to 1897.* Newberry, S.C.: Elbert H. Aull, Publisher and Printer, 1897.

Clement, Maude Carter, ed. *The History of Pittsylvania County, Va.* Lynchburg, Va.: 1929.

Conklin, Eileen F. *Women at Gettysburg 1863.* Gettysburg: Thomas Publications, 1993.

Connelly, Thomas L. *The Marble Man: Robert E. Lee and His Image in American Society.* Baton Rouge: Louisiana State University Press, 1977.

Crozier, Emmet. *Yankee Reporters 1861–65.* 1956. Reprint, Westport, Conn.: Greenwood Press, 1973.

DePeyster, John W. *Decisive Conflicts of the Late Civil War.* New York: MacDonald & Co., 1867.

Fishel, Edwin C. *The Secret War for the Union: The Untold Story of Military Intelligence in the Civil War.* Boston: Houghton Mifflin Company, 1996.

Folsom, James Madison. *Heroes and Martyrs of Georgia*. Macon, Ga.: Burke, Boykin & Company, 1864.

Freeman, Douglas Southall. *Lee's Lieutenants*. 3 vols. New York: Charles Scribner's Sons, 1944.

Furgurson, Ernest B. *Chancellorsville 1863: The Souls of the Brave*. New York: Alfred A. Knopf, 1992.

Gold, Thomas D. *History of Clarke County, Virginia, and Its Connection with the War between the States*. Berryville, Va.: Chesapeake Book Company, 1962.

Lowenfels, Walter, ed. *Walt Whitman's Civil War*. New York: Alfred A. Knopf, 1961.

Moore, Frank, ed. *The Rebellion Record: A Diary of American Events*. 12 vols. 1861–1866. Reprint, New York: Arno Press, 1977.

Nolan, Alan T. *Lee Considered: General Robert E. Lee and Civil War History*. Chapel Hill, N.C.: University of North Carolina Press, 1991.

Palmer, Michael A. *Lee Moves North*. New York: John Wiley & Sons, Inc., 1998.

Rodenbough, Theodore F. *The Bravest Five Hundred of '61*. New York: G. W. Dillingham, 1891.

Schildt, John W. *Roads to Gettysburg*. Parsons, W.V.: McClain Printing Company, 1978.

———. *Roads from Gettysburg*. Chewsville, Md.: Published by the author, 1979.

Sears, Stephen W. *Chancellorsville*. New York: Houghton Mifflin Company, 1996.

Snyder, Charles. *Oswego County, New York in the Civil War*. Oswego County Historical Society, 1962.

Starr, Louis M. *Reporting the Civil War*. New York: Collier Books, 1962.

Starr, Stephen Z. *The Union Cavalry in the Civil War*. 3 vols. Baton Rouge: Louisiana State University Press, 1981.

Stine, J. H. *History of the Army of the Potomac*. Washington, D.C.: Gibson Brothers, 1903.

Swinton, William. *Campaigns of the Army of the Potomac*. 1866. Reprint, Secaucus, N.J.: Blue and Grey Press, 1988.

Tap, Bruce. *Over Lincoln's Shoulder: The Committee on the Conduct of the War*. Lawrence, Kans.: University Press of Kansas, 1998.

Wert, Jeffry D. *A Brotherhood of Valor: The Common Soldiers of the Stonewall Brigade, C.S.A., and the Iron Brigade, U.S.A*. New York: Simon & Schuster, 1999.

Williams, T. Harry. *Lincoln and His Generals*. New York: Vintage Books, 1952.

Wills, Garry. *Lincoln at Gettysburg: The Words That Remade America*. New York: Simon & Schuster, 1992.

Wise, Jennings Cropper. *The Long Arm of Lee*. 2 vols. 1915. Reprint, Lincoln: University of Nebraska Press, 1991.

Woodworth, Steven E. *Davis and Lee at War*. Lawrence, Kans.: University Press of Kansas, 1995.

NEWSPAPERS

Aberdeen (Mississippi) *Examiner*
Advertiser and Register (Mobile)
Atlanta Journal
Brooklyn Daily Eagle
Buffalo Evening News
Burlington Free Press

Cattaraugus (New York) *Freeman*
Charleston News and Courier
Charlotte (North Carolina) *Observer*
Charlottesville (Virginia) *Progress*
Columbus (Georgia) *Daily Enquirer*
Detroit Free Press
Daily Intelligencer (Doylestown, Pennsylvania)
Gettysburg Compiler
Grand Rapids (Michigan) *Democrat*
Hunterdon (New Jersey) *Republican*
The Index
The Irish American (New York)
Lenoir (North Carolina) *News Topic*
Mauston (Wisconsin) *Star*
Memphis Weekly Appeal
Milwaukee (Sunday) Telegraph
Minneapolis Journal
Missouri Republican
Mobile (Alabama) *Advertiser and Register*
National Tribune (Washington, D.C.)
New Haven (Connecticut) *Journal and Courier*
New Orleans Picayune
New York Dispatch
New York Herald
New York Times
New York World
Norfok (Massachusetts) *County Journal*
Norwich (Connecticut) *Morning Bulletin*
Philadelphia Evening Bulletin
Philadelphia Inquirer
Philadelphia Record
Philadelphia Weekly Press
Philadelphia Weekly Times
Pittsburgh Evening Chronicle
Portage County (Ohio) *Newspaper*
Raleigh Observer
Richmond Daily Dispatch
Richmond Enquirer
Richmond (Indiana) *Palladium*
Richmond Times Dispatch
Richmond Whig
Rochester (New York) *Daily Union & Advertiser*
Rochester (New York) *Evening Express*
St. Paul (Minnesota) *Pioneer*
Savannah Morning News
Savannah Republican
Schenectady (New York) *Evening Star and Times*
Semi-Weekly Standard (Raleigh, North Carolina)
Southern Banner (Athens, Georgia)

Star and Sentinel (Gettysburg)
Syracuse (New York) *Standard*
Waco Daily Times-Herald
Winchester (Indiana) *Journal*
Winston-Salem Sentinel

INDEX

African-Americans, 79; seizure of civilians, 79; slaves escape into Federal lines, 59

Alabama troops: artillery (Jeff Davis Artillery, 466); infantry (3rd Regiment, 210), (4th Regiment, 346, 518), (5th Battalion, 159, 166, 168), (8th Regiment, 310), (10th Regiment, 308–10), (11th Regiment, 308–10), (13th Regiment, 158–59, 166, 168, 179, 182, 185–86), (15th Regiment, 339, 340, 347–48, 353–54, 359–60, 371, 519), (44th Regiment, 343, 344–45), (47th Regiment, 336, 340, 347–48, 350–51), (48th Regiment, 336, 339, 344, 345, 360–62)

Aldie, Va., 53, 73

Alexander, Edward Porter, 20–21, 28, 95, 133, 273–74, 297, 312, 328–30, 380–81, 427, 466–68, 484, 485–86, 522, 557; designs July 3 bombardment, 445–46, 452–53, 471; exchange with Longstreet, 459, 460, 461–63, 474–75

Allen, Nathaniel, 385n

Ames, Adelbert, 397, 401

Ames, John W., 95

Ammunition. *See* Armament

Amsberg, George von, 205

Anderson, George T. "Tige," 343

Anderson, Richard H., 192, 247, 458, 510, 557; command decisions, 394

Aquia Landing, Va., 41

Archer, James J., 158, 179, 185–86; captured, 182; command decisions, 182

Arkansas troops: infantry (3rd Regiment, 324, 337, 341)

Armament, Union cavalry arms July 1, 163n

Armistead, Lewis A., 501, 506–7, 512; wounded, 507–8

Army of Northern Virginia, brigades (Stonewall Brigade, 373–75, 397, 428, 438, 447, 449) (Texas Brigade, 324, 331, 334, 335–36); executions, 75; forages in Pennsylvania, 55, 82, 90–92, 123; General Orders No. 73, 90; reorganized by Lee, 17–19

Army of the Potomac, brigades (Irish Brigade, 302–3), (Iron Brigade, 36–37, 162, 163, 173, 174, 181, 182–84, 185–86, 188, 196, 203, 224, 226–28, 230–31, 232, 260) (Philadelphia Brigade, 495–96, 525); executions, 36–37, 59; forages in Virginia, 54; morale after Chancellorsville, 11–12; northward march, 41, 44–45, 50, 54, 58–59, 70–71, 72–73, 80, 95–96, 108–9, 118–20, 136–37

Arrowsmith, George, 149, 229

Artillery Reserve (Army of the Potomac), 476; ammunition supply carried, 286

Ashby's Gap, Va., 58

Aughinbaugh, Nellie, 283, 303–4, 554

Avery, Isaac E., 298, 404
Ayres, Romeyn B., 365

Bacon, Elijah W., 511n
Balson, Edwin H., 36
Baltimore, Md., 81, 94, 101, 105, 111,
    115, 118, 119, 122, 125, 132, 138,
    154, 266, 284, 398, 414, 432, 540
Baltimore and Ohio Railroad (B&O),
    116
Baltimore Pike, 221, 255, 256, 260,
    264, 267, 270, 278, 296, 378, 398,
    417, 431, 433, 437–38, 516
Baltimore Street, 240, 251, 282, 317,
    337, 450, 532
Barksdale, William, 359, 367–68,
    386–89, 417; described, 321
Barlow, Arabella, 249, 258, 418–19,
    523
Barlow, Francis C., 214, 418, 557;
    command decisions, 217–18,
    222–24; wounded, 224, 249
Barlow's Knoll. See Blocher's Knoll
Barnes, James, 359; wounded, 469
Barr, Agnes, 106
Baxter, Henry, 206
Bayly, Harriet, 167–68
Bayly, William H., 429, 532
Beauregard, P. G. T., army in effigy, 63,
    71–72, 113
Beecham, Robert K., 11, 14, 184
Bell, Robert, 65, 79, 84
Benedict, George G., 500
Benett, John W., 518
Benner's Hill, 277, 278, 313, 331, 372,
    373, 397, 437, 465
Benning, Henry L., 342
Berdan, Hiram, 310
Berkeley, Henry Robinson, 62
Betts, A. D., 62
Beveridge, John L., 165, 170
Biddle, Chapman, 200
Biesecker's Woods, 327
Big Round Top, 289, 321, 337, 338,
    339–40, 347–51, 353, 359–60,
    371, 410–11, 430, 447, 456, 517,
    518–19
Bigelow, John, 275, 384–85, 386–87
Bingham, Henry H., 499, 512

Birney, David B., 294–96, 384, 415;
    succeeds Sickles, 376–77
Bisbee, George D., 149
Black, John L., 460, 471
Black Horse Tavern, 200, 417
Blackford, Eugene, 437
Blackford, William W., 108
Blair, John A., 194, 195
Bliss farm, 284–85, 290–91, 300–301,
    317, 335, 339, 393–94, 440, 443,
    449; burned, 451–52
Blocher's Knoll, 217, 223, 225, 241, 307
Bormann fuse, 452
Bowen, George D., 335
Bradwell, I. G., 91
Brady, John L., 285, 290, 502–3
Brainard, Henry C., 364
Brandy Station, Va., Battle of, 30–32
Breck, George, 202
Brewster, William R., 379
Brian farm. See Brien farm
Brickyard Lane, 311–12, 401, 403, 404,
    405, 409
Brien farm, 494
Bright, Robert A., 495, 500
Brinkerhoff's Ridge, 373–74
Broadbent, George, 355
Broadhead, Sarah "Sallie" R., 65, 75,
    84, 99, 106, 123, 129, 143, 154,
    171, 268, 283, 303, 356, 414, 429,
    437, 464, 532, 542, 557
Brockenbrough, John M., 163, 480,
    485, 487–88
Brooke, John R., 365
Brooks, James M., 504
Brown, G. Campbell, 170, 212, 216,
    218, 274, 284
Brown, J. Thompson, 274
Brown, Philip, 209
Brown, William, 79
Brown Jr., Morris, 511n
Bryan farm. See Brien farm
Buck, Daniel W., 165
Buckingham, Lynde W., 60
Buckles, Abram, 186
Bucklyn, John K., 328, 367
Buehler, Fannie, 65, 85
Buford, John, 24, 30, 32, 127–28, 135,
    176, 557; analysis of performance,

272; comments on July 1
    leadership, 264; departs Gettysburg,
    306; sets Gettysburg defense,
    141–43, 147–48, 166–67, 170
Bulger, Michael J., 350–51
Bull Run, Va., (battlefield), 58–59
Burbank, Sidney, 380
Bureau of Military Information,
    described, 14–15
Burgwyn Jr., Henry K., 17, 39, 55, 107,
    224, 226–28, 231–32
Burling, George C., 314, 349
Burner, John, 438
Burns, John, 203, 248
Bushman farm, 337
Bushman Hill, 336, 339
Bushwhackers, 72
Butterfield, Daniel, 53, 100, 292, 557;
    polls commanders, 415; wounded,
    469
Byington, Homer, 432–33, 523
Bynum, G.W., 48

Cabell, Henry C., 320
Caldwell, John C., 354–55
Calef, John H., 166–67, 168, 171, 182,
    202
Camp, Norman H., 508
Carey, Hugh, 396n
Carlisle, Casper R., 368n
Carlisle, Pa., 96, 262–63, 278
Carlisle Road, 154, 204, 228, 251, 261
Carlton, Henry H., 453
Carroll, Samuel, 409
Carter, Thomas H., 205, 206
Cashtown, Pa., 128, 135, 139, 324
Cashtown Gap/Pass, 133, 162, 165,
    175, 192, 252, 258, 333, 441, 536;
    Confederate troops ambushed, 83
Cashtown Pike. See Chambersburg Pike
Casler, John O., 20, 91
Casualties, Brandy Station, 32; Culp's
    Hill, 440, 449; Gettysburg (July
    1–3), 529; Hunterstown, 331; July
    1, 272; July 2, 421; July 3, 524–25;
    McPherson Ridge (July 1 A.M.),
    186
Cemetery Hill, July 1: 197–98, 205,
    208, 215, 218, 235–36, 240,

244–45, 247–48, 249–50, 255,
    258, 260, 261–62, 266, 272; July
    2: 277–78, 280–83, 285, 288, 293,
    298, 302, 307, 311, 313, 316, 317,
    372–73, 392, 397, 401–2, 405–8;
    July 3: 428, 436–37, 450, 452,
    455, 458, 466, 472, 486, 488, 490,
    496, 510, 526
Cemetery Ridge, 181, 280, 283, 285,
    288, 290–92, 294, 300–301, 304,
    314, 317, 320, 326–27, 368, 377,
    380, 383, 385–86, 388, 392–94,
    396–97, 398, 402–03, 404, 416;
    July 3: 430, 436, 439, 443, 449,
    451–52, 455, 458, 461, 466, 468,
    469, 471–72, 474, 477, 484, 486,
    488, 493–95, 497, 499, 501, 504,
    505, 506, 508, 512–14, 518, 520,
    522, 525–26, 529
Chamberlain, Joshua, 11–12, 305,
    410–11, 557; defends Little Round
    Top, 340–41, 357, 359–61,
    364–65, 368–71
Chambersburg, Pa., 46–48, 95, 121
Chambersburg Pike, 156, 159, 166,
    167, 168, 170, 171, 176, 180, 182,
    187, 188, 191, 193–94, 199, 203,
    204, 213, 216, 219, 232, 233, 246,
    247, 252, 297, 333, 411, 429, 465,
    466, 537
Chancellorsville, Va., Battle of, 6, 8
Chandler, Zachariah, 546
Chapman, Orrin, 148, 195
Christian, William S., 79, 488
Clark, A. Judson, 380
Clark, Harrison, 389n
Clarke, John J., 279
Clopp, John E., 511n
Cocke, William Henry, 121, 332–33
Codori farm, 169, 174, 200, 353, 438,
    416, 454, 490, 498, 501
Coffin, Charles Carleton, 112, 125, 138,
    433, 457, 522, 558
Colgrove, Silas, 439–40
Columbia, Pa., 104
Colvill, William, 73, 392–93
Committee on the Conduct of the War,
    98, 546–49
Connally, John K., 180

Connecticut troops: infantry (14th
    Regiment, 11, 25–26, 54, 503),
    (17th Regiment, 218, 223, 403)
Cook, Thomas M., 60
Cooper, Samuel, 113
Copse of Trees, 455, 495, 496, 499,
    502, 505, 506, 507, 508
Corby, William, 303
Coster, Charles R., 157, 240–41
Couch, Darius N., 34
Council of War, 414–15
Cox, A. S., 187
Crawford, Samuel W., 57, 86, 522n
Crenshaw Mill, 1
Cromwell, James, 343
Cross, Edward E., 108–9, 354–55, 363
Crounse, Lorenzo L., 263–64, 285–86,
    419
Cullum, Washington, 94
Culp, E. C., 268
Culp, Peter, 172
Culp, Wesley, 449
Culp's Hill, 249, 256, 257, 259–61,
    267, 268–69, 279, 281, 282, 287,
    292, 306–7, 313, 372–73, 375,
    378, 395–96, 397–400, 401–2,
    404, 408–9, 421, 428, 430–31,
    434–35, 439–40, 443–44, 447–49,
    450, 455, 458, 473, 484, 526, 529,
    534, 538
Cummings, C. C., 28, 82
Curtin, Andrew G., 34
Curtis, William, 403
Cushing, Alonzo H., 276, 478, 496;
    killed, 498
Custer, George A., 118, 330, 456–57
Cutler, Lysander, 162, 169, 173, 178

Dana, Amasa E., 162, 164
Dana, Edmund C., 217, 233
Daniel, Junius, 210, 213, 216, 219, 428
Davis, Jefferson, 4–5, 113, 545
Davis, Joseph R., 178, 487, 490,
    520–21
Dawes, Rufus R., 149, 163, 188,
    192–96, 239, 246, 248, 258, 558
Dawson, Francis W., 72
Dearing, James, 467, 485
De Castro, Joseph H., 511n

Delaware troops: infantry (1st
    Regiment, 285, 290, 301, 439,
    443, 502)
DeLeon, Thomas Cooper, 113
Dement, William F., 372
Devereux, Arthur F., 499
Devil's Den, 314, 315, 322, 325, 328,
    337–39, 341–46, 349, 355–56,
    358, 366, 371
Devil's Den Ridge. See Houck's Ridge
Devin, Thomas C., 170
Dilger, Hubert, 208–9
Doles, George C., 204, 215, 217, 218,
    225–26, 271, 407
Donaldson, Francis Adams, 95–96, 119
Dooley, John, 49, 333, 425–26, 430,
    451, 453, 464, 467, 470, 476, 489,
    502, 558
Dore, George H., 494n
Doubleday, Abner, 156, 182, 188, 196,
    244, 286, 558; command decisions,
    206, 213, 219, 236, 240;
    observations about Howard, 201,
    215; testifies against Meade, 547;
    wounded, 469
Douglas, Henry Kyd, 61, 97, 245;
    wounded, 439
Douglass, Robert T., 20
Dudley, William, 149
Duffy, James, 496
Duke, J. W., 321, 419
Dungan, R. H., 428n
Dwight, Walton, 213

Eagle Hotel, 147, 254
Early, Jubal A., 25, 111, 140, 251,
    256–57, 261–62, 511; orders
    Wrightsville bridge captured, 97
Edward's Ferry, 73
Elder, Samuel S., 516
Ellegood, Martin W.B., 290–91
Ellis, Augustus van Horne, 343
Emmitsburg, Md., 120–21, 123,
    127–28, 136, 141, 152, 157, 168,
    180, 182, 191, 217, 221, 260, 280,
    284, 296, 459
Emmitsburg Road, 180–81, 200, 280,
    284, 288, 289, 295, 301, 302, 310,
    314, 315, 318, 322–24, 326–27,

332, 337–38, 348, 353, 359, 367, 371, 377, 381, 383, 385, 388, 391, 394, 411, 416, 430, 455, 459, 461, 485, 486, 489–90, 491, 494, 495, 496–98, 499, 501, 503, 504, 506, 511, 516–19, 522, 533
Enderlin, Richard, 419n
Eshleman, Benjamin F., 463
Everett, Edward, 554
Evergreen Cemetery, 277, 337
Ewell, Richard S., 27–28, 42, 82, 169–70, 293, 412, 522, 558; at Carlisle, 96–98; command decisions, 54–55, 138–40, 191, 204–5, 215–16, 245, 251–52, 256–57, 259, 261–62, 267, 269, 316, 372–73, 401–2, 428, 443, 484; described, 18; ordered to withdraw, 123–24; plans Winchester attack, 42, 43–44

Fahnestock, Gates D., 84, 187, 531–32
Fairchild, Lucius, 183–84
Fairfax, John W., 114, 322
Fairfield (Millerstown), Pa., 127
Fairfield Road, 182, 200, 219, 237, 239, 284, 288, 537, 540, 541
Falling Waters, Wv., 544
Falls, Benjamin F., 511n
Falmouth, Va., 48
Farnsworth, Elon J., 118, 518–19
Fassitt, John B., 391n
Fastnacht, Mary, 79, 129
Featherstone, Daniel, 470
Ferguson, Milton J., 437
Fisk, Wilbur, 12
Fite, John A., 153
Fleetwood Hill, 32
Fletcher, William A., 360
Flynn, Christopher, 511n
Foster, Catherine, 107, 143, 215
Fountaindale, Md., 126, 127
Fowler, Edward B., 178, 191, 244
Frederick, Md., 138, 548
Fredericksburg, Va., fight at Franklin's Crossing, 26–27, 29, 36, 38–39
Fremantle, Arthur J. L., 112–13, 133, 258–59, 316, 411, 491, 520, 535, 540, 558

Frick, Jacob, 104
Fry, Birkett D., 158–59, 457–58, 481, 496–97
Fuger, Frederick, 498n
Funk, John H.S., 97
Furman, Chester S., 390n

Gamble, William, 165–66, 240
Garlach, Anna, 317
Garlach, Catherine, 283, 532
Garnett, Richard B., 458, 463, 476, 479, 484, 496–97; killed, 505
Garrish, Theodore, 11
Geary, John W., 255, 287, 398, 431
Georgia troops: artillery (Sumter Battalion, 464), (Troup Artillery, 453); infantry (2nd Battalion, 308), (3rd Regiment, 396), (8th Regiment, 347), (9th Regiment, 519), (10th Regiment, 460), (13th Regiment, 225), (20th Regiment, 349), (35th Regiment, 491), (38th Regiment, 62, 146), (59th Regiment, 347), (61st Regiment, 223, 229)
Gettysburg, Pa., 65, 99; cemetery dedication, 552; Gettysburg Address, 555; June 26 skirmish, 84–85; probed June 30, 129, 130
Gerald, George B., 443
Gibbon, John, 14, 207, 327, 353, 402–3, 455, 477; wounded, 509, 558
Gibson, St. Pierre, 125
Gilligan, Edward L., 212n
Gilsa, Leopold von, 223, 311–12
Glasscock Gap, 67, 70, 73
Godwin, A. C., 407
Gordon, John B., 110–11, 146, 225, 230, 245; Gordon-Barlow Incident, 249n
Graham, Charles K., 380
Greene, George S., 287, 558; defense of Culp's Hill, 395–96, 400
Gregg, David McMurtrie, 30, 32, 437–38, 447, 456–57, 558; July 3 actions, 473, 514–16
Gregg, Joseph, 408
Grey, T. C., 105–6

Griffin, Arsenal H., 478
Grover, Andrew J., 173, 180
Grover, Ira, 260, 268–69

Hagerstown Road. *See* Fairfield Road
Hahn, Henry, 83–84
Haley, John, 12, 54, 71, 109–10, 347
Hall, Daniel, 181
Hall, James A., 176, 190
Hall, James O., 156, 160
Hall, Norman J., 499
Halleck, Henry W., 26, 35;
    communications with Meade, 105,
    265, 319, 522, 532, 534, 541, 549,
    559; feud with Hooker, 15–16, 52,
    86, 92–93
Haller, Granville O., 78, 104
Hampton, Wade, 69, 330
Hancock, Winfield S., 34, 266, 327,
    383–84, 386, 392, 403, 413, 416,
    455, 559; actions on Cemetery
    Hill, 244–45, 249–50; actions on
    Cemetery Ridge, 499–500;
    designated Meade's surrogate, 207;
    disagreement with Hunt, 472;
    wounded, 500
Hanover, Pa., June 30 fight, 130,
    133–35
Hanover Road, 255, 304, 307, 313,
    373, 375, 397, 400, 437–38, 447,
    455–56, 473, 515, 533
Hardie, James A., 100–101, 102
Harmon farm, 230
Harper's Ferry, Wv., 46, 50, 52–53, 58,
    65–66, 86, 92–93, 106
Harris, Andrew L., 401, 403, 409
Harris, Edward P., 285, 290, 335
Harris, Loyd G., 148, 173, 188, 194
Harrisburg, Pa., 104, 123
Harrisburg Road. *See* Heildersburg Road
Harrison, Henry T., 100, 114–15, 559
Harrison, Walter, 333, 463
Harshbarger, A. J., 269
Hart, John W., 390n
Hart, Patrick, 472, 486
Hartwell, John F. L., 58
Haskell, Frank A., 12, 423–24, 455,
    464, 476–77, 484, 489, 499, 507,
    512–13, 559

Haskell, John Cheeves, 514
Haymarket, Va., 73
Hays, Alexander, 86, 291, 451, 469,
    502, 511
Hays, Harry T., 407
Hazard, John G., 276
Hazlett, Charles E., 348, 410
Heath, Francis E., 393
Heildersburg, Pa., 138, 140, 164
Heildersburg Road, 222
Heintzelman, Samuel P., 74
Herbst, Samuel, 123
Herbst Woods, 166, 168, 179, 182,
    184, 186, 203, 224, 230–31, 232,
    236, 248
Herbster, Charles W., 355
Herr's Ridge, 165–66, 168, 170, 179,
    200, 201, 209, 212, 213, 216, 224,
    225, 226, 233, 236, 237, 247
Heth, Henry, 121, 128, 140–41, 212,
    220, 279, 441–42, 559; analysis of
    performance, 271; command
    decisions, 153, 162–63, 166, 170,
    176, 179, 201–2; wounded, 236
Hill, Ambrose P., 25, 140–41, 146–47,
    192, 201–2, 212, 233, 247, 279,
    282, 316, 412, 441–42, 458, 466,
    522; described, 19; strategic
    decisions, 153, 237
Hincks, William B., 511n
Hirst, Benjamin, 12, 25–26, 54
Hofmann, William, 176, 178
Hoke, Jacob, 48, 81
Hollinger, Liberty, 254, 283–84, 414
Hood, John B., 289, 318, 334, 559;
    described, 113; modifies attack plan
    July 2, 322–23; unhappy with
    assignment, 321–23, 332;
    wounded, 336–37, 417
Hooker, Joseph, 7–10, 59, 62–63, 70,
    74–75, 92–93, 96, 100, 109, 559;
    communications with Lincoln, 26;
    feud with Halleck, 15–18, 51,
    86–87, 92–94; orders Union army
    across Potomac, 66; performance at
    Chancellorsville, 11, 14; relieved,
    105; resignation, 93, 98–99;
    strategic analysis, 63
Horan, Thomas, 385n

McPherson's Ridge, 143, 147, 165, 166, 170, 172, 173, 174, 176, 177, 179, 185, 188, 196, 197, 198–200, 202–3, 205, 206, 213, 215, 219, 224, 226, 228, 230, 232–34, 236, 237, 247, 257, 272, 321, 324
McPherson Woods. *See* Herbst Woods
Macy, William W., 231
Mahone, William, 394, 458
Maine troops: artillery (2nd Artillery, Battery B, 174, 176, 190), (5th Artillery, Battery E, 402); infantry (3rd Regiment, 309–10), (4th Regiment, 341–42, 345, 355), (16th Regiment, 36, 149, 234–35), (17th Regiment, 54, 109–10, 341, 347), (19th Regiment, 59, 393), (20th Regiment, 11–12, 305, 340–41, 349, 353–54, 357, 359–60, 364–65, 370–71)
Marsh Creek, 135, 136, 144, 148, 156, 158, 163, 180, 200, 267, 324, 333, 537
Marshall, Charles, 16, 104–5, 114–15, 247, 267
Marshall, John K., 483, 497
Martin, Rawley W., 506
Martin, Stephen E., 73
Marye, John L., 274–75, 467, 484
Maryland troops (Confederate): artillery (1st Battery, 372); infantry (1st Battalion, 447)
Maryland troops (Union): infantry (1st Potomac Home Brigade, 398)
Massachusetts troops, artillery (5th Artillery, Battery E, 328), (9th Artillery, 36, 328, 384–85, 386–87); infantry (2nd Regiment, 439–40), (12th Regiment, 136, 235), (15th Regiment, 353), (28th Regiment, 302), (33rd Regiment, 398, 406), (37th Regiment, 294)
Mayberry, John B., 511n
Mayo, Joseph, 502, 510
Mayo, Robert M., 163, 485, 488
Medal of Honor, 186n, 196n, 210n, 212n, 217n, 233n, 254n, 282n, 356n, 368n, 379n, 389n, 388n,

390n, 391n, 396n, 397n, 411n, 417n, 419n, 471n, 494n, 498n, 500n, 509n, 511n, 516n, 519n, 522n
Medical treatment, 257–58
Meade, George G., 9, 96, 106, 118, 125, 175, 292, 306, 413, 455, 469, 505, 512–13, 536–37, 561; analysis of performance July 2, 467, July 3, 527; appointed Army of the Potomac commander, 102; briefs corps commanders July 2, 319; command decisions, 280–81, 283, 299, 319, 326, 377–78, 444, 472, 492–93, 520; communications with Halleck, 158, 319, 413, 522, 532, 534, 541; confronts Sickles, 325–26; confusion with Slocum, 394–95; described, 112, 286, 305–6, 522; July 2 P.M. conference (council of war), 414–15; July 3 P.M. conference, 540–41; monitors events at Gettysburg July 1, 197, 207, 264–66; offers to resign, 546–49; reaches Gettysburg, 277–78; strategic decisions, 112, 118–19, 131–32, 135–36, 150–51, 175
Meade, George G., Jr., 292, 294, 413
Mears, George W., 390n
Melcher, Homer, 370
Meredith, Solomon, 173, 174, 183, 224, 228, 230
Merritt, Wesley, 118, 459–60, 470–71
Messersmith's Woods, 81
Meysenburg, Theodore A., 181
Michigan troops: cavalry (1st Regiment, 330), (5th Regiment, 106), (6th Regiment, 106, 330), (7th Regiment, 473); infantry (16th Regiment, 95, 305, 340, 360–61), (24th Regiment, 54, 163, 185, 227, 251, 257)
Military intelligence, 106; balloon surveillance, 22, 23–24; Confederate failures, 420; shadowing Lee in Pennsylvania, 51–52
Miller, John, 511n

Miller, Merritt B., 463
Miller, William E., 375, 516n
Milroy, Robert H., 38, 42, 45–46
Minnesota troops: infantry (1st
    Regiment, 45, 73, 392–393, 419,
    511)
Mississippi troops: infantry (2nd
    Regiment, 48, 156, 166, 180, 190,
    194), (11th Regiment, 16, 156,
    424–25, 453), (13th Regiment,
    321, 371), (16th Regiment, 335),
    (17th Regiment, 321, 368, 371),
    (18th Regiment, 371), (19th
    Regiment, 335), (21st Regiment,
    368, 371–72, 384–85, 386–87,
    390–91), (42nd Regiment, 156,
    166, 178, 180, 189), (48th
    Regiment, 335)
Mitchell, William G., 513
Monocacy River, 95
Moritz Tavern, 148, 156, 169, 199, 260
Morrill, Walter, 349, 370–71
Morrow, Henry A., 226, 251
Mosby, John S., 64, 88, 118, 561
Mudge, Charles, 439–40
Muffley, J. W., 58
Muhlenberg, Edward D., 434
Mummasburg Road, 178, 205, 206,
    208, 209–10, 214, 233–35
Munsell, Harvey May, 345, 355–56
Murray, John W., 125
Myers, Salome, 171, 253

Nadenbousch, John Quincy Adams, 375
New Hampshire troops: infantry (2nd
    Regiment, 380), (5th Regiment,
    108)
New Jersey troops: artillery (2nd
    Artillery, Battery B, 380); infantry
    (6th Regiment, 349), (12th
    Regiment, 301, 335, 339, 439,
    443, 494, 503–4), (15th Regiment,
    45, 535)
New York troops: artillery (1st Artillery,
    Battery B, 479), (1st Artillery,
    Battery I, 405), (1st Artillery,
    Battery L, 202), (1st Independent
    Battery, 496), (4th Independent
    Battery, 276, 296, 314–15, 345);

cavalry (5th Regiment, 131, 517),
    (8th Regiment, 132), (9th
    Regiment, 154), (10th Regiment,
    375); infantry (39th Regiment,
    300, 390–91), (40th Regiment,
    349), (41st Regiment, 157, 260,
    282, 311, 398, 406), (44th
    Regiment, 96, 305, 327, 340, 346,
    361), (45th Regiment, 205, 208),
    (54th Regiment, 217), (58th
    Regiment, 532), (64th Regiment,
    535), (68th Regiment, 217), (76th
    Regiment, 173, 174, 178, 189),
    (80th Regiment, 163, 230), (82nd
    New York, 353), (84th Regiment,
    aka 14th Brooklyn, 162, 178, 182,
    191), (86th Regiment, 50), (95th
    Regiment, 175, 182, 191, 194–95),
    (97th Regiment, 206), (111th
    Regiment, 388–89), (119th
    Regiment, 533), (120th Regiment,
    379), (124th Regiment, 315, 342,
    343, 344–45), (125th Regiment,
    300, 301, 388–89, 502), (126th
    Regiment, 300, 388–89), (134th
    Regiment, 241), (136th Regiment,
    80, 157, 535), (137th Regiment,
    395, 404–5, 408), (140th
    Regiment, 358, 361–62), (147th
    Regiment, 175, 177, 180, 189–90),
    (149th Regiment, 408), (150th
    Regiment, 398), (154th Regiment,
    50, 137, 150, 157, 163, 240–41,
    260), (157th Regiment, 149, 209,
    226, 228–29)
Newspapers and reporting, 59–60, 111,
    322, 419, 432–33
Newton, John, 286
Nichols, George W., 22, 38, 223
Niemeyer, John C., 506
North Carolina troops: artillery (Rowan
    Artillery, 336); cavalry (1st
    Regiment, 88, 473); infantry (2nd
    Battalion, 233), (7th Regiment,
    503), (11th Regiment, 248), (13th
    Regiment, 259), (14th Regiment,
    80), (16th Regiment, 504), (20th
    Regiment, 211), (23rd Regiment,
    145, 211), (26th Regiment, 17, 39,

107, 135, 144, 226–28, 230–32, 257, 504), (34th Regiment, 17, 239), (38th Regiment, 239), (43rd Regiment, 257), (45th Regiment, 213), (47th Regiment, 129, 230), (52nd Regiment, 230), (55th Regiment, 121, 156, 166, 178, 190)
Norton, Oliver W., 12, 335

Oak Hill, 204, 205, 206, 208, 209, 212, 213, 214, 245, 465
Oak Ridge, 170, 171, 187, 189, 205, 209, 210, 214, 233–35, 245, 246
Oates, William C., 49, 340, 561; Little Round Top attack, 347–48, 353–54, 357, 359–61, 364–65, 368–71
Oberlin, William Penn, 58
Ohio troops: artillery (1st Artillery, Battery I, 163, 208–9); infantry (4th Regiment, 25), (7th Regiment, 444, 526), (8th Regiment, 455, 488, 534), (25th Regiment, 268), (66th Regiment, 438), (75th Regiment, 403, 405), (107th Regiment, 70, 137)
O'Brien, Henry D., 509n
Odell, W. S., 269
O'Kane, Dennis, 496, 497; killed, 508
O'Neal, Edward A., 209–11, 443–44
O'Rorke, Patrick H., 358, 362, 410
Osborn, Thomas W., 465, 486–87, 488
Owen, Edward, 61
Oyster's Point, Pa., 124

Page, Richard C. M., 205
Paine, William H., 280–81, 319
Painter, Uriah H., 125, 154, 432
Parsons, Henry, 518
Patrick, Marsena R., 29, 50, 53–54, 57, 70, 92, 106, 524, 561
Paul, Gabriel R., 233
Peach Orchard, 173, 181, 288, 289, 296, 302, 310, 314, 318, 320, 321, 324, 325, 327, 336, 347, 351–52, 359, 367–68, 371, 376, 379–80, 384, 419, 421, 427, 439, 442, 446, 463, 466, 495, 534

Peel, William, 424–25, 453, 464, 470, 476, 490; captured, 494, 561
Pegram, William J., 158
Pender, W. Dorsey, 17, 48, 55, 61, 407, 545
Pendleton, William N., 279, 442, 461, 474, 486, 561
Pennsylvania troops: artillery (1st Artillery, Batteries F & G, 405–6), (1st Artillery, Battery B, 331); cavalry (3rd Regiment, 375, 516), (4th Regiment, 533), (17th Regiment, 126, 154), (18th Regiment, 131, 517); emergency infantry (26th Regiment, 77–79, 85); infantry (11th Regiment, 206), (26th Regiment, 71), (27th Regiment, 240), (49th Regiment, 296), (56th Regiment, 178, 180, 189), (61st Regiment, 332), (69th Regiment, 495, 497–99, 506, 507), (71st Regiment, 404, 496, 499, 505, 507), (72nd Regiment, 496, 507), (73rd Regiment, 240), (74th Regiment, 532), (83rd Regiment, 305, 340, 346, 351), (90th Regiment, 136), (99th Regiment, 267, 345, 355), (102nd Regiment, 12), (106th Regiment, 335, 496, 497, 532), (116th Regiment, 110, 302), (118th Regiment, 59, 95–96, 119), (140th Regiment, 54), (143rd Regiment, 233), (147th Regiment, 438, 534), (148th Regiment, 45, 58, 362), (149th Regiment, 213, 216, 233), (150th Regiment, 233), (151st Regiment, 233), (153rd Regiment, 157, 217, 282, 311)
Pergel, Charles, 167, 181, 182, 185
Perrin, Abner M., 61, 145, 164, 237, 239, 246
Perrin, Walter, 469
Perry, William F., 344
Pettigrew, J. Johnston, 128–29, 130, 135, 140, 158, 451, 471, 482–83, 545; wounded, 504–5
Philadelphia Brigade. See Army of the Potomac

Phillips, Charles A., 328, 472
Pickett, George E., 457, 462, 471, 473, 476, 489–90, 520–21, 562
Pierce, Tillie, 85, 132, 268, 337–38, 414, 450, 562
Pipe Creek Line, 131, 150–51, 175, 222, 547
Pipes, James M., 379n
Pitzer Woods, 302, 308–9
Platt, George C., 471
Pleasonton, Alfred, 30–32, 57, 306, 437–38, 456, 562
Plum Run, 314, 336, 340, 341, 344, 345, 349, 356, 360, 388, 392, 518
Plum Run Gorge, 314, 338, 340, 341, 342, 344, 345, 349, 355, 360
Point of Rocks, 92
Pontoon bridge, 70
Posey, Carnot, 335, 393–94
Postles, James Parke, 452
Potomac River, 45, 49, 55, 56–57, 60, 61, 62, 64, 70–73, 99, 103–4, 543
Powell, Lewis T., 514n
Powers Hill, 399, 431, 434, 469, 492, 493
Prisoners of war, 266–67, 524, 535, 539–40
Purman, James J., 379n
Pye, Edward, 194

Railroad cut, 171, 178, 187, 194–96, 204, 216, 239
Railroads, protection, 51; destruction, 116
Ramseur, Stephen D., 246, 407
Randolph, George E., 292, 314, 376–77
Rapidan River, 27
Rappahannock River, 7, 9, 11, 16, 21, 25, 27, 32, 38
Ray, William P., 329
Raymond, William H., 494n
Reagan, John H., 5
Reed, Charles, 388
Reid, Whitelaw, 111, 124, 138, 154–55, 263–64, 285–86, 305–6, 457, 468, 522, 536–37, 562

Reisinger, J. Monroe, 217
Reynolds, Gilbert H., 202
Reynolds, John F., 120, 137, 152, 156, 159, 169, 175–76; analysis of performance, 271–72; command decisions, 172–73, 181–82; described, 13–14; killed in action, 184; meeting with Lincoln, 14
Rhode Island troops: artillery (1st Artillery, Battery A, 469, 478,) (1st Artillery, Battery B, 478), (1st Artillery, Battery E, 327, 367)
Rice, Edmund, 509n
Rice, James C., 361
Richardson, H. B., 123
Richmond, James, 511n
Richmond, Va., 1
Rickets, R. Bruce, 405–6
Riley, Frank, 443
Riley, John E., 75
Rittenhouse, Benjamin F., 488
Robertson, Beverly H., 69, 77, 89–90, 116–18
Robertson, Jerome B., 337
Robinson, John C., 200–201, 234
Robinson, John H., 511n
Rock Creek, 208, 217, 223, 255, 282, 307, 332, 400, 402, 428, 431, 437, 524
Rockville, Md., 108
Rodes, Robert E., 251, 510; command decisions, 198, 204–5, 209–211, 259, 261–62, 407
Rogers, E. Clayton, 37
Rogers farm, 467, 490, 501
Rood, Oliver P., 511n
Roosevelt, George W., 385
Root, Adrian R., 233
Rorty, James M., 479
Rose farm, 295, 365, 377
Rose's wheat field. See Wheatfield
Rosengarten, Joseph G., 169
Ross, Fitzgerald, 133, 322, 537, 541–42
Roush, J. Levin, 390n
Rowley, Thomas A., 248
Rowser's Ford, 99, 102–3
Ruger, Thomas H., 439–40
Rupp, John, 465
Rutter, James M., 233n

Saint Joseph Academy, 136
Salem, Va., 67
Sandoe, George W., 85
Scales, Alfred M., 237, 239
Scheibert, Justus, 284
Schimmelfennig, Alexander, 205, 226, 248, 532
Schuricht, Hermann, 48
Schurz, Carl, 197–98, 205, 218, 240–41, 244, 278, 409, 538
Schwenk, Martin, 471n
Scripture, Clark, 208
Seddon, James A., 3–4
Sedgwick, John, 270, 378
Sellers, Harry, 332
Seminary. See Lutheran Theological Seminary
Seminary Ridge, 130, 175, 176, 187, 188, 190, 192, 199, 213, 231, 232, 233, 236, 237, 239, 240, 243, 246, 247, 251, 252, 257, 267, 271, 279, 284, 288, 290, 293, 297, 308, 316, 381, 439, 450, 461, 464, 465, 466, 481, 490, 491, 495, 504, 510, 520, 522, 533, 537, 539
Semmes, Paul J., 363
Setley, George, 355
Seymour, William J., 298
Sharpe, George H., 14–15, 24, 38, 50, 57–58, 120, 562; assesses July 2 enemy strength, 413; decides entire Rebel army is north of the Potomac, 66; difficulties gathering intelligence, 57–58; predicts Rebel cavalry raid, 29; relationship with Hooker, 58
Shepherdstown, Wv., 55, 56, 65, 66, 69
Sherfy, John, 173
Sherfy's peach orchard. See Peach Orchard
Sherman, Marshall, 511n
Sherrill, Eliakim, 455, 525
Shotwell, Randolph, 55
Sickles, Daniel E., 109–10, 119, 221, 277, 310, 367–68; analysis of performance July 2, 421; command decisions, 313–14; relationship with Meade, 119, 132, 280, 294, 299, 319, 325–26; testifies against

Meade, 547; unhappy with assigned position, 301–2; wounded, 376–77, 417
Skelly, Daniel, 106, 141–43, 171, 187, 254, 283, 303, 414, 418, 429, 532, 554, 562
Slaughter Pen. See Plum Run Gorge
Slocum, Henry W., 221–22, 277–78, 281, 533, 562; command decisions, 254–55, 378, 395, 431, 439–40
Slyder farm, 336, 339
Small, Abner R., 149
Smith, James E., 276, 296, 314–15, 335–36, 341–42, 345
Smith, James Power, 251, 253, 256
Smith, Jane, 304, 418, 429, 437
Smith, Richard Penn, 496
Smith, Thaddeus S., 390n
Smith, William "Extra Billy," 218, 255, 428, 438, 440, 449
Smyth, Thomas A., wounded, 469
Sorrel, G. Moxley, 114
South Carolina troops: infantry (1st Regiment Provisional Army, 145), (1st Regiment, 239), (2nd Regiment, 352), (12th Regiment, 239), (13th Regiment, 146, 240), (14th Regiment, 239)
Spangler farm, 485, 490
Spangler's Woods, 308, 446
Spear, Ellis, 353–54, 357, 370–71
Stafford Court House, Va., 45
Stannard, George J., 86, 499–500
Stanton, Edwin M., 98–99
State Line, Pa., 82
Steinwehr, Adolph von, 180
Stephenson's Depot, Va., Battle of, 46
Steuart, George H., 82, 404–5, 408, 447–49
Stevens, George, 184
Stevens, George T., 269–70
Stevens, Thaddeus, 83
Stevens Run, 241
Stone, John M., 194
Stone, Roy, 213
Stonewall Brigade. See Army of Northern Virginia
Stony Hill, 351, 352, 358–59, 362, 365, 376, 377, 379

Stoughton, Homer S., 336
Stragglers, 138
Stratton Street, 240, 241
Stuart, J. E. B., 330, 412, 543, 562;
    commands at Brandy Station,
    31–32; July 3 actions, 437–38,
    455–57, 473–74, 514–16; plan to
    ride around Union army, 64–65,
    67–70; rejoins army, 316; ride
    around Union army, 73–74, 77,
    88–89, 99, 102–4, 107–8, 116,
    125, 130, 137–38, 157, 262–63,
    278; stages reviews at Brandy
    Station, 24, 28
Susquehanna River, 97, 104, 110–11,
    112, 118, 135, 138
Sweitzer, Jacob B., 347, 365,
Sykes, George, 326, 415, 540–41

Taneytown, Md., 155, 173, 175, 191,
    197, 207, 250, 263, 266, 270, 277,
    292, 418
Taneytown Road, 180, 197, 249, 264,
    277, 283, 292, 338, 417, 450, 468
Tate, Samuel McDowell, 404
Taylor, Isaac Lyman, 73
Taylor, O. B., 329
Taylor, Walter H., 17, 122, 247, 251,
    253, 441, 442
Tennessee troops: infantry (1st
    Regiment, 166, 179, 182, 185),
    (7th Regiment, 153, 166, 182,
    185, 186), (14th Regiment, 166,
    182, 184, 185)
Terrell, Leigh R., 334, 348
Texas Brigade. See Army of Northern
    Virginia
Texas troops: infantry (1st Regiment,
    332, 334, 337, 341, 343, 517),
    (4th Regiment, 324, 332, 334,
    337, 338, 346), (5th Regiment,
    337, 338, 346, 360–61)
Thomas, Daniel Boone, 504
Thomas, Edward L., 490
Thompson, James, 472
Thompson, James B., 522n
Thorn, C. Elizabeth, 84
Thoroughfare Gap, 59, 64, 73
Tilden, Charles W., 234–35

"Tout le Monde," 121
Tozier, Andrew J., 411n
Tremain, Henry E., 280, 376–77
Trepp, Casper, 310
Triangular Field, 343, 344, 349
Trimble, Isaac R., 94–95, 139–40, 256,
    293, 480, 563; wounded, 504
deTrobriand, Philippe Regis, 358
Trostle farm, 376, 384
Tshudy, Martin, 496
Turney, Jacob B., 179, 185
Two Taverns, Pa., 192, 221
Tyson, Charles J., 203

United States troops: artillery (1st
    Artillery, Battery I, 478), (2nd
    Artillery, Battery B, 148), (3rd
    Artillery, Batteries F & K, 391),
    (4th United States, Battery A, 465,
    478), (4th Artillery, Battery E,
    516), (4th Artillery, Battery G,
    223), (5th Artillery, Battery C,
    416), (5th Artillery, Battery D,
    348), (5th Artillery, Battery I,
    390–91); sharpshooters (1st
    Regiment, 12, 308–10), (2nd
    Regiment, 336, 338, 346)
Upperville, Va., 57, 60

Vallandigham, Clement, 61
Veazy, Wheelock G., 500n
Veil, Charles H., 169, 172–73, 184
Venable, Andrew R., 157, 216, 218–19
Venable, Charles S., 279, 293
Vermont troops: cavalry (1st Regiment,
    517–18); infantry (2nd Regiment,
    12), (13th Regiment, 397, 499,
    511), (14th Regiment, 499, 513),
    (16th Regiment, 500, 513–14)
Vicksburg, Miss., 3, 544
Vincent, Strong, 305, 326–27, 335,
    340–41; killed, 361
Virginia troops: artillery (Amherst
    Artillery, 62), (Bath Artillery, 329),
    (Charlottesville Horse Battery,
    456), (Fredericksburg Artillery,
    161, 171, 467), (Richmond
    Battery, 439, 467, 533), (2nd
    Richmond Howitzers, 466),

(Rockbridge Artillery, 313); cavalry (7th Regiment, 90), (35th Battalion, 82); infantry (1st Regiment, 333, 425, 470), (2nd Regiment, 373), (4th Regiment, 124), (6th Regiment, 534), (7th Regiment, 333), (8th Regiment, 485, 498), (9th Regiment, 332, 451, 506), (10th Regiment, 405), (11th Regiment, 487), (14th Regiment, 470), (18th Regiment, 487), (22nd Battalion, 480, 488), (23rd Regiment, 428), (24th Regiment, 502), (33rd Regiment, 20, 438), (38th Regiment, 92, 487), (40th Regiment, 480, 488), (42nd Regiment, 269), (47th Regiment, 20, 163, 480), (53rd Regiment, 506), (55th Regiment, 129, 480, 488)

Wade, Benjamin, 546
Wade, Mary Virginia "Jennie," 450
Wadsworth, James S., 37, 156, 169, 174, 176, 202, 260, 286
Wainwright, Charles S., 159, 198–99, 202, 236, 237–38, 243, 331, 372, 405
Walker, Elijah, 344
Walker, James A., 373–75, 428, 438, 444, 447
Walker, R. Lindsay, 297, 486
Wall, Jerry, 511n
Waller, Francis A., 196
Walton, John B., 273, 463
Ward, J. H. Hobart, 341, 355
Warfield Ridge, 288, 315, 318, 336, 342, 348, 351, 381, 436, 466
Warren, Gouverneur K., 131, 266, 292, 319–20, 348–49, 357–58, 362, 415, 563; scouts Union right flank, 299; surveys Little Round Top, 324–25
Warren, Leander, 154, 171–72
Washington, Department of, furnishes reinforcements to Hooker, 57, 74
Watson, Malbone F., 390–91
Waud, Alfred, 60
Way, W. C., 163

Weakley, J. W., 235n
Webb, Alexander S., 478, 496, 507, 511n
Weed, Stephen H., 410
Weikert, Beckie, 268
Weikert (George) farm, 302, 326, 383, 398, 417
Weikert (Jacob) farm, 337–38, 370, 414
Weir, Gulian V., 416–17, 509–10, 563
Welch, Norval E., 360
Welch, Spencer Glasgow, 146
Weld, Stephen M., 172, 197
Welles, Gideon, 45, 75, 80–81, 114, 261, 418, 523, 549
Wells, William, 518
West Virginia troops: cavalry (1st Regiment, 518–19)
Westminster, Md., 125
Wheatfield, 347, 348, 351, 355, 358–59, 362–63, 365, 380, 385, 417
Wheatfield Road, 325, 351, 359, 372, 380, 384
Whitaker, John H., 88
White, Elijah V., 82
Whitman, Walt, 538–39
Wiedrich, Michael, 405–7, 408
Wilcox, Cadmus M., 308–9, 382, 392–93, 463, 500–1, 513–14, 521, 563
Wiley, James, 511n
Wilkeson, Bayard, 223
Wilkeson, Samuel, 124, 154, 457, 468
Willard, George L., 299–300, 383–84, 388–89, 391–92; killed, 392
Williams, Alpheus S., 255, 398, 430–431, 434
Williams, Erasmus, 470
Williams, Jesse M., 400
Williamsport, Md., 45, 47, 55, 56, 66, 69, 71–72, 81, 531, 543, 548
Wills Woods, 170, 176, 189, 200, 206, 209, 234, 235
Willoughby Run, 170, 174, 176, 178–79, 182, 185, 186, 224, 228, 230, 237, 239, 287, 312, 417, 436
Wilson, LeGrand, 258, 537
Winchester, Va., Battle of, 42–44

Winebrenner's Run, 298, 401, 409

Wisconsin troops, infantry (2nd
    Regiment, 163, 182–85, 228), (6th
    Regiment, 37, 148, 163, 174, 188,
    192–93, 239, 246, 260, 408), (7th
    Regiment, 163, 186, 203), (26th
    Regiment, 136)

Wister, Langhorne, 216–17

Witcher, Vincent A., 437, 456

Wofford, William T., 377, 379

Wolf Hill, 281, 282

Wolf Run Shoals, 77

Wood, Andrew J., 186

Wood Jr., George, 403

Woods, John P., 36–37

Woollard, Leander, 180

Worley, C. L. F., 166

Wright, Ambrose R., 396–97, 460, 462,
    563

Wrightsville, Pa., skirmish at, 110–11

York, Pa., 97, 110, 124, 130, 131, 133,
    136, 138

York Road, 256, 316

Young, Louis G., 128–29, 130, 140–41,
    158, 451, 504–5

Zachry, Alfred, 79

Ziegler, Lydia Catherine, 84, 107, 154,
    187

Ziegler's Grove, 469, 478, 505

Zook, Samuel K., 363